THE PRIMACY OF THE BISHOP OF ROME AND ECUMENICAL DIALOGUE

ADRIANO GARUTI, O.F.M.

THE PRIMACY OF THE
BISHOP OF ROME
AND
ECUMENICAL DIALOGUE

Translation edited by Michael J. Miller

IGNATIUS PRESS   SAN FRANCISCO

Cover art: *The Calling of Saint Peter*
Uffizi, Florence
Hans Suess von Kulmbach (ca. 1480–1522)
Photo credit: Alinari

Cover design by Riz Boncan Marsella

ISBN-0-89870-879-6
Library of Congress Control Number 2003115833
Printed in the United States of America ♾

CONTENTS

PRESENTATION

I am pleased to present this new book by Father Adriano Garuti, O.F.M., the author of two previous works that were very well received: on the Pope as Patriarch of the West (1990) and on the Petrine primacy in the light of the 1647 Decree of the Holy Office (1993). The present volume thus completes a kind of trilogy on the universal ministry of the Successor of Peter, a subject currently of great interest, which is treated in depth under various aspects—here, specifically, with regard to ecumenical dialogue—by means of an analysis and an evaluation of the documents published by the several commissions established by the Catholic Church with the Orthodox, the Lutherans, and the Anglicans, respectively.

The conclusion which emerges is not very comforting. Even though the historical context may have changed and with it the tenor of the discussion (from polemics to a dialogue of charity), the theological dialogue being carried on by the Catholic Church with the Orthodox Churches and with the ecclesial communities born of the Reformation on the fundamental theme of the primacy of the Roman Pontiff is still far from obtaining satisfactory results. Indeed, for a number of reasons, including the methodology employed in the dialogue, the subject has not been directly approached, nor has it received the more extensive study it deserves. I believe that this may explain why the title of this book is not "The Primacy of the Bishop of Rome *in* Ecumenical Dialogue" but rather "Primacy *and* Dialogue".

As a result, in the Catholic-Orthodox dialogue, which has been substantially structured on the principles of Orthodox ecclesiology, for years now, the discussion of the problem has been on the agenda, but then precedence has been given to questions of manifestly less importance. The dialogue itself is going through a difficult period regarding the resumption of the work.

As for Catholic-Lutheran dialogue, notwithstanding the willingness on the part of these Protestants to accept a universal ministry in the Church, there has been no real success in overcoming the traditional difficulties.

The most positive result seems to be the overcoming of the polemical tone of the critique of the papacy that was characteristic of the Reformation and Counter Reformation periods. The direct and deeper study of the question, begun in 1995, has not yet produced documents of any kind.

More promising results seem, however, to have been obtained in the Catholic-Anglican dialogue, above all in the recent document *The Gift of Authority,* where the topic is treated explicitly. Here the need for a universal ministry has been recognized, which de facto has been handed down to the Bishop of Rome, although there is no reference to the question of *ius divinum.* Furthermore the problem of the concrete exercise of such a primacy, in the context of collegiality and synodality, remains an open question.

Finally the author's decision to publish his earlier article on "sister churches" as an appendix to the text is to be applauded; in it he makes some interesting and important points, especially regarding the unicity of the Church. It is undeniable, however, that the ministry of the Successor of the Apostle Peter remains a point of debate, that ministry which, as Pope John Paul II has reaffirmed, "among all the Churches and ecclesial communities, the Catholic Church is conscious that she has preserved" (*Ut unum sint,* 88).

At this point, it is to be hoped that a groundbreaking work has been completed as a step toward the attainment of the truth in all its fullness, because ecumenism itself has the obligation to search out the whole truth once it has been only partially discovered. Every activity aimed at restoring the unity of Christians without sufficient clarity would prove to be at best an unconscious celebration of the separations.

Father Umberto Betti, O.F.M.
Rector Emeritus
Pontifical Lateran University
2000

FOREWORD

Official Catholic participation in ecumenical activity since the Second Vatican Council has brought many and various blessings, not only to Christian peoples but to society generally throughout the world. It is one of the best fruits of the Council.

One example of these fruits is the officially sponsored dialogues: Orthodox and Catholic, Lutheran and Catholic, Anglican and Catholic. The English translation of Father Garuti's *Primato del Vescovo di Roma e Dialogo Ecumenico* is an important contribution to this dialogue in the English-speaking world providing us with accurate snapshots of the progress achieved and the difficulties which remain, while enabling us to fit the pieces together.

The most important dialogue is between the Catholic Church and the Orthodox Churches. Progress greater than anything since the Council of Florence has been achieved, but the highest hopes have been disappointed and the Catholic-Orthodox dialogue itself is intellectually less satisfactory than the others.

Providentially the long appendix on "Sister Churches" enables many of the difficulties scarcely touched in the dialogues to be listed and reviewed. Important consequences follow from the autocephalous nature of the Orthodox Churches, the autonomy and fundamental equality of local churches. To ascribe the rise of the five patriarchates simply to sociology or history is also inadequate. The scriptural evidence on Peter (the rock-man) and the other apostles has to be confronted constructively. History moves on, as the story of Jerusalem demonstrates as well as the terrible pressures on the Christian community in Constantinople today and the rise of the Moscow patriarchate.

Neither can the long term influence of Emperors and Kings in the histories of the Churches of East and West be ignored in any study of the Papacy.

The Lutheran and Anglican dialogues demonstrate what good will, scholarship and a willingness to go beyond and behind established positions can achieve, and how much further we need to travel.

The mounting stresses on unity in the Anglican communion from the ordination of women and the ordination of homosexually active bishops provide a new backdrop for all ecumenical discussion.

The author follows Pope Paul VI and Pope John Paul II in believing that the Pope is "the greatest obstacle on the path of ecumenism". But ecumenism is only one important part of the Christian task today.

The early ecumenical optimism about reunion has long passed. We face new challenges from radical Islam and more importantly, in the Western world at least, from the assaults of radical liberalism, a barely disguised neo-paganism, more superstitious than secular, on many aspects of the Bible's teaching on faith and morals. But this is another larger story.

Father Garuti's work is an invaluable reminder to us of the importance of the Roman primacy in retaining Catholic self awareness that it remains primarily and substantially the one true Church, that the Papacy has an indispensable role of world-wide Christian leadership, and that the successor of St. Peter is also the servant of all the servants of God in the Gospel-mandated work of ecumenical prayer, cooperation, joint service and mutual dialogue.

✠ George Cardinal Pell
Archbishop of Sydney
Sydney, Australia
6 January 2004

PREFACE

The results of the ecumenical dialogue—both real and apparent—have made it clear, at any rate, that the primacy of the Bishop of Rome remains the single most serious obstacle on the path of ecumenism, as Pope Paul VI himself stated in an address to the Secretariat for the Unity of Christians (1967) and as Pope John Paul II repeated in his encyclical letter *Ut unum sint* (1995).

John Paul II's invitation to the leaders of other Christian communities and to their theologians to engage in a "patient and fraternal dialogue on this subject" (*Ut unum sint*, 96) prompted a spate of new studies on the subject, as well as two symposia here in Rome. The first of these was organized in Vatican City by the Congregation for the Doctrine of the Faith in December 1996, with a purpose that was doctrinal rather than ecumenical, aimed at delineating the essential points of Catholic doctrine on the Petrine primacy. A second symposium, with a specifically ecumenical purpose, was organized by the Franciscan Friars of the Atonement at the *Angelicum* in December 1997.

In articles published in these years in the journal *Antonianum*, I, too, have sought to explore the subject in greater depth, in the light of the Catholic-Orthodox and Catholic-Lutheran dialogues. I thought it would be useful to gather these articles into a single volume—without substantial modification, though with an updated bibliography—together with a new chapter on the Catholic-Anglican dialogue. Furthermore, given the current interest in the question of "sister Churches", not only within the parameters of Catholic-Orthodox dialogue but also in the dialogues with Anglicans and Lutherans, I decided to include, as an appendix, an earlier article I had written on the subject entitled "Sister Churches: Reality and Questions" which had also been published in *Antonianum* (1996).

In this way I hope to contribute to the investigation of these important issues and to shed some light on a subject which is both sensitive and timely.

Adriano Garuti, O.F.M.

Rome, Pontificio Ateneo Antonianum

February 22, 2000

The Feast of the Chair of Saint Peter

ABBREVIATIONS

ARC   Documents on Anglican/Roman Catholic Relations. Washington, 1972ff.
ARCIC   Anglican-Roman Catholic International Commission.
AS   Ecumenical Second Vatican Council, *Acta Synodalia*.
BE   *The Quest for Unity. Orthodox and Catholics in Dialogue.* Edited by J. Borelli and J. H. Erickson. Crestwood, N. Y.–Washington, D. C., 1996.
BG   *Building Unity. Ecumenical Dialogues with Roman Catholic Participation in the United States.* Edited by J. A. Burges and J. Gros. New York/Mahwah, N. J., 1989.
DEM   *Dictionary of the Ecumenical Movement.* Edited by N. Lossky, J. Míguez, J. Pobee, T. Stransky, G. Wainwreight, and P. Webb. Grand Rapids, Mich., 1991.
EOE   *Enchiridion Œcumenicum.* Bologna, 1986ff.
GMR   *Growth in Agreement II. Reports and Agreed Statements of Ecumenical Conversations on a World Level, 1982–1998.* Edited by J. Gros, H. Meyer, and W. G. Rusch.
HY   *Anglicans and Roman Catholics: The Search for Unity.* Edited by C. Hill and E. Yarnold. London, 1994.
Ins   *Paolo VI e Giovanni Paolo II, Insegnamenti.* Tipografia Poliglotta Vaticana, 1963ff. From the context it is evident which Pope is being cited.
IS   *Information Service, The Pontifical Council for Promoting Christian Unity* (Vatican City, 1967–   ).
JRCLC   Joint Roman Catholic Lutheran Commission in the USA.
JWG   Joint Working Group between the Catholic Church and the Ecumenical Council of Churches.
LCD   Lutherans and Catholics in Dialogue.
LRCIC   Lutheran-Roman Catholic International Commission.
MV   *Growth in Agreement I. Reports and Agreed Statements of Ecumenical Conversations on a World Level.* Edited by H. Meyer and L. Visher. New York/Ramsey, 1984.
O-RCC   Orthodox-Roman Catholic Consultation in the USA.
ORCIC   Orthodox-Roman Catholic International Commission.
Stormon   *Towards the Healing of Schism.* New York, 1987.

SELECT BIBLIOGRAPHY

Ablondi, A. "Il 'servizio di Pietro' e le grandi novità". *Vita e pensiero* 78 (1995): 562–81.

Afanassieff, N. "La doctrine de la primauté à la lumière de l'ecclésiologie". *Istina* 4 (1957): 401–20.

Alberigo, G. "L'Atto di Supremazia del 1534 nel contesto dell'ecclesiologia del tempo". In Alzati, *L'anglicanesimo*, 53–69.

———. "La koinonia, voie et âme de l'Église une". In J.-L. Leuba. *Perspectives actuelles sur l'oecuménisme*. Louvain-la-Neuve, 1995, pp. 17–43.

Alzati, C., comp. *L'anglicanesimo. Dalla Chiesa d'Inghilterra alla Comunione Anglicana*. Genoa, 1992.

Alzati, C., and P. Locati, comp. *L'unità multiforme. Oriente e Occidente nella riflessione di Giovanni Paolo II*. Milan, 1991.

Antón, A. "'Ministerio petrino' y/o 'Papado' en el diálogo con las otras Iglesias cristianas: algunos puntos de convergencia y divergencia". *Il primato del successore di Pietro. Atti del Simposio teologico (Rome, dicembre 1996)*. Vatican City, 1998, 386–453.

Arnott, F. "I 39 Articoli: genesi, significato e ruolo nella storia dell'Anglicanesimo". In Alzati, *L'anglicanesimo*, 145–61.

Assimakis, G. "L'ecclesiologia nei documenti della Commissione mista di dialogo teologico tra la Chiesa cattolica romana e la Chiesa ortodossa nei primi dieci anni della sua attività (1980–1990)". *Oriente Cristiano* 33/I (1993): 5–38, and 33/II (1993): 3–34.

Basdekis, A. "Das Papsttum aus der Sicht der orthodoxen Theologie und Kirche". *Orthodoxes Forum* 9 (1995), 65–85.

Beinert, W. "Stand und Bewegung des ökumenischen Geschehens". *Catholica* 37 (1983): 1–35.

———. "Endechrist oder Zeichen der Barmherzigkeit. Die Möglichkeit einer ekklesiologischen Konvergenz zwischen Lutheranern und Katholiken über das Papsttum". *Catholica* 50 (1996): 121–43.

———. "Ökumene und Ökumenismus 30 Jahre nach dem Vaticanum II". *Theologie der Gegenwart* 39 (1996): 242–55.

Betti, U. "Chiesa di Cristo e Chiesa cattolica. A proposito di un'espressione della 'Lumen gentium'". *Antonianum* 61 (1986): 726–45.

Birmilé, A. "*Status quaestionis* de la théologie de la communion à travers les dialogues oecuméniques et l'évolution des différentes théologies confessionelles". *Cristianesimo nella storia* 16 (1995): 245–84.

Borras, A. "Ut unum sint. Une encyclique pour les chrétiens en voie de réconciliation". *Ephemerides theologicae lovanienses* 72 (1996): 349–70.

Böttigheimer, C. "Von der ökumenischen Relevanz des Papsttums". *Internationale katholische Zeitschrift Communio* 27 (1998): 330–44.

Bouwen, F. "Balamand 1993. VIIe session de la Commission internationale pour le dialogue entre l'Église catholique et l'Église orthodoxe". *Proche-Orient Chrétien* 43 (1993): 91–112.

_____. "Ouverture du dialogue théologique entre l'Église catholique et l'Église orthodoxe". *Proche-Orient Chrétien* 29 (1979): 314–41.

_____. "Uusi Valamo 1988. Cinquième session de la Commission internationale pour le dialogue théologique entre l'Église catholique et l'Église orthodoxe". *Proche-Orient Chrétien* 38 (1988): 281–96.

Bouyer, L. *The Church of God. Body of Christ and Temple of the Spirit*. Chicago, 1982.

Bria, I. "La Koinonia comme communauté canonique. Perspectives actuelles". *Istina* (1975), 116–26.

Brosseder, J. "Vers quelle unité des Églises?" *Concilium*, no. 271 (1997): 161–70.

Brun, M. *Orthodoxe theologische Stimmen zum Zweiten Vatikanischen Konzil. Ein Beitrag zur Überwindung der Trennung*. Freiburg, 1987.

Buchanan, C. "Comunione anglicana". *Dictionary of the Ecumenical Movement* (DME). Ed. Nicholas Lossky, et al. Grand Rapids, Mich., 1991. 210–12.

_____. " 'Evangelicalism' e 'Catholicism' nello sviluppo storico dell'Anglicanismo". In Alzati, *L'anglicanesimo*, 179–88.

Buckley, M.J. " 'Perpetuum utriusque unitatis principium ac visibile fundamentum'. The primacy and the episcopate: towards a doctrinal synthesis". In *Il primato del successore di Pietro*, 281–339.

Burgess, A. ed. *Lutherans in Ecumenical Dialogue. A Reappraisal*. Minneapolis, 1990.

Butler, S. "Authority in the Church: Lessons from Anglican-Roman Catholic Dialog". *Theology Digest* 45 (1998): 337–53.

Bux, N. "Unità e cattolicità della chiesa universale nelle chiese particolari". *Nicolaus* 18 (1991): 161–74.

_____. *Il quinto sigillo. L'unità dei cristiani verso il terzo millennio* (Vatican
City, 1997).

Carrasco Rouco, A. *Le primat de l'évêque de Rome. Étude sur la cohérence
ecclésiologique et canonique du primat de juridiction.* Fribourg, 1990.

_____. "Der päpstliche Primat und das Zweite Vatikanum". *Internationale
katholische Zeitschrift Communio* 27 (1998): 310–29.

Celada, G. "La 'Una Santa' en el diálogo católico-ortodoxo". *Nicolaus* 23
(1996): 121–62.

Cereti, G. *Per un'ecclesiologia ecumenica.* Bologna, 1997.

Chadwick, H. "La continuità della Chiesa in Inghilterra e l'Atto di Supremazia". In Alzati, *L'anglicanesimo*, 43–52.

_____. "Ministero papale e unità dei cristiani dal punto di vista angli-
cano". In Hünermann, *Papato ed ecumenismo*, 63–70.

_____. "Unfinished Business". In Hill and Yarnold, *Anglicans and Roman
Catholics*, 211–21.

Chitarin, L. "L'ecclesiologia di Francis A. Sullivan. Analisi bibliografica".
Ricerche teologiche 7 (1996): 221–31.

_____. "Note sull'attuale dibattito ecclesiologico". *Ricerche teologiche* 8
(1997): 187–93.

Chittleborough, K. S. "Towards a Theology and Practice of the Bishop-
in-Synod". In Sykes, *Authority in the Anglican Communion*, 144–62.

Cioffari, G. *L'ecclesiologia ortodossa. Problemi e prospettive.* Bari, 1992.

Clément, O. *La Chiesa ortodossa.* Brescia, 1989.

Clifford, C. "Reception of the *Final Report*: Beyond Strengthened Agreement". *One in Christ* 32 (1996): 130–48.

Cobb, P. "La continuità cattolica della Chiesa d'Inghilterra nel pensiero
del Movimento di Oxford". In Alzati, *L'anglicanesimo*, 189–202.

Colombo, G. "Il primato petrino tra Parola divina e storicità umana". In
Il primato del successore di Pietro, 171–82.

_____. "Tesi per la revisione dell'esercizio del ministero petrino". *Teolo-
gia* (1996): 322–39.

Congar, Y. "Le développement de l'évaluation ecclésiologique des églises
non-catholiques. Un bilan". *Revue de droit canonique* 25 (1975): 168–98.

_____. *Diversity and Communion.* London, 1982.

_____. *Essais oecuméniques. Le mouvement, les hommes, les problèmes.* Paris,
1984.

————. *Ministères et communion ecclésiale*. Paris, 1971.

Coppola, R., "Primato papale ed ecumenismo". *Nicolaus* 14 (1986): 3–4.

Daley, B. E. "Position and Patronage in the Early Church: The Original Meaning of 'Primacy of Honour'". *Journal of Theological Studies* 44 (1993): 531–53.

Dallari, C. *Chiamati all'unità*. Padua, 1993.

Davey, C., "Chiesa Anglicana e Oriente Ortodosso". In Alzati, *L'anglicanesimo*, 265–79.

de Halleux, A. "La collégialité dans l'Église ancienne". *Revue théologique de Louvain* 24 (1993): 433–54.

————. "Les deux Rome dans la définition de Chalcédoine sur les prérogatives du siège de Constantinople". *Patrologie et oecuménisme. Recueil d'études*. Louvain, 1990, 504–19.

————. "Fraterna communio". *Irénikon* 58 (1985): 291–309.

————. "L'institution patriarcale et la pentarchie. Un point de vue orthodoxe". *Revue théologique de Louvain* 3 (1972): 177–99.

————. "Une nouvelle étape du dialogue catholique-orthodoxe: le texte de Valamo". *Revue théologique de Louvain* 19 (1988): 459–73.

————. "Orthodoxes orientaux en dialogue". *Irénikon* 64 (1991): 332–57.

de Vries, W., *Ortodossia e cattolicesimo*. Brescia, 1983.

Delmotte, M. "Le dialogue entre anglicans et catholiques". *Istina* 27 (1982): 278–92.

Deneaux, H., and W. J. Dick, eds. *From Malines to ARCIC: The Malines Conversations Commemorated*. Louvain, 1997.

Dentin, P. *Les privilèges des Papes devant l'Écriture et l'histoire*. Paris, 1995.

Denzler, G., ed. *Papsttum—heute und morgen. Eine Umfrage*. Regensburg, 1975.

Donneaud, H. "Note sur l'Église comme 'communion' dans le Catéchisme de l'Église catholique". *Revue thomiste* 103 (1995): 665–71.

Doyle, D. M. "Möhler, Schleiermacher, and the Roots of Communion Ecclesiology". *Theological Studies* 57 (1996): 467–80.

Dubasque, B. "Il dialogo con le Chiese orientali ortodosse". *La Chiesa cattolica oggi nel dialogo. Aggiornamento: 1988–1995. Corso breve di ecumenismo*, X. Rome, 1995, 27–59.

Dunstan, G. "Common Law e Diritto Canonico". In Alzati, *L'anglicanesimo*, 129–43.

Duprey, P. "La structure synodale de l'Église dans la théologie orientale". *Proche-Orient Chrétien* 20 (1970): 123–45.

_____. "Une étape importante du dialogue catholique-orthodoxe. Balamand, 17–24 juin 1993". In Evans and Gourgues, *Communion et Réunion*, 115–23.

Edwards, M., and G. Tavard, *Luther. A Reformer for the Churches: An Ecumenical Study Guide*. New York, 1983.

Empie, P. C., and T. A. Murphy, eds. *Papal Primacy and the Universal Church* (LCD V). Minneapolis, Minn., 1974.

Erdö, P. "Conseguenze canoniche di una ecclesiologia eucaristica". *Periodica de re canonica* 83 (1994): 293–312.

Evans, G. R., and M. Gourgues, eds. *Communion et Réunion: Mélanges Jean-Marie Roger Tillard*. Louvain, 1995.

Evdokimov, P. *L'Ortodossia*. Bologna, 1981.

Fahey, M. A. "Ecclesiae sorores ac fratres: Sibling Communion in the Pre-Nicene Christian Era". *Proceedings of the 36th Annual Convention of the Catholic Theological Society of America*, 36 (1982): 15–38.

Falbo, G. *Il primato della Chiesa di Roma alla luce dei primi quattro secoli* (Rome, 1989).

Farmer, W. R., and R. Kereszty. *Peter and Paul in the Church of Rome: The Ecumenical Potential of a Forgotten Perspective*. New York, 1990.

Fontbona i Missé, J. *Comunión y sinodalidad. La eclesiología eucarística después N. Afanasiev en I. Zizioulas y J.-M. R. Tillard*. Rome, 1994.

Fortino, E. "La 'communio-koinonía' nel dialogo cattolico-ortodosso". In P. Rodríguez, comp. *L'ecclesiologia trent'anni dopo la "Lumen gentium"*. Rome, 1995, 181–99.

_____. "Il dialogo fra la Chiesa Cattolica e la Chiesa Ortodossa". *Religioni e Sette nel mondo* 1/4 (1995): 127–52.

_____. "Il dialogo teologico fra la Chiesa Cattolica e la Chiesa ortodossa 1979–1987". In *La Chiesa cattolica oggi nel dialogo. Corso breve di ecumenismo*, IX. Rome, 1988, 7–20.

_____. "Il dialogo tra cattolici ed ortodossi: Panorama e prospettive". In *La Chiesa cattolica oggi nel dialogo. Corso breve di ecumenismo*, IV. Rome, 1982, 7–17.

_____. "Le fasi più recenti del dialogo Cattolico-ortodosso 1988–1995". In *La Chiesa cattolica oggi nel dialogo. Corso breve di ecumenismo*, X. Rome, 1995, 7–26.

Freitag, J. "Vorrang der Universalkirche? Ecclesia *in* et *ex* Ecclesiis— Ecclesiae *in* et *ex* Ecclesia? Zum Streit um den Communio-Charakter der Kirche aus der Sicht einer eucharistischen Ekklesiologie". *Ökumenische Rundschau* 44 (1995): 74–92.

Frost, F. "Orthodoxie". In *Catholicisme: Hier—aujourd'hui—demain*. Paris, 1985, 10: 286–304.

Gahbauer F. R. *Die Pentarchie-Theorie. Ein Modell der Kirchenleitung von den Anfängen bis zur Gegenwart*. Frankfurt am Main, 1993.

Galeota, G., and A. Mancia, "La comunione anglicana in dialogo. Sulla Lambeth Conference 1988". *Asprenas* 36 (1989): 50–68.

Galitis, G. "Gli aspetti ecclesiologici del dialogo teologico nella Commissione mista internazionale cattolico-ortodossa". *Nicolaus* 19 (1992): 191–99.

Garijo-Guembe, M. M. "Die Antwort der Glaubenskongregation auf die Dokumente der anglikanisch/römisch-katholischen internationalen Kommission". *Ökumenische Rundschau* 42 (1993): 32–51.

_____. "Schwesterkirchen im Dialog". *Catholica* 48 (1994): 279–93.

_____. "Unità nella diversità. Riflessioni sui modelli di unità alla luce dei recenti accordi ecumenici". *Studi ecumenici* 13 (1995): 167–83.

Garuti, A. *Il Papa Patriarca d'Occidente. Studio storico dottrinale*. Bologna, 1990.

_____. *S. Pietro unico titolare del primato: A proposito del decreto del S. Uffizio del 24 gennaio 1647*. Bologna, 1993.

Garvey, J. "Orthodox/Roman Catholic Relations Today". *Doctrine and Life* 45 (1995): 140–47.

Gherardini, B. *Creatura Verbi. La Chiesa nella teologia di Martin Lutero*. Rome, 1994.

Ghikas, E. "Comment 'redresser' les définitions du premier concile du Vatican". *Irénikon* 68 (1995): 163–204.

Gianazza, P. G. "Documenti del dialogo ecumenico ufficiale cattolico-ortodosso". *Nicolaus* 23 (1996): 319–57.

Gómez-Iglesia, C. U. "Il ministero petrino alle soglie del terzo millennio". *Ius Ecclesiae* 8 (1996): 629–62.

Gonzáles Montes, A. "Dos propuestas de eclesiología ecuménica". *Diálogo Ecuménico* 31 (1996): 421–35.

_____. "Il tema nel dialogo della Chiesa cattolica con le confessioni protestanti". In Rodríguez, *L'ecclesiologia trent'anni dopo la "Lumen Gentium"*, 237–50.

Granberg, G. "Prospettiva luterana sul Vescovo di Roma". *Il Vescovo di Roma nella Chiesa universale. Breve Corso di ecumenismo*, VIII. Rome, 1987: 93–98.

Grandfield, P. *The Papacy in Transition*. Dublin, 1981.

Greatrex, J. "*Koinônia* as the Key to the Church's Self-Understanding and to Ecumenical Rapprochement". In Evans and Gourgues, *Communion et réunion*, 149–56.

Greenacre, R. T. "Lettre ouverte à quelques amis catholiques". *Istina* 38 (1993): 117–33.

———. "La signification des Églises orientales catholiques au sein de la communion romaine dans la perspective de 'l'Église anglicane unie non absorbée'". *Irénikon* 65 (1992): 339–51.

Haase, W., ed. *Rome and the Anglicans. Historical and Doctrinal Aspects of Anglican-Roman Catholic Relations*. Berlin and New York, 1982.

Hale, R. *Canterbury and Rome: Sister Churches*. London, 1982.

Henn, W. "Commentary on the Gift of Authority". IS, no. 100 (1999): 30–42.

———. "Historical-Theological Synthesis of the Relation between Primacy and Episcopacy During the Second Millennium". In *Il primato del successore di Pietro*, 222–73.

Hill, C. "The Fundamental Question of Ecumenical Method". In C. Hill and E. Yarnold, *Anglicans and Roman Catholics*, 222–36.

———. "Récents documents romains et oecumémisme de Vatican II. Perspective anglicane". *Irénikon* 66 (1993): 52–67.

Hill, C., and E. Yarnold. *Anglicans and Roman Catholics: The Search for Unity*. London, 1994.

Hind, J. "Primato e unità. Un contributo anglicano a un dialogo paziente e fraterno". *Studi ecumenici* 17 (1999): 47–72.

Houtepen, A. "Superare la storia con la storia. Verso una revisione degli anatemi del passato". *Studi ecumenici* 13 (1995): 186–93.

Hryniewicz, W. "Labour and Hope. Fifteen Years of Catholic-Orthodox Dialogue". *St. Vladimir's Theological Quarterly* 39 (1995): 339–60.

———. "Reconciliation and Ecclesiology of Sister Churches". *Eastern Churches Journal* vol. 2, no. 3 (1995): 55–72.

Hünermann, P., comp. *Papato ed ecumenismo. Il ministero petrino al servizio dell'unità*. Bologna, 1999.

Jacobsen, I. "Le Chiese luterane dal 1530 ai nostri giorni". *Conosciamo i fratelli. Corso breve di ecumenismo*, II. Rome, 1993, 71–122.

Jäger, D. M. A. "L'autorità del vescovo in prospettiva conciliare: dimensioni sacramentale e comunionale". *Nicolaus* 18 (1991): 89–113.

Karavidopoulos, J. "Le rôle de Pierre et son importance dans l'Église du Nouveau Testament: problématique exégétique contemporaine". *Nicolaus* 19 (1992): 13–29.

Kasper, W. "Das Petrusamt als Dienst der Einheit. Die Lehre des I. und II. Vatikanischen Konzils und die gegenwärtige Diskussion". In *Das Papstamt. Dienst oder Hindernis für die Ökumene*, 113–38.

Kauchtschischwili, N. "La Russia e Roma. Alcune riflessioni sui rapporti ecumenici tra chiese cattolica e ortodossa". *Cristianesimo nella storia* 17 (1996): 121–52.

Kemp, E. "Fede, ordine e strutture ecclesiastiche nell'Anglicanesimo". In Alzati, *L'anglicanesimo*, 237–47.

Klausnitzer, W. " 'Der Papst ... ist zweifelsohne das größte Hindernis auf dem Weg der Ökumene' (Paul VI)". *Catholica* 50 (1996): 193–209.

_____. *Das Papstamt im Disput zwischen Lutheranern und Katholiken*. Innsbruck and Vienna, 1987.

_____. "Das Papstamt—personaler Dienst an der gesamtkirchlichen Einheit. Ein Blick aus der römisch-katholischer Sicht". *Catholica* 51 (1997): 85–97.

Knoche, H. "Der Petrusdienst für die Einheit der Kirche. Biblische Grundlagen und heutiger Stand der ökumenischen Diskussion". *Baustein für die Einheit der Kirche* 36 (1996): 9–19.

Koch, K. "Einheit der Christen—Einheit Europas. Chancen und Grenzen". *Catholica* 48 (1994): 213–29.

Kramer, F. "An Understanding of Papal Primacy". In Empie and Murphy, *Papal Primacy* (LCD V), 127–33.

Kruse, M. "Die ökumenische Zukunft des Petrusdienstes aus lutherischer Sicht". *Theologische Quartalschrift* 178 (1998): 111–17.

Kühn, U. "Gesamtkirchlicher Petrusdienst? Evangelische Erwartungen". *Una Sancta* 53 (1998): 30–39.

_____. "Papsttum und Petrusdienst. Evangelische Kritik und Möglichkeiten aus der Sicht reformatorischer Theologie". *Catholica* 50 (1996): 181–92.

Lago Alba, L. "Y. Congar, Ecumenista. I. Diálogo con el Protestantismo". *Ciencia tomista* 87 (1996): 149–86.

Langevin, G. "Sinthèse de la tradition doctrinale sur la primauté du successeur de Pierre durant le second millénaire". In *Il primato del successore di Pietro*, 147–68.

Lanne, E. "Aspects ecclésiologiques du dialogue théologique mené par la Commission mixte internationale catholique-orthodoxe". *Nicolaus* 19 (1992): 179–89.

_____. "Catholiques et Orthodoxes. Un dialogue exigeant à un tournant capital". *Nouvelle Revue théologique* 107 (1985): 87–100.

_____. "Églises soeurs. Implications ecclésiologiques du Tomos Agapis". *Istina* 20 (1975): 47–74.

_____. "Le mystère de l'Église dans la perspective de la théologie orthodoxe". In *Tradition et communion des Églises. Accueil d'études*. Louvain, 1997, 413–47.

_____. "Présentation du Colloque de Chevetogne 1992. Les Églises orientales catholiques et l'oecuménisme. Aspects ecclésiologiques du thème". *Irénikon* 65 (1992): 307–24.

_____. "Une même foi, une même communion. A propos du dialogue théologique entre Orthodoxes et Catholiques". *Irénikon* 59 (1986): 338–51.

Legrand, H. "Une éventuelle relance de l'uniatisme pourrait-elle s'appuyer sur Vatican II. Quelques enjeux ecclésiologiques de la crise actuelle autour des Églises unies". *Irénikon* 66 (1993): 7–37.

Lehmann, K. "Grundlinien und Probleme des ökumenischen Petrusdienstes". In *Das Petrusamt*, 129–49.

Lehmann, K., and W. Pannenberg, eds. *The Condemnations of the Reformation Era: Do They Still Divide?* Minneapolis, 1990.

Leuba, J.-L., ed. *Perspectives actuelles sur l'oecumenisme*. Louvain-la-Neuve, 1995.

Lindbeck, G. A. "Papacy and *Ius divinum*: A Lutheran View". Empie and Murphy, *Papal Primacy* (LCD V): 193–208.

Loades, D. M., "Relations between the Anglican and Roman Catholic Churches in the 16th and 17th Centuries". In Haase, *Rome and the Anglicans*, 1–53.

Lossky, N. "Conciliarité: Que pourrait être la contribution orthodoxe à l'oecuménisme?" In Leuba, *Perspectives actuelles sur l'oecuménisme*, 131–39.

_____. "L'ecclésiologie dans une perspective orthodoxe". *Science et Esprit* 48 (1996): 7–14.

———. "La présence orthodoxe dans la 'diaspora' et ses implications ecclésiologiques, de même que celles des Églises orientales catholiques".
Irénikon 65 (1992): 354–62.

Lovsky, F. *Un passé de division. Une promesse d'unité.* Paris, 1990.

Lozza, L. "Accoglienza e commenti all'enciclica 'Ut unum sint' da parte delle
Chiese e comunità cristiane non cattoliche". *Unitas* 50 (1995): 154–65.

Lüning, P. "Das ekklesiologische Problem des 'Subsistit in' (LG 8) im
heutigen ökumenischen Gespräch". *Catholica* 52 (1998): 1–23.

Madrigal, S. " 'Proesis ut prosis': Consideraciones en torno a la Encíclica
Ut unum sint". *Miscellánea Comillas* 55 (1997): 391–403.

Maffeis, A. "La giustificazione nel dialogo ecumenico. Chiarificazioni e
nodi irrisolti". *Rassegna di teologia* 37 (1996): 623–45.

Magrassi, M. "Monaco: una risposta cattolica". *Nicolaus* 11 (1983): 345–46.

Manna, S. *Il dibattito sul primato romano. Il papa segno di unione fra chiesa
locale e chiesa universale.* Bari, 1985.

———. "La koinonia nei documenti della Commissione mista cattolico-
ortodossa". *Studi ecumenici* 12 (1994): 331–41.

———. "L'oecuméniste. Les colloques catholiques-orthodoxes de l'institut
de théologie oecuménique Saint-Nicolas de Bari—La contribution du
P. Tillard". In Evans and Gourgues, *Communion et réunion*, 47–59.

———. "Quale la recezione effettiva seguita ai dialoghi della Commissione mista cattolico-ortodossa?" *Nicolaus* 20 (1993): 56–76.

Martensen, D. F. "Ministry". In Burgess, *Lutherans in Ecumenical Dialogue*,
123–35.

Maviiri Ndidde, J. C. *Primacy in the Communion of Churches.* Rome, 1987.

Maxime de Sardes, Metropolitan. *Le patriacat oecuménique dans l'Église orthodoxe.* Paris, 1975.

McAdoo, H. R. "Anglican/Roman Catholic Relations, 1717–1980: A
Detection of Themes". In Haase, *Rome and the Anglicans*, 143–281.

McDonald, K. M. "Appendice. Comunione anglicana e Chiesa Cattolico-
Romana negli anni 1985–1991". In Alzati, *L'anglicanesimo*, 373–84.

McDonnell, K. "A Year Afterwards: The Vatican Response to ARCIC, a
Slammed Door?". *One in Christ* 29 (1993): 113–17.

McHugh, J. "Marginal Notes on the Response to ARCIC I". In Hill and
Yarnold, *Anglicans and Roman Catholics*, 324–31.

McNeil, J.-T. "The Ecumenical Idea and Efforts to Realize It, 1517–
1618". In R. Rouse and S. C. Neill, eds., *A History of the Ecumenical
Movement 1517–1948*, Philadelphia, 1954, 27–62.

McPartlan, P. "La papauté dans le dialogue entre catholiques et ortho-doxes". *Communio* 21/2 (1996): 111–20.

Mehl, R. "Protestantism". In DEM 830a–37b.

Melia, E. "La Pentarchie". *Istina* 32 (1987): 341–60.

Melling, D. J. "The Right Path". *Eastern Churches Journal* 2, no. 2 (1995): 165–73.

Meyendorff, J. "Églises soeurs. Implications ecclésiologiques du Tomos Agapis". *Istina* 20 (1975): 35–46.

Meyer, H. "La Chiesa Popolo di Dio, Corpo di Cristo, Tempio dello Spirito Santo, nel dialogo tra la Chiesa cattolica romana e le confessioni protestanti. Una prospettiva luterana". In Rodríguez, *L'ecclesiologia trent'anni dopo la "Lumen Gentium"*, 65–111.

———. "Ein evangeliumsgemäßes Papstampt. Kritik und Forderung aus reformatorischen Sicht". In *Das Papstamt: Dienst oder Hindernis für die Ökumene?* Regensburg, 1985, 65–111.

———. "Das Problem des Petrusamtes in evangelischer Sicht". In K. Lehmann, ed., *Das Petrusamt. Geschichtliche Stationen seines Verständnisses und gegenwärtige Positionen.* Freiburg, 1982, 110–28.

———. "L'ufficio papale nella visuale luterana". In *Papato e servizio petrino*. Alba, 1976, 61–80.

Mikulanis, D. L. *Authority in the Church from the Perspective of Recent Anglican / Roman Catholic Dialogue* (Rome, 1986).

Morerod, C. "Réflexions sur l'Accord de Porvoo entre Anglicans et Luthériens". *Nova et Vetera*. No. 3 (1997), 71–103.

Neill, S. C. "Division and Search for Unity Prior to the Reformation". In *A History of the Ecumenical Movement 1517–1948*. Philadelphia, 1954, 1–24.

Neumann, B. "Das Papstamt in den offiziellen ökumenischen Dialogen". *Catholica* 50 (1996): 87–120.

Neuner, P. *Ökumenische Theologie*. Darmstadt, 1997.

Nichols, A. *The Panther and the Hind: A Theological History of Anglicanism.* Edinburgh, 1993.

Ols, D. "Diversités et communion. Réflexions à propos d'un ouvrage récent". *Angelicum* 60 (1983): 122–80.

Pannenberg, W. "Le ministère ecclésial et l'unité de l'Église". *Istina* 40 (1995): 190–201.

———. "Riflessioni evangeliche sul ministero petrino del Vescovo di Roma". In Hünermann, *Papato ed ecumenismo*, 39–53.

———. *Systematic Theology*. Vol. 3. Grand Rapids, Mich., 1998.

Papadopoulos, A. "L'istituzione conciliare. Il suo carattere carismatico e unificatore: una considerazione ortodossa". *Nicolaus* 19 (1992): 285–96.

Papandreu, D. "Riflessioni sulla questione del primato". In *Papato e servizio petrino*, 81–86.

Papathomas, G. D. "Les différentes modalités d'exercice de la juridiction du Patriarcat de Constantinople". *Istina* 40 (1995): 369–85.

Patsavos, L. J. "The Synodal Structure of the Church". *St. Vladimir's Theological Quarterly* 39 (1995): 71–98.

Peri, V. "All'alba del terzo millennio, abbiamo il diritto di rimanere divisi? Cronaca ecclesiologica di un quindicennio ecumenico tra Cattolici ed Ortodossi". *Anuario de Historia de la Iglesia* 5 (1996): 467–79.

————. *Orientalis Varietas. Roma e le Chiese d'Oriente—Storia e Diritto canonico*. Rome, 1994.

————. *Lo scambio fraterno tra le Chiese. Componenti storiche della comunione*. Vatican City, 1993.

Pesch, R. "Was an Petrus sichtbar war, ist in den Primat eingegangen". In *Il primato del successore di Pietro*, 22–114.

Phidas, V. "La notion de primauté papale dans la tradition canonique orthodoxe". *Nicolaus* 19 (1992): 1–41.

Pié i Ninot, S. *La sinodalitat eclesial*. Barcelona, 1993.

Piepkorn, A. C. "Ius divinum and Adiaphoron in Relation to Structural Problems in the Church: The Position of the Lutheran Symbolica Books". In Empie and Murphy, *Papal Primacy and the Universal Church* (LCD V), 119–27.

Pottmeyer, H. J. "Papato e communio ecclesiarum. Il Vaticano I nel Vaticano II—vie per un'intesa ecumenica". In *Papato e istanze ecumeniche*, 127–46.

————. *Towards a Papacy in Communion. Perspectives from Vatican Councils I & II*. New York, 1998.

Poustooitov, J. "La justification ecclésiologique de l'idée 'Nation chrétienne' et coexistence des Églises dans un même lieu". *Irénikon* 65 (1992): 387–99.

Purdy, W. A. "Il dialogo tra cattolici e anglicani. Panorama e prospettive". *La Chiesa cattolica oggi nel dialogo. Corso breve di ecumenismo*, IV. Rome, 1982, 27–40.

Radano, J. A. " 'Ut unum sint'. The Ministry of Unity of the Bishop of Rome". *Angelicum* 73 (1996): 325–59.

Radu, D. "Autorité et conciliarité dans la pratique actuelle de l'église: convergences et tensions". *Nicolaus* 18 (1991): 277–304.

Raem, H. A. "Dialog ohne Ende? Hermeneutische Überlegungen zur 'Gemeinsamen Erklärung des Lutherischen Weltbundes und der römisch-katholischen Kirche zur Rechtfertigungslehre'". *Catholica* 50 (1996): 232–46.

_____. "The Third Phase of the Lutheran/Catholic Dialogue (1986–1993)". IS, no. 86 (1994): 189–97.

Ramsey, M. *The Gospel and the Catholic Church.* London, New York, and Toronto, 1936.

Ratzinger, J. "Anglican-Catholic Dialogue: Its Problems and Hopes". *Insight* 1 (1983): 2–11.

_____. *Called to Communion. Undersanding the Church Today.* San Francisco, 1996.

_____. *Church, Ecumenism and Politics. New Essays in Ecclesiology.* Middlegree and Slough, 1988.

_____. *Principles of Catholic Theology. Building Stones for a Fundamental Theology.* San Francisco, 1987.

Rausch, T. P. "Present State of Anglican-Roman Catholic Relations: An Assessment". *One in Christ* 29 (1993): 118–25.

Reinhardt, H. J. F. "Zur Frage der (Selbst-) Beschränkung des päpstlichen Jurisdiktionprimats im Hinblick auf die nichtkatholischen Christen. Kanonistische Erwägungen". *Catholica* 51 (1997): 255–63.

Ricca, P. "La Papauté en discussion. Attentes et perspectives pour le III millénaire". *Irénikon* 70 (1997): 30–40.

Riedel-Spangenberger, I. "Im Wesentlichen einig? Die Primatausübung des Papstes im ökumenischen Gespräch". *Herder Korrespondenz* 49 (1995): 658–64.

Robertson, R. G. *The Eastern Christian Churches,* Rome, 1990.

Rodríguez, P., comp. *L'ecclesiologia trent'anni dopo la "Lumen Gentium".* Rome, 1995.

Romita, A. "Criteri per la recezione ecclesiale dei documenti del dialogo teologico tra la Chiesa Cattolico-Romana e la Chiesa Ortodossa". *Nicolaus* 22 (1995): 175–89.

Root, H. "Gli anglicani", *Conosciamo i fratelli. Corso breve di ecumenismo,* II. Rome, 1993, 169–88.

_____. "Prospettiva anglicana sul Vescovo di Roma". *Il Vescovo di Roma nella Chiesa universale. Corso breve di ecumenismo,* VIII. Rome, 1987, 85–92.

————. "Some Remarks on the Response to ARCIC I". In Evans and Gourgues, *Communion et Réunion*, 165–76.

Salachas, D. *Il dialogo teologico ufficiale tra la Chiesa Cattolico-romana e la chiesa ortodossa. Iter e documentazione*. Bari, 1994.

————. "Les Églises soeurs Catholique-Romaine et Orthodoxe en dialogue théologique officiel. Réflexions.—Perspectives—Problèmes". *Nicolaus* 9 (1982): 105–6.

Sartori, L. "Battesimo e unità della Chiesa. Un unico battesimo, un'unica Chiesa?". *Studi ecumenici* 13 (1995): 59–72.

————. "Ecumenismo nel terzo millennio. Considerazioni sull'enciclica 'Ut unum sint'". *Studia patavina* 42 (1995): 627–50.

Schatz, K. *Papal Primacy. From Its Origins to the Present*. Collegeville, Minn., 1996.

————. "Primat und Kollegialität. Eine geschichtliche Skizze ihres Verhältnisses". *Internationale katholische Zeitschrift Communio* 27 (1998): 289–309.

Scheffzyk, L. *La Chiesa. Aspetti della crisi postconciliare e corretta interpretazione del Vaticano II*. Milan, 1998.

Schneider, T. "The Dialog Report in the Present Ecumenical Context: A Comment on 'Church and Justification'". Pontifical Council for Promoting Christian Unity, IS, no. 86 (1994): 182–88.

Schultze, B. "Il Vaticano II e Paolo VI di fronte al dilemma: 'Chiese sorelle o Chiese unite?'". *Unitas* 31 (1976): 81–106.

Schulz, H. J. "Église locale et Église universelle. Primauté, Collégialité et Synodalité". *Proche-Orient Chrétien* 31 (1981): 3–22.

Schütte, H. *La Chiesa nella comprensione ecumenica*. Padua, 1995.

————. "Das 'revolutionäre Angebot' in der Ökumene-Enzyklika. Gedanken zu einer Verständigung über das Dienstamt der Einheit". *Bausteine für die Einheit der Christen* 36 (1996): 19–24.

Spiteris, J. *La Critica Bizantina del Primato Romano nel secolo XII*. Rome, 1979.

Spiteris, Y. "La Chiesa ortodossa riconosce veramente quella cattolica come 'Chiesa sorella'? Il punto di vista della tradizione teologica ed ecclesiale greca". *Studi ecumenici* 14 (1996): 43–82.

Stacpoole, A. "Cordial Relations between Rome and Canterbury. First Phase, 1944–1945". *One in Christ* 23 (1987): 212–34.

————. "Pre-ARCIC Conversations between Anglicans and Roman Catholics, 1950". *One in Christ* 23 (1987): 298–323.

Stavridis, B. "L'Autorité du patriarche oecuménique dans la vie de l'Église orthodoxe". *Istina* 40 (1995): 357–68.

Stewart, R. "Il dialogo tra Comunione Anglicana e Chiesa Cattolico-Romana nel quadro del movimento ecumenico". In Alzati, *L'anglicanesimo*, 353–72.

Stirnimann, H. "Papato e servizio petrino. Riflessioni critiche". *Papato e servizio petrino*, 15–40.

Stirnimann, H., and L. Vischer, comps. *Papato e servizio petrino*. Alba, 1976.

Stormon, E. J., ed. *Towards the Healing of Schism*. New York, 1987.

Strukelj, A. "La comprensione ecumenica nell'ecclesiologia ortodossa del teologo serbo Justin Popovic". *Nicolaus* 23 (1996): 73–116.

Sullivan, F. "The Vatican Response to ARCIC I (1992), *Gregorianum* 73 (1992): 489–90.

———. "Per un rinnovamento del ministero del Vescovo di Roma: principio di legittima diversità, collegialità, sussidiarietà". *Nicolaus* 19 (1992): 43–53.

Suttner, E. C. "Warum getrennte Schwesterkirchen?". *Stimmen der Zeit* 120 (1995): 271–77.

Sykes, S. W. (ed.). *Authority in the Anglican Communion*. Toronto, 1987.

Tanner, M. "The Anglican Position on Apostolic Continuity and Apostolic Succession in the Porvoo Common Statement". *Louvain Studies* 21 (1996): 114–25.

Tavard, G. "ARCIC-I on Authority". In Evans and Gourgues, *Communion et Réunion*, 185–98.

———. "Considerations on an Ecclesiology of *Koinonia*". *One in Christ* 31 (1995): 42–51.

———. *La poursuite de la catholicité. Étude sur la pensée anglicane*. Paris, 1965.

———. *The Quest for Catholicity. A Study in Anglicanism*. New York, 1964.

———. "What Is the Petrine Function?" In Empie and Murphy, *Papal Primacy* (LCD V), 208–12.

Tillard, J.-M. R. "Canterbury and Rome: So Near, So Far". *One in Christ* 25 (1989): 139–52.

———. *Church of Churches: The Ecclesiology of Communion*. Collegeville, Minn., 1992.

———. "Église catholique et dialogues bilatéraux". *Irénikon* 56 (1983): 5–19.

————. *L'Église locale. Ecclésiologie de communion et catholicité.* Paris, 1995.

————. "L'expression de la foi". *Proche-Orient Chrétien* 28 (1978): 193–201.

————. "Faire émerger la Communion: L'option de l'ARCIC-I". In Denaux and Dick, *From Malines to ARCIC*, 165–66.

————. "La juridiction de l'évêque de Rome". *Irénikon* 51 (1978): 358–73.

————. "Le ministère d'unité". *Istina* 40 (1995): 202–16.

————. "The Presence of Peter in the Ministry of the Bishop of Rome". *One in Christ* 27 (1991): 101–20.

————. "La primauté romaine . . . jamais pour éroder les structures des Églises locales". *Irénikon* 50 (1977): 291–325.

————. "Une seule Église de Dieu: l'Église brisée". *Proche-Orient Chrétien* 30 (1980): 3–13.

————. "La tension entre primauté du Siège romain et conciliarité". *Nicolaus* 19 (1992): 275–83.

Valentini, D. "Il ministero di unità del Papa nei testi ufficiali di 'consenso' ecumenico". In *Dialoghi ecumenici ufficiali: Bilanci e prospettive.* Rome, 1993, 101–32.

————. *Il nuovo Popolo di Dio in cammino: Punti nodali per una ecclesiologia attuale.* Rome, 1984.

Van De Pol, W. H. *La Communion anglicane et l'oecuménisme d'après les documents officiels.* Paris, 1967.

Various authors. *Konziliarität und Kollegialität: Das Petrusamt—Christus und seine Kirche.* Pro Oriente, Innsbruck, 1975.

Various authors. *Papsttum als ökumenische Frage.* Munich and Mainz, 1979.

Various authors. *Das Papstamt: Dienst oder Hindernis für die Ökumene?.* Regensburg, 1985.

Vercruysse, J. *Introduzione alla teologia ecumenica.* Casale Monferrato, 1992.

Villar, J. R. "La teologia ortodossa della Chiesa locale". In Rodríguez, *L'ecclesiologia trent'anni dopo la "Lumen Gentium"*, 201–23.

Vischer, L. "Pietro e il Vescovo di Roma. I loro rispettivi servizi nella Chiesa". In *Papato e servizio petrino*, 41–59.

von Allmen, J. J. "Ministero papale ministero di unità". *Concilium* 11 (1975): 1362–70.

————. *Il primato della Chiesa di Pietro e di Paolo.* Brescia, 1982.

Wainwright, G. "La confession et les confessions: vers l'unité confessionnelle et confessante des chrétiens". *Irénikon* 57 (1984): 5–25.

Ware, K. T. "L'exercice de l'autorité dans l'Église orthodoxe". *Irénikon* 54 (1981): 451–71, and 55 (1982): 25–35.

_____. *The Orthodox Church*. New York, 1993.

Wenz, G. " 'Est autem ...' . Lumen Gentium 8 und die Kirchenartikel der Confessio Augustana". *Catholica* 52 (1998): 24–43.

Wright, J. M. "An Anglican Comment on Papal Authority in Light of Recent Developments". In Sykes, *Authority in the Anglican Communion*, 236–63.

Zoghby, E. *Tous schismatiques?* Beirut, 1981.

INTRODUCTION

Pope John Paul II, in his address to the World Council of Churches in Geneva on June 12, 1984, stated that the Catholic Church "is convinced that in the ministry of the Bishop of Rome it has preserved the visible pole and guarantee of unity in full fidelity to the apostolic tradition and to the faith of the Fathers", while acknowledging frankly that this conviction constituted "a difficulty for most of you".[1] Three years later, on December 6, 1987, in St. Peter's Basilica in Vatican City, in the course of his homily at a Mass celebrated in the presence of the Ecumenical Patriarch Demetrios I, after declaring emphatically this same conviction, the Holy Father proposed a joint inquiry into forms of exercising this ministry which would allow it to be recognized by all.[2]

Both of these concepts are taken up again in the encyclical letter *Ut unum sint* (May 25, 1995). While noting that the Catholic Church is aware that "she has preserved" among all the Churches and ecclesial communities "the ministry of the Successor of the Apostle Peter, the Bishop of Rome", the Pope recalls what he said at the World Council of Churches about the difficulty constituted by this ministry[3] and declares himself ready to heed the request made to him "to find a way of exercising the primacy which, while in no way renouncing what is essential to its mission, is nonetheless open to a new situation". Then, taking up again the words spoken to Patriarch Demetrios,[4] he concludes with an invitation to patient fraternal dialogue—expressed more emphatically in the form of a question:

---

[1] IS, no. 55 (1984), 39a–b.

[2] "I am aware that, for a great variety of reasons and against the will of all concerned, what should have been a service sometimes manifested itself in a very different light.... Thus, in view of this perfect communion which we wish to reestablish, I insistently pray the Holy Spirit to shine his light upon us, enlightening all of the pastors and theologians of our churches, that we may seek—together, of course—the forms in which this ministry may accomplish a service of love recognized by all concerned" (IS, no. 66 [1988], 25b).

[3] *Ut unum sint*, no. 88.

[4] Cf. ibid., no. 95.

"Could not the real but imperfect communion existing between us persuade Church leaders and their theologians to engage with me in a patient and fraternal dialogue on this subject, a dialogue in which, leaving useless controversies behind, we could listen to one another, keeping before us only the will of Christ for his Church . . . ?" [5]

In the General Audience of January 17, 1996, the Holy Father returned again to this invitation, explaining that it was meant to "solve the obvious anomaly of partial communion".[6]

Aware as he is that he cannot relinquish the office of Successor of the Apostle Peter, willed by Christ, since that would be infidelity to the Gospel and to tradition, the Holy Father has made this humble and courageous gesture. Unfortunately, the initial reactions were not terribly encouraging;[7] indeed, some were not very "ecumenical". Apart from L. Vischer's complaint that there had not been prior ecumenical consultation,[8] it was also suggested, for example, that the encyclical did nothing

---

[5] Ibid., no. 96.

[6] IS, no. 93 (1996), no. 4, 136a–b. See also *L'Osservatore Romano*, 18 gennaio 1996, p. 4. The constant concern of Paul VI for ecumenism, especially vis-à-vis the Orthodox Churches, is described in A Garuti, " 'Sister Churches': Reality and Questions" (see Appendix, p. 269, note 41). See also C. Alzati and P. Locati, eds., *L'unità multiforme. Oriente e Occidente nella riflessione di Giovanni Paolo II* (Milan, 1991).

[7] A. Ablondi, "Il 'servizio di Pietro' e le grandi novità", *Vita e pensiero* 78 (1995): 576–77: "Il pastore Pocenscki, segretario generale dell'Alleanza riformata mondiale, dichiara che è impossibile accettare il Papato come simbolo di unità fra i cristiani: mentre Luca Fischer, presidente di Fede e Costituzione, definisce l'enciclica 'un dilemma'. Da una parte, egli dice, la lettera corrisponde alle condizioni accolte dal Consiglio ecumenico delle Chiese, dall'altra la centralità del Papa per l'unità è veramente discutibile. . . . Ancora Teona Spakalis, rappresentante della diocesi greco-ortodosso in Italia, ha espresso l'apprezzamento per l'enciclica, che rappresenta un incoraggiamento al movimento ecumenico fondato sulla verità e sull'amore. Egli ha inoltre precisato che il Primato in campo ortodosso viene visto essenzialmente come Primato d'amore nel servizio. . . . Douglas Brown del Centro anglicano di Roma ha ammirato la necessità di confessione di peccato e di riforma come richiamo continuo alla Chiesa. Non accetta però che la Chiesa cattolica continui a ritenersi l'unica vera e pura Chiesa di Cristo e vede, fra gli altri problemi aperti, quello del Primato papale. . . . Infine Paolo Ricca, preside della Facoltà valdese di Roma . . . con un'affermazione ecumenicamente ardita . . . pensa alla possibilità di una trasformazione in senso ecumenico del Papato, certo a condizione che in qualche modo l'attuale Papato 'muoia e risorga.' "

[8] "Nell'enciclica si affronta la questione del 'ministero dell'unità' del successore di Pietro. Questo, come noto, è proprio uno dei temi più controversi della discussione. Eppure non si è pensato di avviare alcuna considerazione ecumenica prima di intervenire sull'argomento. . . . Questo tema è stato discusso in più occasioni all'interno di varie commissioni di dialogo bilaterale. E tutti sono arrivate alla conclusione che un qualche tipo di 'ministero di unità' può essere utile. A una condizione: che l'accento fondamentale venga posto sul concetto di

more than reaffirm the Roman Catholic perspective on the Petrine ministry[9] and, notwithstanding its openness, manifested in reality a diplomatic and rhetorical way of proceeding.[10] Above all, it became apparent that, on this particular question, the issue is not so much "the manner in which the ministry of the Successor of Peter is to be exercised as much as the existence itself of a particular ministry of the Bishop of Rome with regard to all the churches".[11] It is still said repeatedly that the necessity—by divine right—of communion with Rome as an essential condition for full and visible communion cannot be accepted either by the Orthodox or by the Protestants.[12]

In the light of these reactions, which certainly do not present a very reassuring picture,[13] and in order to gain a perspective on the current situation, which is necessarily the point of departure for the invitation by Pope John Paul II, a presentation and evaluation of the results achieved thus far by the theological dialogue on the problem of the primacy of the Bishop of Rome will be helpful.

'comunione di chiese' e che il ruolo del vescovo di Roma sia reinterpretato alla luce del carattere 'conciliare' della Chiesa.... Dopo la pubblicazione di questa enciclica, insomma, bisognerà riflettere sulla differenza esistente tra il modo in cui il primato del Papa è esercitato oggi nella Chiesa cattolica e la visione ecumenica del ministero dell'unità" (*Jesus*, July 1995, 21).

[9] J. Moltmann, "Has the Papacy an Ecumenical Future?" *Concilium*, English edition 1995, no. 5, 135–37. It is hard to understand how the author can continue to wonder, "Does the papacy have an ecumenical future as long as the Pope is at the same time a head of state?" (p. 136).

[10] Cf. J. Panagopulos, "*Ut unum sint*: Remarks on the New Papal Encyclical from an Orthodox Perspective", ibid., 137–40.

[11] Cf. the editorial in *La Civiltà Cattolica*, 1995 II. Also in the editorial in *Irénikon* 69 (1996): 162, beyond the attractiveness of the invitation, strong reservations were noted "car on estime que ce n'est pas seulement la manière d'exercer la primauté. Telle est, en particulier, la réaction de nombreux Orthodoxes."

[12] Cf. P. Ricca, "La Papauté en discussion: Attentes et perspectives pour le IIIe millénaire", *Irénikon* 70 (1997): 34.

[13] According to W. Seibel, the first reactions to the Pope's invitation "geben leider wenig Hoffnung"; see "Eine Chance der Ökumene", *Stimmen der Zeit* 36 (1995): 505; even less optimism is shown by the author (F. K.) of the comment entitled "Commitment to Ecumenism", which appeared in *New Blackfriars* 76 (1995): 366–67. On a more hopeful note are the contributions of J. A. Radano, "*Ut unum sint*: The Ministry of Unity of the Bishop of Rome", *Angelicum* 73 (1996), 327–29; P. McPartlan, "La papauté dans le dialogue entre catholiques et orthodoxes", *Communio* 21/2 (1996): 111–20, and most of all L. Lozza, "Accoglienza e commenti all'enciclica '*Ut unum sint*' da parte delle Chiese e comunità cristiane non cattoliche", *Unitas* 50 (1995): 154–65.

In order to give our study the proper structure, it is necessary to begin with a general presentation of the problem connected with the topic of the primacy[14] together with the proposals put forward by Catholic, Orthodox, and Protestant authors for overcoming it (Chapter I). Then follows an exposition of the results which have come from the various ecumenical dialogues: Catholic-Orthodox (Chapter II), Catholic-Lutheran (Chapter III), and Catholic-Anglican (Chapter IV). Each of these will be presented in more or less the same format: a description of how the primacy is viewed in the respective Churches or non-Catholic ecclesial communities, followed by an analysis of the documents of the ecumenical dialogue, and a critical evaluation of the results that have been obtained.

---

[14] I limit my discussion to the question of the primacy of jurisdiction.

CHAPTER I

THE PRIMACY AS AN ECUMENICAL PROBLEM

IT WAS PAUL VI who, with great incisiveness, highlighted the problems posed by his own ministry along the path of ecumenism. However, he was also the true initiator of the "dialogue of charity" and of the "dialogue of truth". In fact, in his address to the members of the Secretariat for the Unity of Christians (April 28, 1967) he openly stated, "The Pope, as we well know, is undoubtedly the greatest obstacle on the path of ecumenism." [1]

These words generated a great deal of comment in special issues of journals and reviews,[2] and above all in interconfessional inquiries and

---

[1] IS, no. 2 (1967), 4. Already in the encyclical *Ecclesiam suam* (March 6, 1964), the same Pope had said, "That We, who promote this reconciliation, should be regarded by many of Our separated brothers as an obstacle to it, is a matter of deep distress to Us. The obstacle would seem to be the primacy of honor and jurisdiction which Christ bestowed on the Apostle Peter, and which We have inherited as his Successor. Are there not those who say that unity between the separated Churches and the Catholic Church would be more easily achieved if the primacy of the Roman Pontiff were done away with?": *The Pope Speaks* 9 (1964): 289–90. See also General Audience of January 18, 1967 (Ins. V 679); Angelus of January 18, 1970, and General Audience of January 21, 1970 (Ins. VIII 50 and 60).

Already before him, Patriarch Maximos IV Saigh of Antioch of the Melchites, during the general assembly of the Council on October 7, 1963, asked that the Roman Catholic Church renounce the "abusive interpretations" of the dogma of the primacy of the Roman Pontiff, that she liberate herself from the "doctrinal and practical exaggerations", so that this dogma might cease to be the "main stumbling block" on the path of the unity of Christians. See AS II/II, 238. Cited by J.J. von Allmen, "Ministero papale ministero di unità", *Concilium* (Ital. ed. 1975, no. 8), 131. On the role played by Paul VI in the field of ecumenism, cf. Garuti, "Sister Churches", Appendix pp. 268–72 below.

[2] Cf., for example, *Concilium* (French ed.), no. 54 (1970); *Concilium* (Italian ed.), no. 8 (1975); *Catholica*, no. 3/4 (1976) and no. 1 (1977).

symposia.[3] These produced an "awareness of the difficulty arising from the existence of the papacy, and it was repeatedly affirmed that the role of the papacy in the Catholic Church constituted the greatest obstacle on the path toward the unity of Christians".[4] In fact, it is often repeated, as a refrain, that the primacy is regarded by all confessions as constituting the main doctrinal difficulty for the union of Churches,[5] a sort of boulder that blocks its path,[6] insofar as it has sometimes "played a decisive role, fraught with responsibility, in the rise of the fatal divisions which are found within the bosom of Christianity".[7] It is "a particularly controversial issue, and consequently as long as this divergence of opinion is not dealt with and clarified, all dialogues about the differences between the Churches will have something of a fictitious nature, but especially because the differing notions about this issue impede the common testimony of the Churches".[8]

---

[3] Cf., for example, "Das Petrusamt in ökumenischer Sicht", *Konziliarität und Kollegialität. Das Petrusamt. Christus und seine Kirche* (Pro Oriente, Innsbruck, 1975), 111–72; G. Denzler, ed., *Papsttum—heute und morgen. Eine Umfrage* (Regensburg, 1975); *Papsttum als ökumenische Frage* (Munich and Mainz, 1979), Acts of a Congress held in Heidelberg in October 1977; *Das Papsttamt: Dienst oder Hindernis für die Ökumene?* (Regensburg, 1985).

[4] Cf. G. Cereti, "Il riconoscimento dei ministeri delle altre chiese", *il regno-att. 6/80*, 141.

[5] B. Tierney, "Modelli storici del papato", *Concilium* 11 (1975): 88: "Il papato moderno è un'istituzione paradossale. Il papa è simbolo dell'unità della chiesa, ma le rivendicazioni della Sede di Roma sono l'ostacolo principale per la riunione delle chiese."

[6] H. Küng, W. Kasper, and J. Remmers, "L'unanimité dans les espoirs et les doléances", an evaluation of the different answers to the question: *Qu'est-ce qui nous sépare encore de l'Église catholique romaine? La papauté, difficulté principale pour l'union oecuménique*: "On ne peut malheureusement pas taire l'unanimité de nos correspondants sur ce point. Rien dans la doctrine ni dans la pratique ne crée, selon eux, autant de difficultés que la papauté pour une union oecuménique des Églises. Elle semble bien être un énorme rocher barrant la voie de la compréhension. Tout en reconnaissant les réformes accomplies sur ce point, l'orthodoxe se plaint de l'évolution du système papal, juridique et centralisateur, surtout depuis le moyen âge, tant dans la production des dogmes que dans la discipline ecclésiastique. Malgré toute sa prédilection pour la tradition catholique, l'anglican critique les structures autoritaires de l'Église catholique dans la doctrine et dans la pratique, structures dont le pape apparaît comme le gardien et le promoteur. En dépit de toute sa compréhension de la situation de l'Église catholique, le luthérien se demande si le pape actuel, dans la mesure où précisément il s'oppose, même dans la doctrine, au renouveau conciliaire par des actes isolés posés en vertu de son pouvoir personnel, peut réellement être considéré comme la voix représentative et seule valable de l'Église catholique" (*Concilium*, French ed. [1970], 52).

[7] Cf. H. Stirnimann, "Papato e servizio petrino. Riflessioni critiche", *Papato e servizio petrino* (Alba, 1976), 17.

[8] Cf. L. Vischer, "Pietro e il Vescovo di Roma. I loro rispettivi servizi nella Chiesa", *Papato e servizio petrino*, 41.

The obstacle constituted by the primacy has been emphasized also in various monographs by individual authors who have pointed out the various aspects of its seriousness[9] and have indicated the crux of the problem by identifying its basis.[10] They have also underscored the unanimous and categorical concurrence of non-Catholics in their rejection of the idea that the exceptional privileges of the primacy can be reserved for one single person.[11] The conclusions that emerge from this are not very promising: "[As a result], the ecclesiology which we [have] presented can—at least in its essentials—be accepted by these Churches [of the East]. But from the time that the chapter on Roman Primacy is opened up, everything is spoiled. It is evident that the problem is complicated because of the groups which were born of the Reformation and its [s]pirit." [12]

At the same time, however, historical and theological studies have helped to create a new atmosphere, one that is less aggressive and polemical, in dealing with the obstacle.[13] This has produced results, both within the

---

[9] R. Coppola, "Primato papale ed ecumenismo", *Nicolaus* 14 (1986): 3–4: Primacy is "una controversa questione, che costituisce un punto nodale nell'ambito dell'odierna teologia ecumenica. Una questione scottante e non facile, con aspetti fondamentali inerenti all'esegesi biblica, all'interpretazione storica ed a quella giuridica, in un insieme che non si esaurisce nella sfera del diritto canonico, ivi compreso il diritto pubblico ecclesiastico esterno."

[10] S. Manna, "L'impegno dell'Istituto ecumenico 'S. Nicola' di Bari nel dialogo", *Nicolaus* 19 (1992): 315: "Il vero nodo della questione, lo si è ripetuto, rimane il *fondamento* del primato del Vescovo di Roma, che, in quanto tale, costituisce un grave ostacolo fra Cattolici, da una parte, Ortodossi e Protestanti, dall'altra." Cf. Manna, *Il dibattito sul primato romano. Il papa segno di unione fra chiesa locale e chiesa universale* (Bari, 1985), 14–24.

[11] P. Dentin, *Les privilèges des Papes devant l'Écriture et l'histoire* (Paris, 1995), 250–51: "Pour les orthodoxes, les luthériens, les réformés, les anglicans, les baptistes, etc., le point de convergence, unanime, catégorique, de tous leurs rejets, c'est la primauté de juridiction universelle du pape et son infaillibilité personnelle. C'est donc essentiellement de la papauté qu'il s'agit, des privilèges exceptionnels réservés à un seul homme." Cf. also L. M. Bermejo, who entitles the first chapter of his book *Infallibility on Trial* (Pune, 1990), "Ecumenical deadlock on the papacy".

[12] J.-M. R. Tillard, *Church of Churches. The Ecclesiology of Communion* (Collegeville, Minn., 1992), 256–57. A. Filippi is no less explicit: "I testi di consenso teologico, elaborati dalle commissioni bilaterali o multilaterali di dialogo, fanno toccare con mano 'una costante': il consenso fra la chiesa cattolica e le altre chiese si è andato via via allargando su quasi tutti i temi, che però si imbottigliano tutti nella strettoia del primato" ("Dopo le divisioni e i dialoghi, mutuo arricchimento", *il regno-att.* 12/95, 368–69).

[13] S. Vartalidis, "Conclusioni del IX colloquio cattolico-ortodosso", *Nicolaus* 19 (1992): 163–64: "un nuovo contesto sembra essersi creato per affrontare questa problematica. Infatti appare smorzata l' 'aggressività' delle Chiese non cattoliche contro il primato romano. Si avverte sempre più la necessità di uscire insieme dalla difficoltà in cui tale argomento sembra essere stato confinato." Tillard also emphasizes the will to reopen the "papacy" dossier,

Catholic Church[14] and outside, at least with regard to the necessity and the existence of the primacy, if only for historical reasons and sociological needs.[15] A distinction is thus made between the reality and its practice: "What is under discussion is not the Papacy in itself (its *Daß*) but the way in which it is exercised (its *Wie*). In other words, the prejudice is no longer against the Papacy, but efforts are now directed towards a new and different kind of Papacy, towards its 'refounding', with emphases that betray, in more than one case, disaffection or opposition to the institution, or which reveal, on the contrary, real scruples about its unthinkableness, or else a more balanced view." [16] Suspicions and hostilities, in any case, still persist, to the point of considering its abolition to be the most effective way to achieve the reunion of Churches.[17]

---

made official by the fifth World Conference on Faith and Constitution: "On est dorénavant fort loin des polémiques sur le pape *Antichristus magnus*. . . . On ne dit plus à la papauté, abruptement, 'nous te refusons'. On lui dit: 'montre-nous si tu es le ministère d'unité que Dieu a donné à son Peuple dans sa *divina providentia'*" ("Le ministère d'unité", *Istina* 40 [1995]: 202).

[14] Cereti, "Il riconoscimento dei ministeri", 141: "Dal punto di vista interno della chiesa cattolica, molti dei rinnovamenti voluti dal Vaticano II hanno cominciato a portare i loro frutti. Il papa ha riscoperto che innanzitutto egli è il vescovo della chiesa locale di Roma. . . . Infine, il servizio papale ha cominciato ad essere purificato mediante la riforma della curia e una prima attuazione del principio della collegialità, mediante la restituzione ai vescovi di molte competenze che nel corso dei secoli erano state avocate da Roma e mediante un sempre maggiore riconoscimento della legittima autonomia delle chiese locali, a livello diocesano, regionale, nazionale."

[15] Ibid., 141–42: "Nel corso degli anni settanta, e per la prima volta nella storia, alcune chiese luterane, riformate e anglicane hanno cominciato a fare oggetto di riflessione e di dialogo con la chiesa cattolica il ruolo e la funzione del 'servizio petrino', come ministero al servizio della comunione della chiesa universale. . . . Le chiese cristiane . . . tendono a riconoscere il ruolo della chiesa di Roma per ragioni storiche e soprattutto per necessità di ordine sociologico: un centro visibile di comunione per la chiesa universale appare necessario, e nessun luogo e nessuna persona può avere titolo a compiere questo ufficio tanto quanto la chiesa di Roma col suo vescovo. L'unica condizione che si pone è che esso sia veramente al servizio dell'evangelo e dell'unità, e che non comprometta la legittima libertà cristiana."

[16] Cf. Coppola, "Primato papale ed ecumenismo", 19. The author refers to K. Barth, *Kirchliche Dogmatik*, I/1 (Zürich, 1947), 106.

[17] J. Macquarrie, "The Papacy in a Unified Church", *Pacifica* 2 (1989): 123–24: "In ecumenical discussion, the Papacy is almost bound to present itself as something of a paradox. . . . Whether we are thinking of the great Orthodox Churches of the East or the Reformed Churches of the West, we have to recognise that among them there remains, even today, considerable suspicion of the Papacy and even hostility toward any such institution. To some people at least, it might seem that the abolition of the Papacy would be the best way to open the door to a drawing together of the Churches."

This conclusion, which has been reached by the various proposals for a renewal of the primacy, insists today on the necessity of freeing it from any confessional connotation, in the sense that it is characteristic of only one ecclesial tradition, and rendering it "universal" in the light of the "double conciliar principle that guides the ecumenical efforts of Catholics and which the Pope himself takes up in *Ut unum sint*: that of the *hierarchy of truths* (no. 37) and that of the *distinction between the deposit of faith and the formulation in which it is expressed* (no. 81, see nos. 18, 19, 36, 38, 78, 81)",[18] so as to arrive at a truly ecumenical way of exercising the primacy.[19]

This recognition is, in any case, linked with precise conditions and concrete proposals for renewal, in "an authentic dialogue within the Catholic Church and between her and the other Churches".[20] Indeed, a rereading of the First Vatican Council—which represents a stumbling block in its formulations[21]—is proposed, and a new view of the primacy is suggested: a transition from the primacy as it has developed historically to one which is understood as a ministry of communion in the context of collegiality and conciliarity[22]; the papacy as a historical phenomenon—which could even

---

[18] Cf. Manna, "Quale primato dopo la 'Ut unum sint'?", *O Odigos* 14, no. 4 (1996): 2.

[19] Ibid., 3: "L'imperativo emergente già da tempo in ambito ecumenico suona così 'Occorre de-confessionalizzare il papato'. Non a caso K. Schatz nel suo testo: *Il Primato del Papa. La sua storia dalle origini ai nostri giorni* (Brescia, 1996), intitola così la IV parte del volume: *Il primato punto di identità confessionale nell'epoca moderna* [pp. 179ff.]. D'altronde lo stesso Giovanni Paolo II parla di 'forma ecumenica di esercizio del primato'. Cosa vuol significare questa affermazione? Luigi Sartori nell'introduzione all'edizione italiana dello Schatz così si esprime: 'E' come se il papa riconoscesse che la forma di esercizio invalsa finora nella chiesa cattolica non è ancora 'ecumenica', e cioè quella che d'obbligo può dirsi già adeguata a tutti ed essere proposta a tutti ... E' come se ammettesse che essa è ancora e in certa misura 'confessionale', nel senso di espressione limitata, così come essa appare nei suoi aspetti storici e culturali, ossia umani; in altre parole, di una parte della chiesa e non della chiesa intera."

[20] Cf. Cereti, *Per un'ecclesiologia ecumenica* (Bologna, 1997), 258.

[21] Cf. Tillard, "La juridiction de l'évêque de Rome", *Irénikon* 51 (1978): 358.

[22] Y. Congar, "Cinquant'anni di ricerca dell'Unità": "Un papato come la storia l'ha strutturato, centralizzatore, imperiale, strettamente autoritario: no. Un ministero papale che presieda alla comunione e all'unità in un regime collegiale e conciliare: perché no? E' stato il presidente Kennedy a sottolineare che non ci si deve chiedere: 'Why not?'. Questo cambia la prospettiva, evidentemente siamo alla soglia di nuove possibilità. Tuttavia, esse sono davanti a noi" (*il regno-doc.* 15/88, 387). G. Alberigo, too, in the editorial of *Concilium* 1975, after having underscored the need for ecclesiological decisions, continues: "In particolare è nodale la possibilità di esercitare la responsabilità suprema nella chiesa universale attraverso un'azione abitualmente ed effettivamente collegiale ... Come per secoli si è

disappear—is supposed to make way for a "renewed" papacy, namely, a Petrine ministry of service to all the Churches.[23] As L. Sartori writes, "there is no longer a prejudice against the papacy; there is, however, a refusal to accept the way in which the papacy was understood and exercised for centuries in the Catholic tradition; efforts are now being directed towards a new and different form of papacy."[24]

The conditions for the renewal of the primacy have been formulated in a more detailed manner by J. J. von Allmen. Having specified that the Pope cannot disown the responsibility which belongs to him,[25] he enunciates the following four principles, which ought to inform the exercise of the papal ministry[26]: the Pope should exercise his ministry as the bishop of the Church of Peter and Paul[27]; he should earnestly respect collegial-

---

avuta una prevalenza di esercizio personale, così ora sembra desiderabile un esercizio abitualmente collegiale delle responsabilità relative alla comunione ecclesiale" (pp. 25 and 32). Cf. Cereti, *Per un'ecclesiologia ecumenica*, 252–59.

[23] Stirnimann, "Papato e servizio petrino", 27–28: "Papato, no; Servizio petrino, sì; o in termini più sfumati: Il papato, quale fenomeno storico, può scomparire, senza danno per la fede, al fine di permettere una nuova espressione del servizio petrino ... quale servizio dell'unità di tutte le Chiese singole."

[24] "Introduzione", *Papato e istanze ecumeniche* (Bologna, 1984), 7. The author continues, "Basti un richiamo: in occasione della visita del papa in Germania (RFT) è stato diffuso un memorandum di esponenti evangelici, in cui si riconosce che ... si può pensare al papa 'come a un simbolo dell'unità della chiesa, a sostegno del pluralismo nella chiesa', e quindi anche 'come rappresentante di tutti i cristiani' (e non solo dei cattolici); ma non per questo si è disposti ad accettare i due dogmi papali del Vaticano I, anzi si accoglie solo la formula 'comunione *col* papa, non *sotto* il papa'."

[25] "Ministero papale ministero di unità", *Concilium*, no. 8 (1975), 133: "Il problema ecclesiologico ed ecumenico non è dunque 'un papa o niente papa', ma 'quale papa per quale chiesa?' ... Il papa mancherebbe al suo ministero di unità se pensasse di porre fine alla divisione, semplicemente invitando a ritornare a Roma le chiese che non sono in comunione con la sua sede. E ugualmente mancherebbe se rinnegasse la responsabilità primaziale che gli compete."

[26] Cf. ibid., 114–35.

[27] The author further develops the theme in his book *Il primato della Chiesa di Pietro e di Paolo* (Brescia, 1982). Cereti too ("Il riconoscimento dei ministeri", 141) writes, "Come vescovo della chiesa di Roma, che conserva la memoria del martirio e la tomba non soltanto dell'apostolo Pietro, ma anche dell'apostolo Paolo, egli ha rivalorizzato la pienezza della propria identità apostolica, come successore non soltanto di Pietro (responsabilità della comunione cattolica), ma anche di Paolo (apertura missionaria ed ecumenica)." Cf. Tillard, *L'Église locale. Ecclésiologie de communion et catholicité* (Paris, 1995), 535–43; Manna, "L'oecuméniste. Les colloques catholiques-orthodoxes de l'institut de théologie oecuménique Saint-Nicolas de Bari—La contribution du P. Tillard", *Communion et réunion, Mélanges Jean-Marie Roger Tillard*, 56–57. But cf. Garuti, *S. Pietro unico titolare del primato. A proposito del decreto del S. Uffizio del 24 gennaio 1647* (Bologna, 1993). Curiously enough, Cereti

ity which binds him to other bishops[28]; he should, above all, be the Bishop of the local Church of Rome[29]; and he should continue energetically to resist the temptation to "secularize" his ministry.

Furthermore, a *return to the pentarchy* has been suggested as a model for the government of the Church.[30] This would mean that, in the first place, a distinction is made, in the person of the Roman Pontiff, between his role as Patriarch of the West and his role as Primate of the universal Church,[31] in order to regulate relations with the other patriarchal Churches

---

continues to consider the decree of the Holy Office "poco più che una curiosità storica" (*Per un'ecclesiologia ecumenica*, 238, no. 87).

[28] This in particular is the condition that has been most insisted upon in the past and continues to be insisted upon in the present: "Per essere convincenti è necessario modificare l'esercizio del primato del Papa, attuando una maggiore decentralizzazione e rendendo più effettiva la collegialità episcopale" (E. Lanne, "A piccoli passi oltre gli ostacoli", *Jesus*, giugno 1995, 76). Cf. Tillard, "La tension entre primauté du Siège romain et conciliarité", *Nicolaus* 19 (1992): 275ff. Tillard, "Le ministère d'unité", 213; H. Legrand, "Une éventuelle relance de l'uniatisme pourrait-elle s'appuyer sur Vatican II?", *Irénikon* 66 (1993): 14ff.

[29] Cf. R. La Valle, "Impegno del papa come vescovo di Roma", *Concilium*, no. 11 (1975), 101–15. It is further claimed that, according to the authentic tradition of the Church, primacy "appartient à l'Église locale de Rome, et non à une personne, le pape, lequel ne jouit de la primauté au sein de l'épiscopat universel que parce que son siège jouit de cette primauté, et non l'inverse" (E. Ghikas, "Comment 'redresser' les définitions du premier concile du Vatican", *Irénikon* 68 [1995]: 201). Cf. Cereti, "Il riconoscimento dei ministeri", 142; G. Falbo, *Il primato della Chiesa di Roma alla luce dei primi quattro secoli* (Rome, 1989), 384ff.

[30] Cf. F. R. Gahbauer, *Die Pentarchie-Theorie. Ein Modell der Kirchenleitung von den Anfängen bis zur Gegenwart* (Frankfurt am Main, 1993); J. Fontbona i Missé, *Comunión y sinodalidad. La eclesiología eucarística después N. Afanasiev en I. Zizioulas y J.-M. R. Tillard* (Rome, 1994), 431–32; W. Klausnitzer, " 'Der Papst ... ist zweifelsohne das größte Hindernis auf dem Weg der Ökumene' (Paul VI)", *Catholica* 50 (1996): 206–9; Cereti, *Per un'ecclesiologia ecumenica*, 238–39. But cf. Garuti, *Il Papa Patriarca d'Occidente. Studio storico dottrinale* (Bologna, 1990); Garuti, "Ancora a proposito del Papa Patriarca d'Occidente", *Antonianum* 70 (1995): 31–45.

[31] A. de Halleux, "La collégialité dans l'Église ancienne", *Revue théologique de Louvain* 24 (1993): 446: "Depuis le VIe siècle, c'est l'unanimité de la 'pentarchie' des Patriarches dans 'la prédication de la foi et de la tradition apostolique' que la conscience ecclésiologique orientale considère comme le rempart de l'unité de 'la sainte Église de Dieu catholique et apostolique' contre toutes les hérésies.... Voilà pourquoi l'Orient orthodoxe n'a jamais véritablement compris et accepté le pape de Rome autrement que comme le premier des cinq patriarches.... Mais, comme l'estiment beaucoup d'oecuménistes, il se peut qu'une meilleure distinction des trois niveaux de la juridiction supra-épiscopale de l'évêque de Rome: métropolite de l'Italie, patriarche de l'Occident et, de par son ministère pétrinien particulier, centre de la communion des Églises, ouvre une voie prometteuse au difficile dialogue sur la primauté romaine." See H. Legrand, "Une éventuelle relance de l'uniatisme", 34; B. Sesboüé, "Le ministère de communion du Pape", *Études*, June 1996, 805–8; W. Seibel, "Petrusamt und Ökumene", *Stimmen der Zeit* 122 (1997): 2.

of the East. Consideration will also have to be made for a new form of
the papacy within the "crown of patriarchs", where the primacy of the
prima sedes would no longer be absolute and would cease to be exercised
in an abnormal manner.[32] But within the Western patriarchate too, the
Pope would have to renounce "the rights of jurisdiction over the protestant Churches" and would have to move in the direction of an auto-
cephality modeled on that of the Orthodox Churches; in exchange, "the
protestant Churches and communities would agree on the existence of
seven sacraments and on the constitution of rites." One could add that
they would also come to an understanding "of the role of the bishop of
Rome as the primate of the universal communion of churches", a role
which would not, however, be linked with "the power of jurisdiction,
which concerns the Patriarchate alone".[33]

Within this context of pentarchy it would be possible today to acknowledge that the Bishop of Rome has a primacy of honor, even though the
most productive way for an eventual reconciliation would be the application of collegiality within the institutional structures of the Catholic

---

[32] Tillard, "Le ministère d'unité", 203–4: "En effet, l'évêque de Rome aura alors retrouvé
sa place au sein de ce que la Tradition appelle 'la couronne des patriarches', des *apostolikoi
thronoi*, traduisons pour l'Occident 'la solidarité hiérarchisée des primats'.... La primauté
du premier siège (*prima sedes*) est une primauté cernée par la responsabilité des autres
primautés. Ce n'est pas une primauté absolue, bien que ce soit celle qui exerce la *prima
potestas*. *Prima*, par définition, s'oppose à *unica* puisque pour être premier, il faut un sec-
onde, un troisième. Dans l'hypothèse d'une pleine *koinonia* entre l'orthodoxie et Rome, il
est clair que la primauté romaine ne se superposera pas à celle des autres sièges patriarcaux
mais s'inscrira à sa vraie place (avec ses attributs et ses privilèges propres) au sein de la
synergie hiérarchique. Elle cessera de s'exercer de façon anormale."

[33] Cf. W. Pannenberg, "L'unità possibile", interview edited by A. Filippi and F. Strazzari: *il regno-att.*, 20/93, 606–7). Tillard also writes, "La question se posera: ces groupes
confessionnels entreront-ils en communion avec l'Orient via leur appartenance à la *pars
occidentalis Ecclesiae* dont l'évêque de Rome est le patriarche, ou de façon directe? ... On
le voit, la question de la primauté romaine ... implique aussi ce que nous avons souvent
décrit comme une reconstitution de la carte de l'*oikoumenè*.... Si elle n'avait pas été désen-
chantée par la réponse de Rome à son *Final Report*, l'ARCIC ... se serait déjà appliquée
à réfléchir sur ce difficile problème de l'emboîtement de la 'primauté intra-confessionnelle'
(celle de l'archévêque de Cantorbéry) dans la 'primauté universelle' (celle de l'évêque de
Rome), qu'on ne peut pas concevoir selon le modèle commandant les relations au sein de
la pentarchie des premiers siècles" ("Le ministère d'unité", 203–4). There are also those
who attribute a "grand intérêt oecuménique" to the "éventualité d'une reviviscence de
l'institution patriarcale dans l'Église latine": A. Borras, "Ut unum sint. Une encyclique
pour les chrétiens en voie de réconciliation", *Ephemerides theologicae lovanienses* 72 (1996):
366–69.

Church, which would bring out the true nature of the primacy: a ministerial power at the service of the universal communion of local Churches, necessary for the maintenance and growth of the communion itself.[34]

Finally, it was Paul VI, the very same person who had so clearly underlined the obstacles placed by the primacy, who was responsible for the "rediscovery" of the category of "sister Churches".[35] This is generally understood as the way to the reestablishment of full communion[36]; it has assumed, however, a specific meaning in relation to the solution of the problem of the primacy.

The category arose as a context within which the Christians of the East acknowledged that Rome has a primacy of honor among equal Churches, "united among themselves by bonds of communion and not of dependence",[37] and as a model for describing the relations among the Churches, within which it was recognized that the "sister" Church of Rome possesses a certain "presidency in love".[38] The category was taken up again "to designate the relations between the Greek Church and the Latin Church" even though "in this context of ecclesial 'fraternitas' there can be no room for papal primacy."[39] It implies taking a new look at the

---

[34] F. Frost, "Orthodoxie", in *Catholicisme. Hier—aujourd'hui—demain* (Paris, 1985), 10: 301: "Aujourd'hui on accorderait encore ce privilège à l'évêque de Rome, mais en le situant comme premier patriarche d'une pentarchie.... Il ne s'agirait alors que d'une primauté d'honneur.... Dans le contexte actuel, il semble que la voie la plus feconde vers une réconciliation éventuelle entre les points de vue oriental et occidental soit une mise en oeuvre effective, dans les structures institutionnelles de l'Église catholique, de la collegialité enseignée par Vatican II. C'est ainsi que la primauté romaine aurait plus de chances de paraître aux yeux des orientaux pour ce qu'elle doit être: un pouvoir ministériel au service de la communion universelle des Églises locales et nécessaire au maintien et à l'approfondissement de celle-ci."

[35] Cereti, "Il riconoscimento dei ministeri", 142: "in una prospettiva di ecclesiologia di comunione nella quale le diverse chiese locali del mondo vengono viste come 'chiese sorelle', alla chiesa di Roma sarà sempre più riconosciuto da tutti il ruolo, non tanto di 'madre', quanto di 'sorella maggiore', quella che è chiamata a presiedere nella carità alla comunione di tutte le chiese.... Il suo compito dovrebbe comunque essere svolto più con la sua esemplarità e con il servizio che essa offre a tutte le chiese, che con forme di intervento diretto, che dovrebbero costituire soltanto l'ultima istanza nel pieno rispetto del principio di sussidiarietà; più con la promozione della ricerca teologica e la animazione della vita ecclesiale, che con funzioni di repressione o di condanna."

[36] Cf. J. Brosseder, "Vers quelle unité des Églises?", *Concilium*, no. 71 (1997), 169.

[37] Cf. J. Spiteris, *La Critica Bizantina del Primato Romano nel secolo XII* (Rome, 1979), 106.

[38] Cf. G. Wainwreight, "La confession et les confessions: vers l'unité confessionnelle et confessante des chrétiens", *Irénikon* 57 (1984): 17.

[39] Cf. J. Spiteris, *La Critica Bizantina*, 299.

problem of the role of the Church of Rome and her Bishop[40] and renouncing the forms in which the primacy has been exercised since the rupture of canonical communion; or rather, a common rethinking of the nature of the particular authority that the East recognizes in the See of Peter.[41] On the basis of this reality, the sister Churches of the East and the West will have to clarify that which was left unsaid by the First and the Second Vatican Councils about the role and functioning of the central authority.[42] The Church of Rome in particular should understand the true relationship between the primacy and the local episcopate and the fundamental constitutive function of the latter, a function that should not lose its essential prerogatives, even if relations with the See of Rome are necessary in order to attain full communion in a single profession of Christ and in a single Eucharist.[43]

In any case, the primacy would be considered under the aspect not of a person, but of a sister Church endowed with a particular dignity,[44] with-

---

[40] Wainwreight, "La confession et les confessions", 21: "Avec la notion d' 'Églises soeurs' . . . nous sommes arrivés à l'endroit où il est opportun de refaire face au rôle de l'Église de Rome et de son évêque, tels que l'histoire nous les donne, avec tout ce qu'ils ont de positif, de problématique, et de prometteur."

[41] Lanne, "Églises-soeurs. Implications ecclésiologiques du Tomos Agapis", *Istina* 20 (1975): 73: "L'ecclésiologie de la fraternité des Églises soeurs requiert donc . . . une vue nouvelle sur les relations entre Rome et les Églises de l'Orient orthodoxe, une redécouverte qui implique que l'on repense ensemble, et non sans l'Orthodoxie, quelle est la nature de l'autorité particulière que l'Orient reconnaît au siège de Pierre."

[42] Tillard, "Église catholique et dialogues bilatéraux", *Irénikon* 56 (1983): 10–11: "depuis la roupture avec sa soeur d'Orient, l'Église d'Occident a, sans contrôle, lourdement hypertrophié le rôle et le fonctionement de l'autorité centrale. Elle a fait de l'évêque de Rome 'plus qu'un pape'. . . . Il est clair que ni Vatican I ni Vatican II n'ont prononcé en ce domaine le dernier mot. Il faudra que l'Orient dise ce qu'il a à dire et, surtout, que l'Église-soeur d'Occident en tienne compte concrètement."

[43] Tillard, "La primauté romaine . . . jamais pour éroder les structures des Églises locales", *Irénikon* 50 (1977): 322–23: "A la lumière des vues de Vatican II sur la collégialité et sur la situation des Églises-soeurs en Orient (dans le décret sur l'oecuménisme), l'usage de la formule implique . . . que la primauté du siège de Rome n'est pas constitutive de l'ecclésialité à un degré aussi essentiel que l'épiscopat local. . . . Affirmer cela, c'est reconnaître à l'épiscopat où qu'il soit, s'il est dans la succession apostolique, une fonction constitutive fondamentale. Et bien que, pour aboutir à son fruit parfait qui est la communion horizontale de toutes les Églises en une seule confession du Christ et une seule eucharistie, elle ait besoin de la relation au siège romain, cette fonction ne saurait d'aucune façon perdre alors ses prérogatives essentielles."

[44] Lanne, "Églises-Soeurs. Implications ecclésiologiques", 61: "Si, selon la doctrine catholique, la primauté et l'infaillibilité du pontife romain trouvent un fondement dans les documents anciens et en particulier chez Ignace et Irénée, il est sûr, par contre, que l'optique

out any mother-to-sister relationship and without any hierarchical type of dependence.[45]

The problematic character of the primacy of the Bishop of Rome has been emphasized by the study document *The Church: Local and Universal* (1990) of the Joint Working Group of the Catholic Church and the World Council of Churches as follows: "The office of the papacy remains a controversial issue in ecumenism, but there are signs of better reciprocal understanding. On the Orthodox side the Ecumenical Patriarch Demetrios I, following a deliberation and resolution of his Synod, and convinced that it expressed the mind of the early Church, declared that the Bishop of Rome is marked out as the one who has the presidency of charity and is the first bishop in rank and honor in the whole Body of the Lord. The Pope can be called *primus inter pares* (first among equals), because this apostolic see has exercised a primacy of love from earliest time. In bilateral dialogues, the Lutherans speak of the value of the 'Petrine function [ministry]', and Anglicans have agreed that 'a universal primacy will be needed in a reunited church and it should appropriately be the primacy of the Bishop of Rome'. The Joint Roman Catholic/World Methodist Council Commission noted: 'Discernment of the various factors in Scripture and history might contribute to an agreed perception of which functions the see of Rome might properly exercise in a ministry of universal unity, by what authority, and on what conditions' (§ 40). Despite these positive statements, the problems of *ius divinum* (divine right), primacy of jurisdiction, infallibility and the papal teaching authority remain subjects of intense ecumenical dialogue."[46]

---

dans laquelle elles se situent pour ceux qui les perçoivent est essentiellement celle d'une Église-soeur et non d'une personne—revêtue d'une autorité particulière, mais soeur quand même." A detailed critique of the positions held by Lanne, especially regarding the connection between sister-Churches and primacy, is found in B. Schultze, "Il Vaticano II e Paolo VI di fronte al dilemma: 'Chiese sorelle o Chiese unite?'", *Unitas* 31 (1976): 81–106.

[45] A. de Halleux, "Fraterna communio", *Irénikon* 58 (1985): 307: "Reste à en tirer toutes les implications ecclésiales et canoniques. Deux Églises soeurs ne se trouvent pas dans le rapport de mère à fille; la pleine communion à restaurer entre elles ne saurait donc revêtir le caractère hiérarchique d'une dépendance." Cf. Tillard, *L'Église locale*, 546–47.

[46] IS, no. 74 (1990), no. 47, 83b.

CHAPTER II

THE PRIMACY AND CATHOLIC-ORTHODOX DIALOGUE

I. THE ORTHODOX VIEW OF THE PRIMACY

TO UNDERSTAND THE PERSPECTIVE of the Chalcedonian Orthodox Churches[1] on the primacy, it is necessary to examine their ecclesiology, which is structured on a eucharistic view of the Church and places the emphasis on the reality of the local Church gathered in the name of Christ in the celebration of the Eucharist and under the guidance of the bishop.[2] It is here that the Church is realized in her totality: "As each particle of the Holy Gifts is truly the Body of Christ, in which all of Christ is present and not just a part of Him, in like manner each local Church is the true Catholic Church."[3] The foundation of Orthodox ecclesiology is therefore "the local eucharistic community", which "is not a *part* of the Church universal but the *expression* of the Church universal".[4]

---

[1] We limit ourselves to the Orthodox Confederation. The ancient Oriental Churches have the same difficulty with regard to primacy: Cf. C. Kostantinidis, "Le dialogue entre l'Église orthodoxe et les Églises de l'ancien Orient. Appréciations et Perspectives", *Proche-Orient Chrétien* 30 (1980): 51; G. Mar Osthathios, "Oriental Orthodox Churches", DEM, 755b–57a; N. Lossky, "L'ecclésiologie dans une perspective orthodoxe", *Science et Esprit* 48 (1996): 7–14.

[2] J. Zizioulas: "Il vescovo, come capo della Chiesa locale, riassume in se stesso l'intera comunità, diventando così l' 'immagine di Cristo' che tutto assomma in sé.... Poiché l'autorità del vescovo deriva in definitiva dal fatto di presiedere l'eucaristia, la sua funzione consiste nel realizzare, a livello non solo locale ma anche universale, la cattolicità della Chiesa, implicata nell'eucaristia": cited by D. Salachas, "Les Églises soeurs", *Nicolaus* 9 (1982): 124–25. Cf. O. Clément, *La Chiesa ortodossa* (Brescia, 1989), 62–64.

[3] Filaret of Kiev, "Paper Read at the Solemn Meeting on Occasion of Celebrations of the 35th Anniversary of the 1946 Lvov Church Council", *The Journal of the Moscow Patriarchate* 10 (1981): 9. Cf. P. Evdokimov, *L'Ortodossia* (Bologna, 1981), 173ff.; K. Koch, "Einheit der Christen—Einheit Europas. Chancen und Grenzen", *Catholica* 48 (1994): 219–20; P. Dentin, *Les privilèges des Papes*, 220.

[4] Lossky, "Orthodoxy", DEM, 776b.

Given the fundamental equality of all the local Churches and of all the bishops who preside over them,[5] each Orthodox Church has its own internal autonomy.[6] To the Oriental mind, therefore, it is a "primary datum" that the Church is constituted by a multiplicity of local Churches. Included, however, in the essentials of Orthodox ecclesiology is a kind of dynamic of universal unity, whereby each local Church "receives" the testimony of the others, and this reciprocal testimony bears witness to the fact that they are, individually and all together, the universal Church.[7] Although in the early centuries, "the Church consisted of a number of communities, completely isolated and independent, without any canonical ties among them, in the sense in which we understand that today", her unity nevertheless was not impaired, since "the concept of one single Church was not merely an idea, but a living reality". This model of "Church unity in plurality, unity in diversity, is the only one which corresponds to the nature of the Church".[8] The totality of the local Churches thus constitutes a fraternity or communion of Churches whose internal unity consists above all in internal harmony and solidarity, and in reciprocal spiritual bonds.[9]

This unity "is expressed in the college of bishops, analogous to the company of the Apostles", and finds its concrete expression in the conciliarity which is realized in local or ecumenical councils and, above all, in a permanent form, in the "'reception' by all the Churches—that is, by the college of bishops as a whole—of a local decision which thus becomes part of the patrimony of the universal Church".[10]

Early in the Church's history, certain centers of agreement began to appear, whereby the living communion of the Churches was manifested in a concrete way. These enjoyed a significant moral authority, which did

---

[5] Filaret of Kiev, "Paper", 10a: "The Orthodox Church teaches that bishops are equal among themselves. This teaching is based on the fact that each bishop heads the one and the same Catholic Church in a given place, and that not one Local Church, including the Roman Church, can be more Catholic than another." Cf. F. Frost, "Orthodoxie", 300–301.

[6] Lossky, "Eastern Orthodoxy", DEM, 312a: "Thus the Eastern Orthodox churches are united in the faith, and each one has internal autonomy under the primacy of the patriarchate of Constantinople, the 'first among equals'."

[7] Clément, *La Chiesa ortodossa*, 62. Cf. E. Melia, "La Pentarchie", *Istina* 32 (1987): 341–42.

[8] Filaret of Kiev, "Paper", 10.

[9] It was precisely to underline this unity that the notion of "eucharistic ecclesiology" was ultimately replaced by that of "ecclesiology of communion": cf. Lossky, "Ecclésiologie et orthodoxie," 9.

[10] Clément, *La Chiesa ortodossa*, 62.

not imply any power, but was based instead on the size and administrative importance of those cities which very early on had witnessed the growth of vigorous Christian communities."[11] This grouping around the principal Churches was the only form of ecclesial organization, which later gave rise to the patriarchates.[12]

Subsequently, on the model of civil organization and under the influence of the Empire, the patriarchal institution gradually asserted itself and was sanctioned by the councils and officially ratified by the legislation of Justinian. Thus was recognized "the existence of the five classical Patriarchates, with the respective order of precedence and relative jurisdiction: Rome, Constantinople, Alexandria, Antioch and Jerusalem".[13] The individual patriarchs were recognized as the new autocephalous authority in the administration of the universal Church[14]; to the Bishop of Rome was assigned the task of presiding in charity, a task which passed over to the patriarch of Constantinople after the break between the East and the West. He too, however, is "a *primus inter pares* who receives certain privileges from his 'brothers', especially through the confirmation of episcopal ordinations. But he himself cannot act alone without the consent of the other bishops or of a synod which represents them."[15]

---

[11] Ibid., 63.

[12] Cf. Lossky, "Orthodoxy", DEM, 766a–768a.

[13] A. Garuti, *Il Papa Patriarca d'Occidente?*, 226.

[14] Cf. V. Phidas, "La notion de primauté papale dans la tradition canonique orthodoxe", *Nicolaus* 19 (1992): 34.

[15] Cf. Clément, *La Chiesa ortodossa*, 63. The role of the Patriarch of Constantinople after the "schism of Rome" is thus described in the Editorial of *Istina* 32 (1987): 337–38: "Quant à la conciliarité orthodoxe, elle a instauré une primauté du siège de Constantinople, primauté de suppléance du fait du 'schisme romain' et qui doit durer jusqu'au jour où Rome retrouvera sa 'primauté d'honneur' dans le concert des Églises. L'Orthodoxie souligne que cette primauté de Constantinople n'est pas une suprématie mais un service, un souci exercé au sein d'une structure de concertation et de communion, la pentarchie, à laquelle elle se plaît à reconnaître une origine très ancienne, voire apostolique. Ainsi dans l'Orthodoxie, la communion entre les différentes parties de l'Église s' exprime normalement et régulièrement par la voix de ces hiérarques, égaux entre eux, que sont les anciens patriarches." Cf. also Metropolitan Maxime de Sardes, *Le patriacat oecuménique dans l'Église orthodoxe* (Paris, 1975): the patriarchal organization is described at great length, especially in chapter 2 (pp. 53–95), whereas chapter 3 (pp. 97–154) is dedicated entirely to the demonstration of the primacy of Constantinople. On the synodal structure of the Church according to the Eastern view cf. P. Duprey, "La structure synodale de l'Église dans la théologie orientale", *Proche-Orient Chrétien* 20 (1970): 123ff.; J. Meyendorff, "Églises-soeurs. Implications ecclésiologiques du Tomos Agapis", *Istina* 20 (1975): 46; M. Brun, *Orthodoxe theologische Stimmen zum Zweiten Vatikanischen Konzil. Ein Beitrag zur Überwindung der Trennung* (Freiburg, 1987), 185–97; A. Papadopoulos, "L'istituzione conciliare. Il

Within the context of the ecclesiological view described above, there gradually developed the Orthodox teaching on the primacy. The "disagreement about origins" between the East and the West, evident especially in the different concepts of the Church and her organization, finds its culmination precisely in this sphere. In fact, in the West, and particularly in Rome, an awareness of the primacy of the Bishop of Rome was present from the very beginning of the Church, albeit in embryonic form. This primacy is not simply one of honor, but "is situated in the order of jurisdiction" and entails the solicitude of the Bishop of Rome for all the Christian communities, which results in a unique jurisdictional position with respect to the universal episcopate.[16] Thus developed a juridical view of ecclesial relations, which places the emphasis on the rights and duties of the Pope vis-à-vis the universal Church. In the East, in contrast, the attention was focused on the relationship of communion among the Churches, limiting the juridical relations almost exclusively to the area of the councils, especially the ecumenical councils.[17] The prevailing idea, therefore, is that of the fundamental equality of all Churches, based on the vision of the Church present in a given locality and constituted through the celebration of the Eucharist and presided over by the Bishop; these Churches are nevertheless in reciprocal communion.[18]

---

suo carattere carismatico e unificatore: una considerazione ortodossa", *Nicolaus* 19 (1992): 285ff.; Lossky, "Ortodossia", 820a.

[16] Cf. Garuti, *Il Papa Patriarca d'Occidente?*, 25–26. This gradual development is also to be found in the work of K. Schatz (*Papal Primacy*), influenced though it is by "common reductive filters" and characterized by "a certain minimism": cf. the review (French ed.) by A. Marchetto in *Rivista di storia della Chiesa in Italia* 47 (1993): 162–69.

[17] E. Lanne, "Il vescovo locale nei canoni dei primi sette concili", *Nicolaus* 18 (1991): 35: "sin dall'epoca subapostolica viene riconosciuto al vescovo dell'antica Roma una autorità singolare che egli interpreta in termini anche giuridici mentre i padri dei sette primi concili ecumenici, tutti riuniti in Oriente, non hanno fatto passare nei canoni questa dottrina."

[18] Not unlike the communion within a local Church, the communion of Churches within the one single Church is also founded on the Holy Trinity: "La Chiesa vien significata con l'Eucaristia; quanti prendono parte all'Eucaristia sono pietre viventi che edificano la Chiesa. La Chiesa viene edificata dal Padre sul fondamento vivo di Gesù Cristo (1 Pt 2,4.5), col quale i partecipanti all'Eucaristia si uniscono e vivono nello Spirito Santo. Così essi prendono parte alla vita della Santa Trinità.... Lo stesso vale anche per la comunione delle chiese locali tra loro; esse sono molte, ma tutte costituiscono la Chiesa una cattolica. Ciascuna Chiesa locale rappresenta tutta la Chiesa cattolica, in quanto si trova in comunione con le altre chiese locali, che sono manifestazioni della Chiesa una cattolica. Come l'unico Dio è comunione di tre persone, così l'unica Chiesa cattolica è comunione di molte chiese locali" (G. Galitis, "Monaco: una risposta ortodossa", *Nicolaus* 11 [1983]: 336–37).

Consequently, "no bishop of the Christian Church has a universal privilege, given by God or by man, over the One, Holy, Catholic, and Apostolic Church of Christ", and "a hierarchical order among the episcopal sees, as useful as that may be, does not depend at all upon the essence of the Church." [19]

We find ourselves, then, confronted with two different concepts of *plenitudo potestatis* in the Church: Rome tends toward a juridical view of ecclesial relations and emphasizes, along personal lines, the rights and duties of the Pope with regard to the universal Church. The East focuses its attention on the relationships of communion among the Churches, limiting the juridical relations almost exclusively to the sphere of the councils, especially the ecumenical councils, with a view that is centered on synodality within which—and never apart from it—the primatial *potestas* is to be exercised. [20] Each of these notions betrays a certain "radicalism". [21]

In the same way, the patriarchal institution, which arose out of the need for a "proper ordering of the Churches", does not imply any supraepis-

---

[19] Patriarch Demetrios, *Address to Card. Willebrands* (November 30, 1973: E.J. Stormon, 260, no. 311). The Patriarch subsequently specified, "We are all, whether in Rome or in this city of Constantinople, or any other city whatsoever, regardless from the Church's point of view of its hierarchical or political position, purely and simply fellow bishops under the one supreme High-Priest and Head of the Church [our Lord Jesus Christ, according to the hierarchical order that has existed and been recognized in every age by the Church], in a holy system of rank and order that has been always received by the Church since the earliest days" (ibid.).

[20] J.-M. R. Tillard, *L'Église locale*, 455–56: "L'Occident accentuera juridiquement, dans une ligne personnelle, la *plenitudo potestatis* de l'évêque possédant ces prérogatives de la primauté. L'Orient, tout en lui accordant beaucoup plus qu'un rang dans la Liturgie et un prestige moral, résistera à toute théologie qui relativise en faveur du primat la réciprocité synodale. Pour lui, la *potestas* spécifique de l'évêque de Rome n'existe et ne s'exerce que *dans* la synodalité, jamais *sans* elle, jamais en 'humiliant' la *potestas* (sacramentellement conférée) des autres évêques."

[21] A. de Halleux, "La collégialité dans l'Église ancienne", 450: "L'autorité reconnue à l'évêque de Rome par l'Orient patristique était celle d'un témoin et d'un garant ou, si l'on veut, d'un 'régulateur' et d'un 'modérateur', bref d'un centre décisif de l'unanimité dans la communion des Églises. L'interprétation de cette autorité a varié selon les circonstances: on la tenait généralement pour plus qu'une simple préséance d'honneur, mais sans jamais aller jusqu'à l'accepter comme la 'plenitudo potestatis' d'un évêque universel, ce qui aurait paru incompatible avec la conception orientale d'une réciprocité interactive entre primauté et synodalité. La définition de la primauté au concile de Florence elle-même, dont s'est inspiré le Ier concile du Vatican, résulta d'un compromis (au sens noble du terme, c'est-à-dire sans compromission) entre le 'papalisme' radical des Latins, qui considéraient le successeur de Pierre comme la source 'iure divino' de toute ecclésialité, et le 'synodalisme' radical des Grecs, qui ne reconnaissaient à l'évêque de Rome que le premier rang canonique parmi les cinq Patriarches."

copal authority of divine right; hierarchy is always subject to synodality, and no primate can lay claims to a power different from the one received by all bishops through their sacramental ordination.[22]

Given this context, what then is the role of the Bishop of Rome as acknowledged in the East during the first millennium? The positions taken by historians on this issue are quite diverse.

Even if there is no question that the Bishop of Rome was acknowledged to have a certain *principalitas* with respect to the other apostolic sees, the nature of it is rather difficult to establish.[23] According to Jan Spiteris, the Bishop of Rome was accorded a primacy which went beyond a simple primacy of honor, and a particular competence, for which reason great importance was attached to communion with him.[24] Schatz, in contrast, is more nuanced; he distinguishes between Rome's "primacy of jurisdiction" and the recognition of Rome "as the ultimate norm of ecclesial *communion*": the former aspect was never accepted; with regard to the latter, on the contrary, the positive testimonies are opposed by others that are negative.[25] It was commonly held that communion with Rome ("*cum*

---

[22] De Halleux, "L'institution patriarcale et la pentarchie. Un point de vue orthodoxe", *Revue Théol. de Louvain* 3 (1972): 198: "Aussi l'organisation métropolitaine et patriarcale du gouvernement ecclésiastique ne saurait-elle impliquer aucune autorité supra-épiscopale de droit divin. La hiérarchie demeure toujours soumise à la synodalité, au point qu'aucun primat ne puisse revendiquer un pouvoir autre que celui que tous les évêques ont également reçu par leur ordination sacramentelle." The author presents the ideas of the Orthodox theologian Biagio J. Pheidas. In reference to the actual role of the Ecumenical Patriarch cf. Garuti, "Sister Churches", Appendix, pp. 321–23.

[23] Cf. Tillard, *L'Église locale*, 510.

[24] *La Critica Bizantina*, 4: "L'Oriente ha generalmente riconosciuto nel vescovo di Roma un'autorità e un primato che non si può ridurre ad un semplice primato d'onore. La Sede Romana è la prima delle sedi patriarcali e a lei spetta una competenza particolare nel proclamare la retta fede di Pietro e nel rappresentare l'unità ecclesiale per cui la comunione col vescovo di Roma è considerata di grande importanza."

[25] Schatz, *Papal Primacy*, 60: "If it is understood to mean a 'primacy of jurisdiction' in the sense of a leadership of the Church that is somehow effective and applicable in normal times, the answer must certainly be negative.... The answer would be different if we were to ask whether Rome was acknowledged as the ultimate norm of ecclesial communion. It would not be difficult to find a continuing series of witnesses in the Eastern Church throughout the centuries who give a clear acknowledgment of that principle, and who speak in one way or another of the Roman church, or even the Roman bishop, as the head or president over all churches.... On the other hand, there are also witnesses on the opposite side expressing a very different opinion. Often Rome is only the first see in the series of the patriarchs, but its preeminence does not seem to be qualitatively different from that of the other patriarchates. In the latter [In a later] theory of the Pentarchy the issue is mainly

Roma") was a necessary element in ensuring orthodoxy in the faith and the orderly life of the Church; this need, however, certainly did not imply a dependence ("*sub* Roma").[26] The line of demarcation is the distinction between *potentior principalitas*, accepted as a datum of tradition, and the nature and scope of the authority that derives therefrom.[27] In any case, it is not a question of the power of jurisdiction connected with consecration, but rather of a *taxis* determined by the need for good order: of a primacy of honor which entails, more than anything else, a moral *leadership*, even if it implies a concrete jurisdiction connected with the role of *prima sedes*.[28]

In reality, it is the nature of the primacy that constitutes the crucial point of divergence.[29] According to the definition of the First Vatican

---

that of harmony among the five patriarchs, and not simply union with Rome. Rome is especially important for communion, but it alone is not decisive."

[26] L. Sartori, "Il papato domani: considerazioni ecumeniche", Introduction to the Italian edition of *Papal Primacy* by Schatz, 16: "Ma il 'cum Roma' implica il 'sub Roma'? Ecco il nodo cruciale della questione.... Potremmo dire che il modello del primo millennio sottolinea con chiarezza il *cum* della necessaria comunione con Roma, non altrettanto il *sub*." Cf. S. Manna, "Quale primato dopo la 'Ut unum sint'?", 2.

[27] V. Peri, "All'alba del terzo millennio, abbiamo il diritto di rimanere divisi? Cronaca ecclesiologica di un quindicennio ecumenico tra Cattolici ed Ortodossi", *Anuario de Historia de la Iglesia* 5 (1996): 478: "Non si tratta tanto, come volgarmente si suole ripetere, del cosiddetto primato romano, che la Chiesa del primo millennio accettò spontaneamente come dato della Tradizione e, in quanto tale, non mise in discussione; quanto dell'esercizio della potestà connessa ad un ufficio non solo onorifico nella Chiesa universale."

[28] Tillard, *L'Église locale*, 484: "Certes, il est clair que pour l'Orient, il s'agit essentiellement de *taxis*, de bon ordre, puisque rien ne saurait surpasser le pouvoir donné par le sacrement de l'ordination (*cheirotonia*). On parle donc d'une primauté d'honneur, avec un certain flou. En fait, cette notion de primauté d'honneur est, en elle-même, loin d'être claire." Referring to the study of Br. E. Daley ("Position and Patronage in the Early Church: The Original Meaning of Primacy of Honour", *Journal of Theological Studies* 44 [1993]: 529–53), the same Tillard recognizes that the greater part of modern commentators understand the "privileges" granted by canon 28 of Chalcedon as "une position de leadership moral, un signe d'*autorité* ou de prestige traditionnellement reconnus mais distincts ... d'un *pouvoir* de juridiction", but, on the other hand, he stresses that they "ne sont pas sans impliquer une juridiction concrète, ne serait-ce qu'en accordant à son évêque le droit de consacrer les métropolitains du Pont, d'Asie, de Thrace et d'exercer son autorité sur les 'régions barbares'". Pope Leo the Great also seems to have seen in them "une atteinte à des droits (*jura*), non une simple question de prestige." He therefore concludes: "Mais s'il en va ainsi pour la 'Rome cadette', on peut en déduire que la 'Rome aînée' jouit de prérogatives identiques. Puisqu'elle est le 'premier siège', on peut même penser que son 'patronat' est à la mesure de son rang, donc aussi son influence" (ibid., 487).

[29] Peri, "All'alba del terzo millennio", 478: "A costo di sorprendere qualcuno e di sfatare un inveterato luogo comune occidentale ed orientale, la Chiesa bizantina del primo

Council, taken up again by the Second Vatican Council, the Roman Pontiff has ordinary jurisdiction, which is truly episcopal and immediate, over all the other Churches, which binds the pastors and the faithful of whatever rite or dignity to the duty of hierarchical subordination and true obedience.[30] In the East, in contrast, the jurisdiction of the Pope was never understood as "an exercise of juridical power", but "rather as the power of jurisdiction of a judge, the highest judge in matters of faith and, at times, also of discipline. Rome was recognized as a center of communion of faith and hence of ecclesial communion and unity.... The authority of the bishop of Rome was always understood within the limits and in the light of a collegial context which was made manifest during the councils and, in ordinary times, in the institution of the Pentarchy."[31] In fact, "the Eastern view does not leave room for the idea of a primacy with a hierarchical character. Within the communion of the Churches, Rome has a particular function and occupies a special position, the first, as the 'basis and foundation' of the Church of God and as 'the greatest' among them; and it is recognized that its bishop 'has the role of *custos fidei et unitatis*, of supreme moderator of the *communio*, of guardian of the rights of the faithful and of the individual Churches, not as his own exclusive prerogative deriving from the primacy, but as a function with which the episcopal college itself has invested him.' Clearly, we are here dealing with a concept quite different from the one that has gradually emerged in the living consciousness of the West right from the very beginning of the Church. Rather than speak of primacy, one should speak, therefore, of an exceptional authority, which is nevertheless not a 'jurisdictional power of dominion, but the privilege of coordination, of counsel, of witness.' It is a special moral authority, understood as a charismatic function of constructing and safeguarding ecclesial communion, and the unity and communion of faith,

---

millennio non ha contestato la potentior principalitas della Chiesa dell'Antica Roma, testimoniata da sant'Ireneo, o il suo 'presiedere alla carità', attestato da sant'Ignazio di Antiochia. Tuttavia le due Chiese non sono finora riuscite ad esprimere un'unanime interpretazione circa la natura e l'ambito di potere della stessa autorità ecclesiale e circa gli strumenti e i modi canonici propri per il suo esercizio nella Chiesa universale."

[30] On the evaluation by Orthodox theologians of the teaching on the primacy proposed by the Second Vatican Council cf. Brun, *Orthodoxe theologische Stimmen*, 98–158.

[31] J. Spiteris, *La Critica Bizantina*, 8. The emperor alone possesses a true and proper juridical power, and he alone can give the force of imperial law to the conciliar decrees: cf. ibid., 12–15; G. Zananiri, "Orthodoxie", *Catholicisme* 10:293–95.

which entails neither a supreme authority nor a jurisdictional power over the universal Church." [32]

If it is maintained that this authority belongs to the Pope by reason of the historical circumstance of his being the Bishop of the See of Peter and Paul, princes of the apostles, and not by divine right, it is difficult to see how the Eastern concept can be deemed compatible with the doctrine of the First Vatican Council on the jurisdictional nature of the primacy of the Roman Pontiff.

The same incompatibility is to be noted also with respect to the exercise of the primacy, qualified by the principles of synodality and pentarchy, which in practice end up granting to the Bishop of Rome a true jurisdiction only in his own patriarchate. [33]

However, there still remains the conviction, expressed earlier in another context, that beginning with the sixth century, when the pentarchy assumed its extreme expression, the Bishop of Rome was considered in the East merely as the patriarch of the West: "His primacy is understood within the context of the college of the five Patriarchs. He is its head and can substitute for it under exceptional circumstances, but he does not enjoy a privileged voice within it. His primary greatness as the custodian of faith and unity, and as the supreme moderator of the *communio* is not an 'exclusive prerogative that derives from the primacy' by divine right, but a 'function with which he has been invested by the episcopal college' in its highest expression: the Ecumenical Council. Furthermore, this function does not represent a supreme jurisdictional authority of the Bishop of Rome over the universal Church, but merely the role of guide within the communion of autonomous Churches, which does not go much beyond

---

[32] Garuti, *Il Papa Patriarca d'Occidente?*, 243–44; cf. A. Carrasco Rouco, *Le primat de l'évêque de Rome. Étude sur la cohérence ecclésiologique et canonique du primat de juridiction* (Fribourg, 1990), 112–17; Fontbona i Missé, *Comunión y sinodalidad*, 65.

[33] Garuti, *Il Papa Patriarca d'Occidente?*, 245–46: "Nonostante la sua speciale funzione, il Papa non agisce mai solo nella Chiesa, almeno moralmente, ma nell'ambito della collegialità e sinodalità dell'episcopato.... Pertanto il principio della collegialità si riconduce in ultima analisi al sistema della pentarchia: 'le decisioni che riguardano la fede e la disciplina e che interessano la Chiesa universale devono essere prese, almeno normalmente, dai cinque patriarchi rappresentanti l'intero collegio dei vescovi, in comunione con il papa, capo del collegio e primo dei patriarchi'.... Ne è risultato che al di là del suo ruolo preminente di 'primo dei patriarchi', il Vescovo di Roma non gode di una vera giurisdizione sulla Chiesa universale, ma solo sul suo patriarcato; al monarchismo papale che sottolinea il primato di giurisdizione di Roma su tutta la Chiesa, si oppone il policentrismo patriarcale, che si esprime nella comunione sinodale di chiese sorelle, uguali ed autonome."

the primacy of honor. The Pope is thus considered to be on the same level as the other Patriarchs. More precisely, he is 'the Patriarch of the Church of the West' who, together with the other four Patriarchs (Constantinople, Alexandria, Antioch and Jerusalem), forms 'τὸ πεντακόρυφαον σῶμα τῆς ἐκκλησίας' [the body of the Church having five leaders]. He has direct jurisdiction in the West, but with regard to the East, he has simply the primacy of honor that is due to a *primus inter pares*." [34]

One could therefore conclude that "despite the 'prestige' of Rome, always considered as the first among the Patriarchal Sees, and despite the importance attributed to its Bishop in the proclamation of the faith of Peter and in representing the unity of the Church, the East does not appear to have ever acknowledged that he has a true primacy of jurisdiction. In any case, his authority in the East was scaled back considerably by conciliarity and, above all, by the ecclesiological importance attributed to the Emperor, and by the theory of the Pentarchy. For this reason, he was considered the Patriarch of the West, with an authority in the Church which did not go beyond that of a *primus inter pares*." [35] Prescinding from the Eastern understanding in the past, however, the fact remains that, from the Orthodox perspective, when the Church of Rome "separated itself from the Orthodox Church with the change of the Creed, it also lost the primacy".[36]

Consequently there is a need for a less romantic and demythologized view of the first millennium. Much is said about the relations between the West and the East in terms of peaceful coexistence, in the so-called undivided Church; the break is said to have followed with the definitive negation of the primacy of Rome by the Eastern Christians. This split is supposed to have come about "perhaps also because this primacy was presented to the Greeks with elements of human law, elements that could easily make them unwilling to accept such a primacy".[37] Indeed, at times,

---

[34] Cf. ibid., 28–29. Schatz himself affirms, "Within this pentarchy, Rome certainly had the undisputed first place. But if we ask whether Rome was seen merely as first among equals or first in a series, or whether it had a quantitatively different and more prominent function, the eastern witnesses cannot be summarized under a single heading. There were variations according to time and interest. The relationship of equality between the bishop of Rome and the other patriarchs was more common than any kind of subordination" (*Papal Primacy*, 49).

[35] Garuti, *Il Papa Patriarca di Occidente?*, 269.

[36] G. Cioffari, *L'ecclesiologia ortodossa Problemi e prospettive* (Bari, 1992), 36.

[37] W. de Vries, *Ortodossia e cattolicesimo* (Brescia, 1983), 21. Cf. H.J. Schulz, "Église locale et Église universelle. Primauté, Collégialité et Synodalité", *Proche-Orient Chrétien* 31 (1981): 14–15; W. Beinert, "Stand und Bewegung des ökumenischen Geschehens", *Catholica* 37 (1983): 24.

while pointing out the different emphases, it is affirmed that the two ecclesiologies "did not present themselves as antithetical and contradictory, but rather were complementary" and that "only in the twelfth century did the Greeks become conscious of that point in the rupture within the Church which had the papacy as its epicenter".[38] The Eastern Christians, too, were well aware of the need for ontological communion with Rome, but not of canonical communion, which had assumed primary importance in the Western view of the Church.[39] But this is not sufficient to allow us to present the first millennium as a model for the exercise of primacy.[40]

The same view of primacy is reflected among the present-day Orthodox theologians, even though, according to von Allmen,[41] the primacy of Rome is a given, an indisputable fact. Granting, in line with Orthodox tradition, the primacy of Peter among the apostles, as "the first among them", there still remains the problem of his successors. In keeping with classical ecclesiology, all bishops are fundamentally equal among themselves;[42] they are all in equal measure direct successors, not merely of

---

[38] J. Spiteris, *La Critica Bizantina*, 23–24.

[39] Cf. Duprey, "Une étape importante du dialogue catholique-orthodoxe. Balamand, 17–24 juin 1993", G. R. Evans and M. Gourgues, eds., *Communion et réunion. Mélanges Jean-Marie Roger Tillard* (Louvain, 1995), 118–19.

[40] Sartori, "Il papato domani: considerazioni ecumeniche", 15: "Gli studi storici (e K. Schatz è esplicito su questo punto; pp. 103–5) *dubitano* che esista realmente *un modello preciso e condiviso* da tutta la chiesa". Sartori himself stresses that the problem becomes complicated when one insists upon proposing the exercise of primacy in the first millennium as a model: "E' vero che questo riferimento, a motivo della sua ufficialità (almeno nel dialogo tra chiesa cattolica e chiese orientali), ha significato di stimolo immediato, forte e concretissimo. Ma giustamente da parte di interlocutori evangelici vengono sollevate *riserve e dubbi* sulla sua attualità" ("Ecumenismo nel terzo millennio. Considerazioni sull'enciclica 'Ut unum sint'", *Studia patavina* 42 [1995]: 644). Cf. N. Bux, *Il quinto sigillo. L'unità dei cristiani verso il terzo millennio* (Vatican City, 1997), 91–95.

[41] *Il primato della Chiesa di Pietro e di Paolo*, 50: "il primato d'onore della Chiesa patriarcale di Roma è riconosciuto non solo come ipotesi rigorosamente accettabile, ma come un fatto che si basa su un principio indiscutibile. In breve, per riprendere la formula barthiana: il *daß* del papato come struttura ecclesiologica non suscita un problema."

[42] Filaret of Kiev, "Paper", 10: "Therefore, not one bishop (the Bishop of Rome is one of the bishops) can be more of a bishop than any other bishop who heads the same Catholic Church in another place." Cf. Papadopoulos, "L'istituzione conciliare", 295–96; Cioffari, *L'ecclesiologia ortodossa*, 56–57.

Peter, but also of all the other apostles.[43] Even if, by analogy with the primacy of Peter among the apostles, "there must exist a first bishop within the episcopal college", still, "no locality is *a priori*, by 'divine right', destined to have this primacy",[44] just as no bishop in postapostolic times has the exclusive right to this primacy.[45] Historically, "for years Rome exercised the function of *primus inter pares*; after its separation from the Orthodox Communion, this honor was inherited by Constantinople."[46]

The Catholic and Orthodox doctrines on the relationship of communion between the local Churches and, consequently, on the communion among the bishops themselves and with the Bishop of Rome differ essentially even today, inasmuch as the Orthodox do not accept any developments in the formulation of the Catholic faith after the separation: at the most they might accept these as *theologoumena* of the Latin Church.[47] Hence, for the Orthodox, primacy is simply unacceptable, for the classical reason of the equality among the bishops.[48] It is the result of a doctrinal

---

[43] Clément, *La Chiesa ortodossa*, 64–65: "I Padri greci, i teologi di Bisanzio e la liturgia ortodossa sottolineano il primato di Pietro fra gli apostoli", nevertheless "il potere delle chiavi fu confidato a tutti gli apostoli". Their successors are all the bishops: "Attori della mutazione eucaristica, custodi privilegiati della verità, pastori del gregge di Cristo, i vescovi costituiscono dunque, per l'ecclesiologia ortodossa, i successori di Pietro nel senso più preciso.... Per questo l'immagine della 'roccia' nella tradizione ortodossa, designerà la funzione episcopale." Citing St. Cyprian, the author concludes, "tutti i vescovi, ciascuno nella sua chiesa e tutti insieme, seggono sulla *cattedra di Pietro*"; P. Evdokimov, *L'Ortodossia* (Bologna, 1981), 189: "Ogni vescovo ... è successore diretto di Pietro, del potere apostolico di celebrare l'Eucaristia". Cf. D. Papandreu, "Riflessioni sulla questione del primato", *Papato e servizio petrino*, 82, 84–85.

[44] Clément, *La Chiesa ortodossa*, 65.

[45] Cioffari, *L'ecclesiologia ortodossa*, 34: "Il passo evangelico di Mt XVI, 18 dava una certa priorità a Pietro, ma fra gli Apostoli, non fra i vescovi dei tempi successivi. L'Apostolo non va confuso col vescovo. Egli era qualcosa di unico e irripetibile, era itinerante, si disperdeva nel mondo. Il vescovo invece ha la sua cattedra, che è anche il limite della sua giurisdizione."

[46] Evdokimov, *L'Ortodossia*, 186–87. Cf. Clément, *La Chiesa ortodossa*, 65–66.

[47] J. Panagopoulos, "Ut unum sint", 139: "As the Orthodox understand it, papal primacy can only be accepted as a theologumenon of the Latin church, not as an essential principle of the *una sancta*." Cf. D. Salachas, "Les Églises soeurs", 113. It is still difficult, however, to explain how a Catholic bishop, Bishop Boustros, could have affirmed that the Melchites have the same common faith as the Greek Orthodox of Antioch and that they consider all other points on which there is discord, including the primacy, "come dei theologoumena, che possono continuare a essere oggetto di discussione in campo teologico" (interview given to F. Strazzari, *il regno-att.* 6/97, 165).

[48] N. Afanassieff, "La doctrine de la primauté à la lumière de l'ecclésiologie", *Istina* 4 (1957), 401–2: "Nous ne pouvons pas imaginer un catholicisme sans doctrine de la primauté,

and institutional development unique to the West, devoid of dogmatic significance, and determined by political and social factors,[49] and—as it is understood in the Latin Church—"it has never existed in the Eastern tradition".[50] Furthermore, it is not "a constitutive element for the unity of the Church", but an alteration of her episcopal structure,[51] a juridical structure which has prevailed over the sacramental order.[52] For this reason, as in the past, the "claims" and the "pretenses" of Rome will never be accepted by the great Eastern Churches, and thus, "far from promoting the unity of the Church", they continue to be "always and irremediably a cause of division".[53] Despite "intimations of consensus and moments of acceptance, even officially", the Eastern Churches in fact "declare themselves impervious and alien to the form of primacy that has taken root in the 'Latin Church' . . . , and this precisely on the basis of their tradition;

---

alors que pour l'orthodoxie cette doctrine est absolument inacceptable.... Aux yeux de l'Église Orthodoxe, le Christ a donné le pouvoir sur l'Église à l'assemblée des apôtres et c'est d'eux qu'il est passé à l'assemblée des évêques, dont chacun se trouve être le successeur d'un apôtre." Despite the new climate ushered in by dialogue, the Orthodox "tuttora rifiutano il primato giuridico di Roma" (Manna, "Quale primato dopo la 'Ut unum sint'?", 2).

[49] Frost, "Orthodoxie", 301: "Une telle conception de l'Église-communion ne peut qu'opposer une fin de non-recevoir à la primauté romaine telle que, dans sa forme actuelle, elle résulte du développement doctrinal et institutionel qu'a connu l'Occident catholique séparé de l'Orient. Certains théologiens orthodoxes vont jusqu'à lui dénier toute signification dogmatique, pour n'y voir qu'un fait historique déterminé par la place qu'avait occupée Rome dans l'empire romain: l'évêque de Rome serait devenu le premier de toute la chrétienté uniquement parce que Rome était devenue la première ville de l'empire."

[50] Lanne, "A piccoli passi oltre gli ostacoli", 76. Cf. J. Karavidopoulos, "Le rôle de Pierre et son importance dans l'Église du Nouveau Testament: problématique exégétique contemporaine", *Nicolaus* 19 (1992): 28.

[51] Salachas, "Les Églises sœurs", 115–16: "La divergence théologique consiste dans le fait que Rome conçoit la primauté du siège romain comme un facteur constitutif de l'unité ecclésiale, tandis que l'Orthodoxie voit en cette prétention une mutation de la structure épiscopale de l'Église." Cf. Papandreu, "Riflessioni sulla questione del primato", 82. Taken up again in *Irénikon* 55 (1982): 468.

[52] J. Ratzinger, *Principles of Catholic Theology. Building Stones for a Fundamental Theology* (San Francisco, 1987), 194–95: "For such a view, the Church in the West ... is seen, rather, as a centrally organized monolith in which the new legal concept of a 'perfect society' has superseded the old idea of succession in the community.... The old sacramental structure seems overgrown, even choked, by this new concept of law: the papacy is not a sacrament; it is 'only' a juridical institution; but this juridical institution has set itself above the sacramental order."

[53] S. C. Neill, "Division and the Search for Unity Prior to the Reformation", *A History of the Ecumenical Movement. 1517–1948* (Philadelphia, 1954), 1: 8–9.

hence, it is as if they were affirming that the present concrete form of papacy cannot count on their 'reception'".[54]

Especially unacceptable is the doctrine of primacy as formulated by the First Vatican Council, which, not having found corroboration in the faith of the universal Church and having no equivalent in the structure of the local Church,[55] will continue to constitute the one genuine obstacle to unity,[56] until the Catholics take into account the decisions of the preceding ecumenical councils.[57] Whereas for Catholics the Pope is the visible foundation of Church unity, for the Orthodox "he is only the first bishop of Christianity".[58] Or else, with the definition of primacy, never before proclaimed in any other council, the Roman Church explicitly broke away from tradition.[59]

Even today, what separates the East from Rome is above all the concept of the primacy as a supreme juridical authority, which the Pope, as the universal superbishop, "claims" to exercise, as successor of Peter and Vicar of Christ, over the whole people of God, with a universalistic and centralized system which is opposed to the autonomous autocephalous system of the local Churches[60] and relativizes or at times ignores the

---

[54] Sartori, "Il papato domani: considerazioni ecumeniche", 14.

[55] I. Bria, "La Koinonia comme communauté canonique. Perspectives actuelles", *Istina* 20 (1975): 122–23: "Il est évident que le dogme de la primauté et de la juridiction universelle du siège romain reste encore l'obstacle principal entre les deux Églises, d'abord parce qu'il ne repose pas sur la foi de l'Église universelle et puis parce qu'il n'a pas de correspondant dans la structure de l'Église locale."

[56] T. Ware, *The Orthodox Church* (New York, 1993), 316: "The crucial issue between Orthodoxy and Rome is certainly the understanding of the Papal ministry within the Church. We Orthodox cannot accept the definitions of the First Vatican Council, promulgated in 1870, concerning the infallibility and the supreme universal jurisdiction of the Pope."

[57] E. Ghikas, "Comment 'redresser' les définitions du premier Concile du Vatican", 182: "Ce sont là des affirmations que l'Orient ne saurait jamais accepter telles quelles et sans doute constitueront-elles une barrière infranchissable à toute tentative de réunion des deux Églises aussi longtemps que les théologiens catholiques s'obstineront à les considérer isolément, sans tenir compte des décisions des conciles antérieurs que l'Occident reconnaît comme oecuméniques, décisions avec lesquelles elles se doivent de former un tout logiquement cohérent."

[58] Bux, *Il quinto sigillo*, 34.

[59] Evdokimov, *L'Ortodossia*, 187.

[60] N. Nissiotis, "Qu'est-ce qui nous sépare encore de l'Église catholique romaine? La réponse d'un orthodoxe", *Concilium* no. 54 (1970), 23–25: "Les Orthodoxes n'ont jamais nié la vraie dimension de la primauté d'amour et d'honneur de l'évêque de Rome, mais en tant qu'évêque de Rome et non en tant que super-évêque universel, revêtu d'une autorité juridique suprême en tant que successeur de Pierre et Vicaire du Christ.... Le système

authority of the bishops, which has a sacramental origin.[61] Thus the primacy is no longer understood as presiding in charity, but as "supreme power, making the bishop of Rome a *principium, radix et origo* of the unity of the Church itself", the "sole Bishop" and the "sole doctor",[62] whereas "Christ remains, immediately, the sole 'principle, root, and origin' of the Church."[63]

As summarized well by Phidas, the Orthodox canonical tradition has always considered the primacy of the Pope within the framework of eucharistic ecclesiology, which favors the local Church as opposed to a universalistic ecclesiology. This canonical tradition considers the primacy in the context of the privileges—which are of an ecclesiastical nature and not of divine right—that belong to the first See within the institution of the pentarchy, excluding every direct relationship of the Pope to the episcopal body of the universal Church, and consequently in the context of conciliarity, which expressed perfectly the privileges of the first See within the framework of canonical relations between the pentarchy of the patriarchs and the ecumenical council.[64]

The difficulty of the past persists in the present: whereas for Catholics primacy is a constitutive element of the unity of the Church, the Orthodox see in this claim a change in the episcopal structure of the Church herself, a change which some have not hesitated to describe as *heretical*.[65]

---

universaliste et centraliste s'oppose au système autocéphale autonome des Églises locales, basé sur une administration synodale et conciliaire."

[61] Tillard, "Le ministère d'unité", 206–7: "L'Orient refuse une primauté conçue comme celle *du* Siège apostolique et non '*du premier des* sièges apostoliques'.... L'Orient refuse une régence de l'Église conçue comme un gouvernement central et autocratique, relativisant et parfois même ignorant le pouvoir des évêques, dont l'origine est sacramentelle." Pages 207–9 describe the two "deviations" in the Roman way of exercising primacy: confusion between supremacy and primacy, and doctrinal innovations, defining the truth without regard for conciliar authority.

[62] J.J. Von Allmen, *Il primato della Chiesa di Pietro e di Paolo*, 51, who cites A. Schmemann, "La notion de primauté dans l'ecclésiologie orthodoxe", *La Primauté de Pierre dans l'Église orthodoxe*, 141, and Y. Congar, *Ministères et communion ecclésiale* (Paris, 1971), 107.

[63] Clément, *La Chiesa ortodossa*, 66.

[64] Phidas, "La notion de primauté papale", 41.

[65] J. Garvey, "Orthodox/Roman Catholic Relations Today", *Doctrine and Life* 45 (1995): 145: "The idea that the power of the papacy is more or less absolute became particularly strong in the West during the eleventh century ..., and there are Orthodox who would argue that it is not only a distortion but, with the nineteenth century declaration of papal infallibility, heretical."

Orthodoxy especially has difficulty in reconciling the full and supreme authority of the Roman Pontiff with the episcopal, ordinary, and immediate jurisdiction of the bishop in his particular see and his role in the ecumenical council.[66] In the final analysis, it comes down to the question of the relationship between the monarchical structure and the collegial structure of the Church.[67]

The same view is found in the thought of some Orthodox exponents over the past few years. From the very beginning of the dialogue in charity, Patriarch Athenagoras has called Paul VI "the first in honor among us" and "the great and worthy Bishop of the Church of Rome, Pope and Patriarch of the Holy Roman Catholic Church of the West".[68] Similarly, Patriarch Demetrios does not go beyond recognizing him as the "first Bishop and Patriarch of the West" and "elder brother".[69]

The exact importance of these designations is to be found in the thinking of Metropolitan Meliton of Chalcedon. He too, in his address on the occasion of the solemn celebration of the tenth anniversary of the lifting of the anathemas (December 14, 1975), greeted Paul VI as the one who presides over the Church "in love and in honor" and assured him of the readiness of the Orthodox to promote the unity of Christians[70]; but then, in an interview given to La Croix (1984), he declared that, precisely in

---

[66] Salachas, "Les Églises soeurs", 115–16: "L'ecclésiologie orthodoxe se pose des problèmes sérieux ... (a) Comment concilier le pouvoir plein et suprême de l'évêque de Rome sur toute l'Église avec la juridiction—elle aussi épiscopale, ordinaire et immédiate—de l'évêque de chaque diocèse? (b) Comment peut-on concilier la place du Pape dans le Concile oecuménique, en dehors et au-dessus du Concile?"

[67] P. Dentin, Les privilèges des Papes, 231: "La question la plus radicale que pose l'orthodoxie est la suivante: 'La structure de l'Église chrétienne est-elle, d'après l'Évangile, monarchique ou collégiale'? ... La reconnaissance de l'idée collégiale mène précisément à reconnaître un évêque comme premier parmi des évêques, c'est-à-dire à lui attribuer la primauté, jamais cependant dans le sens d'un 'Pontife suprême' mais comme le 'premier entre des égaux'." Cf. also J. G. Pagé, Qui est l'église?, III: L'église, peuple de Dieu (Montreal, 1979), 454–56.

[68] Address of welcome (Stormon, 159, no. 173); Letter to Pope Paul VI (Stormon, 170, no. 186).

[69] Address to Card. Willebrands (November 30, 1973): Stormon, 260, no. 311.

[70] Cf. Stormon, 277–78, no. 330. In an interview granted to the newspaper Ekklesiastiki Alithia (December 1979), the same Metropolitan describes the primacy of the Pope as follows: "The fact is that the Pope came to meet the other head of Christians as equal to equal. What I mean by that is that we acknowledge the Pope's primacy of honor, just as the other Orthodox Churches recognize a similar primacy in the Ecumenical Patriarchate" (Stormon, 381, no. 411).

view of unity, it would be necessary to reinterpret the dogmas defined by the First Vatican Council which are unacceptable from the Orthodox point of view[71]; the primacy of honor attributed to the Pope should be equivalent to that attributed by other Churches to the ecumenical patriarch.[72]

Even Metropolitan Chrysostomos of Peristerion, referring to the dialogue, states that "the outcome of the dialogue will depend, in the first place, on whether or not a solution is found to the highly disputed question of excessive powers and the authority of the Pope within the Church, an authority which the Orthodox cannot accept for ecclesiological, historical, biblical, canonical and traditional reasons."[73]

For his part, the present ecumenical patriarch, Bartholomew I, aside from his reaction to the invitation of John Paul II,[74] in an address to the Swiss bishops (December 1995), denies that Christ entrusted to Peter a pastoral role superior to that of the other apostles and consequently affirms that the responsibility of steering the ship of the Church is common to all bishops.[75] He openly recognizes the existence of two different ecclesi-

---

[71] Cf. *Irénikon* 57 (1984): 66–67.

[72] When reminded that "*it has been said that this journey of the Pope has heightened the prestige of the Ecumenical Patriarchate*", he responds, "It is not for me to comment on what people say. The fact is that the Pope came to meet the other head of Christians as equal to equal. What I mean by that is that we acknowledge the Pope's primacy of honor, just as the other Orthodox Churches recognize a similar primacy in the Ecumenical Patriarchate" (Stormon, 381, no. 411). The same Metropolitan subsequently defined the Pope as "chief pastor of the Roman Catholic Church and first Bishop of Christendom": *Address during the papal audience* (June 28, 1979: Stormon, 350, no. 393).

[73] Cf. "Il dialogo teologico tra le chiese ortodossa e cattolica romana", *il regno-doc.* 19/86, 601. Even more drastic is Panagopoulos in his affirmation that "despite the intensive theological conversation we have not got one step further" ("Ut unum sint", 139).

[74] "Salutiamo positivamente questo passo del papa Giovanni Paolo II e auspichiamo che seguano altri sviluppi positivi in questa direzione. E' noto che nella questione dell'interpretazione del primato la chiesa ortodossa dissente dalla dottrina della chiesa cattolica. Discutibile è il trasferimento del ruolo personale di Pietro fra i primi apostoli a tutti i vescovi di Roma. Il problema in questione è, per la pratica dei rapporti fra i cristiani, il più grave dal punto di vista teologico fra quelli che oggi in pratica ci dividono, e per questo non potremmo che salutare positivamente l'inizio di un dialogo teologico su questo tema adesso, alle soglie del giubileo del cristinesimo del duemila" (*il regno-att.* 20/95, 579–80).

[75] "Le Seigneur n'a confié à Pierre aucune tâche pastorale supérieure": "[L]'idée selon laquelle le Seigneur, en choisissant les douze Apôtres, confia à l'un d'eux la tâche de les gouverner, n'a aucun fondement dans l'Écriture Sainte ... Cela n'avait donc pas le sens de confier à celui-ci une tâche pastorale supérieure vis-à-vis de celle des autres disciples. Le Seigneur 'donna le nom d'Apôtres' (Lc 6, 13) à tous ses disciples à titre égal et sans discrimination aucune. ... Il en découle que chacun de nous, évêques, est tenu personnellement pour responsable de contribuer ou d'entraver la route de la nef de l'Église, de la

ologies[76] and hence characterizes the primacy and infallibility of the Roman Pontiff as "theologically erroneous claims" that constitute "the greatest and most scandalous stumbling block" for Catholic-Orthodox dialogue.[77]

Hence Orthodox theologians wonder what sort of results dialogue can produce, if the Catholic side continues to be faithful, in an uncompromising way, to its concept of primacy and remains closed to a new interpretation that might enable the other Churches involved in the dialogue to accept it.[78]

On the basis of such a view it is not surprising that the primacy constitutes the most critical point in Catholic-Orthodox dialogue. "If it is true that many present-day Orthodox theologians demonstrate an openness while debating this central theme, we must at the same time note that the representatives of the traditional line of thinking have made no move forward." For the Orthodox, "the papacy and especially the infallibility of the Roman Pontiff represent a stumbling block".[79]

There is nothing else to do, then, but to go through the various phases of the dialogue, both at the local level and at the official level, in order to analyze the documents and evaluate them.

II. THE PRIMACY IN CATHOLIC-ORTHODOX DIALOGUE

The question of the primacy of the Bishop of Rome did not figure on the agenda of the World Council of Churches, which was established in

---

bonne ou de la mauvaise tenue de cette route" (*La documentation catholique*, February 4, 1996, no. 3, 135).

[76] "We have different ecclesiologies, and the place of the Bishop of Rome in the Universal Church of Christ constitutes the principal obstacle" (*Eastern Churches Journal* 3, no. 1 [1996]: 11).

[77] Interview given to the Catholic periodical of Krakow, "Tygodnik Powszechny": cf. *Irénikon* 59 (1996): 231, under the title "Relations entre les communions". A similar declaration was made by the same Patriarch in an interview given to a group of journalists (Phanar, February 6, 1997): cf. *Episkepsis*, 28 (1997): 2–3, no. 541.

[78] Salachas, "Les Églises soeurs", 115–16: "À quoi aboutira le dialogue officiel ... si la théologie catholique reste fidèle et intransigeante à sa conception sur la primauté juridictionelle et si les Églises orthodoxes seraient appelées d'accepter cette thèse ecclésiologique romaine? En conséquence les théologiens orthodoxes se demandent: Faut-il exclure, dans ce cas, une éventuelle nouvelle modification ou interprétation de la primauté juridictionelle du Pape ... dans le but d'une éventuelle acceptation par les autres Églises en dialogue avec Rome?"

[79] A. Strukelj, "La comprensione ecumenica nell'ecclesiologia ortodossa del teologo serbo Justin Popovic'", *Nicolaus* 23 (1996): 110–11. Cf. A. Basdekis, "Das Papsttum aus der Sicht der orthodoxen Theologie und Kirche", *Orthodoxes Forum* 9 (1995): 69–70.

Amsterdam in 1948. It was not even introduced with the entry of the Catholic Church into the ecumenical movement starting with the Second Vatican Council. As Gassmann has correctly argued, "the ecumenical mentality and strategy [of dialogue] led the Catholic party to believe that it would be inadvisable for them, at the outset of their collaboration ... with the World Council, and in the intense official bilateral discussions with numerous important Christian confessions, to put the 'most burning issue' on the carpet. The dialogue with the new Roman Catholic interlocutor, therefore, was centered at first on those questions concerning which there was hope of arriving at a consensus or indeed at a broad identity of views." [80]

Only in recent times has the primacy become a theme that is actually discussed in ecumenical dialogue, reflecting the conviction that "if it is not resolved, it is bound to remain an impediment and a barrier", since it is even clearer that "the other Christian Churches will not accept the papal office as formulated by the First Vatican Council". [81] Probably it was precisely this realization that led John Paul II to take the initiative in placing the subject on the agenda. [82]

The theological dialogue between the Catholic Church and the Orthodox Churches was preceded by a long period of preparation through the so-called *dialogue of charity*, which has profoundly marked the reciprocal relations. With the call to unity addressed to all Christians by John XXIII in his first Christmas message (December 23, 1958), [83] a new era was ushered in, which found concrete expressions of fraternity in the case of Paul VI and Patriarch Athenagoras: visits by Catholic and Orthodox del-

---

[80] G. Gassmann, "L'ufficio papale. Una prospettiva ecumenica?", *Papato e servizio petrino*, 7–8. Cf. D. Valentini, *Il nuovo Popolo di Dio in cammino. Punti nodali per una ecclesiologia attuale* (Rome, 1984), 127ff.

[81] H. J. Pottmeyer, "Papato e communio ecclesiarum. Il Vaticano I nel Vaticano II—vie per un'intesa ecumenica", *Papato e istanze ecumeniche*, 127.

[82] Sartori, "'Ut unum sint': verso quale futuro?". Editorial of *Studi ecumenici* 13 (1995), 428: "Il tema del primato costituisce ... il punto più nuovo e più importante dell'enciclica. Non che la teologia ecumenica in questi ultimi tempi l'avesse snobbato. ... Soltanto, non ne hanno trattato direttamente i dialoghi ecumenici più ufficiali; il tema in essi è stato affrontato solo parzialmente e non in modo esplicitamente decisivo ... questa volta è il papa stesso che prende l'iniziativa di porlo all'ordine del giorno."

[83] Cf. Stormon, 28–29, no. 4. The appeal was received "with a fraternal welcome" by Patriarch Athenagoras (Stormon, 30, no. 5).

egations to Phanar and Rome; the presence of Orthodox observers at the Second Vatican Council; the "fraternal meeting" crowned by the "kiss of peace"; the lifting of the reciprocal anathemas of 1054; the promulgation of the papal brief *Anno ineunte* (July 26, 1967); and the publication of the *Tomos agapis*, which contains the exchange of messages, letters, telegrams, and the texts of addresses delivered by the Pope and by the patriarch or by their emissaries. As pointed out in E.J. Storman's preface, these texts "give evidence of a common life which is being taken up again in increasing measure, and of a new awareness of unity and of our communion in the mystery of Christ".[84]

This direct connection between "the dialogue of charity" and "theological dialogue" is explicitly underlined by the Catholics[85] as well as by the Orthodox,[86] and both sides have also provided precise guidelines on its purpose[87] and methodology.[88]

In fact, the theological dialogue first found concrete expression at the local level; indeed, as we shall see, it is precisely on this level that we find the first references to the question of the primacy of the Bishop of Rome. Yet there was a steadily growing conviction as to the need for initiating a

---

[84] Stormon p. 24. Cf. Garuti, "Sister Churches", Appendix, p. 269.

[85] Paul VI, *Reply to Metropolitan Meliton of Heliopolis* (February 16, 1965): "We must, by means of more numerous and fraternal contacts, restore step by step what the time of isolation has undone, and create anew, at all levels of the life of our Churches, an atmosphere which will allow us, when the time comes, to set about a theological discussion likely to yield good results" (Stormon, 88, no. 88). Cf. Card. A. Bea, *Address to Patriarch Athenagoras* (April 3, 1965) (Stormon, 93, no. 93).

[86] Metropolitan Meliton of Heliopolis, *Address to Paul VI* (February 16, 1965): "By means of this dialogue may we labor together, removing the accumulated obstacles that stand in our way and preparing the ground on all sides, so that we may be soon brought into theological dialogue" (Stormon, 86–87, no. 87). In his response to Cardinal Bea, Patriarch Athenagoras says that the dialogue of charity is a "careful preparation for the theological dialogue" (Stormon, 95, no. 94).

[87] The purpose is essentially to restore full communion by overcoming the doctrinal and disciplinary differences that still persist and prevent the common celebration of the Eucharist: cf. under respective sections, for example, Stormon, 52, no. 33; 54, no. 35; 63, no. 49; 288, no. 334; 291, no. 335; 315, no. 358; 316–17, no. 359; 353, no. 394; 359, no. 401; 365, no. 403.

[88] Metropolitan Meliton of Chalcedon: "The ecclesial dialogue is now beginning. There will be no concessions on essential matters, but only a search for a common basis. We Orthodox do not accept any sacrifice of truth. All we are doing is to seek an interpretation of the truth with love as a criterion. In this dialogue there will be no compromise; there will be no agreements of a political sort that are signed today and rescinded tomorrow. We are dealing here with a reality that enters into living experience" (Stormon, 380, no. 411).

dialogue on the official level.[89] Through the work of two parallel preparatory commissions and a joint coordinating committee, a common Plan
was eventually drawn up regarding the purpose and the methodology of
the dialogue and regarding the topics to be dealt with in the first phase.[90]
After the approval of the document by the respective Catholic and Orthodox authorities (November 30, 1979) on the occasion of the visit of John
Paul II to the Ecumenical Patriarch Demetrios in Constantinople, the
official announcement of the dialogue was made, and a Joint International Commission was established which, in its first plenary session
(Patmos-Rodi, May 29–June 4, 1980), further defined the procedure and
organization of the work, and the topic for the first phase.[91]

During the subsequent plenary sessions, preceded by the work of the
coordinating committee or of the subcommissions, the following documents were elaborated:

    1. *The Mystery of the Church and of the Eucharist in the Light of [the
       Mystery of] the Holy Trinity* (II assembly: Munich, 1982)[92]

    2. *Faith, Sacraments and the Unity of the Church* (IV assembly: Cassano
       Murge, Bari, June 16, 1987)[93]

---

[89] On the procedure of the dialogue through its different phases, cf. F. Bouwen, "Ouverture du dialogue théologique entre l'Église catholique et l'Église orthodoxe", *Proche-Orient
Chrétien* 29 (1979): 314–47; E. Fortino, "Il dialogo tra cattolici ed ortodossi. Panorama e
prospettive", *La Chiesa cattolica oggi nel dialogo. Corso breve di ecumenismo*, IV (Rome, 1982):
7–17; idem, "Il dialogo teologico fra la Chiesa Cattolica e la Chiesa ortodossa 1979–1987",
ibid., IX (Rome, 1988): 7–20; idem, "Le fasi più recenti del dialogo Cattolico-ortodosso
1988–1995", ibid., X (Rome, 1995): 7–26; idem, "Il dialogo fra la Chiesa Cattolica e la
Chiesa Ortodossa", *Religioni e sette nel mondo* 1/4 (1995): 127–52; idem, "La 'Communio-
Koinonía' nel dialogo teologico cattolico-ortodosso", P. Rodríguez (ed.); *L'ecclesiologia trent'anni
dopo la "Lumen gentium"* (Rome, 1995), 181–99; G. Assimakis, "L'ecclesiologia nei documenti della Commissione mista di dialogo teologico tra la Chiesa cattolica romana e la
Chiesa ortodossa nei primi dieci anni della sua attività (1980–1990)", *Oriente Cristiano* 33/1
(1993): 5–38, and 33/2 (1993): 3–34; D. Salachas, *Il dialogo teologico ufficiale tra la Chiesa
Cattolico-romana e la chiesa ortodossa. Iter e documentazione* (Bari, 1994); P. G. Gianazza, "Documenti del dialogo ecumenico ufficiale cattolico-ortodosso", *Nicolaus* 23 (1996): 319–57.

[90] "Plan to Set Underway the Theological Dialogue between the Roman Catholic and
the Orthodox Churches"; cf. Salachas, *Il dialogo*, 25–30.

[91] Cf. IS, no. 44 (1980), 102b–112a; BE 47–52.

[92] IS, no. 49 (1982), 107–12.

[93] IS, no. 64 (1987), 82–87. The theme was also dealt with in the III assembly (Crete,
May 30–June 8, 1984): cf. IS, no. 55 (1984), 67. Two articles that appeared in the review
Irénikon (1988, no. 61), one by Lanne, "Foi, Sacrements et Unité", and the other by De
Halleux, "Foi, Baptême et Unité", both of whom are among the chief draftsmen of the
Bari Document, provide us with extensive knowledge about the serious difficulties that
arose in this regard during the discussions.

3. *The Sacrament of Order in the Sacramental Structure of the Church* (V assembly: Valamo, June 19–27, 1988)[94]

4. *Uniatism, Method of Union of the Past, and the Present Search for Full Communion* (VII assembly: Balamand, June 17–24, 1993)[95]

In none of these documents is the question of the primacy of the Bishop of Rome confronted directly. The first three, in conformity with the plan proposed by the Joint Preparatory Commission, describe "the common Catholic and Orthodox concept of the mystery of the Church as a communion of faith and of sacraments, manifested eminently in the celebration of the Eucharist", and the structure of the Church herself, which is "expressed in the sacramentality of the ordinations of bishops, presbyters and deacons".[96] As for the primacy, the documents limit themselves to stressing that the *episkopé* of the universal Church is traditionally expressed in the "conciliar practice" and that it can be studied within the "perspective of communion among local churches".[97]

In reality, during the session of Valamo the theme was also chosen for the next document, which would be discussed at Freising in 1990: "The ecclesiological and canonical consequences of the sacramental structure of the Church; conciliarity and authority in the Church".[98] At its meeting in Moscow in February 1990, the coordinating committee also drew up a schema for the text, but it was never studied, because of the insistence of the Orthodox in wanting to give precedence to the problem of uniatism (the Balamand Document).[99] This was supposed to be taken up

---

[94] IS, no. 68 (1988), 173–78. Cf. Salachas, *Il dialogo*, 132–45.

[95] IS, no. 83 (1993), 96–99. Cf. Salachas, *Il dialogo*, 149–54.

[96] Cf. Salachas, *Il dialogo*, 134.

[97] Cf. the Munich Document (IS, no. 49 [1982], 112a); the Valamo Document (IS, no. 68 [1988], 178b).

[98] In the press-communiqué of Valamo (June 27, 1988), it was said, "Both Churches have traditions of conciliarity or synodality which will be examined in the expectation of finding areas of agreement and in the hope that areas of divergence do not create any more obstacles to full communion. Authority in the Church, especially episcopal authority, will be considered not only in the communion of Churches as a whole [and] within particular areas but also within the individual or local Church" (IS, no. 68 [1988], 161b). Cf. O–RCC, *Reaction to the Document of Valamo on the Sacrament of Order* (Brighton, Mass., 1989), no. 27: *St. Vladimir's Theological Quarterly* 34 (1990): 355.

[99] According to the communiqué of Freising (June 15, 1990), the Joint Commission, meeting to draw up its fourth document, was able to draw up, before the defection of some Orthodox members, only a communiqué on "the problem of the origin and present existence of the Catholic Churches of the Byzantine rite" with the connected questions related to their so-called proselytism. A special subcommission for study of the issue was finally established, since both sides had recognized that, "given the situation of conflict

again in June 1996 at the meeting in Baltimore, which did not take place, however, because of the rift created between the patriarchates of Constantinople and Moscow on account of the Orthodox Church of Estonia.[100] The plenary session, too, which had been planned for June 1999, did not take place on account of the war in the Balkans.[101]

An overview, limited though it may be, of the results attained by the Catholic-Orthodox dialogue with regard to the primacy of the Bishop of Rome can be had only through a well-reasoned synthesis of the different elements present in the various local and official documents and in light of the ecclesiological concept underlying them.

Taking its inspiration from the notion of the Church which is typical in the East, the ecumenical dialogue, too, places the emphasis first and foremost on the *reality of the local Church*, which is realized in the celebration of the Eucharist and which, in its turn, is the sacramental realization and manifestation of the presence of the one and only Church of Christ in a given place.[102] In the New Testament "the church describes a 'local' reality", and she "exists in history as local church".[103]

---

which prevails in some regions between the Eastern Catholic Churches of the Byzantine Rite and the Orthodox Church, the problem of 'Uniatism' is urgent and should have priority over the other subjects to be discussed in the dialogue" (quoted by Salachas, *Il dialogo*, 214–16; cf. IS, no. 73 [1990], 52). Cf. Bouwen, "Balamand 1993. VIIe session de la Commission internationale pour le dialogue entre l'Église catholique et l'Église orthodoxe", *Proche-Orient Chrétien* 43 (1993): 91–112.

[100] Patriarch Bartholomew I himself acknowledges this in an interview with the *Catholic News Service*: cf. *Irénikon* 69 (1996): 230.

[101] Cf. Letter of John Paul II to Cardinal Cassidy: IS, no. 103 (2000), 61b. The meeting finally took place at Baltimore in July 2000. However, no agreement was reached, and hence "it was decided not to have a common statement at this time": IS, no. 104 (2000), 148a.

[102] (U.S.A.) O–RCC, Joint Declaration *Primacy and Conciliarity*: "The mystery of Christ's church, in its fullness, is therefore most directly and clearly encountered in the eucharistic community. Each local church, recognized in its celebration of the eucharist, is a full sacramental realization of the one church of Christ" (*Origins* 19 [1989]: 471, no. 4); French Joint Roman Catholic-Orthodox Committee, *The Roman Primacy within the Communion of Churches* (January 11, 1991), *One in Christ* 29 (1993): 157: "The eucharistic body of Christ is the source of this ecclesial body; eucharistic celebration is therefore the highest manifestation of the Church. Because this celebration, in which the mystery is present each time in all its fullness, is always the celebration of a local Church, it is a local Church which is truly the presence, in one place [i.e., in any particular place], of the one Church of Christ."

[103] The Munich Document (II, 1: IS, no. 49 [1982], 109a).

Consequently, the role of the bishop in the local Church is also emphasized: "Because it is in the eucharistic memorial that the Church manifests its fullness, it is equally in the presiding at the Eucharist that the role
of bishop appears in its full light".[104] "In the eucharistic celebration, in
fact, believers offer themselves with Christ as a royal priesthood. They do
so thanks to the ministerial action which makes present in their midst
Christ himself who proclaims the word, makes the bread and the cup
become through the Spirit his body and blood, incorporating them in
himself, giving them his life."[105]

The eucharistic celebration thus becomes the "modus *par excellence*"
through which is expressed "the independent existence of the local church"
in her communitarian dimension, as an individual Church,[106] which has
the Bishop as her center, "whose communion realizes the unity of all and
expresses the fullness of the church".[107] It follows that there is a fundamental equality among all local Churches and all bishops.[108]

At the same time, the eucharistic celebration realizes the unity of the
entire Christian community: "The eucharist ... also manifests the unity
of all churches which truly celebrate it and [furthermore, through the
centuries] the unity of all the churches with the apostolic community
from the beginnings up to the present day.... Indeed, as the central act
of episcopal ministry, [the Eucharist] makes clearly present the world to
come: the church gathered in communion, offering itself to the Father,
through the Son, in the Holy Spirit."[109]

---

[104] Commission of Orthodox and Roman Catholic Theologians, *Reflections on Ministries*
(Chambésy, December 15, 1977, no. 9): *One in Christ* 14 (1978): 292. Cf. the Valamo
Document (no. 34: IS, no. 68 [1988], 176b); French Joint Roman Catholic-Orthodox Com-
mittee, *The Roman Primacy*, 157.

[105] The Valamo Document (no. 35: IS, no. 68 [1988], 176b).

[106] [U.S.A.] O–RCC, *An Agreed Statement on the Church* 4 (New York, December 4,
1974: BE 84).

[107] The Valamo Document (no. 25: IS, no. 68 [1988], 175b).

[108] Cf. [U.S.A.] O–RCC, *The Church*, 6 (BE 85).

[109] The Valamo Document (no. 36: IS, no. 68 [1988], 176b). It takes up a text of the
Commission of Orthodox and Roman Catholic Theologians, *Reflections on Ministries*, no. 10,
293. On the Church-Trinity relationship cf. O–RCC, *The Church*, 2: "The Church is
the communion of believers living in Jesus Christ and the Spirit with the Father. It has
its orgin and prototype in the Trinity, in which there is both distinction of persons and
unity based on love, not subordination" (BE 84). Cf. the Munich Document (II, 1: IS,
no. 49 [1982], 109a) and the French Joint Roman Catholic-Orthodox Committee (EOE
IV 936).

The unity of the local Church, constituted by the eucharistic celebration and guaranteed by the bishop, is therefore "inseparable from the universal communion of the churches", because for one Church "it is essential to be in communion with the others".[110] In this respect, too, the role of the bishop is central; he "becomes in his church the guarantor of apostolicity, the one who represents it within the *communion* of churches, its link with the other churches",[111] In fact, through the sacrament of ordination the bishop "is made minister of a church which he represents in the universal communion".[112]

If the local Churches were isolated and if they lived in self-sufficient autonomy, the universal Church would be reduced to an abstraction: they should therefore be in reciprocal communion through a living process of recognition and exchange.[113] There exists, therefore, a reciprocity between eucharistic communion and ecclesial communion in the person of the bishop, who presides at the Eucharist in his Church and constitutes the bond of communion with the other Churches.[114] The mission of every bishop entrusted with a local Church entails, constitutively, the "solicitude for the totality of Churches which form the universal communion".[115]

---

[110] The Valamo Document (no. 26: IS, no. 68 [1988], 175b). Cf. Commission of Orthodox and Roman Catholic Theologians, *Reflections on Ministries*, no. 14, 293–94.

[111] The Valamo Document (no. 47: IS, no. 68 [1988], 177b).

[112] Ibid. (no. 26: IS, no. 68 [1988], 176a).

[113] French Joint RC-Orthodox Committee, *The Roman Primacy*, 157: "All local Churches gathered together by the Eucharist are in principle the full manifestation in each place of the one catholic and apostolic Church of Christ, but they are so not in isolation nor through an autocratic autonomy that reduces the universal Church to an abstraction: they can be the full manifestation only by maintaining living and active bonds of communion with other local Churches which, just like they themselves and for the same reasons, are the Church of God. The very same elements constitutive of each of the Churches—the Spirit, the gospel and sacraments, pastoral ministry—require that they must be in communion with each other through a living process of recognition and interaction. The one and only Church is thus a communion of local Churches which must be linked to one another by the very elements that make each of them exist as Church."

[114] Ibid., 158: "Because of the reciprocity of eucharistic communion and ecclesial communion, the one who presides at the Eucharist of a particular Church also has the responsibility of being the bond of communion with other Churches. Bishops therefore represent their Church in the communion of Churches and they insert their Church into this communion, just as, conversely, they represent within their own Church the apostolic faith in which all Churches share. For this reason one can speak of a 'college' of bishops: their 'collegiality' is rooted in episcopal ordination, and it is inseparable from what is first, the communion of Churches."

[115] Ibid., 159.

Concretely, the communion of Churches "is expressed and realized in and through the *episcopal college*".[116] In fact, when with the sacrament of ordination the bishop "receives the charism of the Spirit for the *episkopé* of one local church, his own, by that very fact he receives the charism of the Spirit for the *episkopé* of the entire church.... The *episkopé* for the universal church is seen to be entrusted by the Spirit to the totality of local bishops *in communion with one another*."[117]

The communion of the episcopal college in the course of history has known, in the East as well as in the West, "various forms" of practice: "by exchange of letters, by visits of one church to another, but principally by synodal or conciliar life".[118] The most explicit form, therefore, is that of the synods or councils, "privileged places where the communion of Churches is manifested and realized, through those who represent them".[119]

These were joined very soon by the patriarchates. In fact, even while safeguarding the fundamental equality of all local Churches, a *hierarchy* among the Churches gradually developed: "in response to the demands of the mission of the church",[120] from the very first centuries "a distinction and a hierarchy was established between churches of earlier foundation and churches of more recent foundation, between mother and daughter churches, between churches of larger cities and churches of outlying areas."[121] A relationship of interdependence was thus established between him who is "first" and the other bishops, which "mirrors the church's prototype: the Trinity, which the Church can only approach".[122] This hierarchy, or *taxis*, which in an early phase is manifested on a regional level in the "communion in the same patriarchate or in some other form

---

[116] Commission of Orthodox and Roman Catholic Theologians, *Reflections on Ministries*, 294.

[117] The Munich Document (III, 4: IS, no. 49 [1982], 112). In this connection the observation of the O–RCC in its *Commentary on the Munich Document* (New York, 1983) is interesting: "The way in which the document focuses on the 'local church' through eucharistic ecclesiology does not readily correspond to the actual situation of bishops and their churches today. Although this model offers some useful insights, the character, numerical size, and geographical extent of most local churches makes application problematic" (BE 67).

[118] The Valamo Document (no. 52: IS, no. 68 [1988], 178a).

[119] French Joint Roman Catholic-Orthodox Committee, *The Roman Papacy*, 158.

[120] O–RCC, *The Church*, 6 (BE 85).

[121] The Valamo Document (no. 52: IS, no. 68 [1988], 178a).

[122] O–RCC, *The Church*, 5 (BE 84–85).

of regional unity" [123] and which entailed the dependence of the bishops on a primate, [124] later found its canonical expression formulated by the councils, which attributed to the bishops of these sees "a place and prerogatives recognized in the organization of the synodal life of the church. Thus was formed the pentarchy: Rome, Constantinople, Alexandria, Antioch and Jerusalem, even if in the course of history there appeared apart from the Pentarchy other archbishops, metropolitans, primates and patriarchs." [125]

The fundamental forms of exercising the responsibility of maintaining the communion of the totality of the Churches, therefore, were, and still are, the synodal institution and the patriarchal institution. [126] Even though the forms have changed according to the places and times, the principle of the synodal activity of the bishops "is to manifest and make efficacious the life of the church by joint episcopal actions, under the presidency of the one whom they recognized as the first among them [*primus inter pares*]", [127] for example, with regard to the controversial questions which were of more interest to the local Churches or to the totality of Churches or in situations of crisis. [128]

---

[123] The Munich Document (III, 3b: IS, no. 49 [1982], 111b).

[124] O–RCC, *The Church*: "The dependence of local churches on the territorial bishops found its counterpart in the dependence of bishops on the 'first' bishop (archbishop, metropolitan, patriarch) as territories were divided among bishops" (BE 84).

[125] The Valamo Document (no. 52: IS, no. 68 [1988], 178b). Cf. O–RCC, *The Church* (BE 85). The Orthodox position in this connection is well expressed by the Joint Orthodox-Old Catholic Theological Commission (Chambéry, 1983), *Ecclesiology*, in *Koinonia auf Altkirchlicher Basis* (ed. Urs von Arx), 203: "Even though the bishops are equal to one another in episcopal authority, the life of the Church during the first three centuries evidenced a differentiation in the positions of honour granted to the various episcopal sees. The bishops of certain local Churches, who had gained greater authority for various reasons, held a special position of honour and exercised a greater influence in ecclesiastical matters. The position of honour of the bishops of these sees was unfolded in Ecumenical Synods since the 4th century to a presidency of honour (*presbeia times*) in the Church (3rd canon of the 2nd Ecumenical Synod)."

[126] O–RCC, *Primacy and Conciliarity*: "The two institutions, mutually dependent and mutually limiting, which have exercised the strongest influence on maintaining the ordered communion of the churches since apostolic times, have been the gathering of bishops and other appointed local leaders in synods and the primacy or recognized preemenence of one bishop among his episcopal colleagues" (no. 6, 471b). Cf. French Joint Roman Catholic-Orthodox Committee, *The Roman Primacy*, 158.

[127] The Valamo Document (no. 53: IS, no. 68 [1988], 178b).

[128] Ibid., no. 54, 178b. "He only takes a decision in agreement with the other bishops and the latter take no important decision without the agreement of the first."

Nevertheless, on the basis of Canon 34 of the apostles, the primate is simply the *primus inter pares* in order that the independence and interdependence between the "first" and the other bishops may be safeguarded: "In ecumenical councils, convened in the Holy Spirit at times of crisis, bishops of the church, with supreme authority, decided together about the faith and issued canons to affirm the tradition of the apostles." [129] His role should always be conceived "as complementary to the function of synods". [130] The Churches are in fact "bound together neither by a centralized organization nor through a single official" charged with an ecclesial ministry; hence the primates and the patriarchs, in virtue of their function, are "signs of the unity of their churches", and the ecumenical patriarch of Constantinople "does have a priority of honor as 'first among equals', *'primus inter pares'*"; nevertheless, "the Orthodox churches are unified in love and peace only through communion in faith and sacraments". [131]

The supreme authority of the Church, therefore, is not entrusted to any individual person but is constituted by the ecumenical council, [132] which, however, "is 'not an authority equipped with power to rule over the church', but rather a witness to the Church's self-consciousness": it has an ecumenical dimension and hence is definitive and authoritative "only after its decisions have been received as true by the whole of the people of the Church." [133]

The view of the nature and structure of the Church that has emerged from the Catholic-Orthodox dialogue provides the perspective within which the topic of the primacy of the Bishop of Rome could be approached, a topic which constitutes a serious difference of opinion [134] and is still the

---

[129] Ibid., 54. Cf. French Joint Roman Catholic-Orthodox Committee, *The Roman Primacy*, 160.

[130] O–RCC, *Primacy and Conciliarity* (no. 6, 471b). The text further specifies, "It is the primate (*protos*) who convenes the synod, presides over its activities and seeks, together with his colleagues, to assure its continuity in faith and discipline with the apostolic church; yet it is the synod which, together with the primate, gives voice and definition to the apostolic tradition."

[131] Institute for Ecumenical Research, *Communio/Koinonia* (Strasbourg, 1990), 18.

[132] Cf. the Valamo Document (no. 54: IS, no. 58 [1988], 178b); Old Catholic-Orthodox Conversations (Chambésy, 1981), *Ecclesiology*: MV 416.

[133] Institute for Ecumenical Research, *Communio/Koinonia*, 18 .

[134] Cf. the Valamo Document (no. 55: IS, no. 58 [1988], 178b).

principal point of debate and an obstacle to full reciprocal communion, for example, with respect to the manner in which it has been exercised.[135] The presentation of the Catholic view has led to a better clarification of the problem, which nevertheless has yet to be resolved beginning with the ministerial function of "presiding", which is specific and common to all bishops,[136] in light of the communion which is expressed and actualized among the local Churches and within the episcopal college.[137]

The two concepts of the primacy still remain extremely diverse. It is true, indeed, that the See of Rome was recognized as the first among the "centers of communion" constituted by the major sees,[138] but this recognition was qualified by various restrictions. In reality, the diversity of forms assumed by the primatial function of the Roman Pontiff was highly accentuated,[139] distinguishing "between his solicitude for the commu-

---

[135] O–RCC, *Primacy and Conciliarity*: "The particular form of primacy among the churches exercised by the bishops of Rome has been and remains the chief point of dispute between the Orthodox and Roman Catholic churches and their chief obstacle to full ecclesial communion with each other. Disagreement has often centered on the way in which the leadership exercised by Peter in expressing and confirming the faith of the other disciples (Mt. 16:17f; Lk. 22:32; Jn. 21:15–19) is to be realized in church life" (no. 7, 471b). Cf. V Russian Orthodox-Roman Catholic Conversation (March 1980): IS, no. 44 (1980), 112–15.

[136] French Joint Roman Catholic-Orthodox Committee, *The Roman Primacy*, 158: "Only from this perspective, and based on and in function of the ministry of 'presiding' which is specific and common to all bishops, is it possible to consider together the question of the function of primacy exercised by the centres of accord known as the major sees, among which the see of Rome, in the period we are considering, was recognised as the first of these centres."

[137] Cf. Commission of Orthodox and Roman Catholic Theologians, *Reflections on Ministries*, no. 14, 294.

[138] French Joint Roman Catholic-Orthodox Committee: "The primacy of the Church of Rome and of its bishop is inscribed within a fabric of regional primacies, of 'centers of communion', recognized as such by the other churches, both in the East and in the West" (EOE IV 929, translated from Italian). The Joint Orthodox-Old Catholic Theological Commission expresses the idea more precisely: "The Bishop of Rome enjoyed such an honorary position because the see of Rome took the first place in the order of episcopal sees: Rome was the capital of the empire and its Church preserved the apostolic tradition.... So the Bishop of Rome possesses the presidency of honour in the Church. But with regard to episcopal authority, he does not differ [in any way] whatsoever from his brother bishops. The same is valid for the other bishops who hold honorary rank in the Church" (*Ecclesiology*, 203).

[139] This diversity is expressed "especially with regard to his relationship with the councils and his 'interventions' in the affairs of one or the other Church": cf. French Joint Roman Catholic-Orthodox Committee, *The Roman Primacy*, Introduction (cf. EOE IV 929).

nion of all churches in the same faith and his more direct responsibility with regard to the churches under his jurisdiction" and highlighting the difference in legitimization in the East and the West, which nevertheless did not cause a rift in the communion or become a subject of debate in principle.[140] Furthermore, the primatial function is linked with the primacy of Peter, which has not been inherited exclusively by the Bishop of Rome, however, but is common to all bishops *in solidum*[141]; indeed, according to the Orthodox, "the role of Peter within the apostolic college is reflected principally in the role of the bishop within the local church", whereas the Catholics have attributed to the Bishops of Rome "not only the first place in honor among their episcopal colleagues but also the 'Petrine' role of proclaiming the church's apostolic tradition and of ensuring the observation of canonical practices."[142]

In any case, this function is to be considered "equally in the wider context of the exercise of diverse primacies"[143] and in reference to the "regional hierarchies, expressed in the Pentarchy", which "remains a point of reference to the extent that it assured the transition toward an ecclesiology of communion and toward encounters between sister churches".[144] Finally, the particular primacy of the Bishop of Rome "is connected with the fact that Rome was the place where both Peter, apostle of the profession of faith, and Paul preached, were martyred, and were united in offering their life for the Church", but also "with the fact that Rome, capital of the Roman Empire, was the center of the Christian diaspora in the pagan Empire before becoming the center of a Christianised Empire".[145]

The most glaring divergence, however, is seen with regard to the nature of primacy. Indeed, according to the Catholic Church, "the position of

---

[140] Cf. ibid. (EOE IV 930). In reality, at the Photian council of Constantinople (A.D. 879), "this primacy was still accepted in common by the Byzantine East and the Roman West, even if it was often interpreted with different emphases and by reference to distinctive legislative codes" (ibid., 161A).

[141] Ibid., 162E: "Our [two] Churches are unanimous in confessing that every primacy in the Church rests upon the personal confession of the faith of Peter who, within the college of the apostles, received special promises made to him by Christ for the care of the entire Church. This primacy of Peter is transmitted equally to every bishop in as much as [in the measure in which] he accomplishes the ministry of unity for his see. All bishops inherit this primacy *in solidum*. This is true, in the first place, for the bishop of Rome."

[142] O–RCC, *Primacy and Conciliarity* (no. 7, 471b–72a).

[143] French Joint Roman Catholic-Orthodox Committee, *The Roman Primacy*, 161–62D.

[144] Ibid., 163H.

[145] Ibid., 162E.

Peter in the college of the apostles finds visible expression in the Bishop of Rome, who exercises those prerogatives defined by Vatican Council I within the [entire] Church of Christ in virtue of this primacy". In the Orthodox view, in contrast, such primacy "appears to destroy the tension between independence and collegiality".[146] The Orthodox, therefore, "do accept the notion of universal primacy, speaking of it as a 'primacy of honor' accorded to a *primus inter pares*", but at the same time "they cannot accept an understanding of the role of the primate which excludes the collegiality and interdependence of the whole body of bishops and in consequence continue to reject the formulations of papal primacy found in Vatican I's constitution *Pastor aeternus*".[147]

Even the supreme authority of jurisdiction of the Bishop of Rome, ordinary and immediate with regard to all Churches and all the members of the faithful, is somewhat toned down: "Every primatial function—and particularly one which would be recognized in the bishop of the Church 'which presides in love' for fostering communion among sister Churches—has as its purpose the service of edification and communion among the Churches: its service is to watch over the unity of the Churches in the faith and to give expression to this faith, to witness to their communion, and not to allow the Churches to become isolated and to jeopardize the bonds of catholic communion. As such this function of a primate does not place him above the Churches but at the heart of their bonds of communion." [148]

Thus reemerges, in its logical consequence, the fundamental concept of Orthodox ecclesiology, centered upon the local Church, which celebrates the Eucharist under the presidency of the bishop. Indeed, it is emphasized that "the existence of primatial functions, including that of Rome, does not [call into] question the equality of all the bishops", because "whatever may be said about the ways in which the primatial function has been exercised, which are connected with Church law, it has no other

---

[146] O–RCC, *The Church*, 7 (BE 85).

[147] O–RCC, *Primacy and Conciliarity* (no. 7, 472a). Much more explicit is the Joint Orthodox-Old Catholic Theological Commission: having recognized the primacy of honor of the Bishop of Rome, it affirms that "all the decrees of later dates, therefore, which ascribe a monocratic and absolute authority over the whole Church to the Bishop of Rome and which regard him as infallible when he defines doctrine in the exercise of his office ... are regarded as unacceptable" (*Ecclesiology*, 203).

[148] French Joint Roman Catholic-Orthodox Committee, *The Roman Primacy*, 159.

theological foundation except the episcopacy itself; the more particular ministry of universal communion is nothing else but the particular exercise of a solicitude for the Churches and the promotion of communion in the Churches which belongs to the episcopal function, and which every bishop is expected to exercise personally." [149]

The *honor* attributed to the primatial function implies, however, a "real responsibility and a real authority". Even if "the Primate" is "*inter pares*", he is "nonetheless truly *primus*" [150] and always safeguards the communion among the Churches and among the bishops: "there should be interdependence between the one who is the 'first' and the other bishops." [151]

Still, commentators have not failed to underscore one considerable difference between the Catholic Church and the Orthodox Churches, namely, an opposition between "a universalistic ecclesiology (which would see the local Church only as a 'part' of the universal Church) and a local Church ecclesiology (which would see the local Church as a whole reality)". [152] From this follows a different definition of the structure of the Church: "the Church of Rome evolving toward a governance of a Church one and universal, the Byzantine Church toward a communion of local Churches. The former came together according to a unifying principle of jurisdiction, the latter in accepting autonomies and then autocephalies. What took place was as if the Church of Rome developed to an exaggerated degree only a pontifical law, and the Church of Byzantium only a conciliar law." [153]

On the question of authority in the universal Church, the Catholic-Orthodox dialogue has therefore remained focused on highlighting the conciliar structure, based on the concept of the communion among all the Churches, fundamentally equal among themselves, while acknowledging a role "of honor" for the *primus inter pares*.

Looking to the *future*, the dialogue is called to study more carefully the importance of this role: not only with respect to the centers of harmony, for the purpose of determining the exact nature of the authority of the

---

[149] Ibid.
[150] Ibid.
[151] Ibid., 160.
[152] Ibid., 157.
[153] Ibid., 163I.

major sees in relation to the ministry of presidency of the other bishops,[154] but also as it regards the totality of the Church, in order to specify
"the function of the Bishop of Rome with respect to the other bishops".[155]

As we have already noted, plans were made to discuss the topic,[156] but
they never materialized on the official level. Only the oft-cited Document
of the Joint Catholic-Orthodox Committee in France deals with the topic
directly, yet it offers no noteworthy solutions. In fact it puts forward, in the
first place, the hypothesis that the opposition between primacy of honor and
primacy of jurisdiction "could be viewed in a new light" if Rome "were to
take more seriously into account, in that connection, the second part of that
canon [Canon 34 of the Apostles]" and "were to define more precisely the
nature and content of its jurisdiction, and were to accept the differentiated
exercise of jurisdiction in cases dealing with Churches of the West as opposed
to the universal Church"; for their part, the Orthodox Churches would have
to define more precisely the "competencies deriving from the primatial function in cases dealing with regional primacies as opposed to universal primacy".[157] It thus expresses the conviction that until the Photian Council
of Constantinople (879), Roman primacy was still unanimously accepted
by the Byzantine East as well as by the Roman West, although it was often
interpreted with different accentuations and in relation to distinct bodies
of law;[158] in the course of the second millennium, therefore, despite the
various conflicts, the unity of the Church "has not been destroyed even if
from disunion there emerged different conceptions of the Church and of
the episcopacy in relationship to the Church, and finally of the Roman primacy".[159] It then concludes with the hope of a common reception of the
Photian Council, which would constitute "a gesture which could have a

---

[154] Ibid.: "Only [1] within this framework and [2] taking as the point of departure the
ministry of 'presidency' which is characteristic of and common to all the bishops, and [3]
in view of this ministry, is it possible to address together the question of the primatial
function exercised by those centers of harmony which are the principal sees" (EOE IV
946, translated from Italian).

[155] Cf. Orthodox and Roman Catholic Theologians, *Reflections on the Ministries*, 294,
no. 14; cf. the Valamo Document (no. 55: IS, no. 68 [1988], 178b).

[156] Cf. above, pp. 33–34, notes 98–101.

[157] French Joint Roman Catholic-Orthodox Committee, *The Roman Primacy*, 160 (EOE
IV 953).

[158] Ibid., EOE IV 956.

[159] French Joint Roman Catholic-Orthodox Committee, *The Roman Primacy*, 161B (EOE
IV 957).

profound significance by emphasizing that the conciliar way is the preferred way for overcoming divisions". Having been effectively a council of
reconciliation and unity, it "could constitute a point of departure for the
resumption of dialogue about the meaning of primacy by establishing it on
common ecclesiological bases".[160] The different primates have the task,
"within the specific conciliar bodies over which they preside", of resolving
the remaining differences. In particular, "they should consider their role above
all as one of vigilance, as a service for unity in view of maintaining and
re-establishing communion among the Churches, rather than as an arbitrary power of initiative and intervention which risks leading us to new
dispersions".[161]

III. THE ECCLESIOLOGY UNDERLYING THE DIALOGUE

In the encyclical *Ut unum sint*, John Paul II, to illustrate the "substantial
progress" made by the Joint Commission, declares that "it has concluded
'that the Catholic Church and the Orthodox Church can already profess
together that common faith in the mystery of the Church and the bond
between faith and sacraments'."[162]

The same observation has been voiced rather frequently, often taking
refuge in the generic expression of "substantial harmony", which is all
too common in ecumenical dialogue.[163] At the basis of this there is said
to be an "ecclesiological mutation" taking place in the Catholic Church

---

[160] Ibid., 163H.

[161] Ibid., 163–64I.

[162] *Ut unum sint*, no. 59. The Pope cites the Joint Declaration with the Ecumenical
Patriarch (December 7, 1987). Also in the joint declaration at the conclusion of a more
recent visit to Rome by Patriarch Bartholomew, it is acknowledged that from the dialogue
"*a common sacramental conception of the Church* has emerged": IS, no. 90 (1995), 123b.

[163] According to Bishop Fortino, the Munich Document expresses "una sostanziale comune
concezione sacramentale delle Chiese ... affermata ora insieme da cattolici e ortodossi"
("Il dialogo teologico fra la Chiesa cattolica e la Chiesa ortodossa 1979–1987", 8–9). Among
the results attained, he enumerates "*la fede comune sulla concezione sacramentale della Chiesa,
sul mistero dell'eucaristia e sull'inscindibile rapporto tra Eucaristia e Chiesa alla luce del
mistero della Santa Trinità*", "una concezione comune della Chiesa locale e del necessario
e articolato rapporto tra *Chiesa locale e Chiesa universale*", and "una visione dell'unità come
comunione di Chiese locali" (ibid., 16). Elsewhere he speaks of "sostanziali affermazioni comuni"
("Le fasi più recenti del dialogo cattolico-ortodosso 1988–1995", 11–12). Cf. Cardinal J.
Willebrands, *Address to the Extraordinary Synod of the Russian Orthodox Church* (June 6–9,
1988): IS, no. 68 (1988), 138–41.

since Vatican II, which has led to an agreement on the fundamentals of ecclesiology;[164] for this reason, notwithstanding the millennium-long lack of canonical communion, a common concept of the mystery of the Church as a communion of faith and of sacraments has been reached,[165] and progress has been made "from a situation in which each Church claimed to be the only means of salvation to the conviction that the two Churches are 'sister' Churches".[166] An ecclesiology of communion is expressed, jointly,[167] and this communion, "true and real, almost complete, although imperfect", is at the basis of the "noteworthy progress" that has been made.[168]

Much more realistically, the Orthodox side is not always seen to place the same emphasis on the common profession of faith which has been reached in the documents of the ecumenical dialogue, for instance, in the fields of ecclesiology and sacramental theology,[169] and they acknowledge

---

[164] According to Lanne, thanks to this change, the Joint Commission has tried "d'établir d'abord les bases d'une ecclésiologie commune—ce que firent les trois textes produits par le dialogue théologique à Munich, Bari et Valamo" ("Présentation du Colloque de Chevetogne 1992. Les Églises orientales catholiques et l'oecuménisme. Aspects ecclésiologiques du thème", *Irénikon* 65 [1992]: 308–9, 314).

[165] Idem, "Aspects ecclésiologiques du dialogue théologique", 182: "On peut dire à bon droit que, malgré une absence de communion canonique, hélas! presque millénaire, les deux Églises s'accordent sur les fondements de l'ecclésiologie." Cf. Manna, "La koinonia nei documenti della Commissione mista cattolico-ortodossa", *Studi ecumenici* 12 (1994): 338; G. Celada, "La 'Una Santa' en el diálogo católico-ortodoxo", *Nicolaus* 23 (1996): 124.

[166] Press release of the Joint Commission (Ariccia 1991: cf. IS, no. 78 [1991], 204a). The concept was later formulated in the Balamand Document (nos. 13–14: IS, no. 68 [1988], 174b–75a).

[167] Assimakis, "L'ecclesiologia nei documenti della Commissione mista", I, 33: "Notiamo allora [nel documento di Monaco] una ecclesiologia di comunione che si esprime 'insieme' dalla Chiesa cattolica e dalla Chiesa ortodossa". According to Lanne too, the results of the dialogue "se manifestent d'abord dans l'accord mutuel sur une ecclésiologie eucharistique" ("Aspects ecclésiologiques du dialogue théologique mené par la Commission mixte internationale catholique-orthodoxe", *Nicolaus* 19 [1992]: 182).

[168] Editorial of *La Civiltà cattolica* 138 (1987): 6.

[169] For example, Konstantinidis considers "un po' avanzata" and "un po' forte e un po' fuori del tempo" the declaration according to which, in the Munich Document, "i teologi in dialogo 'vogliono mostrare che esprimiamo insieme una fede che è la continuazione di quella degli Apostoli'" ("Valutazione del V colloquio", *Nicolaus* 18 [1991]: 362). Even Metropolitan Damaskinos "si interroga sul senso che hanno i testi firmati dai diversi promotori del dialogo, come quello su *I sacramenti del battesimo, dell'eucaristia e dell'ordine,* quando ogni chiesa li intende, li spiega e li vive in un contesto ecclesiologico differente": cited by Y. Spiteris, "La Chiesa ortodossa riconosce veramente quella cattolica come 'Chiesa sorella'? Il punto di vista della tradizione teologica ed ecclesiale greca", *Studi ecumenici* 14 (1996): 65. With regard to the common understanding of the sacraments, Salachas points out, "La Chiesa cattolica, pur nella sua piena certezza che in essa sussiste la Chiesa di Cristo, riconosce senza riserve la validità dei sacramenti della Chiesa ortodossa, quindi la sua struttura eccle-

the need for a rapid and effective clarification on ecclesiology in order to take a real step forward in reciprocal relations.[170] Rather, the Orthodox underline, with obvious satisfaction, the influence of Orthodox theology, which is clearly reflected in the declarations emerging from the dialogue.[171] Above all, they remain firm in the assurance that "Orthodoxy, and nothing else, is the true Church", with the "deep conviction that renouncing this truth would represent a true betrayal of [their] own faith".[172] It alone "can be called *catholic*", whereas the Western Church "should be called papist or Latin or Roman".[173] Consequently, communion can be reestablished only "through a return to the sole Church which has remained faithful to the true orthodox faith".[174]

In order to shed light on the doctrine of the primacy of the Bishop of Rome in the Catholic-Orthodox dialogue—which is the aim of the present study—it will be necessary to examine more closely, from the Catholic point of view, the salient features of the ecclesiology underlying the various documents, through a systematic analysis of the texts and their respective commentaries, with particular attention to those of the members of the Joint Commission, both Orthodox and Catholic.[175]

---

siale e sacramentale, mentre, come si è notato durante le discussioni a Bari, la Chiesa ortodossa non ha preso nel suo insieme, in un sinodo panortodosso, posizione sulla questione del riconoscimento dei sacramenti delle altre Chiese e comunità cristiane, e di conseguenza del grado della loro ecclesialità e sacramentalità" (*Il dialogo*, 186). Cf. Lanne, "Catholiques et Orthodoxes. Un dialogue exigeant à un tournant capital", *Nouvelle Revue Théologique* 107 (1985): 87–100; Cioffari, *L'ecclesiologia ortodossa*, 57–59.

[170] A. Basdekis, "Das Papsttum", 66: "Denn die Orthodoxe Kirche ist davon überzeugt, daß ein Fortschritt in den ökumenischen Beziehungen zwischen beiden Kirchen von einer möglichst raschen und effektiven Klärung der ekklesiologischen Frage abhängig ist."

[171] In the text of the Munich Document Konstantinidis finds "delle dichiarazioni teologiche molto positive dal punto di vista della teologia tradizionale—e per il mio caso di teologo ortodosso—molto ortodossa" ("Valutazione del V colloquio", 363–64). Assimakis too acknowledges that in the Bari Document "[si] intravvede chiaramente ... l'influenza della teologia orientale" and that the Munich Document "privilegia la teologia ortodossa in maniera eccessiva" ("L'Ecclesiologia", II, 10 and 31).

[172] Cioffari, *L'ecclesiologia ortodossa*, 24, 44–47.

[173] Y. Spiteris, "La Chiesa ortodossa", 61–63.

[174] J. Vercruysse, *Introduzione alla teologia ecumenica* (Casale Monferrato, 1992), 95.

[175] The relationship between the question of the primacy and the ecclesiology underlying the dialogue is expressed by Duprey as follows: "Dans le dialogue avec l'orthodoxie la question de la primauté du Pape est une conséquence. Ce qui est premier c'est la rencontre et l'intégration de deux ecclésiologies, ce qui ne veut pas dire évidemment un alignement des théologies, dont la diversité peut être une bienfaisante richesse" ("La structure synodale", 141).

Especially in the Munich Document, which in the first part deals with the mystery of Christ and studies the Eucharist specifically within the perspective of eucharistic ecclesiology, the accent is placed predominantly on the reality of the *local Church*—endowed with all the elements of catholicity—which is realized in the *Eucharist* and is constituted under the presidency of and around her bishop. The perspective on which the dialogue is structured is "the role of the Eucharist in the constitution of ecclesial communion":[176] it is "the sacrament of the Church and of its unity",[177] and hence "the search for unity should have eucharistic ecclesiology as its model".[178]

Now, it is true that this eucharistic vision of the Church is "a perspective shared by both Catholics and Orthodox".[179] Although it developed mainly in Orthodox circles, it is a reality that is attested to in Scripture and by the entire tradition[180] and taken up also by the Catholics, especially after Vatican II, which defines full and active participation in the same liturgical celebrations, especially in the same Eucharist, as "the principal manifestation of the Church",[181] for which reason the universal Church is present in all particular Churches.[182] A similar acknowledgment is found also in the more recent documents of the Magisterium: for example, the letter *Communionis notio* declares that "the ecclesial communion has its root and center in the Holy Eucharist", which is the place where "the Church expresses herself permanently in her most essential

---

[176] E. Fortino, "La 'communio-koinonía' nel dialogo cattolico-ortodosso", P. Rodríguez (comp.), *L'ecclesiologia trent' anni dopo la "Lumen gentium"* (Rome, 1995), 186.

[177] Ibid., 186–87.

[178] Assimakis, "L'Ecclesiologia", II, 23.

[179] Fortino, "Il dialogo fra la Chiesa Cattolica e la Chiesa Ortodossa", 133.

[180] Ibid., 134: "Va notato che se questa visione è stata di recente riattualizzata essa di fatto si trova presente in tutta la tradizione cristiana. Da S. Paolo in poi non si è mai dimenticato che la Chiesa è corpo di Cristo e che i cristiani sono pienamente incorporati in Cristo per mezzo dell'Eucaristia."

[181] Constitution *Sacrosanctum Concilium*, no. 41. Péter Erdö, "Conseguenze canoniche di una ecclesiologia eucaristica", *Periodica de re canonica* 83 (1994): 295: "Nella dottrina del Concilio Vaticano II l'Eucaristia viene presentata come centro e vertice della celebrazione di tutti i sacramenti (AG 9,2), fonte e apice di tutta la vita cristiana (LG 11; cf. c. 897), fonte e culmine di tutta l'evangelizzazione (PO 5, 2)."

[182] Bux, *Il quinto sigillo*, 102: "L'unica e medesima eucaristia viene celebrata in vari luoghi: per questo l'unica e universale Chiesa è presente veramente in tutte le chiese particolari (*Christus Dominus*, 11), e queste sono formate a immagine della Chiesa universale in modo tale che l'unica Chiesa cattolica esiste in e attraverso le chiese particolari (*Lumen gentium*, 23)."

form. While present everywhere, she is yet only *one*, just as Christ is *one*."[183]

It is equally true that the Eucharist *makes the Church*, in the sense that in every local celebration of the Eucharist, the Church is actualized and realized as a local as well as universal reality, in conformity with the two "registers" of Catholicity.[184] In other words, the Church exists in history as a local Church or as a communion of eucharistic communities united around their bishop,[185] which make present the universal Church, not as a kind of sum of individual realities, but because the presence of the apostolic Church is realized in each of them.[186]

One should nevertheless avoid an excessive and distorted accentuation of the presence of the Church in each community that celebrates the Eucharist and thus avoid the risk of a sort of presumption, rejected by Vatican II, that the local Church is self-constituted and self-sufficient, with the resulting antithesis between local Church and universal Church,[187]

---

[183] *Communionis notio*, 5. Cf. *Christifideles laici*, 19a; CCC, nos. 1142, 1324, 1396. On the principle "the Eucharist makes the Church" in the light of CCC cf. P. McPartlan, "La papauté dans le dialogue entre catholiques et orthodoxes", *Communio* 21, no. 2 (1996): 114–16. It nevertheless seems an exaggeration to say that "le *Catéchisme* reprend à son compte celle [the statement of the Munich Document I, 6)] du dialogue catholique-orthodoxe" (p. 114). McPartlan himself, after declaring that the eucharistic vision of the Church is "musique pour les oreilles orthodoxes", cannot but raise the questions of the reciprocal relations between the local Churches and of the papal ministry (p. 116). Cf. also H. Donneaud, "Note sur l'Église comme 'communion' dans le *Catéchisme de l'Église catholique*", *Revue thomiste* 103 (1995): 665–71; D. M. Doyle, "Möhler, Schleiermacher, and the Roots of Communion Ecclesiology", *Theological Studies* 57 (1996): 467.

[184] Tillard, *L'Église locale*, 393–94: "En l'Église locale *subsiste* l'Église de Dieu, selon le double registre de la catholicité ... : registre de la *plénitude* présente *en ce lieu et aujourd'hui*, registre de l'*ensemble* des lieux et des temps qui sont dans leur réalisme humain le domaine illimité de la 'visite de Dieu' '*per orbem terrarum*' et '*jam ab Abel justo, usque ad adventum Domini*'." Cf. "Chiesa cattolica e ortodossa", editorial of *La Civiltà cattolica*, 9; A. Romita, "Criteri per la recezione ecclesiale dei documenti del dialogo teologico tra la Chiesa Cattolico-Romana e la Chiesa Ortodossa", *Nicolaus* 22 (1995): 183.

[185] Fortino, "Il dialogo fra la Chiesa cattolica e la Chiesa Ortodossa", 135: "Il documento [Monaco] rileva tuttavia che quando la Chiesa si manifesta, già secondo il NT, come 'realtà locale', '*la Chiesa esiste nella storia come Chiesa locale*'".

[186] Tillard, *L'Église locale*, 553: "De même que les Eucharisties célébrées en une multitude de lieux et de temps ne multiplient pas l'Eucharistie apostolique mais la rendent présente ... ainsi les Églises locales ... ne la constituent pas [la Cattolica] en formant la somme de ses réalisations. ... L'Église ne se multiplie pas."

[187] Such a risk is present in Afanassieff, as pointed out by Fontbona i Missé: "Por otra parte, subraya que cada Iglesia local, como Iglesia de Dios en Cristo, no sólo es independiente porque no existe un poder por encima de ella, sino también autónoma porque tiene

which ends up diminishing the importance of the visible unity of the Church.[188]

The Orthodox Churches themselves are not entirely unanimous in identifying the Church with the Eucharist[189] and in accepting the eucharistic ecclesiology, which, on the contrary, represents "a novelty even for Orthodox ecclesiology itself, in which the universality of the Church has traditionally occupied a central place".[190] Evidently, then, there is a danger of isolation or of independence of the local Church with regard to the others;[191] there has been no lack of efforts, some of them presently under way, to overcome the view of a self-enclosed local Church, by means of an openness toward a Catholic, universal view.[192]

----

lo necessario para su vida ecclesial" (*Comunión y sinodalidad*, 41). Furthermore, this has been recognized by other Orthodox theologians as well (cf. ibid., 64). As underlined by A. Smith in his review of the doctoral thesis of McPartlan (*The Eucharist Makes the Church: Henri de Lubac and John Zizioulas in Dialogue*, Edinburgh, 1993), practically "Afanassieff is seen as perpetuating, rather than overcoming, the division between the local church and the universal Church": *St Vladimir's Theological Quarterly* 39 (1995): 110.

[188] In this regard, Cardinal J. Ratzinger, after having affirmed that "from the starting-point of eucharistic ecclesiology there follows that [ecclesiology] of the local church, which is characteristic of Vatican II and which provides the inward sacramental foundation of the doctrine of collegiality" (*Church, Ecumenism and Politics: New Essays in Ecclesiology* [Middlegreen, 1988], 9), makes it clear that the Council "does not say simply: 'The Church exists completely in every community celebrating the eucharist' but uses the formulation: 'The Church is really present in all *legitimately organized* local groups of faithful, which *in so far as they are united to their pastors*, are . . . called Churches.' Two elements are important here: the community must be 'legitimately organized' for it to be the Church, and it is legitimately organized 'in union with its pastors'. . . . Hence the unity among themselves of the communities that celebrate the eucharist is not an external accessory for eucharistic ecclesiology but its inmost condition: it is only in unity that it is one. In this respect the Council evokes the community's responsibility for themselves while excluding self-sufficiency." Cf. Ratzinger, *Called to Communion: Understanding the Church Today* (San Francisco, 1996), 77–78.

[189] Ratzinger: "Anche esse [Chiese ortodosse] ritengono che identificare la Chiesa con l'Eucaristia, trascuri importanti punti di vista. Naturalmente l'Eucaristia resta il centro effettivo [però] . . . non esiste in alcun modo una generale adesione alla sopra ricordata ecclesiologia eucaristica" (cited by Salachas, *Il dialogo teologico*, 62).

[190] J. R. Villar, "La teologia ortodossa della Chiesa locale", Rodríguez, *L'ecclesiologia trent'anni dopo la "Lumen Gentium"*, 201.

[191] Lossky, "L'ecclésiologie dans une perspective orthodoxe", 9: although in every eucharistic celebration the Church is present in her fullness, nevertheless "on ne peut se contenter de cela sans risquer de tomber dans le piège d'une conception tout-à-fait étrangère à une saine orthodoxie en matière d'ecclésiologie. Il s'agit de l'idée—qui malheureusement n'est pas absente chez certains—d'une 'indépendance' d'une Église locale (Patriarcat, diocèse, voire même paroisse) par rapport aux autres."

[192] N. Kauchtschischwili, "La Russia e Roma. Alcune riflessioni sui rapporti ecumenici tra chiese cattolica e ortodossa", *Cristianesimo nella storia* 17 (1996): 132–34: "La sua [Solov'ev]

With the exception of the document of the Joint Catholic-Orthodox Committee of France, which underlines the opposition between the universalistic ecclesiology and the ecclesiology of the local Church—typical of the respective Churches—and the differing views of the very structure of the Church which result, one notices in the other documents a marked insistence on the eucharistic ecclesiology. Despite assurances to the contrary,[193] one gets the impression that this insistence is unilateral and ends up, under the influence of some Orthodox theologians, granting privileges to the reality of the local Church, with the consequent risk of fragmenting the unity of the Church through the plurality of Churches.

In fact, the tendency is to diminish the reality of the universal Church, conceived as a "secondary" reality (not as an "ontological priority"), as though she resulted from a confederation of local Churches which together constitute the unique Church of Christ.[194] The Church founded by Christ is, on the contrary, the universal Church, which is expressed and made manifest in the local Churches,[195] which "are not above the universal Church, nor is the latter the outcome of adding them together".[196]

---

idea di universalità nasce dal tentativo di superare l'accezione di chiesa 'locale' come entità chiusa in sé.... A queste delimitazioni Solov'ev contrapponeva la plurinazionalità della chiesa cattolica che riteneva fondamentale per una visione ecclesiale di dimensioni universali.... Questa constatazione è valida ancora oggi. In seno alla chiesa russo-ortodossa si sta lentamente facendo strada una tendenza, seppure ancora tenue, che va nella direzione di Vladimir Solov'ev e si sta aprendo verso una visione cattolico-universale."

[193] Celada, "La 'Una Santa'", 130: "La importancia de la Iglesia eucarística está muy presente en ambas tradiciones y está en estrecha relación con la iglesia local.... Es claro que con ello no se quiere negar la catolicidad, sino que per el contrario la eucaristía es la que le da su verdadero significado. Es éste un punto importante del diálogo, porque con frequencia se ha querido oponer esta visión, como exclusiva del Oriente, en contraposición al universalismo latino."

[194] John Paul II, Ai vescovi della Campania ricevuti in visita "ad limina": "[i] teologi eviteranno pertanto quelle enfatizzazioni unilaterali e insostenibili per le quali la Chiesa sarebbe originariamente e prioritariamente la Chiesa locale. Come già ho sottolineato al convegno di Loreto: 'Le Chiese particolari ... trovano infatti il loro senso autentico e la loro consistenza ecclesiale solo come espressioni e realizzazioni della 'catholica', della Chiesa una, universale e primigenia'" (Ins. IX/2, 1921). Cf. Paul VI, Evangelii nuntiandi, no. 62.

[195] Bux, Il quinto sigillo, 24: "La Chiesa insomma non è innanzitutto particolare, perché l'evento della sua nascita a Gerusalemme la vede universale e concreta ad un tempo.... Le singole comunità locali possono scomparire, come è avvenuto in Asia Minore e nell'Africa del nord, non la Chiesa universale.... Questo è l'evento: la Chiesa universale nelle diverse parti e luoghi della terra."

[196] Ibid., 114.

Hence, a uniquely eucharistic ecclesiology is insufficient,[197] and it reflects a "romantic" and idealistic view.[198] Above all, it does not give due consideration to the other essential elements required in order for the eucharistic celebration to be truly an ecclesial act par excellence: orthodoxy, without which the Eucharist *cannot* build up the Church in her fullness, and canonical communion with the local bishop and with the other local Churches. Indeed, a local Church separated from universal canonical communion "is not a full Church, even though the Eucharist may be celebrated in it".[199]

Despite the accentuation of eucharistic ecclesiology, with the resulting insistence on the consideration of the Church in her local dimension, the problem of the *relationship between the local Church and the universal Church* could not be avoided. It was even said to be "one of the major latent concerns of Catholic-Orthodox dialogue",[200] which in its documents constitutes "an attempt to combine the viewpoint of a eucharistic ecclesiology with that of a universalistic ecclesiology".[201]

The solution was perhaps already offered by the Munich Document, which "henceforth contains the theological and ecclesiological foundation" of the dialogue "and expresses its general orientation": the third chapter, indeed, deals with the relations between local Church and universal Church, "always centered on the theme of the Eucharist and its

---

[197] Cf. Bux, "Unità e cattolicità della chiesa universale nelle chiese particolari", *Nicolaus* 18 (1991): 171–72. Fontbona i Missé, too, emphasizes the limitations of *eucaristicomonism* and concludes that "*sola Eucaristía no basta para explicar la comunión y la sinodalidad*" (*Comunión y sinodalidad*, 433).

[198] De Halleux, "La collégialité dans l'Église ancienne", 436: "Il faut donc se garder de toute vision romantique de l' 'ecclésiologie eucharistique' de l'Orient. Le P. Nicolas Afanassieff a aidé les Pères du Concile à redécouvrir la théologie de l'Église locale, qui n'avait jamais cessé d'affleurer à la conscience ecclésiale de l'Orthodoxie. Mais son inspiration combinait avec la tradition ancienne un idéalisme et un populisme hérités des slavophiles du XIXe siècle."

[199] Salachas, *Il dialogo*, 63. Cf. Manna, "La koinonia nei documenti della Commissione mista cattolico-ortodossa", *Studi ecumenici* 12 (1994): 332.

[200] Cf. Fortino, "La 'communio-koinonía' nel dialogo cattolico-ortodosso", 193.

[201] Cf. Manna, "La koinonia nei documenti", 332. The author continues, "Per la comprensione fra oriente e occidente la difficoltà non sta tanto nella comunione, quanto nell'articolazione della comunione. E' qui che si pone in termini non facilmente componibili il problema di un'autorità nella chiesa che faccia da raccordo fra le chiese locali."

celebration", and has provided the basis for the ecclesiology of communion which is said to have inspired the dialogue during its various
phases.[202]

In the light of eucharistic theology, which in the person of the bishop
assures unity within the local Church and with the primitive Church of
the apostles, the universal Church is presented as a *communion of local communities* which celebrate the same Eucharist.[203] The various local Churches
"are not autonomous monads"; they do not live in isolation, but are in
communion with the others to the extent that they form that great communion which is the one, holy, Catholic, and apostolic Church.[204] Thanks
to the reciprocal recognition between the different Churches and between
the respective bishops, based on the radical identity of all the eucharistic
assemblies, there arises a substantial correlation and communion among
all the Churches, regardless of the later institution of interecclesial structures.[205] Hence the Church is essentially *"church of churches . . . communion*

---

[202] W. Hryniewicz, "Labour and Hope. Fifteen Years of Catholic-Orthodox Dialogue",
St. Vladimir's Theological Quarterly 39 (1995): 342–43: "All the statements of the Orthodox-
Roman Catholic dialogue are permeated by the categories of *koinonia*, i.e. communion.
They present an ecclesiology of communion, of local Sister Churches sharing the same
faith. . . . What is striking in the dialogue is its evident focus on the Eucharist." Cf. For-
tino, "Progressi nel dialogo tra Cattolici e Ortodossi", *Oriente Cristiano* 22 (1982): 2 and 7;
de Halleux, "Une nouvelle étape du dialogue catholique-orthodoxe: le texte de Valamo",
Revue théologique de Louvain 19 (1988): 459.

[203] Assimakis, "L'Ecclesiologia", II, 31: "Ecco allora che il documento di Monaco
orienta il dialogo in una prospettiva comunionale. . . . A partire da ciò la Chiesa (universale) non è altro che una comunione di comunità eucaristiche, ossia di Chiese
particolari (o locali)." According to Bishop Fortino, too, "La Chiesa così non è
nient'altro che una *'comunione di comunità eucaristiche'* [Monaco II, 4]. L'identità di
una comunità eucaristica con un'altra proviene dal fatto che tutte, con la stessa fede,
celebrano un medesimo memoriale" ("La 'communio-koinonía' nel dialogo cattolico-
ortodosso", 188).

[204] Fortino, "Il dialogo fra la Chiesa cattolica e la Chiesa Ortodossa", 137–38. Among
the Catholic theologians, the one who most developed the doctrine of the Church as
communion is undoubtedly Tillard, who, in his last book, wrote, "Aucune Église locale ne
saurait donc être l'Église de Dieu dans l'isolement. Elle l'est, par nature, avec d'autres, en
communion" (*L'Église locale*, 394). His stand in this regard is presented in a detailed manner
by Fontbona i Missé, *Comunión y sinodalidad*, 245–74.

[205] Tillard, *L'Église locale*, 395: "L'épiscopat n'existe et ne s'exerce qu'en *communion* parce
que les Églises locales n'existent et ne vivent qu'en *communion*. . . . L'identité radicale de
toutes les synaxes eucharistiques fonde cette corrélation essentielle." Ibid., 409: "Résumons-
nous. Avant l'apparition des synodes interecclésiaux, une Église locale se sait dans la *communion* catholique parce que son évêque reste en *communion* avec les évêques de toutes les
Églises inscrites dans la *communion* aux Églises des Apôtres."

of communions, appearing as a *communion* of local churches, spread throughout the world".[206]

As has been pointed out in connection with the eucharistic ecclesiology, the ecclesiology of communion has also become without doubt "the real core of Vatican II's teaching on the Church".[207] Often the two terms are even identified with each other. The ecclesiology of communion can legitimately be considered the central and fundamental idea of the ecclesiology developed by the Council[208] and the key both for the Church's self-understanding and for ecumenical rapprochement.[209]

The results and perspectives of the dialogue are manifested above all in the agreement upon an ecclesiology of communion,[210] as was already mentioned; in the documents of the dialogue, however, one notices in the background an antithesis between eucharistic ecclesiology and universalistic ecclesiology, which essentially takes up again the thought of the Russian theologian Afanassieff, who is considered the founder or "father" of eucharistic ecclesiology.[211] Salachas points out that, according to Afanassieff, in the universalistic view "the Church is a single organism in which every ecclesial unit is included", for which reason the different local Churches "are considered parts of the universal Church". Indeed, it

---

[206] Tillard, *Church of Churches*, 29.

[207] Ratzinger, *Church, Ecumenism and Politics*, 7.

[208] Cf. A. Birmilé, "*Status quaestionis* de la théologie de la communion à travers les dialogues ecuméniques et l'évolution des différentes théologies confessionelles", *Cristianesimo nella storia* 16 (1995): 257; G. H. Tavard, "Considerations on an Ecclesiology of *Koinonia*", *One in Christ* 31 (1995): 42–51; S. Pié i Ninot, *La sinodalitat eclesial* (Barcelona, 1993). However, it should be pointed out that "il termine è emerso solo sommessamente e quasi inavvertitamente . . . nei testi del Concilio. . . . Inoltre parve necessario, contro possibili interpretazioni ritenute pericolose, precisarlo nei termini più completi di 'comunione gerarchica', che in realtà non risulta altrettanto gradito alla letteratura che esalta la Chiesa 'comunione'": G. Colombo, "Tesi per la revisione dell'esercizio del ministero petrino", '*Teologia*' 21 (1996): 327.

[209] Cf. J. Greatrex, "*Koinônia* as the key to the Church's self-understanding and to ecumenical rapprochement", *Communion et réunion*, 150–56; G. Alberigo, "La koinonia, voie et âme de l'Église une", in J.-L. Leuba, ed., *Perspectives actuelles sur l'oecuménisme* (Louvain-la-Neuve, 1995): 18–43.

[210] G. Cereti, "Contributo dei dialoghi fra le chiese per un trattato di ecclesiologia", *Studi ecumenici* 6 (1988): 178: "Infine, come mostrano diversi documenti del dialogo ecumenico, la stessa *chiesa universale* può essere concepita solo come una *comunione di chiese locali*." Cf. Lanne, "Aspects ecclésiologiques du dialogue théologique", 182.

[211] Cf. Fontbona i Missé, *Comunión y sinodalidad*, 33. In contrast, Zizioulas and Tillard, prominent members of the Joint Commission, can be seen "como dos modelos de *recepción* de la intuición eclesiológica de Afanasiev" (ibid., 35); it seems an exaggeration, however, to say that Afanassieff also influenced no. 26 of *Lumen gentium* (cf. ibid., 34).

is not "in every local Church that the *Catholic* Church is found", but rather it is "the ensemble of all the local Churches which form the universal Church". The unity of the Church is then guaranteed by the unity of the episcopate, which "is one because the *chair of Peter 'on which God has established the origin of every unity'* is one". In the eucharistic concept, in contrast, the accent is placed on the local Church, which "enjoys all the fullness of the Church of God in Christ", without thereby diminishing the unity of the Church of God: "the plurality of the eucharistic assemblies does not destroy the unity of the Eucharist in time and space." Hence "every local Church which celebrates the Eucharist is fully Catholic, namely, it is the whole Christ, not just a part. This internal unity and catholicity of every local Church is manifested through the communion among the local Churches spread across the world."[212]

Commentators on the documents of the dialogue underscore the reciprocal integration and simultaneity of the "two movements that lead from the local Church to the universal Church",[213] by virtue of the oneness of the Eucharist despite the multiplicity of celebrations.[214] The two aspects are said to be included "in the fundamental notion of 'koinonia'",[215] thanks to the presence of the same Christ and to the entire gift of salvation in every local celebration of the Eucharist,[216] in which the universal Church becomes a reality and is actualized,[217] and in virtue of the

---

[212] *Il dialogo*, 60–61. Cf. Lanne, "Le mystère de l'Église dans la perspective de la théologie orthodoxe", *Tradition et communion des Églises. Accueil d'études* (Louvain, 1997), 425ff.

[213] M. Magrassi, "Monaco: una risposta cattolica", *Nicolaus* 11 (1983): 345–46.

[214] Ibid., 351: "La molteplicità delle celebrazioni locali non divide la Chiesa, ma al contrario ne manifesta l'unità in modo sacramentale.... L'universale e il locale sono simultanei." Also Fontbona i Missé, presenting the thought of Zizioulas, underlines the simultaneity of the local Church and the universal Church precisely "pues sólo hay una *única* Eucaristía, siempre ofrecida en nombre de la 'Iglesia una, santa, católica y apostólica'" (*Comunión y sinodalidad*, 144).

[215] Assimakis, "L'Ecclesiologia", II, 19.

[216] Ratzinger, "Theological Notes", Congregation for the Bishops, *Directory for the 'Ad limina Visita'* (Vatican City, 1988), 17: "The Church not only celebrates communion; the Church is communion.... The concrete subject of the Eucharistic celebration is the local community, which, in receiving the presence of the Lord [the presence of Christ], receives the complete gift of salvation and thus becomes the realization of the Church."

[217] Magrassi, "Monaco: una risposta cattolica", 345–46: "Perciò l'Eucaristia, come evento locale non si attua soltanto nella Chiesa, ma è la Chiesa stessa, nel senso forte della parola, che diventa evento nella celebrazione locale della Eucaristia.... Non è soltanto una filiale dell'unica Chiesa universale, è l'evento stesso di questa Chiesa universale." Cf. Galitis, "Gli aspetti ecclesiologici del dialogo teologico nella Commissione mista internazionale cattolico-ortodossa", *Nicolaus* 19 (1992): 193.

role of the bishop, who, "through the apostolic succession received in his episcopal consecration, establishes his Church in communion with the Church of the Apostles and, *hic et nunc*, with the universal Church".[218] "The particular Church and the Universal Church interpenetrate in an indissoluble *perichoresis*";[219] the one and only Church is born as *Catholic* and as *local*, inseparably.[220]

The Eucharist thus becomes "the source and the expression of the unity of the Church".[221] This unity is necessary for the catholicity of the local Church, so much so that it cannot be the Church of God unless it is in communion with the other Catholic Churches, with the one and only body of Christ in the whole world;[222] but it is founded on reciprocal recognition, which consists in the fact that each bishop, head of a local Church, is recognized by the other bishops, who are also heads of local Churches, which is implied by the recognition of each local Church by the other local Churches.[223]

Furthermore, every juridical bond is excluded: in fact, the existence of other principles of unity and universality is ignored, or at least underestimated, with the resulting risk of "self-sufficiency" of the local Church.[224] On the basis of an accentuated "episcopalism",[225] unity is reduced to something moral.[226] In fact, among the various provisos for the claim

<hr />

[218] "Chiesa cattolica e ortodossa", editorial of *La Civiltà cattolica*, 9. Magrassi, "Monaco: una risposta cattolica", 350: "Questo collegamento con la Chiesa degli Apostoli è considerato nel documento [Monaco] un elemento costitutivo della Chiesa".

[219] Ratzinger, "Theological Notes", 18.

[220] Cf. Tillard, "Église catholique ou Église universelle?", *Cristianesimo nella storia* 16 (1995): 357.

[221] P. Erdö, "Conseguenze canoniche di un'ecclesiologia eucaristica", 296–97.

[222] Cf. J. Fontbona i Missé, *Comunión y sinodalidad*, 114.

[223] Ibid., 271: "Así pues, la *Iglesia de Dios* es la koinonia de las Iglesias locales que se *reconocen* unas a otras como Iglesia de Dios." The author refers to the thoughts of Zizioulas and Tillard, respectively.

[224] *Communionis notio*, 11: "It is claimed that, where the Eucharist is celebrated, the totality of the mystery of the Church would be made present in such a way as to render another principle of unity or universal inessential. . . . These and other similar errors do not take sufficiently into account that it is precisely the Eucharist that renders all self-sufficiency on the part of the particular Churches impossible."

[225] Konstantinidis, "Valutazione del Colloquio", 362: "La seconda e la terza parte [Documento di Monaco] . . . si sforzano di dare un'interpretazione storico-tradizionale . . . del concetto episcopocentrico dell'ecclesiologia basata sull'elemento eucaristico, sotto l'influsso di alcuni teologi ortodossi (Afanassief, Zizioulas ed altri . . . e non so, però, se tutta la teologia ortodossa odierna accetta questi concetti)". Cf. also ibid., 362–63.

[226] Fontbona i Missé, *Comunión y sinodalidad*, 103–4: "Así pues, si cada asamblea eucarística episcopal está en plena unidad con las demás, es porque el Cristo total está presente en

that the local Church which celebrates the Eucharist is truly part of the ecclesial communion, one does not speak of a communion of *hierarchy* or of *government* (which are indispensable elements of Catholic doctrine),[227] but simply of communion *in ministry*.[228]

Despite these efforts at clarification, the relationship between the local Church and the universal Church does not seem to be expressed clearly or interpreted in the documents of the dialogue. Certainly, the universality of the Church and the concept of her unity was put in second place. In any case, it is a question of an ecclesiological view which is in overt conflict with the doctrine of *Communionis notio*, which, not without reason, was the object of bitter criticism in ecumenical circles.[229] Indeed, the letter recognizes that in the local or particular Churches "the universal Church becomes present in them with all her essential elements", for which reason they are "constituted '*after the model of the universal Church*' and each of them is '*a portion of the People of God entrusted to a bishop to be guided by him with the assistance of his clergy*'".[230] Hence, "it is possible to apply the concept of communion in *analogous fashion* to the union existing among particular churches, and to see the universal Church as a communion of Churches." It denounces, however, as unilateralism an inadequate understanding of the concept of communion which weakens the concept of unity, when the particular Church is considered "a subject complete in itself" and the universal Church is thought to be the "result of a *reciprocal recognition* on the part of the particular Churches".[231] Finally, the letter recalls that the term "communion" can be applied to the totality of Churches only in an analogical sense, because the Church "is not the result of the communion of the Churches, but, in its essential

---

cada una de ellas. No se trata de una *unidad en la colectividad*, sino de una *unidad en la identidad*, de una unión de todos los obispos como cabezas de las Iglesias locales 'en la mente de Cristo'." This concept, dear to Zizioulas, is substantially adopted by the documents of Munich (III, 2: IS, no. 49 [1982], 111a) and of Bari (no. 21: IS, no. 64 [1987], 85a): cf. J. Freitag, "Vorrang der Universalkirche? Ecclesia *in* et *ex* Ecclesiis—Ecclesiae *in* et *ex* Ecclesia? Zum Streit um den Communio-Charakter der Kirche aus der Sicht einer eucharistischen Ekklesiologie", *Ökumenische Rundschau* 44 (1995), 79.

[227] John Paul II, *Letter to the Bishops of Europe* (May 31, 1991): "The unity which is sought—and must be sought—with these [Orthodox] Churches is full communion in one faith, in the sacraments and in ecclesial government" (IS, no. 77 [1991], 38a).

[228] Cf. the Munich Document (III 4: IS, no. 49 [1982], 111a).

[229] Cf. Garuti, "Sister Churches", Appendix, pp. 302–3, note 205. Cf. also Birmilé, "*Status quaestionis*", 258–59.

[230] *Communionis notio*, no. 7. Cf. CCC, nos. 832–33.

[231] *Communionis notio*, no. 7.

mystery, it is a reality *ontologically* and *temporally* prior to every *individual particular Church*". It is thus affirmed that the local Churches have derived their origin and their ecclesial status from the universal Church,[232] with a valuable interpretation and integration of the famous *Ecclesia in et ex Ecclesiis* of *Lumen Gentium* 23.[233]

The expression of communion between the local Churches which emerges from the documents of the Catholic-Orthodox dialogue is constituted by *conciliarity*, or synodality, considered to be "the key-point for the transition from the notion of local Church to that of universal Church".[234] This is the natural outcome of eucharistic ecclesiology,[235] on the level of the local Church as well as on the level of the regional or universal Church.[236]

In this regard too, Catholics and Orthodox might express a common understanding of the Church:[237] in reality, the concept is rooted more in Orthodox ecclesiology,[238] and the statutes and authority of the synods and councils are interpreted differently.[239] In any case, despite the posi-

---

[232] Ibid., 9: "From the Church, which in its origins and its first manifestation is universal, have arisen the different local Churches, as particular expressions of the one unique Church of Jesus Christ. Arising *within* and *out of* the universal Church, they have their ecclesiality in her and from her."

[233] Ibid.: "Hence the formula of the Second Vatican Council: *The Church in and formed out of the Churches (Ecclesia in et ex Ecclesiis)*, is inseparable from this other formula: *The Churches in and formed out of the Church (Ecclesiae in et ex Ecclesia)*." Cf. Garuti, "Sister Churches", Appendix, pp. 303–5.

[234] Magrassi, "Monaco: una risposta cattolica", 353.

[235] Fontbona i Missé synthesizes the ecclesiology of Zizioulas and Tillard in the following manner: "La Eucharistía crea un dinamismo comunional que constituye a la Iglesia en una *koinonía* y la configura sinodalmente" (*Comunión y sinodalidad*, 404).

[236] Fortino, "Il dialogo fra la Chiesa cattolica e la Chiesa Ortodossa", 140: "L'organismo di espressione e anche di costituzione di tale comunione à la prassi sinodale a livello regionale (*concili locali*) o a livello universale (*concili ecumenici*)".

[237] Fortino, "Dialogo tra cattolici ed ortodossi", 11. Assimakis limits his remarks to the "convergenze fra cattolici ed ortodossi" ("L'Ecclesiologia", II, 22).

[238] L. J. Patsavos, "The Synodal Structure of the Church", *St. Vladimir's Theological Quarterly* 39 (1995): 71: "Basic to the ecclesiology of the Orthodox Church is the concept of conciliarity. The Church is, in fact, at her core always synod, the literal meaning of the word 'Ekklesia'. The concept of conciliarity ... includes every expression of ecclesiastical life." In the pages that follow (72–98), the author traces the historical development of conciliarity and describes the synodal structure of the autocephalous Churches and of the patriarchates today, with special reference to the role of the Primate.

[239] F. Bouwen, "Uusi Valamo 1988. Cinquième session de la Commission internationale pour le dialogue théologique entre l'Église catholique et l'Église orthodoxe", *Proche-Orient Chrétien* 38 (1988): 289: "Les deux Églises connaissent le régime des synodes et des conciles, même si leur statut et leur autorité sont interprétés de manière différente."

tive aspects, the difficulties cannot be ignored, such as those concerning the role of the Bishop of Rome.[240]

First of all, there is the problem of the relations between the various Churches. The synodal dynamism has its source in the Eucharist and in baptism, and thus in the local Church, within which it is realized in the first place.[241] However, with the institution of metropolitans and patriarchates, the local Church and her bishop are, in a certain sense, sacrificed in their *sollicitudo omnium ecclesiarum*.[242] Therefore, within the same Orthodox camp is perceived the need for a closer examination,[243] especially with regard to autocephalism and the exercise of the primacy.[244]

But undoubtedly the thorniest issue is that of the relations between the various patriarchates within the context of the universal Church.[245] Indeed,

---

[240] In the Orthodox camp, Metropolitan Chrysostomos Konstantinidis acknowledges that the structuring of the Communion as it was done traditionally "non è di facile soluzione, anche per il problema, non ancora affrontato, della funzione del Vescovo di Roma", and when asked as to how the Communion of local Churches could be realized, he responds, "Questa è la soggiacente problematica nell'ecclesiologia di ambedue le parti e questo è, forse, il punto più difficile della stessa" (cited by Salachas, *Il dialogo*, 66). In the same way, Cardinal Ratzinger affirms, "Avrei desiderato che nel documento [Monaco] venisse dichiarato chiaramente che il problema sorge a riguardo della realizzazione della comunione reciproca delle chiese e della conciliarità delle chiese" (ibid., 66–67).

[241] Tillard, *L'Église locale*, 440: "On sait qu'elle [koinonia] vient de la mise en oeuvre du dynamisme synodal dont la source est eucharistique et baptismale. Or cette source est dans l'Église locale"; hence "Cette synodalité se vérifie d'abord à l'intérieur de chaque Église locale" (ibid., 554).

[242] Ibid., 426–27: "La *'sollicitudo omnium ecclesiarum'* de chaque Église locale et de chaque évêque perd ainsi de sa spontanéité . . . confiné dans les responsabilités de son Église locale, l'évêque soit moins eveillé aux besoins des Églises voisines, le métropolite s'en chargeant." Consequently, "La synodalité de l'Église locale se trouve enserrée dans une synodalité de plus en plus large" (ibid., 433).

[243] As Cioffari remarks, the hierarchical structure within the episcopate "continua ad essere fedelmente osservata"; nevertheless, "taluni moderni sviluppi canonici della Chiesa sembrano minacciare questo principio". Therefore, Orthodoxy "deve affrontare questi problemi in modo da salvaguardare la sua ecclesiologia, altrimenti rischierà di creare una dicotomia tra ecclesiologia e diritto canonico" (*L'ecclesiologia ortodossa*, 57–58).

[244] Lossky, "Ecclésiologie et orthodoxie", 12: "Les Orthodoxes sont tentés par deux écueils ecclésiologiques. D'une part, une conception 'individualiste' des Églises autocéphales. . . . A l'opposé de cet 'autocéphalisme' mal compris, se trouve l'autre écueil ecclésiologique. Il existe des défenseurs d'une conception excessive de la primauté qui serait parfois à la limite d'un 'papisme' universaliste. Cet excès est souvent fondé sur une mauvaise lecture du fameux 28e Canon du Concile de Chalcédoine, lecture qui tendrait à donner au Siège de Constantinople une juridiction pratiquement universelle sur tous les territoires dit 'de diaspora'."

[245] De Halleux, "Une nouvelle étape du dialogue catholique-orthodoxe: le texte de Valamo", 470–71: "L'ecclésiologie du document de Valamo englobe le particulier et l'universel dans la notion fondamentale de 'koinônia'. . . . L'histoire atteste cependant que la dialectique

it is evidently necessary to explore in greater depth not only the question of the "first in the Church" at various levels, but above all the question of the role of the Bishop of Rome in the context of conciliarity or synodality.[246] In the documents of the ecumenical dialogue, and on the part of a number of ecumenists, an appeal is made to the model of the pentarchy, which would be applied on the basis of Canon 34 of the apostles.[247] Despite the recognition, on the part of the Orthodox, of the ministry of the *episkopé*, on the local as well as universal level,[248] in actual ecumenical debate there remains an antithesis between Petrine primacy and the primacy of the [ecumenical] council.[249] In reality, "the Catholic Church has developed a primatial law, whereas the Byzantine Church has developed a conciliar law", and thus the task of the dialogue "is that of overcoming this difference and of harmonizing the two ecclesiologies".[250]

The documents of the ecumenical dialogue, through a closer examination of the eucharistic and communal reality of the Church, which finds its expression in conciliarity, intended to prepare the ground for considering the primatial role of the Roman Pontiff. One does get the impression, however, that this role will be considerably redefined, when one notes with surprise that both the Codes of Canon Law limit them-

---

ecclésiologique du particulier et de l'universel passe normalement par des réalités intermédiaires (n. 52).... La réflexion ecclésiologique de la commission mixte se trouve ainsi engagée dans l'étude des primautés au sein de l'Église universelle."

[246] Fortino, "Progressi nel dialogo", 8–9: "Il presente documento [Monaco] ha parlato del ruolo del vescovo nella Chiesa locale, ha accennato alla 'comunione in un patriarcato', ma non ha parlato del ruolo del Patriarca nel patriarcato, ha indicato la comunione universale dei vescovi nella pratica conciliare, ma non ha parlato del *ruolo del vescovo di Roma* in questa prassi e nella Chiesa universale. Rimane aperta pertanto la questione del primato del Papa nella Chiesa e del rapporto fra 'Primato, collegialità e conciliarità'.... E' il passo obbligato che questo dialogo non può evitare di fare."

[247] The canon reads, "The bishops of every region ought to know who is the first (*protos*) among them, and so esteem him as their head, and not to do any great thing without his consent; but every one ought to manage only the affairs that belong to his own diocese and the territory subject to it. But let him (i.e., the first one) not do anything without the consent of all the other (bishops); for it is by this means that there will be unanimity, and God will be glorified through Christ in the Holy Spirit." Text in F. X. Funk, *Didascalia et constitutiones apostolorum* (1905), 572–74.

[248] Fontbona i Missé, *Comunión y sinodalidad*, 146: "Así pues, la visión ortodoxa de la Iglesia require una institución que exprese su *unicidad* constituida por su *multiplicidad*, con lo cual debe poseer un doble ministerio: 'el ministerio del *protos* (el primero) y el ministerio de la *multitud* (los "cabezas" de las Iglesias locales)'. De aquí la importancia del ministerio de la *episcopé*, tanto a nivel local como universal."

[249] Cf. Bux, *Il quinto sigillo*, 114.

[250] Cereti, *Per un'ecclesiologia ecumenica*, 257.

selves to reaffirming the ordinary power of the Bishop of Rome over the universal Church and over all the particular Churches, of the West as well as of the East, without mentioning the need for a healthy exercise of conciliarity.[251] In any case, the fundamental principles of Orthodox ecclesiology—autocephaly and synodality—which have been emphasized so much in dialogue, make it impossible for the Orthodox to acknowledge a primacy of jurisdiction which does not derive from the consensus of the Church.[252]

It therefore seems that the ecclesiology underlying the documents of the Catholic-Orthodox dialogue is far from expressing a common conception of the Church: it deals rather with the Joint Commission's own view, which not only questions several aspects of Catholic doctrine, but also fails to find complete acceptance even on the part of Orthodox theology, even though it was largely inspired by it.

Obviously, then, there is a need to recover the ecclesiology which understands the Church as universal mother and communion with the Bishop of Rome as the principle and foundation of the unity of the Church.[253] The documents of the dialogue, due to the influence of Orthodox ecclesiology,[254] do not consider the importance of a primatial role, not only

---

[251] Tillard, "La tension entre primauté du Siège romain et conciliarité", *Nicolaus* 19 (1992): 277–79: "On ne peut donc pas s'étonner que le canon 333 du code latin, repris ... dans le canon 45 § du code des Églises orientales, se borne à affirmer que, en vertu de sa charge, le Pontife romain non seulement a pouvoir sur l'Église universelle mais possède aussi une *primauté de pouvoir ordinaire* sur *toutes* les Églises particulières et Éparchies, ainsi que sur les regroupements. Il nous semble donc qu'un sain et paisible exercice de la conciliarité exige que soit scrutée en profondeur et précisée la relation entre l'*exousia* de chaque évêque *en* son Église et *pour* son Église, et l'*exousia* de l'*évêque de Rome* en toutes les Églises et *pour* ces mêmes Églises."

[252] Basdekis, "Das Papsttum", 72: "Die grundsätzliche Eigenständigkeit jeder einzelnen Ortskirche mit der Eucharistie als Zentrum und die Dokumentation der Einheit aller Ortskirchen, die in einem Konsens aller Bischöfe auf einem Ökumenischen Konzil besteht, macht es den Orthodoxen unmöglich, einem Jurisdiktionsprimat, der aus sich heraus und nicht aus dem Konsens der Kirche hervorgeht, anzuerkennen."

[253] Bux, *Il quinto sigillo*, 51: "La lettera [*Communionis notio*] evidenzia in sostanza il rapporto delle chiese particolari col primato romano. Qui si tocca il nodo dell'ecumenismo. Come ho detto, siamo in presenza, dopo il Concilio, di un'ecclesiologia delle chiese sorelle priva dell'ecclesiologia della Chiesa madre universale."

[254] Even Lanne acknowledges this fact: "Le mode d'envisager l'Église est ... plus familier à la tradition orthodoxe qu'à celle de l'Église catholique où la vision universaliste et le rôle de la papauté se profilent habituellement à l'horizon quand il s'agit de traiter de la communion dans la foi" ("Aspects ecclésiologiques du dialogue théologique", 183).

with regard to the unity and communion of the universal Church,[255] but also with regard to the full catholicity of the local Churches themselves.[256] In fact, "the bishops are in communion with the faithful, with the other Churches and the other bishops, to the extent to which they are in communion with the Pope, 'the perpetual and visible principle and foundation of unity'".[257]

To the questions emphasized above, one could add another concerning reciprocal recognition that "what Christ has entrusted to his Church—profession of apostolic faith, participation in the same sacraments, above all the one priesthood celebrating the one sacrifice of Christ, the apostolic succession of bishops—cannot be considered the exclusive property of one of our churches".[258] Indeed, this leads to the conclusion that the active presence of these gifts in one or the other Church realizes in each of them the sacramental structure of the Church, and therefore they are in "almost complete" *ontological* communion,[259] as if they were "two universal *sister* Churches" which cannot subsist otherwise.[260]

In reality, considering the lack of identity of faith and the importance of *canonical* communion with the See of Rome, the Orthodox Churches (not *Church*) draw their existence and salvific efficacy from the one Church of Christ, which subsists in the Catholic Church.[261] With the statement that neither of the two sister Churches can consider herself the exclusive depository of salvation, the oneness and unity of the Church are placed in jeopardy: this leads to the view that after the first millennium, the Church "no longer exists as one in history, but is *in fieri* [in a state of

---

[255] *Communionis notio*, 11: "For this reason too, the existence of the Petrine ministry, which is a foundation of unity of the episcopate and of the universal Church, bears a profound correspondence to the Eucharistic character of the Church."

[256] CCC 834: "Particular Churches are fully catholic through their communion with one of them, the Church of Rome 'which presides in charity'."

[257] Cf. Bux, *Il quinto sigillo*, 29. It is precisely with regard to acknowledging this principle and foundation that the disparity with the Orthodox Churches is encountered (cf. ibid.).

[258] The Balamand Document (no. 13: IS, no. 83 [1993], 97a).

[259] Duprey, "Une étape importante du dialogue catholique-orthodoxe", 122: "Ces dons constituent l'Église comme communauté de salut. Il sont actifs et mis en oeuvre dans l'une et l'autre Église.... Il y a Églises soeurs parce que la structure sacramentale de l'Église est réalisée dans l'une et l'autre Église. L'expression suppose ce niveau de communion ontologique que Paul VI et Jean-Paul II ont plusieurs fois qualifiée de 'presque totale'." The author recognizes, however, the importance of canonical communion and the need to pursue it with a view to unity.

[260] Bux, *Il quinto sigillo*, 110.

[261] Cf. Garuti, "Sister Churches", Appendix, pp. 301–5.

becoming] in the convergence or reunification of the two sister Churches, hoped for and promoted by the dialogue."[262]

On the basis of this ecclesiology, which prefers the local reality of the Church to the universal reality and thus leads to questions concerning the unity and oneness of the Church herself, our task now is to examine more closely what sort of attention the Catholic-Orthodox dialogue is paying to the primacy of the Roman Pontiff.

IV. THE SPECIFIC QUESTION OF THE PRIMACY

As we have already seen, the theme of the primacy has not been dealt with directly in the documents of the Catholic-Orthodox dialogue; however, its importance has been underlined along with the need to resolve the question in order to reestablish full communion.[263] This is "the greatest problem that has to be dealt with in dialogue with the Orthodox",[264] and not merely—as is sometimes affirmed—in relation to the extent and manner of its exercise, but also and especially with regard to its necessity and nature,[265] where the respective positions still diverge.[266]

---

[262] Cf. ibid., 313. Cf. Bux, *Il quinto sigillo*, 12–13.

[263] As Bishop Eleuterio Fortino emphasizes, there are "several other questions" underlying the problem dealt with at Munich, including that of the relation between the local Church that celebrates the Eucharist and the communion of all local Churches within the One Church of God, and therefore "non si può evitare d'affrontare il problema del ruolo primaziale del vescovo di Roma, del Papa, in questa comunione" ("Dialogo tra cattolici ed ortodossi", 15). Cf. idem, "La 'communio-koinonía' nel dialogo cattolico-ortodosso", 194.

[264] Fortino, "Il Dialogo tra cattolici ed ortodossi", 15. It still remains "une pierre d'achoppement" (Birmilé, "*Status quaestionis*, 268).

[265] V. Gómez-Iglesia, "Il ministero petrino alle soglie del terzo millennio", *Ius Ecclesiae* 8 (1996): 644–45: "La sintonia tra Ortodossia e Roma sul tema della successione apostolica è amplissima. Non si verifica altrettanto ... nei confronti della successione di Pietro da parte del Vescovo di Roma e per quanto riguarda il Primato del Romano Pontefice, che non è solo un Primato d'onore, ma anche di giurisdizione." Cf. P. Gefaell, "Doctrinal Principles and Norms for Sharing in Sacramental Life", *Eastern Churches Journal* 3, no. 1 (1996): 37, n. 26.

[266] Salachas, *Il dialogo*, 144: "I cattolici hanno reclamato per i vescovi di Roma, fin dal IV secolo, non solo il primo posto di onore tra i loro colleghi nell'episcopato, ma anche il ruolo *petrino* di proclamare la tradizione apostolica della Chiesa e di assicurare il rispetto dell'ordine canonico. Gli ortodossi accettano la nozione di un primato universale, chiamandolo *primato di onore* accordato *al primus inter pares;* al tempo stesso, non accettano una concezione del ruolo del primate che escluda la collegialità e l'interdipendenza dell'intero corpo dei vescovi e quindi continuano a respingere la formulazione *Pastor Aeternus* del Vaticano I."

In effect, the plan drawn up by the Preparatory Commission antici-
pated that the dialogue would focus first on the common points, the
"documents concerning the possibility of arriving at ecumenically acceptable solutions on these important points of divergence", the first among
them being the theme of the role of the Bishop of Rome,[267] which in a
way had already been introduced in the Munich Document and was placed
on the agenda for the Valamo Document, even though the discussion did
not take place for various unexpected reasons.[268]

Furthermore, it is claimed that the results achieved so far constitute
"the ecclesiological framework within which it will be possible to discuss
the question":[269] indeed, it is said that they have already laid "the necessary groundwork and the indispensable premises" for the discussion
itself.[270] But it is precisely in this area that doubts arise as to the possibility of arriving at a solution, if one keeps in mind the ecclesiology that
underlies the dialogue, elucidated in the preceding discussion.

In the final analysis, the question of the primacy of the Bishop of Rome
consists of the relationship between the local Church and the universal
Church, and between collegiality and primacy. As we have seen, the documents of the dialogue examine in progressively greater depth several concepts: the *local Church*, in close interdependence with the other local
Churches, so that together they constitute the *communion of Churches*, which
finds its expression in *conciliarity* or *synodality*. In this context the problem

---

[267] Metropolitan Anthony of Transylvania, *Telegraful Roman*, 25/1984, 7. Cf. Cardinal
Willebrands, "Discorso al Sinodo straordinario della Chiesa ortodossa russa (6–9 giugno
1988)", IS, no. 68 (1988), 161.

[268] De Halleux, "Catholicisme et orthodoxie. Une étape dans le dialogue", *Revue théol.
de Louvain* 13 (1982): 334: "[L]e document de Munich se termine par une phrase lourde
d'implications [III,4]. La partie catholique avait émis le souhait qu'il fût fait mention ici,
entre autres questions à discuter, du rôle de l'évêque de Rome au sein de la communion
des évêques.... Finalement, on se rangea à l'avis de la partie orthodoxe: un texte qui se
voulait l'expression de la foi commune pouvait, en effet, difficilement se conclure par un
rappel de la divergence dogmatique la plus grave peut-être, qui sépare encore les deux
Églises." E. Lanne too acknowledges that the text of Munich does not deal with the problem and that, practically speaking, at the moment "on ne pouvait faire plus" ("Une même
foi, une même communion", *Irénikon* 59 [1986]: 339). Cf. Lanne, "Aspects ecclésiologiques du dialogue théologique", 182ff., and "Présentation du Colloque de Chevetogne
1992", 307; Fortino, "Le fasi più recenti del dialogo cattolico-ortodosso", 11–12.

[269] Fortino, "Il dialogo fra la Chiesa Cattolica e la Chiesa Ortodossa", 142–43.

[270] Cf. Metropolitan Anthony of Transylvania, *Telegraful Roman*, 25/1984, 7; Metropol-
itan Chrysostomos of Mira, interview given to F. Strazzari, *il regno-att.* 12/86, 339; Fortino,
"Dialogo cattolico-ortodosso. Difficoltà e Problemi", *L'Osservatore Romano*, 15 giugno 1986;
Lanne, "Présentation du colloque de Chevetogne 1992", 307–8.

of the various primacies, especially that of the Bishop of Rome, should have been addressed next. Posing the question about the primacy in the perspective of the communion of Churches and of conciliarity would have facilitated "a new approach to the problem of the two Churches involved in the dialogue".[271]

We have also seen, however, that the eucharistic ecclesiology, which is fundamental to the reality of the local Church, despite its traditional value, is not fully shared even within Orthodox circles, on account of the risk of self-sufficiency that it entails, when it is accentuated unilaterally at the expense of the unity of the Church. Above all—as Cardinal Ratzinger pointed out in his comments on the Munich Document, based on his firsthand experience as a member of the Joint Commission—behind the accentuation of eucharistic ecclesiology was "the notion that the Eucharist builds the Church and this means, consequently, that wherever the Eucharist is found, there the Church is entirely present". Indeed, in the background—the cardinal added—there was above all "the eucharistic ecclesiology developed by the Russian theologian, Afanassieff, which, in his view, would necessarily represent a rival to the Catholic ecclesiology centered on the figure of the Pope, and which is expressed in the following thesis: Catholics maintain that a Pope is required in order for a Church to exist; we [Orthodox], however, hold that the Lord and his body are present wherever the Eucharist is celebrated and this means that every local Church is itself the Church and nothing else is required." [272]

In reality, the eucharistic ecclesiology proposed by the Russian theologian excludes any sort of power of one bishop or of one given local Church over the other local Churches. The possibility of a universal primacy as the power of one bishop over the whole Church of God in Christ is thus rejected by Afanassieff, who insists, therefore, that this primacy is not of a *juridical* character.[273] It is only with the affirmation of a

---

[271] Salachas, *Il dialogo*, 145.

[272] Cited by Salachas, *Il dialogo*, 59. Later on, the same cardinal stressed that, as a consequence of eucharistic ecclesiology in opposition to the presumed centralization of Rome, "the external unity with the other communities is not constitutive for the Church.... This kind of unity is good ... but it does not really belong to the essence of the Church, because one cannot add anything to the completeness of Christ" (*Church, Ecumenism and Politics*, 9). This influence seems to be underlined also by Freitag, "Vorrang der Universalkirche?", 76: "Afanasieff unterscheidet letztlich zwei Typen von Ekklesiologie: die universale und die eucharistische Ekklesiologie. Das erlaubt ihm, primatiale Rechtsansprüche, besonders den Anspruch des römischen Primats, wirklich *ekklesiologisch fundiert* zurückzuweisen."

[273] Cf. Fontbona i Missé, *Comunión y sinodalidad*, 47–49, 62.

universalistic ecclesiology that papal monarchy appears on the scene to make its claim.[274]

According to the Catholic doctrine, in contrast, "the existence of the Petrine ministry, the foundation for the unity of the episcopate and of the universal Church", is not only not excluded, but it also "bears a profound correspondence to the Eucharistic character of the Church".[275] In fact, "every celebration of the Eucharist is performed in union not only with the proper bishop, but also with the pope, with episcopal order, with all the clergy, and with the entire people", and it "expresses this universal communion *with Peter* and with the whole Church, or *objectively* calls for it, as in the case of the Christian churches separated from Rome".[276] Hence, in virtue of the Eucharist itself, the Church is local community, but, above all, people of God and body of Christ in the universal sense, whose visible center of unity is the Bishop of Rome.[277]

The presentation of the trinitarian view of the Church could also assume an analogous anti-Roman bias. It has been thoroughly reexamined by the Second Vatican Council,[278] but always against the background of the thought of Orthodox theologians, who derive the conciliar view of Church unity, or treat the question of Roman primacy, within the trinitarian model of the Church;[279] even in the documents of Catholic-Orthodox dialogue,[280] one notices a sort of recourse to this model in order to affirm that "in the Church there are no positions of preeminence and subordination; rather, the unity of the Church should be understood in terms of the Trinitarian model and consists simply in the reciprocal communion of the many Churches."[281]

---

[274] Cioffari, *L'ecclesiologia ortodossa*, 22: "Purtroppo, commenta Afanas'ev, a questa ecclesiologia primitiva che era eucaristica (e qualitativa), subentrò con Cipriano di Cartagine un'ecclesiologia universalistica (e quantitativa), ove la Chiesa locale diveniva *parte* della Chiesa cattolica universale. Un tipo di ecclesiologia che, alla lunga, non poteva se non sfociare nella monarchia papale."

[275] *Communionis notio*, 11.

[276] Ibid., 14. Ratzinger, "Theological Notes", 18: "Finally the Eucharist is celebrated 'una cum Papa nostro et cum antistite nostro'. Historical research has shown that these formulas are found in the Roman Liturgy at least by the Third Century; this expression of the presence of the universal Church in the particular Church belongs in fact to the essence of Christian consciousness."

[277] Cf. Bux, *Il quinto sigillo*, 102.

[278] Cf. *Lumen gentium*, nos. 1–4.

[279] Cf. Salachas, *Il dialogo*, 63–64.

[280] Cf. the Munich Document (no. II, 2: IS, no. 49 [1982], 109b).

[281] Cardinal Ratzinger (cited by Salachas, *Il dialogo*, 50–60).

To avoid self-sufficiency and isolation of the local Church, understood as the Church in her fullness, the dialogue documents make it a point to emphasize how each of them is essentially connected to the ensemble of the other local Churches, with which it constitutes the communion of Churches. In reality, the concept of the communion of Churches still does not resolve the delicate problem of the primacy of the Bishop of Rome, considered by Catholics to be a constitutive element of full communion.[282] The Church is indeed a communion of Churches, which nevertheless "calls for the existence of a Church that is head of the Churches", namely, the Church of Rome, and "the unity of the Episcopate involves the existence of a Bishop who is head of the Body or College of bishops, namely the Roman Pontiff".[283] Communion with him is an "essential requisite", not only for the very existence of a particular Church, since we are dealing with one of its internal constitutive elements,[284] but also in order for the bishops to be in communion with their own faithful and with the other Churches[285]—which is to say, in order to guarantee full and visible communion[286] and the subsistence of the Church herself.[287] In other words, "There is communion among the Churches if the pastors are in communion with Peter."[288]

---

[282] Birmilé, "Status quaestionis", 268: "Nous avons déjà noté ... que pour les catholiques la pleine communion des Églises inclut comme élément constitutif indispensable, le primat de l'évêque de Rome. Cette problématique très délicate pour les relations entre orthodoxes et catholiques-romains n'a pas encore été abordée dans le dialogue."

[283] Communionis notio, 12.

[284] Birmilé, "Status quaestionis", 273: "La communion avec l'Église universelle, représentée par le successeur de Pierre, n'est pas un complément extérieur à l'Église, mais un de ses éléments constitutifs internes' (Communionis notio, nos. 4 and 17).... Vu la correspondance entre le ministère de Pierre et le caractère eucharistique de l'Église, on peut même douter de la réalité de la communion eucharistique lorsque le lien avec l'Église de Rome n'est plus donné (nos. 11 and 13)." Cf. D. M. A. Jäger, "L'autorità del vescovo in prospettiva conciliare: dimensioni sacramentale e comunionale", Nicolaus 18 (1991): 108.

[285] Bux, "Unità e cattolicità", 166–67: "Quindi i vescovi sono in comunione con i fedeli e con le altre chiese e gli altri vescovi, nella misura in cui sono in comunione col papa perpetuo e visibile principio e fondamento dell'unità." Cf. Fontbona i Missé, Comunión y sinodalidad, 273; A. Borras, "Ut unum sint", 354.

[286] C. U. Gómez-Iglesia, "Il ministero petrino", 656–57: "Pertanto, la 'Chiesa cattolica—dichiara Giovanni Paolo II—sia nella sua praxis che nei testi ufficiali, sostiene che la comunione delle Chiese particolari con la Chiesa di Roma, e dei loro Vescovi con il Vescovo di Roma, è un requisito essenziale—nel disegno di Dio—della comunione piena e visibile'."

[287] Bux, "Unità e cattolicità", 167: "La Chiesa di Cristo pertanto deve la sua sussistenza senza possibilità di essere perduta nella Chiesa Cattolica per il ministero del Vescovo di Roma."

[288] Cf. ibid., 142. The author further specifies, "Tutto questo contrasta con una immagine di communio decapitata, priva di un centro."

In the commentaries on the documents of the ecumenical dialogue, in contrast, among the conditions necessary for participation in ecclesial communion—identity in time and identity in space[289]—hierarchical communion is not mentioned; it is even claimed that the Munich Document has already made explicit what is included in this communion,[290] yet the bond of communion in government, which is indispensable in the Catholic view, does not figure among the essential bonds.[291]

No less problematic is the great prominence given in the documents of Catholic-Orthodox dialogue to conciliarity or synodality as an expression of the communion of Churches, presented as "the theological and ecclesiological principle which the two Churches involved in the dialogue acknowledge as being still valid".[292] In reality, it is characteristic of the Catholic view that it requires that collegiality be reconciled with the role of the Bishop of Rome, whereas the Orthodox view is centered on the principle and praxis of the pentarchy[293]; indeed, according to the Orthodox, in the Catholic Church the sense of the communion of the Churches has been lost or at least weakened, because the doctrine of primacy prac-

---

[289] Fortino,"Il dialogo fra la Chiesa cattolica e la Chiesa Ortodossa", 139: "Due condizioni devono verificarsi perché ciascuna Chiesa locale faccia veramente parte della comunione ecclesiale universale. E cioè: a) L'identità del mistero vissuto nella Chiesa locale con il mistero della Chiesa vissuto dalla Chiesa primitiva—*la cattolicità nel tempo*; b) Il reciproco riconoscimento, oggi, tra questa Chiesa locale e le altre Chiese. Ciascuno deve riconoscere negli altri, attraverso le particolarità locali, l'identità del mistero della Chiesa—*la cattolicità nello spazio*.... E' da queste due dimensioni che risulta la comunione ecclesiale."

[290] Cf. ibid., 140. These constitutive elements are said to be "communion in faith, hope and love, communion in the sacraments, communion in the diversity of charisms, communion in the reconciliation, communion in the ministry" (the Munich Document: IS, no. 49 [1982], 111b).

[291] Cf. above, p. 57, nn. 227–28.

[292] Salachas, *Il dialogo*, 135.

[293] Editorial in *Istina* 32 (1987): 337–38: "La conception catholique de la conciliarité est liée à la primauté de l'évêque de Rome. Certes, elle inclut depuis Vatican II la conscience retrouvée de la collégialité épiscopale, mais le lien direct de chaque évêque avec le pape continue de marquer cette collégialité. Quant à la conciliarité orthodoxe, elle a instauré une primauté du siège de Constantinople, primauté de suppléance du fait du 'schisme romain' et qui doit durer jusqu'au jour où Rome retrouvera sa 'primauté d'honneur' dans le concert des Églises. L'Orthodoxie souligne que cette primauté de Constantinople n'est pas une suprématie mais un service, un souci exercé au sein d'une structure de concertation et de communion, la pentarchie, à laquelle elle se plaît à reconnaître une origine très ancienne, voire apostolique. Ainsi dans l'Orthodoxie, la communion entre les différentes parties de l'Église s'exprime normalement et régulièrement par la voix de ces hiérarques, égaux entre eux, que sont les anciens patriarches."

tically speaking makes communion impossible, and unity communion has been replaced by universality.[294]

In any case, the problem of the conciliarity or synodality of bishops "is intimately connected with that of authority, of primatial character, inasmuch as no synodal form can work without the function of the *protos*";[295] it is therefore necessary to examine more closely this function in the synodal praxis at various levels. This is not an easy task, given the differences in this regard between Catholic ecclesiology and Orthodox ecclesiology.[296]

It is nevertheless difficult to imagine how the work of maintaining Church unity can be founded upon the communion of the five major patriarchates.[297] Besides the difficulty of conceding, from the historical and doctrinal point of view, the very institution of pentarchy,[298] and of determining whether or not it jeopardizes the primacy of the See of Rome,[299] this structure has preserved, even in the East, the Petrine foundation of unity, and union with the Bishop of Rome remains the fundamental condition for conciliarity.[300] In the dialogue documents and in

[294] D. Radu, "Autorité et conciliarité dans la pratique actuelle de l'église: convergences et tensions", *Nicolaus* 18 (1991): 291: "Dans l'Église Catholique Romaine, ce sens de la catholicité en tant que communion s'est perdue ou en tout cas s'est affaiblie, car la doctrine du primat papal et du magistère ecclésial rend impossible la communion de tous les membres de l'Église à tous les égards."

[295] Salachas, *Il dialogo*, 135.

[296] Melia, "La Pentarchie", 342: "Dans la tradition orthodoxe, cette cohésion épiscopale, gage de la communion des Églises, s'effectue au moyen des structures collégiales assurant des regroupements d'Églises locales.... Ce schéma ne semble pas correspondre à l'ecclésiologie catholique-romaine. Y a-t-il une opposition radicale entre celle-ci et la vision orthodoxe? Cette question exprime un des points sensibles du dialogue oecuménique."

[297] Tillard, *L'Église locale*, 441: "Le maintien de l'Église de Dieu dans son unité catholique se jouera maintenant sur le plan de la *communion* des cinq grands patriacats."

[298] Cf. Garuti, *Il Papa Patriarca d'Occidente?*; Garuti, "Ancora a proposito del Papa Patriarca d'Occidente", 31–45.

[299] According to de Halleux, no. 52 of the Valamo Document does not jeopardize this primacy, which "serait de droit ecclésiastique conciliaire, à l'exclusion de tout fondement évangélique. La discussion sur ce point ... devrait normalement faire ressortir que les 'prérogatives de l'honneur' que le 28ᵉ canon de Chalcédoine a reconnues à la 'Rome aînée' ne sont d'origine politique qu'au titre de son évêque au patriarcat de l'Occident, tandis que la priorité du siège romain dans le témoignage et la communion à la foi et à la tradition apostoliques s'origine essentiellement dans la 'confessio' des apôtres Pierre et Paul, dont il est le gardien privilégié" ("Le texte de Valamo", 471).

[300] Ratzinger, "Theological Notes", 19: "It is evident that the historical basis of this construction is very weak as far as Alexandria and Constantinople are concerned. What is important is that with this structure the East too has maintained the idea of a Petrine

the respective commentaries, conciliarity is presented as the ideal for the communion of Churches. It is therefore legitimate to ask: What is the role of the Bishop of Rome in such a context?

The pronounced ecclesiological doctrine, which is centered on the reality of local Churches, and the absence of a universal perspective have somehow jeopardized the discussion on primacy within the context of Catholic-Orthodox dialogue. In the official documents, the universal Church is conceived exclusively as a communion of particular Churches, and by way of a transitional formula, the perspective of conciliarity has pointed out the only approach capable of extricating the question of the primacy from the polemical rut.[301]

As possible solutions to the problem, theologians have proposed specific conditions and concrete plans for renewal. The proposals have ranged from a return to the pentarchy as a model for governing the universal Church by the five major patriarchs[302] to an emphasis upon the primacy of the local Church of Rome, founded by Peter and Paul, who were joined not only in founding that particular Church, but also in transmitting the primacy itself;[303] another proposal has been to promote the the-

---

foundation of unity and of the concreteness of the unity and universality of the Church in the succession of St. Peter. Unity does not result from some vague harmony of a polite conciliarism of different local Churches among themselves; unity has a name: Peter, and a See: Rome. Thus, we celebrate Mass not only in union with the local bishop, but also 'una cum Papa nostro'."

[301] De Halleux, referring to no. 55 of the Valamo Document, notes that the assembly preferred a "formule de transition, qui annonce la question assurément la plus épineuse du dialogue catholique-orthodoxe, tout en indiquant la seule approche susceptible de la dégager des ornières de l'ancienne polémique" ("Le texte de Valamo", 472).

[302] Tillard, "Le ministère d'unité", 203–4: "En effet, l'évêque de Rome aura alors retrouvé sa place au sein de ce que la Tradition appelle 'la couronne des patriarches', des *apostolikoi thronoi*, traduisons pour l'Occident 'la solidarité hiérarchisée des primats'.... Dans l'hypothèse d'une pleine *koinonia* entre l'orthodoxie et Rome, il est clair que la primauté romaine ne se superposera pas à celle des autres sièges patriarcaux mais s'inscrira à sa vraie place (avec ses attributs et ses privilèges propres) au sein de la synergie hiérarchique." Cf. F. R. Gahbauer, *Die Pentarchie-Theorie*; W. Klausnitzer, "Der Papst ...", 206–9; Cereti, *Per un'ecclesiologia ecumenica*, 238–39; de Halleux, "La collégialité dans l'Église ancienne", 446; W. Seibel, "Petrusamt und Ökumene", 2.

[303] It is underlined, for example, that von Allmen "assieme alla trasmissibilità dell'ufficio di Pietro, parla di una trasmissibilità dell'ufficio di Paolo, su cui la Chiesa cattolica ha posto meno l'accento, ma che è ugualmente fondamentale per la Chiesa di Roma. Pietro e Paolo hanno dunque trasmesso il loro ufficio a una Chiesa locale: quella di Roma; è in essa, perciò, che tale primato sussiste." For his part, Tillard is said to have identified "storica-

ology of "sister Churches", a category taken up again "to designate the relations between the Greek Church and the Latin Church", even though "in this context of ecclesial *'fraternitas'* there can be no room for a papal primacy",[304] which would not be constitutive of ecclesiality in the same measure as the local episcopate,[305] and which in any case would be viewed under the aspect, not of a person, but rather of a sister Church endowed with a particular dignity,[306] without any mother-daughter relationship and without any hierarchical dependence.[307]

Returning to earlier studies of some of these proposals[308] and obliged as a chronicler of these developments to mention a perspective

---

mente la dipendenza del primato del vescovo di Roma da quello della Chiesa locale di Roma, fondata da Pietro e Paolo" (G. Falbo, *Il primato della Chiesa di Roma*, 6–9). Cf. von Allmen, *Il primato della Chiesa di Pietro e di Paolo*; Tillard, *Il vescovo di Roma*. For a more complete, and hence even more current, exposition of the thought of Tillard, cf. also his *Church of Churches* and the article "The Presence of Peter in the Ministry of the Bishop of Rome", *One in Christ* 67 (1991): 101–20; W. R. Farmer and R. Kereszty, *Peter and Paul in the Church of Rome: The Ecumenical Potential of a Forgotten Perspective* (New York, 1990).

[304] Spiteris, *La Critica Bizantina*, 299.

[305] Tillard, "La primauté romaine", 322–23: "A la lumière des vues de Vatican II sur la collégialité et sur la situation des Églises-soeurs en Orient (dans le décret sur l'oecuménisme), l'usage de la formule implique ... que la primauté du siège de Rome n'est pas constitutive de l'ecclésialité à un degré aussi essentiel que l'épiscopat local.... Affirmer cela, c'est reconnaître à l'épiscopat où qu'il soit, s'il est dans la succession apostolique, une fonction constitutive fondamentale. Et bien que, pour aboutir à son fruit parfait qui est la communion horizontale de toutes les Églises en une seule confession du Christ et une seule eucharistie, elle ait besoin de la relation au siège romain, cette fonction ne saurait d'aucune façon perdre alors ses prérogatives essentielles." The same Tillard, in another context, adds, "Il est clair que ni Vatican I ni Vatican II n'ont prononcé en ce domaine le dernier mot. Il faudra que l'Orient dise ce qu'il a à dire et, surtout, que l'Église-soeur d'Occident en tienne compte concrètement" ("Église catholique et dialogues bilatéraux", *Irénikon* 56 [1983]: 11).

[306] Lanne, "Implications ecclésiologiques", 61: "Si, selon la doctrine catholique, la primauté et l'infaillibilité du pontife romain trouvent un fondement dans les documents anciens et en particulier chez Ignace et Irénée, il est sûr, par contre, que l'optique dans laquelle elles se situent pour ceux qui les perçoivent est essentiellement celle d'une Église-soeur et non d'une personne—revêtue d'une autorité particulière, mais soeur quand même." A detailed critique of Lanne's position, especially with regard to the relation between sister-Churches and primacy, is found in Schultze, "Chiese sorelle o Chiese unite?", 81–106.

[307] De Halleux, "Fraterna communio", 307: "Reste à en tirer toutes les implications ecclésiales et canoniques. Deux Églises soeurs ne se trouvent pas dans le rapport de mère à fille; la pleine communion à restaurer entre elles ne saurait donc revêtir le caractère hiérarchique d'une dépendance." Cf. Tillard, *L'Église locale*, 546–47.

[308] Cf. Garuti, *Il Papa Patriarca d'Occidente?*; Garuti, "Ancora a proposito del Papa Patriarca d'Occidente"; Garuti, *Pietro unico titolare del primato*; Garuti, "Sister Churches", Appendix.

that shows too many signs of "*do ut des*",[309] I consider it necessary to devote more space to an assessment of canon 34 of the apostles, which also has been presented as an attempt to resolve the problem of primacy.

Found in a collection of canons compiled in Cilicia not long after 381 by the compiler of the "Apostolic Constitutions", Julian the Arian, based on the apocryphal letter of Clement to James and on the canons of the councils of Antioch and Laodicea,[310] it is presented, especially but not exclusively, in Orthodox theology, as the key to ecumenical dialogue on the primacy,[311] inasmuch as it establishes the perfect model for the exercise of primacy, because it could help us to understand the relationship between primacy and conciliarity.[312] Indeed, reestablishment of full communion will be possible only when Catholics recognize this model.[313]

---

[309] Papandreu, "Riflessioni e prospettive", 20: "Ritengo, da parte mia, che due fatti potrebbero qui venire in aiuto: I—Se Roma ristabilisse senza condizioni preliminari la comunione con l'Oriente—naturalmente previo accordo pan-ortodosso—ciò costituirebbe un espresso ... riconoscimento che l'Oriente non debba essere obbligato ad assoggettarsi alla pretesa struttura di primato affermata dall'Occidente. II—L'Oriente, viceversa, verrebbe così da parte sua a riconoscere che l'Occidente, malgrado la dottrina del primato, non ha in via di principio abbandonato il funzionamento della struttura episcopale della Chiesa antica, pur avendo accolto un fattore accessorio, la cui necessità non può essere riconosciuta dalla Chiesa dell'Oriente."

[310] Cf. P. Nautin, "Canons apostoliques", *Dictionnaire encyclopédique du christianisme ancien* (Paris, 1990), 1: 407; Duprey, "La structure synodale", 123–24; M. Metzger, ed., *Les Constitutions apostoliques* (Sources Chrétiennes, 336), 12; Tillard, *L'Église locale*, 428ff. According to Lanne, these were probably known to the legislation of Nicea I ("Il vescovo locale nei canoni dei primi sette concili ecumenici", 26).

[311] Cf. de Halleux, "La collégialité dans l'Église ancienne", 443.

[312] According to Lossky, the said canon has always been the most cited by the Orthodox "comme le modèle parfait de l'exercice de la primauté", precisely because it "devrait nous faire comprendre que la conciliarité *implique* de façon obligatoire la Primauté (exercée dans l'esprit de ce Canon, bien entendu) et que la Primauté à son tour, *implique*, de façon non moins obligatoire, la conciliarité qui n'est autre que l'esprit de communion par excellence" ("Ecclésiologie et orthodoxie", 13–14). Cf. Lossky, "Conciliarité: Que pourrait être la contribution orthodoxe à l'oecuménisme?", *Perspectives actuelles sur l'oecuménisme*, 138.

[313] De Halleux, "La collégialité dans l'Église ancienne", 452: "Tant que cette réciprocité [entre le synode et le 'premier'] n'aura pas été ecclésiologiquement et canoniquement reconnue par l'Église catholique à l'Église soeur orthodoxe, la pleine communion entre elles ne pourra malheureusement pas être rétablie."

Two of the dialogue documents also refer to it,[314] but it is more commonly mentioned by the theologians in their respective commentaries.[315]

Despite the affirmation by the Valamo Document that it is present in the "canonical tradition of our Churches",[316] in reality it has had authority particularly in the East, where the Council of Constantinople in 394 already makes reference to the apostolic canons,[317] which later "became the ecumenical law with the Council in Trullo (canon 2)".[318] These canons, however, had a pragmatic and administrative character; their purpose was to regulate juridical questions, by means of a *fiction* based on the alleged legislation of the apostles, and to provide some distance from the imperial Church of Antioch, which was officially Arian. It cannot be denied that this is how the juridical grounds for the patriarchates and for the autocephalous Churches were laid.[319] In the West, in contrast, it had

---

[314] The Valamo Document (no. 53: IS, no. 68 [1988], 178b). Commenting on numbers 52–53 of the Valamo Document, Bouwen affirms, "Ces pratiques différentes de la vie synodale et de la communion entre évêques forment le meilleur tremplin pour aborder la question de la conciliarité et de l'autorité dans l'Église, thème retenu pour l'étape suivante du dialogue. Dans la ligne du canon 34 des apôtres, qui parle de l'harmonie entre le premier des évêques et les autres dans un synode ou dans une région ecclésiastique, la question du primat, au niveau tant local que régional, y est indissolublement liée" ("Uusi Valamo 1988", 296).

[315] Reference is made in particular to no. 53 of the Valamo Document: "Plus généralement, les primautés intermédiaires apparaissent comme un mode historique essentiel d'expression de la conciliarité et de l'autorité dans l'Église. Le principe communionnel qui les gouverne a été excellemment formulé dans le 34e canon apostolique" (de Halleux, "Le texte de Valamo", 471). Cf. also Fortino, "La 'communio-koinonia'", 194.

[316] Lanne too considers it "commun à nos deux traditions" ("Aspects ecclésiologiques du dialogue théologique", 187). In the Decalogue proposed to the respective Churches by a group of Catholic and Orthodox theologians meeting in Belgium (October 8, 1996), it is specified, "Questo canone, caro all'ecclesiologia ortodossa, appartiene alla nostra tradizione canonica comune ed è citato come normativo da papa Giovanni VIII l'anno stesso della riconciliazione tra Roma e Costantinopoli, l'879 (Ep. 223: PL 126, 837)" (G. Mc, "Una supplica alle chiese sorelle", *il regno-att.* 4/97, 110).

[317] Nautin, "Canons apostoliques", 407.

[318] Lanne, "Il vescovo locale nei canoni dei primi sette concili ecumenici", 26.

[319] De Halleux, "La collégialité dans l'Église ancienne", 442–43: "On a un peu l'impression que les affaires (de nature judiciaire, cf. le 9e canon de Chalcédoine) que les évêques ont à régler dans la capitale provinciale intéressent tout autant le gouverneur civil que le métropolite ecclésiastique.... C'est dans un esprit bien différent que le compilateur antiochien du 34e canon des Apôtres reprend, vers 380, celui de 327/341 en l'adaptant aux besoins et aux aspirations d'une Église encore déchirée par le schisme mais en même temps éprise, comme tout l'Orient, de renouveau spirituel et apostolique." Thus was furnished "sans le

hardly any authority: apart from the nonacceptance of the Council in Trullo,[320] it is cited by only a few Popes and canonists.[321] Furthermore, it had a predominantly disciplinary character,[322] which, as noted by Peri, was meant to "fill a legislative lacuna, which by then seemed incomprehensible to the new canonical mentality, which was positive and centralist", through the promulgation of "specific *Decreta Romanorum Pontificum*, capable of formulating for the entire Church—in much the same way as the capitularies of Charlemagne, which were valid for his whole Empire—the rights and duties of every archbishop and of every metropolitan with respect to those of the bishops who made up their respective synods".[323]

Prescinding from the debate as to whether it was accepted as a whole or in part, could the canon in question be effectively considered a model for putting conciliarity into practice in the Church and for ordering the relationship between the primacy of the Bishop of Rome and the solicitude of the entire episcopate for all the Churches?

Undoubtedly, as an expression of a particular ecclesiological viewpoint, in antiquity it had an influence on the organization of the Church and on

---

prévoir, leur base juridique aux Patriarcats et aux Églises orthodoxes autocéphales médiévales et modernes.... C'est plutôt la fiction d'une législation des Douze (ils sont d'ailleurs pour lui treize!) qui l'avait porté à répartir l'Église universelle entre les 'nations' dont chacun des Apôtres avait présidé la mission. Peut-être voulait-il aussi éviter la dénomination civile de la Province de manière à prendre ses distances vis-à-vis de l'Église impériale d'Antioche, officiellement arienne."

[320] Duprey, "La structure synodale", 123–24: "Même si la question de la réception du concile in Trullo par Rome reste obscure, il est certain que le canon 34 dont nous allons parler était accepté aussi en Occident." Duprey himself admits, however, that the importance and the theology expressed by the canon "sont malheureusement loin d'être comprises et encore moins appliquées dans la vie de l'Église aujourd'hui, non seulement dans l'Église catholique mais aussi dans l'Église orthodoxe" ("Une étape importante," 116, n. 4). Tillard, too, acknowledges that "Rome ne 'reçoit' pas ce concile" (*L'Église locale*, 441, no. 2). Cf. B. Dupuy, "Les recherches contemporaines sur le concile In Trullo", *Istina* 41 (1996): 229ff.

[321] Nautin, "Canons apostoliques", 407: "Le *Decretum Gelasii* ... les range parmi les livres apocryphes parce qu'ils contredisaient sur plusieurs points la tradition de l'Église latine, mais cela n'a pas empêché les papes Jean VIII [PL 126, 836–837], Léon IX, et de grands canonistes comme Yves de Chartres et Gratien de se référer expressément à eux."

[322] Indeed, the compilation in which it is found is a collection of canons "qui concernent surtout les sanctions à prendre contre les fautes du clergé et traitent aussi du baptême, du divorce etc" (Nautin, "Canons apostoliques", 407).

[323] Peri, *Lo scambio fraterno tra le Chiese. Componenti storiche della comunione* (Città del Vaticano, 1993), 341.

the Church's Eastern theology.[324] Originally, however, it regulated the relations between bishops on the *regional* level, and is often cited even today, together with Canon 9 of Antioch, mainly as "an attractive and theologically profound image of the communion among the bishops of a region" and as an example "of a period of full authority for the local bishop in his own Church and of close communion among the bishops and hence among the Churches of the same region".[325] Furthermore, it is said to be the first and fundamental expression of the synodal government in the East.[326]

Nevertheless, an application of it on the level of the *universal* Church is considered to be in harmony with the spirit that inspired it,[327] and therefore it could constitute the principle of communion which governs the intermediate primates as an essential historical means of expressing conciliarity and authority in the Church,[328] inasmuch as, on the one hand, it reaffirms that every ministry or institution in the Church is expressed in the form of communion and, on the other hand, it calls to mind not only the multiplicity but also the oneness of the Church.[329] It is natural, then, that it should be proposed also "as a possible solution for the relationship between collegiality and primacy".[330] The reciprocity underlying the canon, as an expression of synodality on the local and universal levels, would reconcile "centralization" and the "democratic requirement" with one another, eliminating in either case the two tyrannies or caricatures of ecclesial *exousia* which would ruin the *koinonia*: ridiculous authoritarianism and arrogant imperialism.[331]

---

[324] Cf. Duprey, "La structure synodale", 126.

[325] Lanne, "Il vescovo locale nei canoni dei primi sette concili ecumenici", 26.

[326] Cf. Duprey, "La structure synodale", 123.

[327] Duprey, "Une étape importante", 116, n. 4: "Ce canon a en vue directement l'organisation d'une 'province' ecclésiastique. Cependant il est tout à fait indiqué pour régler la vie de l'Église à tous ses niveaux jusqu'au niveau universel. Il semble que ce serait une application élargie en harmonie avec l'esprit qui l'a inspiré." Cf. Lossky, "Ecclésiologie et orthodoxie", 13–14; Tillard, *L'Église locale*, 431.

[328] De Halleux, "Le texte de Valamo", 471: "les primautés intermédiaires apparaissent comme un mode historique essentiel d'expression de la conciliarité et de l'autorité dans l'Église. Le principe communionnel qui les gouverne a été excellemment formulé dans le 34e canon apostolique."

[329] Cf. Fontbona i Missé, *Comunión y sinodalidad*, 188.

[330] Fortino, "Il dialogo fra la Chiesa Cattolica e la Chiesa Ortodossa", 140.

[331] Tillard, *L'Église locale*, 430: "On coupe ainsi court à deux tyrannies qui ruineraient la *koinônia*. La première est celle de l'évêque gouvernant son Église comme bon lui semble.... L'autre, tout aussi nuisible, est celle du hiérarque régnant en maître sur les autres

We are aware that the real problem arises in the actual exercise of conciliarity, when the *exousia* of the individual bishop *in and for his* Church
comes into conflict with the *exousia* of the Bishop of Rome, who represents the center, *in and for* all the Churches.[332] It is maintained, however, that the only hope for finding common ground with the East, in
conformity with Vatican I,[333] would be through an exercise of authority
along the lines inspired by this canon—with two modalities, one collective and the other personal—and that the problem of authority within
the Church can be resolved only in the light of the experience canonized
therein, because it is in this sense that communion with Rome would be
accepted.[334] Hence the invitation to take canon 34 as the model for *reciprocal reception* between the center and the local Churches in order that the
rights of all bishops and of each of them vis-à-vis the *protos* be guaranteed.[335] In this way one could arrive at an *ecumenical reception* of the Catholic doctrine on the primacy of the Bishop of Rome.[336]

Excluded, nevertheless, would be a primacy of jurisdiction, as something contrary to Orthodox ecclesiology, which even today is unanimous
in underscoring the sacramental equality of all bishops and simply accepts
a primacy based on the communal-relational model proposed by canon 34
of the apostles.[337]

évêques.... Autoritarisme ridicule du roitelet, impérialisme hautain du despote, telles sont
les deux caricatures de l'*exousia* ecclésiale que le canon 34 des Apôtres entend éliminer."

[332] Cf. Fontbona i Missé, *Comunión y sinodalidad*, 384.

[333] Duprey, "La structure synodale", 143: "Mais il semble bien qu'il n'y a pas d'espoir de
rencontre avec l'Orient si on ne considère pas le sujet de l'autorité suprême dans l'Église
comme *unique*: le collège épiscopal comprenant le pape, mais avec deux modalités d'exercice
de cette autorité, l'une collective, l'autre personnelle, deux modalités en interdépendance,
dans la ligne du canon 34 des Apôtres. Cette position semble compatible avec le premier
concile du Vatican et est tenue par plusieurs théologiens catholiques."

[334] Cf. Manna, "La koinonia nei documenti", 340.

[335] Fontbona i Misse, *Comunión y sinodalidad*, 385.

[336] Ibid., 402–3: "En efecto, este canon 34 institucionaliza la relación *inclusiva* entre el
Obispo 'reconocido' (se trata de una *recepción*) como *protos* (la cabeza de la Iglesia recono-
cida como el *centro de unidad* de la comunión de todas la Iglesias locales) y el resto de los
obispos (cabezas de estas Iglesias locales). Con ello, afirma el primado del *protos* de la sede
de Pedro y Pablo, garantiza la *conspiratio in unum* de las diversas Iglesias locales que habla el
Vaticano II (LG 23), y brinda una recíproca *re-recepción*, por parte de las Iglesias de Oriente
y de la Iglesia católica romana, de la noción de primado del Obispo de Roma."

[337] Ibid., 65–66: "La eclesiología ortodoxa actual es unánime en resaltar la igualdad
sacramental de todos los obispos y, por eso, non acepta un poder juridico (el primado) de

This solution evidently reflects the Orthodox conception of a primate who is *"primus inter pares"*, which cannot be shared by the Catholic Church. In fact, what is proposed is the model of primacy exemplified by the ecumenical patriarchate, as opposed to the papal primacy.[338] Recognized as *"primi inter pares"*, both the Pope in Rome and the patriarch in Constantinople held and still hold "the distinguished position of elder brothers. This eminent position, however, did not bring about a change in the essence of the Church. It never bestowed a superior office or any substantial privileges with respect to the other bishops."[339]

This way of framing the issue does not take into account the necessary distinction between the patriarchal role of the bishop of Constantinople, which is of ecclesiastical institution, and the primatial role of the Bishop of Rome, which is of divine institution. The former does not constitute the principle of unity of the Church, but confers a particular task and responsibility—acknowledged by the councils—in the canonical ordering which regulates the interdependence of the Churches.[340] Despite the attempts to present the function of the *protos* not merely as a primacy of honor, but as a true primacy (albeit not absolute, because it is controlled and moderated by the other bishops,[341] with effective

---

in obispo (el de Roma) sobre todos los demás. Pero, al mismo tiempo, acepta un primado en el seno de la comunión de todas la Iglesia locales, como fruto de la comunión y de la sinodalidad, y por eso debe fundarse en el modelo *comunional/relacional* propuesto en el canon 34 de la colección denominada *Cánones de los Apóstoles*."

[338] Radu, "Autorité et conciliarité", 302–3: "La conception orthodoxe du primat est nettement différente de celle catholique. Tous les évêques sont fondamentalement égaux, de sorte que si l'un d'eux peut être nommé 'primat', sa position doit être comprise en tant que 'primus inter pares'. C'est la conception du primat impliquée par le canon 34 apostolique.... Mais le patriarche oecuménique n'intervient pas dans les affaires internes d'une Église Orthodoxe Autocéphale sans que celle-ci le lui demande expressément. Le primat papal est la conséquence directe de l'ecclésiologie universaliste promue par l'Église Occidentale, dans les circonstances historiques de son développement."

[339] Papadopoulos, "L'istituzione conciliare", 292.

[340] Melia, "La Pentarchie", 358–59: "La tradition est ici bien exprimée par le célèbre canon 34 des *Canons* dits *apostoliques*.... Cela ne signifie pas que le Patriarcat oecuménique soit la source de l'unité inter-ecclésiale: il ne dispose que d'un souci reconnu conciliairement et d'une responsabilité particulière dans l'ordre canonique de la concertation inter-ecclésiale à ses différents niveaux."

[341] Cf. Fontbona i Missé, *Comunión y sinodalidad*, 189. The author quotes the opinion of Zizioulas. Cf. also J.R. Villar, "La teologia ortodossa della Chiesa locale", 218–19.

power both on the metropolitan level[342] and on the patriarchal level),[343] in reality, within the Orthodox world itself, it is recognized not as true power, but rather as a "service ordered to communion, admitted in principle, but debated as to its real importance".[344]

By the same token, the Bishop of Rome, whose primacy, in contrast, is of divine institution, would also be bound by the consensus of all the other bishops of the Catholic Church, and, even though he was acknowledged as *protos*, he could make decisions only with the consent of the other bishops of the *Catholic* Church, and they, in turn, would not decide on anything of importance without the consensus of him whom they acknowledge to be the first among them. In fact, he is inseparable from his brother bishops, just as Peter (the *one*) was inseparable from the apostles (the *many*). This implies the existence of one supreme authority in the Church, the episcopal body with the Bishop of Rome, as was confirmed by the Second Vatican Council with the conclusive formula *una cum patribus*.[345] In his case too, one speaks of "primacy of honor", which would not be reduced to a mere expression of respect; the expression should also include the recognition of a *de fide* authority within the evangelical communion.[346] The peculiarity of the Church of Rome is conceived as a service for the unity and communion of all the Churches. Therefore this ecclesiological conviction, common to Zizioulas and Tillard, proposes an *ecumenical reception* of the ministry of the Bishop of Rome in the bosom of a communion between the East and the West and hence inscribed in the *conspiratio in unum* of the diversity of Churches.[347]

---

[342] Lanne, "Il vescovo locale nei canoni dei primi sette concili ecumenici", 30: "il metropolita della provincia è sì il vescovo locale per la propria Chiesa, ma *in quanto vescovo locale spetta anche a lui una funzione diversa* da quella degli altri vescovi della sua provincia. Di certo è il *primus inter pares*, ma i suoi colleghi non hanno la medesima funzione della sua." Cf. Tillard, *L'Église locale*, 423–31.

[343] Daley, "Position and Patronage in the Early Church", 551: "The purpose here has simply been to illustrate the original point: that what was at stake in these first discussions of 'primatial' privilege and power in the Church was not simply ceremonial or even 'moral' authority alone, but jurisdiction—practical leadership—in a very real sense." Cf. Tillard, *L'Église locale*, 436ff.

[344] Garuti, "Sister Churches", Appendix, p. 321. Cf. furthermore B. Stavridis, "L'Autorité du patriarche oecuménique dans la vie de l'Église orthodoxe", *Istina* 40 (1995), 357–68; G. D. Papathomas, "Les différentes modalités d'exercice de la juridiction du Patriarcat de Constantinople", ibid., 369–85.

[345] Cf. Fontbona i Missé, *Comunión y sinodalidad*, 425 and 429.

[346] Cf. Manna, "L'oecuméniste", 54.

[347] Cf. Fontbona i Missé, *Comunión y sinodalidad*, 404–5.

Primacy, on the contrary, "involves, in essence, a truly episcopal power, which is not only supreme, full and universal, but also *immediate*, over all, whether Pastors or the faithful",[348] which includes a juridical ranking[349] and excludes all restrictions or qualifications whatsoever.[350] While it is necessary to harmonize this with the principle of synodality, the personal and independent power of the Roman Pontiff must still remain unchanged. "It is true that Roman primacy cannot be considered apart from the one and undivided episcopate, namely, from the totality of the bishops in their communion, and that the authority of the Bishop of Rome is to be understood within the framework of the authority of the episcopal college, which also is the subject of supreme authority within the Church; but it is equally true that the Roman Pontiff personally possesses this same power and can exercise it freely. If, as Congar wrote, on the one hand, the ecclesiology of the universal Church must be 'harmonized with an ecclesiology of the Church as communion', on the other hand, if we were to stop at this, 'the Pope would only be the image and guarantor of unity. He would have no other authority than that of a court of final appeal, capable of adjudicating the controversies that put unity at stake, but only in accordance with tradition and the holy canons. His power would be of an executive not a constitutive nature; power *within*, not power *over*, the Church.' Therefore, while it must be exercised in communion, pontifical power is a qualitatively superior 'episcopal power' over the totality of the Churches and over the faithful."[351]

The ministry of the Bishop of Rome, then, is a service to be carried out in a context of affective and effective collegiality, but it is also "a ministry of a *primus* not *inter* but *super pares et partes*".[352]

It is therefore legitimate to ask whether the appeal to the model of canon 34 of the apostles does not entail, at least in practice, a redefining of the

---

[348] *Communionis notio*, 14.

[349] Gómez-Iglesia, "Il ministero petrino", 657: "Il Romano Pontefice adempie questo servizio di unità 'con il potere e l'autorità senza i quali tale funzione sarebbe illusoria' [UUS 94]. Giovanni Paolo II esclude così non soltanto un mero primato di onore, ma anche un primato unicamente pastorale privo di rango giuridico e passa ad elencare diversi compiti del ministero primaziale."

[350] This was the *intentio profundior* of Vatican I, which proposed "inequivocabilmente di garantire al Papa la giurisdizione piena" (Colombo, "Tesi", 330).

[351] Garuti, *Il Papa Patriarca d'Occidente?*, 246.

[352] Bux, *Il quinto sigillo*, 50.

exercise of the primatial power of the Roman Pontiff[353] or even a questionable view of its very nature. In fact, the Western and Eastern views of Church government are contrasted, with a clear preference for the latter, despite the acknowledgment that both can lead to excesses.[354] Some commentators openly express surprise that the two Codes of Canon Law limit themselves to reaffirming the primacy of ordinary power of the Roman Pontiff over the universal Church and over all the particular Churches or their groupings, whereas conciliarity would demand a further examination in order to specify the relationship between the *exousia* of the individual bishops and that of the Bishop of Rome.[355] Concretely, the model of the Roman synods, inaugurated by Paul VI, is described as a cause for "frustrations" because in the promulgation of the postsynodal instructions, the authority of the *primus* has absorbed that of the other bishops, even if the documents reflect the actual discussions during the general assembly.[356]

Therefore, on account of its origin and its aim, it does not seem that the canon can be adopted as the model for regulating the exercise of the primacy of the Bishop of Rome in safeguarding the rights of other bish-

---

[353] Fontbona i Missé, *Comunión y sinodalidad*, 386: "De este modo, Tillard *redimensiona* el problema del ejercicio del ministerio del obispo de Roma, cabeza de este centro, sin negar con ello que 'comporta una potestad no sólo suprema, plena y universal, sino también *inmediata*, sobre todos, tanto los Pastores como sobre los demás fieles'. Precisamente porque, situando el ejercicio ministerial del obispo de Roma en *sunergía* con el conjunto de todos los obispos y con cada uno de ellos, recalca más la compenetración entre ellos que su complementariedad, más su inseparabilidad que su pluralidad, más su unidad infrangible que la suma de sus influencias."

[354] Tillard, *L'Église locale*, 439–40: "De toute évidence, l'esprit du canon 34 des Apôtres n'imprègne pas la forme romaine du gouvernement de la même façon qu'en Orient, surtout face aux autres 'primats'.... En Orient, la dimension confraternelle, co-associative, concertante, com-pagnonne, de l'activité synodale est la plus accentuée.... En Occident, on privilégie la dimension primatiale *personelle*, participative, hiérachique.... En un cas, la garantie de l'authenticité des décisions prises est cherchée dans l'unanimité des évêques, en l'autre cas, dans leur 'réception' par le primat. Ce sont là deux esprits, pouvant conduire de part et d'autre à des excès, par oubli de ce que l'autre esprit traduit d'essentiel."

[355] Cf. Tillard, "La tension entre primauté du Siège romain et conciliarité", 278–79.

[356] Ibid., 279–80: "Le modèle selon lequel se structurent les synodes romains, réinstaurés par Paul VI, n'est pas sans causer de par cette impression, des frustrations.... Nous ne sommes pas sans modèle. Tel était, en effet, l'esprit du canon 34 des Apôtres.... La belle *communion* ou *symphonie* du *una cum patribus* est brisée, l'autorité du *prôtos* absorbant celle des autres évêques même si le fruit de leur discussion se retrouve dans le mots du document promulgué."

ops; it is even less likely that it could serve as the antithesis to the so-called theologumena of Vatican I, which were taken up again by Vatican II.

It seems legitimate to ask: What results can the much-heralded reexamination of the role of the Bishop of Rome possibly produce, if it is founded upon the ecclesiology underlying the dialogue and, above all, if its point of reference is the principle of conciliarity, which constitutes the pivotal element thereof?

V. CONCLUSION

In the Catholic-Orthodox dialogue, the theme of primacy is being dealt with above all on the local level and generally with a mere mention of the theme, the exception being the more organic treatment of it in the document of the Joint Committee in France.

The official documents speak of it "in a rather transversal manner" and within a future perspective.[357] This corresponds, moreover, to the method agreed upon in the pertinent plan of the Joint Coordinating Committee.[358] Hence, even the treatment of the Church's sacramental structure, which was placed on the *agenda* for the first phase, was adopted as a strategy for laying the groundwork for a closer study of the differences, chief among which was that of the primacy of the Bishop of Rome. In fact, it is said that there is "a close connection and a logical sequence among the first three documents published by the Joint Commission",[359] which allows them to be considered as "an introduction and an indispensable preliminary to the question of the role of the Bishop of Rome in the Church".[360]

In reality, it would have been necessary to refer to the question directly in the various documents. For example, when it was affirmed in the Munich Document that the *episkopé* of the universal Church has been entrusted

---

[357] Sartori, "Il papato domani: considerazioni ecumeniche", 6, no. 2. Cf. *Ut unum sint*, no. 89, note 149.

[358] The Plan determined the principle: "Il dialogo deve partire dagli elementi che uniscono la Chiesa ortodossa e la Chiesa cattolico romana." Furthermore, it specified: "Quanto ai temi che devono costituire l'oggetto del dialogo nella sua prima fase, si pensa che lo studio dei sacramenti della Chiesa è proprizio per esaminare a fondo e in modo positivo i problemi del dialogo": cf. Salachas, *Il dialogo*, 27 and 29.

[359] Ibid., 133.

[360] Fortino, "Dialogo cattolico-ortodosso", *L'Osservatore Romano*, 15 giugno 1986.

to the totality of bishops, in communion with one another expressed through the practice of conciliarity, the Catholic side made known its desire that mention be made of the role of the Bishop of Rome within the bosom of this communion; as it turned out, they gave in to the Orthodox side. In this way they avoided making clear that the real problem "arises with respect to the realization of reciprocal communion and conciliarity of the Churches": by limiting themselves to underlining the positive aspects, they created "the false impression that problems no longer existed".[361]

The Bari Document too, while describing the relationship between the universal Church and the local Churches, insists simply on the reciprocal recognition of the Churches in the person of their bishops, without any mention of the function of the supreme ministry in the universal Church and, in particular, of the Petrine ministry as the principle and as the visible and perpetual foundation of the unity of faith and communion, the guarantor and judge of the unity among the different local Churches. Hence the impression that the universal Church is being viewed as a sum total or confederation of local Churches that recognize each other reciprocally.

Only in the final part of the Valamo Document is there any reference to the question of the primacy, which "could be approached" within the perspective of the communion between the local Churches. It limits itself, however, to saying that the question "constitutes a serious divergence among us and will be discussed subsequently". This time, too, the Orthodox side prevailed, with its ecclesiology that overlooks the universalistic ecclesiology founded on the ministry of unity of the successor of Peter. A discussion of apostolicity would have demanded a precise statement on this ministry, which figures as an essential part in the structure of the apostolic college: instead it limits itself to the possibility of attributing to the Bishop of Rome the role of *primus inter pares*.[362]

Nor does the Balamand Document make any mention of Petrine primacy as the internal principle of unity for the episcopate; rather, it is implicitly called into question by the condemnation of uniatism.

The documents thus present a certain "tendency to relativize the major theological differences between the two Churches and to speak at length

---

[361] Cardinal Ratzinger used these terms in speaking about the Munich Document (as cited by Salachas, *Il dialogo*, 66–67).
[362] Cf. Salachas, *Il dialogo*, 144–45.

in generic 'platitudes' [*'opinioni'*], using a terminology that is ambiguous and at times incomprehensible".[363] The predominant line of thinking in these documents is vitiated by abstractionism and irenicism and takes concrete form in a preoccupation with creating new theological syntheses, rather than adhering substantially to the actual doctrines of the respective sides. One might ask, therefore, whether it would not be more appropriate to speak of a "dialogue of theologies" rather than a "doctrinal dialogue".

In the light of these various elements, it does not seem baseless to conclude that the function of the successor of Peter is not considered to be essential to the nature of the Church, and that the lack of its formal acceptance need not exclude a unity of communion between Catholics and Orthodox. Such a conclusion suggests itself all the more, given that the pentarchy is spoken of, almost unanimously, as an institution willed by Christ, whereas it was an imperial creation specifically aimed at considering Rome as [merely] one among the patriarchal sees. There is also an insistence on conciliarity, with the ecumenical council being presented as the court of appeal in which the supreme authority of the Church resides.

After more than fifteen years of experience, now, it would seem legitimate to ask whether the time has not come to review the method of dialogue, taking as a model the method followed in other dialogues, where the parties have been much more explicit in pointing out not only where their respective views converge, but also where they differ.[364]

While mutually acceptable per se, in practice the present method of the Catholic-Orthodox dialogue has not been free from difficulties. There is in fact an almost tangible presupposition that the faith is "composed"

---

[363] Assimakis, "L'ecclesiologia", II, 30. Celada expresses the same impression, although with a more positive assessment: "El hecho de que los documentos puedan aparecer, a una primera aproximación, prevalentemente descriptivos y genéricos, no debe quitarles su gran valor eclesial. En efecto, se trata de una serie de constataciones de las tradiciones de ambas iglesias. En esos textos se ha preferido afirmar la situación de las cosas, sobre todo de las que son iguales más que de las que son diferentes" ("La 'Una Santa' en el diálogo católico-ortodoxo", 121). Cf. de Halleux, "Le texte de Valamo", 460.

[364] It was in this sense that Metropolitan Chrysostomos of Peristerion, in a text presented to the Holy Synod of the Church of Greece, proposed that the dialogue face "soprattutto le 'numerose' e profonde differenze di ordine teologico che ci sono tra le due chiese" ("Il dialogo teologico tra le chiese ortodossa e cattolica romana", *il regno-doc.*, 19/86, 598).

of elements that are interdependent and extraneous to each other, whereas the faith has its own structure. Furthermore, even on the basis of an erroneous conception of the hierarchy of truths, in an attempt to agree upon a lowest common denominator, which in reality does not adequately represent all the elements of the faith, some aspects of the faith itself end up being considered marginal, including that of the Petrine ministry. The danger looms larger precisely in the dialogue with the Orthodox Churches, which are effectively the ones closest to the Catholic Church with regard to the profession of faith. Rather than seeking compromises or proposing incomplete and ambiguous theologies, what is required is to set forth the true identity of the faith of the respective Churches, leaving behind every tactical strategy and ploy.

Insufficient attention has been paid in the Catholic-Orthodox dialogue to the problem of the primacy of the Bishop of Rome; however, this is due not only to the choice of methodology but also and above all to the underlying ecclesiological point of view. As we have seen, the documents seem to be composed predominantly—if not exclusively—in an Orthodox key, or, to put it more precisely, they reflect the theses of several present-day Orthodox theologians, who are joined by some Catholic theologians as well. For example, such a marked insistence on eucharistic ecclesiology—taken in effect as a unilateral emphasis on the local Church, which is said to be endowed with all the elements of Catholicity—leads to a fragmentation of the unity of the Church among the plurality of Churches. Thus there is a tendency to diminish the importance of the universal Church, conceived as a "secondary" reality, as though it were a result of a confederation of local Churches, which together constitute the one Church of Christ. In this way unity is reduced to a moral entity, something deriving from reciprocal recognition and mutual "interdependence".

Consequently, the big question arises about the concept of the Church's oneness. In general the documents lack clarity in describing the relationship between "local (or particular) Churches" and the "Church". The presentation of the local Churches as the concretization of the *Una Sancta*, even in the light of the context of autocephaly, does not seem to give due consideration to the fact that these are *Churches* only in the measure in which they are found within the *Church*, which is one by virtue of the bonds of the profession of faith, the sacraments, ecclesiastical government, and communion.

Furthermore, the Orthodox Churches are erroneously considered to be a single Church, while, in contrast, the Catholic Church is considered to be a particular Church. The local Churches are no longer referred to the one Church, but to the two sister Churches, namely, the Catholic Church and the Orthodox Church. Besides the contradiction with the doctrine of *"subsistit in"*, practically speaking the Church of Christ is no longer one but two: she is said to be a transcendent subject with regard to the two sister Churches, and only the totality of the Churches, Catholic and Orthodox, constitutes the Church. Moreover, the Church does not exist as one in history (at least in the second millennium), but exists only in the ideal convergence which the dialogue proposes to achieve.[365]

One of the fundamental and indispensable elements that needs to be taken into account in the dialogue is the awareness of the Catholic Church that the one Church of Christ subsists in her, with the fullness of the means of salvation, despite the acknowledgment that the term *Church* can also be applied, in an analogous and participative sense, to the Orthodox Churches, which are also endowed with the elements of salvation.[366]

Just as indispensable—to keep more closely to our subject—is the recognition of the essential role of the Bishop of Rome as the visible principle of the unity of the universal Church. In virtue of his role he possesses, by divine mandate, the supreme authority over all the Churches, including the Orthodox Churches, which derive their ecclesial character *from* and *in* the universal Church, and precisely because they do not acknowledge this authority they find themselves in an ecclesial condition that is *wounded*, that is to say, irregular.[367]

The ecumenical quest in its diverse expressions, including dialogue, tends precisely to make sure that "all be enabled to recognize the continuity of the primacy of Peter in his successors, the Bishops of Rome, and to see the Petrine ministry fulfilled in the manner intended by the Lord, as a worldwide apostolic service".[368] The invitation of John Paul II, which served as the point of departure for our considerations, concerns simply the "way of exercising the primacy", which, "while in no way renouncing

---

[365] Cf. Garuti, "Sister Churches", Appendix, pp. 311–314.
[366] Cf. ibid., pp. 302–5.
[367] Cf. *Communionis notio*, no. 17.
[368] Ibid., no. 18.

what is essential to its mission",[369] "can find expression in various ways according to the different circumstances of time and place, as history has shown".[370]

Even though there are those who might wish to play down the real import of the problem,[371] it is much more realistic to emphasize that, despite the progress made in reciprocal relations, "Orthodoxy does not accept the Primacy of the Roman Pontiff, especially because of the way in which it was dogmatically defined in the First Vatican Council". Despite the different historical situation and the profound changes in the context of these theological problems (from polemics to dialogue in charity), "the theological dialogue between the Catholic Church and the Orthodox Church ... today still seems to meet with difficulties on the part of some Orthodox Churches".[372]

No doubt the picture that has emerged is far from rosy. At the same time, however, "unity, after all, is a gift of the Holy Spirit".[373] In the ecumenical process, to which the Catholic Church has "committed herself *irrevocably*",[374] even before dialogue the "important priorities are prayer and penance", which are more capable of bringing about "a new conversion to the Lord",[375] which then will facilitate the acknowledgment and the full realization of the Petrine ministry.

---

[369] *Ut unum sint*, no. 95.

[370] *Communionis notio*, no. 18.

[371] Salachas, *Il dialogo*, 52: "Per sé, tra cattolici e ortodossi, non si tratta di discutere se il Papa abbia un ruolo primaziale. Questo, a parte casi di fanatismo polemico, è comunemente accettato anche dagli ortodossi.... Il contenzioso si concentra piuttosto sull'estensione del contenuto del ruolo primaziale: quale è l'autorità del Vescovo di Roma e quali sono le sue modalità di esercizio nella vita della Chiesa intera."

[372] A. Romita, "Criteri per la recezione ecclesiale dei documenti del dialogo", 178–79. Even Tillard, such a typical exponent of Catholic-Orthodox dialogue, writes, "There has as yet been no statement on this subject from the Orthodox-Roman Catholic Commission. However, it is clear that as a result of the warm exchange of words and gestures between Paul VI and Athenagoras.... Orthodoxy is changing the way it looks at the primacy of the bishop of Rome.... But the Orthodox Churches would find it difficult to accept a Roman primacy which differed from that of the first few centuries" (s.v. *Primacy*, DEM, 823).

[373] Apostolic Letter *Tertio millenio adveniente*, no. 34.

[374] *Ut unum sint*, no. 3.

[375] *Communionis notio*, no. 18. Cf. *Ut unum sint*, nos. 15–16, 21–27.

CHAPTER III

THE PRIMACY AND CATHOLIC-LUTHERAN DIALOGUE

I. THE LUTHERAN VIEW OF THE PRIMACY

HAVING ANALYZED THE QUESTION of the primacy with reference to the Catholic-Orthodox dialogue, I consider it useful to take up the subject again with reference to the Catholic-Lutheran dialogue. In this case, too, we will have to frame the question within a larger ecclesiological context, since this specific theme has not been addressed directly in the dialogue, except sporadically and at the national level. After a presentation of the Lutheran view of the primacy over the course of history, we will proceed to a systematic analysis of the documents of the dialogue and a general assessment of the results.

The Lutheran view of the primacy is rooted in the Church's nature,[1] which in turn is closely connected with the problem of justification by faith, the real hermeneutical key for all Christian life and doctrine, which gave rise to the Reformation. Indeed, all of the doctrinal formulae of the

---

[1] Cf. R. Mehl, s.v. "Protestantism", DEM, 830–37; D. Steinmetz, s.v. "Reformation", DEM, 848–50; N. A. Hjelm, "Lutheran World Federation", DEM, 640–41; E. T. Bachmann, s.v. "Lutheranism", DEM, 641–43; J. T. McNeil, "The Ecumenical Idea and Efforts to Realize It, 1517–1618", R. Rouse and S. C. Neill (eds.), *A History of the Ecumenical Movement 1517–1948* (Philadelphia, 1954), 27–62; H. Meyer, "L'ufficio papale nella visuale luterana", *Papato e servizio petrino* (Alba, 1976), 61–80; H. Meyer, "Das Problem des Petrusamtes in evangelischer Sicht", K. Lehmann, ed., *Das Petrusamt. Geschichtliche Stationen seines Verständnisses und gegenwärtige Positionen* (Freiburg, 1982), 110–28; W. Klausnitzer, *Das Papstamt im Disput zwischen Lutheranern und Katholiken* (Innsbruck and Vienna, 1987); I. Jacobsen, "Le Chiese luterane dal 1530 ai nostri giorni", *Conosciamo i fratelli. Corso breve di ecumenismo*, II (Rome, 1993), 71–122; B. Gherardini, *Creatura Verbi. La Chiesa nella teologia di Martin Lutero* (Rome, 1994); H. A. Raem, "The Third Phase of Lutheran/Catholic Dialogue (1986–1993)", IS, no. 86 (1994), 189–97; M. Kruse, "Die ökumenische Zukunft des Petrusdienstes aus lutherischer Sicht", *Theologische Quartalschrift* 178 (1998): 111–17.

traditional creeds must be understood in the light of the central fact of justification,[2] which was considered by Luther and by the Lutheran tradition as the essential point, the *articulus stantis vel cadentis ecclesiae* [the article of faith on which the Church stands or falls], which led to their estrangement from Rome.[3]

An adequate presentation of this view requires, however, some preliminary remarks on the Lutheran concept of the nature of the Church in her various aspects, with particular emphasis on the question of ministries.

1. The nature of the Church

Given the total corruption of human nature in the wake of original sin, and the consequent loss of man's capacity to do good and to cooperate in his own justification, the "fresh reading of the Bible", which was the real novelty of Protestantism, led Luther "to claim that Christians are 'justified' ... not by their works and the merits that derive from them, but by God's grace alone, received in faith and not by means of works.... Only the redeeming work of Christ is pleasing to God, and in His grace God 'reckons' to us [to man's account] the righteousness of Christ."[4] The initial consequences of this way of framing the issue are certitude of his own salvation on the part of the sinner who is justified in Christ and radical rejection of the concept of "merit".[5]

---

[2] M. Edwards and G. Tavard, *Luther. A Reformer for the Churches. An Ecumenical Study Guide* (New York, 1983), 41: "Justification by faith, or, as one can also express it, by grace through faith, becomes in Luther's writings a key to all Christian life and doctrine.... For everything that is formulated in the traditional creeds is to be understood in the light of the central fact of justification."

[3] P. Neuner, *Ökumenische Theologie* (Darmstadt, 1997), 256: "Dabei ist die Lehre von der Rechtfertigung für die Reformatoren ... der *articulus stantis vel cadentis ecclesiae*, die Mitte des Glaubens, 'das Evangelium', mit dem die christliche Kirche steht und fällt. Sie ist das Kriterium, nach dem alle Lehraussagen und jede kirchliche Ordnung und Struktur sich zu richten haben. Weil Luther in der römischen Kirche die biblische Lehre von der Rechtfertigung preisgegeben, einer Werkerei und einer kirchlichen Verfügung über das Heil geopfert sah, mußte er sich von Rom lossagen." Cf. G. Cereti, "Usciti dalla separazione", 455.

[4] R. Mehl, s.v. "Protestantism", DEM, 830a. Cf. F. Lovsky, *Un passé de division. Une promesse d'unité* (Paris, 1990), 65–66.

[5] Ibid., 66: "Deux conséquences en découlaient rapidement. L'une, c'est que le pécheur justifié par la foi en Christ doit donc vivre dans la certitude de son salut. L'autre, c'était un refus si radical de la notion de 'mérites' que la Réforme condamnait les indulgences et les couvents."

A fundamental ecclesiological conflict follows from this. Whereas initially Luther "never dreamed of founding a new church, or even substantially modifying the Catholic Church", in which he had acknowledged that both bishops and priests have a ministerial function, in the second phase of his thought, not only "did he appeal from the visible hierarchical and authoritarian Church to the invisible Church of the pure *communio sanctorum*, but in the *De Captivitate Babylonica* he was to stigmatize the whole of traditional Catholicism as a radical corruption of the Gospel".[6] This change of outlook was motivated precisely by his doctrine of justification: neither the individual nor the Church is able to claim a cooperative role in salvation. Hence, the Church's function of interpreting the Scriptures—and hence the authority of her tradition—is radically called into question.[7] The Church, consequently, is not regarded as a salvific institution willed by Christ or a sacrament of salvation organized as a community and endowed with ministries which are the effective means for the communication of grace.[8] Luther held that the only sacrament known in Scripture is Christ himself; the doctrine of the Church as sacrament destroys the immediacy that exists between God and man as well as the principle of salvation by grace alone. This leads to the antithesis,

---

[6] L. Bouyer, *The Church of God* (Chicago, 1982), 47–48.

[7] N. Lovsky, *Un passé de division*, 66–67: "Luther insistait sur la foi personnelle, les Catholiques sur la foi de l'Église. Rome maintenait la possibilité que l'homme justifié par le Christ puisse 'coopérer' d'une certaine manière à son salut, et l'Église 'coopérer' à celui des Chrétiens. C'était poser toute une série de questions qui concernaient les oeuvres du croyant, le rôle de l'Église ... La divergence spirituelle se transformait en conflit ecclésiologique quand les Réformateurs ... s'appuyaient sur une lecture en quelque sorte directe des Saintes Ecritures.... L'Église Catholique n'accepta pas d'être dépossédée de sa fonction séculaire: interpréter les Écritures. Autrement dit, le XVIe siècle se demandait si l'autorité de l'Église avait une seule source ou deux. Les Protestants affirmaient que l'Église est soumise à la Bible. Les Catholiques répliquaient que l'Église est l'interprète de la Bible. En fait, la Réforme sous-entendait, mais avec des nuances, que la Tradition était réformable, parce qu' elle était humaine, ce que l'Église Catholique n'acceptait pas: elle ne refusait pas de se réformer, mais elle n'admettait pas que son magistère fût contesté."

[8] L. Lago Alba, "Y. Congar, ecumenista. I. Diálogo con el Protestantismo", *Ciencia tomista* 87 (1996): 176: "El Protestantismo no admite esta concepción católica de una Iglesia querida por Cristo como institución de esa salvación con la facultad de comunicar, sacramental y causativamente, con una causalidad ministerial, real, la salvación otorgada una vez para siempre por Jesucristo. Para el Protestantismo ... no existe el cuerpo místico como una institución, organizada comunitariamente, como gran sacramento de la salvación, ni existen, por consiguiente, los ministerios o sacramentos como medios eficaces de la comunicación de la gracia."

"Church or Justification?" which characterizes the essence of Catholicism or Protestantism, since all the differences between them, in the final analysis, were based on this fundamental difference.[9]

Furthermore, this outlook was favored by the ecclesial situation of the times: since the Church offered no assurance of salvation—indeed, Luther regarded her as the "enemy of salvation" because she was devoid of all theological content and positive meaning—the one thing necessary, then, was "the true Church", which was extraneous to the institution. As Cardinal Ratzinger emphasizes, "Luther had found himself no longer able to recognize the Spirit of Christ in the universal Church and indeed regarded it as the tool of the Anti-Christ. He could not even regard the Protestant national Churches that arose from the Reformation as the Church in the proper sense of the word. They were merely functional machines that were sociologically and politically necessary under the direction of the political authorities, and nothing more. For him the Church withdrew into the local community. Only the congregation that hears the word of God on the spot is the Church. Hence he substituted the term congregation or community for that of the Church, which became a negative concept." [10]

Devoid of all institutional character, according to Luther, the Church— still abiding by the principle of the uniqueness of the salvific encounter between God and man in Christ—is said, though, to preserve a few

---

[9] Neuner, *Ökumenische Theologie*, 261–62: "Viele Kontroversen in der Ekklesiologie bündeln sich in der Vorstellung von der Sakrametalität der Kirche.... Die Lehre von der Kirche als Sakrament stelle das 'Solus Christus' und damit die Botschaft von der Rechtfertigung allein aus Gnaden in Frage. Doch 'nur ein einziges Sakrament kennt die Heilige Schrift, das ist Christus der Herr selbst' [WA 6, p. 86], darum könne man sich gegen eine solche über Gott verfügende Ekklesiologie nur wehren. Die evangelischen Christen stünden vor der Frage: Kirche oder Rechtfertigung.... An dieser Stelle wurde das Wesen des Katholizismus im Gegensatz zum Wesen des Protestantismus greifbar. Alle anderen Differenzen gründeten in dieser Grunddifferenz."

[10] *Church, Ecumenism and Politics*, 9. J. Ratzinger, *Principles of Catholic Theology*, 196–97: "It is against this background of a profoundly shaken ecclesial consciousness that we are to understand that Luther, in the conflict between his search for salvation and the tradition of the Church, ultimately came to experience the Church, not as a guarantor, but as the adversary of salvation. The concept of the Church was limited, on the one hand to the local community; on the other, it embraced the community of the faithful throughout the ages who are known only to God. But the community of the whole Church as such is no longer the bearer of a positively meaningful theological content. Ecclesial organization is now borrowed from the political realm because it does not otherwise exist as a spiritually significant entity."

ministerial and sacramental functions, in that she makes the salvific work of Christ present and efficacious. It is the *locus* of the encounter with God who saves, thanks to its special relationship with Christ, by whose Word it is generated and therefore considered the *Creatura Verbi*,[11] the communion of the saints called together by the Holy Spirit under one head, who is Christ.[12] The vital relationship between Christ as head and the Church as body gives rise to the idea of the spousal[13] and maternal character[14] of the Church.

This appears, then, to revisit the debate concerning the invisibility or visibility of the Church. Indeed, for Luther, the Church is first of all a mystery, an invisible reality, before being a visible institution.[15] As Gherardini observes, however, "the famous diatribe [dispute] between the visible and the invisible Church is a poorly framed theological problem", inasmuch as Luther considered the Church to be "the instrument of the

---

[11] Gherardini, *Creatura Verbi*, 106: "L'incarnazione e la redenzione ... hanno una vera continuità nella Chiesa, in particolare nella sua predicazione e nei suoi sacramenti.... È anzi proprio questo il compito della Chiesa; in tale compito e per mezzo di esso l'opera salutare di Cristo è attuale ed efficace, cosicché la Chiesa è il *luogo* dove l'incontro con il Cristo della Parola e dei sacramenti è l'incontro con Dio che salva." Ibid., 331: "La ragione per la quale la Chiesa è così intimamente radicata in Cristo vien da Lutero individuata nel fatto ch'essa è generata dalla Parola di Lui: è *creatura Verbi*, sotto la signoria dello Spirito Santo che nella Chiesa ripete oggi quanto già operò nell'umanità assunta dal Verbo. Donde una *communicatio idiomatum* che, dai rapporti fra l'umanità assunta e il Verbo assumente, s'allarga ai rapporti tra la Chiesa-corpo e Cristo-capo, o fra la Chiesa-sposa e il Cristo sposo."

[12] Ibid., 149. Other definitions of Church are also found in Luther: people of God, in perfect harmony with the word of God; earthly Christianity, but also: spiritual, intimate Christianity of the heart and of the soul; the assembly of all believers in Christ; the communion of saints and the kingdom of God. The most frequently recurring term, however, is *Gemeinde*, indicating not only a particular church, but also, and perhaps above all, the concrete historical reality of the Church, which both patristic and medieval writers had synthesized in the concept of *societas*: cf. ibid., 146ff.

[13] Ibid., 179–80: "La capitalità, ovviamente, non è né soppressa, né superata, né sottaciuta: della *Gemeinde* Cristo è e resta il capo e il signore.... La capitalità, tuttavia, viene come temperata ed insieme integrata dal fatto nuovo ch'emerge dal predetto rapporto vitale: Cristo-capo è lo sposo, e tutt'i cristiani, in quanto *Gemeinde* son la sua sposa."

[14] Ibid., 181–83: "Lutero riconosce che in essa [Chiesa] ... sono presenti i mezzi 'esteriori' della grazia, per i quali s'avvia e si completa il processo 'interiore' della rinascita." Hence there is a strong emphasis on "la strumentalità che la Chiesa mette in atto nell'annuncio della Parola e nella dispensazione dei sacramenti. Su codesta strumentalità si fonda la sua maternità; essa è la madre dei santi perché dà loro la vita con la Parola e li sostenta con i mezzi della grazia."

[15] Cf. P. Dentin, *Les privilèges des Papes*, 236.

presence and saving action of Christ in the world", which is by nature visible. "If there is a polemic against the so-called visible Church, it has as its object the institutionalism of the 'papist' Church, which Rome is said to substitute for the aforementioned action and presence." [16] Invisibility and visibility are both constitutive elements of the Church: "one *spiritual*, in which can be discerned the profound, ineffable and hidden essence of the *Gemeinde*, the other *corporeal*, which comprises its exterior, historical and concrete aspect, and which coincides with its visible extension in space and time, from the first moment of existence to the end." [17] Hence we can conclude, "There is no difficulty, then, not even for Luther, in speaking of the visible church, or in recognizing or admitting its visibility, so long as visible church deos not mean a counter church, or a subspecies of church, but the one *'creatura Verbi et Spiritus Sancti'*, which is at once holy and sinful, the spiritual living in 'the corporeal', under and in the concrete visible form of the *Gemeinde*. The 'exterior reality' of this church is visible; its institutional existence is visible; visible is the historical reality in which it is incarnate, in which it lives, preaches and works." [18] Undoubtedly, the need for a visible institution and for ecclesiastical organization became more apparent when confronted with the danger of "as many creeds as believers", [19] and this need was formulated concretely, especially in the works of Melanchthon, yet the elements "were very much Lutheran, and Luther would not hesitate to make this work his own". [20]

The signs which distinguish the Church from the "Synagogue of Satan" (the "papist" Church) are the word and the sacraments.

The word is the "sign of signs", in other words, "the first and last, the decisive and fundamental element, the one toward which all the others are ordered, and therefore It is indispensable for the certification and recognition of the Church itself". The word, indeed, "makes the Church what It wishes the Church to be; therefore where the Word is, there too is a sure sign, indeed the only infallible sign of the Church itself". This is due to the "connection between the Word and Christ", indeed, to "its identification with the Word incarnate.... Christ is in his Word. Indeed,

---

[16] *Creatura Verbi*, 103.
[17] Ibid., 191.
[18] Ibid., 222–23.
[19] Cf. Dentin, *Les privilèges des Papes*, 235–36.
[20] Bouyer, *Church of God*, 52.

He is his Word and comes with It. Consequently, while the Word authenticates and guarantees the Church, it reveals Christ [es treibt den Christus, puts Christ forth, like a shoot]." Hence, should someone wish to know Christ, he must "turn to the Church, attend it, and ask the Church, for the simple reason that outside of the Church there is neither truth nor Christ. . . . The true Church is found where the true tradition flourishes, which is the immutable and genuine continuity of the divine Word."[21]

To the extent that the word is decisive "in authenticating the Church, the sacraments have a similar function in virtue of their intimate connection with the same Word". Thus the one holy Church of Christ is found "only where the Sacraments are found also (but these are found together with the Church only if the Word of God is there), because with the sacraments Christ and his Spirit are always found". In conclusion, "Luther regards the Gospel on the one hand, and on the other hand the administration of the sacraments in conformity with the Gospel, as the distinctive signs of authentic ecclesiality. In the final analysis, however, the Gospel is always the only sign. . . . Purity of evangelical doctrine, i.e. 'true knowledge of Christ and the faith', constitutes the foundation and hence the mark of the Church; in their turn, the sacraments play an identical distinctive role, because—far from the efficacy of 'ex opere operato' so cherished by the papists—evangelical doctrine views them as tokens of grace, of the promise, and of the remission of sins."[22]

Notwithstanding the ministerial and sacramental function of the Church and her visible character, the difference between the Catholic view of the Church and the Lutheran view is all the more pronounced with regard to the role of the Church and her ministries, her authority, and her relationship with Christ.[23] Indeed, "while retaining a ministry with sacerdotal functions and even 'ordination' to this ministry by the laying on of hands, which was called evangelical, Luther and Lutherans always maintained a characteristic hesitation between its restabilization in a traditional spirit and [a refusal] to see a proper sacramental element in it which would be constitutive to the Church." This derives from two considerations: "The first is the devolution of Church authority to the secular authority

---

[21] Gherardini, Creatura Verbi, 191–99.
[22] Ibid., 200–206.
[23] Cf. Lovsky, Un passé de division, 68.

which now was impossible to change. Obviously, the second is the 'radical' interpretation of the universal priesthood which Luther reached, in what we have described as the second and ultraspiritualized phase of his ecclesiology, which left almost no room for a return to the traditional view of ministry." Behind these two factors lies "the outline of an episcopacy that was completely degenerate in its exercise, a legacy of the late Middle Ages, particularly in Germany. This fact was too facilely persuasive in showing the impossibility of restoring the episcopate to its original spirit."[24] The traditional episcopate, together with the need for an apostolic succession of bishops, had to be rejected.[25] While retaining the episcopal ministry, which in any case was not linked to apostolic succession, its essential characteristics were changed, with foreseeable consequences as to the need for ordained ministries.[26] In this regard we note an attempt to revise the traditional evaluation of Luther's position, while recognizing that his assertions in this field are not always that clear and are still the subject of controversies even within Protestant circles.[27] Indeed,

---

[24] Cf. Bouyer, *Church of God*, 52–53. Neuner, *Ökumenische Theologie*, 220: "So wurde die katholische Kirche zunehmend zu einer Kleruskirche, die vom Amt und seiner Vollmacht her betrachtet wurde, wo Priester und Ordensleute als die wahren und eigentlichen Christen erschienen, Laien dagegen auf die Funktion des Hörens und Gehorchens festgelegt blieben und in dem Maß als Christen verstanden wurden, als sie mit den Klerikern und deren Lebens- und frömmigkeitsstil übereinstimmten. Im Gegensatz dazu wurde in den Kirchen der Reformation die Freiheit eines jeden Christenmenschen und die Gleichheit aller, die 'aus der Taufe gekrochen' sind, verkündet, sie sollte zum Strukturprinzip der reformatorischen Gemeinschaften werden.... Kirchliche Ordnung und Amtsstrukturen verstehen sich in diesen Gemeinschaften ausschließlich aus organisatorischen Notwendigkeiten stammend, ohne daß ihnen eine theologische Relevanz zukommen würde."

[25] Edwards and Tavard, *Luther*, 60–61: "Unable to maintain the traditional episcopal structure ... he [Luther] came to rely on the princes and the political order since he wanted the preachers to devote all their strength to the gospel and to doctrine. What mattered was that the church give itself those structures needed to preach the gospel effectively."

[26] Lovsky, *Un passé de division*, 69–70: "Le désaccord sur la succession apostolique et sur la nature et l'instrumentalité de l'Église aboutit à des différences profondes au sujet des ministères ... l'Église catholique maintient une hiérarchie des ministères ordonnés permanents, du diacre au prêtre, à l'évêque et au Pape; la Réforme récuse plus ou moins cette hiérarchie, refuse totalement le ministère du Pape, et ne voit pas dans l'organisation des ministères une structure indispendable qui serait donnée par Dieu."

[27] W. Pannenberg, *Systematic Theology*, (Grand Rapids, Mich., 1998) 3: 376: "Luther emphasized strongly that he intended to maintain the need for a special calling to discharge publicly the functions of preaching the Word and administering the sacraments, but it is indeed hard to understand how this emphasis relates to what he says about the universal priesthood. Even to this day this issue is debated in the Protestant exposition of Luther and teaching on the ministry."

Mehl frankly acknowledges that "While the Roman Catholic Church maintained that there is no church except where there are priests ordained by a bishop who is within apostolic succession and in communion with the Pope as successor of Peter, the Reformation maintained that the church is wherever the word of God is rightly proclaimed and the sacraments initiated by Christ ... are administered in accordance with the Gospel." This would not imply a rejection of all ecclesiastical institutions, in the sense that when schism became inevitable Protestantism "adopted a variety of institutional forms in its various denominations, but all of these institutions were marked by their collegial character and by the increasing role of the laity in the government of the Church". The understanding of ministry, however, remained different: "that the ministry is an essential is not disputed in churches that resulted from the Reformation. But pastors are not priests, in that they have no special character or power which should distinguish them from lay people." [28]

Pannenberg, in contrast, is no less explicit in maintaining that while attributing "to all Christians the same power (*potestas*) in the proclamation of the word and administration of the sacraments", Luther "emphasized that it does not follow from this that all may equally exercise this ministry publicly in the congregation, in the sphere of their common life. A special calling is needed for this public ministry and Luther finally traces this back to the apostles and to their calling by Jesus Christ himself." [29] Even the Reformation, Pannenberg adds, never contested the need for supralocal ministries, including that of the regional episcopate, for the purpose of preserving the community in unity and apostolic faith. [30] Consequently, while distinguishing "between the direct calling of the apostles to ministry by the Risen Lord and the indirect calling of all later ministers that followed", Luther accepted as immutable "the rule of apostolic succession by way of the bishops as bearers of an office

---

[28] Mehl, s.v. "Protestantism", DEM, 831b–832a.

[29] Pannenberg, *Systematic Theology*, 3: 375–76.

[30] Pannenberg, "Le ministère ecclésial et l'unité de l'Église", *Istina* 40 (1995): 198 and 201: "Malgré son insistance sur le ministère local comme forme fondamentale du ministère de la prédication institué par Dieu, la Réforme luthérienne n'a jamais contesté la nécessité de ministères ecclésiaux supra-locaux dépassant les frontières paroissales." Supralocal ministries, especially episcopal ministry, "furent chargés par la Réforme de la mission qui fut déjà déterminante pour l'émergence du ministère de direction locale des premières communautés chrétiennes, le ministère confié à l'*episkopos*: il s'agit de maintenir les communautés dans l'unité de la foi apostolique."

that came down from the apostles".[31] That succession continues through presbyteral ordination of "pastors by pastors" in the ordained ministry, "which is a continuation of the leadership function of the apostles", although later ministers, "unlike the apostles, are not called directly by the risen Lord".[32]

Catholic circles, however, continue to emphasize the formal rejection by Protestant ecclesiology of the Church's role in salvation, or at least of her *instrumentality* in salvation, along with the profound differences which result as to the nature and hierarchy of ministries.[33] The divine foundation of the ecclesiastical hierarchy "is atomized to the extent in which Luther laicizes the priesthood, deprives it of its specificity, and renders it banal by ratifying it at the level of common Christian life".[34] Protestantism, then, does not recognize any hierarchical mediation. In contrast with Catholic ecclesiology, which sees the Church as an organism which lives by grace, born of the Incarnation and constituted by the joint action of the Holy Spirit and the apostolic ministry, Protestantism views the Church as an assembly which is bound, not to the ordained ministers, but to the word of God: the apostolicity of doctrine replaces the apostolicity of ministry.[35] Ministry, which in the final analysis is described "predominantly as a preaching ministry",[36] "belongs, at least in its origin, to all the baptized, not only by right but also by precept", "because baptism extends the priesthood of Christ to all".[37]

---

[31] Pannenberg, *Systematic Theology*, 3:401.

[32] Ibid., 402.

[33] Lovsky, *Un passé de division*, 69: "Le désaccord sur la succession apostolique et sur la nature et l'instrumentalité de l'Église aboutit à des différences profondes au sujet des ministères. Tout le monde sait que la Réforme refusa de reconnaître la primauté romaine et le ministère du Pape, mais c'était aussi la nécessité absolue d'un ministère ordonné par un évêque pour célébrer les sacrements que la Réforme mettait en cause." The author then proceeds to list the resulting differences concerning the Mass, the distinction between the ordained priesthood and the common priesthood, the hierarchy of the ordained priesthood, and the sacraments.

[34] Gherardini, *Creatura Verbi*, 240.

[35] Lago Alba, "Y. Congar, ecumenista", 177: "Mientras la eclesiología católica es horizontal, pues la iglesia es concebida como un organismo de la gracia, nacido en la encarnación y constituido hoy por la acción conjunta del Espíritu Santo y el ministerio apostólico, la Iglesia es entendida por el Protestantismo como una asamblea, ligada no a la sucesión de los ministros ordenados sino a la palabra de Dios."

[36] Pannenberg, *Systematic Theology*, 3:384.

[37] Gherardini, *Creatura Verbi*, 246.

Notwithstanding the rite of imposing hands and its concomitant prayer, ordination no longer entails anything sacramental.[38] Rather it becomes a simple symbolic action, which the Church describes as a "sacrament", by virtue of which the minister is called to discharge *publicly* the mandate entrusted to him,[39] without any conferral of grace or of a particular character.[40] As Bishop Gherardini concludes, "From the community the candidate receives, not an appointment to an ordained class, as in the doctrine and practice of the Roman Church, but rather a simple calling with the official commission to lead worship services. This calling and commission qualify the candidate for ministry but they do not consecrate." Consecration "neither adds anything to baptismal consecration, nor produces sacramental effects". It merely "legitimizes, on the official level, the man called to divine service and service to the brethren".[41] In reality "Luther retains [at least in part] the Catholic terminology relating to the apportionment of ministry: *bishop, pastor, minister.* He did not, however, preserve the contents [of that terminology], which ... he radically alters.... [For him] the priestly terminology has reference merely to lay realities, and the competencies that it signifies derive from the community." For Luther "Ordination is simply a politico-administrative act by which a Christian is chosen by other Christians ... who, in the name of Christ and of the Church, empower him to exercise the *ministerium verbi.* The source of this empowerment lies, then, in the community and not in any arcane sacralizing powers."[42]

---

[38] Pannenberg, *Systematic Theology,* 3:393: "Luther refused to call ordination a sacrament. He wrote in 1520 that the New Testament makes no promise of grace (promissio gratiae) to this call and even that it makes no mention at all of the action."

[39] Ibid., 388: "In the Reformation tradition this precise feature of the pastoral ministry comes out in the fact that it is public.... The idea of 'public' arrives within the thought of a relation to the totality not merely of the local Church but of the church universal." On the symbolic character of ordination, see ibid., 397.

[40] Ibid., 397–98: "According to Roman Catholic teaching, ordination confers a gift [of grace]. In support Trent appealed to 2 Tim. 1:6, where indeed, as in 1 Tim. 4:14, we read of a charism that is imparted by the laying on of hands. Even in 1522 Luther did not contest the imparting of such a gift, which Trent used as an argument for calling *ordo* a sacrament (DS 1766). Hence Luther constantly attacked the doctrine of an indelible character as the effect of ordination, and in so doing he could sometimes state that a priest who is deposed is a priest no longer."

[41] Gherardini, *Creatura Verbi,* 252–53.

[42] Ibid., 257 and 259.

2. Specific view of the primacy

The difficulty of determining the precise meaning of the Church's visibility and especially of her ministerial role in Luther's view and—
consequently—the nature of ministry naturally affects the Lutheran idea
of the primacy as well. Aside from his initial intentions and attitudes, and
prescinding from later invective, it is difficult to gather Luther's true thinking on this question. F. Kramer's analysis of the Lutheran Confessions, as
elaborated in the various Smalcald articles, reveals conflicting positions,
ranging from that of openness to the possibility of a certain primacy of
the Bishop of Rome, albeit *de iure humano*, to an explicit rejection of the
Church's need for a visible head.[43]

In the earliest phase, notwithstanding the impromptu antipapal polemics, "Luther's campaign for reform did not begin with a critique of the
hierarchical and institutional structure of the Roman Church, much less
with a critique of the papacy. His primary concern was to bring to
light again and to make heard once more the original Gospel message
of God's grace in Christ, which alone and gratuitously reconciles man
with God."[44] Ample proof of this is available in several pronouncements of Luther which clearly support the Pope, his office, and the
fullness of his powers: "At the outset of his struggle [for reform], we
find in Luther's works a whole series of writings in which he expresses
the hope that the papacy might accept the reform, declares his willingness to submit to the Bishop of Rome, acknowledges that the papacy
and the primacy can be perfectly acceptable (God willing), takes issue
with those who oppose Rome without reason, and blames the adversaries of the papacy—in this case the Hussites—for having provoked an
'unpardonable' schism."[45] Luther's fundamental concern was the reform
of the Church, and this did not necessarily involve rejection of the
papacy, provided that it is exercised according to the Gospel.[46] Even in

---

[43] "A Lutheran Understanding of Papal Primacy", LDC V, 130: "There are, however,
passages in the Lutheran Confessions which, theoretically, at least, seem to leave open the
possibility of a certain primacy of the bishop of Rome, though strictly *de iure humano*. On
the other hand the *Smalcald Articles* deny that the church needs a visible head."

[44] Meyer, "L'ufficio papale", 66. Cf. Meyer, "Das Problem des Petrusamtes", 111–14.

[45] J.J. von Allmen, *Il primato della Chiesa di Pietro e di Paolo*, 49–50. Cf. Meyer, "L'ufficio
papale", 66–68.

[46] Kruse, "Die ökumenische Zukunft", 112–13: "Es könnte ja noch immer so scheinen,
als wäre das Zentrum der Bemühung Luthers um eine Reform der Kirche in seiner Zeit

those early years there was no lack of charges leveled against the Pope, including the description of him as the "Antichrist", which was understood thereafter as a key element in the conflict between the word of Scripture and the Pope, who was considered as the adversary of truth.[47] Since Christ had given equal authority to all the apostles, the primacy of the Bishop of Rome was neither an article of faith nor a characteristic sign of the true Church of Christ: inasmuch as the primacy conferred a particular dignity in human law, it was a marginal question and in any case not necessary for salvation.[48] While the Church had to be liberated from the tyranny of the papists, Luther still felt that he belonged to the See of Rome.[49] We can conclude then, with Meyer, "For the Luther of the period 1517–1519 the matter seems clear: he does not think of his own campaign of reform as an attack on the papal office as such. He believes that his demands for reform, which he refused to abandon, were clearly consistent with his own respect for, obedience to, and confidence in the Roman See, even in his confrontations with it. Luther sees no irreconcilable contradiction between the firmness with which he maintains his convictions concerning reform, on the one hand, and his recognition of the papacy, on the other. Consequently, he rejects the claims of his adversaries that his stance involved an irreconcilable contradiction which was a source of ecclesiastical divisions and which, in their eyes, was central to the entire polemic."[50]

---

der Kampf gegen das Papsttum und letztlich dessen Abschaffung gewesen. Als ein völlig gesichertes historisches Faktum kann aber gelten: Luthers reformatorisches Wirken setzt nicht bei einer Kritik des Papsttums an.... Noch zwei Jahre nach dem Thesenanschlag äußerte sich eine gewisse Hoffnung, der Papst werde in dem aufgebrochenen Streit im Sinne des Evangeliums entscheiden.... Und doch muß festgehalten werden: Luther intendierte nicht die Beseitigung des Papstamtes an sich, sondern eine dem Evangelium gemäße Ausprägung und Praxis."

[47] Klausnitzer, *Das Papstamt im Disput*, 136: "Noch bevor die Bulle 'Exsurge Domine' die Luther mit dem Bann bedrohte, promulgiert war, gewann der Konflikt mit dem Papsttum für den Augustinermönch eine neue Qualität. Schon früher hatte er Vermutungen geäußert, daß der Antichrist an der römischen Kurie regiere oder daß gar der Papst persönlich der Antichrist oder sein Sendbote sei."

[48] Ibid., 137–38: "Es gebe nicht elf Boten (die Apostel) und einen Sonderboten (Petrus), der ein Amt über die anderen besitzt, sondern Christus habe alle Apostel mit gleicher Vollmacht in die Welt geschickt.... Auf der Ebene des menschlichen Rechtes könne dem Papst eine besondere Stellung eingeräumt werden ... Das Papsttum ist ihm in dieser Zeit nur eine Randfrage und auf jeden Fall nicht zur Seligkeit notwendig."

[49] Cf. ibid., 139.

[50] "L'ufficio papale", 69.

In reality, at least initially, Luther rejected not the "Petrine function" as such, but rather its concrete historical embodiment.[51] Luther would simply have hoped for a reform of the papacy, to be brought about through an ecumenical council, since he still acknowledged that the Bishop of Rome had legitimate spiritual powers, not only in his diocese, but also at a more general level, albeit as a matter of merely human law.[52] Such powers derived from his succession to the Apostle Peter, to whom the New Testament attributes a preeminence over the other apostles.[53]

Very soon, however, when it became apparent that reconciliation was henceforth impossible[54] and Luther was excommunicated,[55] the primacy itself was rejected in clear terms and often in a tone which went far

---

[51] *Reflections of the Lutheran Participants*, LCD V, 25: "In considering the historic Lutheran position on the papacy, we have become very much aware that the early Reformers did not reject what we have called the 'Petrine function', but rather the concrete historical papacy as it confronted them in their day. In calling the pope the 'antichrist', the early Lutherans stood in a tradition that reached back into the eleventh century." Meyer, "Ein evangeliumsgemäßes Papstampt. Kritik und Forderung aus reformatorischer Sicht", *Das Papstamt: Dienst oder Hindernis für die Ökumene?* (Regensburg, 1985), 69: "*Sofern* das Papsttum diesem Evangelium widerspricht, wird es als antichristlich verworfen. Die Kritik am Papsttum ist also keine Kritik am Papsttum qua Papsttum. Sie richtet sich ihrerseits nach einem übergeordneten Kriterium und ist damit abhängig von diesem Kriterium. Würde das Papsttum diesem übergeordneten Kriterium entsprechen, so würde damit ipso facto die Kritik am Papsttum erlöschen. Die Kritik ist also eine *bedingte* Kritik." Cf. Pannenberg, "Die lutherische Tradition und die Frage eines Petrusdienstes an der Einheit der Christen", *Il primato del Successore di Pietro*, Atti del Simposio teologico (Rome, December 1996; Libreria Editrice Vaticana, 1998), 472–75.

[52] *Reflections of the Lutheran Participants*, LCD V, 26: "We need to remember that the earliest Lutherans hoped for a reform of the papacy precisely for the sake of seeing the unity of the church preserved. Melanchthon held that 'for the sake of peace and general unity among the Christians' a superiority over the other bishops could be conceded to the pope. Many Lutherans kept hoping for an ecumenical council to reform the papacy. Despite their often violent antipapal polemics, Lutherans continued to concede to the pope all the legitimate spiritual powers of a bishop in his diocese, in this case, Rome. They even granted the propriety of his exercising a larger jurisdiction by *human* right over communities that had by their own will placed themselves under him."

[53] Ibid., 27: "Even theologians of the era of classic Lutheran orthodoxy conceded that in the New Testament Peter possessed a preeminence among the Twelve as a leader (*coryphaeus*), spokesman (*os*), chief (*princeps*) and the one who proposed what was to be done. In rejecting the monarchical authority of the bishop of Rome in the church, they were careful not to exclude a primacy of Peter among the apostles based on honor, age, calling, zeal, or order, nor did they deny that in a broad sense Peter could be called a 'bishop' of Rome." Cf. ibid., 29.

[54] Edwards and Tavard, *Luther*, 34: in the Augsburg Confession (1530), "No mention was made of the pope. Seven years later, when the possibility of reconciliation seemed remote

beyond the polemical, especially in opposition to the teaching of *Unam Sanctam* (drawn from the Fifth Lateran Council) on the need for every human being to be a subject of the Bishop of Rome in order to be saved.[56] The point of rebellion was reached with the refusal to accept the Pope's primacy of jurisdiction and to submit to his authority.[57] The appearance of several antipapal books aggravated this situation over the years. As Luther gradually lost hope as to the possibility of reforming the Roman Church of his day, and his confidence in the Petrine office as a service to the Gospel and to the true unity of the Church of Jesus Christ waned, he launched a swift and intensifying critique and polemic against the Pope, which eventually culminated in an identification of the Pope with the Antichrist. This not only sealed the definitive break with Rome but also gave rise almost automatically to blind hatred, imprecations of the lowest order, and even the invocation of fire and sword.[58] Henceforth, the

---

and the need for diplomacy less urgent, a new section was added rejecting papal claims of authority within the church and the world and identifying the papacy with the antichrist."

[55] Klausnitzer, *Das Papstamt im Disput*, 140: "Der offizielle Bruch des Papsttums mit Luther ist jedenfalls die Bulle 'Decet Romanum Pontificem' (15. Januar 1521), die die in 'Exsurge Domine' angedrohte Exkommunikation vollzieht."

[56] J.-M. R. Tillard, "Le ministère d'unité", 209-10: "Quand Luther dans la *Préface des oeuvres latines* (1545) écrit que 'le pape est nécessairement du diable', ou quand il déclare dans le *Commentaire de l'épître aux Galates* (1535) 'le pape est antichrist et vicaire de Satan', il faut lire, sous les formules excessives qu'inspire la passion et qui dépassent la pensée, beaucoup plus que le refus d'un certain exercice de la primauté. La papauté comme telle, comme institution se trouve en cause, quoi qu'il en soit de la qualité personelle de celui qui exerce cet office.... Luther y voit l'instrument diabolique de l'asservissement des consciences que l'Évangile déclare libres, par une sorte de tyrannie qui lie la Parole de Dieu en niant la justification par la foi seule. Car le pape exige qu'un observe en les considérant comme nécessaires au salut ses décrets, ses traditions, ses 'oeuvres'. Ainsi la papauté est 'comme une chambre de tortures pour les consciences' et donc l'ennemie du Christ libérateur.... La question de la papauté relève donc, selon Luther, directement de la théologie du salut.... Là où elle est sous le pape, l'Église n'a plus la possibilité de croire ce qui est au coeur de la foi chrétienne, la justification gratuite, l'imputation des mérites du Christ." Similar comments by the early Protestants and Anglicans may be found in P. Grandfield, *The Papacy in Transition* (Dublin, 1981), 18–20. On the equations papacy/kingdom of Babylon and Pope/antichrist, see also Gherardini, *Creatura Verbi*, 88–92.

[57] *Reflections of the Lutheran Participants*, LCD V, 26: "Because of these factors, from the 1520s on, Lutherans regarded themselves as in fact outside the pope's spiritual jurisdiction. They saw themselves as being on a par with those parts of the church, especially in the East, which did not recognize the jurisdictional primacy of the bishop of Rome."

[58] Cf. Meyer, "L'ufficio papale", 70–71. In the following pages the author attempts a benign reading of this identification, which, nonetheless, accurately reflects Luther's view of the papacy. Cf. Meyer, "Das Problem des Petrusamtes", 114–19.

admission of a primacy *iure humano*, with its consequent obligation of obedience, was excluded, while opposition to such an institution was fomented on the basis that it was contrary to the divine wisdom and the will of God.[59] Those who continued to obey the Pope were said consequently to be jeopardizing their own salvation.[60] Since the papacy came from the devil, it was considered a Christian duty to oppose it, and defending it was the source of every evil in the Church.[61] The Church had her foundation and her identifying mark in the word of God, which all pastors have the duty to preach. By his exaggerated pomp and incredible expenditures on luxurious living and liturgical ceremonies, the Pope proved that he was at variance with the Gospel, a tyrant and the Antichrist.[62] Luther declared that henceforth it would be senseless and useless for the Church of the Reform to take up the papal office, even in the event that that office had shed her "hostility to the Gospel" and thus lost her character of being the "anti-Christ".[63]

The critique of the papacy became more systematic in the Smalcald articles of 1537, especially in the fourth. That critique has been summarized as follows: "The Bishop of Rome boasts that by divine right he is superior to all bishops and pastors, and adds that by the same divine law he possesses the two swords, that is, the authority to confer and transfer

---

[59] Klausnitzer, *Das Papstamt im Disput*, 141: "Das Papsttum ist nicht nur bloß 'iure humano' und damit letztlich doch von Gott wenigstens toleriert: Langsam zeichnet sich eine neue Argumentation ab, die das Papsttum als gegen Wissen und Willen Gottes enstanden versteht."

[60] Cf. ibid., 146.

[61] Ibid., 154: "Sich dem päpstlichen System zu widersetzen sei eine christliche Tat (WA 7,7.45). Umgekehrt wird die Verteidigung der päpstlichen Gewalt zur Quelle alles Bösen in der Kirche (WA 7,6.44f; vgl. 2,22; 7,9f.47f). Der Hauptvorwurf an den Papst lautet, daß er sich über die Schrift erhebt und keine kritischen Rückfragen vom Evangelium her zuläßt (z. B. WA 7,177)."

[62] Ibid., 142–44: "Aufgabe (und Erkennungszeichen) der Hirten in der Kirche ist die Verkündigung des Evangeliums mit einer lebendigen Stimme (viva voce) (WA 7,721)... Das Antichristliche des Papsttums zeige sich in dem Übermaß an Pracht und dem unglaublichen Aufwand im Lebensstil und im Kult (WA 7,732–734) sowie der Mißhandlung deutscher Fürsten durch den Papst (WA 7,748f).... Der Papst sei ein Bekämpfer des Evangeliums, ein Tyrann und der Antichrist." The polemic intensifies with the passage of time: "Die Verbindung von Papsttum und Teufel, die in der Antichristpolemik hergestellt wird, wird zum beherrschenden Thema seiner späteren Papstkritik.... Bereits 1537 ist Luther der sicheren Überzeugung: Das Papsttum sei auf Lügen gegründet und teuflisch geworden; der Papst sei Beelzebuls getreuer Untertan (WA 50,128), des 'Teuffels vol', er gehöre mit seinen Dekreten 'in des Teuffels Reich' (WA 50,671)."

[63] Cf. Meyer, "L'ufficio papale", 74.

kingdoms. He further claims that it is necessary to believe this in order to be saved. For this reason the Bishop of Rome calls himself the Vicar of Christ on earth. We believe and confess that these three articles are false, impious, tyrannical and pernicious for the Church." [64] Thus developed the categorical denial that the Pope is *iure divino* the head of Christendom,[65] because, in his diabolical wickedness, he has brought ruin to the entire Church and destroyed the principal article of faith in salvation through Jesus Christ.[66] Despite attempts at a more benign interpretation of the foregoing,[67] we are nevertheless confronted with a total juridical degradation of the Bishop of Rome. "Luther replaced apostolic succession with the successive proclamation of the Gospel, indeed of the 'pure' Gospel, which was not necessarily linked to the successors of the apostles. . . . The most drastic consequence which Luther deduced [from that substitution] concerned the release [of Christians] from the 'potestas clavium' by reducing it to a merely disciplinary authority, and the jurisdictional reduction of the Bishop of Rome. . . . History provides examples of popes who had

---

[64] Cf. von Allmen, *Il primato della Chiesa di Pietro e di Paolo*, 47.

[65] Kruse, "Die ökumenische Zukunft", 113: "In den (von Luther verfaßten) *Schmalkaldischen Artikeln* ... wird die Frage nach der Autorität des Papstes dahingehend beantwortet, daß sie nicht als 'iure divino' anerkannt werden könne."

[66] Klausnitzer, *Das Papstamt im Disput*, 147–48: "Zur Begründung für die Ablehnung eines Papstprimates 'iure divino' wird angegeben, der Papst verderbe die ganze christliche Kirche und zerstöre den Hauptartikel von der Erlösung Jesu Christi. . . . Luther hätte gefunden, daß der Rechtfertigungsartikel und die Lehre vom Primat des Papstes als Glaubensartikel und in der praktischen Ausübung des Primates ... sich nicht miteinander vereinbaren lassen. Nach seiner Auffassung stößt sich die Christusunmittelbarkeit des Glaubens mit dem Gehorsamsanspruch des Papstes, der als Gehorsamsinstanz Christus im Evangelium verdrängt." Cf. A. C. Piepkorn, "*Ius divinum* and *Adiaphoron* in Relation to Structural Problems in the Church: The Position of the Lutheran Symbolical Books" (LCD V, 119).

[67] Significant in this respect is Meyer ("L'ufficio [Il servizio] papale", 77–79): referring to Luther's tract on "The Power and the Primacy of the Pope" he writes, "Tutta l'argomentazione di esso in fondo è imperniata sulla questione del carattere 'iure divino-iure humano' dell'ufficio papale. Quando con argomenti biblici e storici ivi si respinge la pretesa di 'ius divinum' del primato papale e si afferma il suo carattere di 'ius humanum', è del tutto chiaro che non s'intende con ciò squalificare in linea di principio il primato e dimostrare che si tratta di qualcosa di secondario o addirittura di inesistente. Il suo senso piuttosto consiste nel respingere una concezione esagerata e massimalistica del potere papale. . . . Possiamo addirittura dire: Vista alla luce del trattato, l'insistenza riformatoria sul carattere 'iure humano' dell'ufficio papale in fondo non è altro che una correzione di una concezione esagerata e massimalistica del carattere 'iure divino' di tale ufficio. . . . Tutta questa argomentazione sta ad indicare che il trattato non intende contestare in maniera assoluta e radicale il carattere 'iure divino' del primato papale, ma che lo concepisce e vorrebbe vederlo concepito in maniera diversa da come faceva la teologia cattolica contemporanea."

been unworthy of their exalted position, which Luther exploited in his argument against the primatial and magisterial function of the Petrine office." In his argument one notes "a sudden leap from his consideration of Peter to his reflections on the Bishop of Rome ... such that, despite the homage that he pays to the primatial and magisterial authority of Simon, son of Jonah, he does not acknowledge it at all in [Peter's] successors".[68] No doubt various other factors entered into play, but the fundamental position always remained bound up with a particular concept of justification in Christ and of the salvific mediation of the Church. Only in the wake of an admission that justification comes from God alone in Christ,[69] and of the rejection of apostolic succession according to the Roman theory, which was deemed contrary to the Gospel,[70] would it have been possible to reflect on a Petrine ministry and to recognize the Pope as the Supreme Pontiff.[71] As it happened, though, the papacy "added to the word of God several propositions and demands of its own, new and false ways of worshipping God, and it set them on a par with the commandments and words of God; it formulates 'new articles of faith', devises 'other doctrines' and claims to do so 'by divine right'". In this way the Pope " 'destroys the primary and fundamental article of faith concerning redemption through Jesus Christ', that is to say, the principle of justification 'by the love of Christ ... unmerited ... through faith', on which 'is based everything that we teach and practice against the Pope, the devil, and the world' ", and thus the papacy has cast Christ and his Gospel out of the government of the Church.[72] Since no one holds author-

---

[68] Cf. Gherardini, *Creatura Verbi*, 353–56.

[69] H. Schütte, *La Chiesa nella comprensione ecumenica* (Padua, 1995), 186: "Ancora nel 1531, nel commento alla lettera ai Galati, egli [Lutero] si è dichiarato pronto a ritirare il suo no al papato, 'se il papa ammette che solo Dio giustifica, per pura grazia attraverso il Cristo'". Cf. Klausnitzer, *Das Papstamt im Disput*, 155; G. Chantraine, "Nécessaire papauté", *Communio*, no. XVI, 3 (1991): 15; Meyer, "L'Ufficio papale", 66f; Meyer, "Das Problem des Petrusamtes", 111.

[70] Cf. Gherardini, *Creatura Verbi*, 216–17.

[71] Pannenberg, "Le ministère ecclésial", 201: "C'est dans ce cadre qu'il s'agit de réfléchir à frais nouveaux à la relation entre le ministère qui aurait la responsabilité constante de veiller à l'unité de toute la chrétienté dans la foi en l'Évangile apostolique, et l'autorité des conciles oecuméniques. Pareil service pétrinien pourrait se concevoir comme service de médiation entre les Églises particulières de la chrétienté: il aurait le souci particulier de préserver leur unité dans la foi apostolique." Cf. Mehl, "Protestantism", 830a–31b.

[72] Cf. Meyer, "L'Ufficio papale", 72–73. H. Schütte, "Das 'revolutionäre Angebot' in der Ökumene-Enzyklika. Gedanken zu einer Verständigung über das Dienstamt der Einheit", *Bausteine für die Einheit der Christen* 36 (1996): 21: "Der eigentliche Grund für Martin Luthers

ity in the Church but Christ alone and his Gospel, the presence of bishops and pastors in the Church has no particular juridico-sacramental relevance. Hence as the implications of the doctrine on justification were brought to bear on the papacy, it was reduced to an institution of human law and regarded not only as useless for salvation, but even as superfluous[73] or positively harmful, since the same papacy had shut the gates of the kingdom of heaven on the faithful.[74]

It is evident, then, that "a sacramental and juridical concept [of the papacy], like that of the Catholic Church, not only met with little sympathy from Luther, but was vilified by him as being the subversion of the entire Gospel. Indeed, he considered as contrary to the Gospel the Pope's claim to be above everyone else and every other ecclesiastical authority, and invested with the power to judge and to forgive or retain sins."[75]

The ecclesiology of the community of the baptized "led Luther to maintain that all the baptized were equal and to abolish all distinctions and differentiations of condition or state (sacerdotal equality)". What follows is a vision of "a completely lay Church, in the sense that it has been radically declericalized".[76]

The same basic vision persists down to the present day, accompanied by a sort of allergy to the papacy.[77] "Radical rejection of the papal ministry therefore remains one of the defining elements which to this day

Ablehnung des Papstes war die Meinung, dieser verleugne das Evangelium von der Rechtfertigung 'allein durch Christus, allein aus Gnade, allein durch Glauben' . . . ; weil der Papst sich der Erlösung durch Christus wiedersetze, sei er der 'Antichrist'".

[73] Klausnitzer, *Das Papstamt im Disput*, 155: "Luther konkretisiert also die Rechtfertigungslehre auf das Papsttum hin. Drittens folgt aus der Rückführung des Papsttums in den Bereich des Ius humanum, und der äußeren Kirchenstruktur nicht nur seine Nichtteilsnotwendigkeit, sondern auch seine Veränderbarkeit und sogar . . . seine Überflüssigkeit."

[74] Neuner, *Ökumenische Theologie*, 239: "Er [Luther] gipfelte in der Aussage, daß der Papst das Evangelium nicht zulasse, daß er den Menschen die Tür zum Himmelreich verschließe, daß er nicht wolle, daß jemand ohne ihn selig werde und daß er darum der Antichrist sei."

[75] Cf. Gherardini, *Creatura verbi*, 277. Pannenberg, *Systematic Theology*, 421–22: "Luther himself first turned against the pope, as it seemed, at least to him, the pope was condemning instead of supporting the teaching of the gospel. Against the pope who set his own authority against the authority and teaching of scripture, Luther brought the accusation that he was the antichrist in the sense of 2 Thess. 2:4 because all the features mentioned there applied to him."

[76] Cf. Gherardini, *Creatura Verbi*, 332.

[77] F. Kramer, "A Lutheran Understanding of Papal Primacy", LDC V, 132: "Most Protestant churches are definitely allergic to the idea of the pope."

characterize the Lutheran 'churches' and all the other Protestant 'churches'."
While a thorough examination of this question is still awaited, even today
radical condemnation of the papacy is encountered among the Protestant
"churches", and "it has become more and more a prejudice simply handed
down from generation to generation".[78] In any case, uncertainty prevails:
the same author, Meyer, has written more recently that the issue is still
open in the Lutheran churches,[79] whereas Lukas Vischer continues to
assert the incompatibility of the papacy with the New Testament and
maintains that the positions adopted by the Pope and the Catholic Church
continue to be obstacles to Christian unity.[80]

II. ANALYSIS OF THE DIALOGUE DOCUMENTS

In the Catholic-Lutheran dialogue, at least on the official level, the theme
of the primacy of the Bishop of Rome has not been directly addressed.
Therefore it is necessary to gather materials that are scattered in various
documents and to preface them with a presentation of the underlying
ecclesiology.[81]

---

[78] Cf. Meyer, "L'Ufficio papale", 62. Cf. also ibid., 63–67, 74–75, and Meyer, "Das
Problem des Petrusamtes in evangelischer Sicht", 110–28.

[79] *Irénikon* 70 (1997): 554, under the entry *Chronique des églises*: "Le Pr Harding Meyer
... a indiqué que 'la question de la primauté papale en tant que nécessaire ("iure divino")
ne se pose plus comme une nécessité de salut, mais plutôt comme une nécessité ecclésiologique'. Il a ajouté que le ministère de Pierre est une question aujourd'hui ouverte dans
les Églises luthériennes."

[80] Ibid., 556: "Le Dr Lukas Vischer ... affirma que pour les Réformés tous les ministères sont égaux et la papauté est incompatible avec le Nouveau Testament. La situation
de chef d'État reconnue au pape, son infaillibilité, ses positions en matière de morale, mais
aussi l'opposition de l'Église catholique aux ministères féminins sont autant d'obstacles,
selon lui, à l'unité des chrétiens."

[81] In addition to the bibliography already cited (cf. p. 87, n. 1, above) cf. M. Root,
"Dialogo cattolici luterani", DME 365–68; Tillard, s.v. "Primacy", DEM, 822a–85; J. A.
Burgess, ed., *Lutherans in Ecumenical Dialogue. A. Reappraisal* (Minneapolis, 1990); A. Maffeis,
Il ministero nella Chiesa. Uno studio del dialogo cattolico-luterano (1967–1984) (Milan, 1991);
D. Valentini, "Il ministero di unità del Papa nei testi ufficiali di 'consenso' ecumenico",
Dialoghi ecumenici ufficiali. Bilanci e prospettive (Rome, 1993), 101–32; B. Neuman, "Das
Papstamt in den offiziellen ökumenischen Dialogen", *Catholica* 50 (1996): 87ff.; C. Böt-
tigheimer, "Von der ökumenischen Relevanz des Papsttums", *Internationale katholische
Zeitschriftcommunio* 27 (1998): 330–44; A. Antón, "'Ministerio petrino' y/o 'Papado' en el
diálogo con las otras Iglesias cristianas: algunos puntos de convergencia y divergencia", *Il
primato del successore di Pietro. Atti del Simposio teologico (Roma, dicembre 1996)* (Città del
Vaticano, 1998), 386–453; E. Herms, "Der Dialog zwichen Päpstlichen Einheitsrat und

1. The ecclesiology underlying Catholic-Lutheran dialogue

As it became quite evident in the foregoing presentation of Luther's view of the primacy, ecclesiology is always closely connected with the problem of justification. Therefore it is necessary to consider first of all how this question is approached in the texts of the Catholic-Lutheran dialogue.

Apart from a brief reference in the Malta Declaration (1972) [*The Gospel and the Church*], in which a "far reaching consensus is developed in the interpretation of justification",[82] the problem was confronted more directly in the third phase of the dialogue, which concluded with the publication of *Church and Justification* (1993 [Eng. trans. 1994]) by the Joint Roman Catholic-Evangelical Lutheran Commission. As the subtitle indicates, the document confronts the question of *Understanding the Church in the Light of the Doctrine of Justification*.

The first three chapters contain the *points of agreement* between Catholics and Lutherans (justification and Church, the permanent origin of the Church, the Church of the one and triune God). The document's point of departure is an explicit declaration that, on the basis of the New Testament, "the justification of sinners and the existence of the Church are indissolubly linked with the triune God and are founded in him alone."[83] Before all else, therefore, the Church is founded on Christ and upon the saving work of God accomplished in him. On the basis of this "fundamental principle of ecclesiology", everything that can be said of "the origin, nature and purpose of the Church must be understood as an explanation [and clarification] of this primary principle", and unity itself

---

LWB, 1965–1998. Ausgangsperspektiven, Verlauf, Ergebnis", *Theologische Literaturzeitung* 123 (1998): 657–714.

[82] MV 174, no. 26.

[83] LRCIC, *Church and Justification*, no. 6: IS, no. 86 (1994), 132b. The text makes explicit the christological and trinitarian foundation of the Church in the following terms: "Accordingly, the Church has its foundation in the sacrifice of the Son and the sending of the Spirit. God 'obtained' his church 'with the blood of his own Son' (Acts 20:28). Christ has 'saved' the Church 'for it is his body' (cf. Eph. 5:23). 'Christ loved the Church and gave himself up for her, that he might sanctify her, having cleansed her by the washing of water with the word' (Eph 5:25–26). By virtue of the sending of the Holy Spirit the young church appears publicly on the day of Pentecost (cf. Acts 2). Especially in Paul's letters the relation of the Church to the triune God becomes clear, when he describes it as the pilgrim people of God the Father, as the body of Christ, the Son, and as the temple of the Holy Spirit" (ibid., no. 7, 132b).

"is to be understood solely" in reference to it.[84] At the same time, the Church has a profound relationship with the Trinity. "This relationship of the Church to the triune God is both causal and substantive [*essenziale*], involving the differentiated yet reciprocal unity of Father, Son and Holy Spirit."[85] This is the biblical vision of the Church, which is perpetuated both in the Catholic and Lutheran views.[86]

In concrete terms, the Church is constituted by the proclamation of the Gospel, which "produces" her, and because of which the Church is called "the creature of the Gospel" or "Creatura Verbi".[87] This permanent relationship with and subordination to the Gospel "was the main ecclesiological concern of the Reformation" and also "determines the Roman Catholic understanding of the Church".[88] Although divergent understandings and forms of this ministry persist, there is, nevertheless, a *fundamental agreement* between Catholic and Lutheran doctrines in this regard.[89]

The fourth chapter, which is the heart of the document, treats the more delicate problem of the Church as "recipient and mediator of salvation", highlighting from the outset the different emphases that have

---

[84] Ibid., no. 10, 133a.

[85] Ibid., no. 48, 139b.

[86] That biblical vision of the Church, which was quite familiar to the early Church and which lives on in the present-day Roman Catholic concept, "is at home [also] in the reformation view of the church" (ibid., no. 50, 140a). The point has been underlined several times in the Catholic-Lutheran dialogue as it has developed thus far (cf. *Ways to Communion*, nos. 9–13: MV 216–19, I, 1317–21; *Facing Unity*, no. 3, 88–90: IS, no. 59 [1985], 45a, 59a–b). The declaration of the Plenary Assembly of the World Lutheran Federation of 1984 (*L'obiettivo dell'unità*) also affirms, in speaking of the Church and of her unity, that the latter "participates in the unity of the Father, the Son and the Holy Spirit".

[87] LRCIC, *Church and Justification*, no. 34: "As on earth the Lord called and gathered people by the proclamation of the 'good news of the kingdom' (Mt 4:23; 9:35; 24:14; Mk 1:14), so too after Pentecost the calling and the fresh gathering of God's people is continued by the proclamation of the 'good news of Christ' (Rom 1:16; 15:19; cf. 1:1–9). For this purpose the risen Lord chooses his witnesses and sends them into the world (cf. Mt 28:19; Mk 16:15; Acts 1:8; Jn 20:21). When they proclaim the gospel of 'Jesus the Messiah' (Acts 5:42) and people hear that gospel and accept it in faith as a promise of salvation, congregations are constituted from Jerusalem as far as Rome. The commission laid upon the apostles is 'to proclaim the gospel' (Rom 1:15; 1 Cor 1:17; 9:16). This gospel, as 'God's word' (1 Thess 2:13) or the 'word of the Lord' calls people to be 'imitators of . . . the Lord' (1 Thess 1:5–8) and brings the church into being (cf. 1 Cor 15:1f.)" (IS, no. 86 [1994], 137).

[88] Ibid., nos. 36–37, 137b–38a.

[89] Ibid., no. 40, 138b.

come about over the course of history: "While Lutherans see the church mainly as the recipient of salvation, as the 'congregation of faithful', the *congregatio fidelium*, contemporary Catholic theology emphasizes more the Church as the mediator of salvation, as the 'sacrament' of salvation." [90]

Such differences, however, are somewhat attenuated in the presentation of the different points of view,[91] and throughout the *common statement*, practically, the Church is spoken of only as the recipient of salvation (and not as "mediator"): "Both Lutherans and Catholics understand the Church as the assembly of the faithful or saints which lives from God's Word and the Sacraments. Seen thus, the church is the fruit of God's saving activity. . . . Christ who acts in his saving word and sacrament, confronts the church which is the recipient of his and the Holy Spirit's activity. The presence of Christ marks the church as *the place where salvation takes place*. The gift of salvation, however, becomes a task and mission of the church as the community which has received salvation. Thus the church is taken by its Lord into *the ministry of mediating salvation*." [92]

The difference emerges especially with regard to the Church as *sacrament of salvation*. After presenting several points of view on this question,[93] the document stresses the difficulty which such a doctrine poses for Lutherans: "There are certainly Lutheran theologians who apply [the concept of] 'sacrament' to the Church. Yet reservations about references to the Church as 'sacrament' remain in [the heart of] Lutheran theology." [94]

The *basic question* as to the relationship between justification and Church is formulated in the document itself as follows: "Catholics ask whether the Lutheran understanding of justification does not diminish the reality of the Church; Lutherans ask whether the Catholic understanding of church does not obscure the gospel." [95] In turn, this question requires an answer to the following problems: "1) the institutional continuity of the church; 2) the ordained ministry as ecclesial institution; 3) the teaching function of the church's ministry; and 4) the jurisdictional function of the church's ministry".[96]

---

[90] Ibid., no. 108, 149b.
[91] Ibid., nos. 109–16, 149a–51b.
[92] Ibid., no. 117, 151b.
[93] Ibid., nos. 120–29, 152a–54a.
[94] Ibid., no. 130, 154a.
[95] Ibid., no. 166, 159a.
[96] Ibid., no. 173, 160a.

Here we shall dwell only on the subject of the ordained ministry and its jurisdictional function.

The question of ministries

In order to frame the question, we must mention the relationship between the Church's visible/institutional form and her hidden, essentially spiritual nature, which is comprehensible only in faith. The admissibility of a visible character for the Church is indeed decisive for the Lutheran idea of ordained ministry.

In this regard, the document *Ecclesial Communion in Word and Sacrament* (1984) published by the Bilateral Working Group of the German Episcopal Conference and the United Evangelical Lutheran Church explicitly recognizes that, no doubt, "clear differences can be identified in the traditions of both of our Churches. From the outset, the Reformers stressed that the Church was not tied to any particular times, places, or persons, while the Catholic position highlighted the constitutive importance of its episcopal office and of the *papacy*. In this manner, a situation was reached in which unilateral concerns emphasized either the hidden aspect (*Verborgenheit*) of the Church or its visible aspect (*Sichtbarkeit*)." However, an important clarification follows: "In Lutheran doctrine, this does not imply that the Church is only an invisible reality, a *civitas platonica*, since the true Church is identifiable by word and sacrament, for the administration of which an ecclesial ministry has been instituted.... On the other hand, Catholic theology does not hold that the visible Church is to be identified simply with its pneumaticological essence which is only understood in faith. Indeed *the sacramental vision of the Church worked out by the Second Vatican Council* tries to maintain the reciprocity between the Church's visible form and its spiritual essence which is understandable only in faith, while avoiding any absolute identification of the two aspects." [97]

The subject is raised again in the document *Communio/koinonia*, published by the Strasbourg Centre for Ecumenical Research, which explicitly

---

[97] The document is originally entitled *Kirchengemeinschaft im Wort und Sakrament* and has not been translated into English. The various quotations from it, however, have been translated into English and are cited according to the internal numeration of the text and its subdivisions as printed in *Enchiridion Oecumenicum* (EOE 1313–14, n. 9).

recognizes the invisible and at the same time visible nature of the Church,[98] together with the ministry which is consequently required.[99] Subsequently, the document *Church and Justification* (1993) presents the disagreement on this point as the result of reactions to reciprocal polemical accusations based on an excessive insistence on these various aspects: invisibility on the part of the Lutherans and visibility on the Catholic side.[100] In reality it was ascertained that these recriminations were utterly unfounded, since each party continued to deny that it taught what the other party condemned.[101] Hence,

---

[98] "As the assembly of all who participate in Christ through faith, the Church is a 'fellowship [which] is *inward, spiritual, and invisible for it is in the heart*' . . . which extends through space and time. As such a 'spiritual communion', the church is not however simply invisible. The Church is not 'some Platonic republic (*Apol. Conf. Aug.* 7.20) which is nowhere to be found'. As a 'spiritual communion' the Church is simultaneously a '*fellowship [which] is outward, physical, and visible*'. The Church can be seen and experienced [thanks to certain outward signs], particularly in the community's concrete preaching of the Gospel and its celebration of the sacraments. In these easily perceivable events, the Church comes to be; without them the Church cannot exist. The communion which is the Church is thus a *a visible communion in the proclamaion of the Word and the celebration of the sacraments.* . . . At the inter-congregational or inter-church level, this communion finds expression in what would later be called '*altar and pulpit fellowship*'" (p. 15).

[99] Ibid., 15–16: "Such 'altar and pulpit fellowship' includes communion or fellowship in the divinely instituted office of ministry. This office is commissioned to proclaim the Gospel in Word and sacraments and at the same time to help to protect and maintain communion. Thus the office, exercised by pastors or bishops, is, by divine right, to exclude from and admit to the visible communion (CA 28.21; Treatise 60–62)."

[100] LRCIC, *Church and Justification*, no. 135: "The view has often been advanced that the terms 'visible Church' and 'invisible Church' point to a disagreement between Roman Catholic and Lutheran ecclesiologies. Often one appeals to Luther's saying, 'the holy church is invisible, dwelling in the Spirit, in an unapproachable place'. Post-Reformation Catholic ecclesiology reacted polemically to such an understanding of the Church, and focused almost exclusively on the Church as an external, visible entity marked out by creed, sacramental structure and hierarchical leadership. . . . In the nineteenth century especially Lutherans and Catholics both thought that this was the essential difference in their ecclesiologies" (IS, no. 86 [1994], 155a).

[101] The text reads, "Thus Melanchthon in the Apology for the Augsburg Confession utterly rejected the reproach that the church was, in the Lutheran Reformation view, only a kind of 'platonic republic.' Nor—in the light of the pronouncements of Vatican II—can the reproach be sustained that the one holy church is equated undialectically on the Catholic side with its empirical historical form. For there it is said of the church that 'while the visible assembly and the spiritual community' are indeed 'not to be considered as two realities,' they are nevertheless linked together asymetrically: '. . . [T]he communal structure of the church serves Christ's spirit, who vivifies it by way of building up the body' (cf Eph. 4:16)" (ibid., no. 136, 155a).

the Lutheran concept of the Church also acknowledges the visible character of the Church.[102]

This acknowledgment, expressed in the constitutive elements of the Church's unity (word and sacrament), leads also to a certain agreement on the need for a ministry in the Church.[103]

However, the question of ministries remains extremely delicate, one reason being the difficulty of determining what the sixteenth-century reformers actually thought in this regard. Indeed, *Eucharist and Ministry*, published by the Catholic-Lutheran Commission in the U.S. (1970), notes that "the Book of Concord itself affirms the desire of the Lutheran reformers to preserve, if possible, the episcopal polity that they have inherited from the past".[104] According to the common declaration, *All under One Christ*, published by the Joint Roman Catholic/Evangelical Lutheran Commission (1980), "the Augsburg Confession affirms a ministry of unity and leadership set over the local ministries (CA XXVIII) as essential for the Church, even if the usual form to be given to this ministerial office remains open".[105]

Yet *The Ministry of Communion in the Universal Church* (1985), a document produced by the Dombes Group, expressed a contrary view: "For the Lutherans, the institution of a particular type of ministerial organization was never regarded as an essential or normative element for the authenticity and unity of the Church." [106] The Joint Roman Catholic/Evangelical Lutheran Commission, in its document *(Pastoral) Ministry in the Church* (Lantana, 1981), emphasizes that being a ministry in line with

---

[102] Ibid., no. 138, 155b: "That the term 'church' also indicates a visible assembly is clearly borne out by the existence of 'signs of the church', for example, the Word, the confessions of faith, and the sacraments, all of which are eminently visible realities."

[103] Bilateral Working Group of the German Episcopal Conference and the Evangelical Lutherans of Germany, *Ecclesial Communion in Word and Sacrement* (1984): "Both churches agree that word and sacrament are constitutive elements for the church's unity, and that [an ordained] ministry has been instituted to preach the word and administer the sacraments, and that ministries are necessary in the church" (EOE II, 1315, no. 9).

[104] LCD IV, 19, no. 28.

[105] MV 345, no. 22.

[106] EOE II, 1076, no. 70. No English translation of this document appears to have been made. Given the frequent references to this document, it is regarded as necessary to undertake one that retains the numeration and subdivision of the text as contained in the *Enchiridion Oecumenicum* (II, 1002–1174).

the New Testament,[107] "the Lutheran confessions wanted to retain the episcopal polity of the Church and with it the differentiation of the ministerial office on the condition that the bishop grant freedom and opportunity for the right proclamation of the Gospel and the right administration of the sacraments." Still, the existing order was forcibly rejected when it became impossible to agree on doctrine and when bishops refused to ordain evangelical ministers. In turn, this led to "the installation of ministers by non-episcopal ministers or even by the congregation, provided it took place *rite*, that is publicly and in the name of the whole church". In this situation, "the Lutheran confessions avoided prescribing any specific form for the *episkope*, in the sense of regional Church leadership", even though the Augsburg Confession mentions the episcopal ministry as a normal structure in the Church. Since, then, "the office of pastor, comparable to that of presbyter, has [among the Lutherans] really taken over the spiritual functions of the bishop's office", the two offices came to be identified with each other in their theological speculation. Therefore the "function of *episkope* was retained as necessary for the Church; but its concrete ordering was taken to be a human and historical matter".[108]

Even today considerable differences can be observed. The document *Eucharist and Ministry* (USA, 1971) cited above recalls that "some Lutherans have episcopacy with a formal 'apostolic succession' (e.g. [Sweden] Norway, Denmark, Iceland, and Germany)",[109] while the Lantana document specifies that "the holders of this superior grade of ministry [today] have different titles: bishop, president of the Church, superintendent. Where such was possible, some Lutheran areas have preserved a continuity of episcopal ministry."[110] Furthermore, according to the document *Ways to Communion* (1980), published by the Joint Roman Catholic/Evangelical Lutheran Commission, in the Lutheran concept "the individual congregation is

---

[107] "The New Testament shows how there emerged from among the ministries a special ministry which was understood as standing in the succession of the apostles sent by Christ. Such a special ministry proved to be necessary for the sake of leadership in the communities. One can, therefore, say that according to the New Testament the 'special ministry' established by Jesus Christ through the calling and sending of the apostles 'was essential then—it is essential in all times and circumstances'" (MV 252–53, no. 17).

[108] MV 262–63, nos. 42–43.

[109] LCD IV, 19, no. 28.

[110] MV 263, no. 43.

essentially related to the Church as a whole, and in addition to the office of parish pastor, there is a place for supracongregational ministries in the Church." Although "Lutherans do not regard the historic episcopate as based on an explicit irrevocable command from the Lord, valid for all times and situations, yet this polity arose through the work of the Holy Spirit, and there are biblical and ecumenical reasons for seriously considering its restoration in Lutheran Churches."[111]

There is, then, some consensus that ministry is "essential for the Church". This is understood, however, in various ways. As distinct from Catholics, "Lutherans can give a theological definition of the Church without express reference to ministry, because it is either 'presupposed' by or implied by the proclamation of the word and the administration of the sacraments."[112] The document *Communio/koinonia* published by the Centre for Ecumenical Studies (Strasbourg, 1990) remarks that, while some decisive steps have been taken toward effecting Catholic-Lutheran ecclesial communion, "the most difficult problem remains the still incomplete communion in ministerial office."[113]

The more recent 1993 document *On Justification* approaches the subject in a more systematic manner. First of all, it radically denies the claim that the very existence of the ministry is a contradiction of the doctrine of justification, even though "the Reformation doctrine of justification and its emphasis on the unconditionality of the gift of salvation has at times been understood as questioning the necessity of the ordained ministry and the legitimacy of its institutional ecclesial form."[114] The dialogue is said, then, to have demonstrated that for the Reformation "there is no contradiction between the doctrine of justification and the idea of ordained ministry instituted by God and necessary for the Church—quite the opposite".[115] As already recognized in *Pastoral Ministry in the Church*, the exis-

---

[111] MV 219, no. 23.

[112] JRCLC, *Facing Unity*, no. 96: IS, no. 59 (1985), 60a.

[113] *Communio/Koinonia*, 24.

[114] LRCIC, *Church and Justification*, no. 184: IS, no. 86 (1994), 161b.

[115] Ibid., no. 185. The text continues, venturing the opinion that "the Augsburg Confession already makes this clear, with its characteristic transition from the article on justification [AC 4] to that on the church's ministry [AC 5]. There justifying faith is grounded in the gospel which the ordained ministry is to proclaim in word and sacraments. Article 14 of the Augsburg Confession excludes the idea, which only arose in the nineteenth century, that 'the church's ministry' or the 'preaching ministry' could mean anything other than the ecclesial institution of the ordained ministry. For Luther and the Lutheran Con-

tence of a particular ministry "is bindingly constitutive for the Church",[116] and it is possible to show how the institution of ministry is consonant with the Gospel and can be understood in accord with the doctrine of justification. Thus both the early Reformers and contemporary Lutherans admit the existence of an ordained ministry as an institution necessary for the Church. Therefore the institution of ordained ministry "not only does not contradict the Gospel as it is explicated by the doctrine of justification, but corresponds to it, and in the last analysis, receives its character of indispensability for the Church from that correspondence"[117] and is inserted into apostolic succession.[118]

The obvious differences between Catholics and Lutherans could not be overlooked "in the theological and ecclesiological evaluation of the episcopal office seen in terms of apostolic succession". Indeed, while Lutherans cannot accept the view that this historical form of ministry of leadership in the Church is something whose existence determines the very essence of the Church, Catholics see a "divine institution in the organization of the ministry as it has developed through history, i.e. a development led, willed and [approved] by divine providence", by which "the episcopate is, in the Catholic view, a necessary service of the Gospel which is itself necessary for salvation."[119] Such differences with regard to

---

fessions, the church's ministry and the gospel are so closely united that they can both be spoken of in identical terms and can let the church be founded on the ministry [i.e., the Confessions go so far as to say that the church is founded upon ministry]. In a similar sense Lutheran orthodoxy taught that the triune God is 'the primary efficient cause' of the church and that the church's ministry is the 'efficient cause which God uses to gather his church'."

[116] Ibid., no. 186, 161b.

[117] Ibid., no. 189, 162a. In support of this, reference is made to the Accra document, which by then was hardly new, and to the later BEM statement that the presence of ministers "reminds the community of the divine initiative, and of the dependence of the Church on [the authority of] Jesus Christ, who is the source of its mission and the foundation of its unity" (MV 485).

[118] Ibid., no. 191, 162b: "The development of the ministry into an episcopate standing in historic succession, i.e., the continuity of apostolic succession which occurred already very early in history, was fully affirmed by the Lutheran Reform and emphatically championed."

[119] IS, nos. 192–97, (1994) 162b–163b. The dialogue does not appear therefore to have overcome the differences already outlined in *Ecclesial Communion in Word and Sacrament* (1984) published by the Bilateral Working Group of the German Episcopal Conference and the United Evangelical Lutheran Church of Germany: "The question crystallizes with the problem of apostolic succession understood as the historical transmission of the episcopal ministry. According to Catholic doctrine, *communio* in word and sacrament is linked

the epsicopate are not "so radical that a Lutheran rejection or even indifference towards this ministry stands in opposition to the Catholic assertion of its ecclesial indispensability". It is said, rather, to be a matter of "a clear gradation in the evaluation of this ministry, which can be and has been described on the Catholic side by predicates such as 'necessary' or 'indispensable' and on the Lutheran side as 'important', 'meaningful', and even 'desirable'".[120] To understand these differences "it is necessary to observe that behind it lie two different correlations of salvation and Church".[121] Indeed, within the framework of the Lutheran conception of the Church, "nothing good and 'profitable' for ecclesial communion which exists alongside the Gospel proclaimed in word and sacraments may be considered ecclesially necessary, in the strict sense of the word, lest the one thing necessary for salvation—the Gospel—be endangered". According to the Catholic understanding, however, there is "a correlation between salvation and Church consisting not only in the church membership of those who hear the word in faith and receive the sacraments fruitfully, but there is also an [ordering] to the church on the basis of the visible and hidden saving work of God's grace outside the church which can lead to saving faith".[122]

Divergent views as to the relation between justification and Church are also evident with respect to the "necessity of the episcopal office in apostolic succession [with reference to the Church], something which is not necessary for the salvation of the individual person",[123] even though that necessity would lose much of its importance in the event of a mutual recognition of ministries.[124]

---

to *communio hierarchica* (hierarchical communion) (CD 4; PO 7, 15; LG Nota praevia 2, 4 ...). This understanding of hierarchical communion is foreign to evangelical Lutheran theology. A joint reply capable of opening up the possibility of further reflection is possible only when based on a global understanding of those elements which both churches regard as constitutive for ecclesial communion, that is, word, sacrament and the pastoral ministry ordained to their service" (EOE II, 1315, n. 9).

[120]LRCIC, *The Church and Justification*, no. 197: IS, no. 86 (1994), 163b.
[121]Ibid., no. 198.
[122]Ibid., nos. 200–201, 163b–64a.
[123]Ibid., no. 202, 164a.
[124]Ibid., no. 204, 164a–b: "The difference in the theological and ecclesiological evaluation of the episcopal office in historic succession loses its sharpness when Lutherans attribute such a value to the episcopate that regaining full communion in this office seems important and desirable, and when Catholics recognize that 'the ministry in Lutheran churches exercises essential functions of the ministry that Jesus Christ instituted in his church'."

On the basis of "common fundamental convictions" with regard to Church ministry, the above mentioned document on justification approaches the question of the jurisdictional function pertaining to this ministry. It would seem that the Reformation, too, recognized such a function, even though it emphasized the primacy of the Gospel. Article XXVIII of the Augsburg Confession admits as much in its enumeration of the following duties specifically belonging to a bishop: "'to preach the Gospel,' 'to administer ... the sacraments,' 'to forgive ... sins' (absolution), 'to condemn doctrine that is contrary to the Gospel' and to 'exclude from the Christian community.' They can be summed up in the terms 'power of the keys,' 'the office of preaching' or 'jurisdiction'." These functions, which are "necessary for salvation" and therefore of "divine right", imply "a duty of obedience on the part of the community".[125] Hence the conclusion that "it is a Lutheran conviction that there is a legitimate jurisdictional function of the ordained ministry in this context which is defined by the doctrine of justification."[126]

However, as is clear from the document itself, there are considerable differences of opinion on the question, the most prominent being contrary conceptions of the Church, whether at the local or universal level.

Certain ambiguities persist with regard to the first level. While in the *Catholic conception*, the Church in her full sense "is the local Church led by its bishop",[127] the *Lutheran* idea insists on the full realization of the *communio sanctorum* in the local Church, which lacks nothing at all that is essential to the Church, not even ministry, which guides the community simply by the proclamation of the word and the administration of the sacraments. In any case the term *bishop* is not used.[128]

---

[125] Ibid., nos. 230–32, 168a–b.

[126] Ibid., no. 234, 168b–69a.

[127] Ibid., no. 84, 145b.

[128] Ibid., no. 85: "Lutherans understand the *una sancta ecclesia* to find outward and visible expression wherever people assemble around the gospel proclaimed in sermon and sacrament. Assembled for worship the local congregation therefore is seen, according to the Lutheran view, as the visible church, *communio sanctorum*, in the full sense. [It lacks nothing that makes a gathering of people the Church: neither the preaching of the Word and the distribution of the sacraments, a reality by means of which the faithful experience communion with Christ in the Holy Spirit, nor the ministry which, at Christ's command and in his place, proclaims the word, administers the sacraments, and thus guides the community.]" [The bracketed part of the citation was translated from Italian.]

The same can be said for the Church at the universal level. Certain types of regional, national, or diocesan Churches have developed among the Lutherans from the clustering of several local communities. These have their own juridical structures and are united to each other by different expressions of communion. Such structures, however, are juridically autonomous and are regarded as united among themselves by communion with Christ.[129]

In either case, it becomes clear what, "according to the Lutheran understanding of the Church as *koinonia*, is constitutive, irrespective of whether the expression is congregational, territorial/national or global: the common understanding and confession of the apostolic faith (confessional communion) and communion in preaching and sacraments, pulpit and altar fellowship, including, by implication, the ministry of proclamation and the administration of the sacraments (recognition of ministries)".[130]

It is not possible, therefore, to overlook a certain persistent lack of clarity in Lutheran doctrine concerning ministry, which is alternately described as "necessary" or "desirable", which does not imply, however, a leadership function at either the local or the universal level. Indeed, the chapter devoted to "ordained ministry as a Church institution" ends with the following disconcerting conclusion: "The difference in the theological and ecclesiological evaluation of the episcopal office in historic succession loses its sharpness when Lutherans attribute such a value to the episcopate that regaining full communion in this office seems important and desirable, and when Catholics recognize that the ministry in the Lutheran Churches exercises essential functions of the ministry that Jesus Christ instituted in his Church and do not contest the point that the Lutheran Churches are Churches." [131]

This statement, in reality, raises two major problems: the recognition of ministries and the recognition of the ecclesial character of the Lutheran "Churches".

---

[129] Ibid., no. 87: "Lutheran congregations are part of larger fellowships which are themselves constitutionally structured. According to geographical, historical, national, or political realities they form dioceses or juridically autonomous provincial or national churches. These larger communities are held together by communion in Christ, and that shows itself in their common understanding of the apostolic faith (confessional communion), in word and sacrament (pulpit and altar fellowship), and in a mutually recognized ministry."

[130] Ibid., no. 89, 146a.

[131] Ibid., no. 104, 149a.

The document *Ways to Communion* (Augsburg, 1980), published by the Joint Roman Catholic–Evangelical Lutheran Commission, explicitly acknowledges that Catholics and Lutherans "continue to be troubled by non-recognition of ministry". Whereas Lutherans "have never denied the existence of the office of the ministry in the Roman Catholic Church", Vatican II "speaks of a *defectus* of the sacrament of order in the transmission of the ministry in the Reformation Churches". The dialogue might have arrived at the conviction that "it is not a matter of a total absence, but instead as a lack of the 'fullness of ministry' and it is not denied that the ministry in Lutheran Churches exercises essential functions of office which, according to Roman Catholic conviction, Jesus Christ instituted for his Church." Hence, given the current state of ecumenical reflection, it is necessary to "take whatever steps are possible towards full recognition of ministries in the context of mutual reception by the Churches as a whole".[132]

Facing Unity (Rome, 1984), published by the Joint Roman Catholic–Evangelical Lutheran Commission, returns to the same subject. Emphasizing the current partial common exercise of ecclesial ministry in various forms of collaboration, "for example, in the area of social responsibility, in the ethical and charitable fields, or in evangelization", it is recognized that progress toward "full common exercise" of this ministry requires that three facts be borne in mind: "1) the statement of Vatican II which, regarding the ordained ministry of the Reformation churches, speaks of a 'lack of the sacrament of Orders'; 2) a certain 'asymmetry' in the more precise definition of the theological values assigned to the ministry, particularly of the historic episcopacy in the understanding of the Church; 3) the close bond that exists in the Catholic Church between the bishops and the Pope".[133]

While on the Lutheran side, indeed, "the existence of ministry in the Catholic Church is not to be called into question, Catholics cannot yet fully recognize [Lutheran ecclesial ministry], because according to their view, [it does not have] the fullness of the ordained ministry since [it lacks] the sacrament of orders". Such recognition would require "acceptance of full church communion", "of which fellowship in the historical episcopate is an essential part". While there is a common "conviction

---

[132] MV 234–35, no. 87.
[133] IS, no. 59 (1983), 60a, nos. 93–94.

that the ordained ministry of the Church is essential for the Church", for Lutherans (unlike Catholics) it is possible "to give a theological description of the Church without making explicit mention of the ministry, because it is either 'presupposed' or implied by the proclamation of the Word and the administration of the sacraments".[134] Furthermore, while Lutherans can recognize as "the action of the Spirit the historical differentiation of the one apostolic ministry into more local ministry or more regional forms" and "the function of the *episkope* as necessary for the Church", they in fact regard themselves as "free to face up to the call for communion with the historical episcopal office, i.e., the historical evolved pattern of episcopal ministry in the form of the office of bishop standing in apostolic succession".[135]

However, contrary to what is asserted by the Catholic-Lutheran Commission in the USA, *Eucharist and Ministry* (1970),[136] and the *Dombes Group*,[137] the problem of ministries and of the possibility of reciprocal recognition remains to this day unsolved in Catholic-Lutheran dialogue. On the one hand, there is said to be "agreement that a special ministerial office conferred by ordination is constitutive for the Church" and a common recognition that the Augsburg Confession "affirms a ministry of unity and leadership set over the local ministers (CA XXVIII) as essential for the Church, even if the actual form given to this ministry or office remains open".[138] On the other hand, it is recognized that, notwithstanding their intentions, they ended up "forsaking continuity with the previous order"

---

[134] Ibid., nos. 95–96.

[135] Ibid., no. 97. Cf. also *The Ministry in the Church* by the Roman Catholic-Lutheran Joint Commission (Lantana): MV 251ff.

[136] "The episcopal structure and polity of the Roman Catholic church does not in itself constitute a problem for Lutherans. Indeed the Book of Concord itself affirms the desire of the Lutheran reformers to preserve, if possible, the episcopal polity that they had inherited from the past.... Within their own community some Lutherans have episcopacy with a formal 'apostolic succession' (e.g. Norway [Sweden], Denmark, Iceland, and Germany). Lutherans also have or have had churches governed by synods, by consistories, and by ministries" (BG, no. 28).

[137] "By reason of the situation created by the rupture in the sixteenth century, we recognize that we are deprived, not of apostolic succession, but of the fulness of the sign of this succession. This results in a splintering off to form various national churches and loss of the sense of the unity of the church in time and space. With a view to the unity of the Church and its ministries we recognize the necessity to return to the fulness of the sign of the apostolic succession": *Modern Ecumenical Documents on the Ministry* (London, 1973), 104.

[138] JRCLC, Common declaration *All under One Christ* (MV 244, no. 18; 245, no. 22).

that existed in the Church.[139] On this basis the function of the *episkope* was regarded as necessary for the Church, but the concrete form that it took was considered the result of historical and human factors. "The holders of this superior grade of ministry [today] have various names: bishop, president of the Church, superintendent. Where such was possible, some Lutheran areas have preserved a continuity of episcopal ministry."[140] It follows that reciprocal recognition of ministries has not yet been attained because of a sacramental "defect" in the transmission of ministry in the Churches of the Reformation.[141]

In its statement *Eucharist and Ministry* (1970), The Catholic-Lutheran Commission in the USA makes a somewhat surprising claim on the subject of recognizing the validity of Lutheran ministry and the ecclesial character of their respective communities: "As Roman Catholic theologians we acknowledge in the spirit of Vatican II that the Lutheran communities with which we have been in dialogue are truly Christian Churches, possessing the elements of holiness and truth that make them organs of grace and salvation. Furthermore, in our study we have found serious defects in the arguments customarily used against the validity of the eucharistic ministry of the Lutheran Churches. In fact we find no positive reason to deny the possibility of the Roman Catholic Church recognizing the validity of this ministry. Accordingly we ask the authorities of the Roman Catholic Church whether the ecumenical urgency flowing from Christ's will for unity may not dictate that the Roman Catholic Church recognize the validity of the Lutheran ministry and, correspondingly, the presence of the body and blood of Christ in the eucharistic celebrations of the Lutheran Churches." While not contesting "the age-old insistence of ordination by a bishop within our own Church" and hoping that "the episcopacy in apostolic succession, functioning as the effective sign of Church unity, [might be] acceptable to all", it is considered a duty "to

---

[139] JRCLC, *The Ministry in the Church* (MV 262, no. 42).

[140] MV 263, no. 43.

[141] "Before the Second Vatican Council there were no official pronouncements in Catholic teaching on the question of validity or invalidity of the ministries in the Lutheran Church. It was theoretically assumed that they were invalid. The Second Vatican Council speaks of a *defectus* in the sacrament of orders in the churches deriving from the Reformation" (MV 271, no. 75).

envisage a practical and immediate solution in a *de facto* situation where episcopacy is not yet seen in that light".[142]

The same hypothesis is advanced in the document *Gospel and Church*, which is part of the Malta Report,[143] and in *Ecclesial Communion in Word and Sacrament* (1984), which was published by the Bilateral Working Group of the German Episcopal Conference and the United Evangelical Lutheran Church of Germany.[144]

On the other hand, recognition is given to the relative importance of persistent differences with regard to episcopal ministry,[145] and the hope is expressed that the Lutheran ecclesial communities might be recognized as *sister* Churches.[146]

Notwithstanding the absence of apostolic succession in the ecclesial communities deriving from the Reformation and the consequent impossibility of recognizing their ecclesial character, the documents produced by the present dialogue frequently recall the reality of the *Church as commu-*

---

[142] LCD IV, 31–32, no. 54 and 32–33, no. 57.

[143] "Although there are considerable differences of opinion on this matter in the Catholic Church, it is pointed out on the Catholic side that there is no exclusive identity between the one Church of Christ and the Roman Catholic Church. This one church of Christ is actualized in an analogous manner also in other churches. That also means that the unity of the Roman Catholic Church is not perfect but that it strives toward the perfect unity of the Church. In this sense the eucharistic celebration in the Catholic Church also suffers from imperfection. It will become the perfect sign of the unity of the Church only when all those who through baptism have been invited in principle to the table of the Lord are able in reality to partake" (MV 185, no. 71).

[144] "The sacramental vision of the Church worked out by the Second Vatican Council (LG 1, 9, 48; GS 42, 45; AG 1–5) tries to maintain the unbreakable reciprocity between the visible form of the Church and its spiritual essence which is perceived only in faith, and at the same time to avoid an absolute identification of these two dimensions. This vision also allows for the recognition of essential elements of the true Church outside of the Roman Catholic Church (LG 8; UR 3 f.)" (EOE II, 1314, n.9).

[145] Cf. above, p. 120, notes 134–35.

[146] The Catholic-Lutheran Commission in the U.S., *Papal Primacy* (1974): "Likewise, we ask the Roman Catholic Church: . . . if, in the expectation of a foreseeable reconciliation, it is ready to acknowledge the Lutheran churches represented in our dialogue as sister-churches which are already entitled to some measure of ecclesiastical communion" (LCD V, 23, no. 33). The Joint Roman Catholic–Evangelical Lutheran Commission, also, in the Common Declaration, *All under One Christ* (1980) fosters the hope that it might be possible to give the most unified answer thus far possible to the questions and problems which are still open, so that our Churches might take a further step forward so as to become, instead of separated Churches, sister Churches (MV 245, no. 25).

nion, founded on the indissoluble communion (*koinonia*) of the three Divine Persons. Such communion exists not only among the faithful[147] but also between the Churches. In referring to a concept which is typical of the New Testament and the early Church, "Lutherans and Catholics agree that the Church is a *koinonia-communio* rooted in the mystery of the Holy Trinity. Proof of that assertion is found both in the Lutheran confessions and in the documents of Vatican II."[148] This communion "is shown and realized in the proclamation of the Gospel, baptism and the Lord's Supper".[149] It is manifested concretely in the communion of the Churches: "the One, Holy Catholic, and Apostolic Church, the *Una Sancta* of the *Credo* is realized in the *communio ecclesiarum* as local, regional, and universal communion and so as church fellowship".[150]

As the Joint Roman Catholic–Evangelical Lutheran Commission emphasizes in its document *Facing Unity* (Rome, 1984), the one Church of Jesus Christ "assumes concrete form in local churches.... The Church is therefore a communion (*communio*) subsisting in a network of local churches." This is a crucial concept both for the primitive Church and for life and the ecclesiology of the Orthodox Churches and is "particularly stressed in Catholic ecclesiology" as well. The idea of the Church as communion, the document continues, "is also in accord with Lutheran ecclesiology. The local communities gathered around word and sacrament do not remain isolated as visible forms of the Church of Jesus Christ, but rather live in such large and organically united communities as regional churches, national churches, folk churches, etc. The worldwide Lutheran community, which has the Lutheran World Federation as an instrument, is made up of Churches that are bound together by a common understanding of the Gospel and by participation in the sacraments which that includes."[151]

The previously cited document by the Centre for Ecumenical Studies in Strasbourg (located in a Lutheran region) is concerned in particular

---

[147] LRCIC, *Church and Justification,* no. 65: "It is not primarily the communion of believers with each other which makes the church *koinonia;* it is primarily and fundamentally the communion of believers with God, the triune whose innermost being is *koinonia.* And yet the communion of believers with the triune God is inseparable from their communion with each other" (IS, no. 86 [1994], 142b, n. 65).

[148] Ibid., no. 75, 144a.

[149] Ibid., no. 66, 143a.

[150] Ibid., no. 79, 145a.

[151] IS, no. 59 (1985), 45b–46a.

with the theme of the Church as communion, especially Chapter Three, which is devoted to the concept of communion in the context of contemporary ecumenism. The Catholic view of communion is presented as follows: "As in New Testament and ancient theology, Catholic ecclesiology emphasizes the believers' participation in grace and the divine life and [their] participation in the communion of the church. Personal communion with God always creates a 'communion of the faithful' one with another. . . . At the local level, this 'communion of the faithful' is made concrete in the particular or local churches (dioceses) grounded in the Eucharist and led by the Bishop. At the universal level, communion is made concrete as the 'communion of local churches', in which there is room for a legitimate diversity." [152]

The idea of *communion* is fundamental in the Lutheran view of the Church also: "When the *Augsburg Confession*, art. 7, describes the 'holy Christian Church' as *'an assembly of all believers'*, this 'assembly' is identified with the *'communion of saints'* spoken of in the Apostles' Creed (*Apol. Conf. Aug. 7, 8*). The *Great Catechism* explains the concept of the 'communion of saints' (*communio sanctorum*) in the early Church as follows: it concerns 'the assembly of the saints', 'the holy remnant of the community' (II. I, 49–51). The specific emphasis of the Reformation—that the Church is an assembly, people, or community of believers, and not primarily a hierarchiacal institution (*Apol. Conf. Aug. 7.23*)—does not reduce the Church to a mere gathering of individuals. Article 7 of the *Augsburg Confession* states this clearly when it specifies that the church is 'the assembly of all believers *among whom the Gospel is preached in its purity and the holy sacraments are administered according to the Gospel.*' An assembly or community is Church because of an event that occurs within it, the proclamation of the Gospel in Word and sacraments. Through this proclamation of the Gospel Christ is present in his saving power and is grasped by faith. [Because] faith unites believers with Christ, they are justified before God, freed from the power of sin, and made members of Christ's body, the Church." [153] This communion is founded upon "our common faith in the one proclaimed Gospel, because of which communion in preaching and the sacraments is essential to communion between churches". In the Lutheran view, however, "communion between churches does not

---

[152] *Communio/Koinonia*, 17.
[153] Ibid., 15.

require uniformity in merely human structures, forms of worship, or church practices, but calls for freedom and legitimate diversity in these areas". Hence, "within the Lutheran communion can be found differ-ent church structures (both episcopal and non-episcopal), different litur-gical traditions, different theological streams, and different forms of piety." [154]

In Catholic-Lutheran dialogue, as in Catholic-Orthodox dialogue, the idea of Church as communion immediately gives rise to differences with regard to the concept of the local Church. Among the Lutherans the local Church is understood as "Church in the full sense" and as a visible realization and "concrete manifestation of the Church as *communio sanc-torum* in the full sense of the term: Nothing is missing which makes a human assembly Church: the preached word and the sacraments, gifts through which the faithful participate in Christ through the Holy Spirit, but also the ministers who preach the Word and administer the sacra-ments in obedience to Christ and on his behalf, thus leading the con-gregation." [155] According to the Catholic view, in contrast, "each of the constitutive elements of the local Church (*portio* of the people of God, Holy Spirit, Gospel, Eucharist and presidency of the Bishop) and their presence together show that the local Church is indeed the Church of God in the full sense, but that it cannot be regarded as the whole Church of God. 'The local Church is not a free-standing, self-sufficient entity. As part of the network of communion, the local Church maintains its reality as Church by relating to other local Churches.' Part of its nature is to be in real fellowship with other local Churches and with the Church as a whole." [156]

In the final analysis, differences arise concerning the relationship between the local Church and the universal Church. *Koinonia*, both for Catholics and Lutherans, can be expressed at different levels, [157] and individual local Churches should not isolate themselves, but rather should exhibit a visible

---

[154] Ibid., 21.

[155] LRCIC, *Church and Justification*, nos. 84–85: IS, no. 86 (1994), 145b.

[156] Ibid., no. 94, 147a.

[157] Ibid., no. 79, 145a: "Catholics and Lutherans together understand that the commu-nion with God mediated through word and sacrament leads to communion of the faithful among themselves. This takes concrete shape in the communion of the churches: the one holy catholic and apostolic church, the *una sancta* of the creed, is realized in the *communio ecclesiarum* as local, regional and universal communion, and so as church fellowship."

communion with one another.[158] In practice the local Lutheran communities are grouped into larger communions, and since the middle of the nineteenth century they have become increasingly conscious of "the global dimension of the ecclesial communion".[159] However, they consider themselves Churches in the full sense of the term, as lacking nothing in their ecclesial nature.[160] Therefore the visible Church unity which is being sought is understood by them as a "communion of churches".[161]

According to Catholic doctrine, on the other hand, "the local Church is certainly a Church of God in the full sense of the term, but it cannot be regarded as the whole Church of God"; "it is not a self-standing, self-sufficient reality"; because of its very nature it must be in "real fellowship with other local churches and with the universal Church as a whole".[162] In virtue of a relationship of "reciprocal inherence" or of "mutual indwelling" which exists between the local Church and the universal Church, the Church is "a body of churches [*corpus ecclesiarum*]; or a communion of churches".[163]

2. The specific view of the primacy

If, for Protestants, the problem of the primacy is fundamentally rooted in their view of the nature of the Church, which in turn is connected to the problem of justification, the question is more immediately associated with their lack of apostolic succession and, consequently, of a ministry of unity.[164]

---

[158] Ibid., no. 86, 145b: "The understanding of the Church as communion of persons based on communion with the [one] Lord includes the communion of separate congregations bound together in true communion with Christ. Therefore congregations may not distance themselves nor isolate themselves from one another. The communion they have in Christ must be visible."

[159] Ibid., no. 88, 146a.

[160] Cf. above, p. 125, note 156.

[161] IS, no. 86, no. 86, (1994), 145b.

[162] IS, no. 86, no. 94 (1994), 147a.

[163] IS, no. 86, no. 96 (1994), 146a–b, no. 86.

[164] *Ecclesial Communion in Word and Sacrament* (1984) of the Bilateral Working Group of the German Episcopal Conference and the United Evangelical Lutheran Church of Germany: "The question crystallizes with the problem of apostolic succession understood as the historical transmission of the episcopal ministry. According to Catholic doctrine, *communio* in word and sacrament is linked to *communio hierarchica* (hierarchial communion)

Conflicting statements on the subject are to be found in the documents deriving from Catholic-Lutheran dialogue. While emphasizing the profound relationship between the ministry and the nature of the Church as well as the need for ministry at different levels,[165] it is asserted, on the one hand, that in the Lutheran tradition also "apostolic succession is necessary and constitutive for both the Church and for its ministers" and that "the Lutheran Reform affirmed and intended to preserve the historical continuity of church order as an expression of the unity of the apostolic Church among all peoples and throughout all centuries".[166] On the other hand, however, Lutherans maintain that because of the break in the sixteenth century they lack "not apostolic succession, but the fullness of the sign of that same apostolic succession" and consequently that they have "lost a sense of the universal unity of the Church in space and time". Hence it is necessary to attain the fullness of the sign of apostolic succession, and "the question of unity in the universal Church immediately arises".[167]

It is recognized, however, that among the problems remaining unresolved is that of the primacy, and the Augsburg Confession made no pronouncement on it.[168] Furthermore, it is recognized that "for the Lutherans apostolic

---

(CD 4; PO 7, 15; LG Nota praevia 2, 4 . . .). This understanding of hierarchical communion is foreign to evangelical Lutheran theology. A joint reply capable of opening up the possibility of further reflection is possible only when based on a global understanding of those elements which both churches regard as constitutive for ecclesial communion, that is, word, sacrament and the pastoral ministry ordained to their service" (EOE II, 1315, no. 9).

[165] JRCLC, *The Ministry in the Church* (Lantana, 1981): "The development of the one ministry of the church into different ministries can be understood as having an intimate connection with the nature of the church. The church is actualized at different levels: as the local church (congregation), as the church of a larger region or country, and as the universal church. At each of these levels, albeit in different forms, it is essential that the ministry be both 'in and over against' the ecclesial community" (MV 263, no. 45).

[166] MV 269, nos. 63 and 65. JRCLC, *All under One Christ* (February 1980): "As far as the question of the episcopal office is concerned, here again it has to be noted that, in accord with the historic truth [i.e., precedent], the *Confessio Augustana* specifically affirms its desire to maintain the episcopal structure. The assumption here was that the true proclamation of the gospel is helped not hindered by this office. The *Confessio Augustana* affirms a ministry of unity and leadership set over the local ministers (CA XXVIII) as essential for the church, therefore, even if the actual form to be given to this ministerial office remains open" (MV 245, no. 22).

[167] Cf. above, p. 120, note 137; EOE II, 770–74.

[168] JRCLC, *All under One Christ*: "Honesty in our dialogue on the Augsburg Confession also compels us to admit that there are still open questions and unresolved problems, among them the following: the *Confessio Augustana* does not adopt a position on the number of

succession came to focus on the right preaching of the Gospel, which always included the ministry, and on faith and the testimony of a Christian life".[169] However, while it is affirmed that, for the Lutherans, the Catholic position on the ministry in other Churches "does not depend directly on the question of primacy, as is shown by its view of ministry in the Orthodox Churches",[170] it is held that the Lutheran tradition would have "willingly accepted the ministries as they existed prior to the 16th century, including the episcopal ministry, indeed even the papal ministry, and it is acknowledged that such ministries had positive historical results" and that some contemporary Lutheran theologians, "basing themselves on the evangelical ministry of Peter, have declared their acceptance of a ministry of unity that would be exercised by the Bishop of Rome".[171] The question of the papacy is approached, moreover, from the false presupposition of a "fundamental agreement" on the doctrine of ministry.[172]

Given this ambiguity, we must first turn to a detailed analysis of the various documents from the dialogue in order to determine whether and what progress has been made with regard to this delicate question.

---

the sacraments, the papacy, or even on certain aspects of the episcopal order and the church's teaching office; The *Confessio Augustana* naturally makes no mention of dogmas which have only been promulgated since 1530: the primacy of jurisdiction and the infallibility of the Pope (1870); the gracious preservation of the Virgin Mary from 'original sin' (1854) and her bodily assumption into heaven (1950)" (MV 245, no. 23).

[169] MV 268, no. 64.

[170] MV 272, no. 78. The text goes on to specify, however, "Yet for a full recognition of ministries in a reconciliation of churches, according to Catholic understanding, the Petrine office must also be taken into consideration."

[171] The Dombes Group, *The Ministry of Communion in the Universal Church* (1985) (EOE II, 1076, no. 70).

[172] Catholic-Lutheran Commission in the USA, *Papal Primacy* (1974), "As we Lutheran and Roman Catholic theologians turned in our discussions to the need for visible unity in the universal church, we were assisted by the fundamental accord stated in an earlier report on the doctrine of ministry. We there agreed that, by the will of God, 1) the general ministry of proclaiming the gospel devolves upon the whole people of God, and 2) the ministry of the Word and sacrament serves to unify and order the church for its mission in and to the world. Our previous discussions had centred on the service rendered to the local communities by the Ministry. Now we focus on the unifying and ordering function of this ministry in relation to the universal church, the manner in which a particular form of this Ministry, that is, the papacy, has served universal church unity in the past and how it may serve it in the future" (LCD V, 10–11, no. 2).

Evaluation of the position of the early reformers

The first reference to the primacy is found in the document *Eucharist and Ministry* published by the Catholic Lutheran Commission in the USA (1970). While pointing to the need for further research and study on the subject, this mention of the primacy merely states the Lutheran position of the sixteenth century as contained in their creedal books. These "recognize the Bishop of Rome as a lawful pastor of the Church in that city" and did not exclude "the possibility that the papacy might have a symbolic or functional value in a wider area as long as its primacy is seen as being of human right",[173] since, according to the Lutheran view, "a ministry serving the unity of the Church as a whole is ... in accord with the will of the Lord, but without its concrete form having been fixed once and for all".[174]

The greatest difficulty for the Lutherans with regard to primacy was the definition made by Boniface VIII in the bull *Unam Sanctam* (1302) that being subject to the Roman Pontiff is a *"necessitas salutis"*. A note contains an assertion to the effect that the bull conflicts with twentieth-century Catholic thought and specifically with a letter of the Holy Office to the bishop of Boston (August 8, 1949).[175] Furthermore, it is suggested that the bull had been "revised" due to the acknowledgment of Vatican II that Churches and ecclesial communities not in communion with Rome are not "deprived of significance or importance in the mystery of salvation". They emphasize that, according to LG 15, "communion under the successor of Peter" is not regarded as necessary to be "honored with the name of Christian" and "unite[d] ... to Christ". Indeed, despite their persistent denial of the primacy, the ecclesial nature of the Oriental Churches is recognized.

An evaluation or "reevaluation" of the early reformers' thought is included also in the declaration *Papal Primacy and Universal Church*, published

---

[173] LCD IV, 19–20, no. 29. The Reformation did, however, raise the subject of the primacy only at a later stage. Originally the universal Church was understood as "a purely spiritual reality which did not seem to need any particular recognisable structure" (Document of the Dombes Group: *The Ministry of Communion in the Universal Church*: EOE II, 1158, no. 152).

[174] JRCLC, *Ways to Communion*: MV 219, no. 23.

[175] DS 3866–73.

by the American commission, according to which they "did not totally reject all aspects of the papal expression of the Petrine function, but only what they regarded as its abuses", in the hope of a conciliar reform of the papacy that would secure the unity of the Church. They "continued to concede to the Pope all the legitimate spiritual powers" inherent in his position as Bishop of the diocese of Rome, as well as "the propriety of his exercising a larger jurisdiction over communities that had by their own will placed themselves under him". Such jurisdiction, however, was merely of human right.[176]

The Bilateral Working Group of the German Episcopal Conference and the United Evangelical Lutheran Church of Germany, in their statement *Ecclesial Communion in Word and Sacrament* (1984), offer some clarifications with regard to the positions assumed by the initial reformers, and above all reject the terms which the reformers used to describe the papacy. While noting that the "doctrine on the *papal ministry* is one of the most controversial points between our Churches, especially in the wake of Vatican I", it is acknowledged "with gratitude that it is discussed to-day amongst us, and it would seem possible to formulate new common positions on the subject, although no consensus had yet been reached". Most importantly, it is admitted that "none of the statements contained in the confessional books of the evangelical Lutherans can be applied to-day to the various historical forms taken by papacy in the course of history, nor to any individuals holding that ministry. . . . Such is a requisite of theological rectitude and not merely a courtesy extended in inter-Church diplomacy." [177] The same document goes as far as to recognize the "beneficial role" played by the papacy in the course of history.[178]

While acknowledging that "the Reformers were not able to see the primacy of the Bishop of Rome as a divine ordinance founded on the Lord's commission to Peter" and some came "to the point of terming the Pope the Antichrist", the *Final Report on the Examination of the Sixteenth-Century Condemnations* (Maria Laach, 1985), published by the Catholic/Evangelical Commission of the Federal Republic of Germany, states that "through the softening of antitheses in the doctrine of justification and in

---

[176] LCD V, 12, no. 5. Cf. also *Reflections of the Lutheran Participants* on the same document, LCD V, 26 and 32.

[177] Cf. EOE II, 1431–32, no. 74.

[178] Cf. LCD V, 21, no. 28.

the doctrine of the Eucharist . . . the reason for the Reformation judgement about the papacy now no longer applies, and the Protestant Churches can accept that to term the Pope the Antichrist, who sets his own authority above the Scripture and the Gospel, is not appropriate." Significantly, the statement concludes, "To-day both Churches have cause to look back with shame to the history of vilification, which found expression in this term for the papacy and in corresponding judgements about the Reformation. Protestant Christians too can understand today that in the Roman Catholic Church the papal office is understood and lived as a ministry for the unity of the church, a unity which has its foundation in the gospel. The critical judgement of the Reformation about the pope can find no application to a papacy whose office is subordinated to the gospel." [179]

Possibility of and need for the primacy

The Report *The Gospel and the Church*, published by the Joint Lutheran–Roman Catholic Study Commission (Malta, 1972), directly confronts the question and reaches the conclusion that it has not been possible to arrive at a consensus on it. The Lutheran side, however, acknowledges the importance of a service for the communion of the churches and underlines the disadvantages deriving from its absence. In practical terms, though, this document does not go beyond stating that the "office of the papacy as a visible sign of the unity of the Churches was therefore not excluded in so far as it was subordinate, by theological reinterpretation or practical structuring, to the primacy of the Gospel". [180] The divergence of opinion on whether the papacy is necessary for the Church or simply a possible function is expressly mentioned in the statement. [181]

Similar divergence is to be noted in the common declaration of the Catholic Lutheran Commission of the USA, which directly addressed the

---

[179] *The Condemnations of the Reformation Era: Do They Still Divide?*, ed. K. Lehmann and W. Pannenberg (Minneapolis, 1990), 185.

[180] MV 184, no. 66.

[181] "The question, however, which remains controversial between Catholics and Lutherans is whether the primacy of the pope is necessary for the church, or whether it represents only a fundamentally possible function." However, there is a surprising agreement "that the question of altar fellowship [intercommunion] and of mutual recognition of ministerial offices should not be unconditionally dependent on a consensus on the question of the primacy" (MV 184, no. 67).

question in *Papal Primacy and Universal Church* (1974). The declaration states at the outset that "there is a growing awareness amongst Lutherans of the necessity of a specific ministry to serve the Church's unity and universal mission . . . while Catholics increasingly see the need for a more nuanced understanding of the role of the papacy" which could "envision possibilities of concord".[182] However, in the reflections of the Lutheran participants, the clarification was made that such a possibility implied not a sole form of primacy but rather a diversity of forms which could develop today, as it happened in the past; in any case the question of the powers of a single person who would exercise the Petrine office remained open.[183] Furthermore, at the conclusion, the document notes that "the traditional distinctions between divine institution and human institution are no longer relevant", and it states that, for Catholics, the institution of the primacy "is in accord with God's will", while for Protestants it remains "a secondary question".[184]

Ministry in the Church (Lantana, 1981), published by the Joint Roman Catholic/Evangelical Lutheran Commission, takes a similar view on the

---

[182] LCD V, 10: Introduction.

[183] *Reflections of the Lutheran Participants*, LCD V, 30: "To be sure, there is for Lutherans no single or uniquely legitimate form of the exercise of the Petrine function. At every stage, the Petrine function developed according to the possibilities available at that time. Councils, individual leaders, specific local churches, credal statements and the papacy have all in various ways ministered to the unity of the church. Further, the papal form of the universal Ministry has not always involved the centralized, juridical apparatus which now exists, nor need we assume that it will always continue to do so. Even if it should be desirable that the Petrine function be exercised by a single individual, the question of his powers would still be open."

[184] The Lutheran participants explain further on: "We have found in our discussion however, through a series of careful historical investigations, that the traditional distinction between *de iure humano* and *de iure divino* fails to provide usable categories for contemporary discussion of the papacy. On the one hand, Lutherans do not want to treat the exercise of the universal Ministry as though it were merely optional. It is God's will that the church have the institutional means needed for the promotion of unity in the gospel. On the other hand, Roman Catholics, in the wake of Vatican II are aware that there are many ways of exercising papal primacy. Some are willing to consider other models for the exercise of the Petrine function. They recognize the dangers of ecclesiastical centralism, and realize the limitations of a juridical description of the Petrine function. Rather than using the traditional terminology of divine and human right, therefore, both Lutherans and Roman Catholics have been compelled by their historical studies to raise a different set of questions: In what way or ways has our Lord in fact led his church to use particular forms for the exercise of the Petrine function? What structural elements in the church does the gospel require for the ministry which serves the unity of the empirical church?" (*Reflections of the Lutheran Participants*, LDC V, 31).

possibility of a ministry in the universal Church. Having outlined Catholic doctrine and noting that the papacy "remains to this day for many Christians one of the greatest obstacles on the road to unity", the statement emphasizes that "for the Lutheran Churches it is essential to be aware of the relationship of the individual local and regional Churches" and that "questions arise regarding the visible forms of Church fellowship which represent a world-wide bond of faith." Such awareness has led to the discussion of "various models for the unity of the universal Church, including first and foremost the model of conciliar fellowship of the Churches". The Reformation "never surrendered the view that the council is the locus for the expression of the consensus of all Christendom, and, therefore, of universal Church unity", while it appeared to the Reformers that "the papacy suppressed the Gospel and was to this extent an obstacle to true Church unity". Today, however, in diverse dialogues and among theologians, "the possibility begins to emerge that the Petrine office of the Bishop of Rome also need not be excluded by Lutherans as a visible sign of the unity of the Church as a whole", with the condition, already formulated in the Malta Report, that the primacy be "subordinated to the primacy of the Gospel by theological reinterpretation and practical restructuring".[185]

Ways to Communion (Augsburg, 1980), published by the Joint Roman Catholic/Evangelical Lutheran Commission, moves from considering the possibility of a ministry of unity in the universal Church to considering a certain need for such ministry. The document acknowledges that such a ministry is in accordance with the will of the Lord (albeit implicit), but has no determined concrete form.[186] In order to be credible, such ministry

---

[185] MV 270, no. 72.

[186] "According to the Lutheran notion as well, the individual community is necessarily connected with the whole church. Corresponding to this are the leadership ministries at a level higher than that of the local congregation (*episkope*), which have a spiritual responsibility for the preaching, the sacraments and the unity of the church. According to this notion, besides the ministry of the pastor of the parish community, the church has other supra-parochial ministries. Although Lutherans do not regard the historic episcopate as based on an explicit irrevocable command from the Lord, valid for all times and situations, yet this polity arose through the work of the Holy Spirit, and there are biblical and ecumenical reasons for seriously considering its restoration in Lutheran Churches. According to the Lutheran view, a ministry in the service of universal church unity would also be in keeping with the Lord's will, but its practical form has not been established once and for all" (MV 219, no. 23).

"must avoid the dangers of bureaucracy and anonymous administrators" and "be understandable [transparent], and have concern for cooperation with all who serve in the Church. A certain quality of spiritual power— and not mere jurisdictional competence—must be present. In these ways the discussions and decisions of those who exercise oversight (or *episkope*) will be visible and related to what actually is needed and their words will possess an intrinsic authority." [187]

On the other hand, it is recognized that the Lutheran-Catholic dialogue "has emphasized the same constitutive elements of [ecclesial] communion but does not speak of the necessity of an universal office of unity": communion has already been achieved "in the unity of faith, hope and love and seek[s] a visible form. [Unity] does not require uniformity but rather allows for legitimate diversity", even if "the complete visible expression and normative character" of that communion can only be found in a common ecclesial ministry. [188]

The primacy of Peter

In the joint declaration *Papal Primacy and Universal Church*, the Catholic-Lutheran Commission in the USA takes "the image of Peter" as the point of departure for its dialogue on the primacy and concludes that it has discovered, on the basis of the New Testament texts, that "it was appropriate to speak of a 'Petrine function'", that is, "a particular form of ministry exercised by a person, office holder or local Church with reference to the Church as a whole". It explains furthermore that "the Petrine function of the ministry serves to promote or preserve the oneness of the Church by symbolizing unity, and by facilitating communication, mutual assistance or correction, and collaboration in the Church's mission." [189]

The Lutherans, however, when confronting the problem of the Petrine succession, "have minimized Peter's role in the early Church and denied that this role continued in the Church in later periods". This has led to what seems to be the common opinion that "terms such as 'primacy' and

---

[187] MV 235, no. 88.

[188] Institute for Ecumenical Research (Strasbourg, January 1, 1990), *Communio/ Koinonia*, 24. The question of communion in ecclesial ministry is central in the JRCLC documents *Facing Unity* (IS, no. 59 [1985], 58ff.) and *Church and Justification* (IS, no. 86 [1994], 144ff.).

[189] LCD V, 11–12, no. 4.

'jurisdiction' are best avoided when one describes the role of Peter in the New Testament".[190] As a result, to the question "What role does Peter play in this ministry directed to the Church at large?" the answer is given, "There is no simple or uniform New Testament outlook on such a question." [191] Although it is not always easy to say to what extent he carried on a ministry with respect to the universal Church and to what extent his influence remained regional, "Peter was very important as a companion of Jesus during Jesus' public ministry; he was one of the first of the disciples to be called and seems to have been the most prominent among the regular companions. . . . Clearly he was the most prominent of the twelve and took an active part in the Christian missionary movement." [192] From the various images associated with Peter, it is possible to trace an evolution which, while it "does not constitute papacy in the later technical sense", allows for "the possibility of an orientation in that direction when shaped by favouring factors in the subsequent [history of the] Church". A preminence emerges "that can be traced back to Peter's relationship to Jesus in his public ministry and as the risen Lord".[193] "The relative silence of the New Testament about the career of Peter [after] the Jerusalem meeting (A.D. 49) makes it difficult to find a biblical basis for affirmations about his continuing role in the Church." There is no "trustworthy evidence that Peter ever served as the supervisor or bishop of the local Church of Rome". In conclusion, "from the New Testament we know nothing of a succession to Peter in Rome".[194] The question, therefore, of "whether Jesus appointed the first Pope has shifted in modern scholarship to the question of the extent to which the subsequent use of the images of Peter in reference to the papacy is consistent with the text of the New Testament".[195]

The Dombes Group, having examined several interpretations of Matthew 16:17–19, note in their document *The Ministry of Communion in the Universal Church* (1985), that the churches born of the Reformation "see in this rock both a confession of faith in Christ and Peter as the first to

---

[190] LCD V, 12, no. 6, and 13, no. 9.
[191] LCD V, 14, no. 11.
[192] LCD V, 15, no. 13.
[193] LCD V, 15–16, no. 13.
[194] LCD V, 14, no. 11.
[195] LCD V, 16, no. 3. Previously (cf. LCD V, 13, no. 9) the problem was described as an "anachronism".

believe in Christ. In reaction to the claims of the Bishop of Rome, they rejected the idea that this text has any institutional consequences as far as the 'successors of Peter' are concerned. . . . Equally, these Churches, in a polemic reaction to the Catholic insistence on Peter, point to Paul as a witness to the freedom of the Gospel and one capable, when necessary, of open disagreement with Peter (Gal 2:11)." [196]

On the basis of exegetical research of the last few decades, "all accept the fact that, with regard to the people of God, Peter received a special mission from the Lord". Concerning the most controversial passage in Matthew 16:17–19, it is now acknowledged that the [usual] objection (i.e., that its vocabulary seems to come not from Jesus but from a later tradition which arose in the Matthean community) "is not decisive, for a special mission could [very] well have been consigned to Peter by the Lord before or after the resurrection, even if these words reflect a later ecclesial context". [197] An *exegetical* analysis of this passage alone will not provide a definitive answer to the question of whether this text is to be applied only "to the historical Simon or whether it has implications also for the Church", by pointing "to a universal ministry of communion". Taken together as a whole, various episodes make it possible "to deduce both the figurative importance and the ecclesiological implications of Mt 16:17–19" without broaching the question "of the form of the ministry of communion which it demands". [198] In conclusion, "The New Testament does not claim to say everything about the organization of the early communities nor about the forms which communion took at that time. It merely states the essential components of that communion . . . without which Church unity would be reduced to empty words." [199]

Successors to Peter

Practically the only place where this problem is addressed is the document *The Ministry of Communion in the Universal Church* (1985) of the Dombes Group. [200]

---

[196] EOE II, 1113, n. 9.

[197] EOE II, 1132–33, n. 17.

[198] EOE II, 1135 36, nn. 18–19.

[199] EOE II, 1138, n. 20.

[200] Previously, the most significant note was struck in the common declaration *Papal Primacy* published by the mixed Catholic-Lutheran Commission in the USA: "The disputes

Based on the testimonies of Clement of Rome, Ignatius of Antioch, and Ireneus,[201] the fact is acknowledged that as early as the end of the second century "the Church of Rome enjoyed a greater authority in virtue of its foundation", and her Bishop was regarded as "first amongst the Bishops": "In the Bishop of Rome, Peter is in some way continually present in the Church: this Bishop is called the 'successor of Peter' but he is also the 'vicar of Peter', in that he exercises the ministry in Peter's stead. Unfortunately, an almost exclusive reference to the 'see of Peter', which is Rome, has resulted in the relative oblivion of that Church's relationship with the Apostle Paul.[202] From the end of the second century the Bishop of Rome participated in the Church's synodal life and often promulgated the convocation of different regional synods." [203]

The linking of the role of Bishop of Rome with that of Peter, as transmitted by the New Testament, "was a secondary phenomenon in the early Church when compared with the original praxis. Tertullian was the first to refer to Mt 16:18–19 to describe Peter as the font of the episcopate and universal unity. Cyprian, referring to Mt 16:18–19 and John 21:17, developed a theology of the Church's unity based [simultaneously] on the see of Peter and the collegiality of the Bishops gathered in Council. . . . Thus, while Peter, in some way or other, is present in every Church, the unity of the successors of the Apostles is only guaranteed by the see of Peter." [204] References

---

have centered, first, on the question [of] whether the papacy is biblically warranted. Roman Catholics have read the New Testament as indicating that Jesus conferred on Peter a unique role of leadership in the whole church for all times and in this sense provided for successors in the Petrine function, the bishops of Rome. . . . Lutherans, in contrast, have minimized Peter's role in the early church and denied that this role continued in the church in later periods or that the Roman bishops could be considered his successors in any theologically significant sense" (LCD V, 12 no. 6).

[201] Cf. EOE II, 1026, no. 20. On the development of the *Petrine function* in the postbiblical period, see also the document *Papal Primacy*, produced by the mixed commission in the USA (LCD V, 16, nos. 14ff.).

[202] Note 23 explains more precisely, "Notwithstanding this link between Peter and the succession of the bishops of Rome, the church of the capital remains that of Peter and Paul. The feast every June 29 demonstrates sufficiently that the testimonies of Clement, Ireneus and Gaius, as well as the graffiti in the catacombs of Saint Sebastian could not pass into oblivion. At least one papal text referring to both apostles can be cited: the letter of Adrian to Irene (772–95) refers to the popes as the vicars of Peter and Paul (J. D. Mansi XII, 1078–84)."

[203] EOE II, 1027, no. 21.

[204] EOE II, 1028, no. 22.

to the Petrine succession reach their apogee during the reign of Leo I in the middle of the fourth century.[205]

This broad historical overview concludes as follows: "During the entire patristic period the Churches lived their own communion based on the same fixed reference points of the faith, and had the same ministerial forms, that is, the episcopate and synods, at first local, but subsequently regional and ecumenical. These are the facts of tradition. The Churches also took the view that the Church of Rome, the Church of Peter and Paul, is the first among the Churches, not in a chronological sense (Jerusalem being the mother of all Churches), and not always in a political sense (Constantinople would gradually become the new Rome),[206] but according to apostolic order, since this was the Church of the Prince of the Apostles and of the Apostle to the Gentiles. The traditional precedence given to Rome among all the Churches constitutes a primacy. A primacy of honour is acknowledged which also implies not only a precedence but also a duty to exercise a presidency of charity, [that is to say,] of the communion of the Churches."[207]

Only the Bishop of Rome can exercise this presidency of charity which is proper to the Church of Rome: "There is a Bishop who, as Bishop of Rome, is responsible for his part for what that Church is: namely, this Church is *apostolic*, its Bishop cannot accede to any rupture in communion between the Churches. This is the *first* of the Churches and its Bishop is obliged to have a solicitude for all of the other Churches which befits the Apostle Paul. This Church is the *See of Peter*, and its Bishop responds with the faith of Peter to the Lord's promise to build his Church on this rock. All of these responsibilities are exercised by the Bishop of Rome in virtue of his presiding over this Church."[208]

---

[205] JRCLC, *Papal Primacy*: "With Leo I the correlation between the bishop of the Roman Church and the image of Peter, which had already been suggested by some of his predecessors, became fully explicit. According to Leo, Peter continues his task in the bishop of Rome, and the predominance of Rome over other churches derives from Peter's presence in his successors, the bishops of the Roman see" (LCD V, 17, no. 18).

[206] The sociopolitical factor must not be underestimated, however: "The prestige and centrality of Rome as the capital city, combined with the wealth and generosity of Roman Christians, quite naturally led to a special preeminence of the Roman Church" (LCD V, 17, no. 16).

[207] The Dombes Group, *The Ministry of Communion*: EOE II, 1047, no. 41.

[208] EOE II, 1048, no. 42.

This structure endured up to the ninth century, in keeping with the principles of an ecclesiology of communion: "However, grave signs of decadence began to emerge in the Church, even in the institution of the papacy, during the Middle Ages."[209]

The conclusion, however, throws cold water upon the entire historical survey: "But the New Testament never says that another Church has succeeded the Church of Jerusalem: the Roman primacy of the Church of Peter and Paul is a phenomenon subsequent to the New Testament."[210]

The nature of the primacy

The issue of the necessity or possibility of a primacy crystallizes in the question of *ius divinum* or *ius humanum*, already raised by the early Reformers and now revisited by the Catholic-Lutheran dialogue. The divergences with regard to the conferral of a primacy upon Peter and upon those who succeed him as the Bishop of Rome are reflected in different concepts of the nature of primacy itself. The following declaration of the Lutheran Catholic Mixed Commission in the United States (1974) amply illustrates the point: "Roman Catholics have tended to think of most major aspects of papal structure and function as divinely authorized.... [The Pope's] jurisdiction over the universal Church is, in the words of Vatican I, 'supreme', 'full', 'ordinary' and 'immediate'. This authority is not subject to any higher human jurisdiction, and no pope is absolutely bound by disciplinary decisions of his predecessors. This view of the exercise of papal power has been vehemently repudiated by Lutherans and viewed by them as leading to intolerable ecclesiastical tyranny."[211]

The "considerable progress" said to have been made in the course of the discussions, which would enable the parties to the dialogue to make "a fresh approach to the structure and operations of the papacy", remains very generic and vague. In practical terms, there is agreement in saying that "the centralization of the Petrine function in a single person or office results from a long process of development", and, therefore, "the papal office can be seen both as a response to the guidance of the Spirit in the Christian community, and also as an institution which in its human

---

[209] EOE II, 1050, no. 44.
[210] EOE II, 1123, no. 117.
[211] *Papal Primacy:* LCD V, 13, no. 8.

dimensions, is tarnished by frailty and even unfaithfulness."[212] The various differing positions are acknowledged in the final conclusion, together with a common admission that the forms of exercising the primacy can be adapted or modified so as to be more responsive to the needs of the Church.[213]

Even more misleading is the document *The Ministry of Communion in the Universal Church* (1985), published by the Dombes Group. In it, the primacy attributed to the Church of Rome by the early Church "primarily implied deference or respect for the See of Peter". It does not exceed "recognition of 'a primacy of honour'", even if inseparable from an actual responsibility, consisting in "maintaining a unanimity of faith amongst the Churches and a communion of charity".[214] It had authority therefore to receive appeals from other Churches,[215] for example, but excluded any government of the Church.[216] It was a ministry which could not be distinguished from episcopal ministry, which has sometimes been *confused* with it by the Bishop of Rome during the course of history. "But the Pope has sometimes confused solicitude for the Churches and abusive interference, the western patriarch and universal supremacy, the Roman episcopate and pontifical monarchy."[217]

The greatest obstacle to consensus on the nature of the primacy is ultimately the problem as to its divine or human origin. The early Reformers[218] posed the question in these terms in their writings, and so

---

[212] LCD V, 19, no. 21.

[213] "The Catholic members of this consultation see the institution of the papacy as developing from New Testament roots under the guidance of the Spirit [LG, chap. III]. Without denying that God could have ordered the church differently, they believe that the papal form of the unifying ministry is, in fact, God's gracious gift to his people. Lutheran theologians, although in the past chiefly critical of the structure and functioning of the papacy, can now recognize many of its positive contributions to the life of the church. Both groups can acknowledge that as the forms of the papacy have been adapted to changing historical settings in the past, it is possible that they will be modified to meet the needs of the church in the future more effectively" (LCD V, 19, no. 21).

[214] EOE II, 1029, no. 27.

[215] Cf. JRCLC, *Papal Primacy* (LCD V, 17, no. 17).

[216] EOE II, 1029, no. 27: "The primacy therefore includes an authority in the church, but not government of the church. This is the reason why its exercise is always exceptional in one or more churches that are in grave difficulties, either by recourse or by appeal from other churches for an arbitrator. Unity in faith should not be confused with uniformity of practise."

[217] EOE II, 1051, no. 45.

[218] JRCLC, *Papal Primacy*: "They continued to concede to the pope all the legitimate spiritual powers of a bishop in his diocese, in this case, Rome. They even granted the

it continues to be framed in the present dialogue: "Closely linked to historical question regarding the institution of the papacy by Christ is the theological issue of whether the papacy is a matter of divine law (*ius divinum*).
Roman Catholics have affirmed that it is and consequently have viewed it
as an essential part of the permanent structure of the Church. Lutherans have
held, in opposition to this, that the papacy was established by human law,
the will of men, and that its claims to divine right are nothing short of
blasphemous."[219] The discussion, nonetheless, arrived at an agreement to
abandon traditional terminology in favor of more general terms.[220]

Conditions for acceptance of the primacy

It is possible and, in a certain sense, even necessary that the Bishop of
Rome play a role, which constitutes "a charism proper to the Catholic
Church"; yet, as the document of the Dombes Group emphasizes, "in
the context of [fully] restored unity, it would have to become the common property of all Christians."[221]

propriety of his exercising a larger jurisdiction by human right over communities that had
by their own will placed themselves under him" (LCD V, 12, no. 5). A Lutheran-Roman
Catholic Statement, *Eucharist and Ministry* (1989), remarks, "The confessional texts, in fact,
do not exclude the possibility that the papacy might have a symbolic value or function
over a wider area, provided its primacy is not seen as anything other than of human law"
(BG 109, no. 29).

[219] LCD V, 12–13, no. 7.

[220] *Reflections of the Lutheran Partcipants*, LCD V, 30–31: "Lutherans and Catholics alike
have often doubted that a reconciliation of the two standpoints would be possible. We have
found in our discussion however, through a series of careful historical investigations, that
the traditional distinction between *de iure humano* and *de iure divino* fails to provide usable
categories for contemporary discussion on the papacy. On the one hand, Lutherans do not
want to treat the exercise of the universal Ministry as though it were merely optional. It is
God's will that the church have the institutional means needed for the promotion of unity
in the gospel. On the other hand, Roman Catholics, in the wake of Vatican II, are aware
that there are many ways of exercising papal primacy. Some are willing to consider other
models for the exercise of the Petrine function. They recognize the dangers of ecclesiastical centralism, and realize the limitation of the juridical description of the Petrine function. Rather than using the traditional terminology of divine and human right, therefore,
both Lutherans and Roman Catholics have been compelled by their historical studies to
raise a different set of questions: In what way or ways has our Lord in fact led his church
to use particular forms for the exercise of the Petrine function? What structural elements
in the church does the gospel require for the ministry which serves the unity of the empirical church?" Cf. ibid., 34–35.

[221] EOE II, 1139, no. 133.

Recalling the most common charges leveled by the Reformers against the papacy, namely, that it had strayed from the Gospel on the question of justification, together with the consequent willingness to accept the papacy on the condition that it returned to the Gospel,[222] the same condition is reiterated in the Catholic-Lutheran dialogue: "But in various dialogues, *the possibility* begins to emerge that the Petrine office of the Bishop of Rome also need not be excluded by Lutherans as a visible sign of the unity of the Church as a whole 'in so far as [this office] is subordinated to the primacy of the Gospel by theological reinterpretation and practical restructuring'."[223] It particular, this would involve a change or adaptation of the papacy to the historical context, as has occurred in the past.[224]

The Catholic-Lutheran Commission in the United States offers further details on these general conditions in its research on "basic principles of renewal, and on questions facing Roman Catholics and Lutherans in view of the possibilities of rapprochement".[225]

The principles of *legitimate diversity*,[226] *collegiality*,[227] and *subsidiarity*[228] would imply, in a Catholic perspective, "a greater participation of pastors,

---

[222] JRCLC, *The Ministry in the Church*: "It seemed to Lutherans that the papacy suppressed the Gospel and was to this extent an obstacle to true Christian unity" (MV 270–71, no. 73). *The Final Report* on the review of the sixteenth-century condemnations by the Joint [Catholic-Evangelical] Ecumenical Commission [of the Federal Republic of Germany] notes, "The Reformation did not fundamentally reject the possibility of a supreme office of leadership in the church, although the Reformers were not able to see the primacy of the bishop of Rome as a divine ordinance founded on the Lord's commission to Peter. Their rejection of the papacy, to the point of terming the pope Antichrist, must be viewed as a reaction to the condemnation of the Protestant doctrine of justification by Rome, in which the Reformers saw the rejection of the gospel itself" (*The Condemnations of the Reformation Era*, 185).

[223] MV 271, no. 73. Cf. JRCLC [USA], *Papal Primacy* (LCD V, 21–23, nos. 29–32).

[224] Cf. above, p. 140, note 213.

[225] LCD V, 19, no. 22.

[226] "Even the exercise of the Petrine function should evolve with the changing times in keeping with a legitimate diversity of ecclesial types within the church" (LCD V, 20, no. 23).

[227] "Collegial responsibility for the unity of the church, as emphasized by Vatican II, is of utmost importance in protecting those values which excessive centralization of authority would tend to stifle.... The collegial principle calls all levels of the church to share in the concern and responsibilities of leadership for the total life of the church" (LCD V, 20, no. 24). Cf. the Malta Report (MV 184, no. 66).

[228] "The principle of subsidiarity is no less important. Every section of the church, each mindful of its special heritage, should nurture the gifts it has received from the Spirit by exercising its legitimate freedom" (LCD V, 20, no. 25).

scholars, and all believers in the direction of the universal Church"[229] and "voluntary limitations by the pope on the exercise of jurisdiction" which will "accompany the growing vitality of the organs of collegial government, so that checks and balances in the supreme power may be effectively recognised".[230] In the Lutheran view, "papal primacy will no longer be open to many traditional Lutheran objections",[231] and agreement may be reached that the papacy "is (God's) gracious gift to his people", provided that the "primacy in which the pope's service to unity in relation to the Lutheran Churches would be more pastoral than juridical, be so structured and interpreted that it clearly serve the Gospel and the unity of the Church of Christ, and that its exercise of power not subvert Christian freedom."[232] Having underlined the convergence already reached[233] and noted the remaining differences,[234] some questions are put both to the "Lutheran Churches"[235] and to the Catholic Church.[236]

---

[229] LCD V, 21, no. 26.

[230] Ibid., no. 27.

[231] Ibid., no. 28.

[232] Ibid.

[233] "Such a responsibility for the universal church cannot be ruled out on the basis of the biblical evidence; the bishop of Rome, whom Catholics regard as entrusted by the will of Christ with this responsibility, and who has exercised his ministry in forms that have changed significantly over the centuries, can in the future function in ways which are better adapted to meet both the universal and regional needs of the church in the complex environment of modern times" (LCD V, 22, no. 29).

[234] "We do not wish to understate our remaining disagreements. While we have concluded that traditional sharp distinctions between divine and human institution are no longer useful, Catholics continue to emphasize that papal primacy is an institution in accordance with God's will. For Lutherans this is a secondary question. The one thing necessary, they insist, is that papal primacy serve the gospel and that its exercise of power not subvert Christian freedom" (LCD V, 22, no. 30).

[235] "Therefore we ask the Lutheran churches: if they are prepared to affirm with us that papal primacy, renewed in the light of the gospel, need not be a barrier to reconciliation;—if they are able to acknowledge not only the legitimacy of the papal Ministry in the service of the Roman Catholic communion but even the possibility and desirability of the papal ministry, renewed under the gospel and committed to Christian freedom, in a larger communion which would include the Lutheran churches;—if they are willing to open discussion regarding the concrete implications [of the papacy] for them" (LCD V, 22–23, no. 32).

[236] "Likewise we ask the Roman Catholic Church:—if in the light of our findings, it should not give high priority in its ecumenical concerns to the problem of reconciliation with the Lutheran churches;—if it is willing to open discussions on possible structures for reconciliation which would protect the legitimate traditions of the Lutheran communities and respect their spiritual heritage;—if it is prepared to envisage the possibility of a reconciliation which would recognize the self-government of Lutheran churches within a

The document of the Dombes Group, too, insists on the renewal of the papacy and formulates a number of proposals on the subject both for the Catholic Church and for the *Churches* of the Reformation.

As for the Catholic Church, it is absolutely necessary that there be an "authentic conversion" of the Petrine ministry and its exercise, so as to eliminate all those historical factors that have caused "solicitude for unity to become a force for uniformity, by which the service of communion gives rise to an exaggerated centralization of the Church" and "the personal role of the pope has obscured other instances of the same ministry of communion".[237] In concrete terms, the conversion of the Catholic Church requires "a balance between the *community, collegial,* and *personal* dimensions of this ministry, in which this last dimension cannot be authentically exercised unless it becomes, in some way, the consequence of the other two dimensions".[238]

The question of the Western patriarchate assumes great significance in the group's description of collegiality. Since the break between the East and the West, "the Catholic Church has coincided with the earlier patriarchate of the west, or more precisely with the Latin Church", and the Bishop of Rome, in the ensuing practical confusion, "has exercised a double responsibility in this Church, consisting of a ministry of communion and that of the western patriarch, which has resulted in an increasing centralization. This is an 'anomaly' that has compromised the image of the papacy and mistaken it for a monstrous conflation of that which it no longer is." Consequently, for as long as "the distinction between these two functions is not rendered visible in the living organs of the Church, the need for a ministry of communion as exercised by the Bishop of Rome cannot be accepted by our Orthodox, Anglican and Protestant brethren." Only "an internal decentralization of the Catholic Church can offer them a concrete idea of the commitment they would assume in reestablishing full communion with the Catholic Church."[239]

It follows that, with regard to the personal dimension of this question, the Catholic members of the group—"while adhering fully to the Catholic Church's doctrine of the faith on the ministry of communion of the universal Church conferred on the Bishop of Rome" and maintaining

---

communion;—if, in the expectation of a foreseeable reconciliation, it is ready to acknowledge the Lutheran churches represented in our dialogue as sister-churches which are already entitled to some measure of ecclesial communion" (LCD V, 23, no. 32).

[237] EOE II, 1139, no. 133.
[238] EOE II, 1140, no. 134.
[239] EOE II, 1148–49, nos. 142–43.

that "the Pope exercises his ministry to the universal Church as Bishop of Rome and that this ministry is structurally necessary for the Church"— desire a "renewal of the concrete *forms* of the papal ministry of communion", which would involve a distinction between the [Pope's] primatial and patriarchal roles and "the creation of large continental Churches endowed with substantial autonomy". A further desire is expressed for a reevaluation of the exercise of authority by the Bishop of Rome in his own particular Church: "A pope who would assume his episcopal responsibilities to a greater degree where he is so obliged and able to, would greatly assist in modifying the image of the papacy. He would then appear as a pastor, the servant and leader of his brethren in an authentically common and joint ministry of *episkopé*." [240]

On their side, the *Churches* of the Reformation recognize first of all that they are, for historical reasons, incapable "of clearly expressing or manifesting at a universal level a visibly lived 'catholicity'". [241] Noting or presupposing the *metanoia* of the Church of Rome in her renunciation "of the privileges of a primacy of power and centralization" and her commitment "to a primacy of service and unity in the faith", they realize that this is a crucial and unavoidable question for all the Churches, for which an answer can be found by pursuing developments in three areas: at the community level, at the collegial level, and at the personal level. [242] Given the possible risks at the community or collegial level, [243] the will to *metanoia* must take account "of the spiritual need for a harmonious development of community, collegial and personal expression in the very structures by which our Churches express communion at local and regional levels". [244] The *Churches* of the Reformation, conscious that "any visible expression of the universal Church requires a ministry of communion", should question "the reasons which now prevent them from conceiving of, or recognizing that such ministry can be positively exercised for the communion of the whole Church" [245] and raise this question of a personal

---

[240] EOE II, 1154 and 1156, nos. 148–49.

[241] EOE II, 1158, no. 152.

[242] Cf. EOE II, 1159–60, nos. 153–54.

[243] "At a *community level* ... this locus for dialogue always runs the risk of not involving the diverse separated churches sufficiently.... At a *collegial level* ... the emphasis on this collegiality has sometimes had the effect of atrophying the community and personal exercise of the ministry of communion within our churches" (EOE II, 1162, no. 156).

[244] Ibid.

[245] Ibid., 1163, no. 157.

ministry. A ministry of communion would have to respond, then, to the following ecclesiological demands: "be assumed only in vigilant obedience to the word of God"; "be exercised only on the basis of a personal *episkope* in a particular Church, thereby assuring its community dimension"; "be exercised collegially" through "councils, synods, reciprocal consultation not only of the *episcopi* but also of presbyters, deacons and laity"; "ensure ... an [arbitrating] role in episcopal collegiality and in the conciliar assemblies that would function as a universal *episkope* so as to encourage unity among the particular Churches, and act as a prophetic service opening up new prospective for the Church".²⁴⁶

In expressing their final common desire, the Dombes Group touches on the primacy's role in communion. For each particular Church fully realizes itself as Church only "when in communion with all other Churches". Such communion "demands a community (*comunitario*), collegial and personal ministry". Hence the invitation is offered "realistically and imaginatively to search for instances that could be established to articulate the communitarian, collegial and personal aspects of communion which are accepted by all".²⁴⁷

In the same vein, the document on *justification* published by the Joint Roman Catholic/Evangelical Lutheran Commission (1993) expresses the hope that "Catholic-Lutheran dialogue on the Church would concentrate on the theme of a directional ministry in the universal Church within the context of an ecclesiology of communion." ²⁴⁸

---

²⁴⁶ Ibid., 1164, no. 158.

²⁴⁷ Ibid., 1167–68, nos. 161–62.

²⁴⁸ "According to the belief of the Catholic Church, of course, the primatial function of the bishop of Rome is an essential element of the Church, with the consequence that each local church must be related to the primacy of the church of Rome and its bishop in order to be in full communion of churches. But on the other hand it must not be forgotten that the Roman primacy is also related [ordered] to the koinonia of local churches. The Catholic-Lutheran dialogue must deal with the question of the ministry of oversight in the whole church in the context of ecclesial koinonia in general, but also in the particular context of the Roman Catholic understanding of the relationship between the episcopal college and the papal office. To be sure a problem thereby arises in regard to the Catholic ecclesiology of communion to which the ecumenical dialogue has, in various ways, called attention. In spite of Catholic adherence to the principle of a ministry of unity in the universal church, the challenge of self-criticism cannot be ignored. The doctrine of primacy must be further developed, and primatial practice must be shaped accordingly" (IS, no. 86 [1994], 149a).

III. EVALUATION OF THE RESULTS OF THE DIALOGUE

As in the analysis of the documents of the Catholic-Lutheran dialogue, so too in our evaluation of the results thereof, it is necessary to proceed in terms of the usual distinction between ecclesiology in general and the specific question of the primacy, with their respective subcategories (justification and Church, questions concerning ministries, the ecclesial character of the Lutheran communities). This allows us to determine whether and to what extent these individual problems have been dealt with and resolved. In order to gain such an overall perspective, we must take into account also, besides the texts already mentioned, the theological literature which precedes, accompanies, or is derived from the documents themselves.

1. The ecclesiology underlying the dialogue

The results of the dialogue on justification are often greeted with enthusiasm, inasmuch as they would allow us to consider the doctrine of justification as no longer being an obstacle to Catholic-Lutheran unity, other persistent differences notwithstanding.[249] Indeed, the "Response of the Catholic Church to the Joint Declaration of the Catholic Church and the Lutheran World Federation on the doctrine of Justification" recognizes that the declaration itself "represents significant progress in mutual understanding and in coming together in dialogue of the parties concerned; it shows that there are many points of convergence between the Catholic position and the Lutheran position on a question that has been for centuries so controversial" and that it can be stated with certainty "that a high degree of agreement has been reached, as regards both the approach to the question and the judgement it merits". It is therefore true to say that "a consensus on the basic truths of the doctrine of justification" has been reached. Yet the same official response of the Catholic Church explains that, with regard to the doctrine of *justification in se*, "on some points the

---

[249] A. Gonzáles Montes, "Dos propuestas de eclesiología ecuménica", *Diálogo Ecuménico* 31 (1996), 435: "[L]a doctrina de la justificación podría dejar definitivamente de ser obstáculo para la unidad católico-luterana, aunque según lo dicho, quedasen pendientes cuestiones bien centrales. Rectamente entendida, la doctrina de la justificación ya no podría ser utilizada para oponerse de principio a una teología de la 'potestad' de la Iglesia enfrentada a su misión diacónica."

positions are, in fact, still divergent". By way of overcoming these, the reply offers a list of points "that still constitute an obstacle to agreement between the Catholic Church and the Lutheran World Federation on all the fundamental truths concerning justification".[250]

Above all it must not be forgotten that the Joint Declaration does not address the ecclesiological aspects of the question of justification,[251] to which the dialogue had alluded, at least to some extent, when it recognized that "consensus on the doctrine of justification—if it is nuanced—must prove itself ecclesiologically".[252] Indeed, since the sixteenth century the controversy surrounding the doctrine of justification has moved into ecclesiology, and the greater part of recent dialogue has been concerned with ecclesiological questions, since these were perceived as the fundamental problem and the major obsctacle impeding the reestablishment of unity.[253] However great the extent of that attention, regrettably, it has not been sufficient to resolve most of these questions.

The central problem remains the sacramentality of the Church in relation to the question of the sole mediatorship of Christ; in this tension, as in the respective traditional views of the Church, we continue to see two conflicting ecclesiologies: justification by faith alone in the Lutheran view

---

[250] IS, no. 98 (1988), 93a.

[251] In note 43 of the Declaration itself the need for further clarification is stressed: "In this respect, there are still questions of varying importance which need further clarification. They include, among other topics . . . as well as ecclesiology, authority in the church, ministry, the sacraments. . . . We are convinced that the consensus we have reached [in this declaration] offers a solid basis for this clarification" (ibid., 86b). This need is again confirmed by the Official Common Statement of October 31, 1999: cf. IS, no. 103 (2000), 4b.

[252] LRCIC (IS, no. 86 [1994], 131–32), Church and Justification. This need had already been noted by the Memorandum comune on the manner of proceeding in the third phrase of the dialogue: "It can be observed that . . . Catholics and Lutherans keep coming back to the question about the understanding of the church, more precisely to the central question and the nature of its centrality in the divine plan of salvation (church as sign and instrument; 'sacramentality' of the church). . . . This question immediately raises again, especially for the Lutheran side, the question of the doctrine of justification. It is less a matter of the understanding of justification as such . . . rather it is a matter of the implications of the mutual relationship of justification and the church" (ibid., foreword, 130).

[253] Cf. Maffeis, "La giustificazione nel dialogo ecumenico. Chiarificazioni e nodi irrisolti", Rassegna di teologia 37 (1996): 624. Raem is more explicit when he notes that the third phase of the dialogue "had to focus attention on the question, to what extent the far-reaching agreement on justification could be verified by drawing its ecclesiological consequences" ("The Third Phase", 190a).

and the Catholic view of the Church's sacramentality.[254] "The question of the Church's sacramentality has assumed major importance especially in the discussions on the 'fundamental difference', since many regard it as central for understanding the Churches' function in the process of making salvation concretely accessible."[255] As in the past, the fundamental reason for persistent differences continues to be the doctrine of justification, which is crucial for ecclesiology.[256] Indeed, there is no unanimity with regard to the results of the dialogue. Opinions range from a recognition that the problem might be resolved by developing the pneumatological basis for the Church and the idea of the Church as the sacrament of intratrinitarian communion[257] to an emphasis on the ongoing Protestant reservations about making salvation conditional upon institutional structures.[258] The parties then have recourse to the interpretation that

---

[254] Gonzáles Montes, "Dos propuestas", 433: "La misión de la Comisión católico-luterana ... era lograr poner en relación dos doctrinas históricamente confrontadas a partir de la Reforma: la doctrina luterana de la justificación por la sola fe con la doctrina católica de la sacramentalidad de la Iglesia"; Meyer, "La Chiesa Popolo di Dio, Corpo di Cristo, Tempio dello Spirito Santo, nel dialogo tra la Chiesa cattolica romana e le confessioni Protestanti. Una prospettiva luterana", P. Rodríguez, ed., *L'ecclesiologia trent'anni dopo la "Lumen Gentium"* (Rome, 1995), 232: "In questo dialogo si possono trovare due comprensioni della Chiesa: da una parte quella della Riforma, spesso nella sua deformazione Protestante, una visione fortemente determinata dalla relazione 'parola di Dio-fede dell'uomo' e, d'altra parte, la comprensione cattolica, una visione invece sacramentale e istituzionale." Cf. Gherardini, *Creatura Verbi*, 102.

[255] Cf. Maffeis, *Il ministero nella Chiesa*, 296–97.

[256] T. Schneider, "The Dialogue Report in the Present Ecumenical Context. A Comment on 'Church and Justification'": "In this final remark (n. 242) the dialogue-text once again repeats emphatically its basic agreements with the theological conviction that criterion for ecclesiology is the doctrine of justification" (IS, no. 86 [1994], 186b).

[257] Gonzáles Montes, "Dos propuestas", 433: "el éxito del trabajo de la Comisión ... tiene su llave de comprensión en el virtualismo siguiente: hablar de la sacramentalidad de la Iglesia profundizando en el contenido teológico implicado en la identidad de la Iglesia como creatura y ministra de la Palabra. Esto lo logran los teólogos de la Comisión primero mediante el desarrollo del fundamento pneumatológico de la Iglesia: es el Espíritu el que capacita a la Iglesia para el servicio de la Palabra y, al hacerlo, garantiza tanto la apostolicidad de la predicación como la vida de fe que da origen a la Iglesia (nos. 41–43). Luego, ya en el cap. 3, la exploración de la *koinonía* de la Trinidad sirve a la comprensión de la Iglesia como sacramento de la comunión intradivina, cuya vida emana de ella. La predicación sirve así a esta *koinonía*, a la que se llega por el bautismo y la Cena del Señor (nos. 66–72)."

[258] Maffeis, "La giustificazione nel dialogo ecumenico", 628, no. 12: "Pur riconoscendo in linea di principio che la Chiesa riceve la salvezza e ha un ruolo attivo nella sua trasmissione, da parte luterana rimangono delle riserve circa la posizione cattolica quando p. es. questa considera necessarie determinate strutture istituzionali.... Queste concezioni

there is a "differentiated consensus", which distinguishes between a complete agreement on the fundamental truths of the faith and the legitimacy of differing theological formulations.[259]

Given that the Joint Declaration made no reference to the problem of the sacramentality of the Church, one might ask whether such a "differentiated consensus" exists. During the course of the various dialogues a recurring question was asked as to whether the remaining ecclesiological differences were not really a reflection of fundamental differences in the understanding of salvation and that consequently the agreement which had been reached on justification might not be more apparent than real.[260] It would seem that this possibility is all too real and unfortunately cannot be resolved by recourse to a "differentiated consensus".

Furthermore, it is premature to speak of a "full consensus" signifying that traditional disagreements had been overcome.[261] While it must be recognized that substantial progress has been made in understanding individual important aspects of the doctrine of justification, it cannot be said that the parties have arrived at a global agreement with regard to the meaning of this doctrine in its entirety. Above all, there is no agreement

---

suscitano nella teologia luterana il timore che venga compromesso il carattere assolutamente *incondizionato* della salvezza e che questa venga invece legata a 'condizioni' umane e a istituzioni che sono ispirate alla logica della legge non del vangelo."

[259] Raem, "Dialog ohne Ende?", 235–36: "Sowohl das Dialogdokument 'Kirche und Rechtfertigung' als auch die 'Gemeinsame Erklärung zur Rechtfertigungslehre' operieren mit dem Begriff des differenzierten Konsenses. ... Was ist unter einem 'differenzierten Konsens' zu verstehen? ... Der differenzierte Konsens beschränkt sich darauf, die Anliegen der beiden Seiten und damit das gemeinsame Glaubensgut zu sichern, während im Bereich der theologischen Formulierung Unterschiede fortbestehen können, solange das gemeinsame Glaubensgut gesichert ist. Entscheidend ist, daß auf diese Weise trotz unterschiedlicher theologischer Formulierungen kirchentrennende Gegensätze zu überwinden sind. ... Die Idee des differenzierten Konsenses unterscheidet damit bei der Bewertung einer Glaubensaussage zwischen zwei Arten von Übereinstimmung: 1. es muß im Dialog Übereinstimmung erzielt werden, was zum Grundlegenden einer bestimmten Glaubensaussage gehört, und im Bereich des Grundlegenden muß es volle Übereinstimmung geben; 2. es muß im Dialog Übereinstimmung erzielt werden, daß die verbleibenden Differenzen bezüglich der betreffenden Glaubensaussage nicht nur legitim, sondern sogar bedeutungsvoll sind und die erzielte Übereinstimmung im Grundlegenden nicht in Frage stellen." Cf. K. Hünerbein: "Differentierter Konsens. Wichtiger Schritt zur Kirchengemeinschaft: 1997 wollen Lutheraner und Katholiken ihre Beziehungen auf eine neue Basis stellen": *Bausteine für die Einheit der Kirche*, no. 144 (1996), 24ff.

[260] Cf. Maffeis, "La giustificazione nel dialogo ecumenico", 626.

[261] Schütte, *La chiesa nella comprensione ecumenica*, 186: "Nel dialogo ecumenico si è riconosciuto che nella dottrina della giustificazione non ci sono contrasti che separino le chiese."

on the role of the Church in salvation. According to Catholic doctrine, the Church is not only the communion of saints but also a "sacrament" and a salvific reality in herself. Not only is she the "locus" (recipient) in which Christ alone saves, but her very existence and activity are decisive for the very nature of justification, which, by Christ's will, is given to mankind in the Church, with the Church, and through the Church. This doctrine is presented, however, merely as a Catholic tendency against which a Protestant critique can be legitimately advanced. It is recognized that the latter can rightly appeal to Vatican II, but it is then maintained that the sacramentality of the Church, as taught by *Lumen Gentium* I, is circumscribed by the reference to Christ, the true "light of the nations [of humanity]", for whom the Church is a sacrament insofar as she is a sign and instrument for the mediation of the invisible salvation which God grants to mankind. The depiction of the Church as sacrament emphasizes an ecclesiology which understands the Church not primarily as an institution but as divinely instituted. Sacramentality underscores the efficacy of God which foresees all human activity, and thus it contrasts with the concepts of the Church understood as a *societas* or as *Christus prolongatus*, by accentuating the concept of sacrament, that is to say, a sign and instrument of intimate union with God and of the unity of all mankind.[262] Therefore the idea of the Church's sacramentality, as used by the council, simply takes up the fundamental desire of the ecclesiology of

---

[262] Neuner, *Ökumenische Theologie*, 262–63: "Gegen diese Tendenzen richtet sich die Protestantische Kritik mit Recht. Sehr wohl aber ist zu bestreiten, daß diese Tendenzen sich legitimerweise auf das Konzil berufen und daß sie die rechte Interpretation der Aussage von der Sakramentalität der Kirche darstellen. In der dogmatischen Konstitution 'Lumen Gentium' des Zweiten Vatikanischen Konzils lauten die ersten Worte in fast definitorischer Weise: 'Christus ist das Licht der Völker. . . .' Als Grundaussage ist hier festzuhalten, daß die Kirche nicht in sich, sondern von Christus her verstanden wird, er, nicht sie, ist Licht der Völker, sein, nicht ihr eigenes Licht erstrahlt auf ihrem Antlitz. Diese Christusbezogenheit wurde durch den Begriff der Sakramentalität umschrieben"; ibid., 264–65: "Die Vorstellung der Kirche als Sakrament prägte eine Ekklesiologie, die Kirche primär noch nicht als Institution, sondern als göttliche Stiftung, getragen vom Heiligen Geist, verstand. Sakramentalität betont die jeder menschlichen Aktivität zuvorkommende Wirksamkeit Gottes. . . . Die Auseinandersetzung mit der Reformation verstärkte diese Tendenz. Kirche erschien kaum noch als geistliche Wirklichkeit, sondern fast ausschließlich als *societas*. Ihre Grundlegung im göttlichen Heilsplan reduzierte sich auf die Stiftung ihrer Ämter, besonders des Papsttums. . . . Das II. Vatikanum wollte mit seiner Aussage von der Sakramentalität der Kirche zunächst die Engführung von Kirche auf Institution und Hierarchie aufbrechen. Kirche gründet in der Zuwendung Gottes zum Menschen, in seinem Heil, nicht in der Perfektion ihrer Ämter. Darüber hinaus sollte aber auch einer unkritischen Identifizierung

the Reformation: the Church is a sacrament precisely because she is sinful. This concept was criticized by the conservatives, who regarded it as a Protestantization of the Church. It also raised objections on the part of polemical Protestant theologians. In any case the controversy over the sacramentality of the Church would no longer necessarily be a source of division for the Churches.[263]

With good reason, many commentators hold that, on the basis of data already available from discussions on other topics, a common declaration on the nature and mission of the Church should be made, even if the existence of a "basic consensus" is still disputed and "fundamental differences" between the Churches persist.[264] Apart from what has already been

---

mit Christus ein Riegel vorgeschoben werden. Die Kirche wurde nicht mehr als *Christus prolongatus* verstanden, sondern 'nur' als Sakrament, als Zeichen und Werkzeug."

[263] Ibid., 265–66: "Somit hat das Konzil im Wort von der Sakramentalität der Kirche Grundanliegen der reformatorischen Ekklesiologie aufgegriffen: Gerade als sündige Kirche ist sie Sakrament. Wegen dieser Konnotation wurde die Vorstellung beim Konzil von konservativen Kreisen kritisiert.... Diese Argumentationsfigur hat sich inzwischen verschiedentlich fast in ihr Gegenteil verkehrt. Angesichts mancher Versuche, die Kirche unter Berufung auf LG 1 einer quasi- sakramentalen Verehrung zuzuführen, wurden nun aber auch längst überwunden geglaubte Einwände Protestantischer Kontroverstheologie gegen das katholische Sakramentsverständnis und die Ekklesiologie wieder ausgegraben. Es kann ökumenisch nicht förderlich sein, eine richtige und legitime Konzilsaussage gleichsam zum Wesen des Katholizismus hochzustilisieren, wenn sie in unmittelbarer Gefahr steht, innerhalb der katholischen Theologie weithin im Gegensatz zur Intention der Konzilsväter interpretiert zu werden und in der Konsequenz fast unausweichlich neue Barrieren zwischen den Kirchen aufzurichten. Die mit dieser Aussage ursprünglich verbundenen Inhalte sind unverzichtbar und systematisch fruchtbar, und dies für alle christlichen Kirchen. Sie lassen sich aber auch in einer Sprachgestalt formulieren, die weniger Gefahren birgt, neue ökumenische Konflikte zu schüren und mißbräuchliche Verwendungen zu eröffnen. Soweit evangelische Theologen diese Terminologie für angemessen erachten und sie in bilaterale oder multilaterale Texte aufgenommen wurde, wird jedenfalls eine Interpretation beigegeben, die ein angemessenes Verständnis sicherstellt. Daß dies möglich ist, beweist, daß diese Kontroverse um die Sakramentalität die Kirchen keineswegs notwendigerweise trennt."

[264] Schneider, "The Dialog Report", 182b: "[M]any commentators on the ecumenical situation have almost unanimously maintained in recent theological literature: that agreements achieved about important specific themes need to be linked and grounded in a common statement about the nature and the mission of the Church. This important insight grew mainly out of the lively discussions of the eighties, around the question of whether there existed, between the Christian churches, a 'basic consensus' or whether there remained a church-dividing 'basic difference' to be reckoned with." Also, the press release issued by the Commission (1993) states, "The document reveals a large measure of consensus on the topics it discusses while not attempting to paper over differences which still remain. Significant, however, is whether the churches will judge these remaining differences as necessarily church dividing, or whether they will assign them to the realm of legitimate diversity."

said on the question of justification,[265] the problem with such a declaration is that the results supposedly obtained from the dialogue continue to raise major questions.

The *problem of ministry*, and especially episcopal ministry, remains a stumbling block for Catholic-Lutheran dialogue.[266] It has been examined in several texts of that dialogue. The dilemma persists of the substantial unity of the Churches in their faith in Christ and disagreement on differing concepts of ministry.[267] G. Turbani, addressing a symposium in Milan (April 16–18, 1998) on the subject of the primacy in ecumenism, summed up the current situation as follows: Protestant theology, unlike its Catholic counterpart, does not understand the ministry of ordination immediately in terms of apostolicity, because that concept is based primarily on the transmission of the content of faith, which is proper to the entire community of believers, and is measured according to the criterion of fidelity to its scriptural content, rather than to apostolic succession. The sacramental work of the Church, understood as an encounter of divine and human action, necessarily and theologically requires an ordained ministry that can express the oneness of the priesthood of all the faithful. The distinction between the common priesthood and the ordained ministry is connoted by the public role of the latter and by its signification of unity. Even the "churches" of the Reformation regard ordination as not simply deriving from the consent of the community, but also from a design of divine grace, according to which the ordained ministry must be regarded as instituted *iure divino*.[268]

---

[265] In Chapter 4 (nos. 107–242), Schneider, commenting on the Church as recipient and mediatrix of salvation, maintains that the Church "first brings together questions which used to be considered controversial but which, after carefully sifting the different confessional points of wiew, can largely be discussed in agreement in this document: 'Church as Congregatio fidelium' (nos. 108–17); 'Church as Sacrament of Salvation' (nos. 118–34); 'The Church Visible and Hidden' (nos. 135–47); and 'Holy Church, Sinful Church' (nos. 148–65). In each of these themes the commission finds theologically-based solutions for understanding the different confessional standpoints as complementary and therefore reconcilable" ("The Dialogue Report", 186ab). Cf. Raem, "The Third Phase", 192a.

[266] Cf. Neuner, *Ökumenische Theologie*, 219; Mehl, s.v. "Protestantesimo", 897.

[267] Ibid., 221: "Trotz aller ökumenischen Bemühungen tun sich, so wird immer wieder behauptet, 'in der Amtsfrage keine neuen Horizonte auf'. Es bleibt vorerst bei dem Dilemma: Die Kirchen sind sich im Glauben an Christus wesentlich eins, aber sie sind uneins über das, was sie von sich selbst und ihren Ämtern glauben."

[268] Cf. "Un primato per l'unità", *il regno-att.* 10/98, 354.

Evidently several questions remain open, even though according to Pannenberg, "in principle there is no difference any more between the Roman Catholic and the Reformation view of Church office or ministry and the priesthood of all believers."[269] At the same time, however, Pannenberg also asserts that "as regards the nature and commission of the Church's ministry the Roman Catholic and Reformation views no longer have insurmountable differences" while recognizing that the "current state of divisions, which fragment Christianity into a plurality of churches that are not in full communion with one another is mainly based on differences concerning ecclesial ministry".[270] Therefore the same Lutheran writer poses the following question: "What is this defect? It might be based on the Reformation refusal to call ordination a sacrament; or it might be related to an imperfection in the act of ordination itself, to different understandings of its effects, or finally to different answers to the question of who is qualified to confer ordination."[271]

An initial question that remains open concerns the very existence and the necessity of ministry, notwithstanding claims to the effect that this question has been resolved in recent ecumenical documents.[272]

In the first place, there has been no clarification as yet of the *relationship* between *the universal priesthood* of the faithful and the *ordained ministry*. While an essential distinction is made between the two, it is regarded as deriving not from a particular state of grace, but rather from the public character of the ministry. Hence it is declared that there is complete equality among all the baptized as to their status as Christians,[273] even though

---

[269] *Systematic Theology*, 374.

[270] Ibid., 392.

[271] Ibid., 417. Neuner poses an analogous question: "Dabei stellt sich die Frage, ob die lateinische Formulierung *'propter sacramenti Ordinis defectum'* mit 'Fehlen' angemessen übersetzt ist oder ob *defectus* nicht mangelhafte Verwirklichung bedeutet, wobei dann im einzelnen zu prüfen ist, worin der *defectus* besteht bzw. ob er heilbar ist" (*Ökumenische Theologie*, 220).

[272] Pannenberg, *Systematic Theology*, 386: "Modern ecumenical reports on ministry give sharper emphasis to the idea that church leadership is linked to the task of teaching (and presiding at the celebration of the Eucharist) than was the case in the Reformation tradition, especially the Lutheran."

[273] Neuner, *Ökumenische Theologie*, 222–23: "Auf bilateraler Ebene wurde formuliert: 'In der Lehre vom gemeinsamen Priestertum aller Getauften und vom Dienstcharakter der Ämter in der Kirche und für die Kirche besteht heute für Lutheraner und Katholiken ein gemeinsamer Ausgangspunkt' [BEM n. 6]. Auf der Ebene des Christ-Seins gibt es zwischen den Getauften und dem Amtsträger keine Differenz."

there are special functions or ministries in the community.[274] Such ministries are not conferred simply through delegation by the community, but by means of an *ordination*.[275] But what is the significance of this ordination? Having emphasized that public ministry is carried out, not in one's own name, but by the mandate of Jesus Christ, Pannenberg, referring to Luther, reiterates the symbolic nature of ordination, which can be regarded as a sacrament: "even if, unlike Baptism, it does not impart justifying grace to the recipients or their institution as children of God, but presupposes already the relationship to Christ and his Church that has its basis in Baptism".[276] Neuner, too, underscores the difference between the Catholic Church and the Lutheran communities in their views of ordination, but then maintains that, for Protestants as well, ordination is not without significance, and, hence, both views would seem equivalent. On the basis of *Ministry in the Church*, the question might be asked whether the differences which have divided the Church up to now have ever been so small.[277]

Neuner comes to a similar conclusion with regard to the question of the indelible *character* of ordination. Despite traditional differences, he claims, this doctrine is no longer unquestioned among the Catholics themselves, while Lutherans admit, in practice, that ordination is not repeatable.[278] In support of his thesis, Neuner cites Pannenberg, who maintains that today

---

[274] Pannenberg, *Systematic Teology*, 374–75: "According to Roman Catholic teaching the grace conferred by ordination, as a grace of office, relates to the authority and function of the office bearer but does not lift this individual as a person above the relationship with Jesus Christ that is common to all Christians. The latter view is what the Reformation had in mind when it criticized the limiting of the term priesthood to the church's ordained ministers. All Christians are priests by baptism and are thus of the same spiritual standing."

[275] Ibid., 223–24: "Zu dieser Aufgabe wird durch 'ordentliche Berufung', durch eine 'Ordination' bestellt.... In der Verhälnisbestimmung von Amt und Gemeinde wird betont, 'daß das Amt sowohl gegenüber der Gemeinde wie in der Gemeinde steht. Insofern das Amt im Auftrag und als Vergegenwärtigung Jesu Christi ausgeübt wird, steht es der Gemeinde in Vollmacht gegenüber.... Die Vollmacht des Amtes darf deshalb nicht als Delegation der Gemeinde verstanden werden'."

[276] Pannenberg, *Systematic Theology*, 397.

[277] Cf. Neuner, *Ökumenische Theologie*, 227, citing no. 33 of the document *Ministry in the Church*.

[278] Ibid., 228: "Nun ist aber die Interpretation des sakramentalen Charakters, so wie ihn die Reformatoren kritisierten, in der katholischen Theologie keineswegs unbestrittene Lehre. Die Konzeption vom sakramentalen Charakter wurde für die Sakramente entwickelt, die nach kirchlicher Praxis keine Wiederholung zulassen: die Taufe, die Firmung und die Ordination.... Die Praxis, die die Lehre vom sakramentalen Charakter begründet, nämlich die

it is already an accepted common idea that the *character* signifies "once-for-all ordination that rules out repetition.... As the baptized are baptized once and for all, so the ordained are permanently called to the church's public ministry even though they may cease to exercise their ministry or be inhibited from its exercise."[279] Again on this point, Neuner concludes that *Ministry in the Church* represents "an objective consensus".[280]

An analogous consensus is deemed to have been reached as well on a question which has divided the Churches until now: the specific role of the ordained ministry in the administration of the sacraments and the preaching of the word.[281]

Regarding the problem whether the "term *defectus* means that the sacrament of ordination is incomplete or totally missing at ordination in the Reformation Churches", a lack that "has to do with a defect in commissioning, in ordination",[282] Pannenberg, again referring to traditional Lutheran doctrine, does not deny that difficulties still persist in identifying the subject of a valid ordination. Still, he recognizes the requirement that the ministry must be conferred by an already ordained minister in order to ensure the unity of the universal Church.[283] Indeed, he states that "it has become a regular feature that the holders of high office in the Church should ordain. In any case, however, an essential part of ordina-

---

Einmaligkeit und Unwiederholbarkeit der Ordination, wird auch im evangelischen Bereich geübt."

[279] *Systematic Theology*, 398–99.

[280] Cf. *Ökumenische Theologie*, 229. Cf. also MV 261, no. 39.

[281] Ibid., 224–25: "In der katholischen Theologie wurde der Träger des geistlichen Amts oft als 'Mann der Sakramente' verstanden, während im Bereich der evangelischen Kirchen diese Funktion zugunsten der Wortverkündigung eher in den Hintergrund trat. Inzwischen hat die ökumenische Theologie gezeigt, daß dieser Gegensatz keineswegs der genuinen Lehre beider Kirchen entspricht.... Inzwischen ist diese Gegenstellung weithin überwunden. Das II. Vatikanische Konzil hat es als 'erste Aufgabe' des Bischofs und des Priesters bezeichnet, 'allen die frohe Botschaft Gottes zu verkunden'. Andererseits hat das evangelische Amtsverständnis die Dimension des Sakraments wiederentdeckt." Referring to the Lima Document (cf. EOE I, 3125) he concludes, "Mit dieser Aussage sind Gegensätze überbrückt, die die christlichen Kirchen bisher getrennt hatten." Pannenberg, in contrast, is much more realistic; he simply notes that, after the positions taken by the Second Vatican Council, the contrast between the two positions has been much attenuated (*Systematic Theology*, 384).

[282] *Systematic Theology*, 393.

[283] Cf. ibid., 399–400.

tion is that it should take place in preservation of the unity of the whole Church that is represented by the ministers who participate."[284] The expectation that the Roman Catholic Church might recognize the state of emergency invoked by the Reformers and accept their ministries as valid presupposes that "the Protestant churches view their practice of ordination along the lines of the Lutheran confessional witness, i.e., as the expression of an emergency rule, and do not trace it back to the priesthood of all believers as the source of authority by delegation." From this it follows that "it is not just for ecumenical reasons, but for the sake of their own understanding of ordination that the Reformation Churches should hold strictly to the fact that individual public preaching of the Word and administration of the sacraments should be on the condition of prior ordination".[285] That requirement is justified by the simple fact that the minister is a representative of the whole Church and by the public nature of his office.[286]

The lack of clarity with regard to the existence and nature of an ordained ministry becomes even more evident when approaching the question of *apostolic succession*, on which the entire doctrine of ordained ministry is based. It is asserted that the ordained ministry is necessary and theologically justifiable. Protestant theology, as distinct from its Catholic counterpart, does not connect ministry with apostolic succession.[287] At the same time it is held, even from a Catholic perspective, that the communities

---

[284] Ibid., 403.

[285] Ibid., 404.

[286] Ibid., 381–82: "Handing down the office from one bishop to another makes good sense in so far as the bishops represent the whole church and the task of proclaiming the Gospel that is committed to the church, but it should not lead to the setting up of an independent clerical church apart from the faith awareness of the churches." Consequently, "we can maintain that God instituted the ministry only on the premise that such a ministry of teaching and preserving the church in the faith of the people, which is public in as much as it pertains to the whole fellowship of believers (cf. CA 28, 20–22), standing in a material relation to the sending out of the apostles to preach the Gospel."

[287] Neuner, *Ökumenische Theologie*, 229: "Apostolizität bedeutet Ursprungstreue. Diese wird katholischerseits eng mit dem Amt zusammengesehen. Demzufolge ist die Kirche apostolisch, weil ihr Amt in einer ununterbrochenen Sukzession steht.... Demgegenüber verstehen die evangelischen Kirchen die Apostolizität zumeist als Identität mit der Lehre der Apostel. Die Kirche ist dadurch apostolisch, daß sie in ihrer Botschaft, eventuell auch in ihrem Leben, das weitergibt, was ihr von den Aposteln her überkommen ist ... Von hier aus wird der katholischen Kirche vorgeworfen, durch die Einführung menschlicher Traditionen die apostolische Botschaft verdrängt und verfälscht, also die Apostolizität preisgegeben zu haben. Die Kontroversen zwischen den Kirchen bündelten sich im gegenseitigen Vorwurf mangelnder Apostolizität."

deriving from the Reformation, both initially and presently, did not lose their apostolic character, which is constituted by fidelity to the teaching of the apostles.[288] In the recent debate, succession in ministry is considered to be a secondary question.[289]

The problem becomes even more acute with regard to episcopal ministry. The Reformation, in fact, understood the *defectus ordinis* to mean that there was no doubt but that in the sixteenth century the succession in episcopal service was interrupted, and therefore continuity with the early Church no longer existed either. In turn, this led to a dismembering of the Church into opposing ecclesial communities and at the same time to a break with the apostolic message, which consequently gives rise to the question of episcopal ministry in the ecumenical dialogue, since the evangelical "Churches" from the time of the Reformation have not had bishops, only pastors. The theory is that the chain of succession was not disrupted, however, but only the episcopal structure of the Church. As a result of recent research, it is maintained that tangible convergence can be achieved in this area as well, in the sense that Protestant ordination is conferred by ordained ministers, thereby giving rise to the possibility of seeing a kind of chain of succession in ordained ministry going back to the Reformers, whose own ordinations have never been contested by the Catholic Church. Hence, only the episcopal structure of the Church has been broken, but not succession as such.[290]

---

[288] Ibid., 231: "Die Kirchen der Reformation haben auch nach katholischem Verständnis nicht mit der Apostolizität gebrochen; gegebenenfalls ließe sich argumentieren, daß sie die personale Zuspitzung der apostolischen Überlieferung, die das Amt bedeutet, nicht beibehalten haben. Wenn nun aber das Amt so sehr im Dienst der rechten Botschaft steht, wie hier vorausgesetzt, dann ist in einer ökumenischen Erschließung die Frage zu stellen, ob nicht immer dann, wenn das Amt die rechte Lehre verkündigt, es damit auch als rechtes Amt anerkannt werden könnte, und das selbst dort, wo die Art und Weise, wie die Amtsübertragung erfolgte, nicht nach den Regeln verlief, die die katholische Theologie für den Normalfall aufstellt. Wenn ein Amtsträger die rechte Lehre verkündet, dann, so die These, wäre sein Amt legitimierbar."

[289] Cf. Pannenberg, *Systematic Theology*, 403.

[290] Neuner, *Ökumenische Theologie*, 232: "Neuere Untersuchungen haben auch in dieser Problematik deutliche Konvergenzen sichtbar werden lassen. Auch im evangelischen Bereich werden die Ordinationen von Ordinierten durchgeführt, so daß damit auch hier so etwas wie eine Kette von Amtssukzessionen nachgewiesen werden kann, die zurückreicht bis zu den Reformatoren, deren Ordinationen innerhalb der katholischen Kirche nie in Zweifel gezogen wurden. Damit läßt sich, so eine verbreitete katholische Interpretation, auch im evangelischen Bereich eine Kette von Ordinationen und damit eine Sukzessionsreihe erkennen, die auf der katholischen Amtssukzession aufruht. Allerdings, so die Argumentation,

The evident contradiction between these two positions[291] is confirmed by the persistent refusal on the Protestant side to consider the episcopate as the primary and original ministry in the Church.[292] Instead, the very origin of this ministry is presented in a manner that indicates serious reservations. It is said to have emerged late, after a period of uncertainty concerning who it was that held the authority exercised by the apostles, which at any rate was not directly connected to the appointment of their successors by an apostolic arrangement.[293]

The question of the recognition of orders arises against this background and must be considered in the light of a *sacramenti Ordinis defectus*, because of which, for both Catholics and Orthodox, the communities deriving from the Reformation "have not preserved the proper reality of the eucharistic mystery in its fullness".[294] The ministry "does not fittingly represent the Church's unity"[295] in such communities, which cannot be called "Churches" because they lack apostolicity.[296] The ancient Churches of

---

stehe diese Sukzession nicht auf episkopaler, sondern auf presbyterialer Ebene. Denn in den evangelischen Kirchen haben seit der Reformation nicht mehr Bischöfe, sondern Pastoren, also nicht-bischöfliche Amtsträger ordiniert. Damit sei aber nicht die Sukzessionskette als solche gebrochen, sondern lediglich deren bischöfliche Struktur."

[291] L. Chitarin, "Note sull'attuale dibattito ecclesiologico", *Ricerche teologiche* 8 (1997): 190: "Il ministero episcopale nella successione apostolica è da parte luterana qualificato 'importante, significativo, e perciò desiderabile', ma non 'necessario o indispensabile'." The author comments on no. 197 of *Church and Justification* (cf. above, p. 116, note 120).

[292] Pannenberg, "Le ministère ecclésial et l'unité de l'Église", 190–91. "Il faut donc refuser la conception selon laquelle 'le ministère supra-paroissial de l'évêque serait le ministère premier et originel de l'Église', conception proposée par le second Concile du Vatican."

[293] Pannenberg, *Systematic Theology*, 378 and 379: "After the death of the apostles it would seem that in the second and third generations of the early church a phase of uncertainty developed as to how to maintain this function.... The other ministers, the elders based on models from Judaism, the local teachers mentioned by Paul (1 Cor 12:28; Rom 12:7; cf. Eph 4:11), the leaders of the house churches (episkopoi), and the supporting deacons obviously did not have at first the authority that was needed for succession in the apostolic function.... This historic development is an important and momentous one as regards the doctrine of ministry. It means first that the authority and form of church leadership in terms of the office of bishop cannot be based directly on an order that the apostles set up to appoint successors."

[294] *Unitatis redintegratio*, 22. Cf. Neuner, *Ökumenische Theologie*, 220.

[295] Pannenberg, *Systematic Theology*, 393.

[296] Neuner, *Ökumenische Theologie*, 231: "Damit ist jedenfalls eine mechanistische Konzeption der Amtssukzession überwunden, selbst wenn sie in manchem kirchlichen Dokument noch nachwirken mag ... daß die Kirchen der Reformation im 16. Jh. die Sukzession

the East and the communities deriving from the Reformation evaluate the problem in different ways; the former regard a sacramental ministry, handed down by apostolic succession, as essential, while the latter simply deem it irrelevant for adequate proclamation of the Gospel and administration of the sacraments. Consequently, one finds also different degrees of willingness to give reciprocal recognition to orders.[297]

Attempts have been made to resolve the problem by proposing various models and determining various conditions (although no unanimous consensus has been reached); it is said that the heightened agreement attained through the ecumenical dialogue renders continued nonrecognition of ministries illegitimate and that the Catholic Church could recognize the ministries of the Reformed Churches and thus remove any possibly subsisting "defectus".[298] In reality, however, aside from the models that have

---

preisgegeben haben, damit kein gültiges Amt mehr verwirklichen und deshalb den Titel 'Kirche' nicht mehr verdienen, weil ihnen die Apostolizität fehlt."

[297] Ibid., 235: "Die Anerkennung der Ämter ist vor allem ein Problem der bischöflich verfaßten Kirchen.... Demgegenüber ist das Problem des Amts für die Kirchen der Reformation zunächst weniger gewichtig, es erscheint kaum als in sich relevant, sondern allein Teilaspekt in der Frage angemessener Evangeliumsverkündigung und Sakramentenspendung. Darum ist es für die Kirchen der Reformation keine Schwierigkeit, das Amt in den alten Kirchen anzuerkennen, soweit es nur dem Wort und dem Sakrament dient, während diese in der Anerkennung der Ämter in den Reformationskirchen den entscheidenden Schritt auf dem Weg zur Versöhnung der Kirchen als Schwesterkirchen sehen. Der Anerkennung oder der Gültigmachung der nicht-bischöflich verfaßten Ämter kommt nach dem Verständnis dieser Kirchen entscheidende Bedeutung im Prozeß der ökumenischen Annäherung zu."

[298] Ibid., 235–37: "Für diesen Akt wurden unterschiedliche Modelle entwickelt. Traditionellerweise gingen die bischöflichen Kirchen davon aus, daß die nicht-bischöflich ordinierten Amtsträger die Priesterweihe empfangen müßten, um als Amtsträger anerkannt werden zu können.... Verschiedentlich wurde vorgeschlagen, lediglich bedingt (*sub conditione*) eine bischöfliche Ordination zu spenden, also mit der Intention, nur dann zu ordinieren, wenn der Empfänger nicht bereits gültig geweiht sei.... Besonders intensiv wurde das Modell der gegenseitigen Handauflegung diskutiert. Dabei sollten bei einem Versöhnungsgottesdienst die (bischöflichen) Repräsentanten der beteiligten Kirchen sich gegenseitig die Hände auflegen.... Eine pragmatische Lösung wurde im südindischen Modell entwickelt, in dem nicht-bischöfliche Kirchen mit der anglikanischen Gemeinschaft eine Union eingingen. Hier wurde beschlossen, alle Amtsträger, bischöflich oder nicht-bischöflich ordiniert, grundsätzlich anzuerkennen, mit Beginn der Union aber alle Ordinationen bischöflich zu vollziehen.... Die traditionelle katholische Argumentation, durch die Unterbrechung der Sukzessionskette sei in diesen Kirchen kein gültiges Amt verwirklicht, wird damit zunehmend brüchig.... Die in der ökumenischen Theologie aufgezeigten Konvergenzen offenbaren ein Maß an Gemeinsamkeit, das es jedenfalls schwer macht, die Nichtanerkennung weiterhin zu legitimieren.... Angewandt auf die Anerkennung der Ämter ließe sich hier

been proposed, which are *courtesy* gestures more than anything else, the first order of business is to overcome the doctrinal differences that still exist with regard to ministry.

Naturally some maintain that, with regard to those doctrines on which there is still no agreement, "an understanding can be sought that robs the remaining differences of their divisive significance".[299] However, the *Catholic Response to BEM* (July 21, 1987) seems much more realistic in noting that "the problem of the mutual recognition of the ordained ministry" remains "a crux in the endeavors towards Christian unity". At the heart of it stands "the very concrete issue of the sacrament of ordination related to the issue of historic episcopal succession.... It must be clear that the recognition of ordained ministry cannot be isolated from its ecclesiastical context. The recognition of ordained ministry and of the ecclesiastical character of a Christian community are indissolubly and mutually related. To the extent that it can be recognized that communion now exists between Churches and Christian communities, however imperfect that communion may be, there is implied some recognition of the ecclesial reality of the other. The question that follows is what does this communion imply for the way we perceive the ministry in the other? This perhaps is one question that should be taken up when attention is given to the fundamental ecclesiological dimension of the problem of recognition of ordained ministry. Since, in our view, ordained ministry requires sacramental ordination in the apostolic succession, it is premature to make pronouncements on the form a public act of mutual recognition of Churches and ministries would have. Rather, it is necessary now to work toward unity in faith on this central ecclesiological issue."[300]

A further question to emerge from the Catholic–Lutheran dialogue and from the commentaries is that of the *ecclesial character* of the communities deriving from the Reformation and the related possibility of attributing

---

folgern: Diese Vollmacht im sakramentalen Zeiche könnte die (katholische) Kirche auch in einer Anerkennung der Ämter in der Kirchen der Reformtion ausüben. Die könnte diese als gültig anerkennen und damit einen gegebenfalls noch bestehenden '*defectus*' tilgen."

[299] Pannenberg, *Systematic Theology*, 403–4.

[300] IS, no. 65 (1987), 137b–38a.

to them the title of *Churches*.[301] In contrast to the traditional thesis, which does not recognize such an ecclesial character,[302] there has been a gradual recognition not only of the Anglican Communion[303] but also of the Lutheran communities.[304] In fact, it has been called into question whether a specific form of ministry, in this case the episcopate, can determine the ecclesial character of a community, i.e., its existence as a Church in the full sense of the term. Indeed, the question is asked whether the Catholic Church recognizes that the ministry in the Protestant Churches has fulfilled and fulfills "the essential functions of the ministry which Jesus Christ instituted in his Church"; furthermore, if the Catholics acknowledge the presence of the Lord in these communities, through the proclamation of his word and the celebration of his memory (*anamnesis*) in the Supper, are not these things the prerequisites for defining them as Churches?[305]

Some assert that the nonacceptance of the primacy would not constitute an obstacle to such recognition. The primacy could be maintained and at the same time renounced by the recognition of the autonomy of the Churches or ecclesial communities.[306] The ecclesiological basis for

---

[301] Klausnitzer, *Das Papstamt im Disput*, 456: "An der Frage der apostolischen Sukzession entscheidet sich letztlich die Frage der wechselseitigen Anerkennung der Ämter und damit der Kirchen als Kirchen im Vollsinn." Cf. above, pp. 120–22, notes 138–46.

[302] Tillard, *Church of Churches*, 38: after the break "the West has preserved the conviction that the Church continued to exist in the East" and "continued to call Churches these eastern communities separated from them, whereas it avoided doing [so] for those which rose out of the Reformation."

[303] Cf. R. T. Greenacre, "La signification des Églises orientales catholiques au sein de la communion romaine dans la perspective de 'l'Église anglicane unie non absorbée'", *Irénikon* 55 (1992): 344–51; C. Hill, "Récents documents romains et oecumémisme de Vatican II. Perspective anglicane", *Irénikon* 66 (1993): 65–66.

[304] It must be noted that these "non riconoscono a nessuna delle 'chiese' esistenti la vera unità e identità con Cristo, bensì sono dell'opinione che la chiesa ... esista (nonostante tutte le divisioni), ma esista come 'nascosta identità in Cristo'. Tra le comunità cristiane visibili e realmente esistenti, nessuna può concepirsi quale 'vera' chiesa di Cristo e quale 'centro' attorno a cui si muovono le altre 'chiese', per diventare infine come questa": L. Scheffzyk, *La Chiesa. Aspetti della crisi postconciliare e corretta interpretazione del Vaticano II* (Milan, 1998), 138.

[305] Cf. M. Garijo-Guembe, "Unità nella diversità. Riflessioni sui modelli di unità alla luce dei recenti accordi ecumenici", *Studi ecumenici* 13 (1995): 181–83.

[306] H. J. F. Reinhardt, "Zur Frage der (Selbst-)Beschränkung des päpstlichen Jurisdiktionsprimats im Hinblick auf die nichtkatholischen Christen. Kanonistische Erwägungen", *Catholica* 51 (1997): 262: "[D]ie Anerkennung der Kirchen und Gemeinschaften vice versa nicht abhängig gemacht worden ist von der Anerkennung des päpstlichen Jurisdiktionsprimats durch diese Kirchen und Gesellschaften. Kann nicht der päpstliche Jurisdiktions-

such a renunciation could be the consequence of renouncing the identification of the Catholic Church with the Church of Christ,[307] on the basis of an *exact* interpretation of the term *"subsistit in"* as mentioned in *Lumen gentium*[308] and of a *new concept* of the Church as the communion of the local Churches.[309] Even outside of communion with the See of Rome, the action of the Holy Spirit makes itself felt. Thus for the separated Churches there is no "ecclesial void", but rather the presence of the one Church of Christ is at work. Therefore, "there is no longer any hesitation in stating: 'It is not that beyond the boundaries of the Catholic Church there is an ecclesial vacuum' (*UUS* n. 13). For, because of the elements of sanctification and truth that have their source in the Spirit, even in what is lived in those communities separated from Rome, 'the one Church of Christ is effectively present' (*UUS* n. 11). The Spirit himself

---

primat aufrechterhalten und zugleich auf die Inanspruchnahme dieses Primats verzichtet werden? Dieser Verzicht könnte ausdrücklich oder durch die Weiterführung des eingeschlagenen Weges der Anerkennung der Autonomie der nichtkatholischen Kirchen und kirchlichen Gemeinschaften erfolgen."

[307] Ibid., "Die ekklesiologisch-dogmatische Grundlage dieses Verzichts auf die Ausübung der päpstlichen Jurisdiktion gegenüber nichtkatholischen Christen kann aus dem Verzicht der absoluten Identifikation der Ecclesia Jesu Christi mit der Ecclesia Catholica in 'Lumen Gentium' (Art. 8) abgeleitet werden."

[308] W. Beinert, "Ökumene und Ökumenismus 30 Jahre nache dem Vaticanum II", *Theologie der Gegenwart* 39 (1996): 244–45: "Wie kann sich Rom selber zurücknehmen? Das Zauberwort, das den Weg zeigen sollte, war das berühmte und umstrittene Verbum *subsistit*, das allerdings nicht im Ökumenismusdekret, sondern in der Kirchenkonstitution 'Lumen gentium' steht . . . Es liegt uns fern, die ganze Debatte aufzurollen. Als Ergebnis kann man in etwa festhalten: auf keinen Fall will das Konzil die von Christus gewollte Kirche und die römisch-katholische Kirche schlankweg und vorbehaltlos identifizieren. Es gibt echte Kirchlichkeit auch in den anderen Konfessionen. Elemente des Kircheseins existieren dort, wird audrücklich festgehalten—und sie exitieren so, das muß man schließen, daß sie zwar nach Einbeziehung in die katholiche Kirche verlangen, daß sie aber auch außerhalb ihrer ihren Wert in sich haben." The Catholic Church "ist nur eine geschichtlich bedingte Gestalt der Kirche Christi". Cf. Cereti, "L'enciclica 'Ut unum sint'", *Rassegna di teologia* 36 (1995): 683–84; P. Lüning, "Das ekklesiologische Problem des 'Subsistit in' (LG 8) im heutigen ökumenischen Gespräch", *Catholica* 52 (1998): 1–23; G. Wenz, " 'Est autem . . .'. Lumen Gentium 8 und die Kirchenartikel der Confessio Augustana", ibid., 24–25.

[309] Wenz, " 'Est autem . . .' ", 25: "Die Annahme eines wirklichen Kircheseins nichtkatholischer Kirchen erscheint von daher ebenso folgerichtig wie der Hinweis, daß die römisch-katholische Kirche der communio mit den anderen Kirchen um der bestimmungsgemäßen Realisierung katholischer Einheit willen in ekklesiologisch konstitutiver Weise bedarf. Letzeres impliziert, wie mit Recht hervorgehoben wird, daß offenbar auch die römisch-katholische Kirche letzlich doch nicht alle ekklesialen Elemente besitzt, die für die noch erstrebende bzw. noch ausstehende vollständige sichtbare Einheit der Kirche erforderlich sind."

maintains a real, 'albeit imperfect' *communion* among all the communities of the baptized (n. 11)."[310] Indeed, the term *sister Churches* is even applied to such ecclesial communities, or at least it is said that they are called to be such.[311]

Concerning the interpretation of the term *subsistit in*—which is in fact "the foundational and essential principle upon which ecumenism is based"[312]—it should be explained that the Second Vatican Council effectively recognizes the presence of some elements of holiness and truth in the separated Churches and ecclesial communities, which are, however, "gifts belonging to the Church of Christ" which, "constituted and organized as a society in the present world, subsists in the Catholic Church, which is governed by the successor of Peter and by the bishops in communion with him".[313] It is true therefore to say that all the baptized are "Christians" and "united to Christ"; but fully incorporated into Christ are only those who "accept all the means given to the Church together with her entire organization and who—by the bonds constituted by the profession of faith, the sacraments, ecclesiastical government, and communion—are joined in the visible structure of the Church of Christ, who rules her through the Supreme Pontiff and the bishops".[314] The replacing of "*est*" with "*subsistit in*" has given the impression that the Church has renounced her claim to be the true Church of Christ. In reality, though, this is not an abandonment of her traditional claim but rather the Church's opening to the particular demands of ecumenism and of the separated ecclesial communities. In virtue of the elements of holiness and truth present in such communities, it cannot be denied that they have "a certain ecclesial character. But to be 'ecclesial' is not yet to be a 'Church'."[315]

---

[310] Tillard, "Catholic Church Is at Heart of Communio", *L'Osservatore Romano*, English ed., October 25, 1995, p. 8.

[311] Cf. ibid.; Cereti, "L'enciclica 'Ut unum sint'", 684; A. Houtepen, "Superare la storia con la storia. Verso una revisione degli anatemi del passato", *Studi ecumenici* 13 (1995): 190; R. Cantell, "The Ecumenical Witness of the Evangelical Lutheran Church of Finland", *Mid-Stream* 35 (1996): 260; D. F. Martensen, "Ministry", Burgess, *Lutherans in Ecumenical Dialogue*, 131.

[312] Cf. C. U. Gómez-Iglesia, "Il ministero petrino", 637.

[313] *Lumen gentium*, no. 8.

[314] Ibid., no. 14.

[315] Cf. Scheffczyk, *La Chiesa*, 143. The Lutheran Ulrich Kühn is well aware of this while commenting rather freely on no. 10 of the encyclical *Ut unum sint*, and he affirms

Similar distinctions have to be made with regard to the concept of the Church as communion.[316] Ecclesial communion is "at the same time visible and invisible". "Apart from a common faith and Baptism, it is rooted above all in the Eucharist and in the Episcopate." The unity of the episcopate, in turn, implies "the existence of a bishop who is head of the college of bishops, namely the Roman Pontiff", who, "as the successor of Peter, is the perpetual and visible source and foundation"[317] of that unity. The genuine notion of communion, therefore, implies "communion with the universal Church represented by Peter's successors", not as "an external complement to the particular Church" but as "one of its internal constituents". The Eastern Orthodox Churches lack this element, and consequently "their existence as particular Churches is *wounded*." That wound goes "even deeper in those ecclesial communities which have not retained the apostolic succession and a valid Eucharist".[318] Consequently, the term *Church* cannot be applied to these communities. To be united does not mean the same as "to be part of", since there is only one "subsistence" of the true Church, whereas outside of her visible boundaries there are only "*elementa Ecclesiae*", which—as elements of the same Church—tend and lead toward the Catholic Church.[319] Any authentic ecumenical commitment takes this reality as its point of departure in the hope that "all may be enabled to recognize the continuity of the primacy of Peter in his successors, the Bishops of Rome, and to see the Petrine ministry fulfilled, in the manner intended by the Lord, as a world wide apostolic service".[320]

Notwithstanding the existence of many diverse elements, which allow us to recognize a certain communion, albeit imperfect, with non-Catholic Christian Churches and ecclesial communities, and to designate the Orthodox communities as "Churches", the Church of Christ subsists in the Catholic Church, which is therefore identical with the universal

---

that John Paul II "redet von den reformatorischen Kirchen weithin so, als ob sie keine Kirchen seien" ("Gesamtkirchlicher Petrusdienst? Evangelische Erwartungen", *Una Sancta* 53 [1998]: 30).

[316] Cf. Garuti, "Ancora a proposito del Papa patriarca d'Occidente", 40–42; idem, "Sister Churches", Appendix to this volume, pp. 298–300.

[317] *Communionis notio*, 11–12.

[318] Ibid., 17.

[319] Cf. Congregation for the Doctrine of the Faith, *Notificazione sul volume del P. Leonardo Boff*: AAS 77 (1995): 759; also Bux, "Unità e cattolicità", 164–67.

[320] *Communionis notio*, 18.

Church. This is not a matter of preferring a hierarchical ecclesiology over an ecclesiology of communion, since they are not mutually opposed, but rather of fidelity to Catholic doctrine. Nor does this constitute a "step backward" for ecumenism. Rather it expresses the Church's desire that ecumenical dialogue continue on the basis of her proper ecclesiological identity—a stance which "is not only legitimate but indispensable according to the spirit and the letter of the Second Vatican Council".[321]

It is still claimed, however, that recognition of the ecclesial character of non-Catholic communities, coupled with a renunciation of the exercise of any primatial jurisdiction over them, would open the way, in the ecumenical dialogue, for a recognition of a "primacy of honor" or of a "preeminence of love" in the person of the Bishop of Rome. No answer has yet been forthcoming to the question of whether such a proposal is consistent with Vatican I: the Pope, however, should proceed along these lines when he sees that such a self-restriction of his own primacy would promote Church unity.[322] It must be kept in mind, however, that full ecclesial communion and a genuine consensus on ministry cannot be envisaged without considering the primacy.[323] So far, the research necessary

---

[321] Cf. "La Chiesa come Comunione", article published with three asterisks in *L'Osservatore Romano*, 23 giugno 1993, 4.

[322] Reinhardt, "Zur Frage der (Selbst-)Beschränkung", 163: "Eine Nichtinanspruchnahme des päpstlichen Jurisdiktionsprimats gegenüber nichtkatholischen Christen, verbunden mit der schon erfolgten und weiter folgenden Anerkennung der Autonomie der nichtkatholischen Kirchen und kirchlichen Gemeinschaften ... könnte einen Weg aufzeigen, im ökumenischen Diskurs über das Papstamt weiterzukommen. Es wäre schön, wenn mit dieser Nichtinanspruchnahme Anerkennungen des Papstes durch die nichtkatholischen Kirchen und kirchlichen Gemeinschaften korrespondieren würden, und zwar in dem bereits aufgezeigten Sinne etwa durch Anerkennung des 'Ehrenprimats' und 'des Vorsitzes in der Liebe in der Person des Bischofs von Rom für die Gesamtkirche'.... Wie sich eine derartige Entwicklung mit den Definitionen des Ersten Vatikanischen Konzils zusammenlesen läßt, muß m.E. noch nicht jetzt beantwortet werden.... Wenn diesem Ziel der Einheit eine Selbstbeschränkung seines Primatsanspruches dient, wird er diesen Weg gehen, Nichtkatholische Christen könnten dies anerkennen, auch wenn dieser Prozeß noch einige Zeit brauchen wird."

[323] Klausnitzer, *Das Papstamt im Disput*, 457–58: "Genauso richtig ist aber auch, daß eine volle Kirchengemeinschaft und ein echter Konsens in der Ämterfrage ohne ein Bedenken des Petrusamtes nicht zustandekommt. Die Papstfrage hat ihr eigenes Gewicht. Wie es einseitig wäre, die katholische Kirche ausschließlich vom Primat her zu interpretieren und zu strukturieren, so ist es unbedacht, ökumenische Dialoge zu führen, ohne dieses Problem wenigstens im Blick zu behalten. Die katholische Lehre vom Amt und insbesondere vom Bischofsamt kann seit dem 18. Juli 1870 und dem Vaticanum II ohne ein Kapitel über das Papstamt nicht adäquat wiedergegeben werden."

for an eventual agreement on the questions of the episcopacy and the papacy has not been done; the participants have limited themselves to recommending that they be dealt with in the next phase of the dialogue.[324]

2. The question of the primacy

According to one of the Protestants who has been heavily involved in the dialogue, it must be kept in mind that the Lutheran mentality does not attribute crucial importance to the problem of the "papal office" or hypothetically of an ecclesial office which is universal in the strict sense, which in a particular way would be concerned about and at the service of the worldwide communion of all Christians and of all the Churches. It is seen merely as a secondary question within the broader one of ecclesiastical office in general.[325] At the same time, it becomes clear how the present evangelical Lutheran-Catholic dialogues, which have produced positive results in areas such as Scripture and tradition, the doctrine of justification, the conception of the Eucharist, and ecclesiastical office, have also implicitly dealt with the problem of the papacy or the "papal office", thereby setting in motion a resolution of this question, since the other Churches are seriously considering the assumption of this office themselves.[326] As evidence for this position, Meyer cites the general affirmations that they do not exclude the papal office as a visible sign of unity, which would be of human right, however, without implying thereby that

---

[324] Cf. Schneider, "The Dialogue Report", 186a, 187b.

[325] "L'Ufficio papale", p. 63. Meyer continues, "In proposito bisogna notare una duplice cosa. Primo, l'esistenza di un ufficio nella Chiesa è tutt'altro che qualcosa di secondario.... L'esistenza di un ufficio invece è costitutiva per la Chiesa. L'ufficio è voluto da Dio, da lui 'istituito' e quindi di 'diritto divino,' come gli scritti confessionali luterani affermano spesso e abbastanza chiaramente ... Nel medesimo tempo—e questo è il secondo aspetto—tanto la mentalità quanto la prassi delle Chiese luterane fanno sfoggio di una sorprendente libertà e addirittura d'indifferenza di fronte alla configurazione concreta di tale ufficio ecclesiale. La cosa decisiva è solo e sempre una: l'ufficio ecclesiale ... deve conservare il carattere e la funzione di un servizio al vangelo. Da questo punto di vista le Chiese luterane sono del tutto libere di accettare, per amore dell'unità ecclesiale, l'ufficio episcopale o addirittura di inserirsi di nuovo nella successione episcopale dell'ufficio.... Secondo il pensiero luterano perciò la questione di un ufficio ecclesiastico universale ... non è una vera questione controversiale e quindi non dovrebbe neppure essere posta come tale in partenza."

[326] Cf. ibid., 73–74.

it is being "disqualified" as something superfluous or secondary, as a "human invention" or "the work of the devil".[327] In reality, even in the most recent dialogue documents and the respective commentaries on them, the basic ecclesiological questions concerning the very structure of the Church—the assumption being that this was not essentially described in the New Testament[328]—ministry (especially the Petrine ministry),[329] and the relationship between the local Church and the universal Church[330] remain unresolved. Furthermore, the problem in general concerns not only the form in which the primacy is exercised, but also the question of its nature and the necessity for it.[331] The results of the dialogue do not yet seem sufficiently noteworthy, since the subject has not yet been examined in depth, especially at the international level,[332] but has simply been listed on the agendas of several

----

[327] Cf. ibid., 76. The previous page had referred to no. 66 of the Malta Report and to no. 28 of the concluding Report of the Catholic-Lutheran dialogue in the USA.

[328] Klausnitzer, *Das Papstamt im Disput*, p. 491: "Aber gerade auf dem Gebiet der kirchlichen Verfassungsstruktur finden sich im Neuen Testament zu wenig Aussagen, die *unmittelbar* die jetzige Verfassungsstruktur der Kirche legitimieren."

[329] H. Legrand, "Pape", J. Y. Lacoste (ed.), *Dictionnaire critique de Théologie* (Paris, 1998), 845b: "La tradition Protestante, en effet, est peu omogène, dans sa conception de l'*episkopé*/ épiscopat comme instrument de la communion entre les Églises.... Et l'acceptation du ministère papal se révélera encore plus difficile."

[330] For example, as Schneider maintains, in the document on *Justification* the question remains unresolved "concerning how to achieve a consensus regarding the theological concept of the 'local church' and how this relates to the universal Church's claim to primacy" ("The Dialogue Report", 187a).

[331] Kruse, "Die ökumenische Zukunft", 111: "Für einen lutherischen Gesprächsteilnehmer kann es allerdings nicht nur um die Form der Ausübung gehen.... Das 'Wie' ist nicht vom 'Was' zu lösen." Cf. G. A. Lindbeck, "Papacy and *Ius divinum*. A Lutheran View", LCD V; I. Riedel-Spangenberger, "Im Wesentlichen einig? Die Primatausübung des Papstes im ökumenischen Gespräch", *Herder Korrespondenz* 49 (1995): 663b; Pannenberg, "Le ministère ecclésial", 199; U. Kühn, "Papsttum und Petrusdienst. Evangelische Kritik und Möglichkeiten aus der Sicht reformatorischer Theologie", *Catholica* 50 (1996): 181.

[332] Klausnitzer, "Das Papstamt—personaler Dienst an der gesamtkirchlichen Einheit. Ein Blick aus der römisch-katholischer Sicht", *Catholica* 51 (1997): 86–87: "'Unübersichtlich' ist allerdings das letzte Adjektiv, das einem Beobachter in den Sinn käme, wenn er das katholisch/lutherische Gespräch zum Papstamt resümieren müßte. In den bisherigen drei Dialogphasen ... wird die Frage des Papsttums zwar immer wieder angesprochen, aber dies nur sehr vereinzelt und stets im Kontext anderer Problemfelder." The recommendation of an in-depth study, expressed in the document on *Justification* (no. 106), seems to suggest "daß dieses Thema bisher eben noch nicht gründlich erörtert worden ist". Cf. Neumann, "Das Papstamt in den offiziellen ökumenischen Dialogen", 97.

planning meetings.[333] Thus a "reconciliation with the primatial jurisdiction of the Bishop of Rome" is not yet foreseeable.[334] The Lutherans speak of the "possibility" of a Petrine ministry (which, however, goes no farther than nonexclusion of such an office);[335] in their view that ministry belongs not to the Church's being [*esse*] but only to the Church's well-being [*bene esse*].[336] Hence it is useful in avoiding the isolation of local communities; it is possible, but not indispensable.[337] At most it is "necessary for sociological reasons";[338] it must, however, be subject to the primacy of the Gospel.[339] On the other hand, one cannot passively accept "an ecclesiastical ministry which does not explain its function", for no other reason than because, "in spite of everything, the unity of Christians has not been lost, inasmuch as it has its real basis in Jesus Christ,

---

[333] I. Cassidy, "Der päpstliche Rat zur Förderung der Einheit der Christen im Jahre 1995", *Catholica* 50 (1996): 227–28: "Die Frage des Primats wird auch auf der Tagesordnung der vierten Phase des lutherisch-katholischen Dialogs stehen, der vom 10. bis 16. September 1995 in Lärkulla (Finnland) erstmals zusammentrat. . . . Es wurde entschieden, sich auf das Thema der Apostolizität der Kirche zu konzentrieren, um von hier aus die verschiedenen Dimensionem und Aspekte des Themas in bezug auf das Bischofsamt und mögliche Formen und Strukturen eines universalen Dienstes für die Einheit der Christen zu behandeln." The executive meeting of the Commission on Justification (May 1993) decided that the subjects of the episcopate and the primacy should be included among the themes requiring further exploration: cf. Raem, "The Third Phase", 197b.

[334] Cf. A. Houtepen, "Superare la storia con la storia", p. 191.

[335] Martensen, "Ministry", 128: "The dialogue was led quite naturally to a consideration of the question on universal ministry. No conclusions were reached, but the commision could say in various dialogues 'the *possibility* begins to emerge that the Petrine office of the Bishop of Rome also need not to be excluded by Lutherans'."

[336] Klausnitzer, "Das Papstamt", 88: "Die katholische Seite betrachtet das Papstamt als Element des 'esse' der Kirche, die lutherische Position akzeptiert allenfalls eine Diskussion darüber, ob es zum 'bene esse' der Kirche gehören könne."

[337] Gómez-Iglesias, "Il ministero petrino", 646: "I luterani si rendono conto che le chiese locali non possono isolarsi e perciò avvertono la necessità di un servizio efficace di unità a livello universale . . . il primato non è indispensabile, è 'solo una funzione possibile in linea di principio'."

[338] Cf. Cereti, *Per un'ecclesiologia ecumenica*, 234.

[339] Commenting on the Malta Report, Lindbeck sums up the Lutheran position as follows: "1: Lutherans recognize the importance of . . . 'the Petrine function' . . . 2. They are open to the possibility that this needs to be more effectively institutionalized than has been true in Lutheranism up until now. 3. They do not exclude the possibility that the papacy could rightly exercise this function. 4. In order to do this, however, it must be reformed theologically and practically in order to make clear its subordination to the primacy of the gospel. 5. Even if this were to happen, however, Lutherans do not agree that the papacy is the necessary institutionalization of the Petrine function" ("Papacy and *Ius divinum*", LCD V, 195–96).

and continues to exist even within divided Christianity, as long as there is faith in the one Lord". This unity is a given fact, founded upon Christ, "that has to be preserved and renewed". This alone validates the purpose of that service of unity which is entrusted to those who have the office of Church leadership. "That such a service is necessary surely implies that we cannot simply take for granted the existence and continuation of the church's unity, even though it is grounded in Jesus Christ and on this basis constantly renewed also in the church's life."[340]

The three main questions which Lutheranism has raised and continues to pose with regard to the primacy are as follows: Is it of divine right, in other words, founded by Christ (Petrinitas)? Was the power received from Christ by Peter transmitted to his successors (Perpetuitas)? In the event that a successor of Peter exists, does he possess the primacy of jurisdiction over the entire Church, in such a way as to safeguard the character of the episcopate and Christian liberty?[341]

Petrinitas

All contemporary exegetes and historians regard the question of whether Jesus constituted Peter as the first Pope as an anachronism, because it reflects a later model of the papacy. Instead, the question has to be asked whether the successive application of the Petrine typology found in the New Testament to the papacy actually conforms to the New Testament.[342] The New Testament texts merely provide a series of images

---

[340] Pannenberg, *Systematic Theology*, 405.

[341] Cf. Klausnitzer, *Das Papstamt im Disput*, 462; Beinert, "Endechrist oder Zeichen der Barmherzigkeit. Die Möglichkeit einer ekkleiologischen Konvergenz zwischen Lutheranern und Katholiken über das Papsttum", *Catholica* 50 (1996): 123 and 126ff.; Kühn, "Papsttum und Petrusdienst", 185; Böttigheimer, "Von der ökumenischen Relevanz des Papsttums", 332.

[342] W. Kasper, "Das Petrusamt als Dienst der Einheit. Die Lehre des I. und II. Vatikanischen Konzils und die gegenwärtige Diskussion", *Das Papstamt. Dienst oder Hindernis für die Ökumene* (Regensburg, 1985), 130: "Mit Recht wird gesagt, wir könnten heute nicht fragen, ob Jesus den Primat, so wie wir ihn heute verstehen, eingesetzt hat, sondern nur, ob und inwieweit der spätere Gebrauch der neutestamentlichen Petrustypologie in bezug auf das Papsttum übereinstimmt mit der Zielrichtung des Neuen Testaments." Cf. Beinert, "Endechrist", 127: "*Kennt die Bibel ein Petrusamt?* Die Exegese neigt zu einer bejanden Antwort." Cf. Kühn, "Papsttum und Petrusdienst", 187–88.

from which the exceptional importance attributed to Peter emerges, but these passages exclude the concepts of monarchy, *primacy*, and *jurisdiction*.[343] At the same time, they provide useful material for the Catholic-Lutheran dialogue on the Petrine office.[344]

Setting aside the historical debates of the past on the interpretation of these classical texts for the primacy, especially Matthew 16,[345] the research conducted during the dialogue, while relativizing these texts, has been chiefly concerned with tracing the general outlines of the New Testament portrait of Peter. The process has resulted in not one image of Peter but in diverse and sometimes conflicting *images* of Peter. Nonetheless, some important findings have also emerged concerning the preeminent role of Peter, both during the public life and after the death of Jesus. Although the primacy is not directly based on these, Peter's special role in the early Church emerges from the ensemble of these texts, as well as the Church's particular interest in him.[346] It is evident, above all, that this

---

[343] Pannenberg, *Systematic Theology*, 455: "It is true that the prominent role of the apostle Peter in the most varied of primitive Christian writings is a unique phenomenon that has no parallel among the apostles. Peter seems above all to be a paradigmatic figure in virtue of his being a first witness of the resurrection of Jesus, of his faith, of his model confession, and also of his role as the first among the twelve." Cf. Klausnitzer, *Das Papstamt im Disput*, 463, who reprints various passages from the common declaration, *Papal Primacy and Universal Church* of the Catholic-Lutheran Commission in the U.S.A.; Kühn, "Gesamtkirchlicher Petrusdienst?", 34; Kühn, "Papsttum und Petrusdienst", 188; Beinert, "Endechrist", 128.

[344] Klausnitzer, *Das Papstamt im Disput*, 465: "im Neuen Testament Material bereit liegt, das für das Begründung der petrinischen Funktion im Papst verwendet werden kann: eine für das katholisch-lutherische Gespräch sehr bemerkenswerte Einsicht."

[345] Cf. ibid., 493–97; G. Granberg, "Prospettiva luterana sul Vescovo di Roma", *Il Vescovo di Roma nella Chiesa universale. Breve Corso di ecumenismo* (Rome, 1987), 8:96–98; R. Pesch, "Was an Petrus sichtbar war, ist in den Primat eingegangen", *Il primato del successore di Pietro. Atti del Simposio teologico* (Rome, December 1966; Libreria Editrice Vaticana, 1998), 28ff. For an overview of the various positions in this regard, cf. H. Knoche, "Der Petrusdienst für die Einheit der Kirche. Biblische Grundlagen und heutiger Stand der ökumenischen Diskussion", *Bausteine für die Einheit der Kirche* 144 (1996): 10ff.

[346] Klausnitzer, *Das Papstamt im Disput*, 497–98: "So bemüht sich die den ökumenischen Dialog zwischen Katholiken und Lutheranern begleitende Forschung, ein Gesamtbild des Petrus im Neuen Testament zu erstellen.... In anderen Worten: Mit dem Neuen Testament kann man das Papsttum nicht unmittelbar begründen. Aber die Gruppe der Petrustexte und -bilder verweist auf eine besondere Rolle des Apostels Petrus in der Urkirche und auf ein besonderes Interesse der Urkirche an dieser Figur." Pesch, "Was an Petrus sichtbar war", 38: "Ein Durchgang durch die vier Evangelien, der ihren geschichtlichen Standort und ihre unterschiedlichen Sehweisen so weit wie möglich und notwendig berücksichtigt, rückt uns ein genügend deutliches Bild vom Träger, der Vollmacht und den

role proceeds from the fact that he is the representative and head of the college of the apostles. Indeed, this role is so overwhelmingly attested to in the Bible that in the final analysis it cannot be contested.[347] Hence, the Protestant view represents an intermediate between the two classical positions (divine right/human right) by distinguishing between Petrine function and papacy.[348]

If these points, which are mainly the expression of the American dialogue, were to be accepted, the arguments of the past would be profoundly changed, yet it is necessary to take living tradition as a means of interpreting Scripture.[349]

Perpetuitas

In the course of history, especially during the Counter Reformation period, the argument for the succession of the Bishop of Rome in the primacy was based, first, on the proposition that God necessarily ensured that his people would have a guide after the death of Peter, and secondly, on the historical fact of Peter's death. Yet neither Catholics nor Protestants consider this fact as sufficient to establish a Roman succession. The fundamental question, therefore, remains of whether Peter was Bishop of Rome and whether his successor as Bishop in that See also succeeded in the primacy.[350] This same question implies others in turn: the sojourn and

---

Anforderungen des Primats von Augen." Cf. Pannenberg, "Evangelische Überlegungen zum Petrusdienst des römischen Bischofs", *Papstamt und Ökumene. Zum Petrusdienst an der Einheit aller Getauften* (Regensburg, 1997), 53–55.

[347] Knoche, "Der Petrusdienst für die Einheit der Kirche", 14: "Dieser Vorrang des Petrus als Haupt des Apostelkreises ist so massiv biblisch begründet, daß er letzten Endes nicht mehr bestritten werden kann."

[348] Klausnitzer, *Das Papstamt im Disput*, 472: "Die Reformatoren ... gehen einen dritten Weg zwischen der katholischen Position, das Papsttum sei 'iure divino', und der Auskunft der Reformatoren, es sei 'iure humano'.... Die von Petrus ausgeübte petrinische Funktion wird aber nicht auf eine Stiftung Christi in einem ausschließlichen Sinn zurückgeführt. Sie ist keine exklusive Prärogative des Petrus allein. Die Schrift decke, ja fordere geradezu eine petrinische Funktion, aber nicht einen Primat, der auf Petrus beschränkt sei und auf ein Wort Jesu zurückgehe."

[349] Ibid., 498: "Sollten diese Punkte und die Grundthese im katholisch-lutherischen Gespräch weithin rezipiert werden können, würde dies die jeweiligen Argumentationsstrukturen erheblich verändern. Im Grunde ist dies jedoch ... die Position der lebendigen Tradition als Interpret der Schrift."

[350] Ibid., 499–500: "Der Tod Petri sei heilsgeschichtlich qualifiziert (Quo-vadis-Legende). Diese Qualifikation ist aber genau das Problem. Der simple Tod Petri (nuda

martyrdom of Peter in Rome, the authenticity of the lists of Popes maintained by the early Church, the distinction between the Roman episcopate and the primacy, and the juridical title of such a bond [with Peter]. While tradition replies affirmatively to the first question, different opinions concerning the other questions can be found even within Catholic theology.[351] The First Vatican Council, too, while tracing *petrinitas* and *perpetuitas* directly to Christ, left the question of *romanitas* open.[352]

The question was broached by the Catholic-Lutheran dialogue in the United States, where the Protestant parties, referring to the initial period of the Reformation, did not accept that the "Petrine function" was always and everywhere invested in the Bishop of Rome. As A. Gonzáles Montes notes, "even if the Protestant Churches recognize the expediency of 'a supreme directional ministry in the Church', they continue to maintain a Reformation theological position which cannot recognize the primacy of the Bishop of Rome as an arrangement divinely founded upon the Lord's mandate to Peter".[353] Exegesis does not support the view that the particular

---

mors) begründet nach Auskunft der katholischen wie der lutherischen Theologen noch keine römische Sukzession. Aber die entscheidende Frage lautet ... : War Petrus *Bischof von Rom*, und ist mit seinem Tod eine Sukzessionsreihe des römischen Bischofs im Primat begründet worden?"

[351] A. Vanhoye, "Reazione al testo di Rudolph Pesch", *Il primato del successore di Pietro*, 114: "Que la succession de la primauté de Pierre soit attribuée à l'évêque de Rome, parce que Pierre a subi le martyre en cette ville, c'est là une donnée pour laquelle, me semble-t-il, le Nouveau Testament n'apporte aucune indication, ni pour, ni contre. Sur ce point comme sur beaucoup d'autres, c'est à la Tradition de l'Église qu'on doit se fier." Beinert, "Endechrist", 128: "Höchstwarscheinlich war der historische Petrus in Rom; vermutlich hat er die dortige Gemeinde begründet; gute Gründe sprechen für Martyrium und Begräbnis in der Tiberstadt. Nichts ist bekannt über sein Selbverständnis und etwaige Regelungen über eine Nachfolge. Seher wohl aber wissen wir gegenwärtig, daß es in den ersten Jahrhunderten noch kein Papsttum im späteren Sinne gegeben hat. Alles spricht sogar dafür, daß im Gegensatz zu den kleinasiatischen Gemeinden die römische im 2. Jahrhundert nicht einmal einen Monepiskopen gehabt hat.... Entscheidend bleibt nach wie vor die Frage ... ob also auch im zweiten seinerzeit genannten Sinn eine *Perpetuitas* des Petrusamtes im historisch existierenden Papsttum existiert."

[352] Klausnitzer, *Das Papstamt im Disput*, 500: "Die Petrinitas (DS 3055) und die Perpetuitas (DS 3058) werden vom Vatikanum I unmittelbar auf Christus zurückgeführt und als Ius divinum betrachtet. Zum Rechtstitel der Romanitas macht das Konzil keine Aussage (DS 3058). Wie aus den Diskussionen auf dem Konzil deutlich wird, will der Text von 'Pastor aeternus' die Frage offenhalten."

[353] "Il tema nel dialogo della Chiesa cattolica con le confessioni protestanti", Rodríguez, *L'ecclesiologia a trent'anni dopo la "Lumen Gentium"*, 248–49. According to Pannenberg, the issue that is still to be addressed, "always connected to the claims of the Roman Papacy

role of Peter implies a successor invested with a permanent office in Christianity.[354] Indeed, among Catholic exegetes themselves it is generally agreed that "these NT sayings about Peter, no matter how else we might assess them, refer only to Peter, not to any successors in office". Not even the Roman Pontiffs, in justifying their privileged position in the Church, cited "the Petrine sayings of the New Testament". Instead, they used as leverage "the altogether singular importance which the [Christian] community of Rome came to assume in the capital of the empire", a relevance which was accentuated even more by the fact that the two most important apostles had been martyred precisely in this city. Therefore the development of the Roman primacy is really not based on "the historical figure of Peter", even if "this does not mean that the Roman bishops could not find in the depiction of Peter in the NT a model for the function in the Church that they were claiming". Consequently, viewing things through the eyes of the Reformation, "the authority of such an office, and of those who hold it, can be only of human law [of human right] because we cannot trace it back to any express institution by Jesus Christ."[355] The symbolic function of Peter for the unity of the Church which emerges from the New Testament is not restricted to the Bishop of Rome: it can be extended to any bishop.[356] Moreover, in the Lutheran concept of the Petrine succession on the part of the Bishop of Rome, the determining factor is the value that they attribute to apostolic succession, which is considered to be constitutive and necessary for the Church, which the

---

over the entire Church, derives from the statement that the primacy of the Bishop of Rome rests on a divine right—that is, on the fact that the Apostle Peter was invested by Jesus Christ himself according to Mt 16:16–18 and John 21:15–17 as the visible head of the Church (DS 3055, 3068)" (*Systematic Theology*, 429).

[354] Pannenberg, "Das Papsttum und die Zukunft der Ökumene. Anmerkungen aus lutheranischer Sicht", *Das Papstamt: Dienst oder Hindernis für die Ökumene*, 141–42: "Zur Frage einer speziellen Beauftragung des Apostels Petrus durch Jesus Christus selbst ist die heutige Exegese nicht über die Feststellung hinausgekommen, daß Mt 16,18 und Joh 21,15ff. zwar auf einen persönlichen Vorrang des Petrus in den Anfängen der Jerusalemer Gemeinde hinweisen, nicht aber die Einsetzung eines auf Nachfolger zu übertragenden, bleibenden Amtes in der Christenheit berichten." Cf. Pannenberg, "Die lutherische Tradition", 473–74.

[355] Pannenberg, *Systematic Theology*, 429–30. Cf. Pannenberg, "Evangelische Überlegungen", 45, 52–53; idem, "Das Papsttum und die Zukunft der Ökumene", 141–43; Neuner, *Ökumenische Theologie*, 242–43.

[356] Pannenberg, "Evangelische Überlegungen", 54: "[D]ie Symbolfunktion des Apostels Petrus für die Einheit der Kirche, wie sie im Neuen Testament zum Ausdruckt kommt, ist auch nicht beschränkt auf den Bischof von Rom. Jeder christliche Bischof kann die Gestalt des Petrus als vorbildlich für seinen eigenen Auftrag erkennen."

Lutherans identify, however, with continuity in the word, that is to say, in doctrine.[357] The conclusion to be drawn, therefore, is that there is neither convergence nor consensus on the question of the institution of a primacy by the historical Jesus and on the form in which that function was handed down to the Bishop of Rome, and that agreement with regard to the First Vatican Council's formulations on the subject is not necessary.[358] In view of the early Church's interest in Peter following his death and taking into consideration all the constituent elements of the so-called Petrine tradition, the possibility of a biblical basis for Petrine succession in the person of the Bishops of Rome cannot be excluded.[359] The silence of the New Testament is complemented by the general description of the primacy found therein, from which the necessity of a succession emerges.[360] The various testimonies concerning a *handing on* of pastoral functions during the lifetime of the apostles imply a transition to a *succession* following their deaths. Although there is no explicit statement about a transmission of pastoral functions over the entire Church, this still has a foundation in the literary genre and the purpose of the Gospel accounts, which are not simply historical recollections of the past but rather founding texts which authenticate the basis of the Church's life and her apostolic

---

[357] Cf. Gómez-Iglesias, "Il ministero petrino", 647.

[358] Beinert, "Endechrist", 140: "So gehört nicht zur Konvergenz- bzw. Konsensmaterie die Frage einer Stiftung des Primats durch den historischen Jesus und der Form und Geschichte der Weitergabe seiner Funktion an den römischen Bischof.... Keine Übereinstimmung ist somit auch erforderlich mit jenen Formulierungen des Ersten Vatikanischen Konzils."

[359] Klausnitzer, *Das Papstamt im Disput*, 495: "Auffallend ist allerdings, daß im Neuen Testament ein 'eigenartiges Erwachen des Interesses an Gestalt und Amt des Petrus *nach seinem Tod*' nachgewiesen werden kann. 'Petrus' ist mit Petrus nicht gestorben.... Im amerikanischen Gespräch zwischen Katholiken und Lutheranern fiel in diesem Zusammenhang das Stichwort der 'petrinischen Funktion'. Zwar ist damit noch keineswegs eine exklusive petrinische Sukzession der Bischöfe von Rom begründet ... aber die Möglichkeit einer biblischen Begründung eines bestimmten Aspektes des Petrusamtes oder Petrusdienstes eröffnet."

[360] Pesch, "Was an Petrus sichtbar war", 66: "Da das Neue Testament über einen Nachfolger Petri schweigt, kann die Notwendigkeit der Weitergabe des Primats nur aus der Gesamt-Beschreibung des Petrusdienstes, aus dem kirchlichen Autorenwillen, aus dem Richtungssinn des Endtextes gefolgert werden." Kühn, "Papsttum und Petrusdienst", 189: "die Frage eines Nachfolgers des Petrus, die bis hin zu Oscar Cullmanns Petrusbuche immer wieder verneint wurde, ist durch die traditionsgeschichtliche Aufhellung des neutestamentlichen Befundes und die Endeckung des Petrus-'Bildes' der frühen Christenheit sozusagen gegenstandslos geworden. Das Neue Testament kennt in der Gestalt des Petrus so etwas wie einen für die Gesamtkirche wichtigen 'Petrusdienst'."

structure. The importance ascribed to Peter's role leads to the conclusion that such a role is essential to the Church's life and must therefore continue in the Church.[361] The need for continuing this apostolic service, already present in the New Testament, was evident to the postapostolic period; it entailed not only a spiritual continuity in the sense of a "successio fidei" but also an awareness of a historical succession conferred by the imposition of hands. Just as different episcopal sees traced their succession from specific apostles, so too the episcopal See of Rome traced its succession from the Apostle Peter.[362]

It would be auspicious if the Lutherans, too, would recognize that Christ has connected his action, as the foundation of the Church, not only to the apostles as a whole, but also to Peter, the visible head of the apostles and pastor of the universal Church.[363] They, on the other hand, still regard the *ius divinum* character of the primacy of the Bishop of Rome as unacceptable, precisely because it does not have a biblical foundation and hence cannot be regarded as having been instituted by Christ, contrary to what is taught by the First Vatican Council. The special position accorded to Peter ceased with his death; therefore, in their view, there is no evidence in the Bible and in the foundational period of the Church which could prove the continuity of his primacy in the Bishop of Rome by divine right. It would follow that the primacy itself is not necessary for man's salvation and is not essential to the Church, which is ordered to that

---

[361] Vanhoye, "Reazione al testo di Rudolph Pesch", 114: "Du Nouveau Testament lui-même, on peut néanmoins déduire des arguments ... mais on y trouve plusieurs attestations d'une *transmission* de fonctions pastorales faite du vivant des apôtres.... Les récits évangéliques, en effet, ne sont pas de simples récits historiques, écrits pour rappeler des événements passés: ils sont aussi et surtout des textes fondateurs, écrits pour assurer les bases de la vie de l'Église.... Si donc ils attribuent tant d'importance au rôle de Simon-Pierre, il faut en conclure que ce rôle est essentiel pour la vie de l'Église et doit donc y rester présent de façon perceptible."

[362] Knoche, "Der Petrusdienst für die Einheit der Kirche", 15: "Die schon vom Neuen Testament und vom ganzen Sinn und Zweck der Aposteleinsetzung her notwendige Fortdauer der apostolischen Dienstämter war in der nachapostolischen Zeit von vornherein selbstverständlich. Es ging eigentlich niemals nur um eine rein spirituelle Kontinuität im Sinne einer successio fidei, sondern immer auch zugleich um das Bewußtsein einer historischen Nachfolge, die durch Handauflegung vermittelt wurde. In diesem Verständnishorizont beriefen sich wie selbstverständlich auch verschiedene Bischoffsitze auf die Nachfolge bestimmter Apostel, so der Bischofssitz in Rom auf die Nachfolge des Apostels Petrus."

[363] Cf. ibid., 17–18.

salvation.[364] Notwithstanding the progress that has been made by the dialogue, the primacy continues to be regarded as merely possible—given the requisite renewal—but not as a necessary constitutive element of the Church.[365] For the sole purpose of fostering the dialogue, it could be considered as "functionally" necessary, in the sense that such a formulation would satisfy the doctrinal demands of both traditions.[366] In any case, the authority for such a ministry and for its holder can only be one of human right, precisely because it cannot be traced to an explicit institution by Christ himself.[367]

All this notwithstanding, it is still claimed that the Catholic and Protestant positions on *ius divinum* are not irreconcilable in the present circumstances.[368] Even though it is recognized that in the dialogue the description of the fact of papal ministry in terms of "divine right/human right" still remains a fundamental problem, it is thought that the two terms should no longer be used, inasmuch as the element of "divine law" cannot be identified with a direct institution by Christ, and hence the two terms cannot be considered antithetical; indeed, they were not antithetical even for Luther. The two concepts need to be differentiated and reformulated, since they are, in reality, complementary: just as divine right

---

[364] Meyer, "Ein evangeliumsgemäßes Papstamt. Kritik und Forderung aus reformatorischer Sicht", *Das Papstamt: Dienst oder Hindernis für die Ökumene?*, 82–83: "Für eine 'Fortdauer des Primats des heiligen Petrus in den römischen Päpsten' kraft einer Einsetzung Christi und damit für ein in diesem Sinne verstandenes 'göttliches Recht' ... gebe es keine biblische und damit keine aus der apostolischen, kirchenkonstitutiven Epoche herkommende Begründung. Wenn aber eine in Ursprung und Wesen des Christlichen gegebene Begründung des Primats des römischen Bischofs fehle, dann sei der Primat auch nicht zum Heil der Menschen und für das Wesen der diesem Heil zugeordneten Kirche 'notwendig'."

[365] Kasper ("Das Petrusamt als Dienst der Einheit", 129), referring to the Malta Report and to the USA document, states, "Die weitgehende ökumenische Übereinstimmung in der Auslegung der neutestamentlichen Petrusaussagen bedeutet nämlich keineswegs einen Konsens über die biblische Begründung eines irgendwie gearteten fortdauernden Petrusamtes.... In allen Dialogergebnissen betonen die Lutheraner lediglich die Möglichkeit eines praktisch und theologisch erneuerten Petrusamts, während die katholische Seite ein solches Amt als für die Kirche konstitutiv und notwendig anerkennt." Cf. Klausnitzer, *Das Papstamt im Disput*, 473.

[366] Cf. Granderg, "Prospettiva luterana sul Vescovo di Roma", 97.

[367] Cf. Pannenberg, *Systematic Theology*, 429–30.

[368] Lindbeck, "Papacy and *Ius divinum*", LCD V, 195: "[W]e have a situation in which the Reformation denial and the contemporary Catholic affirmation of the *ius divinum* are not irreconcilable."

is always intermingled with human elements, so too human right is always connected with divine impulses and with hearing the word of God.[369] As a result, Catholics would find it difficult to classify all the elements of the ecclesiastical order, including the papal primacy, as irrevocably necessary. For Catholics the Petrine function is part of the Church's fundamental structure. But is it irrevocably necessary that the holder of such an office be the Bishop of Rome? Or that it always be a single person and not a troika instead? In other words, the Catholic side could concede that, while the Petrine function is necessary, it might only be contingently associated with the Bishop of Rome. The Lutheran side, in contrast, while confessionally obliged to deny the Petrine function, could now admit its importance and regard it as contingently necessary.[370] This would not involve a submission to the papacy on their part, but only the obligation to do all in their power to reform the papacy.[371]

---

[369] Lehmann, "Grundlinien und Probleme des ökumenischen Petrusdienstes", *Das Petrusamt*, 141–42: "Wir haben immer wieder gesehen, daß in den Gesprächsergebnissen eine Grunddifferenz bestehen bleibt, nämlich die verschiedene theologische Qualifikation des Faktums des päpstlichen Amtes.... Man hat öfter darauf hingewiesen, dass 'ius divinum' / 'ius humanum' auch nach Auffassung der lutherischen Reformation keine ausschließlichen Antithesen sind.... Wir sehen jedoch heute die Notwendigkeit einer Differenzierung, die jedes einfache Handhaben der überkommenen Kategorie fragwürdig macht. Es gibt kein chemisch reines 'göttliches Recht', dieses wird vielmehr immer schon in menschlichen Gestaltungen entfaltet. Und 'menschliches Recht' ist in der Kirche nicht ohne jeden Zusammenhang mit göttlichen Impulsen und mit einem Hören auf das Wort Gottes, wie es durch die Zeiten im Geist geschieht." Cf. Kasper, "Das Petrusamt als Dienst der Einheit", 129–30.

[370] Lindbeck, "Papacy and *Ius Divinum*", LCD V, 200–201: "The Catholic authors of this Report [Malta] would find it difficult or impossible to identify any concretely specifiable aspect of church order, including the papacy and its primacy, as unchangably or irreversibly necessary.... But is it irreversibly necessary that the occupant of this central office be the bishop of Rome? Or that it always be a single individual rather than, e.g., a troika? Or that the office resemble the historic papacy rather than an ecumenical patriarchate or executive secretaryship? ... Some of these [Catholics] would grant that, while necessary, it is only contingently necessary to associate the Petrine function and office with the Roman pontiff.... Lutherans admit the importance of the Petrine function ..., and there is nothing to prevent them from thinking that now, and perhaps in the foreseeable future, it is contingently necessary for the papacy to exercise this function if it is to be carried out effectively for the church as a whole."

[371] Ibid., 201–2: "Lutherans ... are conscience bound not to 'submit' to the papacy until it has been so thoroughly renewed that the language of submission is totally inappropriate. In the meantime, however, granting the papal primacy is contingently necessary, they are obligated to do everything possible to contribute to that renewal, not, obviously, by destructive or purely condemnatory criticism, but by working together with Catholics

From a much more realistic perspective, it seems necessary to recognize that the question of the divine right of the papacy continues to be a cause of division between the Churches, specifically because, both in the dialogue and in contemporary theology, the concept itself has still not been clarified.[372] It seems that the only point of agreement in this matter is the need to frame the issue in a new way, abandoning the rigid positions of the past (which continue to be operative) and without isolating the problem from the overall context of the mystery of the Church.[373]

Primacy over the universal Church?

Apart from the difficulties relating to *petrinitas* and *perpetuitas*, Lutherans also ask whether there "is needed also at the *universal* level of the Church as a whole ministry to the unity of Christians" which is to be rendered "by the ministry of an individual who can be active as a spokesman for Christianity as a whole"? Faced with the Catholic Church's conviction "that it has such a ministry in the office of the Bishop of Rome", the Lutherans, too, in the documents produced by the dialogue, accept "in principle a ministry to the unity of the Church on the universal level"

---

to the extent that this is possible, and by seeking to change their own structures in order to facilitate reunion."

[372] Klausnitzer, *Das Papstamt im Disput*, 501–2: "Kirchentrennend bleibt die Aussage, das Papsttum sei eine Institution 'iuris divini'. Angesichts dieses Faktums ist es doch erstaunlich, daß bei genauerer Beobachtung der Begriff 'ius divinum' inter- *und* intrakonfessionell in seiner Bedeutung und in seinem Umfang keineswegs eindeutig geklärt ist.... Für die überwiegende Mehrheit der traditionellen katholischen Theologen, aber auch für Luther und die meisten protestantischen Theologen, sofern diese den Ausdruck Ius divinum überhaupt verwenden ... bedeutet Ius divinum 'Stiftung durch Christus' ... Die Aussage in den lutherischen Bekenntnisschriften, das Papsttum sei 'iure humano' ... , kann in diesem Zusammenhang nur den Sinn haben, es sei aufgrund geschichtlicher und sozio-kultureller Faktoren entstanden (und deswegen veränderlich) und könne jedenfalls nicht auf den Stiftungswillen Christi zurückgeführt werden.... Obwohl immer noch gefordert ist, daß auf ein Schriftwort hingewiesen werden kann, bevor eine kirchliche Institution dem Bereich des Ius divinum zugerechnet werden darf, genügt es dann, daß das Neue Testament Spuren und Hinweise in Richtung auf die künftige Entwicklung enthält.... Diese Deutung wird gerade im katholisch-lutherischen Gespräch fruchtbar, da sie die (katholische und lutherische) Fixierung auf die unmittelbare Stiftung des Papstamtes durch Jesus überwindet und die Geschichte als Interpretament neutestamentlicher Ansätze (die Intention des katolischen Traditionsbegriffs!) einführt." Cf. Piepkorn, "Ius Divinum *and* Adiaphoron", LCD V, 121; Neumann, "Das Papstamt in den offiziellen ökumenischen Dialogen", 92–94.

[373] Cf. Antón, " 'Ministero petrino' en el diálogo con las otras Iglesias cristianas", 405–6.

and that "there need not be ruled out the possibility that the Petrine office of the bishop of Rome might be a visible sign of the unity of the whole Church to the degree that by a theological reinterpretation and practical restructuring the office is subordinated to the primacy of the Gospel".[374] Not only is a universal primacy not excluded, it is regarded as vital, especially for the unity of the Church and of mankind, as well as for the *libertas Ecclesiae* in today's world.[375]

There remains, however, a fundamental difference between the Catholic and Protestant views of the primacy: the essential nature of the primacy maintained by the Catholic partners is countered by a simple possibility. Hence, despite a certain convergence which has been reached, one cannot speak of a fundamental agreement.[376] Therefore the very nature of the primacy is at stake. While acceptance of the need/possibility of a *coordinator* or of a *spokesman*, or of a *reference point*, undoubtedly represents a certain rapprochement, the primacy cannot be considered solely from a functional perspective, and reform cannot be taken to mean the creation of something absolutely novel.[377]

Research on the nature of the primacy, both in the dialogue and in theology, concentrates especially on interpreting the definitions of the

---

[374] Pannenberg, *Systematic Theology*, 420–21. Cf. idem, "Das Papsttum und die Zukunft der Ökumene", 140. Cf. above, p. 131, note 181.

[375] Neuner, *Ökumenische Theologie*, 241: "In der Situation einer kleiner werdenden Welt, einer Infragestellung des Christlichen und der Hinordnung der Einheit der Kirche auf die Einheit der Menschheit erscheint ein Amt universaler Einheit nicht nur als möglich, sondern sogar als dringend wünschenswert." Cf. Pannenberg, "Evangelische Überlegungen", 43.

[376] Lehmann, "Grundlinien", 134–35: "Freilich wird durch diese Situation ein wesentlicher Unterschied markiert: Die katholischen Gesprächspartner müssen voraussetzen, daß das Petrusamt nach dem Willen Jesu Christi eine *unerläßliche Notwendigkeit* für die Einheit von Kirchen darstellt. Evangelische Theologen können jedoch nur von der oder gar vor einer *Möglichkeit* sprechen, daß das Papstamt unter gewissen Bedingungen als Amt der Einheit der Christenheit anerkannt werden *kann*. . . . Die erwähnte Grunddifferenz bewirkt auch, daß man bei den bisherigen Gesprächen trotz beachtlicher Konvergenzen im ganzen noch zu keinem fundamentalen Konsens gelangen konnte." In proof of this several sections of the Malta Report and of the 1974 USA document are quoted.

[377] Ibid., 143: "Es geht nicht nur um eine Frage der Kirchenorganisation. Die Formulierungen von einem 'Koordinator', 'Sprecher', von einem 'Dialogzentrum', von einem 'Mittelpunkt für Initiativen' usw. sind Worte der Annäherung. Es kann im Dialog ja nicht nur darum gehen, daß man mit einem vorhandenen, 'fertigen' Amt in irgendeiner Form das Einheitsproblem löst. . . . Wir Katholiken sind uns der Notwendigkeit und der Schwierigkeiten einer Erneuerung des päpstlichen Dienstprimates für ein Amt der ganzen Christenheit bewußt. Aber es hat für uns auch wenig Sinn, über einen solchen Einheitsdienst so zu sprechen, als ob etwas vollkommen Neues geschaffen werden müßte."

First Vatican Council in the light of the Second Vatican Council.[378] The first Council is said to have marked the completion of the transition from the ecclesiology of communion known to the early Church to the ecclesiology of unity under the primacy of the Pope, a transition that began with Pope Gregory VII and extended through the Middle Ages, guided by a determination to counteract the errors of the times.[379] It should be kept in mind, however, that even though this development was conditioned by historical, sociological, and psychological circumstances, it was pursued with an awareness that it was based on the testimony of Scripture and tradition. In this context and with this awareness, the Council defined the dogma of the Pope's primacy of jurisdiction over the universal Church, understood not as a competence of mere supervision but as one of full and supreme power. That same Council, however, did not intend to define that the Pope's power was unlimited, as is demonstrated by the fact that it was unable to deal with the second schema on the Church, and confirmed the joint Declaration of the German Bishops published in 1872 and approved by Pius IX.[380]

---

[378] Kasper, "Das Petrusamt als Dienst der Einheit. Die Lehre des I. und II. Vatikanischen Konzils und die gegenwärtige Diskussion", *Das Papstamt*, 131–32: "Umgekehrt müssen wir aber auch alle geschichtlichen Ausformungen des Petrusdienstes, also auch die Papstdogmen des I. Vatikanischen Konzils vom Ursprungszeugnis der Schrift her einer kritischen *lecture* unterziehen. Dieses Prinzip wahrt einerseits die Kontinuität mit der Tradition, andererseits erlaubt es aber doch, die Tradition vom Ursprung her zu erneuern und auf neue Zukunft hin zu öffnen." It is also necessary "daß wir die Geschichte des Papsttums und speziell die beiden Papstdogmen des I. Vatikanischen Konzils auch im Licht der Erfahrungen tiefer verstehen müssen, die nichtkatholische Kirchen mit diesem Papsttum gemacht haben. Wir müssen also ernst nehmen, was die anderen Kirchen und kirchlichen Gemeinschaften vom Papsttum, so wie es bisher geschichtlich konkret verwirklicht war, abhält, und wir müssen die positiven Anliegen, die hinter solcher Kritik stehen, konstruktiv in die *relecture* unserer katholischen Tradition einbeziehen."

[379] Ibid., 115–17: "Die Entwicklung zum I. Vatikanischen Konzil hat wesentlich zu tun mit dem Übergang von der altkirchlichen communio-Ekklesiologie zu einer Einheits-Ekklesiologie unter dem Primat des Papstes.... Das Paradoxe an dieser Entwicklung war freilich, daß die Kirche im Kampf gegen den Staatsabsolutismus selbst absolutistische Formen annahm.... Damit ist der Hintergrund der Papstdogmen des I. Vatikanischen Konzils (1869/70) deutlich. Papst Pius IX. berief das Konzil ein mit der erklärten Absicht, es solle gegenüber den modernen Irrtümern dasselbe leisten, was das Trienter Konzil gegenüber den Irrtümern des 16. Jahrhunderts geleistet hat." Cf. W. Henn, "Historical-theological synthesis of the relation between primacy and episcopacy during the second millennium", *Il primato del successore di Pietro*, 251–61; H.-J. Pottmeyer, *Towards a Papacy in Communion. Perspectives from Vatican Councils I & II* (New York, 1998), 70–75.

[380] Cf. Kasper, "Das Petrusamt als Dienst der Einheit", 118–21; Lehmann, "Grundlinien", 144–45.

What Vatican I did not manage to bring to completion was developed by Vatican II with the doctrine of collegiality. In a climate which was marked, in contrast, by dialogue and openness to the world, the Second Vatican Council, while reaffirming the definitions of the first Vatican Council, integrated or balanced them in an ecclesial context characterized by a sacramental vision of the Church and the episcopacy.[381] Like the Church, the Petrine office, too, is referred to Christ and understood as a service in the Church and for the Church. Thus the Council returned to the original ecclesiology, emphasizing that the one Church has the character of a communion, constituted *in et ex ecclesiis particularibus*, and that her government has a collegial character.[382] In this manner, a new perspective was found from which to interpret the primacy, considered now in its essentially pastoral dimension.[383] The Council, however, left open the question of the single or double subject of the supreme power in the Church, and consequently the doctrine of collegiality has not yet been entirely clarified, nor has it been put into practice fully.[384]

In the light of this view of communion, some look forward to a self-limitation of the primacy of jurisdiction—based on the principles of conciliarity, synodality, susbsidarity, and diversity in unity, and exploring further the questions left open by the two Vatican Councils—which could open

---

[381] A. Carrasco Rouco, "Der päpstliche Primat und das Zweite Vatikanum", *Internationale katholische Zeitschrift Communio* 27 (1998): 312: "Die wichtigste Neuerung besteht vielmehr darin, daß die gesamte Lehre über das Bischofsamt und den Primat in einen neuen ekklesiologischen Kontext gestellt wurde, der in dieser Hinsicht durch eine von Grund auf sakramentale Auffassung von Bischof und Kirche selbst charakterisiert ist." Cf. G. Langevin, "Synthèse de la tradition doctrinale sur la primauté du successeur de Pierre durant le second millénaire", *Il primato del successore di Pietro*, 167; Henn, "Historical-theological synthesis", 223 and 262–73.

[382] Kasper, "Das Petrusamt als Dienst der Einheit", 124–26: "Vor allem wurde die Kirche insgesamt und alle ihre Ämter, das Petrusamt eingeschlossen, integriert in das, was Grund und Mitte des christlichen Glaubens ist: Sie wurden explizit von Jesus Christus her betrachtet.... Auch das Petrusamt steht nicht freischwebend über der Kirche, es ist im Dienst in der Kirche und für die Kirche.... So lehrte es in der Tradition der alten Kirche, daß die eine Kirche 'in und aus' Ortskirchen besteht und insofern eine communio von Ortskirchen ist, die unter der Leitung des jeweiligen Bischofs steht.... Das bedeutet: Nicht nur der Papst, sondern die gesamte Körperschaft der Bischöfe 'ist gemeinsam mit ihrem Haupt, dem Bischof von Rom, und niemals ohne dieses Haupt gleichfalls Träger der höchsten und vollen Gewalt über die ganze Kirche'."

[383] Cf. Böttigheimer, "Von der ökumenischen Relevanz des Papsttums", 337–38; Beinert, "Endechrist", 137.

[384] Cf. Kasper, "Das Petrusamt als Dienst der Einheit", 127–28.

the way to a consensus in the field of ecumenism, inasmuch as it might allay the fears of the non-Catholic Churches vis-à-vis an absolutist and juridical papacy, i.e., one that is not in keeping with the Gospel.[385] The parties acknowledge the need to refer to the center of unity of the episcopal college, but in the context of an ecclesiology of communion, not of jurisdiction. The result is a vision of the Church in terms of "structured collegiality", which would exclude every sort of "monarchical" regime but also any unspecified collegiality that is not intrinsically related to the Petrine primacy.[386] The definitions of Vatican I would retain their validity, but the non-Catholics would not be obliged to accept them explicitly in their present formulation, but rather in a spirit of *koinonia* and respect for the traditions proper to the particular Churches, the sole concern being to keep them united in faith and *koinonia*.[387] On the Protestant side, too, while expressing disappointment that the Second Vatican Council did not effect any real change, it is recognized that, thanks to the Council and the ensuing dialogue, it has been possible to examine the question of the primacy from a new perspective during the postconciliar

---

[385] Böttigheimer, "Von der ökumenischen Relevanz des Papsttums", 340: "Katholizität, Kollegialität, Konzialiarität und Subsidiarität sind Prinzipien, die aus dem Wesen einer communional verfaßten Kirche erwachsen und mit denen die Vollmachten päpstlicher Amtsführung zu korrespondieren haben, ist doch der Papst wesensmäßig an jene Bedingungen gebunden, die durch die communionalen Kirchenstrukturen vorgegeben sind.... Um die Befürchtung nicht-katholischer Kirchen vor einem 'absolutistischen', nicht-evangeliumsmäßen Jurisdiktionsprimat zu zerstreuen, wäre es notwendig, daß jene Prinzipien ... den Primat nicht nur moralisch, sondern auch rechtlich binden und somit notfalls juridisch einklagbar wären.... Würde die dienende Funktion des Papsttums über dessen Amstvollmachten dominieren, könnte aus dem Jurisdiktionsprimat ein ökumenisches, pastorales Dienstamt werden, ein interkonfessionell anerkanntes Dienst- und Wächteramt." Cf. Lehmann, "Grundlinien", 144; Beinert, "Endechrist", 138–39.

[386] G. Colombo, "Il primato petrino tra Parola divina e storicità umana", *Il primato del successore di Pietro*, 178–79.

[387] K. Schatz, "Primat und Kollegialität. Eine geschichtliche Skizze ihres Verhältnisses", *Internationale katholische Zeitschrift Communio* 27 (1998): 305–6: "Die vom Wesen des Bischofsamtes gegebene 'kollegiale' Einbettung impliziert notwendig eine Beziehung zum Centrum unitatis des Kollegiums, die aber dann primär im Rahmen einer Communio-Theologie und nicht bloß im Sinne einer reinen Ekklesiologie der 'Jurisdiktio' zu verstehen ist.... Hier muß die Frage gestellt werden: Ist Kollegialität nicht auch ein kritisches, begrenzendes Element gegenüber dem Primat? und wie kann sie das wieder werden? Nur wenn dies auch ist, existiert sie nicht letzten Endes doch 'von des Papstes Gnaden', und nur dann hat das kollegiale Element in der Kirche eine Eigenständigkeit gegenüber dem primatialen." Cf. Böttigheimer, "Von der ökumenischen Relevanz des Papsttums", 338–39; Antón, "'Ministero petrino' en el diálogo con las otras Iglesias cristianas", 436–37.

period and in the ecumenical dialogues and that a new interest in the primacy has developed.[388]

It should not be forgotten, though, that the dependence of the bishop and of the local Church on the universal Church and on the college of bishops also implies a dependence on the Bishop of Rome, as defined by the First Vatican Council: A bishop can be head of his Church precisely because he is a witness to the universal Church, and this is possible thanks to his communion with the Pope.[389] Therefore the pastoral and collegial character of the primacy, inasmuch as this can take on great importance in the dialogue, must also safeguard a personal dimension and not be confused with the collective "we" of a college.[390] It is risky to describe the exercise of the supreme power of the Roman Pontiff over all the faithful—including bishops—as an extraordinary form of the Petrine ministry, while saying that its collegial form is the ordinary form.[391] Indeed,

---

[388] Meyer, "Ein evangeliumsgemäßes Papstamt", 84: "Das Konzil als ganzes, sein Charakter als Erneuerungskonzil, seine ausgeprägte ökumenische Dimension, Gestalt und Verhalten der beiden Konzilspäpste, der vom Konzil ermöglichte, ja mit ihm bereits einsetzende, dann offiziell aufgenommene Dialog zwischen katholischer Kirche und evangelischen wie anglikanischen Kirchen und das allgemein intensivierte Fragen und Suchen nach Einheit der Kirche, all das hat zwar die evangelische Kritik am definierten Papstamt nicht beantwortet, aber es hat die Perspektive, unter der man das Papstamt bisher sah, tiefgreifend verändert."

[389] Carrasco Rouco, "Der päpstliche Primat", 321: "Der Bischof kann das Haupt seiner Kirche gerade deshalb sein, weil er Zeichen von etwas ist, das mehr ist als er selbst oder irgendeine menschliche Interpretation, nämlich Zeichen der Gesamtkirche, und eben dies wird durch die Gemeinschaft mit dem Papst ermöglicht."

[390] Kasper, "Das Petrusamt als Dienst der Einheit", 134–35: "Dieser universalkirchliche Dienst der Einheit braucht freilich nicht allein und auch nicht primär juridisch, als Jurisdiktionsprimat verstanden zu werden ... Ein Pastoralprimat ist also nur dann theologisch sinnvoll, wenn er in der Substanz die Intention dessen, was hinter dem Jurisdiktionsprimat steht, als ein Element aufnimmt. Wenn man deshalb in der gegenwärtigen ökumenischen Diskussion ein ökumenisches Petrusamt oft als Sprecher, Symbol, Zeichen, Kommunikationszentrum der Kirche beschreibt, so sind solche Begriffe als Worte der gegenseitigen Annäherung sinnvoll und hilfreich; nach katholischer Vorstellung erreichen sie jedoch die intendierte Wirklichkeit so lange nicht voll, als sie nicht realisieren, daß nach biblischer Vorstellung das kirchliche Amt immer die personale Verantwortung des Zeugen einschließt, des Zeugen, der als einzelner mit seiner ganzen Existenz für seine 'Sache' haftet und deshalb nie in einem kollektiv verstandenen Wir eines Kollegiums untergehen kann. Nur als solch personal verantwortlicher und vollmächtig sprechender und handelnder Zeuge kann das Petrusamt zu einem Symbol werden, das der Kirche Identität verleiht nach innen und nach außen."

[391] S. Madrigal, "'Proesis ut prosis'. Consideraciones en torno a la Encíclica *Ut unum sint.*" *Miscelánea Comillas* 55 (1997): 396: "Esta [capacidad de actuar sobre los obispos]

it is evident that only the Pope (or the Pope together with an ecumenical council) has, as Successor of Peter, the authority and the competence ultimately to determine the modality in which his own pastoral ministry is to be exercised in the universal Church.[392]

Conditions and methodology for a solution

While it would be an exaggeration to say that the parties are gradually delineating an agreement in recognizing the papacy as a ministerial structure for unity in the Church at a universal level (while distinguishing between its essence and the forms in which it is exercised),[393] undoubtedly the ecumenical debate about the primacy is guided, today, by a deliberate change of perspective: on the Protestant side, the question now is only "how", and no longer "why" or "to what purpose". From regarding the papacy as an "obstacle" there has been a move toward recognizing the possibility of a Petrine ministry as a way of fostering unity.[394]

Nevertheless, the condition that the Petrine service be reformed in the light of the Gospel and be exercised in a manner which does not impair Christian freedom[395] is still demanded, just as it had been by the initial

---

debería ser, a tenor de una ecclesiología de comunión, la forma extraordinaria del ejercicio de la autoridad pontificia, no la forma ordinaria. Si esta perspectiva excepcional del primato de jurisdicción se convierte en la forma normal de su ejercicio estaríamos ante una situación de centralismo injustificado, a-colegial, sin límites jurídicos, ante una forma de absolutismo."

[392] *Il primato del Successore di Pietro nel mistero della Chiesa. Considerazioni della Congregazione per la Dottrina della Fede*, in the Appendix to the Acts of the Symposium, 501–2.

[393] Cf. Antón, "'Ministerio petrino' en el diálogo con las otras Iglesias cristianas", 430.

[394] Meyer, "Das Problem des Petrusamtes", 123: "Die ökumenische Papstdebatte ist also heute bestimmt von einer sehr bewußten Veränderung der Fragestellung.... Man schaut Protestantischerseits nicht mehr wie gebannt nur auf das problematische 'Wie' des Papstamtes, so daß man die Frage nach dem 'Warum' und 'Wozu' dieses Amtes gar nicht mehr zu Gesicht bekommt.... Protestanten haben ... ein ganz neues 'Papstgefühl' entwickelt. Es ist die bedeutungsvolle Wende von der bisherigen Fixierung auf das Papstamt als 'Hindernis' hin zum Blick auf das Papstamt als mögliche 'Hilfe' zur Einheit." Cf. Meyer, "Ein evangeliumsgemäßiges Papstamt", 85–87, where this new prospect is explicitly attributed to the results of the Malta Report and of the document by the Commission in the USA.

[395] Ibid., 87: "Das Papstamt ist als positive Möglichkeit, als Dienst an der Einheit der Kirche anzuerkennen, wenn—oder sofern—es dem Evangelium dient, wenn es im Lichte des Evangeliums erneuert ist und wenn seine Ausübung von Macht nicht die christliche Freiheit untergräbt."

Reformers. Thus it is necessary to find suitable forms of a truly ecumenical primacy that are acceptable to all the Churches,[396] a primacy which does not necessarily have to be ascribed to the Bishop of Rome as a characteristic that sets him over all the other bishops.[397]

The chief inspiration for such a new expression of the primacy is collegiality, on the basis of which, through dialogue, ecumenism should redefine the fullness of power vested in the Roman Pontiff, which is odious to the ears of the Protestants, according to whom the possibilities of developing collegiality itself are therefore of vital interest.[398] The result would be a less centralized primatial function which would be more at the service of the unity of the local Churches in the *koinonia* of the universal Church—something that would be of great importance, from an ecumenical perspective.[399] Indeed, precisely by virtue of an ecclesiology of communion it would be possible to overcome the confessional differences that still exist and be open to new prospects for major consensus on a primacy modelled on "reconciled diversity" and on "unity in multi-

---

[396] Kruse, "Die ökumenische Zukunft", 115: "Es müssen neue, wirksamere Formen eines ökumenischen Leitungsdienstes auf Weltebene gefunden werden." Cf. Antón, "'Ministero petrino' en el diálogo con las otras Iglesias cristianas", 431–32, where some texts from the dialogue are reproduced precisely to emphasize Lutheran thought in this regard.

[397] G. H. Tavard, "What Is the Petrine Function?," LCD V, 212: "The exercise of this function by the bishop of Rome is too well attested to be discarded. Yet its attribution to the Roman pontiff as a distinctive mark placing him over and above all other bishops cannot be necessarily and absolutely permanent if the forms and, a fortiori, the exercises of the function are historical variables."

[398] Kruse, "Die ökumenische Zukunft", 116: "Letztlich ist der Papst eigenständig. Er verfügt 'kraft seines Amtes in der Kirche über höchste, volle, unmittelbare und universale ordentliche Gewalt, die er immer frei ausüben kann'.... Das ist eine Machtfülle, die evangelisch geschulten Ohren geradezu unheimlich ist. Wenn dies nach katholischer Überzeugung zum Wesentlichen des Petrusdienstes gehört, was kann dann ein Dialog überhaupt erreichen? ... Eine der Fragen, die lutherischerseits von vitalem Interesse sind, richtet sich also auf die Entfaltungsmöglichkeiten der Kollegialität."

[399] Neuner, *Ökumenische Theologie*, 238–39: "Als Amt der Einheit der Orts- und Teilkirchen hat das Papsttum eine eminent ökumenische Aufgabe und Funktion. Dies ist eine Konzeption des Papsttums, die implizit als Kritik an einer langen Entwicklung zu verstehen ist, in deren Verlauf die katholische Kirche immer mehr zentralisiert wurde, der Papst alle Vollmacht beanspruchte und alle Amtsträger in der Kirche als seine Delegierten ohne eigene Vollmacht erschienen. Gegen ein derartiges Verständnis des Papsttums haben die Kirchen protestiert, es erscheint als der bedeutendste Stein des Anstoßes zwischen den Konfessionen und als der schwierigste Punkt einer ökumenischen Annäherung." Cf. also ibid., 242–43.

plicity".[400] This would mean facing the theological task of reinterpreting the papacy: a transition from a hierarchical and pyramidal view of the Church to a vision of a communion of particular Churches. "Now the possibility is recognized of another theological interpretation of the papacy, based on the concept of the Church as a communion of particular Churches, whose bishops form a college headed by the Bishop of Rome, who as such is also necessarily a member of that college."[401]

It follows from such a view that the exercise of the primacy is understood to be a service, bound by certain structural obligations (collegiality, synods, legitimate pluralism),[402] and distinguishing between *habitual and substitutional* functions.[403] This would assure that primacy and collegiality are not opposed to each other; indeed, it underscores their reciprocal complementarity.[404] Primacy and collegiality would therefore constitute

---

[400] Böttigheimer, "Von der ökumenischen Relevanz des Papsttums", 342: "Eine rechtliche Veränderung der katholischen Primatslehre in der Communio-Ekklesiologie würde jenen Grundkonsens vorbereiten helfen, den das ökumenische Modell der 'versöhnten Verschiedenheit' voraussetzt. Wird ein solcher gefunden, dann bräuchten die Papstdogmen mit ihrem Anspruch auf gesamtkirchliche Verbindlichkeit nicht mehr kirchentrennend zu wirken, weil im Sinne des Ökumeneplans 'Einheit in Vielfalt' ein Maximalkonsens, d.h. eine *explizite* Zustimmung zur Primatslehre des 19. Jahrhunderts keine notwendige Bedingung einer Kircheneinheit darstellt." Cf. Kasper, "Das Petrusamt als Dienst der Einheit", 133.

[401] Cf. F. A. Sullivan, "Per un rinnovamento del ministero del Vescovo di Roma: principio di legittima diversità, collegialità, sussidiarietà", *Nicolaus* 19 (1992), 44–45; Beinert, "Endechrist", 136–37.

[402] Father Antón summarizes the principles for a renewal of the primacy in the light of the Gospel in the following terms: "Dichos principios los han formulado el Vaticano II y los documentos oficiales del diálogo ecuménico: la legitima diversidad de las Iglesias locales y los principios de colegialidad y subsidiariedad de las Iglesias locales en las relaciones vigentes entre el primado y episcopado y entre el gobierno central de la Iglesia y la legitima autonomía de las Iglesias locales a nivel regional, nacional y continental" ("'Ministero petrino' en el diálogo con la otras Iglesias cristianas", 438). He then concludes, "Son prometedoras las posibilidades que se abren por estas tres pistas para la restructuración del papado con el fin de que pueda presentarse verdaderamente como un 'ministerio universal de unidad' en la comunión de las Iglesias" (ibid., 453).

[403] Cf. M. J. Buckley, "'Perpetuum utriusque unitatis principium ac visibile fundamentum'. The Primacy and the Episcopate: Towards a Doctrinal Synthesis", *Il primato del successore di Pietro*, 316–25.

[404] Ibid., 328: "Primacy is not opposed to collegiality in principle; on the contrary, primacy is the servant of collegiality. Further, one can gauge the effectiveness of the primacy by the vitality of collegiality within the Church. If the college of bishops is flourishing ... then the primacy is flourishing. This flourishing of bishops is a term and a reason for the primacy."

"two precious stones with which it is possible to compose the mosaic of an ecumenical primacy."[405]

In the ecumenical field, however, the question still remains open as to the need for the primacy in the Church: not so much in the sense of whether it is necessary for salvation, but whether it is so essential to the Church that if a "Church" does not recognize the primacy, it necessarily lacks ecclesial status.[406]

In an attempt to resolve differences on this point, the dialogue has sought to distinguish between *papacy* and *Petrine service*—in other words, between service to the unity of the Church at a universal level (service or Petrine function) and the historical concretization of that service in the primacy of the Bishop of Rome. While Protestants are prepared to accept the necessity of the former aspect, they deny the latter, which, for them, is merely possible or desirable.[407] A further distinction is made between primacy as constitutive of visible unity and primacy as constitutive of the Church's essence. Lutherans, as well as Anglicans, would be disposed to accept the need for the primacy in the first sense, but

---

[405] Cf. Antón, "'Ministero petrino' en el diálogo con las otras Iglesias cristianas", 434.

[406] Meyer, "Ein evangeliumsgemäßes Papstamt", 89–90: "Daß der Papst in seinem Primatsanspruch und seiner Primatsausübung die kollegialen, synodalen, konziliaren und subsidiaren Strukturen der Kirche stärker berücksichtigt, daß er legitime Vielfalt in der Kirche respektiert und schützt, daß er seinen Primat als pastoralen Dienst versteht, all das ist sicherlich wichtig für die Glaubwürdigkeit seiner Amtsausübung.... Die Frage nach der 'Notwendigkeit' des päpstlichen Primats stellt sich heute sicherlich nicht mehr als Frage nach seiner 'Heilsnotwendigkeit'.... Sie stellt sich aber wohl als durchaus auf die Heilsfrage bezogene, wenn auch nicht mit ihr identische Frage nach der ekklesialen Notwendigkeit des päpstlichen Primats: Gehört der universale Primat des römischen Bischofs zum Wesen der Kirche, so daß eine 'Kirche', die diesen Primat nicht anerkennt, keine Kirche ist oder es ihr an Kirche-sein mangelt?"

[407] Kasper, "Das Petrusamt als Dienst der Einheit", 130–31; "Der Begriff 'Petrusamt' hat gegenüber dem bisher geläufigen, historisch sehr belasteten Begriff 'Papsttum' den Vorteil, daß er auf dessen neutestamentliche Wurzeln verweist und zugleich die späteren historischen Ausgestaltungen kritisch daran mißt. Der relativ junge Begriff 'Petrusamt' stellt also einen kritischen Normbegriff dar, welcher es der neueren katholischen Theologie erlaubt, im Licht des Ursprungs eine *relecture* der geschichtlich gewordenen Ausgestaltungen des Papsttums und der Papstdogmen vorzunehmen. Dieser Begriff stellt freilich auch eine Frage an die nicht-katholischen Kirchen dar. Wo und in welcher Weise wird bei ihnen die neutestamentlich begründete Petrusfunktion, der Dienst der Einheit an der universalen Kirche, wahrgenommen?" Cf. Beinert, "Endechrist", 125; Kühn, "Gesamtkirchlicher Petrusdienst?" 33; Antón, "'Ministero petrino' en el diálogo con la otras Iglesias cristianas", 386–87.

not in the second sense, because that would call into question their own ecclesial character.[408]

The general appeal to collegiality as a principle for a renewal of the papacy often takes the form of concrete proposals. Among them one deserves particular attention: the proposal which sees a possible solution to the problem of the papacy in the distinction between the primatial and patriarchal roles of the Roman Pontiff, a proposal which is set forth in the dialogue documents[409] and is taken up again in theological commentaries on the dialogue. Pannenberg, for example, writes, "A starting point might be the separation of the functions of the Roman bishop as primate of the whole Church and as patriarch of the West." In that instance, his role "within the Latin patriarchate" would be defined in reference to the autonomy of the dioceses. He continues, "The jurisdiction of a universal Christian ministry of leadership ought essentially to mean that the one who discharges this ministry ought to be the chief advocate of unity in interchurch relations." Such a function could be carried out by the Bishop of Rome but as "less a function of power (*potestas*) than of the ability to persuade (*auctoritas*)".[410]

The same question has be examined in the perspective of the Church's unity at an international level, that is, in relation to the other patriarchates, among them the patriarchate of the West.[411] Aside from the rather

---

[408] Meyer, "Ein evangeliumsgemäßes Papstamt", 91: "Auch in dieser Aussage wird … differenziert zwischen Notwendigkeit zur sichtbaren Einheit der Kirche und Notwendigkeit zum Kirche-sein von Kirche. Und zwar würden Lutheraner wie Anglikaner das erste vertreten, ohne damit bereits das zweite auszusagen und aussagen zu können, schon deshalb, weil sie dadurch das eigene Kirche-sein in Frage stellten. *Ein Dienst oder Amt der Einheit für die Gesamtkirche in Gestalt eines universalen Primats wäre dann zwar 'einheitskonstitutiv' aber darum noch nicht 'kirchen-konstitutiv'.*"

[409] Cf. above, pp. 144–45, notes 239–40.

[410] *Systematic Theology*, 428–29. Cf. Pannenberg, "Das Papsttum und die Zukunft der Ökumene", 148.

[411] Pannenberg, "Evangelische Überlegungen", 48–51: "Für die heutigen reformatorischen Kirchen geht es daher beim Gespräch über das Papsttum nicht nur um die gesamtkirchliche Autorität Roms, sondern auch um die formelle Entlassung aus der Jurisdiktionsgewalt des lateinischen Patriarchen. … Im Verhältnis zur geschichtlichen Entwicklung der Ausübung gesamtkirchlicher Autorität durch den Bischof von Rom bedarf eine von der christlichen Ökumene zu akzeptierende Ausübung seines Petrusdienstes heute der klaren Unterscheidung zwischen gesamtkirchlichem Primat und der Patriarchalgewalt des Bischofs von Rom." Cf. Neuner, *Ökumenische Theologie*, 238 and 242; Schütte, "Das 'revolutionäre Angebot'", 22.

curious view that the definitions of both Vatican Councils are restricted to the Latin patriarchate,[412] such a distinction is seen as the completion of the doctrine of the First Vatican Council and as an application of the principle of collegiality as opposed to centralization.[413] The ripple effect of this distinction is evident in the ecumenical field. Paraphrasing Pannenberg: an ecumenically acceptable contemporary exercise of the Petrine ministry requires that a clear distinction be drawn between the universal primacy and the patriarchal power of the Bishop of Rome. This is the most important gain in relation to the doctrine of the First Vatican Council ... for the reformed Churches. A clearer distinction between these two functions of the Bishop of Rome can facilitate agreement on the Petrine ministry of the Bishop of Rome as a service to the unity of all the Christian Churches in faith.[414]

The question automatically arises, however, of whether this distinction safeguards the nature of the primacy of jurisdiction. I refer the reader to other works published on this theme, which conclude that such a distinction is theologically and historically without foundation, precisely because it is incompatible with the definitions of the First Vatican Council, which were taken up again by the Second Vatican Council. It would

---

[412] Cf. Pannenberg, "Das Papsttum und die Zukunft der Ökumene", 147: "Auch die Aussagen der beiden vatikanischen Konzilien über das Papsttum bleiben dann in ihrer Geltung auf das lateinische Patriarchat beschränkt."

[413] Pannenberg., "Evangelische Überlegungen", 51: "Katholische Theologen haben schon seit vielen Jahren darauf hingewiesen, daß das I. Vatikanische Konzil in seinen Aussagen über die Jurisdiktion des Papstes nicht unterschieden hat zwischen der Jurisdiktion, die dem romischen Bischof in seiner Eigenschaft als Patriarch der lateinische Kirche des Abendlandes zukommt, und andererseits seiner Funktion als Inhaber des Vorrangs unter den Bischöfen der Gesamtchristenheit. ... Hilfreich dafür wäre auch eine Reform der Ausübung der Patriarchalgewalt selber nach den Grundzätzen der Kollegialität und der Subsidiarität und der Abbau von der Geschichte der abendländischen Kirche wirksam gewordenen Tendenzen zu einem römischen Zentralismus." Cf. Kasper, "Das Petrusamt als Dienst der Einheit", 133.

[414] Cf. Pannenberg, "Il ministero petrino a servizio dell'unità", *il regno-att.*16/98, 565a–b. Idem, "Das Papsttum und die Zukunft der Ökumene", 148: "Die Amtsgewalt des Papstes als Bischof von Rom und als Patriarch des Abendlandes ist zu unterscheiden von seiner gesamtkirchlichen Autorität, und gerade eine solche Unterscheidung würde die Anerkennung und Wirkung der Autorität des römischen Bischofs in der Ökumene nur fördern können." This distinction cropped up again, along with various prospects, in the symposium held in the Vatican in 1996: cf. *Il primato del successore di Pietro,* 278, 341, 344, 356, 384, 474.

reduce the Roman Pontiff to nothing more than a *primus inter pares.*[415] Subsequent literature draws the same conclusion. Just as in the past, with the classical historical pentarchy, while the Church of Rome and her Bishop were held in particular esteem, they did not enjoy a jurisdictional primacy,[416] so too today such a primacy, while having a certain importance in the ecumenical dialogue,[417] would be limited to the exercise of a pastoral role, which would not oblige non-Catholic Churches to accept Catholic juridical structures.[418]

Apart from the effective psychological results that have been achieved through reciprocal exchange, it would seem that Catholic-Lutheran dialogue is still a long way from agreement on the foundations and of the primacy of the Bishop of Rome, as well as on the concrete forms through which that primacy is exercised.

IV. CONCLUSION

As is the case with the Orthodox in the East, so too with the Protestants of the West, the traditional difficulties continue. Even though the strident

---

[415] Cf. Garuti, *Il Papa Patriarca d'Occidente?*; Garuti, "Ancora a proposito del Papa Patriarca d'Occidente", 31–45.

[416] H.J. Pottmeyer, *Toward a Papacy in Communion*, 28: "The Roman church and its bishop did enjoy a special standing, but not a jurisdictional precedence. As long as the churches of the East and of the West remained united, the East's conception of the church prevented the universal acceptance of the jurisdictional primacy claimed by the popes as the 'representatives of Peter'." According to Kasper, too, in the context of the Patriarchates Rome was the "Kommunikationszentrum, Orientierungspunkt der kirchlichen Gemeinschaft", which certainly implied "mehr als ein äußerlich verstandener Ehrenprimat, aber—vor allem im Verhältnis zum Osten—noch nicht der Jurisdiktionsprimat des I. Vatikanischen Konzils" ("Das Petrusamt als Dienst der Einheit", 114–15).

[417] Cf. Kasper, "Das Petrusamt als Dienst der Einheit", 116–17.

[418] Kühn, "Gesamtkirchicher Petrusdienst?", 39. After recalling the Orthodox idea of the Bishop of Rome as a "Primus inter pares", Kühn comments, "Wenn das aber die Richtung weiteren Nachdenkens wäre, könnte man überlegen, ob etwa der römische Bischof jene beschriebene petrinische Funktion eines Pastoralprimats für die ganze Christenheit ausüben könnte, ohne daß damit die römisch-katholische Rechtsstruktur von den anderen Kirchen übernommen werden müßte.... Aber es bedeutete nicht einfach einen Eintritt der nicht-römischen Kirchen in diese (dann reformierte) Rechtsstruktur, sondern könnte eine offenere Gestalt gewinnen. Es wäre eine Form der Gemeinschaft zugleich 'mit' und 'unter' dem Papst. Auf diese Weise bliebe die Stadt Rom der Ort, an dem die Gesamtchristenheit so etwas wie einen gemeisamen Bezugspunkt hätte—dies wäre ein Anknüpfen an die hohe respektgebietende Tradition der Bedeutung Roms für die Christenheit."

tone of the critique of the papacy during the Reformation and Counter Reformation periods has ceased,[419] non-Catholics insist on the need for a theological reinterpretation of the primacy and for a restructuring, matters which must be clarified by means of ecumenical dialogue.[420]

That clarification does not yet appear to have been achieved by the Catholic-Lutheran dialogue. Study of the preliminary ecclesiological questions necessary for any treatment of the specific question of the primacy (e.g., the sacramentality of the Church, apostolicity, and ministry)[421] has not yet produced sufficient results. In other words, there is still no agreement on a common image of the Church, without which all efforts by theologians to reach agreement on the primacy are destined to fail.[422] Most significantly, there is no agreement on the meaning of the definitions of the First Vatican Council, without which the dialogue operates in a cul-de-sac despite certain dialogue statements that come close to recognizing them.[423] While on the one hand it is commonly admitted that a critical reexamination of the dogmas of the First Vatican Council, in the light of Scripture and tradition, would be possible and useful,[424]

---

[419] Pannenberg, "Das Papsttum und die Zukunft der Ökumene", 139: "Das Papsttum gilt allgemein als eines der schwierigsten Themen des ökumenischen Dialogs zwischen den Kirchen. . . . Das gilt sowohl für das Verhältnis Roms zu den Kirchen des Ostens als auch vom Verhältnis der römisch-katholischen Kirche zu den protestantischen Kirchen. Von beiden Seiten aus wird der wirkliche oder vermeintliche Herrschaftsanspruch des römischen Bischofs mit Mißtrauen betrachtet. Das ist auch heute noch nicht überwunden, obwohl die schrillen Töne Protestantischer Papstkritik, wie sie die Zeit der Reformation und Gegenreformation begleiteten, dann aber auch im Zeitalter nach dem I. Vatikanum wieder auflebten, heute verklungen sind."

[420] Ibid., 140: "Was man sich unter solcher theologischen Reinterpretation und praktischen Umstrukturierung des Papstamtes im eizelnen vorzustellen hat, das ist in der ökumenischen Diskussion noch zu klären."

[421] Cf. above, pp. 110–26.

[422] Beinert, "Endechrist", 136: "Entscheidend für jede Konvergenz und jeden möglichen Konsens ist Konvergenz und Konsens der ökumenischen Partner über das *Kirchenbild*. Weil und solange zwischen Lutheranern und Katholiken . . . keine Einigkeit hierüber herrscht, bleiben alle papsttheologischen Unternehmungen auf der Strecke."

[423] Kühn, "Papsttum und Petrusdienst", 198: "Die erreichten Ergebnisse bleiben bestenfalls in einem extrem labilen Gleichgewicht. Der merkwürdige Befund aufgrund der Durchsicht der offiziellen ökumenischen Konsenspapiere ist nun, daß zwar festgestellt wird, das theologische Gespräch zum Doppeldogma von 1870 befinde sich in einer Sackgasse, andererseits aber Aussagen in den Dokumenten enthalten sind, die diesem Doppeldogma sehr nahe kommen." Cf. Pannenberg, "Das Papsttum und die Zukunft der Ökumene", 146.

[424] Kasper, "Das Petrusamt als Dienst der Einheit", 131: "Umgekehrt müssen wir aber auch alle geschichtlichen Ausformungen des Petrusdienstes, also auch die Papstdogmen

this nevertheless cannot be understood as a simple recognition of a primacy of honor which would exclude any formal obligation to accept these dogmas.[425] It must also be stated that the oft-proclaimed readiness of Lutheranism to accept a universal service in the Church conflicts with the so-called monopolization of decisional competence[426] and continues to be qualified by an almost obsessive recourse to the traditional stipulation of conformity to the Gospel. In spite of a certain rapprochement (which is unthinkable if it is confronted with the theory of the papacy formulated by the First Vatican Council), it is impossible to overlook the controverted points which still exist, especially concerning the *ius divinum* and the fullness of the power of the Bishop of Rome.[427]

A long and difficult road remains, then, in order to overcome this obstacle, which specifically demands further research. At Lärkulla (1995) it was decided to address the topic of the apostolicity of the Church with a view to finding ways to overcome the differences concerning the possible forms of a universal service for the unity of Christians.[428] Thus far no document on the subject has appeared, nor any report whatsoever.

---

des I. Vatikanischen Konzils vom Ursprungszeugnis der Schrift her einer kritischen lecture unterziehen. Dieses Prinzip wahrt einerseits die Kontinuität mit der Tradition, andererseits erlaubt es aber doch, die Tradition vom Ursprung her zu erneuern und auf neue Zukunft hin zu öffnen."

[425] Pannenberg, "Das Papsttum und die Zukunft der Ökumene", 147: "Einer solchen Anerkennung des Bischofs von Rom als des ersten an Ehre und des Vorsitzers in der Liebe in der Christenheit könnten auch die evangelischen Kirchen zustimmen. Das bedeutet, daß auch ihnen nicht eine formelle Anerkennung und Übernahme der Lehren der beiden vatikanischen Konzilien über das Papsttum zugemutet werden sollte und dürfte."

[426] Beinert, "Ökumene und Ökumenismus", 249–50: "Man kann bezüglich des Luthertums heute eine prinzipielle Bereitschaft zur Anerkennung eines universalkirchlichen Dienstamtes vermerken, wie sie beispielsweise in den Kommentaren sur Enzyklika 'Ut unum sint' zum Ausdruck kommt.... Genau aber diese Monopolisierung kirchlicher Entscheidungskompetenz ist gegenwärtig zu beobachten, und zwar durchaus auch dort, wo sie nicht absolut glaubensförderlich zu sein scheint." He cites, for example, "das harsche Schreiben der Glaubenskongregation über einige Aspekte der Communio, das viel Staub aufgewirbelt hat" and other documents which tend toward the danger of bringing the Catholic Church "innerhalb der Ökumene in eine Isolation".

[427] Böttigheimer, "Von der ökumenischen Relevanz des Papsttums", 337: "Der Überblick über die Ökumenediskussion in der Primatsfrage ließ deutlich werden, daß in einigen jüngsten ökumenischen Dialogen eine so weitreichende Annährung erzielt wurde, wie sie, gemessen an der extremen Papaltheorie des I. Vatikanums, niemand zu erhoffen vermochte. Allerdings sind auch die noch bestehenden Kontroversen unübersehbar, die insbesondere die Ius-divinum-Lehre und die päpstlichen Vollmachten betreffen."

[428] Cf. above, p. 169, note 333.

CHAPTER IV

THE PRIMACY AND THE
CATHOLIC-ANGLICAN DIALOGUE

I. THE ANGLICAN VIEW OF THE PRIMACY

ANGLICANS RECOGNIZE MINISTRY as necessary to the structure of the Church; therefore the Catholic-Anglican dialogue on the question of the primacy begins on a different basis from that of the Catholic-Lutheran dialogue.[1] Moreover, at least in the beginning, the Anglican reform did not make a direct reference to justification in the ecclesiological context,[2] or to the questions of ministry and apostolic succession.[3] It

---

[1] B. Neumann, "Das Papstamt in den offiziellen Ökumenischen Dialogen", 103–4: "Der internationale Dialog der katholische Kirche mit der Anglikanischen Gemeinschaft steht im Blick auf die Papstfrage auf einer anderen Basis als der Dialog mit den reformatorischen Kirchen. Denn für die Anglikanischen Kirchen gehört das historische Bischofamt zur Gestalt der Kirche hinzu, so daß die Frage nach der ekklesialen Bedeutung des dreigliedrigen Amtes, die etwa innerhalb des Dialogs mit den lutherischen Kirchen eine besondere Rolle spielt, innerhalb dieser Gespräche nicht zur Diskussion steht. Das dürfte der Grund sein, daß dieser Dialog die inhaltliche Auseinendersetzung über die Stellung des Bischofs von Rom relativ früh angegangen hat und darin weiter gediehen ist als andere internationale Gespräche."

[2] The observation is well founded, even if article 37 of the *Thirty-Nine Articles of Religion*, relative to justification, inclined toward the Lutheran view: cf. A. Gatard, "Anglicanisme", *Dictionnaire de théologie catholique* (Paris, 1909), 1:1284. Only afterward, Cranmer "war bereits in seiner Studienzeit mit den Schriften Luthers in Kontakt genommen, erlebte die Lehre von der Rechtfertigung allein aus Glauben als Befreiung von der Höllen- und Fegefeuerspekulation der zeitgenössischen Buß- und Ablaßprediger" (P. Neuner, *Ökumenische Theologie*, 120).

[3] Ibid., 122: "Der Anglikanismus hat am dreigeteilten kirchlichen Amt von Bishof, Priester und Diakon festgehalten und damit die Sukzessionsreihe gewahrt ... die ungebrochene apostolische Sukzession im Amt sollte keinesfalls preisgegeben werden. Sie ist bis heute für die anglikanischen Kirchen konstitutiv." Three different formulations on the nature of the necessity of apostolic succession are noted in Anglican theology: depending on the sources, the hierarchical structure would belong to the *esse*, to the *plenum esse*, or to the *bene esse* of the Church (ibid., 122–23). Cf. A. Nichols, *The Panther and the Hind: A Theological History*

194

had its origins, in fact, not in problems of a doctrinal nature, but rather in the religious politics of Henry VIII, which was affected in turn by the king's personal situation, that is, by his desire to obtain a divorce.[4] Therefore, it was born from a civil act—not an ecclesial one—to preserve the prerogatives of the crown;[5] not out of a desire to create a Catholicism without a Pope, but rather out of a political compromise[6] in an attempt to justify, in Catholic tradition and in Protestant thinking, the situation in which the Church in England came to find herself.[7]

Even today the Anglican Communion presents itself as a harmony of Catholic and Protestant elements, though the Catholic element seems to grow progressively weaker, to the point of causing Anglicanism to lose its pivotal role among Christians.[8]

Hence it does not seem necessary to frame the problem in a more general ecclesiological context; it will be enough to present briefly the Anglican concept of the primacy in its historical context,[9] to be followed

---

of Anglicanism (Edinburgh, 1993), 82; M. Tanner, "The Anglican Position on Apostolic Continuity and Apostolic Succession in the Porvoo Common Statement", Louvain Studies 21 (1996): 114.

[4] Y. Congar, "Anglicanisme", Catholicisme. Hier Aujourd'hui Demain (Paris, 1948), 562: "À la différence des réformes continentales, la réforme anglicane ne vint pas de la pensée dogmatique d'un réformateur, mais de la politique religieuse d'un prince, elle même conditionnée par sa situation personnelle." Cf. R. Hale, Canterbury and Rome: Sister Churches (London, 1982), 81–83.

[5] Nichols, Panther and the Hind, 9: "The anti-papal legislation of earlier kings had been enacted in order to preserve the prerogatives of the imperial crown of the realm. The jurisdiction of ecclesiastical courts, whether English or Roman, was simply delegated judgment from the king." Cf. H. Chadwick, "Ministero papale e unità dei cristiani dal punto di vista anglicano", in P. Hünermann, ed., Papato ed ecumenismo. Il ministero petrino al servizio dell'unità (Bologna, 1999), 63.

[6] Nichols, Panther and the Hind, XVII: "Anglicanism ... is not so much a theological ideal as a political compromise. It was created by the sixteenth century English monarchy in an effort to avoid religious disunity of the kind so notable in the Continental Reformation."

[7] Cf. G. Leonard, "Foreword", in Nichols, Panther and the Hind, x.

[8] C. Morerod, "Réflections sur l'Accord de Porvoo entre Anglicans et Luthériens", Nova et Vetera (1997/3), 102: "De son coté, l'Église anglicane se présente depuis des siècles comme une harmonie d'éléments catholiques et protestants. On ne peut échapper à l'impression que l'élément catholique s'aminuise progressivement, faisant perdre à l'Anglicanisme le rôle de charnière qu'il pourrait avoir parmi les chrétiens."

[9] Cf. C. Buchanan, s.v. "Anglican Communion", DEM, 18–20; R. Mehl, s.v. "Protestantism", DEM, 833; L. Bouyer, The Church of God, 62–66; J. C. Maviiri Ndidde, Primacy in the Communion of Churches (Rome, 1987), 8–13, in C. Alzati, ed., L'anglicanesimo: Dalla Chiesa d'Inghilterra alla Comunione Anglicana (Genoa, 1992).

by a systematic analysis of the dialogue documents and an evaluation of the results, both by the official spokesmen and by the theologians.

The break with the See of Rome was without a doubt connected to, but not caused by, the divorce of King Henry VIII, or at least that was not the only cause.[10] The break actually found fertile ground in the widespread anticlericalism directed toward the Curia,[11] and even more so in the awareness of the Church in England of its national specificity and its autonomy, already present in the Middle Ages and reinforced in the age of humanism,[12] that brought with it a tendency to take the geopolitical and cultural reality of the island as the point of departure for seeing and living the Church.[13] Indeed, although under Henry VIII the break with Rome did not involve any doctrinal innovations,[14] subsequently the principle of autonomy was the "explosive force which led to more profound and extensive changes. In the reigns of Edward VI (1547–1553) and of Elizabeth I (1558–1603), the Church of England followed largely Protestant ways and separated itself from the Church of Rome in doctrine

[10] D. M. Loades, "Relations between the Anglicans and Roman Catholic Churches in the 16th and 17th Centuries", in W. Haase, ed., *Rome and the Anglicans: Historical and Doctrinal Aspects of Anglican-Roman Catholic Relations* (Berlin and New York, 1982), 9: "The traditional thesis of a complete casual relationship between the 'divorce' and the break with Rome is no longer adequate." Cf. D. L. Mikulanis, *Authority in the Church from the Perspective of Recent Anglican/Roman Catholic Dialogue* (Rome, 1986), 1–17; H. Root, "Prospettiva anglicana sul Vescovo di Roma", *Il Vescovo di Roma nella Chiesa universale. Corso breve di ecumenismo*, VIII (Rome, 1987), 86; Nichols, *Panther*, 1–36.

[11] Cf. Chadwick, "La continuità della Chiesa in Inghilterra e l'Atto di Supremazia", in Alzati, *L'anglicanesimo*, 44.

[12] Neuner, *Ökumenische Theologie*, 116: "Bedingt durch die Insellage am Rande der damals bekannten Welt war England im Mittelalter in hohen Maße selbständig und unabhängig ... So sehr die Kirche in dieser Zeit Teil der universalen Kirche war, so sehr war sie auch von dem Bewußtsein einer nationalen Eigentümlichkeit und Eigenständigkeit durchgedrungen. Im späten Mittelalter und unter dem Einfluß des Humanismus wurde die Spannung gegenüber Rom stärker." Cf. Maviiri Ndidde, *Primacy in the Communion of Churches*, 8.

[13] Cf. G. Alberigo, "L'Atto di Supremazia del 1534 nel contesto dell'ecclesiologia del tempo", in Alzati, *L'anglicanesimo*, 57.

[14] Congar, "Anglicanisme", 563: "Malgré sa rupture avec Rome, Henri VIII n'innova en aucun point de doctrine.... Les différents formulaires de foi édités sous Henri VIII restent catholiques et même antiprotestants.... L'Église anglicane doit à Henri VIII sa séparation d'avec Rome; elle ne lui doit ni sa théologie, ni ses formulaires de prière." Cf. G. Tavard, *The Quest for Catholicity: A Study in Anglicanism* (New York, 1964), 1–21; Mikulanis, *Authority in the Church*, 9f.

and ethos as well as in structure. The cornerstones of the settlement were the *Book of Common Prayer* and the *Thirty-Nine Articles of Religion*, which rooted the Church in the life of the one nation." [15] Together with the *Ordinal*, the said Articles constitute also the definitive doctrinal foundation of the Church of England in the initial period,[16] even though they have never been considered a rule of faith.[17]

Notwithstanding the fact that a large number of the faithful and the clergy, and a great many of the bishops, remained attached to the traditional forms and beliefs, "the Catholic façade of the Church would collapse almost unexpectedly and would appear to be completely transformed into the extreme forms of Protestantism." In the time of Elizabeth, in place of the Zwinglian model, accommodating to the medieval forms "was substituted a more or less strict Calvinism with which the majority of Protestant agitators, who had returned from exile, were impregnated. For these people, Cranmer's 'reform' was merely a sketch of a reformation. For a Church whose structure and ritual were still more or less Catholic a new Church would be substituted, totally remade from top to bottom on the Calvinist model." [18] The Lutheran influence was also strong, to the point that a "common inheritance" was spoken of: "In the early stages of the Reformation close ties existed between the Reformers in Britain and on the Continent. Under Henry VIII and Edward VI many English Reformers were strongly inflenced by Luther's writing. Attempts

---

[15] Buchanan, "Anglican Communion", DEM 18a. *The Book of Common Prayer* was a collection of the Missal, the ritual for the administration of the sacraments, and prayers for the faithful. The "Thirty-Nine Articles" constitute an authoritative exposition of the entire ecclesial body, but they do not assume a normative character with respect to the Anglican faith comparable to that exercised in the Roman Catholic sphere by the decrees and canons of the Council of Trent, and they never claimed to be a complete formulation of the faith of the Church: cf. F. Arnott, "I 39 Articoli: genesi, significato e ruolo nella storia dell'Anglicanesimo", Alzati, *L'anglicanesimo*, 46–48. Together the two texts give evidence of the position of Anglicanism as a *Via Media* between Rome and the reformed Churches (ibid., 149–50). Cf. Chadwick, "Ministero papale e unità dei cristiani", 64.

[16] Cf. Nichols, *Panther and the Hind*, 37.

[17] Ibid., 34: "But the Articles have never been treated by the Anglican church as a rule of faith comparable to the Augsburg Confession or the Westminster Confession."

[18] Bouyer, *Church of God*, 64. As Tavard pointed out, the Queen personally "belonged to neither side ... her religion seems to have been a cross between the non-papal Catholicism of Henry VIII and the moderate Lutheranism of the Augsburg Confession" (*The Quest for Catholicity*, 23); however, during her reign, even among bitter disputes between theologians, "the Church's structure must obviously be affected by this conception of Catholicity as essentially Protestant" (ibid., 30).

were made, though politically motivated, to formulate an official consensus between English and German theologians and churchmen (*The Wittenberg Articles* 1536). This early Lutheran influence has left its mark on the first *Book of Common Prayer* by Archbishop Cranmer, on the *Book of Homilies*, on the English translations of the Bible, and through some of the first doctrinal statements (such as *The Ten Articles* of 1536, *The Bishop's Book* from 1537, *The Thirteen Articles* of 1538), on many of the *Thirty-nine Articles of Religion*." [19] In the legislation introduced by Cranmer in 1571 the Church clearly acquired a synodal foundation.[20]

It cannot be said, however, that the Anglican tradition as a whole intended to break with the greater Catholic tradition with regard to the ministerial hierarchy and its functions:[21] the undeniable break with Rome did not mean a break with catholicity, but rather a desire for reform of the Church from within, with a view to establishing a Church that would be *simul catholica et reformata*.[22] Undoubtedly such a desire experienced fluctuations of a conservative and of a protestantizing tendency—as demon-

---

[19] Anglican-Lutheran Dialogue: *The Report of the Anglican-Lutheran European Regional Commission* (Helsinki, 1982), no. 8, 4. Cf. Anglican-Lutheran Joint Working Group, *Anglican-Lutheran Relations: Report* (Cold Ash, 1983), nos. 8–13.

[20] Neuner, *Ökumenische Theologie*, 121–22: "Die innere Organisation der Kirche förderte Cranmer durch eine neue Gesetzgebung.... Die von ihm vorgelegte Sammlung von Rechtstexten wurde erst 1571 gedruckt. Seine Auswahl gab der Verwaltung der Kirche dabei eine deutliche syndale Prägung, er sah die Teilnahme der Laien an der Regierung der Kirche vor und führte ihre Vertretung in Diözesansynoden ein."

[21] Tanner, "The Anglican Position on Apostolic Continuity", 116–17: "It was the Act of Uniformity in 1662 that formally excluded clergy who had not been episcopally ordained from pastoral office in the Church of England.... The Church's constitution is independent of that of civil society and only by mantaining that constitution—ordination by persons standing in succession to the Apostles—can the Church maintain its identity.... The way was open for a debate between those who see the 'historic episcopate' as belonging to the *esse* of the Church, and those who see it as a matter of *bene esse* or *plene esse*. This is a debate which still rumbles on, though.... Anglicans have never expressed a common mind about this: all three views have been, and still are held within the Church of England and the Anglican Communion today."

[22] J.-M. R. Tillard, "Canterbury and Rome: So Near, So Far", *One in Christ* 25 (1989): 141–42: "If one reads the great theologians of this history one perceives how the breach with the see of Rome, which is evident, does not signify for the mass of Anglicans a breach with the great force-line of catholicity. What was involved, according to the formula which gradually took shape, was a will for reform *within* the *catholica*, not parallel to it, for an *Ecclesia simul catholica et reformata*.... Despite certain of Cranmer's intentions and the adherence of several English reformers to the ideas of the continental Reformation, taken *in globo* it seems clear enough that the general self-understanding of the Church of England did not choose to cut itself off from catholicity."

strated by the different editions of the *Book of Common Prayer*[23]—which have given the Anglican Church the character of a *via media* between Catholicism and Protestantism or as a *bridge Church*[24] that intended to remain "Catholic but not Roman".[25] This became most apparent during the reign of Queen Elizabeth I, who was looking for a *modus vivendi* with the papacy and who was personally inclined toward an Anglo-Catholicism (or a "Lutheran" Catholicism), but was forced by the political situation to a solution of compromise and to make greater concessions to the Lutherans and above all to the Calvinists, who were backed by the noble and merchant classes.[26]

This intermediate position was characteristic of Anglicanism in its subsequent history as well.[27] Especially in the seventeenth century, the so-called *Puritans* were able to overturn completely the ecclesial order established by Elizabeth I;[28] but the Reform which followed remained as though

---

[23] Neuner, *Ökumenische Theologie*, 121: "Die erste Ausgabe dieses nun offiziellen Buches war noch verhältnismäßig konservativ, die zweite von 1552 war dagegen weithin von calvinistischen Einflüßen bestimmt.... Unter Elisabeth I. wurde 1559 eine revidierte Ausgabe des 'Book of Common Prayer' eingeführt, die einen Kompromiß zwischen der ersten und der deutlich protestantischen zweiten Ausgabe dieses Werkes darstellt." Cf. Nichols, *Panther and the Hind*, 11–19.

[24] Nichols, *Panther and the Hind*, XIX: "The theology of the English Reformers was built on both Lutheran and Calvinist foundations, yet it was never systematically either Lutheran or Calvinist. Partly from conviction but mostly from political necessity their theology was poured into an institutional mould which retained large elements of a Catholic structure.... The history of Anglican pluralism derives from the intrinsic difficulty of defining such a *via media*, and from the resultant need to leave open a wide latitude in the construing of doctrine." Cf. Neuner, *Ökumenische Theologie*, 122; P. Dentin, *Les privilèges des Papes*, 243.

[25] Cf. Chadwick, "Ministero papale e unità dei cristiani", 67.

[26] Nichols, *Panther and the Hind*, 17: "Elizabeth entertained some hope of reaching a *modus vivendi* with the Papacy until as late as 1571. But strengthened by the example of the Protestant martyrs under Mary, the pro-Lutheran and pro-Calvinist parties were even more clamant than under Edward VI. Elizabeth disliked Calvinism both for its doctrinal rigorism and for its subjection of the ruler to the judgment of the gathered church. Her personal views were probably those of a Lutheranising Catholicism. She was obliged by the total political situation to come to a compromise solution on more or less everything." Cf. ibid., 38–39.

[27] Ibid., 11: "The result was that the Anglican Church oscillated between Lutheranising and Catholicising positions for the rest of her reign."

[28] Ibid., 40–41: "Such radical Protestants, Calvinist in doctrine, Presbyterian in church order and deeply anti-Erastian in their attitude to the State, are called in the English situation, 'Puritans', and they can be thought of as taking certain elements of Calvin's theology and church practise to their logical extreme.... In the course of the seventeenth

"obsessed" with its Catholic past,[29] and the true *via media* of Anglicanism was still marked by both Catholic and Reformed influences.[30]

It does not seem therefore in keeping with reality to label, as does von Allmen, the Anglican Church as *Protestant*.[31] As a matter of fact, it remained open to the principles of Lutheran ecclesiology, above all when they seemed particularly suited to the demands of the English situation, and appeared not particularly to be connected to the real core of Luther's theology.[32] In reality, the Reform in England, however sensitive to the doctrinal positions of a clearly Protestant matrix, did not seem inclined to renounce the principle based on an episcopal foundation of the apostolicity of the Church.[33] Therefore it cannot be considered as a variant of the phenomenon that took place, for example, in Germany or in Scotland, since the final separation of the Anglican Church from the Church of Rome was, in many respects, more similar to the separation from Rome of the Eastern Orthodox Churches than to that of the Lutheran or Calvinist Churches of Europe. Laden with ambiguities, it was more a political than a theological separation, determined more by the temporal jurisdiction reclaimed from the Bishop of Rome than by the dogmas proclaimed by the See of Rome.[34] In fact, in the seventeenth century the Anglican Church would

---

century they were able in fact to overthrow the Elizabethan settlement, so that from 1649 to 1660 the Anglican church as Elizabeth had fashioned it ceased to exist, or at least only existed as an underground sect."

[29] The Anglican historian Diarmaid McCulloch describes the "later Reformation" as "the building of a Protestant Church which remained haunted by its Catholic past": cited by Nichols, *Panther and the Hind*, 52.

[30] Ibid., 57–58: "as the seventeenth century progressed the Anglican episcopate became more and more convinced that the true *via media* is that between Rome and the Reformation itself."

[31] J. J. von Allmen, *Il primato della Chiesa di Pietro e di Paolo*, 46–47: "La protesta anglicana contro Roma si riassume essenzialmente nei tre punti seguenti: primo, l'anglicanesimo respinge l'infallibilità del papa; secondo, respinge la pretesa della Chiesa di Roma d'essere la sorgente dell'ecclesialità delle altre Chiese: si può dunque essere cristiani senza essere in comunione con Roma; infine, la protesta verte circa la pretesa del vescovo di Roma di tenere le due spade.... Finché la posizione di Roma su questi tre punti non sarà cambiata, la Chiesa anglicana—per riprendere l'idea dell'arcivescovo William Laud (1573–1645)—dovrà restare una Chiesa *protestante*."

[32] Cf. G. Alberigo, "L'Atto di Supremazia", 59.

[33] Cf. Alzati, *L'anglicanesimo*, Introduzione, 18.

[34] Cf. Root, "Gli anglicani", *Conosciamo i fratelli. Corso breve di ecumenismo*, II (Rome, 1993), 171. The author then goes on to state, "La grande ondata di controversie dottrinali e teologiche, ben rappresentata da uomini come Lutero e Calvino, ebbe un impatto molto ridotto sull'Inghilterra" (ibid., 173). Cf. Maviiri Ndidde, *Primacy in the Communion of Churches*, 9–10.

constitute, together with the Eastern Orthodox, a sort of alliance against Rome.[35] Von Allmen himself ends up being in agreement with this position, provided that Rome would change its viewpoint.[36]

The same evolution is also noted with regard to the primacy in particular. The *Act of Supremacy* issued by Parliament in 1534—according to which the king was designated the supreme head of the Church in England, not simply as an honorific title, but with practical implications[37]—concluded and synthesized the rapid evolution, begun only a few years earlier, and in continuity with the characteristics of the Anglican Church in the late Middle Ages.[38]

No doubt this act—a true model of the nationalization of the ecclesiastical body[39]—certainly implied the rejection of any power of the Bishop of Rome over the Anglican Church:[40] it can be seen as the refusal to recognize the Pope as the sign and instrument of unity and continuity in the *Catholic Church*.[41] This rejection became an explicit deprivation of any jurisdiction over the Anglican Church when Queen Elizabeth I was named the sole supreme head of the kingdom in matters both ecclesiastical

---

[35] Cf. C. Davey, "Chiesa Anglicana e Oriente Ortodosso", in Alzati, *L'anglicanesimo*, 265–70.

[36] *La Chiesa di Pietro e di Paolo*, 47: " 'Cristo' infatti—cito un testo di re Giacomo I del 1609—'prima della sua Ascensione, non ha promesso di lasciare con essi Pietro per dirigerli ed istruirli in tutte le cose, mentre a tale scopo ha promesso d'inviare lo Spirito'. Ma se Roma cambiasse, la tendenza dell'Anglicanesimo che su questo punto s'avvicina alla Chiesa ortodossa e sostiene, pur con meno scetticismo, ciò che si trova anche nelle Chiese riformata e luterana sarebbe di riconoscere il primato d'onore del vescovo di Roma, poiché 'La Chiesa d'Inghilterra, per voce dei suoi teologi più rappresentativi, non nega che Pietro sia stato il primo tra gli Apostoli, né che il vescovo di Roma dovrebbe essere, per analogia, il primo tra i vescovi.' "

[37] Maviiri Ndidde, *Primacy in the Communion of Churches*, 12: "By this Act the king/queen of England is the supreme governor of the Church of England. In the same year Parliament passed the Act of Uniformity which constitutionally established the Church of England. The Act also set up the *Book of Common Prayer* and later on (1571) the *39 Articles of Religion* were promulgated, setting up the official standard of Anglican Orthodoxy and the consequent *Ecclesia Anglicana*. The Bishop of Rome was explicitly stripped of the right of jurisdiction over the Church of England." Cf. G. Dunstan, "Common Law e Diritto Canonico", Alzati, *L'anglicanesimo*, 129–41; Neuner, *Ökumenische Theologie*, 117.

[38] Cf. G. Alberigo, "L'Atto di Supremazia", 62.

[39] Cf. Buchanan, " 'Evangelicalism' e 'Catholicism' nello sviluppo storico dell'Anglicanismo", in Alzati, *L'anglicanesimo*, 179.

[40] Cf. G. Alberigo, "L'Atto di Supremazia", 63–66.

[41] Cf. Chadwick, "La continuità della Chiesa in Inghilterra", 46.

and temporal.[42] The subsequent excommunication of the queen by Pius V (1570) heralded the almost complete separation of the Catholic Church and the Church of England.[43] This took place under the influence of an extreme form of conciliarism[44] and of a Protestantism that began to make itself heard not only with regard to the priority of the Scriptures relative to salvation and to the nature of the Church, but also with regard to the doctrine on the primacy of the Bishop of Rome; once again in the ritual of 1662 it was denied that the Pope had any jurisdiction whatsoever over the English realm.[45] In this sense the harsh feelings toward the Pope are understandable, obviously fueled by Protestant influence.[46]

It is nevertheless necessary to bear in mind that the failure to recognize the jurisdiction of the Bishop of Rome over the Church of England con-

---

[42] Neuner, *Ökumenische Theologie*, 119: "Elisabeth erließ nicht mehr als 'Haupt' der Kirche von England, sondern 'oberster Leiter' ('The only supreme governor of this realm, as well in all spiritual and ecclesiastical things or causes as temporal')."

[43] K. M. McDonald, s.v. "Anglican-Roman Catholic Dialogue", DEM 26b: "The decisive event on the part of Rome was the promulgation of the Bull *Regnans in Excelsis* by Pope Pius V, which excommunicated Queen Elizabeth and absolved her subjects of allegiance to her. This series of events and their manifold repercussions led to an almost complete estrangement between the RCC and the Church of England which lasted until the 20th century." Cf. Neuner, *Ökumenische Theologie*, 119.

[44] Tavard, "ARCIC-I on Authority", in G. R. Evans and M. Gourgues, eds., *Communion et Réunion*, 195: "The Elizabethan Settlement, which gave shape and tone to the Anglican communion, maintained the succession of bishops from apostolic times, and admitted the legitimacy of the bishop of Rome in his see. But, following an extreme form of late medieval conciliarist theology, it recognised the Roman primacy only to the extent that the legitimate authorities of each kingdom would permit the Pope to act in their realm. As she was eager to maintain peace with the Puritan faction in England, Elizabeth did not allow any Roman jurisdiction in her kingdom and forbade all appeals to Rome. By contrast, the Roman system of authority during the counter-reformation developed in the opposite direction, away from all forms of conciliarism."

[45] Root, "Prospettiva anglicana sul Vescovo di Roma", 85: " 'Il Vescovo di Roma non ha nessuna giurisdizione sul Regno d'Inghilterra'. . . . É questo l'unico esplicito riferimento al Vescovo di Roma contenuto nel Rituale Anglicano del 1662. Era il frutto, la conclusione di un periodo molto anteriore, che va dal regno di re Enrico VIII a quello della Regina Elisabetta I." Cf. von Allmen, *La Chiesa di Pietro e di Paolo*, 46.

[46] Root, "Prospettiva anglicana sul Vescovo di Roma", 85: "Nel 1662, il Rituale aveva abbandonato parte del duro linguaggio e degli aspri sentimenti dei suoi predecessori del 16° secolo. Per esempio in una precedente versione delle Litanie, il sacerdote diceva: 'Dal Vescovo di Roma e da tutte le sue abominevoli enormità' e i fedeli rispondevano: 'Liberaci o Signore'." J. Hind, too, emphasizes that the expression "down with the papacy" belonged to the popular culture, "Primato e unità. Un contributo anglicano a un dialogo paziente e fraterno", *Studi ecumenici* 17 [1999]: 50.

stituted more of a political than a theological conflict.[47] One could say that, at the most profound level, it was never the idea of the Anglicans to reject the Bishop of Rome, and even at the time of Henry VIII the rejection of papal supremacy was not a rejection of the Bishop of Rome *as such*. It was rather a rejection motivated by the belief that he was virtually the prisoner of those European kings and princes who were determined to destroy England. This places the problem in a somewhat different light.[48] The authority of the Roman Pontiff was considered, however, as more patriarchal than papal[49] and therefore "foreign", irrelevant, and subject to the crown.[50]

Thus it was a matter of a tacit opposition, based on theological and historical motives, to the view—typical of the time—of papal supremacy and of the temporal and spiritual jurisdiction of the Pope, supposedly for lack of a foundation in Scripture, the Fathers, and early Church history that could vindicate the claim that the primacy was *de fide* or necessary to the essence of the true Church.[51]

A critique was leveled against the papacy, from a doctrinal point of view, especially from the seventeenth century on, during which ecclesiology

---

[47] Root, "Prospettiva anglicana sul primato", 85: "Dall'epoca di Elisabetta in poi, dire che il Vescovo di Roma non aveva giurisdizione sul regno d'Inghilterra era la semplice constatazione di un dato di fatto. Questo fatto, tuttavia, non era in se stesso un giudizio teologico nei confronti del Vescovo di Roma, del ministro di Pietro o di qualsiasi altra cosa." It was a "conflitto politico piuttosto che teologico" (ibid., 86).

[48] Cf. ibid., 91.

[49] Cf. Mikulanis, *Authority in the Church*, 14. The patriarchal authority of the Bishop of Rome was limited to the suburbican dioceses and did not extend to all the West, because various provinces, especially Britain, remained autonomous, as was claimed by Anglican theologians in the prolonged discussions on the patriarchate of Rome during the whole of the 17th century: cf. A. Garuti, *Il Papa Patriarca d'Occidente?*, 80–83.

[50] Mikulanis, *Authority in the Church*, 16–17: "The Roman Papacy, viewed as a foreign power on the Island Bastion, no longer influenced, to its benefits, life in England. In effect, the Reformation in England produced a revolution in ecclesiological thinking where the authority of the crown replaced the authority of the pope, causing a debate on the concept and nature of authority in the Church."

[51] H. R. McAdoo, "Anglican/Roman Catholic Relations, 1717–1980. A Detection of Themes", Haase, *Rome and the Anglicans*, 165: "The general attitude of traditional Anglicanism ... was one of unyielding opposition on theological and historical grounds to contemporary concepts of papal supremacy, of temporal and spiritual jurisdiction.... From Jewel's 'Apology' (1562) onwards this is the case. Theologically, the grounds of opposition were broadly that there was no Scriptural basis for the claims which could not therefore be *de fide* or essential to the being of a true Church. Historically, it was held that the claims could not be substantiated from antiquity, the Fathers, and the teaching and practice of the Early Church."

became the dominant theme, especially in the work of the so-called *Caroline Divines*.[52] They represent, however, a great variety of opinions. "On the one hand there are those for whom the papacy was an irremediably defective institution, and among them some even go as far as to identify the Pope with the Antichrist. On the other hand there are those who considered the papacy to be a corrupt institution, but one capable of being reformed." [53] In any case, in their attempt to consolidate the Anglican identity, "which asserted with conviction its full catholicity and apostolicity, regardless of its separation from the See of Rome", the Caroline Divines were "notably free of a gratuitous spirit of polemics and of *odium teologicum*".[54]

Therefore it can be concluded that Anglicanism—except for rare occasions[55]—rejects not the papacy as such, but rather the supremacy of Rome; not the *principalitas*, but the universal sovereignty that concentrates all power in a sort of universal bishop.[56] In reality one of the cardinal

---

[52] Root, "Prospettiva anglicana sul Vescovo di Roma", 85: "Il cosiddetto periodo 'classico' della teologia anglicana è rappresentato dai Teologi carolini, e cioè da questi teologi che prosperarono dopo il periodo dei Tudor. Il loro compito, a loro parere, era quello di tracciare un'immagine della posizione anglicana che evidenziasse le differenze con quella cattolica (romana) di allora, nonché da quella dei riformatori protestanti come Lutero e Calvino." According to these theologians "la Chiesa d'Inghilterra dopo la Riforma era la stessa Chiesa fondata da sant' Agostino: 'lo stesso giardino, ma disinfestato'" (P. Cobb, "La continuità cattolica della Chiesa d'Inghilterra nel pensiero del Movimento di Oxford", in Alzati, *L'anglicanesimo*, 189). For a presentation of the rather diversified thought of the various theologians, see Nichols, *Panther and the Hind*, 54–79; Tavard, *The Quest for Catholicity*, 44–68; Mikulanis, *Authority in the Church*, 10–17.

[53] Cf. Hind, "Primato e unità: Un contributo anglicano", 51. In the pages following the author relates the thought of various bishops and theologians. Cf. McAdoo, "Anglican/Roman Catholic Relations", 273–77, where, in an appendix, he deals with the subject "Anglican Theologians and the Concept of a Roman Primacy", citing various authors of the period.

[54] Cf. Root, "Gli anglicani", 174 and 176. Nichols, *Panther and the Hind*, 59: "Laud and his sympathisers had distanced themselves from the early Anglican perception, expressed in violent imagery drawn from the biblical apocalypses, that the Church of Rome was identical with Antichrist."

[55] Such is the case of Stephen Gardiner, for whom the ideal was a "Catholicism-without-the-pope" (ibid., 81).

[56] Tillard, "Ministère de l'unité", 209–11: "La tradition anglicane, qui utilise elle aussi l'image de l'Antichrist, est infiniment plus souple. Tenant à l'épiscopat, elle a des réactions proches a celles de l'Orient, refusant moins la primauté comme telle que la suprématie romaine, moins *principalitas* que la *universal domination*. . . . Leur grand problème sera d'ordre ministériel plus que soteriologique. (A) Ainsi, Richard Hooker trouve inacceptable la concentration en un seul de la puissance ministérielle qui ferait du primat comme une réplique

principles of the English reform was precisely the identification of the primacy in a regional or, more specifically, a national context.[57]

A primacy of order or of dignity is thus recognized, which nevertheless is not always traced back to the will and direct institution of Christ.[58] Moreover, the papacy must be exercised in a markedly collegial context[59] and is limited to the role of the Roman Pontiff as the Patriarch of the West.[60]

A very decisive development in the Anglican concept of the primacy can be found in the famous Conversations of Malines (1921-1926) between an Anglican delegation and a Catholic one, led by Lord Halifax and by Cardinal Mercier, respectively, and with the tacit agreement between the respective authorities. The immediate purpose was to investigate the possibility of union between the two Churches: naturally the theme of the primacy emerged at the very first meetings, though in connection

---

'sur terre' de ce qu'est le Christ 'à la droite du Père'. L'idée d'évêque 'universel' ... lui apparait modelée plus sur la conception mondaine du pouvoir que sur une fidélité à la notion évangelique d'*exousia* ... (B) William Laud ... fait la distinction que nous avons évoquée entre la *principalitas* (dont parle Irenée) et la *domination universelle*.... Le pouvoir *principal* ... n'équivaut pas nécessairement à *tout* le pouvoir.... (C) Quant à Lancelot Andrewes ... il se montre lui aussi du même avis. Il refuse d'admettre un *universal power* qui se veut de droit divin, les autres degrés hiérarchiques étant simplement *de jure positivo*." A distinction was made, moreover, between *primacy* and *Supremacy*: cf. Cobb, "La continuità cattolica", 192.

[57] Cf. Hind, "Primato e unità: un contributo anglicano", 57.

[58] Nichols, *Panther and the Hind*, 63-64: "However, though Bramhall's ecclesiology thereby provides a category in which to place the pope, Bramhall himself held that this logical category does not correspond to anything in the will and historical institution of Jesus Christ. In this, he was not followed by all the 'right-wing' Caroline divines."

[59] McAdoo, "Anglican/Roman Catholic Relations". 166: "but when we come to the question of a simple Roman primacy, we find instances of a flexibility which arise from the writer's knowledge of Church history and from the fact that there is no inbuilt resistance in Anglicanism to the concept of primacy *per se*. It is noticeable that Wake, like other well-known Anglicans such as Field, Bramhall, Cosin and Laud, could conceive of a primacy of order or dignity within a strongly collegial setting." The distinction between the two primacies is explained by Bramhall as follows: "A primacy of order may consist with an equality of dignity; but a supremacy of power taketh away all parity" (ibid., 275).

[60] Among others, the observations of John Cosin are worth recalling: "Likewise John Cosin, whose path had lain through the Anglican/Roman Catholic polemics of the day, could still write that Anglicans might agree 'in acknowledgment of the Bishop of Rome, if he would rule and be ruled by the ancient canons of the Church, to be the Patriarch of the West, by right of ecclesiastical and imperial constitutions ... without any necessary dependence upon him by divine right'" (reported by A. Nichols, "Anglican/Roman Catholic Relations, 1717-1980", 275).

with the question posed by the Anglicans as to the role of the Archbishop of Canterbury in relation to the Pope should a union come about.
This question was dealt with most directly in the Conversations of 1923.
Naturally the Catholic delegation emphasized that the Pope cannot renounce
his ordinary and immediate jurisdiction, even if the exercise of it might
be restricted.[61] For the time being the question was remanded,[62] but then
taken up again in the third conversation, which was devoted to the foundation for the Petrine succession and to papal primacy, on the basis of a
memorandum prepared by Dom Lambert Beauduin.[63] Its introduction
asserted the equality, by divine right, of all the bishops, except for the
successor of Peter, the Bishop of Rome, who is constituted as supreme
head of the episcopal college, with episcopal jurisdiction over all the
Churches.[64] After a historical survey of the Church of England, and on
the basis of the organization of the uniate Eastern Churches, it was proposed that the traditional patriarchal role of the Archbishop of Canterbury, with his respective rights, be reestablished.[65] As a consequence, the
Church of England would not be *Latin*, but *Roman*, preserving her own
organization and autonomy, but in subordination to the universal Church
with Rome as her center of unity.[66]

---

[61] As it is evident from the Anglican memorandum *L'Église anglicane unie non absorbée* of
1923, the See of Canterbury was compared to a patriarchate. Such a comparison was already
proposed by the Lambeth Conference of 1897, even though it was later discarded: cf. E.
Lanne, " 'L'Église anglicane unie non absorbée' et le contexte oecuménique au moment
des Conversations de Malines", H. Deneaux and W.J. Dick, eds., *From Malines to ARCIC.
The Malines Conversations Commemorated* (Louvain, 1997), 14–18.

[62] Ibid., 21: "La question de la remise du pallium et d'une éventuelle reconnaissance de
la position du siège de Cantorbéry comme équivalant à celle d'un patriacat oriental n'était
pas exclue, mais elle paraissait prématurée pour le moment tant que la question doctrinale
de la primauté n'aurait pas été au clair de façon satisfaisante pour les Anglicans."

[63] The English translation of the text, "The Church of England United Not Absorbed",
is reprinted in Denaux and Dick, *From Malines to ARCIC*, 35–46.

[64] Ibid., 35: "If we only consider divine right, all Bishops are equal among themselves.
One alone, the successor of St. Peter, Bishop of Rome, is constituted the supreme head of
the episcopal body and of the whole Catholic Church. His episcopal jurisdiction is extended
to all individual Churches without exception—he is *Episcopus catholicus*."

[65] Ibid., 43: "In practice, the Archbishop of Canterbury would be re-established in his
traditional and effective rights as Patriarch of the Anglican Church. After receiving his
investiture from the successor of St. Peter by the traditional imposition of the pallium, he
would enjoy patriarchal rights over the whole Church of England."

[66] Ibid., 45: "It would be necessary, then, if the Anglican Church wished to belong to
the unique and visible society of Christ, for her to establish between herself and the Roman
Church a link of dependence and submission to the successor of Peter, in other words she

As can be seen from the minutes of the Anglican and Catholic delegations,[67] the effective Anglican concept of primacy emerged more clearly
in the subsequent discussions. Apart from the call for a new papacy, different from the one in existence then among the Catholics,[68] it was hoped
that in his interventions the Pope would deal directly with the Archbishop of Canterbury, as the head of the Anglican Communion, or with
the metropolitans.[69] From a strictly doctrinal point of view, we should
emphasize the recognition of a *leadership* role among the apostles which
was conferred on Peter by Christ himself. And even though no evidence
of a true jurisdiction was found in the New Testament, but only of leadership,[70] it was said to be not merely a primacy of honor, but of true
responsibility, which was in turn transmitted to the Church of Rome.[71]
Consequently, the recognition of the primacy of the Bishop of Rome is
assumed to be indispensable for reunion, even though a more precise
"definition" of it was still necessary.[72]

The Conversations of Malines, suspended with the explanation that
the Pope, having followed to that point the development of the matter,

---

must become not Latin but Roman; while preserving all her internal organization, all her
historical traditions and her legitimate autonomy, on the model of the Eastern Churches,
she would strongly establish this essential link of subordination to the universal Church
whose centre of unity is in Rome."

[67] Cf. respectively ibid., 47–64 and 65–74.

[68] Ibid., 51: "we should not shrink from the idea of a Papacy acting as a centre of unity;
but, in so saying, we have in view not the Papacy such as it exists in theory and practice
among Roman Catholics at the present time, but a conception of unity such as may emerge
in the future."

[69] Ibid., 54: "They would in any case hope that the Pope might restrict himself to
dealing directly with the Archbishop of Canterbury as recognized leader of the Anglican
Communion, or with the several Metropolitans in Anglican Provinces."

[70] Ibid., 56: "We recognize that St. Peter was the accepted chief or leader of the Apostles, and was so accepted because he was treated so by our Lord.... There is ... no trace
in the New Testament of a jurisdiction of St. Peter over other Apostles, or over churches
founded by them.... On the other hand, the evidence of the New Testament justifies us
in saying that St. Peter was chosen and marked out by our Lord to exercise a primacy of
leadership among the Twelve."

[71] Ibid., 59: "To the objection that a mere Primacy of Honour cannot be admitted by
the Roman Church, it was insisted that this was more than a Primacy of Honour, it was
also a Primacy of responsibility."

[72] Ibid., 62: "Nor can we imagine that any reunion of Christendom could be effected
except on the recognition of the primacy of the Pope. But while we think that both
Eastern Orthodox and the Anglican Churches would be prepared to recognize such primacy, we do not think it likely that they would be ready to define it more closely."

nonetheless had never regarded it as anything more than something that had taken place between private persons without a mandate of any sort,[73] contributed to creating the new climate in Anglican-Catholic relations— encouraged following Vatican II[74]—which made possible the convergence reached with regard to the primacy,[75] and in effect some elements relative to the primacy outlined in them would be taken up again in the Catholic-Anglican dialogue.[76]

Even today the Anglican notion of primacy is more similar to the Eastern concept than to the Protestant view. Having always preserved a historical episcopate, although not valid, the Anglican notion recognizes that every single bishop, even though autonomous, is linked to the other bishops so as to form a unity, in a spirit of collegiality and conciliarity, under the direction of the Archbishop of Canterbury.[77] Nevertheless, among Anglicans the position of the primacy is still not well defined, although various Lambeth Conferences have sought to articulate the complex identity of their communion.[78] Indeed, the relationship between the diverse communions is moral rather than juridical and is expressed in the famous notion of *dispersed authority*,[79] out of a concern to avoid

---

[73] Cf. *L'Osservatore Romano*, 21 gennaio 1928.

[74] R. T. Greenacre, "Lettre ouverte à quelques amis catholiques (Epistola ad Romanos)", *Istina* 38 (1993): 119: "Le Second Concile du Vatican et le dialogue de l'A.R.C.I.C., qui est l'un de ses fruits, ont profondément changé l'attitude à l'égard de Rome d'une majorité ... d'anglicans de tendance catholique. Avant le Concile, une nette majorité d'anglo-catholiques rejetaient la définition donnée à Vatican I de l'infaillibilité et de la primauté universelle; seule une petite minorité (que l'on surnommait 'papaliste') l'acceptaient. Après le Concile et, plus particulièrement après la publication du *Rapport final*, un groupe beaucoup plus important s'est constitué de ceux que, pour la commodité, ont pourrait appeler 'les anglicans pro-A.R.C.I.C.': ceux qui en sont venus à admettre que 'le mantien de l'unité visible au niveau universel inclut l'évêque de Rome ... appartient au dessein de Dieu sur l'unité et la catholicité de l'Église."

[75] Maviiri Ndidde, *Primacy in the Communion of Churches*, 29: "The convergence so far reached on the nature and exercise of primatial authority on a theological level has been possible because of the mutual change of attitude."

[76] Cf. Tillard, "Faire émerger la Communion. L'option de l'ARCIC-I", Denaux and Dick, *From Malines to ARCIC*, 165–66.

[77] Cf. Mikulanis, *Authority in the Church*, 52–66.

[78] Cf. G. Galeota and A. Mancia, "La comunione anglicana in dialogo. Sulla Lambeth Conference 1988", *Asprenas* 36 (1989): 51.

[79] Ibid., 53: "Il rapporto che lega i membri della Comunione è di mutua lealtà, morale. Esso non si esprime e non esprime alcuna realtà giuridicamente configurata. Già la *Lam-*

the risk of a synodal or primatial centralization.[80] Actually, the Archbishop of Canterbury exercises a certain universal primacy, without enjoying however significant power over the other bishops,[81] among whom he is a *primus inter pares* according to the model of the Eastern Orthodox Churches,[82] thus excluding any possibility of his being considered an "Anglican Pope".[83]

As for the Bishop of Rome, he is considered Patriarch of the West[84] and also the pastor of the universal Church.[85] The problem is always the

---

beth Conference del 1948 ha trovato una locuzione caratterizzante il tipo di autorità che le Chiese Anglicane sono venute realizzando nel tempo, la *dispersed authority*."

[80] Ibid., 60: "La *Lambeth Conference* ha cercato di incoraggiare e di promuovere l'autorità episcopale proponendo la crescita del ruolo del *Primate's meeting*. Tale orientamento ha ricevuto il plauso dell'Arcivescovo di Canterbury. Occorre tuttavia inquadrare questa proposta nell'insieme degli strumenti di decisione dei quali la Comunione Anglicana è dotata. Si vedrà allora che l'obiettivo principale è quello dell'equilibrio fra le quattro strutture esistenti, fuori dal rischio di una centralizzazione sinodale—per esempio la proposta di un sinodo pan-anglicano—e dal pericolo di una centralizzazione primaziale facente capo all'Arcivescovo di Canterbury."

[81] Tillard, "Canterbury and Rome: So Near, So Far", 146: "The Archbishop of Canterbury exercises a certain universal primacy within the Anglican Communion, which an Anglican theologian even describes as 'embryonic universal papacy'.... The Anglican Church has always been convinced that to give the Primate too much power over the other bishops would lead to the destroying of his influence. This influence is exercised by persuasion, through dialogue, patient listening, and communicating to everyone solutions discovered in one place or another, and inviting people to share in decision-making." Cf. S. Butler, "Authority in the Church: Lessons from Anglican-Roman Catholic Dialogue", *Theology Digest* 45, no. 4 (1998): 344.

[82] Root, "Prospettiva anglicana sul Vescovo di Roma", 87: "si potrebbe dire che l'attuale modello anglicano assomiglia molto a quello delle chiese ortodosse orientali, nelle loro singole autonomie unitamente alla simbolica deferenza verso il Patriarca di Costantinopoli quale *primus inter pares* tra i vari patriarchi."

[83] Butler, "Authority in the Church", 345: "They (Anglicans) are not about to make the Most Reverend and Right Honorable George H. Carey an Anglican pope."

[84] Root, "Prospettiva anglicana sul Vescovo di Roma", 87: "non ho alcun dubbio sul fatto che la maggior parte degli anglicani che si soffermano a riflettere su questi argomenti non esiterebbe ad accettare uno dei titoli tradizionali attribuiti al Vescovo di Roma, e cioè quello di Patriarca d'Occidente." Cf. Root, "Gli Anglicani", 178; E. Kemp, "Fede, ordine e strutture ecclesiastiche nell'Anglicanesimo", Alzati, *L'anglicanesimo*, 237–44.

[85] Root, "Prospettiva anglicana sul Vescovo di Roma", 91: "Si può giustamente osservare che molti anglicani si sono convinti, con metodi induttivi piuttosto che deduttivi, della necessità di un 'primato universale'. Papa Giovanni Paolo II parla della sua missione qual 'pastore universale' della Chiesa. Ad un orecchio anglicano, l'espressione suona molto più congeniale di altre usate in passato. É chiaro che quando parliamo di pastore universale non può trattarsi che del Vescovo di Roma. Non può esservi altro candidato."

same, that is, the current development in the exercise of the primacy.[86] The traditional disagreements concerning the *ius divinum/humanum* of the primacy and its necessity for the *esse* or the *bene esse* of the Church remain fundamental. As Hind underscores: though there is not a universally accepted interpretation of this expression (*ex ipsius Christi Domini institutione seu iure divino*), everyone asserts that it at least indicates the fact that this primacy is an expression of the will of God for the Church. In this context, *ius divinum* does not necessarily imply that the universal primacy as a permanent institution was established personally by Jesus during his earthly life. Nor does the term signify that the universal primacy is a "source of the Church", such that salvation by Christ would have to be channeled through it, but rather, the Pope must be the sign of visible *koinônia* that God desires for the Church and an instrument through which unity in diversity comes about. The qualification *iure divino* can be applied to a universal primacy thus conceived, within the collegiality of the bishops and the *koinônia* of the whole Church.[87]

The question still remains problematic whether a character of true jurisdiction can be attributed to the primacy, or simply the role of *primus inter pares*,[88] with the consequent rejection on the part of Anglicans of the definitions of Vatican I.[89]

---

[86] J. Arnold, "Rigore confessionale e apertura ecumenica", *il regno-att.* 10/93, 265: "Non il primato in quanto tale ci fa problema, ma come è inteso attualmente, anche se si tenta di presentarlo in maniera più dolce, più gradevole. Siamo pronti ad accettare un primato di amore, come era all'inizio. . . . In particolare, la struttura giuridica della curia romana e il primato del papa così come è inteso adesso, non hanno fondamento né nella Scrittura né nella Tradizione" (interview with F. Strazzari).

[87] Cf. Hind, "Primato e unità: un contributo anglicano", 70. Maviiri Ndidde, *Primacy in the Communion of Churches*, 3: "While the Catholics clearly assert a theological grounding (that is, the universal primatial authority was directly given to Peter by the Lord himself, *de iure divino*), the Anglicans hold that universal primacy is justifiable on historical contingent developments, *de iure ecclesiastico*. For the Anglicans, universal primacy in the communion of Churches will be needed for the '*bene esse*' of the Church, while for the Catholics it necessarily belongs to the '*esse*' of the Church."

[88] Ibid., 4: "The Catholics hold that the universal primate exercises a power of jurisdiction (DS 3055). On the contrary, Anglicans see the universal primate as 'first-among equals' (*primus-inter-pares*). He occupies the seat of a president among his brother bishops but has no jurisdiction outside his diocese." Cf. Hind, "Primato e unità: un contributo anglicano", 61–62.

[89] Maviiri Ndidde, *Primacy in the Communion of Churches*, 82: "This means that the majority of Anglicans (who hold the *39 Articles of Religion* as normative) do not accept the dogmatic Constitution *Pastor aeternus* (DS 3050–3075) of Vatican I on the universal primacy

Chadwick offers a synthesis of the present situation: from the Anglican point of view, the Roman primacy seems to strengthen the claim that the Pope is something more than *primus inter pares*, more than the first of the patriarchs, more than a bishop, more than the president of a conciliar assembly, of which he is the privileged spokesman. Nevertheless, the claim to a universal jurisdiction remains difficult to accept, even when it is readily conceded that the papacy must possess an adequate power basis to be able to serve the unity and harmony of the whole Church and of all of her parts.[90]

Apart from the difficulty of establishing, over the course of history, the causes, the influences, and "the differences of opinion concerning the papacy that have been expressed in the Church of England since the time of the Reformation",[91] the problems still to be overcome today, in the field of ecumenical dialogue, are: "1) whether this ministry is necessary; 2) if so, whether it is required *de iure divino* or for practical reasons; 3) and in what manner it should be exercised (including its relations with the living structures through which it would be exercised)".[92]

II. ANALYSIS OF THE DIALOGUE DOCUMENTS

The Catholic-Anglican dialogue goes back to the meetings held in Madeira (1890) between Lord Halifax and the Vincentian priest Stefano Ferdinando Portal, and to the Conversations of Malines (1921–1926) between Lord Halifax and Cardinal Mercier. Its formal beginning, however, followed the Common Statement (March 24, 1966), in which Paul VI and Archbishop Runcie made public their intention to initiate a dialogue. In fact, the Anglican-Roman Catholic International Commission (ARCIC I) was officially instituted on November 8, 1969, which was followed by ARCIC II.

---

of the Bishop of Rome. According to them (Anglicans) such a teaching cannot be recognized 'as the authentic expression of Christian doctrine and therefore (cannot be accepted to be) part of the deposit of faith'. For Catholics, however, *Pastor Aeternus* is 'recognized as the authentic expression of Christian doctrine and therefore part of the deposit of faith'."

[90] Cf. Chadwick, "Ministero papale e unità dei cristiani", 69–70.

[91] Hind, "Primato e unità: un contributo anglicano", 50.

[92] Ibid., 61.

Naturally, the topics dealt with were varied. It is important to emphasize here that no other commission in all of the worldwide bilateral theological dialogue gave more complete and explicit attention to the questions of the primacy and the papacy than the Catholic-Anglican dialogue.[93] The work of analysis, however, is facilitated also by the fact that at the end of the first phase a Final Report was drawn up that surveys the various texts.

1. The "Final Report" of ARCIC I

As emphasized in the introduction, primacy in the Catholic-Anglican dialogue is considered in the wider context of *koinonia*: primacy is "as a visible link of *koinonia*" and "a necessary link between all those exercising *episkopé* within the *koinonia*". Since the one Church "is a communion of local churches", the primacy, "as a focus within the *koinonia* is an assurance that what [all the ministers of the Gospel] teach and do is in accord with the faith of the apostles".[94]

Recalling the need in the Church, as in every human community, for "a focus of leadership and unity", that is, of a "responsibility for 'oversight' (*episkopé*)" which is an "essential element in the ordained minis-

[93] Maviiri Ndidde, *Primacy in the Communion of Churches*, 5: "But on a world-wide bilateral theological dialogue, no commission has yet so thoroughly and directly confronted the question of universal primacy and the papacy, as ARCIC I has done." For the different phases of the dialogue: from the Lambeth Conferences to the Malines Conversations, to the principles dictated by Vatican II, to the meetings between Paul VI and the Primates of England, up to the work of the Commission, cf. ibid., 13–29; W.H. Van De Pol, *La Communion anglicane et l'oécumenisme d'après les documents officiels* (Paris, 1967); W.A. Purdy, "Il dialogo tra cattolici e anglicani. Panorama e prospettive", *La Chiesa cattolica oggi nel dialogo. Corso breve di ecumenismo*, IV (Rome, 1982), 27–40; A. Stacpoole, "Cordial Relations between Rome and Canterbury. First Phase, 1944–1945", *One in Christ* 23 (1987): 212–34; Stacpoole, "Pre-ARCIC Conversations between Anglicans and Roman Catholics, 1950", ibid., 298–323; R. Stewart, "Il dialogo tra Comunione Anglicana e Chiesa Cattolico-Romana nel quadro del movimento ecumenico", Alzati, *L'anglicanesimo*, 353–69; McDonald, "Appendice. Comunione anglicana e Chiesa Cattolico-Romana negli anni 1985–1991", ibid., 373–83; Tavard, "ARCIC-I on Authority", 185–98. For a more detailed report, see McAdoo, the Anglican co-President of the Commission ("Anglican/Roman Catholic Relations", 174–273). Cf. also the various contributions collected in Denaux and Dick, *From Malines to ARCIC*, especially that of Denaux himself, "Brève histoire de l'ARCIC" (ibid., 111–32).

[94] MV 65–66, no. 6.

try",[95] the Report dealt with the question of the primacy in the joint declaration *Authority in the Church* (Venice, September 1976).[96] The text recalls, first of all, how it was "precisely in the problem of papal primacy that our historical divisions found their unhappy origin" and that the "unresolved questions on the nature and exercise of authority in the Church would hinder the growing experience of unity which is the pattern of our present relations".[97] Hence the need for changes, not only in the Anglican Communion, but also in the Roman Catholic Church.[98]

There followed a presentation on the historical process of the primacy, based on the commission's characteristic method, which is inductive or historical. The need for communion among the individual local Churches[99] was first seen concretely in the local and ecumenical councils[100] and subsequently in the role of oversight entrusted to the bishops of the more important sees in dealings with the other bishops of their region.[101] In

---

[95] Canterbury Statement, *Ministry and Ordination* (September 1973) (MV 80–81, nos. 7 and 9).

[96] The need to treat the topic was already underlined by the Report of the Anglican-Roman Catholic Preparatory Commission (Malta, January 2, 1968): "Real or apparent differences between us come to the surface in such matters as the unity and indefectibility of the Church and its teaching authority, the Petrine primacy, infallibility, and Mariological definitions" (MV 124, no. 20). The Report of the Mixed Commission for Anglican/Catholic Relations in the United States (Boynton Beach, Fla., December 1969) also asserted, "We feel that ARCIC should immediately study the question of orders together with the related topics of episcopal collegiality, the papacy, and the authority and teaching office in the whole church" (ARCIC I, 16–17).

[97] MV 88. The Reports of the Anglican-Roman Catholic Preparatory Commission (Malta 1968) and of the Mixed Commission for Anglican-Catholic Relations in the USA (Boynton Beach, Fla., 1969) had already commented on the primacy as an obstacle to unity and on the need to discuss the topic further: cf. previous note.

[98] "Communion with the see of Rome would bring to the churches of the Anglican Communion not only a wider *koinonía* but also a strengthening of the power to realize its traditional ideal of diversity in unity. Roman Catholics, on their side, would be enriched by the presence of a particular tradition of spirituality and scholarship, the lack of which has deprived the Roman Catholic Church of a precious element in the Christian heritage. The Roman Catholic Church has much to learn from the Anglican synodical tradition of involving the laity in the life and mission of the Church" (MV 89).

[99] Cf. MV 92, no. 8.

[100] "Ever since the Council of Jerusalem (Acts 15) the churches have realized the need to express and strengthen the *koinonia* by coming together to discuss matters of mutual concern and to meet contemporary challenges. Such gatherings may be either regional or world-wide" (MV 92, no. 9).

[101] Cf. MV 92–93, no. 10.

the context of such a process "the see of Rome, whose pre-eminence was associated with the death there of Peter and Paul, eventually became the principal centre in matters concerning the Church universal". The importance of the Bishop of Rome, "explained by analogy with the position of Peter among the apostles", was then "interpreted as Christ's will for his Church".[102]

Vatican I is said to have based its affirmation of the need for this service for the unity of whole Church on the same analogy, which in turn was employed by Vatican II in the context of collegiality.[103] No mention was made, however, of the jurisdictional nature of the primacy; the emphasis was simply on its character of being a service, which over the course of history was not always exercised in an exemplary fashion.[104] Emphasis was given, rather, to the need for the primacy to be an authentic expression of the episcopacy, in the spirit of *koinonia* and collegiality, maintaining a proper balance between primacy and conciliarity, the complementary elements of *episkope* in service of the *koinonia* of the Churches.[105]

---

[102] MV 93, no. 12.

[103] "On the basis of this analogy the First Vatican Council affirmed that this service was necessary to the unity of the whole Church. Far from overriding the authority of the bishops in their own dioceses, this service was explicitly intended to support them in their ministry of oversight. The Second Vatican Council placed this service in the wider context of the shared responsibility of all the bishops" (ibid.).

[104] "The theological interpretation of this primacy and the administrative structures through which it has been exercised have varied considerably through the centuries. Neither theory nor practicum, however, has ever fully reflected these ideals. Sometimes functions assumed by the see of Rome were not necessarily linked to the primacy: sometimes the conduct of the occupant of this see has been unworthy of his office; sometimes the image of this office has been obscured by interpretations placed upon it; and sometimes external pressures have made its proper exercise almost impossible. Yet the primacy, rightly understood, implies that the bishop of Rome exercises his oversight in order to guard and promote the faithfulness of all the churches to Christ and one another. Communion with him is intended as a safeguard of the catholicity of each local church, and as a sign of the communion of all the churches" (MV 93–94, no. 12).

[105] "If primacy is to be a genuine expression of *episkope* it will foster the *koinonia* by helping the bishops in their task of apostolic leadership both in their local church and in the Church universal. Primacy fulfills its purpose by helping the churches to listen to one another, to grow in love and unity, and to strive together towards the fulness of Christian life and witness; it respects and promotes Christian freedom and spontaneity; it does not seek uniformity where diversity is legitimate, or centralize administration to the detriment of local churches. A primate exercises his ministry not in isolation but in collegial association with his brother bishops. His intervention in the affairs of a local church should not be made in such a way as to usurp the responsibility of its bishop" (MV 96–97, no. 21). "Although primacy and conciliarity are complementary elements of *episkope* it has often

The text concludes by acknowledging that "the only see which makes any claim to universal primacy and has exercised and still exercises such *episcope* is the see of Rome"; therefore "it seems appropriate that in any future union a universal primacy such as has been described should be held by that see".[106]

The same commission, though expressing satisfaction at having arrived at "a consensus on authority in the Church and, in particular on the basic principles of primacy"—judged to be "of fundamental importance"—did not obscure the persistence of "problems associated with papal primacy" when treating "the particular claims of papal primacy and its exercise",[107] such as the weight given to Petrine passages,[108] the question of the *divine right* of the successors of Peter,[109] and the claim to the Pope's immediate universal jurisdiction.[110] The difficulties notwithstanding, the

---

happened that one has been emphasized at the expense of the other, even to the point of serious imbalance. When churches have been separated from one another, this danger has been increased. The *koinonia* of the churches requires that a proper balance be preserved between the two with the responsible participation of the whole people of God" (MV 97, no. 22). "If God's will for the unity in love and truth of the whole Christian community is to be fulfilled, this general pattern of the complementary primatial and conciliar aspects of *episkopé* serving the *koinonia* of the churches needs to be realized at the universal level" (MV 97, no. 23).

[106] Ibid.

[107] Ibid., no. 24.

[108] "Claims on behalf of the Roman see, as commonly presented in the past, have put a greater weight on the Petrine texts (Matt 16.18; Luke 22.31–32; John 21.15–17) than they are generally thought to be able to bear. However, many Roman Catholic scholars do not feel it necessary to stand by former exegesis of these texts in every respect" (MV 97, no. 24a).

[109] "The First Vatican Council of 1870 uses the language of 'divine right' of the successors of Peter. This language has no clear interpretation in modern Roman Catholic theology. If it is understood as affirming that the universal primacy of the bishop of Rome is part of God's design for the universal *koinonia*, then it need not be a matter of disagreement. But if it were further implied that as long as a church is not in communion with the bishop of Rome, it is regarded by the Roman Catholic Church as less than fully a church, a difficulty would remain: for some this difficulty would be removed by simply restoring communion, but to others the implication would itself be an ostacle to entering into communion with Rome" (MV 97, no. 24b).

[110] "The claim that the pope possesses universal immediate jurisdiction, the limits of which are not clearly specified, is a source of anxiety to Anglicans who fear that the way is thus open to its illegitimate or uncontrolled use. Nevertheless, the First Vatican Council intended that the papal primacy should be exercised only to maintain and never to erode the structures of the local churches. The Roman Catholic Church is today seeking to replace the juridical outlook of the nineteenth century by a more pastoral understanding of authority in the Church" (MV 98, no. 24d).

conviction remained that "this statement on the authority of the Church represents a *significant convergence*" with far-reaching implications.[111]

The publication of the Venice Statement, besides the understandable expressions of recognition, has also met with a considerable amount of criticism. The two *Responses* of the National Anglican-Catholic Consultation in the United States are of particular significance. The first Response (New Orleans, January 1977) limits itself to contrasting the alleged "consensus" with the difficulty that the principles in the Venice Statement "may not be fully reflected or even recognizable to all readers in the practice of either of our churches at the present time"[112] and to emphasizing that the Statement "appears to treat the question of *episkopé* (oversight) and primacy more fully than certain other expressions of authority, more directly involving laity and clergy."[113]

The second Response, *Authority in the Church: Vital Ecumenical Issue* (New Orleans, January 1978) is even more articulate. First of all, it laments the fact that the "treatment of the authority and responsibility of *episkopé* or 'oversight' is directed mainly toward that exercised by primates and most especially by the bishop of Rome" and "quickly moves into the most crucial ecumenical problem of our sister churches, namely, that of the Roman primacy", with the consequence that "other forms of authority in the church, such as that of the laity and unordained ministries do not, indeed cannot, receive the fuller treatment that they would deserve in a document devoted to the complete exposition of authority in the church".[114] Some questions followed, among them that treating the nature of the primacy of the See of Rome considered in the light of the present Roman Catholic practice and of the contemporary Anglican points of view. Referring to nn. 12 and 21 of the Venice Statement,[115] the text considers the presentation on primacy from a rather idealistic viewpoint rather than from that of concrete lived experience;[116] therefore some clarification of the evolution that took place after the division is needed, on

---

[111] Ibid., no. 25.

[112] ARC, *First Response to the Venice Statement*, IV (Washington, 1979), 17.

[113] Ibid.

[114] ARC, *Second Response to ARCIC Venice Statement*, IV, 18–19, no. 2.

[115] Cf. above, pp. 214 and 215, nn. 103 and 106.

[116] "By its attention to this ideal rather than to the actual lived experience, the Venice Statement calls our attention to the discrepancy between papal primacy considered in principle

the part of both Anglicans[117] and Catholics.[118] It was also noted that while "a particularly troubling question to Anglicans is that raised by the issue of papal jurisdiction", the Venice Statement "is dealing primarily with one specific aspect of ecclesiastical authority—namely the discernment of truth in matters of the church's teaching": in fact, this concern for true doctrine "cannot be separated entirely from the authority exercised in the governance of the church ... but it is mainly in this second sense of authority, which was hardly touched in the Venice Statement, that the troublesome jurisdictional question arises".[119] Nevertheless, it is recognized that "the model for the Petrine Office which prevails throughout the Venice Statement" is valid, because it is that of "a papacy that strengthens and upholds other bishops in their ministry, not one that overrides or bypasses them in their own diocese".[120] It could therefore be the future pastoral model of the primacy.[121]

The same Anglican-Roman Catholic Consultation in the USA, in its report *The Substantial Progress of Anglican-Catholic Dialogue after 12 Years of Ecumenical Work* (December 1977), evaluated, albeit indirectly, the chapter in the Venice Statement dedicated to the relationship between the bishops and the universal Church. Aside from some historical judgments on the Anglican and Catholic concept, in the past, of the ministry of the

---

and flaws in the exercise of this primacy by some bishops of Rome" (ARC, *Second Response to ARCIC Venice Statement*, 21, no. 9).

[117] "Anglicans have moved towards a gradual acceptance of the fact that the quest for church unity cannot ignore a church whose membership includes half the Christians of the world. The entry of Rome into the ecumenical movement has encouraged Anglicans and other Christians in the West to consider the positive values of a universal primacy in a reunited church" (ibid., no. 10).

[118] "Roman Catholics have, since Vatican II, come to value the collegial exercise of authority by the bishops of the church which has been characteristic of the Anglican tradition. The developing role of the Synod of Bishops is one indication of such movement; the role now played by national and regional bishops' conferences is another. Steps towards making the Roman Curia more representative of the worldwide Catholic Church as well as the establishment of new norms for the selection of bishops are still further indications of a general trend to decentralize the governance of the Roman Catholic Church today" (ibid., 22, no. 10).

[119] Ibid., 22–23, no. 11.

[120] Ibid., 23.

[121] "A more appropriate exercise of authority affecting individual jurisdiction might be along the lines of an ultimate court of appeal which could well serve Anglican as well as Roman Catholic churches, much as the papacy served both East and West during the days of the undivided church" (ibid., 22, no. 10).

Bishop of Rome, concerning which there is recognized "a certain degree of convergence",[122] the following recommendation seems to be of particular importance: "In the view of the ARCIC Venice Statement 'Authority in the Church' and recent papers prepared for ARC on authority, the episcopacy, and papacy, we now see the possibility, after some further investigation, of drawing up a set of mutual affirmations about the ministry of the Bishop of Rome. There are points on which we believe there may well be substantial agreement between the Episcopal and Roman Catholic Churches and which should therefore be drafted on paper for further consideration by our respective [ecclesiastical] bodies and authorities."[123]

In the face of commentaries and critiques, the commission felt the need to intervene first of all through the *Elucidation of Windsor* (September 1981), which responded to, among others, the questions concerning the status of the local primates and the nature of the necessity of the primacy.[124]

With regard to the first question, the commission acknowledged that specific terms were avoided; however, it qualified this admission, noting that "in speaking of bishops with a special responsibility of oversight in their regions", it "intended to point to the reality behind the historical terms used for this form of episcopal corresponsibility in both East and West". Moreover, it "pointed to the contemporary development and importance of new forms of regional primacy in both traditions, e.g. the elective presidencies of Roman Catholic episcopal Conferences and certain elective primacies in the Anglican Communion".[125]

Concerning the other objection that recommended the primacy of the Roman See for purely historical reasons, the commission reaffirmed the doctrinal character of its previous statements: "According to Christian doctrine the unity in truth of the Christian community demands visible expression. We agree in maintaining that such a visible expression is the will of God and that the maintenance of the visible unity at the universal level includes the *episkopé* of a universal primate. This is a doctrinal state-

---

[122] Cf. *Origins* 7 (1978): 468a–70a.

[123] Ibid., 471b, no. 1.

[124] "Some questions have been asked about the status of regional primacies—for example, the patriarchal office as exercised in the Eastern Churches. Finally, a recurring question has been whether the Commission is suggesting that a universal primacy is a theological necessity simply because one has existed or been claimed" (MV 99–100, no. 1).

[125] MV 104, no. 7.

ment." This is not to deny that "the way *episkopé* is realized concretely in ecclesial life (the balance fluctuating between conciliarity and primacy) will depend upon contingent historical factors and upon development under the guidance of the Holy Spirit". The very location of the universal primacy in the city of Rome, by virtue of the "original witness of Peter and Paul" and of the "continuing exercise of a universal *episkopé* by the see of Rome", cannot be attributed to mere historical contingencies: "Therefore, while to locate a universal primacy in the see of Rome is an affirmation at a different level from the assertion of the necessity for a universal primacy, it cannot be dissociated from the providential action of the Holy Spirit." [126]

The Venice Statement concluded by reaffirming that "visible unity requires the realization of a '*model* which recognizes the complementarity of the primatial and conciliar aspects of *episkopé*' serving the [universal] 'koinonia of the churches'",[127] which is not to say that "what has evolved historically or what is currently practised by the Roman see is necessarily normative." Therefore, "much Anglican objection has been directed against the manner of exercise and particular claims of the Roman primacy rather than against universal primacy as such." [128]

From a practical point of view, reference is made to the evolution of the role of the Archbishop of Canterbury, as an example of the relationship between primacy and conciliarity in the Anglican Communion.[129] Such a model would admit of the common recognition of a primacy that does not compromise conciliarity, and which would help Anglicans to overcome their fear of extreme centralization and Catholics theirs of doctrinal incoherence.[130]

---

[126] Ibid., no. 8.

[127] Cf. above, p. 215, n. 106.

[128] MV 105, no. 8.

[129] "Anglicanism has never rejected the principle and practice of primacy. Reflection upon it has been stimulated by the evolving role of the bishop of Canterbury within the Anglican Communion. The development of this form of primacy arose precisely from the need for a service of unity in the faith in an expanding communion of Churches. It finds expression in the Lambeth Conferences convoked by succesive archbishops of Canterbury which originated with requests from overseas provinces for guidance in matters of faith. This illustrates a particular relationship between conciliarity and primacy in the Anglican Communion" (ibid.).

[130] "The Commission has already pointed to the possibilities of mutual benefit and reform which could arise from a shared recognition of one universal primacy which does not

In the conclusion of the Venice Statement, the commission itself noted four problems associated with the topic of authority in the Church which still required further study: "the interpretation of the Petrine texts, the meaning of the language of 'divine right', the affirmation of papal infallibility and the nature of the jurisdiction ascribed to the bishop of Rome as universal primate".[131] These were treated in the Windsor Statement *Authority in the Church* (II) (September 1981).

With regard to the *Petrine texts*, it was acknowledged that the New Testament explicitly stresses "Christ's will to root the Church in the apostolic witness and mandate" and "attributes to Peter a special position among the Twelve", a position given to Peter already during the ministry of Jesus, setting aside the question of whether "the Petrine texts contain the authentic words of Jesus or not".[132] Peter, therefore, had a responsibility to lead that was not his exclusively, but extended to all the apostles, in the collegial context of the company of apostles.[133] The "position of special importance" reserved to Peter remains undeniable, not on account of his personal gifts, but because of "his particular calling by Christ" to a "leadership of service".[134]

---

inhibit conciliarity—a 'prospect (which) should be met with faith, not fear' (Co-Chairmen's Preface). Anglicans sometimes fear the prospect of over-centralization, Roman Catholics the prospect of doctrinal incoherence. Faith, banishing fear, might see simply the prospect of the right balance between a primacy serving the unity and a conciliarity maintaining the just diversity of the *koinonia* of all the churches" (ibid.).

[131] MV 106, no. 1 (cf. above, pp. 215–16, nn. 109–11). Cf. Purdy, "Dialogue with the Anglican Communion", *One in Christ* 18 (1982): 212.

[132] MV 106, no. 3. The following is the list of references which, taken as a whole, provide a general picture of Peter's preeminence: "the bestowal on Simon of the name Cephas, his being mentioned first among the Twelve and in the smaller circle of the three (Peter, James and John), the faith which enabled him to confess Jesus' Messiahship (Matt. 16.16; Mark 8.29; Luke 9.20; and John 6.69), and the answer of Jesus (Matt. 16.18) in which he is called rock, the charge to strengthen his brethren (Luke 22.31–32) and to feed the sheep (John 21.16–17) and the special appearance to him of the risen Lord (e.g., Luke 24.34; 1 Cor. 15.5)" (ibid.).

[133] "Although the author of Acts underlined the apostolic authority of Paul in the latter part of his book, he focused in the first part on Peter's leadership. For instance, it is Peter who frequently speaks in the name of apostolic community (Acts 3.15, 10.41), he is the first to proclaim the Gospel to the Jews and the first to open the Christian community to the Gentiles. Paul seems to have recognized this pre-eminence of Peter among the apostles as well as the importance of James (Gal. 1.18–19). He appears also to have accepted the lead given by Peter at the Council of Jerusalem (Acts 15), even though he was prepared to oppose Peter when he held Peter to be at fault (Gal. 2.11)" (MV 106–7, no. 3).

[134] MV 107, no. 5.

Regarding the *succession to Peter*, the New Testament "contains no explicit record of a transmission of Peter's leadership, nor is the transmission of apostolic authority in general very clear". Indeed, "the Petrine texts were subjected to differing interpretations as early as the time of the Church Fathers". Nevertheless, "the Church of Rome, the city in which Peter and Paul taught and were martyred, came to be recognized as possessing a unique responsibility among the churches: its bishop was seen to perform a special service in relation to the unity of the churches, and in relation to fidelity to the apostolic inheritance, thus exercising among his fellow bishops functions analogous to those ascribed to Peter, whose successor the bishop of Rome was claimed to be."[135]

Therefore, "it is possible to think that a primacy of the bishop of Rome is not contrary to the New Testament and is part of God's purpose regarding the Church's unity and catholicity while admitting that the New Testament texts offer no sufficient basis for this".[136] As a consequence, "even if Peter's role cannot be transmitted in its totality, however, this does not exclude the continuation of a ministry of unity guided by the Spirit among those who continue the apostolic mission."[137] This is the common prospect, for the protection of unity in a future reunited Church.[138]

The expression *"iure divino"*, applied by Vatican I to the Roman primacy, poses two questions: "What does the language actually mean? What implications does it have for the ecclesial status of non-Roman Catholic communions?"[139]

For Catholics the expression means that the primacy derives from Christ, though it does not necessarily imply that it was established directly by

---

[135] Ibid., no. 6.

[136] MV 108, no. 7.

[137] Ibid., no. 8.

[138] "If the leadership of the bishop of Rome has been rejected by those who thought it was not faithful to the truth of the Gospel and hence not a true focus of unity, we nevertheless agree that a universal primacy will be needed in a reunited Church and should appropriately be the primacy of the bishop of Rome, as we have specified it (*Authority in the Church* I, 23). While the New Testament taken as a whole shows Peter playing a clear role of leadership, it does not portray the Church's unity and universality exclusively in terms of Peter. The universal communion of the churches is a company of believers, united by faith in Christ, by the preaching of the word, and the participation in the sacraments assured to them by a pastoral ministry of apostolic order. In a reunited Church a ministry modelled on the role of Peter will be a sign and safeguard of such unity" (MV 108, no. 9).

[139] Ibid., no. 10.

him during his earthly life,[140] nor does it mean that the universal primacy is a "source of the Church",[141] and so it cannot be deduced that "a Christian community out of communion with the see of Rome does not belong to the Church of God." Indeed, canonical communion with the Bishop of Rome "is not among the necessary elements by which a Christian community is recognized as a church".[142]

For Anglicans, past relationships notwithstanding, "from time to time Anglican theologians have affirmed that, in changed circumstances, it might be possible for the Churches of the Anglican Communion to recognize the development of the Roman primacy as a gift of divine providence—in other words, as an effect of the guidance of the Holy Spirit in the Church". It would therefore be "reasonable to ask whether a gap really exists between the assertion of a primacy of divine right (*iure divino*) and the acknowledgement of its emergence by divine providence (*divina providentia*)".[143] In any case, developments among Catholics relative to the *status* of the

---

[140] "The Roman Catholic conviction concerning the place of the Roman primacy in God's plan for his Church has traditionally been expressed in the language of *ius divinum* (divine law or divine right). This term was used by the First Vatican Council to describe the primacy of the 'successor in the chair of Peter' whom the Council recognized in the bishop of Rome. The First Vatican Council used the term *iure divino* to say that this primacy derives from Christ. While there is no universally accepted interpretation of this language, all affirm that it means at least that this primacy expresses God's purpose for his Church. *Jus divinum* in this context need not be taken to imply that the universal primacy as a permanent institution was directly founded by Jesus during his life on earth" (MV 108–9, no. 11).

[141] "Neither does the term mean that the universal primate is a 'source of the Church' as if Christ's salvation had to be channelled through him. Rather, he is to be the sign of the visible *koinonia* God wills for the Church and an instrument through which unity in diversity is realized. It is to a universal primate thus envisaged within the collegiality of the bishops and the *koinonia* of the whole Church that the qualification *iure divino* can be applied" (MV 109, no. 11).

[142] Ibid., no. 12. This statement is supported by the following argumentation: "For example, the Roman Catholic Church has continued to recognize the Orthodox churches as churches in spite of division concerning the primacy (Vatican II, *Unitatis redintegratio* 14). The Second Vatican Council, while teaching that the Church of God subsists in the Roman Catholic Church, rejected the position that the Church of God is co-extensive with the Roman Catholic Church and is exclusively embodied in that Church. The Second Vatican Council allows to be said that a church out of communion with the Roman see may lack nothing from the viewpoint of the Roman Catholic Church except that it does not belong to the visible manifestation of full Christian communion which is maintained in the Roman Catholic Church (*Lumen gentium* 8; *Unitatis redintegratio* 13)" (Ibid., no. 13).

[143] Ibid.

other Churches would remove obstacles to the Anglican acceptance of the primacy.[144] Therefore, the expression *"divine right"* can no longer be considered a reason for disagreement.[145]

As for the power of *jurisdiction*, drawing on a comparison with that of the bishop,[146] the Commission asserted that within the universal *koinonia*, "the universal primate (also) exercises the jurisdiction necessary for the fulfilment of his functions, the chief of which is to serve the faith and unity of the whole Church." [147] Recalling the difficulties, the misunderstandings, and the anxieties of Anglicans toward the definitions of Vatican I,[148] the text calls for the exercise of the primacy in a collegial context and in service of the communion of the Churches,[149] within the moral limits

---

[144] "Anglicans have commonly supposed that the claim to divine right for the Roman primacy implied a denial that the churches of the Anglican Communion are churches. Consequently, they have concluded that any reconciliation with Rome would require a repudiation of their past history, life and experience—which in effect would be a betrayal of their own integrity. However, given recent developments in the Roman Catholic understanding of the status of other Christian churches, this particular difficulty may no longer be an obstacle to Anglican acceptance, as God's will for his Church, of a universal primacy of the bishop of Rome such as has been described in the first Statement *on authority* (23)" (MV 110, no. 14).

[145] "In the past, Roman Catholic teaching that the bishop of Rome is universal primate by divine right or law has been regarded by Anglicans as unacceptable. However, we believe that the primacy of the bishop of Rome can be affirmed as part of God's design for the universal *koinonia* in terms which are compatible with both our traditions. Given such a consensus, the language of divine right used by the First Vatican Council need no longer be seen as a matter of disagreement between us" (ibid., no. 15).

[146] "Each bishop is entrusted with the pastoral authority needed for the exercise of his *episcope*. This authority is both required and limited by the bishop's task of teaching the faith through the proclamation and explanation of the word of God, of providing for the administration of the sacraments in his diocese and of maintaining his church in holiness and truth (cf. *Authority in the Church* I, 5). Hence decisions taken by the bishop in performing his task have an authority which the faithful in his diocese have a duty to accept. This authority of the bishop, usually called jurisdiction, involves the responsibility for making and implementing the decisions that are required by his office for the sake of the *koinonia*. It is not the arbitrary power of one man over the freedom of others, but a necessity if the bishop is to serve his flock as its shepherd (cf. *Authority Elucidation,* 5)" (MV 110–111, no. 17).

[147] MV 111, no. 17.

[148] Cf. ibid., no. 18.

[149] "The universal primate should exercise, and be seen to exercise, his ministry not in isolation but in collegial association with his brother bishops (*Authority in the Church I,* 21 and 23). This in no way reduces his own responsibility on occasion to speak and act for the whole Church. Concern for the universal Church is intrinsic to all episcopal

derived from the nature of the Church and of the primatial office[150] and with respect for the legitimate customs and traditions of the local Churches.[151] The defense of these principles will be a guarantee of the Anglican acceptance of the universal primacy of the Bishop of Rome in a future united Church.[152]

The conclusion expresses the conviction of being able to affirm together that "the church needs both a multiple, diverse authority, with which all God's people are actively involved; and also a universal primate as servant and focus of visible unity in truth and love", even though not all differences have been overcome; in fact, "some difficulties will not be wholly resolved until a practical initiative has been taken and our two Churches have lived together more visibly in the one *koinonia*."[153]

---

office; a diocesan bishop is helped to make this concern a reality by the universal jurisdiction of the universal primate. But the universal primate is not the source from which diocesan bishops derive their authority, nor does his authority undermine that of the metropolitan or diocesan bishop. Primacy is not an autocratic power over the Church but a service in and to the Church which is a communion in faith and charity of local churches" (ibid., no. 19).

[150] "Although the scope of universal jurisdiction cannot be precisely defined canonically, there are moral limits to its exercise: they derive from the nature of the Church and of the universal primate's pastoral office. By virtue of his jurisdiction, given for the building up of the Church, the universal primate has the right in special cases to intervene in the affairs of a diocese and to receive appeals from the decision of a diocesan bishop. It is because the universal primate, in collegial association with his fellow bishops, has the task of safeguarding the faith and unity of the universal Church that the diocesan bishop is subject to his authority" (ibid., no. 20).

[151] "The purpose of the universal primate's jurisdiction is to enable him to further catholicity as well as unity and to foster and draw together the riches of the diverse traditions of the churches. Collegial and primatial responsibility for preserving the distinctive life of the local churches involves a proper respect for their customs and traditions, provided these do not contradict the faith or disrupt communion. The search for unity and concern for catholicity must not be divorced" (ibid., no. 21).

[152] "Even though these principles concerning the nature of jurisdiction be accepted as in line with the understanding which Anglicans and Roman Catholics share with regard to the Church's structure, there remain specific questions about their practical application in a united Church. Anglicans are entitled to assurance that acknowledgement of the universal primacy of the bishop of Rome would not involve the suppression of theological, liturgical and other traditions which they value or the imposition of wholly alien traditions. We believe that what has been said above provides grounds for such assurance. In this connection we recall the words of Paul VI in 1970: 'There will be no seeking to lessen the legitimate prestige and the worthy patrimony of piety and usage proper to the Anglican Church'" (MV 112, no. 20).

[153] MV 115, no. 33.

2. The ARCIC II documents

The response of the Lambeth Conference to ARCIC I invited the new commission "to continue to explore the basis in Scripture and Tradition of the concept of universal primacy in conjunction with collegiality as an instrument of unity, the character of such a primacy in practice, and to draw upon the experience of other Christian Churches in exercising primacy, collegiality and conciliarity".[154] Actually, the topic had been merely alluded to, in the more general context of communion, in the document *Church as Comunion* (Dublin, September 1990). It dedicated a section to the ministry of oversight, entrusted to the episcopacy, that "has both a collegial and primatial dimension", specifying that "the episcopal ministry of a universal primate has its role as the visible focus of unity." [155] It limited itself again to underlining the need for further study "of episcopal authority, particularly of universal primacy, and of the office of the Bishop of Rome".[156]

The Joint Statement *Life in Christ: Morals, Confession and the Church* (Venice, September 5, 1993) also limited itself to recognizing that with the Reform, "the Church of England abjured papal supremacy, acknowledged the Sovereign as its Supreme Governor (cf. Article 37)", with the resulting consequences for the life of the Church of England[157] and for the subsequent organization based on autonomy, while maintaining communion.[158] The Catholic Church is credited for resisting the secular power: "This concern of the church to uphold its independence from the state,

---

[154] HY 9, 153, no. 3.

[155] IS, no. 76 (1991), 94b.

[156] Ibid., 96b.

[157] "Thus the life of the church, the culture of the nation and the law of the land were inextricably combined. In particular the lay voice was given, through Parliament, a substantial measure of authority in the affairs of the church. With the growth of the Anglican Communion as a world-wide body, patterns of synodical government developed in which laity, clergy and bishops shared the authority of government, the bishops retaining a special voice and responsibility in safeguarding matters of doctrine and worship" (IS, no. 85 [1994], 59b–60a).

[158] "As the Anglican Communion has spread, provinces independent of the Church of England have come into being; each with its own history and culture. . . . Each province is responsible for the ordering of its own life and has independent legislative and juridical authority; yet each continues in communion with the church of England and with one another. Every ten years since 1867 the bishops of the Anglican Communion have met together at Lambeth at the invitation of the Archbishop of Canterbury, to whom they continue to ascribe a primacy of honour" (ibid., 60a).

together with its need to reaffirm and strengthen its unity in the face of divisive forces, lent to the papal office a renewed significance, and provided the context for the solemn definition of the First Vatican Council which clarified the universal jurisdiction of the Bishop of Rome and his infallibility."[159]

The topic of primacy was given extensive treatment in the more recent document *The Gift of Authority* (May 1999), which, on the basis of the agreements already concluded[160] and of the instructions supplied by the authorities of the two communions, intended to give further consideration to, among other things, "the Petrine ministry of universal primacy in relation to Scripture and Tradition".[161] After a reference to the authority of each bishop in his local Church,[162] the text reaffirmed the necessity of the "mutual interdependence of all churches", which is "integral to the reality of the Church as God wills it to be" in order that no local Church "can regard itself as self-sufficient". This interdependence is expressed in various forms of synodality.[163] The synodal concept of the Church is shared by both Catholics and Anglicans, even though "they express it in different ways",[164] and in the course of history it has been expressed by means of conciliar, collegial, and primatial authority: "Forms of primacy exist in both the Anglican

---

[159] Ibid.

[160] Among these are: "the complementarity of primacy and conciliarity as elements of *episcope* within the Church (cf. *Authority in the Church* I, 22); the need for a universal primacy exercised by the Bishop of Rome as a sign and safeguard of unity within a re-united Church (cf. *Authority in the Church* II, 9); the need for the universal primate to exercise his ministry in collegial association with the other bishops (cf. *Authority in the Church* II, 19); an understanding of universal primacy and conciliarity which complements and does not supplant the exercise of *episcope* in local churches (cf. *Authority in the Church* I, 21–23; *Authority in the Church* II, 19)" (*The Gift of Authority*, no. 1: IS, no. 100 (1999), 18a.

[161] Ibid., no. 3.

[162] Here it takes up no. 17 of *Authority in the Church* II: cf. above, p. 204, note 54.

[163] *The Gift of Authority*, no. 37: "The ministry of the bishop is crucial, for this ministry serves communion within and among local churches. Their communion with each other is expressed through the incorporation of each bishop into a college of bishops. Bishops are, both personally and collegially, at the service of communion and are concerned for synodality in all its expressions. These expressions have included a wide variety of organs, instruments and institutions, notably synods or councils, local, provincial, worldwide, ecumenical. The maintenance of communion requires that at every level there is a capacity to take decisions appropriate to that level. When those decisions raise serious questions for the wider communion of churches, synodality must find a wider expression" (ibid., 24a).

[164] Cf. ibid, 24a–b, nos. 30–40.

Communion and in the churches in communion with the Bishop of Rome. Among the latter, the offices of Metropolitan Archbishop or Patriarch of an Eastern Catholic Church are primatial in nature. Each Anglican Province has its Primate and the Primates' Meeting serves the whole Communion. The Archbishop of Canterbury exercises a primatial ministry in the whole Anglican Communion." [165]

In this context the need for an *episcope* in the service of *koinonia* on a universal level is reaffirmed, as was already acknowledged in previous documents, [166] as well as the effective transmission of this ministry to the Bishop of Rome. [167]

Even though aware that the text of the Joint Statement would have to be submitted to the respective authorities, the commission proceeded to list some of the elements of the agreement arrived at concerning the exercise of authority. Among these were the following: "a universal primacy, exercised collegially in the context of synodality, as integral to *episcope* at the service of universal communion, such a primacy having always been associated with the Bishop and See of Rome (paragraphs 46–48);—how the ministry of the Bishop of Rome assists the ministry of the whole episcopal body in the context of synodality, promoting the communion of the local churches in their life in Christ and the proclamation of the Gospel (paragraphs 46–48);—how the Bishop of Rome offers a specific ministry concerning the discernment of truth (paragraph 47)". [168]

---

[165] Ibid., 25b, no. 45.

[166] "ARCIC has already recognised that the 'pattern of complementary primatial and conciliar aspects of episcope serving the koinonia of the churches needs to be realised at the universal level' (*Authority in the Church* I, 23). The exigencies of church life call for a specific exercise of episcope at the service of the whole Church. In the pattern found in the New Testament one of the twelve is chosen by Jesus Christ to strengthen the others so that they will remain faithful to their mission and in harmony with each other (see the discussion of the Petrine texts in *Authority in the Church* II, 2–5)" (ibid., 25b, no. 46). Cf. above, pp. 215, 222, notes 108, 140.

[167] "ARCIC has also previously explored the transmission of the primatial ministry exercised by the Bishop of Rome (see *Authority in the Church* II, 6–9). Historically, the Bishop of Rome has exercised such a ministry either for the benefit of the whole Church, as when Leo contributed to the Council of Chalcedon, or for the benefit of a local church, as when Gregory the Great supported Augustine of Canterbury's mission and ordering of the English church. This gift has been welcomed and the ministry of these Bishops of Rome continues to be celebrated liturgically by Anglicans as well as Roman Catholics" (ibid., 26a, no. 46). Cf. above, pp. 222–23, notes 141–46.

[168] Ibid., 27b, no. 52.

There followed a reference to significant developments which have been
noted in the Anglican Communion[169] and in the Catholic Church,[170]
notwithstanding the problems that persist within the one[171] and the other.[172]

---

[169] "The Lambeth Conference of 1988 recognised a need to reflect on how the Anglican Communion makes authoritative decisions. At the international level, Anglican instruments of synodality have considerable authority to influence and support provinces, yet
none of these instruments has power to overrule a provincial decision, even if it threatens
the unity of the Communion. Accordingly, the Lambeth Conference of 1998, in the light
of The Virginia Report of the Inter-Anglican Theological and Doctrinal Commission,
resolved to strengthen these instruments in various ways, particularly the role of the Archbishop of Canterbury and of the Primates' Meeting. The Conference also requested the
Primates' Meeting to initiate a study in each province 'on whether effective communion,
at all levels, does not require appropriate instruments, with due safeguards, not only for
legislation, but also for oversight . . . as well as on the issue of a universal ministry in the
service of Christian unity' (Resolution III, 8h). Alongside the autonomy of provinces,
Anglicans are coming to see that interdependence among local churches and among provinces is also necessary for fostering communion" (ibid., no. 53).

[170] "The Roman Catholic Church, especially since the Second Vatican Council, has
been gradually developing synodal structures for sustaining koinonia more effectively. The
developing role of national and regional Episcopal Conferences and the regular holding of
General Assemblies of the Synod of Bishops demonstrate this evolution. There has also
been renewal in the exercise of synodality at the local level, although this varies from place
to place. Canonical legislation now requires lay men and women, persons in the religious
life, deacons and priests to play a part in parochial and diocesan pastoral councils, diocesan
synods and a variety of other bodies, whenever these are convened" (ibid., 27b–28a, no. 54).

[171] "We have seen that instruments for oversight and decision making are necessary at
all levels to support communion. With this in view the Anglican Communion is exploring
the development of structures of authority among its provinces. Is the Communion also
open to the acceptance of instruments of oversight which would allow decisions to be
reached that, in certain circumstances, would bind the whole Church? When major new
questions arise which, in fidelity to Scripture and Tradition, require a united response, will
these structures assist Anglicans to participate in the sensus fidelium with all Christians? To
what extent does unilateral action by provinces or dioceses in matters concerning the whole
Church, even after consultation has taken place, weaken koinonia? Anglicans have shown
themselves to be willing to tolerate anomalies for the sake of maintaining communion. Yet
this has led to the impairment of communion manifesting itself at the Eucharist, in the
exercise of episcope and in the interchangeability of ministry. What consequences flow
from this? Above all, how will Anglicans address the question of universal primacy as it is
emerging from their life together and from ecumenical dialogue?" (ibid., 28a, no. 56).

[172] "The Second Vatican Council has reminded Roman Catholics of how the gifts of
God are present in all the people of God. It has also taught the collegiality of the episcopate in its communion with the Bishop of Rome, head of the college. However, is there
at all levels effective participation of clergy as well as lay people in emerging synodal bodies? Has the teaching of the Second Vatican Council regarding the collegiality of bishops
been implemented sufficiently? Do the actions of bishops reflect sufficient awareness of the
extent of the authority they receive through ordination for governing the local church?

The conclusion expressed the certainty that these problems can be overcome through a "renewed collegiality" that can make "more visible the *koinonia*" already existing. In this way the gift of the universal primacy can be shared, precisely because it is "exercised in collegiality and synodality", safeguarding the "legitimate diversity of traditions", "in a prophetic way": "An experience of universal primacy of this kind would confirm two particular conclusions we have reached:

- that Anglicans be open to and desire a recovery and re-reception under certain clear conditions of the exercise of universal primacy by the Bishop of Rome;
- that Roman Catholics be open to and desire a re-reception of the exercise of primacy by the Bishop of Rome and the offering of such a ministry to the whole Church of God." [173]

III. EVALUATION OF THE RESULTS OF THE DIALOGUE

Of all the various documents of the bilateral dialogues, only the Final Report of ARCIC I has already been officially evaluated by the respective ecclesial authorities. Before considering evaluations on the part of theologians, therefore, it is necessary to take into account the official evaluations, allowing for a consideration of the Observations of the Congregation for the Doctrine of the Faith (March 29, 1982), even though they are regarded not as official, but as a "contribution" to the ongoing dialogue. [174]

Has enough provision been made to ensure consultation between the Bishop of Rome and the local churches prior to the making of important decisions affecting either a local church or the whole Church? How is the variety of theological opinion taken into account when such decisions are made? In supporting the Bishop of Rome in his work of promoting communion among the churches, do the structures and procedures of the Roman Curia adequately respect the exercise of episcope at other levels? Above all, how will the Roman Catholic Church address the question of universal primacy as it emerges from 'the patient and fraternal dialogue' about the exercise of the office of the Bishop of Rome to which John Paul II has invited 'church leaders and their theologians'?" (ibid., 28a–b, no. 57).

[173] Ibid., no. 61.

[174] Concerning the methods of the publication of the text cf. McDonald, "I rapporti cattolico-anglicani e cattolico metodisti", *La Chiesa cattolica oggi nel dialogo. Aggiornamento: 1983–87. Corso breve di ecumenismo*, IX (Rome, 1988), 30–37; T. Gallagan, "La Chiesa cattolica in dialogo con la Comunione anglicana e con il Metodismo mondiale. 1987–1994", *La Chiesa cattolica oggi nel dialogo. Aggiornamento: 1988–95. Breve corso di ecumenismo*,

1. Official appraisals

Observations on the "Final Report" of ARCIC by the Congregation for the Doctrine of the Faith

After having emphasized "the importance of the fact that Anglicans recognize that 'a primacy of the Bishop of Rome is not contrary to the New Testament and is part of God's purpose regarding the Church's unity and catholicity' (*Authority II, 7*)," the Congregation maintained that "it is not possible for the Church to adopt as the effective norm for reading the Scriptures only historical criticism, thus allowing the homogeneity of the developments which appear in tradition to remain in doubt." In fact, precisely on the basis of such a criterion, "what ARCIC writes about the role of Peter ('a special position among the Twelve', par. 3; 'a position of special importance', par. 5) does not measure up to the truth of faith as this has been understood by the Catholic Church, on the basis of the principal Petrine texts of the New Testament (John 1:42, 21:15; Matthew 16:16—cf. DS 3053), and does not satisfy the requirements of the dogmatic statement of Vatican Council I: 'the apostle Peter . . . received immediately and directly from Jesus Christ our Lord a true and proper primacy of jurisdiction' (Constitution *Pastor aeternus*, Ch. 1: DS 3055)."[175]

With regard to the expression "*ius divinum*" used by Vatican Council I in reference to the primacy of the Pope, successor of Peter, the Observations rejected ARCIC's interpretation, according to which "it means at least that this primacy expresses God's purpose for his Church, and that 'it need not to be taken to imply that the universal primacy as a permanent institution was directly founded by Jesus during his life on earth' (*Authority II, 11*)". Such an interpretation does not respect "the exigencies of the word 'institution' in the expression of Vatican Council I: 'by institution of Christ our Lord himself' (Constitution *Pastor aeternus*, 2: DS 3058), which require that Chirst himself provided for the universal primacy".[176]

---

ibid., X (1995), 70–72; Root, "Some Remarks on the Response to ARCIC I", *Communion et Réunion*, 165–76; C. Clifford, "Reception of the *Final Report*: Beyond Strengthened Agreement", *One in Christ* 32 (1996): 130–48.

[175] *Origins* 11 (1982): 754b–55a.
[176] Ibid., 755a.

ARCIC's view as to the ecclesiality of the non-Catholic confessions was also strongly criticized: "In this perspective, one should note that ARCIC is not exact in interpreting Vatican Council II when it says that the 'Council allows it to be said that a church out of communion with the Roman See might lack nothing from the viewpoint of the Roman Catholic Church except that it does not belong to the visible manifestation of full Christian communion which is maintained in the Roman Catholic Church' (12)." Indeed, according to Catholic tradition, "visible union is not something extrinsic, added to the particular churches, which already would possess and realize in themselves in the full essence of the church; this unity pertains to the intimate structure of faith, permeating all its elements. For this reason the office of conserving, fostering and expresing this unity in accord with the Lord's will is a constitutive part of the very nature of the church (cf. Jn 21:15–19)."[177]

There followed also a critique of ARCIC's view with respect to the power of jurisdiction of the Bishop of Rome over all the particular Churches: it is not determined by historical factors, but rather is intrinsic to the primacy; it is "full, supreme and universal" over the whole Church, which he can always exercise unhindered.[178]

With regard to recognizing the need for a primacy in a future reunited Church and agreeing that it could be exercised by the Bishop of Rome, the Observations specified that this "must be regarded as a significant fact in interchurch relations", while at the same time specifying that "there remain important differences between Anglicans and Catholics concerning the *nature* of this primacy".[179]

In its concluding Observations, the Congregation judged that the Final Report of ARCIC, though representing "a notable ecumenical endeavor and a useful basis for further steps on the road to reconciliation between the Catholic Church and the Anglican Communion, does not yet constitute a substantial and explicit agreement on some essential elements of

---

[177] Ibid.

[178] Ibid., 755a–b: "The power of jurisdiction over all particular churches, therefore, is intrinsic (i.e., *iure divino*) to this office, not something which belongs to it for human reasons nor in order to respond to historical needs. The Pope's 'full, supreme and universal power over the whole church, a power which he can always exercise unhindered' (Constitution *Lumen gentium*, 22; cf. DS 3064), which can take different forms according to historical exigencies, can never be lacking."

[179] Ibid., 755b.

Catholic faith".[180] Among the different reasons given for this judgment were the only partial acceptance of the primacy of the Bishop of Rome and the inadequate formulation of the relationship between primacy and the structure of the Church—allowing for interpretations not in harmony with the Catholic faith.

Among the criticisms leveled, in the context of the dialogue, at the Observations of the Congregation for the Doctrine of the Faith were the "Remarks" of the *Anglican-Catholic Working Group of Canada* (April 1983). These followed the same arrangement as the Congregation's Observations, taking into consideration first of all the commentaries on the Petrine texts, underscoring an excessive preoccupation with the possible dangers of historical criticism, while in the case of those texts, "it was precisely the use of historical biblical criticism by Anglicans and Roman Catholics (and, we also acknowledge, particularly the work of the US Lutheran-RC Dialogue) which enabled Anglicans to come to a new interpretation of the texts" and which enabled them to abandon some of their "past objections to the Roman Catholic insistence on the importance of a distinctive Petrine ministry".[181]

More particularly, the "Remarks" denounced the fear expressed by the Observations that "the *Final Report's* formulations do not conform to Vatican I's statement that Peter received primacy of jurisdiction directly from Christ." In reality, "the analysis of scriptural data on Peter's role in the Church yields a convergence of positive explicit indications that this role was one of leadership." [182] Such a role was conferred upon him personally by Jesus, even if "from a strictly historical perspective it is impossible to establish whether or not a full blown universal primacy was actually established as a permanent institution by Jesus during his life on earth." [183]

Over and above similar fears, it is more important "to seize the opportunity of the current dialogue when many Anglicans may sense the hand of God at work in our times, and to believe that a ministry of unity and witness may be offered to the universal Church by Peter's successor".[184]

---

[180] Ibid., 756b.
[181] *One in Christ* 20 (1984): 267.
[182] Ibid., 279.
[183] Ibid., 268.
[184] Ibid.

It then takes up the question of Peter's *succession* by the Bishop of Rome, concerning which the Working Group straightaway made the following clarification: "While the *Final Report* underlines at length the centrality of Peter's role among the twelve, it does not believe that the Scriptures provide a basis sufficient to show the transmission of this role to those who would be later bishops of Rome nor the explicit intention of Jesus during his earthly life that such transmissiom take place." It limited itself to saying that "the development of papal primacy is legitimate and providential", insofar as it is possible to think "that such a development 'is not contrary to the New Testament and is part of God's purpose regarding the church's unity and catholicity'." We find therefore a positive evaluation of the Church's tradition, that even though using "a different language and conceptual structure than do the formulations of Vatican I, its substantial agreement with the reality affirmed by Catholic tradition should not be missed".[185] The insistence of the Observations on the term *institution*, which implies an "action of the historical Jesus during his life on earth", is countered with the thesis that the christological foundation of the primacy "can be achieved securely by locating the institution of papal primacy in the unfolding interpretation of Christ's life in which the primitive Church engaged under the guidance of the Spirit of Christ",[186] just as Catholic theology itself today admits with regard to the institution of the sacraments.[187] It follows that, also using historical and evolutionary language, and not that of Vatican I, the Final Report wants to express the same doctrine: "We believe that the primacy of the bishops of Rome can be affirmed as part of God's design for the universal *koinonía*."[188]

Finally, it dealt with the problem of the ecclesial character of the non-Catholic communions. Even though agreeing with the Observations in considering unity as an organic ecclesial reality and not a juridical imposition extrinsic to the particular churches, the Final Report questions

---

[185] Ibid., 280.

[186] Ibid.

[187] "Current Roman Catholic theology links the institution of some of the seven sacraments not to direct action of Christ during his earthly life, but to the interpretation of the will of Christ and the development of the meaning of the Christ event by the primitive community under the guidance of the Spirit, a point to which the *Observations* draw our attention in the preceding section. If theology does not insist that the historical Christ directly instituted each of the seven sacraments, it can hardly insist on this for the institution of the papal primacy" (ibid.).

[188] Ibid.

whether in reality the Observations undermine not only the traditional identification of the Orthodox Churches with the Church of Christ,[189] but also that of the Anglican and Protestant "Churches" .[190]

The *Executive Committee of the Evangelical Fellowship of the Anglican Communion* (1988) also criticized the Observations of the CDF (B.III.1) for claiming a true and proper primacy of jurisdiction received by Peter directly from Christ, countering that the supreme head of the Church is Christ, and hence no universal Pastor is necessary, other than in the sense of the leadership exercised by the Archbishop of Canterbury and by the Orthodox patriarchs.[191]

The 1988 Lambeth Conference: "Resolution 8" and "Explanatory Note Regarding ARCIC I"

In a brief Resolution, the Lambeth Conference recognized "*Authority in the Church* (*I* and *II*), together with the *Elucidation*, as a firm basis for the direction and agenda of the continuing dialogue on authority, and encouraged ARCIC to continue to explore the basis in Scripture and Tradition

---

[189] "But when the *Observations* speak of the office of unity as a 'constitutive part of the very nature of the Church', denying that there might be a Church which lacks nothing from the viewpoint of the Roman Catholic Church except that it does not belong to the visible manifestation of full Christian communion which is maintained in the Roman Catholic Church, it undermines the longstanding recognition that the Orthodox Churches are in communion with the Church of Christ; in the Roman Catholic view, they lack only a visible sign of this communion" (ibid., 281).

[190] "In addition, Vatican II understands the Church of Christ to be a communion of particular churches, each of which is fully Church in itself and manifests this ecclesial character in a visible way by its communion with other local churches through the Petrine office. Because of its understanding of the Church as a communion of particular churches, Vatican II was able to evaluate more positively the ecclesial status of Anglican and Protestant Churches despite their lack of some ecclesial elements, including a visible sign by which to manifest their communion in the one Church of Christ" (ibid.).

[191] "On the contrary, the church's supreme head is Christ himself, to whom universal authority has been given, and who rules his people by his word and Spirit. We are not at all convinced that an earthly pastor with universal oversight is desirable, let alone necessary." Not incompatible with the New Testament "would be a leadership somewhat similar to the role exercised by the Archbishop of Canterbury in the world-wide Anglican Communion, expressing historical continuity, visible unity, personal affection and a ministry of brotherly support, but not infallibility or universal jurisdiction. Similarly, within the fellowship of autonomous Orthodox Churches the Ecumenical Patriarch possesses neither infallibility, nor universal jurisdiction, nor even 'primacy', but rather a certain 'seniority' which 'is to be understood in terms not of coercion but of pastoral service'" (HY, 295–96).

of the concept of a universal primacy, in conjunction with collegiality, as an instrument of unity, the character of such a primacy in practice, and to draw upon the experience of other Christian Churches in exercising primacy, collegiality and conciliarity".[192] Moreover, in an Explanatory Note it acknowledged "the considerable measure of consensus and convergence which the Agreed Statement represents" and that, generally speaking, "the responses from the provinces to the two Statements on *Authority in the Church* were generally positive", even if they raised questions "about a number of matters, especially primacy, jurisdiction and infallibility, collegiality and the role of laity".[193]

The Holy See, "The Catholic Response to ARCIC I" (December 5, 1991)

The Catholic Response was more articulate. After expressing gratitude to the members of the commission for its "achievement of a point of convergence and even of agreement which many would not have thought possible before the Commission began its work",[194] the Response could not avoid making a necessary clarification: "The Catholic Church judges, however, that it is not yet possible to state that substantial agreement has been reached on all questions studied by the Commission. There still remain between Anglicans and Catholics important differences regarding essential matters of Catholic doctrine."[195]

Among those differences, some pertain to the theme of the primacy. Indeed, in the Explanatory Note it was emphasized that, in general, with regard to the question of Authority in the Church, the Final Report "makes no claim of 'substantial agreement'". Rather, the most that was achieved "is a certain convergence, which is but a first step along the path that seeks consensus as a prelude to unity". Still, there were evident "certain signs of convergence that do indeed open the way to further progress in the future", and, as already pointed out by the Congregation for the Doctrine of the Faith in its Observations, "it is necessary to underline the importance of the fact that Anglicans recognize that 'a primacy

---

[192] HY 153.
[193] HY 154–55.
[194] IS, no. 82 (1993), 47b.
[195] Ibid., 47b–48a.

of the Bishop of Rome is not contrary to the New Testament and is a part of God's purpose regarding the Church's unity and catholicity'".[196]

Taking its cue from the two documents of the Final Report on the infallibility of the Pope,[197] the Response commented, "This statement and several others in the *Final Report* illustrate the need for much more study to be done with respect to the Petrine ministry in the Church." There followed a list of citations from the Final Report itself which on the one hand reflect "the more positive approach of Anglicans in recent times in this connection" and on the other hand "also illustrate the reservations that still exist on the part of the Anglican community".[198]

A further point of difficulty emerges in the position taken regarding the relationship of the *ecclesial character* of a Christian community and its incorporation into Catholic communion through union with the See of Rome. Making reference to *Lumen gentium*, no. 8, and to *Unitatis redintegratio*, no. 13, in a manner not entirely exact, the Final Report stated, "The Second Vatican Council allows it to be said that the church out of communion with the Roman see may lack nothing from the viewpoint of the Roman Catholic Church except that it does not belong to the visible manifestation of full Christian communion which is maintained in the Roman Catholic Church." The Response instead specified, "It is the teaching of the Second Vatican Council that a church outside communion with the Roman pontiff lacks more than just the visible manifestation of unity with the Church of Christ which subsists in the Roman Catholic Church." [199]

---

[196] Ibid., 48b.

[197] Cf. ibid., 48b–49a.

[198] " 'Much Anglican objection has been directed against the manner of the exercise and particular claims of the Roman primacy rather than against universal primacy as such' (AE 8); 'Relations between our two communities in the past have not encouraged reflection by Anglicans on the positive significance of the Roman primacy in the life of the universal church. Nevertheless, from time to time Anglican theologians have affirmed that, in changed circumstances, it might be possible for the churches of the Anglican Communion to recognize the development of the Roman primacy as a gift of divine providence—in other words, as an effect of the guidance of the Holy Spirit in the Church' (AII, 13).

—'In spite of our agreement over the need for a universal primate in a united church, Anglicans do not accept the guaranteed possession of such a gift of divine assistance in judgments necessarily attached to the office of the bishop of Rome by virtue of which his final decisions can be known to be wholly assured before their reception by the faithful' (AII, 31)" (ibid., 49a–b).

[199] Ibid., 49b.

There followed the two most fundamental observations with respect to the definitions of Vatican II concerning the role of Peter among the other apostles[200] and the *ius divinum* of the primacy.[201] There is little wonder then at the resulting conclusion: "As is obvious, despite considerable convergences in this regard, full agreement on the nature and the significance of the Roman primacy has not been reached."[202] One of the reasons for a lack of agreement is indicated by the historical critical method used by the commission in its analysis of the Petrine texts.[203] On the other hand, as specified by the Statement by the Co-Chairmen of the Anglican/Roman Catholic International Commission, the same ARCIC, in reference to the authority of the Church, spoke not of an *agreement*, but of a *convergence*, and both of the "Churches" asked the commission to proceed to a further study of the problem.[204]

While the Resolution of the Lambeth Conference was judged almost unanimously positive, there were many different reactions to the Response of

---

[200] "The manner in which ARCIC I writes in respect of the role of Peter among the Twelve—'a special position' (AII, 3), 'a position of special importance' (AII, 5)—does not express the fullness of the Catholic faith in this regard. The dogmatic definition of the First Vatican Council declares that the primacy of the bishop of Rome belongs to the divine structure of the church; the bishop of Rome inherits the primacy from Peter who received it 'immediately and directly' from Christ" (ibid., 50a).

[201] "From a Catholic viewpoint, it is not possible then to accept the interpretation given in 'Authority in the Church II' concerning the *ius divinum* of the First Vatican Council, namely that it 'need not to be taken to imply the universal primacy as a permanent institution was directly founded by Jesus during his life on earth' (No. 11). The Catholic Church sees rather in the primacy of the successors of Peter something positively intended by God and deriving from the will and insitution of Jesus Christ" (ibid.).

[202] Ibid.

[203] "As is well known, the Catholic doctrine affirms that the historical-critical method is not sufficient for the interpretation of Scripture. Such interpretation cannot be separated from the living tradition of the church which receives the message of Scripture. The Final Report seems to ignore this when dealing with the interpretation of the Petrine texts of the New Testament, for it states that they 'do not offer sufficient basis' on which to establish the primacy of the bishop of Rome" (ibid., 51a–b).

[204] "ARCIC never claimed that its agreement on authority had quite the same quality. What was claimed here was highly significant but more limited: a high degree of agreement 'on authority in the Church and, in particular, on the basic principles of primacy' (Preface to the Final Report). After careful study of the particular issues of papal primacy and infallibility, ARCIC spoke of a 'convergence' which, taken with its earlier agreements, appeared 'to call for the establishing of a new relationship between our churches' (Final Report, Conclusion). Both churches have asked the Commission to continue to work on vital issues connected with authority" (IS, no. 87 [1994], 238a).

the Holy See, not only by Anglicans, but also by Catholics.[205] For now, it suffices simply to mention the criticisms pertaining to the authorship of the text, which—on account of its predominantly critical content—was attributed to the Congregation for the Doctrine of the Faith,[206] and for that reason the Response was said to have a broader theological basis than that of the council, more in keeping with *Communionis notio*,[207] and to reflect only one among the many other current Catholic theologies.[208] Practically speaking, according to its critics, the *Response* is not capable of correctly understanding the terminology of the Final Report[209] and of distinguishing between *consonance* and *identity* in the results of the dialogue with the Catholic faith.[210] Moreover, the *Response* was criticized for concentrating excessively on the Observations of the Congregation

---

[205] ARCIC II also released the document *Clarifications of Certain Aspects of the Agreed Statement on Eucharist and Ministry* (cf. IS, no. 87 [1994], 239–42), but, as is clear from the very title, it did not deal with the reservations relative to the primacy.

[206] Cf. M. M. Garijo-Guembe, "Die Antwort der Glaubenskongregation auf die Dokumente der anglikanisch/römisch-katholischen internationalen Kommission", *Ökumenische Rundschau* 42 (1993): 32; F. Sullivan, "The Vatican Response to ARCIC I (1992)", *Gregorianum* 73 (1992): 489–90.

[207] K. McDonnell, "A Year Afterwards: The Vatican Response to ARCIC, a Slammed Door?", *One in Christ* 29 (1993): 116–17: "Everything that the Response asserts about primacy can be found in the Constitution of the Church of Vatican II. What can be questioned is whether the broader theological posture of the Response is that of the same Council.... The Cardinal's letter [*Communionis notio*] does not relate the Church as a communion to the primacy as presented at Vatican II, but returns to the more primitive vision of Vatican I."

[208] Garijo-Guembe, "Die Antwort der Glaubenskongregation", 47: "Dem katholischen Theologen stellt sich die Frage, ob man in Treue zur vollen römisch-katholischen Tradition in bestimmten Punkten nichts anderes hätte sagen können als die GK und inwieweit diese von einer bestimmten Theologie Gebrauch macht, die letztendlich nur *eine* Theologie unter anderen innerhalb der heutigen katholischen Theologie ist."

[209] Cf. Sullivan, "The Vatican Response", 492: "It would seem correct to say ... that at least to some extent the negative character of the Vatican Response is due to the fact that it criticizes ARCIC I for not achieving results which the Commission itself did not claim to have achieved."

[210] Ibid., 494: "for the authors of this *Response*, to say that an agreed ecumenical statement is *consonant* with the faith of the Catholic Church, means that it must be *identical* with that faith. Further examination of the *Response* shows that an agreed dialogue statement will not be seen as identical with Catholic *faith*, unless it corresponds fully with Catholic *doctrine*, and indeed with the official Catholic formulation of that doctrine." Cf. T. P. Rausch, "Present State of Anglican-Roman Catholic Relations: An Assessment", *One in Christ* 29 (1993): 120; Root, "Some Remarks on the Response to ARCIC", 171–72; C. Hill, "The Fundamental Question of Ecumenical Method", in C. Hill and E. Yarnold, *Anglicans and Roman Catholics*, 225. Only Yarnold recognized that, naturally, "the Catholic

for the Doctrine of the Faith, ignoring the positive evaluations of the episcopal conferences.[211] As a consequence, it is said to have engendered fear, on the part of both Anglicans and Catholics, that the door to dialogue had been closed shut.[212]

It was also pointed out that, on the question of *ius divinum*, while the positions of Catholic authors and of ARCIC are not very far apart, the understanding of the congregation is formulated too strictly[213] and does not properly interpret Vatican I.[214] Moreover, it is said that the *Response* is ambiguous on the ecclesial character of the non-Catholic confessions and their incorporation in the Church[215] and that it is not grounded or at least not completely in agreement with Vatican II in its critique

---

understanding of consonance should be more rigorous than the Anglican" ("Roman Catholic Responses to ARCIC I and ARCIC II", ibid., 243).

[211] Cf. Greenacre, "Lettre ouverte", 124; Hill, "ARCIC-I and II. An Anglican Perspective", Deneaux and Dick, *From Malines to ARCIC*, 141–42.

[212] McDonnell, "A Year Afterwards", 114: "Anglicans might fear that Roman Catholics, although giving lip service to collegiality, do not really believe in any other authority but papal; Roman Catholics might fear that Anglicans, in spite of contrary protests, do not really believe in an effective universal primate."

[213] Garijo-Guembe, "Die Antwort der Glaubenskongregation", 45: after citing Congar and Kasper, the author comments, "Warscheinlich sind solche Bemühungen katholischer Autoren und die Position von ARCIC nicht so weit voneinander entfernt. Eine Gegenfrage scheint mir auch hier berechtigt: Arbeitet die GK hier nicht mit einer Konzeption über das *jus divinum*, die zu eng fixirt ist?"

[214] Chadwick, "Unfinished Business", in HY, 228: "The Response insists that the primacy of the successors of Peter is something positively intended by God (so far ARCIC I and an increasing number of Anglicans are able to concur). It then adds that it is derived from the will and institution of Jesus Christ. By this it seems to mean by Jesus Christ during his time among us on earth, which ARCIC I did not interpret Vatican I as necessarily entailing. *Pastor Aeternus* speaks rather of Peter receiving the primacy 'immediately and directly' from Christ, and the bishops of Rome inheriting the primacy from Peter. The Response collapses this argument unhelpfully. Moreover, it places an unnecessarily tight interpretation upon Vatican I's *de jure divino* Petrine primacy."

[215] Root, "Some Remarks on the Response to ARCIC I", 171: "The Commission had clearly as well as boldly concluded 'The Second Vatican Council allows it to be said that a church out of communion with the Roman See may lack nothing from the viewpoint of the Roman Catholic church except that it does not belong to the visible manifestation of full Christian Communion which is maintained in the Roman Catholic Church (LG 8; UR 13)'. The *Response* replies, 'It is the teaching of the Second Vatican Council that a church outside of communion with the Roman Pontiff lacks more than just the visible manifestation of unity with the Church of Christ which subsists in the Roman Catholic Church'.... There, as we hold our breath, it stops. It does not tell us what the 'more' is. It affirms it as one might affirm that Monday is not Tuesday." Cf. McDonnell, "A Year Afterwards", 116.

concerning the role of Peter among the Twelve.[216] Also, with regard to
the exercise of the primacy, the reviewers affirmed that the Response was
correct to insist on the necessity of further discussion of the reservations
of the Anglicans, but that reflection on the part of Catholics is likewise
necessary.[217]

The document *The Gift of Authority* also was accompanied by a Commentary of Father W. Henn that, though unofficial in character, assumed
a certain importance. With regard to the primacy, first of all, he pointed
out the effort to reaffirm some of the essential doctrines of *Pastor aeternus*,[218] which could lead—the conditional mood is suggested by the recurring use of *it seems*—to the acknowledgment that the primatial ministry
pertains to the *esse* of the Church and that it comes directly from Christ
himself.[219] Then referring to the Considerations of the Congregation for

---

[216] McDonnell, "A Year Afterwards", 116–17: "One thing it is to repeat the longstanding claims of the primacy asserted anew at Vatican II, and another to do so ignoring the
theological development, indeed the faith retrieval, of collegiality and an ecclesiology of
communion, which has taken place since Trent and Vatican I." Root's statement is even
more detailed: "What the *Response* voices is the conviction that nothing said in an 'agreed
statement' should be at variance with, let alone contradicted by anything said before. The
final lines (p. 18) say clearly that the primacy of Peter derives directly 'from the will and
institution of Jesus Christ'. The *Report* did not say this—nor did it deny it—and the ARCIC
language does not satisfy the *Response*. The language of the *Response* is not argued for; it
is simply used. What emerges is that the dissatisfactions of the *Response* cannot be overcome by simple appeal to Vatican II. There is nothing in the *Response* which cannot find
support, even if only the support of silence, in *Lumen Gentium*, most abundantly in its *Nota
praevia*" ("Some Remarks on the Response to ARCIC I", 172).

[217] Chadwick, "Unfinished Business", in HY, 226–27: "In noting a number of Anglican
reservations about the exercise of the Petrine ministry, the Response rightly calls for more
discussion about the practical exercise of authority. But it must also gently be said that
questions about the actual exercise of authority by Rome are surely not limited to Anglicans. To ask such questions about the manner of the present exercise of Roman authority
is not to deny a proprer Petrine ministry."

[218] W. Henn, "A Commentary on *The Gift of Authority*": "Indeed, in what are perhaps
some of the most remarkable paragraphs to appear in ecumenical dialogue to date, there is
an effort to reaffirm some of the essential doctrines of Vatican I's *Pastor aeternus*, on papal
primacy and infallibility (Gift, 45–48)": IS, no. 100 (1999), 30b.

[219] Ibid., 37b: "Thus *The Gift of Authority* seems to be saying that primatial ministry is
of the *esse* and not of the *bene esse* of the Church. It is required. In addition, both the
biblical and the patristic evidence provided presuppose that the initiative in providing the
Church with what she needed came from Jesus himself."

the Doctrine of the Faith[220]—published as an appendix to the Acts of
the symposium on the primacy of the successor of Peter (Rome, December 1996)—he thought it possible to attribute the same teaching also to
ARCIC II, which would therefore "be able to affirm a succint statement
such as: 'The Episcopacy and the Primacy, reciprocally connected and
inseparable, are of divine institution'". Better still, "this statement could
be acceptable to both communities." [221] He concluded, "Within the ecumenical landscape, it is fair to say that no other community has come so
far along with Roman Catholics in common agreement about the primacy of the Bishop of Rome." [222]

In her Commentary, the Anglican theologian M. Tanner, too, while
emphasizing the results achieved, pointed out that what was striking here
was that the Report spoke of a rereception of the universal primacy of
the Bishop of Rome on the part of both "Churches". It is not that the
Anglicans received something anew from the Catholic Church, but that
both "Churches" together received again a renewed ministry of the universal primacy.[223]

2. Evaluation by theologians

The basic results from the Catholic-Anglican dialogue relative to the primacy, especially in light of the statement *Authority in the Church II* (Windsor, 1981), are summed up by Coppola as follows: "1) the primacy of the
bishop of Rome does not contradict the New Testament, and it is part of

---

[220] Ibid.: "The recent considerations by the Congregation for the Doctrine of the Faith
about the primacy of the successor to Peter admit 'doctrinal development' and 'growing
clarity' regarding this ministry. At the same time, the Congregation underlines the continuity in this development, and that the growing clarity concerned a conviction which
the Church had from its origins that 'just as there exists a succession to the apostles in the
ministry of the bishops, so too the ministry of unity, entrusted to Peter, belongs to the
perennial structure of the Church of Christ and that this succession is tied to the see of his
martyrdom'. (16) By affirming its necessity and by referring to biblical and patristic texts
which speak of Jesus' words spoken specifically to Peter, choosing him for a role which
had reference to the Church as a whole, which called upon him to exercise powers entrusted
to the whole, ARCIC II seems to affirm substantially what the Congregation also affirms
regarding the foundation of the primacy in the will of Christ for the Church."

[221] Ibid., 37b–38a.

[222] Ibid., 40b.

[223] Ibid., 384c. Other commentaries, rather critical, always on the part of Anglicans, are
reported in *Catholic Insight* 7 (1999): 20.

God's design for the unity and universality of the Church, even though the New Testament texts do not offer a sufficient basis in this regard; 2) the primacy of the bishop of Rome can be affirmed as part of God's design for the universal *koinonia* in terms which are compatible with both traditions: 3) the universal primacy is not the source from which the diocesan bishops derive their authority, nor does its authority undermine that of the metropolitan or diocesan bishop (the primacy is not an autocratic authority over the Church, but a service, there being moral limits to its exercise); 4) once the primacy of the bishop of Rome is acknowledged, it follows that it is proper to this office, in which the Petrine function is handed down, to possess both a clear responsibility to teach and the appropriate gifts of the Holy Spirit that enable him to carry it out." [224]

It is a question of seeing to what degree such a judgment, substantially positive even in its nuances, has been and is able to be shared among theologians.

Petrinitas

With respect to the considerations already expressed concerning the question of evaluating the results of the Catholic-Lutheran dialogue,[225] we might limit ourselves here to emphasizing the lack of a substantial agreement between Catholics and Anglicans on the interpretation of the Petrine texts. This is the conclusion of Maviiri Ndidde,[226] arrived at after careful presentation of the Catholic and Anglican positions following upon the Observations of the Congregation for the Doctrine of the Faith and the Catholic Response to ARCIC I.[227] It is not clear, therefore, how it is

---

[224] Cf. R. Coppola, "Primato papale ed ecumenismo", 25. Cf. also Maviiri Ndidde, *Primacy in Communion of Churches*, 69; Neumann, "Das Papstamt in den offiziellen Ökumenischen Dialogen", 105.

[225] Cf. above, pp. 170–72.

[226] Maviiri Ndidde, *Primacy in the Communion of Churches*, 141: "The foregoing discussion on the institution of Petrine office has shown the divergence as regards the interpretation of these texts and how they should apply to the living Petrine ministry in a re-united Church. The Anglican counterparts have voiced dissatisfaction over the Catholic tendency to overstress these texts in order to justify the papacy. At the same time Catholics are not prepared to accede to the Anglican tendency to deny any New Testament foundation to justify the papacy. So far there is no substantial agreement as regards the common interpretation of these texts and therefore discussion must continue."

[227] Cf. ibid., 105–16.

possible to maintain that, given the debate over the concept of *ius divinum*, the controversy between Catholics and Anglicans centers no longer on the theological foundation of the primacy, but rather on its exercise.[228] The accusations made against the Congregation, of having gone beyond the documents of Vatican I on the conferral of the primacy on Peter by Christ[229] and of not understanding the intention of ARCIC I concerning the institution of the primacy by Christ,[230] are therefore unfounded.

Perpetuitas

The statement by ARCIC I that there is no biblical evidence to establish the transmission of the role of Peter to a successor[231] was likewise appraised in various ways.

The historical approach adopted by the commission, which lacked a theological justification,[232] was in fact interpreted by Catholic theologians

---

[228] Mikulanis, *Authority in the Church*, 322: "Basically, the theological foundation of a universal primacy is not the question of debate. Rather, the exercise of the primacy is what raises concern. This is evident in the Anglican/Roman Catholic debate over the concept of *ius divinum*."

[229] Hill, "Récents documents", 5: "Tandis que *Pastor Aeternus* (répété par Vatican II) parle de manière biblique et historique plus nuancée, et donc aussi plus acceptable, de Pierre recevant la primauté du Christ et des évêques de Rome héritant la primauté de Pierre, la *Réponse* semble si soupçonneuse à l'égard de l'approche historique de la primauté de Pierre par l'ARCIC qu'elle va au-de-là du texte de Vatican I qui avait été prudemment rédigé et discuté."

[230] Mikulanis, *Authority in the Church*, 323: "Where ARCIC questions whether Christ Himself established a universal primacy as an 'institution', i.e., an office of authority, the SCDF says that ARCIC has completely misunderstood the use of 'institution' in Vatican I and defends the belief that Christ instituted, i.e., established a universal primacy. It appears here that the SCDF is the one confused. ARCIC uses 'institution' as a noun, not as a verb; the SCDF reverses the use and thus misses the whole point of ARCIC's intention." Cf. ibid., 328.

[231] Cf. above, p. 221, note 135. Curiously, the biblical foundation of the Catholic doctrine could have been discerned, given the exegetical expertise of the members of ARCIC: "The members of the Commission, all of them familiar with modern exegetical methods, had no difficulty agreeing that the Roman doctrine on the primacy says more than is found in the New Testament (n. 2–9)" (Tavard, "ARCIC-I on Authority", 197).

[232] Mikulanis, *Authority in the Church*, 243–44: "But unfortunately, the arguments proposed for the primacy of the bishop of Rome in Venice are done so primarily on the basis of historical developments, and any theological foundations for the papacy were merely ignored."

as reducing the primacy to a simple delegation of power on the part of the local Churches, without a heavenly mandate.[233] Even the acknowledgment of the intervention of Providence, which guided the emergence of the primacy,[234] did not dispel the doubt that the commission intended to separate the Petrine from the papal ministry in such a way that the former could not serve as a theological foundation for the latter.[235]

Such an approach, however, confirmed the Anglican theologians in thinking of the primacy as having resulted from different human factors and in denying that the primacy given to Peter by Jesus is perpetuated in his successors.[236] In the hopes of dealing with the problem, a small number of theologians were disposed to accept a Petrine succession,[237] even if they did not believe there to be any evidence of it in Scripture. Therefore, even though according to ARCIC I the universal primacy is constitutive of the *koinonia* of the Churches, its realization is not necessarily

---

[233] Maviiri Ndidde, *Primacy in the Communion of Churches*, 119: "The lack of commitment to a theological justification of Petrine succession of the bishop of Rome ... can only be interpreted as a reduction of the primatial office in the universal Church to 'mere manifestation'. In other words, it is 'a simple delegation of powers by the local Churches, a delegation which does not of itself demand a particular mandate from on high'." Cf. J. Ratzinger, "Anglican-Catholic Dialogue: Its Problems and Hopes", *Insight*, March 2, 1983, 6; J. Dumont, "Authority in the Church; Comment on the Document", *Doctrine and Life* 27 (1977): 122.

[234] Tavard, "ARCIC-I on Authority", 197: "They found likewise no major difficulty in reaching agreement on the canonical and theological meaning of *jus divinum*, if at least Anglicans admit that the Roman primacy did emerge 'by divine providence' and Roman Catholics recognise that this is an acceptable meaning of *jure divino* (no. 13)." Cf. Tillard, "Faire émerger la communion", 165–66.

[235] Maviiri Ndidde, *Primacy in the Communion of Churches*, 157: "But we would raise serious question-marks if by its propositions, ARCIC I intends to separate Petrine ministry from papal ministry in such a way that the emergence of the latter cannot be theologically grounded in the former." Cf. J.M. Wright, "An Anglican Comment on Papal Authority in the Light of Recent Developments", S.W. Sykes (ed.), *Authority in the Anglican Communion* (Toronto, 1987), 246–68.

[236] Chadwick, "Unfinished Business", 124: "Generally, the evolution of thought of Anglicans towards the Roman primacy has not yet superceded historical or pragmatic justifications.... The Roman primacy is recognized as a result of a combination of human factors. Most Anglicans do not equate the 'Petrine office' with the 'Papacy'. They outrightly reject that 'the pope is the successor of Peter. Even theologians who accept Petrine primacy deny any perpetuity in the primacy Jesus granted to Peter'."

[237] Maviiri Ndidde, *Primacy in the Communion of Churches*, 225: "In an effort to tackle the problem, there is a minority group in Anglicanism which holds rather a pro-Petrine succession of the bishop of Rome."

linked to the papacy.[238] This underscores a certain ambiguity in the Final Report: it affirms, on the one hand, that the importance of the Bishop of Rome has been interpreted as being the will of Christ for his Church, and, on the other hand, that the primacy is part of a divine plan;[239] however, even if it can be allowed that Christ did not directly institute the primacy in the concrete way in which it appears today, the fact remains that it cannot be dissociated from the explicit will of Christ which conferred on Peter a primatial role among the apostles.[240] It may be granted that a clear confirmation for the transmission of the Petrine ministry to a successor cannot be found in Scripture and that this constitutes a problem for contemporary exegetes of all Churches,[241] but it is nevertheless necessary to acknowledge that the enduring character of such a ministry implies succession and that it is of divine law, just as the Petrine ministry is of divine law.[242] Nor is it acceptable to say the universal ministry of the Bishop of Rome results from the honor due him as the successor of Peter and *Paul* in that See.[243]

Therefore the Catholic and Anglican positions on the succession of the Bishop of Rome to Peter remain divergent, as the former asserts that it is

---

[238] Ibid., 128: "Universal primacy is constitutive of *koinonia* (that is, the communion of Churches), but the realization of it is not necessarily inherent in the papacy."

[239] Cf. above, p. 221, note 136.

[240] Maviiri Ndidde, *Primacy in the Communion of Churches*, 142–43: "If ARCIC I understands '*jus divinum*' as the explicit will of Christ for his Church, then it is difficult to reconcile the Commission's idea that universal primacy as a permanent institution need not be taken to imply direct foundation by the earthly Jesus.... Of course the earthly Jesus did not leave behind a blue-print ready-made structure for the Church as we know it today. But we believe that the explicit will of Christ cannot be dissociated from the earthly Jesus who allowed to Peter a unique role of primacy among the apostles."

[241] Tavard, "ARCIC-I on Authority", 196: "Do the Petrine texts of the New Testament justify the Roman primacy? This is not a specifically Anglican problem since the point is raised by all contemporary exegesis in all churches."

[242] Maviiri Ndidde, *Primacy in the Communion of Churches*, 158: "But the enduring character of the Petrine office necessarily implies succession. Therefore the oneness of the Church requires that Petrine ministry is perpetually in service of unity. In accordance with ARCIC I's remark that 'The only see which makes any claim to universal primacy and which has exercised and still exercises such *episcope* is the see of Rome', it would be absurd if this claim is merely *de iure ecclesiastico*, and not *de iure divino*. We say 'absurd' because the Petrine ministry is *de iure divino*; how can succession to it be *de iure ecclesiastico*?"

[243] Mikulanis, *Authority in the Church*, 325: "ARCIC has no problem with granting this ministry of universal *episcope* to the bishop of Rome, as a result of the honor which is his by virtue of the fact of his being the successor of Saints Peter and Paul in that city."

by divine law, and the latter that it is by ecclesiastical law.[244] Consequently, it appears that ARCIC has not resolved the question as to the necessity of the primacy as a principle of unity,[245] as is demonstrated by the divergence of opinions among Anglicans and by the doubts on the part of Catholics as to whether or not the primacy proposed by ARCIC truly provides for a degree of jurisdiction capable of preserving the communion of the Church.[246]

In conclusion, just as in the discussion on the need of the episcopacy in general[247]—considered useful but not indispensable[248]—it is not clear,

---

[244] Maviiri Ndidde, *Primacy in the Communion of Churches*, 157: "On this issue Catholics and Anglicans are obviously divided. While the Catholics clearly assert a theological grounding (that is, universal primatial authority was directly given to Peter by the Lord himself and now being perpetuated by his successor, the Roman Pontiff, *de iure divino*), the Anglicans generally hold that universal primacy is justifiable on historical contingent grounds, *de iure ecclesiastico*." It does not seem possible to maintain, as some Catholics have proposed, that the primacy was not instituted *directly* by Christ *during his earthly life*: J. McHugh, "Marginal Notes on the Response to ARCIC I", in HY, 327: "No Catholic therefore may deny that the permanence of the primacy results from the institution of Jesus Christ, or that it belongs to the divine constitution of the Church; but the wording of chapter 2 (of Vatican I) does not appear to decide irrevocably the question whether 'the universal primacy as a permanent institution was *directly* founded by Jesus *during his life on earth*'."

[245] Mikulanis, *Authority in the Church*, 321: "In its treatment of primacy ARCIC asserts the need for a primacy of *episcope* in the Church to watch over and guide this union of local churches with one another.... However, one is left wondering how Anglicans can accept such a position and remain true to their historical freedom from centralized authority. This is a question which ARCIC leaves unanswered."

[246] Ibid., 350: "Both Anglican and Roman Catholic theology provide for the role of a primate in the Church, although with varying degrees of authority. ARCIC cites the need for a primacy of *episcope* in the Church and actually produces a viable plan for such. However, there is such widespread difference of opinion in Anglicanism on the role of primacy, from that held by the Evangelical wing, which disclaims any need for a primate at all, to that held by the Anglo-Catholic wing, which seeks a strong primacy, that one cannot say that an acceptable agreement has been reached on this topic. Furthermore, there are Roman Catholic concerns that the primacy proposed by ARCIC fails to provide a proper degree of jurisdiction to preserve the *koinonia* of the Church. Though members of ARCIC agree that they have reached consensus on this point, and in general they have, they must nevertheless consider the objections raised by those elements of the Churches opposed to it."

[247] Ibid., 349: "As a result of this oversight on ARCIC's part, the controversy on episcopacy as pertaining to the *esse* or *bene esse* of the Church remains unresolved."

[248] Morerod, "Réflexions sur l'Accord de Porvoo", 103: "Et d'ailleurs le Porvoo insiste longuement sur l'importance de l'épiscopat. Mais si celui-ci est réduit à une fonction utile mais non indispensable, et qu'en outre le moyen de sa transmission 'physique' est relativisé, nous craignons fort que l'apostolicité, la relation permanente de l'Église avec les Apôtres, soit mise en cause."

due to the typically Anglican principle of a *dispersed* authority,[249] whether there is a common view concerning the need for a primate at the world-wide level. The Final Report effectively affirmed such a need,[250] but at the same time acknowledged that the primacy of jurisdiction remains an unresolved problem.[251] It is therefore understandable how, even among the different Anglican factions, in the light of the above-mentioned principle of dispersed authority, it can still be maintained that a universal primacy is not necessary, that the immediate power of the Pope contradicts the Anglican notion of conciliarity and collegiality and moreover is not of divine law.[252] The consensus remains therefore conditioned by the demand that freedom from any form of centralization—a historical characteristic of Anglicanism—be respected[253] and that the rights of

---

[249] Mikulanis, *Authority in the Church*, 225: "When one considers the Anglican concept of dispersed authority, it is difficult to see how a universal primacy could be established."

[250] Cf. above, p. 214, note 103.

[251] Cf. above, p. 215, notes 107–10.

[252] P. Lüning, "Anglikanisch/Römisch-katholische Beziehungen aus der Sicht der Kirche von England", *Catholica* 51 (1997): 108–9: "Das anglikanische Prinzip einer "dispersed authority" wird daher von beiden Gruppen unterschiedlich ausgelegt: 'Dispersed' kann für die Nachfolger der Traktarianer nur eine kollegiale Ausübung apostolischer Vollmacht durch weltweit alle Bischöfe bedeuten, ohne dabei einem bestimmten Bischof größere Vollmachten zu verleihen. 'Moderne (Anglo-)Katholiken' verstehen unter dem Begriff 'dispersed authority' eine gemeinschaftliche Verantwortung des ganzen Volkes Gottes für den Glauben der Kirche. Beide kritisieren jedoch die römisch-katholische Lehre über eine päpstliche *potestas immediata*, die dem anglikanischen Verständnis von Konziliarität und Kollegialität widerspräche: Eine 'dispersed authority' mit ihren gegenseitigen 'checks and balances' stehe in fundamentalem Gegensatz zur rechtlich zentralisierten römisch-katholischen Kirche.... Einig sind sich aber beide Theologengruppen, daß weder die Kollegialität der Gesamtkirche noch eine sich auf ausschließlich moralische Autorität berufende kollegiale Leitungsgemeinschaft der 'Ergänzung' durch primatiale Strukturen *iuris divini* bedürfen. Evangelikale Theologen zweifeln grundsätzlich an der Legitimität eines universalen und personalen Primates und verweisen dabei auf das Neue Testament, das von einem einzigen Haupt der Kirche, Jesus Christus, spricht." Cf. Mikulanis, *Authority in the Church*, 225–41, which treats in particular the question of divine right.

[253] Ibid., 321: "In its treatment of primacy ARCIC asserts the need for a primacy of *episcope* in the Church to watch over and guide this union of local churches with one another.... However, one is left wondering how Anglicans can accept such a position and remain true to their historical freedom from centralized authority. This is a question which ARCIC leaves unanswered. The Evangelical criticism and fears of this opinion are evidence enough that Anglicans themselves are not agreed upon the need for a universal primacy of *koinonia* in the Church."

regional primacies[254] be preserved, especially those of local bishops in synod.[255]

The nature of the primacy

Even more ambiguous is the way in which the Final Report treated the nature of the primacy, leaving perplexing questions that required further discussion.[256] Indeed, even if it is admitted that, in principle, there is agreement on the necessity of a universal primacy, the fact remains that its exact nature and concrete realization have yet to be specified: that is, it is not clear whether it involves only a functional, honorific duty or a true jurisdiction, with a theological basis[257] in divine law.[258] It is stated that this would not be a simple primacy of honor, but would have a more prominent role in seeing that the authentic Gospel is preached in all the Churches;[259] however, the type of authority which the Roman Pontiff would need to carry out this role is not defined. The Final Report limits

---

[254] Ibid., 324: "Finally, despite the Evangelical Anglican objections to a primacy of *episcope* in the Church, it seems that the emerging general consensus between Anglicans and Roman Catholics is that a universal primacy is needed, but one which respects regional primacies as well."

[255] K. S. Chittleborough, "Towards a Theology and Practice of the Bishop-in-Synod", Sykes, *Authority in the Anglican Communion*, 155: "The ARCIC Statements on Authority have traced the development of papal primacy very clearly, and they raise the question, Is it possible to *add* centralized to dispersed authority and yet leave the theology of bishop-in-synod intact? The short answer to this question is: Only if it leaves intact the *balance of theological principles* inherent in the bishop-in-synod." The author concludes that in practice "this claim to have discovered an existing consensus between our two churches on the principles of primacy is highly questionable" (ibid., 156).

[256] Mikulanis, *Authority in the Church*, 249: "As most everywhere else in the Authority Statements of ARCIC, the role of the bishop of Rome causes the most anxiety and produces the most discussion."

[257] Maviiri Ndidde, *Primacy in the Communion of Churches*, 4: "While there is agreement, in principle, over the need of universal primacy, the dialogue has not yet produced satisfactory propositions as regards the exact nature and concrete realization of the latter. Is it merely a functional/honorary or theological and jurisdictional primacy?"

[258] Tavard, "ARCIC-I on Authority", 196: "They question the form that the Roman practice of authority acquired in the counter-Reformation: is the universal primacy of divine law (*jus divinum*)? ... Does it include a universal immediate jurisdiction of the primate in all dioceses of the church?"

[259] Maviiri Ndidde, *Primacy in the Communion of Churches*, 95: "ARCIC I envisages a primacy, not just for honor, but as occupying the first place in ensuring that the authentic Gospel is preached in all the local Churches."

itself to saying that it is an authority which effectively enables him to confirm his brothers in the faith.[260]

In particular, there remains a lack of convergence on the questions of the divine institution of the primacy and of its juridical character, which for the Catholic Church are fundamental aspects of the nature and exercise of the primacy.[261] Discussing the issue in the context of the Church as communion,[262] the Final Report emphasized the need to consider the nature and exercise of the primacy, within the sphere of collegiality and conciliarity, and in practice established the principle of complementarity between primacy and conciliarity,[263] which is however not fully accepted among Anglicans, because it would involve attributing to the Archbishop of Canterbury a merely moral-spiritual authority.[264] Postulating an authority on the universal level which is at the same time primatial and conciliar,[265] the Final

---

[260] Ibid., 4: "[T]he Commission does not define the type of authority needed but clearly acknowledges that any future universal primate will have to possess authority in order to effectively strengthen his brethren in the faith."

[261] Ibid., 86: "[A]s a matter of principle, Catholics and Anglicans agree to this function of the universal primate, but theologically and practically disagreements still remain over divine institution and primacy of jurisdiction, aspects which are fundamental to the nature and exercise of universal primacy in the Catholic Church."

[262] Ibid., 2: "The Commission worked on the nature and exercise of primatial authority within the context of a *koinonia* Church. It is worthwhile to note that its *Final Report* is consistent wih this *koinonia* ecclesiology." Cf. Mikulanis, *Authority in the Church*, 199–206.

[263] Maviiri Ndidde, *Primacy in the Communion of Churches*, 92: "For ARCIC I the council and primate stand in a relationship of complementarity. There is no question of one substituting for the other in the exercise of authority in the Church. The mutual union of the two aspects is consistently maintained in the Commission's Report. . . . Primacy is intended to be the focus of *koinonia* in its organic unity and, in practice, it must favour and promote the conciliarity of the Church as much as possible." It must be emphasized that the Anglican idea of conciliarity is not limited to bishops, but involves the entire people of God: cf. Mikulanis, *Authority in the Church*, 59–60; G. White, "Collegiality and Conciliarity in the Anglican Communion", Sykes, *Authority in the Anglican Communion*, 202–19.

[264] Lüning, "Anglikanisch/Römisch-katholische Beziehungen", 107–8: "Daher kritisierten anglo-katholische Theologen die Kommission in ihrem Versuch, den Jurisdiktionsprimat des Papstes aus der Perspektive einer 'Ergänzung' ('complementarity') zu konziliar-kollegialer *episkope* zu deuten . . . Die von ARCIC I geforderte Komplementarität von primatialen und kollegialkonziliaren Strukturen sehen viele anglo-katholische Theologen in vorbildlicher Weise in der Anglikanischen Kirchengemeinschaft verwirklicht, in der der Erzbischof von Canterbury aufgrund des Prinzips einer "limitation of office" nur moralisch-spirituelle Autorität besitze und in der die zahlreiche regionale und überregionale Synoden über die Belange ihrer jeweiligen Kirchen entscheiden."

[265] Greenacre, "Lettre ouverte", 122: "Car le *Rapport final* voyait clairement le besoin d'établir un équilibre entre le respect d'une légitime diversité et d'un degré d'autonomie

Report sought to reconcile the two different ecclesiologies[266] and to overcome the difficulty for Anglicans posed by attributing to the Bishop of Rome
a universal, ordinary, and immediate jurisdiction.[267] The Final Report, sensitive to the Anglican fears, explained the term *universal* in the sense that "it
must enable him to serve the unity and harmony of the *koinonia* as a whole
and in each of its parts."[268] However, this explanation was criticized by the
Congregation for the Doctrine of the Faith, specifying that the power of
jurisdiction of the Bishop of Rome over all the particular churches is "intrinsic to the primacy, it is 'full, supreme and universal power over the whole
church', a power which can be exercised unhindered".[269]

The principle of complementarity between primacy and conciliarity, clearly
supported by ARCIC,[270] needs some clarification. First of all, this is understood as an attempt to define the limits of papal authority on the basis of
contemporary criteria suggested by democracy and by ecumenical expe-

---

au niveau des Églises particulières ou locales, et la reconnaissance de la nécessité d'une
autorité au niveau universel à la fois conciliaire et primatiale, pour maintenir et protéger
l'unité et la communion de ces Églises locales l'une avec l'autre dans l'Église du Christ
une, sainte, catholique et apostolique."

[266] Mikulanis, *Authority in the Church*, 330: "In fact, this topic seems to have produced more
dissent than others, the root of which is a conflict between two ecclesiologies, one of
which is primarily conciliar (Anglican), the other of which is more primatial (Roman Catholic)." There is a diversity of ecclesiological ideas within the Anglican communion itself: "In
der Beschäftigung mit der ekklesiologischen Problematik im Anglikanismus ist deutlich
geworden, daß hinter den zahlreichen anglikanischen Reaktionen auf ARCIC I verschiedene
ekklesiologische Selbstverständnisse stehen, die Ausdruck von unterschiedlichen anglikanischen Identitaten geben": Lüning, "Anglikanisch/Römisch-Katholische Beziehungen", 118.

[267] Lüning, "Anglikanisch/Römisch-Katholische Beziehungen", 110: "Während die
römisch-katholische Kirche auf der theologischen Grundlage eines 'hierarchischen' Kirch-
enverständnisses der Überordnung klerikaler Lehrgewalt über die Laien in der Kirche ar-
beite, hatten Anglikaner eine 'organische' Sicht der Kirche, die auf die Einsicht zurückgehe,
daß alle Glieder des Volkes Gottes aufgrund ihrer Taufe zur gemeinsamen Verantwortung
für die Kirche berufen seien. Dieser Einsicht entspreche das Modell des 'bishop-in-synod',
in dem der Bischof nicht alleiniger 'Repräsentant' einer Lokalkirche, sondern deren bloß
'moralisches' Haupt sei. Daher müßten alle Teile des Volkes Gottes in einer Synode angemessen vertreten sein, um gemeinsam am Entscheidungsprozeß in Glaubensfragen mitzu-
wirken. Eine päpstliche *potestas immediata* als 'Ergänzung' zu dieser synodal-kollegialen Struktur
in der Kirche schränke nicht nur die Freiheit des Geistes Gottes, sondern auch die Glaubens-
freiheit des einzelnen Christen ein und sei darum abzulehnen."

[268] MV III, no. 18.

[269] Cf. above, p. 231, note 178.

[270] Cf. above, p. 214, note 105.

rience.[271] This principle was advanced—along with the interpretation of
subsistit in of *Lumen Gentium* (no. 8)[272]—in order to claim ecclesial character for the Anglican Communion, the lack of union with Rome notwithstanding,[273] and to propose not only that living in communion need
not be postponed by the existing disagreement over primacy, but also that
it might be the means to overcome the disagreement.[274] Contrary to what
is asserted, such a claim is not based on Vatican II, but instead disagrees with

---

[271] Tavard, "ARCIC-I on Authority", 195–96: "In the nineteenth century the authority
of the see and the bishop of Rome was defined by Vatican Council I in ways that went far
beyond the practice and principles of the sixteenth. In these conditions ARCIC's acknowledgement of legitimate 'conciliar and primatial authority' needed to be complemented by
an investigation of the limits of authority.... According to contemporary political principles the source of authority is the people of the land. This authority is delegated to elected
or at least recognised officials whose exercise of power is constitutionally limited, the possibility of recalling unsatisfactory officials being even admitted in some political systems....
Secondly there was the experience of ecumenical dialogue about papal primacy and infallibility. It is impossible in an ecumenical setting to reach agreement on the authority that belongs
in principle to the bishop of Rome without at the same time determining what practical limits must be assigned to its exercise on the basis of Scripture and the tradition. This requirement, however, seems to be at odds with what has been the Roman theory and practice."

[272] Cf. above, p. 239, note 215.

[273] Root, "Some Remarks on the Response to ARCIC I", 170: "In that paragraph [no. 12
in *Authority* II] the Commission wanted to say something about the character, church character, of churches not in communion with the Roman See.... It cites the case of the Orthodox churches, recognised by Rome as churches even though not in communion with the Roman
See. There is then a reference to *Unitatis Redintegratio* 14. That paragraph is very general. It
does not explicitly declare that the 'Churches of the East' are fully churches. A careful reading might suggest that the paragraph does not wish to declare on this question. At the very
least, however, it does not deny that they are churches." McDonnell makes the same critique: "The ARCIC report contends that a Church not in communion with the Holy See
may 'lack nothing' except it does not belong to the visible communion which is maintained
in the Roman Catholic Church. To this the Response takes exception, saying such a Church
'lacks more' than just the visible manifestation of unity. No indication is given of what this
'more' might be. One of the achievements of the Final Report is the very positive evaluation
of the pope as universal primate" ("A Year Afterwards", 116).

[274] Tavard, "ARCIC-I on Authority", 197: "In other words, the *Final Report* of ARCIC-I
proposed that the restoration of communion need not wait until all problems have been solved.
Rather, living together in communion should be the main factor that will bring in the solution of the remaining problems regarding the Roman primacy and its exercise. In spite of Bel-
larmine's ecclesiology such problems of organisation do not belong to the essence of what is
to be the Church of Christ. They may then be tabled for the sake of restoring communion.... This being the case, the idea that communion may be restored before total agreement is reached on the authority of the universal primate implies that the Roman doctrines
of Vatican I that regulate this authority are themselves not to be placed at the level of faith."

Catholic doctrine on the unity of the Church,[275] reaffirmed by *Communionis notio*.[276]

Outlook for the future

Fundamental disagreements are found as well with regard to future prospects as to the necessity of the primacy as a *conditio sine qua non* for the restoration of the full communion of the Churches. Following their traditional distinction between the *plene esse* and the *bene esse* of the Church relative to the episcopacy, Anglicans maintain that the primacy pertains merely to the *bene esse* of the Church: that is, that it is useful, but not constitutive of the Church. Furthermore, they assert that the primacy is not necessarily bound to the Bishop of Rome, though he remains nevertheless the best suited to a legitimate Petrine succession, even without a biblical foundation to support it.[277] In Catholic circles, even if the need

---

[275] Ratzinger, *Church, Ecumenism and Politics*, 74–75: "With such an assertion wrongly claiming the support of Vatican II, Church Unity is debased to an unnecessary, if desirable, externality, and the character of the universal Church is reduced to mere outward representation, of little significance in constituting what is ecclesial. This romantic idea of provincial Churches, which is supposed to restore the structure of the early Church, is really contradicting the historical reality of the early Church as well as the concrete experiences of history, to which one must certainly not turn a blind eye in considerations of this sort. The early Church did indeed know nothing of Roman primacy in practice, in the sense of Roman Catholic theology of the second millennium, but it was well acquainted with living forms of unity in the universal Church which were constitutive of the essence of provincial Churches. Understood in this sense, the priority of the universal Church always preceded that of particular Churches."

[276] The Anglican theologian Hill is very critical of this letter: "Mais la Lettre de la Congrégation pour la Doctrine de la Foi implique que la succession et l'épiscopat ne peuvent exister que si les évêques sont en communion hiérarchique avec Rome. De la même manière, la Lettre dit que 'afin que chaque Église particulière soit pleinement Église (...) le collège épiscopal avec le Pontife romain, son chef (...), doit être présent en elle'. D'un coup toutes les Églises qui ne sont pas en communion avec Rome sont ainsi privées de leur propre ecclésialité ... Mais une fois encore il n'est pas suggéré par là que les évêques qui ne sont pas en communion hiérarchique avec Rome ne sont pas évêques ou que les Églises séparées ne sont pas véritablement Églises" ("Récents documents", 65).

[277] Maviiri Ndidde, *Primacy in the Communion of Churches*, 135: "Anglicans seriously committed to the cause of the unity of the Churches, would undoubtedly acknowledge the primatial leadership of the successors of Peter on the grounds that it belongs to the '*bene esse*' of the Church, but they are not committed to the perpetuity of the papacy. They would not view universal primacy as necessarily linked with the bishop of Rome. For them the latter is seen to be a possible, and probably the most suitable candidate of a legitimate Petrine succession, but they maintain that there is no biblical evidence for it."

for the primacy in the event of reunion is emphasized, there are nevertheless two different approaches to it: the so-called reversibilists, who maintain that the papacy could be replaced by another form of primacy; and
the irreversibilists, who hold that the papacy cannot be removed from the
Church.[278] The first position is based on the contingent historical development of the Petrine ministry, which on scriptural grounds certainly
constitutes an essential part of the Church of Christ, of which the Church
herself can regulate the concrete expressions, distribution, and powers,
exercising it therefore with forms more suitable to the future reunited
Church.[279] The second position, referring explicitly to the will of Christ
and the activity of the Holy Spirit at the origins of the primacy, emphasizes the essential and permanent character of the primacy as bound to
the See of Rome, though it remains always necessary to distinguish between
its immutable essence and its changeable expressions.[280]

Although there are such differences among Catholics, those between
Catholics and Anglicans are far greater. With reference to the idea of the
Church as communion—which Catholics have supposedly not understood well[281]—and in light of the difficulties that the exercise of the primacy has posed in history, Anglicans insist on a primacy of honor in a
specifically corporate context of conciliarity and collegiality,[282] which would
reduce the universal primate to a *primus inter pares* within the context of

---

[278] Ibid., 128: "Miller outlines two main approaches in answer to our question: Is the
papacy *sine qua non* if full communion is to be restored between the Churches? The first
approach pertains to a group of theologians he calls 'reversibilists'. For them the papacy
could be substituted by another form of primacy. But a contrary group is that which
Miller calls 'irreversibilists' who insist that the papacy cannot be detached from the Church."

[279] Cf. ibid., 128–29.

[280] Cf. ibid., 129–32.

[281] Clifford, after a biting critique of *Communionis notio*, states, "Roman Catholics must
ask themselves whether they have truly received the communion ecclesiology of the Second
Vatican Council, whether we have in place the structures which reflect this ecclesiology of
communion and which can make the reception of ecumenical agreement an organically
experienced reality in the life of the Church" ("Reception of the *Final Report*", 143).

[282] Tanner, "The Anglican Position on Apostolic Continuity", 121: "This emphasis on
the personal, the collegial and the communal, the threefold dimension of *episcope*, is familiar to Anglican theology and Anglican experience, though like all Christian churches Anglicans struggle with how best to express the personal, collegial and communal forms of
oversight.... Here it is worth drawing particular attention to two lines of the final paragraph of this Porvoo section: 'The personal, collegial and communal dimensions of oversight find expression at a local, regional and universal level of the Church's life' [Porvoo,
par. 45].... The passage implicitly looks forward to that conversation on ministry of universal

the ancient patriarchal institution,[283] with the duty of being a spiritual guide, but without any jurisdiction over the other Churches, which maintain their autonomy. For Catholics, in contrast, the primacy exercises true jurisdiction over all the Churches.[284] In any case, for Anglicans, acceptance of the universal jurisdiction of the Bishop of Rome is predicated on the indispensable condition of being able to preserve their past heritage,[285] out of respect for the various traditions and on the basis of a reinterpretation of the terminology of Vatican I.[286] This is a logical consequence of the fundamental principal for Anglicans that unity does

---

primacy which is asked for by the Holy Father in *Ut Unum Sint*." Cf. Butler, "Authority in the Church", 350.

[283] McDonnell, "A Year Afterwards", 115–16: "Peter is still founding-rock and stumbling-block. The Final Report never explicitly suggests, but it has been interpreted as proposing, a return to the earlier situation when the Church was organized by patriarchates (Rome, Alexandria, Antioch, Jerusalem), with Rome exercising a presidency in love." Cf. Mikulanis, *Authority in the Church*, 152–53.

[284] Maviiri Ndidde, *Primacy in the Communion of Churches*, 152: "The Anglican counterparts are generally satisfied to accept the primacy of Rome (therefore the papacy) in a future re-united Church more so on this ground than on any other. For Catholics in general this is rather insufficient. Papal primacy is of theological necessity because it was divinely instituted by Christ. . . . The exercise of this function has presented grave difficulties. Anglicans would insist on a primacy of honour with variations, while for the Roman Catholics it is a primacy of jurisdiction (DS 3055) exercised over the whole Church. In this regard the Anglicans seem to push a corporate primacy expressed in conciliarity and in the collegiality of bishops in meetings whereby the universal primate will be the president, in the words of former Archbishop of Canterbury, Michael Ramsey, a special place for a 'primus-inter-pares' as organ of unity and authority." Cf. M. Ramsey, *The Gospel and the Catholic Church* (London, New York, and Toronto, 1936), 233. Cf. Mikulanis, *Authority in the Church*, 75.

[285] Mikulanis, *Authority in the Church*, 329: "Before any form of universal jurisdiction can be acceptable to Anglicans, they must be assured that the past four and a half centuries of the ecclesiastical heritage they have developed will be preserved and retained." The same Anglicans doubt that the Catholic Church could accept "the *Final Report's* interpretation of 'universal, ordinary, and immediate'" in the sense of a *primus inter pares*: Wright, "Papal Authority in the Light of Recent Developments", 249.

[286] M. Delmotte, "Le dialogue entre anglicans et catholiques", *Istina* 27 (1982): 286–87: "La Commission pense que la primauté de l'évêque de Rome comme faisant partie du dessein de Dieu pour la *koinonía* universelle peut être affirmée dans de termes compatibles aves les deux traditions. Elle pense aussi qu'il est possible de pervenir à une interprétation des termes employés par Vatican I pour qualifier la juridiction de l'évêque de Rome (ordinaire, immédiate et universelle) dans sa primauté universelle qui soit acceptable pour les anglicans; car il faut toujours rappeler que cette juridiction est au service de la communion des Églises locales et n'empiète pas sur la juridiction ordinaire des autres évêques; une telle façon de comprendre la juridiction de l'évêque de Rome n'entraîne pas la suppression des traditions théologiques et des coûtumes propres de l'Église anglicane."

not mean absorption.[287] The type of authority that would be enjoyed by the Bishop of Rome in the future remains undetermined, and so the fundamental problem is still not resolved: that is, whether it would involve true jurisdiction, even though exercised on the basis of the principles of nonabsorption and of collegiality.[288]

Thus we find an ambivalent attitude among Anglicans[289] in the sense that they are aware of the need for a Petrine ministry to assist the local bishop in the difficult task of preserving the Church in truth and unity, so much so that if the Pope did not already exist, it would be necessary to invent him—on one condition, however, namely, that Catholics be disposed to review the exercise of the papacy, as suggested by John Paul II in *Ut unum sint*.[290]

A conclusion can be inferred from the comments of the Anglican theologian Hind, which offer some hope without glossing over the difficulties

---

[287] Cf. Mikulanis, *Authority in the Church*, 347.

[288] Maviiri Ndidde, *Primacy in the Communion of Churches*, 159: "The Commission does not concretely define the type of authority required. This is practically the most difficult problem to solve. While the Catholics firmly hold to a power of jurisdiction (DS 3055), the Anglicans insist on a universal primate, *primus-inter-pares*, without jurisdiction outside his diocese. This presents a stalemate. There are no signs on the Anglican side to accede to a primacy of jurisdiction. This is foreign to their tradition of provincial, national and diocesan autonomy. The primate of the Anglican Communion (who is also the Archbishop of Canterbury) is the president of the Lambeth Conference, but has no jurisdiction outside his diocese. In the college of Anglican bishops, he is regarded as first-among-equals and enjoys a primacy of honour in the world-wide Anglican Communion. On the Catholic side, there are no signs of backing down from the primacy of jurisdiction. As regards the present form and exercise of the papacy in the Catholic Church, drastic changes will be needed before it can be accepted as focus of unity of *koinonia* in a re-united Church."

[289] McDonnell, "A Year Afterwards", 116: "Whatever serious disagreements still remain these positive attitudes are surprising when one considers that Anglicans consider themselves a communion of autonomous provincial Churches, and that rejection of the jurisdiction of the Bishop of Rome has been a distinguishing feature of Anglicanism. There is a reason for hope." Hill, "ARCIC-I and II. An Anglican Perspective", 144–45: "Today ARCIC has not convinced everybody for there are still some Anglicans who react like Luther to the Papacy. But it is now *mainstream* to talk about a potential universal Primacy, balanced by conciliarity and collegiality, as an Anglican possibility."

[290] Butler, "Authority in the Church", 350: "[L]ocal bishops cannot, it seems, fulfill their office of maintaining the church in truth and unity (*koinonia*) without the service of a primate who has universal jurisdiction. (Or, if we did not have a pope we would have to invent one!) Is it possible that, having discovered this, Anglicans can 're-receive' the apostolic tradition regarding his primatial office? The question is no longer only theoretical. But if so, Roman Catholics must also be open to re-receiving this ministry—and in the way it may be exercised in the 'new situation' that Pope John Paul II anticipates in *Ut unum sint*."

that still exist: "Certainly, that the problem is posed does not at all imply the approval of a determined form of primacy. On the contrary, there are still Anglicans that profess to be relentlessly opposed to any discussion whatsoever of a universal primacy, whether connected to the Roman See or not. They are at any rate a minority, and on November 13, 1986, the General Synod of the Church of England approved a resolution that acknowledged that the three authority documents of the *Final Report* of ARCIC I 'reveal a sufficient degree of convergence on the nature of authority in the Church to allow our communions to continue to explore together the structures of authority and the exercise of collegiality and of primacy in the Church'.

"A little later, the same day, the Synod approved another motion which expressed the conviction that it was a priority 'to give the utmost attention to the possibility of a universal primacy, situated necessarily in Rome, including the official Catholic claim that the Pope is the Vicar of Christ on earth'.

"Nevertheless, as was said by a senior member of the General Synod of the Church of England during a previous discussion on the *Final Report* of ARCIC I: 'We have only begun, groping and with fear, to imagine what would be an appropriate kind of presidency for the worldwide college of bishops, a position for which, practically speaking, the Bishop of Rome is the only candidate'. . . .

"It is not a coincidence that the worldwide role of the Archbishop of Canterbury and the universal primacy of the Bishop of Rome are presented together in this way. Leaving aside any consideration of the intervention of Providence in the development of the papacy, it is clear that history and politics have had a role to play. And this applies also for Canterbury: the same factors in the 20th century and within a divided church have constrained the Anglican Communion to develop instruments on a global plane. Perhaps the hand of Providence can be seen also here.

"If the prospect of a fully visible unity to which the Anglicans aspire is authentic, it seems improbable that we will end by establishing a parallel or rival papacy. The suggestion is completely absurd. It is more likely that the Anglican churches find themselves looking forward to the experience of a universal primacy which their ancestors had to do without from the time of the Reformation. It is my conviction that things being as they are, and also the way in which it is developing under the watchful eyes of God, *this* worldwide ministry has something to offer to a future papacy which could become a sign and service of a unity more universal than that which is possible in the present situation of division in the Church."[291]

IV. CONCLUSION

Owing to the historical motives that led to the rejection of the papacy by the Anglicans and thanks to the efforts toward reunion already begun in the last century, the Catholic-Anglican dialogue has undeniably attained promising results concerning the issue of the primacy of the Bishop of Rome. If nothing else, the commission has dealt with the topic more directly. Moreover, unlike what has been observed in the other dialogues, the results of the first phase of ARCIC I have been officially scrutinized by the respective ecclesial authorities, which with their reservations and with their specific instructions induced ARCIC II to study the question further.

The fruit of those deliberations can be seen in the document *The Gift of Authority*, which clearly recognizes the necessity of an *episcope* in the service of the universal *koinonia* and the effective transmission of that ministry to the Bishop of Rome, even though no mention is made of the question of *ius divinum*. Also still unresolved is the problem of the concrete exercise of this primacy, in the context of collegiality and synodality, and in the interest of safeguarding the legitimate diversity in each tradition.

The conclusion of that document expresses the certainty that one day the gift of the universal primacy, understood in this way, will be shared by both parties, above all because they are both committed to a renewed reception of it.

Comments by theologians have not yet appeared, much less official position statements. Nothing remains but to wait for future developments, in the knowledge that the necessary foundations are already in place.

---

[291] Hind, "Primato e unità: un contributo anglicano", 67–68.

GENERAL CONCLUSION

From this analysis of the results of the major bilateral dialogues on the question of the primacy of the Bishop of Rome, it becomes evident that up to now great progress has not been made.

This conclusion is particularly evident with regard to the Catholic-Orthodox dialogue, both because of the methodology that has been adopted (though not always actually applied, especially in dealing with the subject of the primacy, which so often is placed on the agenda only to be postponed) and also because of the difficulties resulting from divergent ecclesiological viewpoints. The impression given is that the commission does not consider the issue of the primacy in its true significance.

Turning to the Catholic-Lutheran dialogue, it can be said that the effective disappearance of the strident criticism of the papacy, which was characteristic of the Reformation and Counter Reformation periods, has not been matched by suitable progress on the specific question of the primacy. First of all, the prior ecclesiological questions (the sacramentality of the Church, apostolicity, and ministry) have still not been clarified; furthermore, the much touted Lutheran willingness to accept a service to the universal Church continues to be accompanied by the traditional proviso of conformity to the Gospel and in practice is nullified by the continuing controversy over the *ius divinum* and plenitude of power of the Bishop of Rome.

More promising results, however, seem to have been reached in the Catholic-Anglican dialogue. Thanks to the official evaluation of the documents of the first phase of the dialogue by both Catholic and Anglican authorities and to theological debate, the document of ARCIC II, *The Gift of Authority*, is much more explicit in emphasizing the recognition of and willingness to accept a universal primacy though under very precise conditions, for which the Bishop of Rome is the most natural candidate.

The common denominator, in all these dialogues, continues to be the problem of the concrete exercise of the primacy, in light of the relationship between the universal Church and the local Church and of the principles of collegiality or synodality.

Yet this is the heart of the invitation by Pope John Paul II to a deeper examination of the question. Perhaps there is too much concentration on this particular aspect, but until the fundamental questions of its existence and nature are tackled and resolved, the primacy will continue to be the most serious obstacle in the path of ecumenism.

APPENDIX

SISTER CHURCHES:
REALITY AND QUESTIONS

The expression "sister Churches" has acquired a decisive significance in present-day ecumenical dialogue, inasmuch as the ecclesiology of communion among the sister Churches seems to be the most promising path toward reestablishing unity.[1] Used for the first time by Patriarch Athenagoras of Constantinople in a letter to Cardinal Augustine Bea (April 12, 1962)[2], it eventually became, in the vocabulary of the Roman Church, "a privileged and almost official expression to designate the objective bond between the Orthodox Church and the Roman Church", and its actual use within the context of recent ecumenical rediscoveries is an example of *receptio*, on the part of Rome, of a viewpoint proposed by another Church and fraught with implications.[3] It has become commonplace to speak of a "theology of sister Churches"[4] and of an "ecclesiology of sister Churches".[5] The intention behind such language is the establishment of the reality of sister Churches as a possible way to "envisage reunion among divided traditions as a family reconciliation"[6] and as "a model for

---

[1] It is in these terms that A. de Halleux concluded his review of my book *Il Papa Patriarca d'Occidente?*: see *Revue théologique de Louvain* 23 (1992): 211.

[2] In E. J. Stormon, 36–37, no. 12.

[3] J.-M. R. Tillard, "La primauté romaine", 320–21.

[4] Cf. J. Meyendorff, "Églises soeurs", 44; Lanne, "Implications ecclésiologiques", 58; Tillard, "Catholic Church Is at the Heart of Communion", 8. On the other hand, it is an exaggeration to speak *sic et simpliciter* of the "ecumenical heresy of the 'sister Churches'", *sì sì no no* 21 (1995): no. 8, pp. 1–5.

[5] De Halleux, "Les deux Rome dans la définition de Chalcédoine sur les prérogatives du siège de Constantinople", *Patrologie et oecuménisme. Recueil d'études* (Louvain, 1990), 517.

[6] Joint Commission between the Roman Catholic Church and World Methodist Council, *Towards a Statement on the Church* (The Nairobi Report, 1986: IS, no. 62 [1986], 210a).

pursuing unity"[7], or as a "concrete prospect", founded on eucharistic ecclesiology, for realizing communion.[8] Indeed, the "union between the sister Churches" becomes nothing less than the path to world unity.[9]

One does get the impression, however, that a certain ambiguity and lack of continuity prevail in the use of the term. It seems therefore all the more useful to go back to the origin of the expression, so as to evaluate its real significance and doctrinal implications for each side, for the purpose of determining whether and to what extent it can form the basis for an ecumenical dialogue, for example, with the Orthodox Churches.

I. ORIGIN AND DEVELOPMENT OF THE EXPRESSION

Paul VI speaks of the expression as part of "traditional vocabulary".[10] In reality it does not occur explicitly in Scripture and in the writings of the Fathers despite the emphasis on the profound sentiments of fraternity, that kept the Churches of antiquity united.[11] The primitive local Churches lived in the same spirit of fraternity, and, even though they possessed all the structures required to function in a normal "self-sufficient" way, they noticed the need for a mutual communion through various forms of

---

[7] The subcommission for the study of the problems posed by uniatism (January 26–31, 1989) rejects such a model and affirms that "la recherche de l'unité devrait avoir comme modèle celui des Églises Soeurs": "Relations entre les Communions", *Irénikon* 63 (1990): 64.

[8] In the conclusion to the Acts of the 10th Catholic Orthodox Colloquium (Bari, 1991), S. Manna writes, "Non solo i testi, ma anche i gesti ci consentono di poter dire che vi è una comune tensione verso la comunione che non si può negare: è nella prospettiva concreta delle due Chiese sorelle. La conquista decisa anche da parte cattolica della ecclesiologia eucaristica promossa dal Vaticano II deve essere incarnata dai fatti. Se la definizione delle Chiese come sorelle ha un senso, dobbiamo essere conseguenti. Se no, restiamo dei nominalisti, i quali si contentano delle belle parole, ma tutto rimane immutato. Sarebbe il fallimento degli intenti del dialogo" (*Nicolaus* 19 [1992]: 321).

[9] F. Ossanna, "La Basilica dedicata ai Patroni di Roma: attraverso il linguaggio dell'arte i segni di una profonda devozione", *L'Osservatore Romano*, June 29, 1995, 9.

[10] Papal brief *Anno ineunte*, July 25, 1967: Stormon, 162, no. 176. Cf. also John Paul II, encyclical *Ut unum sint*, no. 56.

[11] Cf. E. Lanne, "Implications ecclésiologiques", 52–62; Y. Congar, "Le développement de l'évaluation ecclésiologique des églises non-catholiques", *Revue de droit canonique* 25 (1975): 194; Congar, *Diversity and Communion* (London, 1984), 85–87; F. Bouwen, s.v. "Churches, Sister", DEM, 186b–87a; B. Dupuy, "L'encyclique *Ut unum sint* de Jean-Paul II", *Istina* 41 (1996): 11.

"coordination".[12] Among the Popes of antiquity too, although it was quite common to address the Eastern patriarchs as "brother", it was only Innocent I who called the Church of Antioch *"velut germana ecclesiae Romanae"*.[13]

The earliest explicit attestations, on the other hand, are found in the letters written by the Eastern patriarchs to the Popes—no longer as an expression of fraternity and communion, but rather in a spirit which is anything but irenic, indeed, decidedly anti-Roman and opposed to the primacy of the Bishop of Rome.

One of the most common formulae used to convey the growing awareness of the primacy of the Church of Rome and of her Bishop was *"Ecclesia Romana mater et caput omnium ecclesiarum"*, with its consequent claim that all Churches "receive their being, their origin, and their continuity from the Roman Church" and for this reason "should follow their mother if they want to live at all".[14] Against this the Eastern Christians propose the category of "sister Churches", "born of the same father and hence worthy of the same honor".[15] The one true head of the Church is Christ, and the one visible head is the emperor.[16]

With the progressive consolidation of the pentarchy came the acceptance of the principle that there are *mother Churches and sister Churches*, according to which (the role of the emperor remaining unchanged) the five patriarchs stand at the head of the entire Church, and the Church of Rome occupies the first place among the patriarchal sister Churches, which are all equal.[17] The principal exponents of this theory were Nicetas, metropolitan of Nicomedia[18], and Patriarch John X Camateros.[19]

---

[12] M. A. Fahey, "Ecclesiae sorores ac fratres: Sibling Communion in the Pre-Nicene Christian Era", *Proceedings of the 36th Annual Convention of the Catholic Theological Society of America* 36 (1982): 36: "We now conclude our overview of major elements that contributed to the coordination of sister churches before Nicaea. Some factors were principally religious, such as the celebration of Eucharist, the sacramental installation of new bishops by the neighboring bishops. Some were organizational and social, such as the convocation of synods or letter writing. Others concentrated coordination within one person or one institution, be it the see of Rome or the imperial court of New Rome."

[13] *Epist. de pace Antiochenae ecclesiae impartita*: PL 20, 546A.

[14] J. Spiteris, *La Critica Bizantina*, 21.

[15] Ibid., 312.

[16] Ibid., 315ff.

[17] Cf. ibid., 76, 94, 106, 276, 296, 299, 302. Cf. also Garuti, *Il Papa Patriarca d'Occidente?*, 23–26, 232–48.

[18] Cf. J. Spiteris, *La Critica Bizantina*, 85–108.

[19] Cf. ibid., 248–99.

In dialogue with Anselm, bishop of Havelberg, who was involved in demonstrating the primacy of the Roman See, Nicetas acknowledged a certain primacy of Rome, inasmuch as even the ancient historical writings of the East testify to the existence of three *sister* patriarchal sees (Rome, Alexandria, and Antioch), among which Rome exercised a primacy over the others and enjoyed the right of appeal. Its Bishop, however, is neither the prince nor the chief priest, but only the bishop of the primary See.[20] In other words, he is not over and above the other patriarchs, and his See, although it has the first place among the *sister* Churches and the primacy of honor at councils, separated itself when the monarchy intruded and divided the bishops and the Churches of the West and the East.[21] Thus, it becomes apparent what sort of primacy the Greeks of that period were ready to acknowledge Rome as having: a "primacy of honor" (*primatus honoris*) "within the context of sister Churches, hence among Churches that are equal and united among themselves through bonds of communion and not of dependence".[22]

It was this same antiprimatial spirit that drove Patriarch Camateros in his polemic against Innocent III. Faced with the problem of the return of the Greek Church into the bosom of the Roman Church, Innocent III emphasizes the need for the Greeks to return to the one sheepfold of Christ, to the one true ark of salvation, to the one pastor, to the one foundation, to the one mother, that is, the Roman Church. She is, in fact, "*cunctorum fidelium mater et magistra*" and "*epitome omnium ecclesiarum*".[23] The patriarch objects to such an affirmation by asking to know the special reasons that would make

---

[20] Cf. Anselm of Havenberg, *Dialogi*: "Primatum Romanae Ecclesiae, quem tam excellentem mihi proponis, ego non nego, neque abnuo, siquidem in antiquis nostrorum historiis hoc legitur, quod tres patriarchales sedes sorores fuerant, videlicet Romana, Alexandrina, Antiochena, inter quas Roma eminentissima sedes imperii primatum obtinuit, ita ut prima sedes appellaretur, et ad eam de dubiis causis ecclesiasticis a caeteris omnis appellatio fieret, et eius iudicio ea quae sub certis regulis non comprehenduntur, diiudicanda subiacerent. Ipse tamen Romanus pontifex, nec princeps sacerdotum, nec summus sacerdos, aut aliquid huiusmodi, sed tantum primae sedis episcopus vocaretur" (PL 188, 216D–17A).

[21] Ibid.: "Verum Romana Ecclesia, cui nos quidem inter has sorores primatum non negamus, et cui in concilio generali praesidenti primum honoris locum recognoscimus, ipsa se propter sui subtilitatem a nobis sequestravit, quando monarchia, quod sui officii non erat, invasit, et episcopos et Ecclesias occidentis et orientis, diviso imperio, divisit" (PL 188, 1919AB).

[22] J. Spiteris, *La Critica Bizantina*, 106.

[23] Cf. ibid., 256.

the Church of Rome the mother of all other Churches.[24] He himself provides the answer: "It is not possible, therefore, that Rome should be the mother of all Churches, for there are five great Churches that possess patriarchal dignity and Rome is the first, as among sisters of the same rank. . . . The Church of the Romans is the first in rank and is worthy of respect only on the basis of its dignity, being the first among sister Churches of the same rank and of the same origin, born of the same heavenly Father from whom every paternity in heaven and on earth derives."[25]

For both, Nicetas and Camateros, it is the "principle of fraternity" that elucidates the relations among the various Churches: "The great patriarchal Churches are sister Churches, with the bishop of Rome enjoying a slight preeminence of honor." The "typical image of sister Churches" henceforth "is part of authentic Oriental ecclesiology".[26]

To find the concept of "sister Churches" in *the modern era*, we must go back to the nineteenth century and, in particular, to the First Vatican Council. A noteworthy occurrence is the appeal of the Armenian bishop, Joseph *Papp-Szílagy*, in favor of the coexistence of the Oriental and Latin disciplines as expressions of the one Catholic discipline, based precisely on the fact that the Eastern Churches and the Western Church differ externally but are two sister Churches, equal daughters of the same mother Church.[27]

In the Second Vatican Council the expression "sister Churches" occurs for the first time in a conciliar text, specifically in the decree "De oecumenismo".[28]

---

[24] Ibid., 267–68: "Ora io domando di conoscere dove precisamente si trovano nei Vangeli le parole che 'la chiesa romana è il capo e la madre, anzi la madre generale di tutte le altre chiese diffuse nei quattro angoli del mondo,' o quale concilio ecumenico ha confermato quelle pretese da voi invocate riguardo alla vostra chiesa."

[25] Ibid., 268, 269–70.

[26] Ibid., 307.

[27] "Aliud quod occurrit in hac secunda paragrapho est commemoratio disciplinae, haud dubie etiam tendentiose ad disciplinam ecclesiasticam ecclesiae orientalis, ut nimirum illa possit de plenitudine potestatis pontificiae etiam mutari, aut disciplinae ecclesiae latinae ex toto assimilari. Disciplina orientalis et occidentalis ecclesiae una est eo respectu, quia et una et alia disciplina catholica est. Ecclesia orientalis et occidentalis sunt sorores duae, quae externa forma et specie ad invicem differunt ... sed tamen sunt sorores, sunt aequales eiusdem dulcis matris ecclesiae filiae" (Mansi 52, 603A–B). For other texts cf. Congar, *Diversity and Communion*, 87.

[28] During the preparatory phase of the Council, there was mention of "Églises soeurs" in the already-cited letter of Patriarch Athenagoras to Cardinal Augustine Bea (cf. above, p. 261, n. 2). The same cardinal limits himself to assuring that every possible effort will be

In the scheme presented to the conciliar assembly on April 22, 1963, n. 13 of chapter III, which describes the character and the distinctive history of the Eastern Christians, first calls to mind the reality of the existence of many particular or local Churches in the East, of which not a few glory in having been founded by the apostles themselves; next, it recalls their great concern and care, in the past and at present, about maintaining the fraternal relations that should exist between the local Churches, as among sisters.[29] The only amendment presented was that of the bishop of Segni, Luigi *Carli*, who, referring only to the current situation (*"praevalet"*), proposed that they speak of *particular* (and not local) Churches, that they qualify the relations as *friendly* (and not fraternal), and that they use the expression "among sisters", omitting the word "as".[30]

No changes figured in the new scheme of April 27, 1964.[31] There was no lack, however, of subsequent proposals for amendments. Nine Fathers, otherwise unidentified, proposed clarifying that the issue was one of existing relations between local Churches, which originate from the same apostolic mother Church. The modus, however, was not accepted, because the text already made it clear that many particular or local Churches in the East were founded by the apostles themselves, and particularly because having fraternal relations should be the concern of all local Churches, regardless of their common apostolic origin.[32]

---

made to continue "fraternal relations" with the Orthodox Churches (Stormon, 42, no. 21) and to hoping for a growth in "brotherly exchanges between our Churches" (ibid., 56, no. 39).

[29] "Quapropter apud Orientales praevaluit atque praevalet sollicitudo et cura illas servandi fraternas necessitudines in fidei communione quae inter locales Ecclesias ut inter sorores vigere debent" (AS II/5, 425).

[30] "Dicatur: praevalet *cura et studium* servandi, *inter particulares Ecclesias, amicales* illas in fidei caritatisque communione necessitudines, quae inter sorores vigere debent" (AS II/5, 462 mode 146. Outline of observations presented in writing: cf. AS II/5, 889).

[31] Cf. AS III/2, 310. The only change was that of the number, from 13 to 14.

[32] "Loco 'inter Ecclesias locales, ut inter sorores vigere debent' dicatur: inter Ecclesias locales, *ab eadem Ecclesia apostolica matrice provenientes*, ut inter sorores, vigere debent.

Ratio adlata: Ecclesiae matrices sunt Ecclesiae principales quae originem ducunt ab aliqua sede apostolica. Inter eas Ecclesia Romana gaudet "potentiori principalitate," quia sedes Principis Apostolorum.

R.—Modus non accipitur ob sequentes rationes:

1) Iam satis provisum in textu linn. 25–27 ubi dicitur: omnibus in mentem revocare non paucas in Oriente particulares seu locales Ecclesias ab ipsis Apostolis originem duxisse

2) Modus non est ad rem, cum cura servandi fraternas necessitudines non sit tantummodo de Ecclesiis quae ab una Ecclesia Apostolica Matrice proveniunt, sed de omnibus Ecclesiis localibus, quid sit de communi vel non communi origine apostolica" (modo 7: AS III/7, 676).

Much more consistent were the remarks made by the minister general of the Dominicans, Fr. Aniceto *Fernandez*. He denounced, first of all, the failure to distinguish between the two different grades of the hierarchy—the supreme pontificate and the episcopate—with the obvious intention of pleasing the separated Eastern Christians, among whom the category of "sister Churches" is prevalent. Despite the laudable effort to draw near to the separated brethren, it was a case of incorrect methodology.[33] With a more direct reference to the relations between the "sister Churches", or rather, applying the category to the Church in general, he asked that the terms *fraternal* and *sister* be changed to *maternal* and *mother*, for it is unusual, in all of tradition, to refer to a Church as the sister of a local community. In working toward ecumenism it is only right that we bear in mind the special sensibility of the Eastern Christians for the *fraternity* that exists among the individual Churches; but when it is a question of the principles on which to build unity, as in the present context, the Church cannot be considered a *sister*, but rather the *Mother* of the local Churches. This is necessary if one is to be consistent with the schema *de Ecclesia*, which, in describing the relations with the separated brethren, calls the Church *mother*.[34]

The only text which seems to apply the concept of "sister Churches" to the relations between the Church of the West and the Church of the East is found in the observations of the titular archbishop of Seleucia, Giulio Giorgio *Kandela*, according to whom revoking the excommunication,

---

[33] "Schema videtur vitare distinctionem utriusque gradus hierarchiae [pontificato supremo et episcopato], a Christo institutae, intentione placendi orientalibus seiunctis, in quibus praevalet 'cura servandi fraternas illas in fidei caritatisque communione necessitudines, quae inter Ecclesias locales, ut inter sorores, vigere debent' (chapter III, no. 14, p. 19, lines 27–30). Fatemur plane conatus accedendi ad fratres seiunctos laudari oportere. Attamen via electa deerat a recto" (observations written from May 21 to September 13, 1964: AS III/2, 862).

[34] "In eadem pag. 7, lin. 19, vocabulum *fraterna* mutandum est in *materna*. Vocabulum electum fuit indubie propter ea quae dicuntur paulo post, lin. 29 atque cap. 3, n. 14, pag. 19, linn. 27–30 ... His non obstantibus, postulo enuntiatam mutationem proper sequentes rationes. Primo, inconsuetum est in universa traditione Ecclesiam uti talem appellare *sororem* alicuius communitatis localis; vocatur semper *Mater*: Mater Ecclesia ... Orientalibus utique placet consideratio *fraternitatis* inter Ecclesias singulas et propterea congruum est ut, cum agitur *de exercitio oecumenismi*, omnes catholici id prae mentem habeant. Sed caput primum est *de principiis*, quibus attentis, unitas efficietur, quam Christus vult. In unitate autem illa Ecclesia est Mater, minime soror, communitatum localium. Mutatio demum est necessaria, ut hic locus aptetur schemati *de Ecclesia*, ubi, loquendo de habitudine inter Ecclesiam et fratres seiunctos, eadem Ecclesia appellatur Mater" (cf. schema *de Ecclesia*, chapter II, no. 15, p. 37, line 14): ibid., 864.

in the case of Eastern Christians who are only materially separated, means breaking down the wall that it has created between two "sister Churches".[35]

Already with Pope John XXIII a new era begins in the relations between the Catholic Church and the Orthodox Churches, for example, with that of Constantinople. In a printed communiqué of October 30, 1958, Patriarch Athenagoras speaks of having learned with great pleasure of the election of the new Pope[36], and in his message on the occasion of New Year's Day 1959 he welcomes with joy the call of John XXIII for unity.[37] Furthermore, 1962 marks the beginning of visits by Catholic and Orthodox delegations to Fanar and Rome, respectively, and the letters of gratitude for the welcome received often express the hope of seeing unity reestablished soon between the two sister Churches. Negotiations were also set in motion to send Orthodox observers to the Second Vatican Council.[38] The negotiations failed, but the fraternal relations did not cease.[39]

It is above all with Paul VI, however, that one observes "an extraordinary reversal of the tendency with regard to the spirit and goals of visible relations between the two sister Churches".[40] In keeping with an

---

[35] "Insuper opinor istam relaxationem auferre pariem quod excommunicatio erexit inter duas Ecclesias sorores credentes unam fidem, unum Dominum, unum Baptisma" (AS II/6, 390).

[36] Cf. Stormon, 27, no. 3.

[37] Cf. Stormon, 30–31, no. 5. There is, however, a polemical note, given that he was apprised of it only "indirectly".

[38] Cf. letters of Bishop Willebrands (Stormon, 36–37, no. 2; 39, no. 17) and especially the official letter of invitation on behalf of the Pope (Stormon, 40, no. 18).

[39] Cf. letter of Cardinal Bea to Patriarch Athenagoras (October 10, 1962: Stormon, 42, no. 21) and the communiqué of the Ecumenical Patriarchate (Stormon, 42–43, no. 22). In the patriarch's statement on the occasion of the death of John XXIII, the Pope is termed the "venerable leader of our sister Church of Rome" (June 4, 1963: Stormon, 45, no. 26).

[40] Cf. V. Peri, *Orientalis Varietas. Roma e le Chiese d'Oriente—Storia e Diritto canonico* (Rome, 1994), 7. Cardinal Jan Willebrands also speaks of "un nuovo periodo della storia delle relazioni fra Oriente e Occidente. L'abolizione delle scomuniche pronunciate nove secoli fa tra Roma e Costantinopoli, solennemente proclamata alla chiusura del Concilio, le visite del Santo Padre al Patriarca Atenagora ad Istanbul nel luglio 1967, così come la visita del venerando Patriarca a Roma tre mesi dopo, le visite di altri Patriarchi d'Oriente, armeni, siro, copto e di alti gerarchi delle Chiese orientali venuti da Istanbul, dalla Russia, dalla Grecia, dalla Romania, dall'Egitto e dal Medio Oriente e da tante altre regioni stanno a comprovare che l'atmosfera è cambiata e che le Chiese di Oriente ci sono diventate più vicine e che da parte nostra le abbiamo nuovamente riscoperte come Chiese sorelle" (Introduction to the April–June issue of *Seminarium*, dedicated to the theme "De Oriente Cristiano": 15 [1975]: 252).

innate tendency in his character, ecumenism remained a key idea through-out his pontificate.[41] With him the ancient praxis of communicating one's own election to the patriarch of Constantinople was resumed,[42] and shortly thereafter (September 20, 1963) the Pope sent a handwritten letter to Patriarch Athenagoras, making known his desire to do everything possi-ble toward reestablishing perfect harmony among Christians.[43]

In this climate preparations were being made for the historical journey of Paul VI to the Holy Land (January 4–6, 1964), crowned by the "fra-ternal meeting" with Patriarch Athenagoras and the kiss of peace. From then on the exchange of letters and telegrams on the most varied occa-sions became more frequent, marked always by *fraternal* relations and often by explicit references to the reality of "sister Churches", for instance, on the part of the Orthodox Church.[44] Furthermore, arrangements were made so that a delegation of Orthodox observers could participate in the work of the Second Vatican Council during the second and third phases.

Such a climate helped, above all, to make possible the abrogation of the mutual excommunications of 1054. After several meetings with the representatives of the patriarchate of Constantinople, Cardinal Augustine Bea, by registered letter dated October 18, 1965, suggested to Patriarch Athenagoras that a mixed commission be established, comprising four members from either side, in order to study the problem and to elaborate

---

[41] Cf. A. Franquesa, "Paul VI et l'Église orthodoxe", *Proche-Orient Chrétien* 30 (1980): 179–210. On the role played by Paul VI in the field of ecumenism cf. Lanne, "Hommage à Paul VI. En mémorial d'action de grâce", *Irénikon* 51 (1978): 299–311; Congar, "L'oecuménisme de Paul VI", *Nicolaus* 6 (1978): 207–19; A. Brunello, "Paolo VI e l'Oriente cristiano. Principali atti e documenti del Pontificato di Paolo VI riguardanti l'Oriente cris-tiano", *Oriente cristiano* 18 (1978): 9–50.

[42] Letter of Cardinal Bea (June 25, 1963: cf. Stormon, 49, no. 29). In his reply, Met-ropolitan Maximos communicates the felicitations and wishes of the Patriarch "for a long and fruitful service [by Your venerable Holiness] in the holy sister Church of Rome" (Stormon, 52, no. 32).

[43] Cf. Stormon, 52, no. 33. The patriarch had the letter published (November 6, 1963) in the bulletin of his patriarchate, *Apostolos Andreas*, significantly entitled, "The Two Sister Churches".

[44] Cf. the telegram of Patriarch Athenagoras (March 27, 1964), in which the Church of Rome is called "Sister Church of the West" (Stormon, 71, no. 58); cf. also a letter and a telegram of the same patriarch (Stormon, 74–75, no. 65 and 76, no. 67); discourse of Metropolitan Meliton of Heliopolis on the occasion of a visit to Paul VI (February 16, 1965: Stormon, 85–86, no. 87); discourse of the archbishop of Crete, Eugenios, on the occasion of his meeting with Paul VI (May 23, 1967: Stormon, 149, no. 156).

a formula to be published contemporaneously in Rome and in Constantinople.[45]

The work of the commission began on November 22, 1965, with an opening address by Metropolitan Meliton, copresident, and a response thereto by His Eminence Cardinal Willebrands;[46] it concluded the following day with the drawing up of a *Joint Document* on the modalities of dialogue.[47] After a joint declaration by Paul VI and Patriarch Athenagoras,[48] the papal brief *Ambulate in dilectione* was published on December 7, 1965, cancelling once and for all from the memory of the Church, the excommunication of 1054.[49] The expression "sister Churches" does not occur in any of these texts; the act in itself, however, was interpreted as an expression of an underlying reality.[50]

The act that signaled in a more definite way the "reversal of the tendency" in the relations between the Catholic Church and the Orthodox Churches and "conferred upon the term its official status"[51] was the brief

---

[45] Cf. Stormon, 115–16, no. 119. On November 16 of the same year, the same cardinal announced the names of the Catholic representatives: His Eminence Jan Willebrands, president; Bishop Michele Maccarone, Fr. Alfonso Raes, Don Alfonso Stickler, and Fr. Christoph Dumont: cf. Stormon, 117–18, no. 121.

[46] It was on this occasion that Metropolitan Meliton explained how the Church of Constantinople "understands its duty of service [diakonia] in the present situation towards our sister Orthodox Churches" (Stormon, 120), and His Eminence (Cardinal) Willebrands used, for the first time on the part of Catholics, the expression "sister Churches" in reference to the Church of Constantinople: "The Church of ancient Rome has taken note of the feelings and desires of its sister Church of [N]ew Rome" (Stormon, 121, no. 123).

[47] Cf. the minutes of the deliberations: Stormon, 123–25, no. 124. A synthesis of the document, which describes the scope, methodology, and theme of the first phase of the dialogue, is found in Salachas, *Il dialogo*, 25–30.

[48] Cf. Stormon, 126–28. The most important text concerns the mutual desire to continue the dialogue "which will lead them with the help of God to live afresh, for the greater good of souls and the coming of God's kingdom, in the full communion of faith, of brotherly harmony, and of sacramental life, which obtained between them throughout the first thousand years." This affirmation would be taken up again by Paul VI in his message to Patriarch Dimitrios I on the occasion of the tenth anniversary of the withdrawal of excommunications (December 14, 1975: cf. Stormon, 288, no. 334).

[49] Cf. Stormon, 128–29, no. 128. For the corresponding "Tomos" of Patriarch Athenagoras cf. Stormon, 130–31, no. 129.

[50] Lanne, "Aspects eccésiologiques du dialogue théologique", 180: "Ce geste a eu une portée ecclésiologique, car il a permis de redécouvrir l'autre Église comme une Église sœur"; M. I. Lubachivsky, "L'unità delle sante chiese", *il regno-doc.* 21/94, 677): "Con questo atto le chiese sorelle si impegnarono a perseguire la restaurazione della piena comunione."

[51] Bouwen, "Churches, Sister", 187a.

of Paul VI, *Anno ineunte*, dated July 26, 1967.[52] It is worth citing its essential features:

"By Baptism 'we are one in Christ Jesus' (Gal 3:28). In virtue of the apostolic succession, we are united more closely by the priesthood and the Eucharist [*cf.* the Decree *Unitatis redintegratio* n. 15]. [In fact we are united with one another by such an intimate and mysterious communion that,] [b]y participating in the gifts of God to his Church we are brought into communion with the Father through the Son in the Holy Spirit. Having become sons in the Son in very fact (cf. 1 Jn 3:1–2), we have become mysteriously but really brothers among ourselves. In each local Church this mystery of divine love is enacted, and surely this is the ground of the traditional and very beautiful expression 'sister Churches,' which local Churches were fond of applying to one another (cf. Decree, *Unitatis Redintegratio*, 14). For centuries we lived this life of 'sister Churches,' and together held the Ecumenical Councils which guarded the deposit of faith against all corruption. And now, after a long period of division and mutual misunderstanding, the Lord is enabling us to discover ourselves as 'sister Churches' once more, in spite of the obstacles which were once raised between us. In the light of Christ we see how urgent is the need of surmounting these obstacles in order to succeed in bringing to its fulness and perfection the already very rich communion which exists between us." [53]

Curiously enough, despite Paul VI's authoritative recognition of the reality and rediscovery of the "sister Churches", in the years immediately following there is a continued emphasis on the progress achieved with regard to *fraternity*,[54] but the expression "sister Churches" occurs explicitly only a few times. Apart from the correspondence gathered in the

---

[52] After recalling that in *Unitatis redintegratio*, 14, the Churches of the East are called "sisters" among themselves, L. Sandri emphasizes, "L'*Anno ineunte*, invece, le chiama *sorelle* anche rispetto alla Chiesa cattolica. Paolo VI non fa questo a caso, per compiacenza o per sentimentalismo. Al contrario, ci sembra piuttosto che tutto il documento sia redatto per poter giungere a questa affermazione basilare" ("Paolo VI a Costantinopoli. Incontro di Chiese sorelle", *il regno-att.* 1967, 319).

[53] Stormon, 162–63, no. 176.

[54] For example, Paul VI in a telegram sent on October 9, 1967 expresses the hope that "the Lord will enable the Synod to contribute by its works to our continued progress in a rediscovered brotherhood" (Stormon, 170, no. 187), and Patriarch Athenagoras, in his discourse of October 26, 1967 in St. Peter's basilica, says, "We have arrived ... to meet Your Holiness as brother to brother" (Stormon, 171–72, no. 189).

Tomos agapis (until 1970)[55] and in the volume edited by Stormon (until 1984),[56] the expression is found in the reply of Paul VI (August 23, 1973) to the greetings sent to him by Patriarch Demetrios I on the occasion of the tenth anniversary of his pontificate[57] and in his discourse to the Pontifical Commission for the revision of the Oriental Code of Canon Law (March 18, 1974). On this last occasion it is emphasized that the designation is no longer limited to the Byzantine Church alone, but is extended to include all Orthodox Churches in general.[58]

Other particular occurrences of the expression are found on the occasion of the tenth anniversary of the abrogation of mutual excommunications and of the papal brief *Anno ineunte*.[59]

The appeal to the reality of the "sister Churches" has continued during the pontificate of *John Paul II* as well. Six days after his election, the new Pope, receiving in an audience the representatives of non-Catholic Churches, expressed his determination to make progress in establishing closer ties with them and in overcoming the *"intolerable scandal* of divisions between

---

[55] Paul VI uses it twice (cf. Stormon, 219, no. 269), and so does Patriarch Athenagoras (cf. Stormon, 159, no. 173 and 219, no. 267), whereas Bishop Willebrands uses it four times (cf. Stormon, 207, no. 245 and 225–26, no. 275). Athenagoras, in the first text cited above, calls Constantinople "younger sister".

[56] Cf. Stormon, 256, no. 308; 257, no. 310; 267, no. 319; 283, no. 332; 285–287, no. 333; 288, no. 313; 313, no. 357.

[57] The Pope prays God to grant "sa grâce à nos Églises Soeurs pour accomplir l'oeuvre commencée en vue du rétablissement de la pleine unité" (Ins. XI 796).

[58] "Magnopere quidem Nos consolamur, cum inter Ecclesiam Catholicam et sorores Orthodoxas Ecclesias contrahi cernimus, impellente Spiritu Sancto, vinculum verae unitatis, hoc est communionem ecclesialem iam valde profectam" (Ins. XII 266). On the other hand, the Pope emphasizes the importance of the Syrian Orthodox Church being "in union with her sister Oriental Orthodox Churches" in order to continue the dialogue aimed at overcoming the misunderstanding of the past (*Address to the Syrian Orthodox Patriarch, Mar Ignatius Jacob III*, October 25, 1971: IS, no. 16 [1972], 3). Fr. Antoine Plolesteanu, too, will speak to the Pope about the "important contacts" of the Orthodox Patriarch of Romania "avec les Églises-soeurs Catholiques-Romaines locales, d'Autriche, d'Allemagne Fédérale" (Saluto a Paolo VI, del 18 marzo 1972; Ins. X 271).

[59] It seems that the final mention is found in the message to the Mechitarists (September 8, 1977) on the occasion of the third centenary of Venerable Mechitar: "Desideriamo noi pure partecipare in qualche modo, alle solenni manifestazioni tre volte centenarie, con il presente messaggio, per onorare, in quest'ora della Chiesa, l'insigne uomo di Dio, consci come siamo che il suo insegnamento echeggerà più che mai attuale alle Chiese sorelle e al mondo in ascolto" (Ins. XV 812).

Christians".[60] In fact, in his opinion, "service of unity is the primordial duty of the ministry of the Bishop of Rome".[61] Pursuing "the opening made by John XXIII" and continuing "the memorable initiatives" of Paul VI, he soon undertook a brief visit to Turkey (November 29–30, 1979) to meet with various Eastern patriarchs. In the greetings that he addressed to them he often recalled the form of life which had characterized the relations between the sister Churches during the first millennium, but was obscured in the second, leaving behind a wound that persists until the present day.[62]

But the fact that in the past "the two forms of Christianity had already developed: the Eastern form, linked with Byzantium, and the Western, linked with Rome, while the Church continued to remain one and undivided" should inflame all the more the "desire for full communion in Christ with these sister Churches" and spur us "to undertake fresh studies and take new steps to favor it".[63] This reality has been rediscovered today even though full communion does not exist:[64] this is a factual observation and not just a polite phrase. "Today we see more clearly and understand better the fact that our Churches are sister Churches. To say 'sister Churches' is not just a polite phrase, but rather a fundamental category of ecclesiology."[65]

---

[60] *Address to Representatives of Other Christian Churches*, October 22, 1978: IS, no. 41 (1979), 1b. Cf. *Address to the Secretariat for Promoting Christian Unity*, November 18, 1978: IS, no. 39 (1979), 1–2.

[61] Cf. General Audience of January 17, 1979: (IS, no. 40 [1979], 1a). Cf. also Encyclical *Ut unum sint*, no. 99.

[62] John Paul II, *Address during the Liturgy at Fanar*: "For nearly a whole millennium, the two sister Churches grew side by side, as two great and complementary traditions of the same Church of Christ, keeping not only peaceful and fruitful relations, but also concern for the indispensable communion in faith, prayer and charity, which they did not at any cost want to imperil, despite their different kinds of sensibility. The second millennium, on the contrary, was darkened, apart from some fleeting bright intervals, by the sense of estrangement which the two Churches felt towards each other, with all the fatal consequences of this. The wound is not yet healed. But the Lord can cure it and he bids us do our best to help the process" (IS, no. 41 [1979], 23b). Cf. also ibid., 20a, 22a–b, 26a.

[63] Apostolic letter *Euntes in mundum*, January 25, 1988 (*Origins* 17 [1988]: 715a–b).

[64] "The Catholic Church and the Orthodox Church have been granted the grace of once again recognizing one another as sister Churches and of journeying towards full communion" (*Homily during Vespers*, December 6, 1987: IS, no. 66 [1988], 20a).

[65] *Address to Representatives of the Orthodox Church in Poland* (Bialystok, June 5, 1991): IS, no. 81 (1992), 68a. Commenting on these words of the Pope, Cardinal Lubachivsky notes, "Apprendiamo così la verità fondamentale che caratterizza le relazioni tra cattolici e ortodossi:

Since "full communion is a gift and will not be solely the result of purely human efforts and desires, even though these latter are indispensable and condition many things",[66] there arises the need for mutual listening in order to arrive at a better understanding of the characteristics of each Church, an indispensable condition for maturing toward full reconciliation and full communion.[67] In reality, the "two sister Churches of the East and the West understand today that without mutually listening to the profound reasons that underlie in each one the understanding of what characterizes it ... the Church of Christ cannot manifest the full maturity of that form received in the Upper Room at the beginning".[68] From this arises also the need for dialogue[69], made fruitful by prayer.[70]

Further, it needs to be underlined that with John Paul II the recognition of sister Church is no longer limited to the Church of Constantinople, the "thousand-year-old sister Church",[71] but is extended to include

la chiesa cattolica e la chiesa ortodossa sono chiese sorelle" ("L'unità delle sante chiese", 677).

[66] Apostolic letter *Euntes in mundum*, no. 11, 716a.

[67] *Oriente e Occidente si uniscono a Bari* (22 febbraio 1984; Ins. VII/1 532). Cf. ibid., 534. Subsequently John Paul II would recall that the Church of Bari is "particularly well prepared to be a bridge between East and West, and to make a decisive contribution to that day which we so much desire, in which the two sister Churches will be able once again to experience themselves as totally united in the peace of Christ" (IS, no. 64 [1987], 62a).

[68] IS, no. 54 (1984), 8a.

[69] John Paul II, *Address to the Roman Curia* (June 28, 1985): "[W]ith the venerable Orthodox Churches, the sister Churches—according to the expression dear to Pope Paul VI (cf. *Tomos Agapis*, 176, 283 and *passim*)—with whom we have the closest bonds of communion, the Catholic Church maintains a dialogue of charity in the context of which theological dialogue grows" (IS, no. 59 [1985], 4b). The same need was stressed the following day in the *Address of the Pope to the Orthodox Delegation*: "Today our Churches are meeting in a true spirit of fraternity which characterizes the relations between sister Churches. After centuries we meet in the dialogue of charity within which blossoms a theological dialogue" (IS, no. 59 [1985], 22b).

[70] John Paul II, *Address of Welcome to the Delegation of Ecumenical Patriarchate* (June 28, 1984): "[T]ogether let us ask the Lord for full reconciliation between our sister Churches for a more effective Christian witness to Christ and for a more incisive spread of his gospel of love and peace" (IS, no. 55 [1984], 66b); "Invito tutti a pregare perché il dialogo aperto tra le nostre Chiese sorelle ci porti finalmente alla piena unità" (*Omilia per la solennità dei Santi Pietro e Paolo*: Ins. X/2, 2375).

[71] Apostolic letter *Euntes in mundum*, no. 15. During the general audience on November 28, 1984, the Pope announced that a delegation of the Catholic Church would be present at the feast of St. Andrew "to participate in the joy of that sister Church" (IS, no. 56 [1984], 85b). The expression occurs particularly in the various addresses to delegations of the Ecumenical Patriarchate of Constantinople on the occasion of the feast of Saints Peter

the Orthodox Churches of Moscow[72] and Alexandria,[73] the "sister Churches of the East"[74] in general, and "our sister Orthodox Church".[75]

The thinking of John Paul II is taken up again in an authoritative manner in the encyclicals *Orientale lumen* (May 2, 1995)[76] and, above all, *Ut unum sint* (May 25, 1995), wherein the reality of sister Churches is presented in accordance with the usage that the Second Vatican Council had established in connection with earlier tradition[77] and which serves as the point of reference for the reestablishment of full communion and unity.[78]

Following the course charted by Patriarch Athenagoras, other representatives of the *Eastern Churches*, the Orthodox as well as ancient Eastern Christians, also began using, in their addresses during visits or in their

and Paul: IS, no. 52 (1983), 77a; IS, no. 71 (1989), 124a. Cf. also *Message to His Holiness Demetrios I*: IS, no. 69 (1989), 15b. For statements made before 1984 cf. Stormon, 358–59, no. 401; 361–63, no. 402.

[72] Apostolic letter *Euntes in mundum*, no. 15: "In a special way, of course, this is the feast of the Russian Orthodox Church, which has its centre in Moscow and which we call with joy 'sister Church'" (*Origins* 17 [1988], 717b–c). Cf. *Omilia nella Basilica di S. Paolo* at the conclusion of the Octave for Christian Unity (January 25, 1988: Ins. XI/1 247); *Address to Congress on the Baptism of Rus'* (November 12, 1988): IS, no. 69 (1989), 5a. In exchange, Patriarch Alexis II, in a press conference (Geneva, June 18, 1995), criticized the Catholic Church for "ne pas se conformer à la déclaration du Concile Vatican II qui avait souligné que les Églises orthodoxes étaient des Églises-soeurs", *Ecumenical News International*, no. 13, July 1995, 2.

[73] *Address to the Greek-Orthodox Patriarch Parthenios III* (September 24, 1990): cf. IS, no. 75 (1990), 152a–b.

[74] Apostolic letter *Euntes in mundum*, no. 16, 717c. *Letter to the Bishops of Europe* (May 31, 1991: IS, no. 77 [1991], 33a).

[75] "I wish to greet the representatives of our Orthodox sister Church, together with Archbishop Chrysostom" (*Homily delivered during the Mass celebrated at "Vingio Parkas" in Vilnius*, September 5, 1993: Ins. XVI/2, 627).

[76] "We know today that unity can be realized by the love of God ... only through the love of the Churches who feel called to manifest ever more fully the one true Church of Christ ... and who wish to be sisters" (no. 20).

[77] "Following the Second Vatican Council, and in the light of earlier tradition, it has again become usual to refer to the particular or local Churches gathered around their Bishop as 'sister Churches'" (no. 56).

[78] "If today, on the threshold of the third millenium, we are seeking the re-establishment of full communion, it is for the accomplishment of this reality that we must work and it is to this reality that we must refer" (n. 57). Commenting on the encyclical, M. Thurian writes, "Grazie a questa comunione ritrovata, sebbene ancora imperfetta, si può parlare nuovamente di *Chiese sorelle*, chiese particolari attorno ai loro vescovi, che desiderano esprimere la loro comunione plenaria come Chiesa una, santa, cattolica e apostolica" ("Apertura e chiarezza. L'ecumenismo di Giovanni Paolo II", *L'Osservatore Romano*, June 2, 1995, 4).

correspondence, the expressions "sister Church of Rome",[79] "the most holy sister Church of the Old Rome",[80] "elder sister".[81] Above all, the already traditional presence of representatives from the respective Churches to celebrate together every year the patronal feast of the apostles Peter and Paul at Rome, and of St. Andrew at Constantinople, became an occasion to greet the "sister Church of Rome"[82] and to recall the existing fraternal relations between the sister Churches of the Old and the New Rome[83] as well as "the duty of love which should unite the sister Churches founded by them".[84]

With particular reference to the succeeding ecumenical patriarchs, we note that the generic description of the Church of Rome as "sister" Church occurs rather frequently in the correspondence and visits of Patriarch Demetrios I.[85] The same patriarch, in his meeting with representatives from the Vatican on the occasion of the feast of St. Andrew (1978), expressed his grief over the death of Paul VI and John Paul I and refers to the election of the new primate of the sister Church of Rome. On the same occasion he looked forward to the continuation of the dialogue toward unity in accord and in collaboration with all the sister Orthodox Churches.[86] This hope had been expressed a little earlier in the message dispatched June

---

[79] *Address of Metropolitan Meliton of Heliopolis* (February 16, 1965: Stormon, 86, no. 87); *Address by Metropolitan Meliton of Chalcedon* (June 30, 1983: Stormon, 454, no. 467). Cf. Stormon, 397, no. 417.

[80] Metropolitan Chrysostomos of Myra, *Address to Pope Paul VI* (June 29, 1987: IS, no. 64 [1987], 63a). The same metropolitan had called Constantinople "sister Church" of the "venerable Church of Rome" (June 29, 1985: IS, no. 59 [1983], 23a).

[81] Archimandrite Cyril Argenti of Marseilles: "[L]a très antique et très vénérable Église de Rome, notre Soeur aînée" ("L'unité des chrétiens", *Irénikon* 49 [1976]: 33).

[82] Cf. Metropolitan Meliton of Chalcedon and Archbishop Stilianos of Australia: Stormon, 397, no. 417; 454, no. 467; 472, no. 480.

[83] The metropolitan of Myra, Chrysostomos, in his address of June 29, 1985, says that he was sent by the Ecumenical Patriarch Demetrios I "so that by the grace of God, there might be maintained this year again, the sacred custom of the reciprocal visits for the patronal feasts of our Churches, and in order to present on this occasion the greetings and the message of the sister Church of Constantinople to the venerable Church of Rome" (IS, no. 59 [1985], 23e). Cf. also Metropolitan Damaskinos (June 29, 1988: IS, no. 68 [1988], 155a).

[84] Metropolitan Bartholomew of Philadelphia (June 29, 1989: IS, no. 71 [1989], 125a).

[85] Cf. Stormon, 267, no. 318; 272, no. 324; 290, no. 335; 327, no. 373; 338, no. 383; 345, no. 389; 396, no. 416; 410, nos. 425–26; 412, no. 428; 425, no. 437; 439, no. 453; 459, no. 471.

[86] Cf. Stormon, 343–46, no. 389.

28, 1984, on the vigil of the feast of Sts. Peter and Paul.[87] Years later it was reiterated on the same occasion (June 29, 1990) with the call to "persevere in the holy effort undertaken to achieve a deeper knowledge, understanding and a reciprocal and ever increasing closeness of our sister Churches through the dialogue of charity and that of theology, with the aim of achieving, when our Lord and Builder of the Church sees fit, unity of faith and its visible expression in the communion of the sacraments".[88]

Even the present patriarch, Bartholomew I, in his message to John Paul II on the occasion of the feast of the apostles Peter and Paul, June 29, 1993, expressed his own happiness that the Pope had underscored the need for honesty in ecumenical dialogue which, when "applied to all the expressions of the relations between our two sister Churches, should certainly produce ever more positive results".[89] After this, his appeal to the "sister" Church of Rome appears only in his greetings to the representatives of the Vatican on the feast of St. Andrew, November 30, 1994 and 1995.[90]

On the Orthodox side too, the designation "sister" is extended to all the sister Orthodox Churches[91] and to those of the ancient Eastern Christians.[92]

---

[87] Among the expressions of fraternity and reciprocal understanding, he in fact mentions the continuation of dialogue "between our sister Churches" (Stormon, 471, no. 47).

[88] IS, no. 75 (1990), 150b. Again, in a telegram sent during a meeting of the Joint International Commission for Catholic Orthodox Dialogue (Freising, June 6–15, 1990), the patriarch blessed "le travail sacré et usant du dialogue théologique entre nos Églises soeurs" ("Relations entre les Communions", Irénikon 63 [1990]: 217).

[89] IS, no. 84 (1993), 145b. Even the metropolitan of France, Jeremias, delegate of the patriarch on that occasion, expressed his own sentiments "because we are aware that this event is henceforth definitively anchored in the tradition of our two sister Churches" (Address to the Pope, ibid., 146a).

[90] Cf. IS, no. 85 (1994), 39–40.

[91] Cf. Address of the Ecumenical Patriarch to the Vatican Delegation on the occasion of the feast of St. Andrew (November 30, 1990): IS, no. 77 (1991), 49b. The Ecumenical Patriarch Bartholomew I, on the occasion of his visit to the Russian Church (July 10–19, 1993), calls it "sister" but at the same time calls the Church of Constantinople "mother": Istina 39 (1994): 284–85.

[92] Chrysostomos of Myra, "Le dialogue entre l'Église orthodoxe et les Églises de l'ancien Orient. Appréciations et Perspectives", Proche-Orient Chrétien 30 (1980): 41 and 57. On his part, the Catholicos of the Syrian-Orthodox Church of India, Moran Mar Baselius Marthoma Mathews I, in his greetings to Pope John II during a visit to Rome (June 3, 1983), hopes for the reestablishment of communion "between our churches, along with our sister Orthodox churches" (IS, no. 52 [1983], 74b).

The use of the expression "sister Churches" acquires a more solemn and quasi-official meaning in some *joint declarations* of the Popes and patriarchs.

During the pontificate of Paul VI it occurs only in the joint declaration with Athenagoras (October 28, 1967) at the end of the patriarch's visit to Rome[93], whereas in the one with the Armenian catholicos, Vasken I (May 12, 1970), there is only a mention of the "fraternity" between the heads of the two Churches[94] and of their rediscovery after two millennia, as though in a reawakening, that they are "brothers".[95] Similarly, the joint declaration of the Pope and the Syrian-Orthodox patriarch of Antioch and the entire East, Moran Mar Ignatius Jacoub III, recognizes "the deep spiritual communion, which already exists between their Churches".[96] However, it is Paul VI alone who speaks of "sister Churches" in his opening address during the first meeting (October 25, 1971), and this in the context of relations between the Assyrian Church and other Orthodox Churches.[97] Expressions such as "bonds of brotherly love",[98] "many bonds which already bind us together",[99] "brotherly love", and "bonds of brotherly affection"[100] were also used during the meeting between Paul VI and Amba Shenouda III, Coptic-Orthodox patriarch of Alexandria (May 5–10, 1973). The next joint declaration, however, does not go beyond acknowledging that they possess "to a large degree, the same understanding of the Church" and stating that, in spite of the differences, "we are rediscovering ourselves as Churches with a common inheritance and are reaching out with determination and confidence in the Lord to achieve the fullness [and perfection] of that which is His gift".[101]

---

[93] The Pope and the patriarch "rejoice in the fact that their meeting was able to contribute to their Churches' rediscovering themselves still more as sister Churches" (IS, no. 3 [1967], 18). Their manner of expression and the context, however, convey the impression that this condition of "sister Churches" has not yet been fully realized.

[94] IS, no. 11 (1970), 10b.

[95] Ibid., 9b. To be noted, however, is the more general statement of the Catholicos: "The Armenian Church is happy to take part in the ecumenical movement and, in agreement with the sister Churches, to progress toward unity in love of Christ" (ibid., 4b).

[96] IS, no. 16 (1972), 5b.

[97] "The Syrian Orthodox Church in union with her sister Oriental Orthodox Churches meeting in Addis Ababa in 1965, has already determined to press forward for a dialogue which will help overcome the misunderstandings of the past" (ibid., 3b).

[98] Opening address of Paul VI during the first meeting (IS, no. 22 [1979], 4a).

[99] Ibid., 7b.

[100] Patriarch Shenouda during the farewell meeting: cf. ibid., 8b–9a.

[101] Ibid., 10a.

In the joint declaration of Pope John Paul II and Patriarch Demetrios (November 30, 1979), the expression is, for the first time, used officially in referring to the scope of theological dialogue as a means to achieving full communion and unity.[102]

An explicit reference to the reality of "sister Churches" is made again later in the joint declaration (June 23, 1984) of John Paul II and the Syrian-Orthodox patriarch of Antioch and the entire East, Moran Mar Ignatius Zakka I Iwas.[103]

Of particular importance is the joint christological declaration of the Catholic Church and the Assyrian Church of the East (November 11, 1994), which takes up the meaning of the expression "sister Churches" in *Unitatis redintegratio*, no. 14, a meaning limited to the particular Churches, insofar as it is applied to the reality of the Western Church as well. No longer are the Catholic Church and the Assyrian Church as such termed "sisters", but rather their respective particular Churches.[104]

Even the more recent joint declaration of Pope John Paul II and the ecumenical patriarch, Bartholomew I (June 30, 1995), makes a reference to the theological dialogue which has enabled the joint Catholic-Orthodox Commission to declare that the two Churches recognize each other as sisters.[105]

---

[102] "This Theological Dialogue envisages not only an advance towards the re-establishment of full communion between the Catholic and Orthodox [sister] Churches, but also a contribution to the multiple dialogues that are pursuing their course in the Christian world as it seeks its unity" (Stormon, 367, no. 404).

[103] The Pope and the patriarch thank the Lord for having brought them together in his love "in order to strengthen further the relationship between their two sister Churches, the Church of Rome and the Syrian Orthodox Church of Antioch". Moreover, the faithful of the respective Churches who have no access to their respective priests are permitted "to ask for the sacraments of Penance, Eucharist and the Anointing of the Sick from lawful priests of either of our two sister Churches, when they need them": IS, no. 55 (1984), 62–63.

[104] "Living by this faith and these sacraments, it follows as a consequence that the particular Catholic churches and the particular Assyrian churches can recognize each other as sister Churches" (IS, no. 88 [1995], 3). The editorial of *Irénikon* (67 [1994]: 450) also points out that "il n'est pas dit que ces deux Églises catholique et assyrienne sont des Églises soeurs, mais bien que les Églises particulières qui forment ces deux Églises peuvent se reconnaître comme Églises soeurs. Il y a là une nuance—subtile—qui mérite d'être notée, car c'est la première fois, à notre connaissance, que dans une déclaration de cette nature cette distinction est formulée aussi nettement." However, in their respective opening addresses, both John Paul II and Patriarch Mar Dinkha IV speak of "sister Churches" in reference to the Catholic Church and the Patriarchate: cf. IS, no. 88 (1995), 3–5.

[105] "Considering that in every local Church the mystery of divine love is realized and this is how the Church of Christ shows forth its active presence in each one of them, the Joint Commission has been able to declare that our Churches recognize one another as

It is in the sphere of *ecumenical dialogue* that reference to "sister Churches" is most often made and, at the same time, is marked by the greatest ambiguity. With its fundamental purpose of strengthening fraternity from a theological perspective, it has enabled the Churches to be aware of the deep communion that unites them, so much so that henceforth they can consider and treat one another as sister Churches.[106] It is therefore presented as "a new method and a new model" for reestablishing full communion between the Catholic Church and the Orthodox Church,[107] whose relations are guided by the theology of sister Churches.[108]

Of course, the theme is present in a special manner in the Catholic-Orthodox dialogue. It is necessary nevertheless to draw attention to a certain confusion in assigning the title of "sister". On the regional level it is generally attributed to the local Church understood "above all as an ensemble of different dioceses" which "took the form of autocephalous patriarchates with their own canonical structure, preserving among themselves communion in faith, sacramental life and brotherly relations".[109]

Sister Churches, responsible together for safeguarding the one Church of God, in fidelity to the divine plan, and in an altogether special way with regard to unity" (IS, no. 90 [1995], 124a).

[106] Metropolitan Meliton, cited by D. Salachas, "Les Églises soeurs", 105–6.

[107] Salachas, "Chiese sorelle: un'ecclesiologia", il *regno-att.* 16/93, 510. The Metropolitan Damaskinos too explains the reality of the sister Churches in the sense of "Églises appelées dans le dialogue et par le dialogue à rétablir la communion parfaite entre elles" (Salachas, "Les Églises soeurs Catholique-Romaine et Orthodoxe", 109).

[108] Cf. Lanne, "Aspects ecclésiologiques du dialogue théologique", 189.

[109] [Fifth] Russian Orthodox–Roman Catholic Conversations (Odessa, March 13–17, 1980), Joint Communiqué (IS, no. 44 [1980], 113b). The document *The Church, the Eucharist and the Trinity* (Munich, June 6, 1982), issued by the Joint International Commission for Catholic-Orthodox Dialogue, also affirms, "This recognition is achieved first of all at the regional level. Communion in the same patriarchate or in some other form of regional unity is first of all a manifestation of the life of the Spirit in the same enclosure [= culture], or in the same historical conditions.... This communion within the same region should extend itself further in the communion between sister Churches" (IS, no. 49 [1982], IIIb). A little farther on, however, it adds, "This mutual recognition, however, is true only under the conditions expressed in the anaphora of St. John Chrysostom and the first Antiochene anaphoras. The first condition is communion in the same kerygma, and so in the same faith.... Permanence through history and mutual recognition are particularly brought into focus in the eucharistic synaxis by the mention of the saints in the Canon and of the heads of the churches in the dyptichs." Since neither of these two conditions has been fulfilled, Spiteris comments, "Queste formulazioni danno chiaramente l'impressione che tutto ciò è stato detto intenzionalmente per lasciare un margine a quella chiesa che si considera come l'unica detentrice di tutta la tradizione e, di conseguenza, *dell'ortodossia*, di ritenere l'altra parte che partecipa al dialogo come priva della pienezza della verità e quindi,

At the same time, it is extended to the relations between the Catholic Church and Orthodox Church in their totality[110] and between the ecumenical patriarchate and the other Orthodox Churches.[111] In fact, what is emphasized is a gradual progress from the level of the patriarchate to the level of the universal Church, which thereby has become a "communion of sister Churches within the universal symphony of the Holy Church of God".[112]

It has now been admitted in the context of ecumenical dialogue that "the appeal to the term 'sister Churches' is unclear. Does it refer to patriarchates or jurisdictions in full communion or to the special relationship between the Orthodox Church and the Roman Catholic Church?"[113] Hence the challenge to explain its practical significance.[114]

In the more recent documents of Catholic-Orthodox dialogue, the appeal to the ecclesiology of communion among sister Churches is found, above all, in the condemnation of "uniatism", a method that is said not to take "into account that, according to ecclesiology, the Orthodox Church is a

automaticamente, priva di quanto precedentemente dichiarato come deposito comune." In other words, the mutual recognition of sister Churches "è impossibile, in quanto mancano determinate condizioni che vengono definite come indispensabili" ("La Chiesa ortodossa", 46). Cf. G. Assimakis, "L'Ecclesiologia", 37.

[110] Russian Orthodox–Roman Catholic Conversations (Odessa, 1980): "Despite their state of separation, the Catholic and Orthodox Churches recognize one another as sister Churches" (IS, no. 44 [1980], 113b).

[111] The Dombes Group, Ministero di comunione (1985), 91: "In 1902 the Ecumenical Patriarch sent a letter to the sister Orthodox Churches concerning relations with the non-Orthodox and the quest for a greater unity with Catholicism and Protestantism" (cf. EOE II, 1097).

[112] De Halleux, "Catholicisme et orthodoxie", 335: "On est sans doute fidèle à l'intention des rédacteurs (of the Munich document) en comprenant, dans cette unique mention qui en soit faite, les Églises soeurs au sens des Églises régionales. On entendra alors le dépassement en question comme le passage du niveau des Églises patriarcales et autocéphales orthodoxes, ou de l'Église catholique romaine, au niveau de l'unique Église universelle." In fact, Cardinal Willebrands, in his response to the address of the metropolitan of Chalcedon on the occasion of the feast of St. Andrew (November 30, 1982), observes that the document of Munich contains fundamental affirmations which demonstrate, among other things, an identical understanding "of the communion between the [sister] Churches in the universal symphony of the Holy Church of God": IS, no. 50 (1982), 126a.

[113] O–RCC, The Munich Document: A Response (New York, May 21–25, 1983), Diakonia 18 (1993), 176.

[114] O–RCC, Declaration on Uniatism (May 28, 1992): "We are challenged ... to explain what mutual recognition as sister churches means in practice and to explore structures needed for achieving communion among the worldwide communities of local churches" (Journal of Ecumenical Studies 29 [1982]: 147).

sister Church which itself offers the means of grace and salvation"[115] and which is said to destroy the progress made toward achieving unity.[116] In fact, acknowledging themselves to be sisters, the Catholic Churches and the Orthodox Churches (or more simply, the Catholic Church and the Orthodox Church) feel that they are "together co-responsible for maintaining the Church of God in fidelity to the divine purpose, especially in what concerns unity" and that "the ecumenical effort of the sister Churches of the East and of the West, founded upon dialogue and prayer, seeks perfect and total communion which is neither absorption nor fusion, but a coming together in truth and in love".[117] (Cf. Slavorum apostoli, n. 2.)

---

[115] O–RCC, The Freising Document (June 15, 1990), 6 (b) (IS, no. 73 [1990], 52b). The Ecumenical Consultative Body CECKEK (Resoconto e raccomandazioni: Geneva, July 6, 1992) specifies, "Sembra legittimo, da una parte che la chiesa di Roma dia testimonianza della sua fede attraverso le diocesi di rito latino entro la giurisdizione di una chiesa sorella ortodossa (...) Invece insediare una chiesa che adotta il rito di un'altra chiesa locale entro la sua stessa giurisdizione è una tentativo di soppiantare tale chiesa, negando in tal modo la sua ecclesialità e contraddicendo la teologia delle chiese sorelle" (il regno-documenti, 17/92, 521–22).

[116] The Ariccia Document, no. 6 (d): "Today, when our Churches meet on the basis of the ecclesiology of communion between sister-Churches, it would be regretful to destroy the important work for the unity of the Churches accomplished through the dialogue, by going back to the method of 'Uniatism'" (IS, no. 73 [1990], 52b–53a).

[117] Instrumentum Laboris of the Ariccia Document, Uniatism, Former Method of Union, and the Present Search for Full Communion (June 15, 1991): cf. EOE III, 1920. Successive paragraphs call attention to the duty of the Catholic Church "to help the Oriental Catholic Churches and their communities so that they too can make their contribution towards meeting the conditions for the full communion between the two sister Churches" (EOE III, 1925), and both sides are called to condemn "the violence exercised by some communities against other communities of a sister Church" (EOE III, 1931). Cf. the Balamand Document, no. 14 (IS, no. 83 [1993], 97a), and the related comment of the O–RCC, A Response on Proselytism and Uniatism, Origins 21 (1995): 571: "We also note the document's use of sister churches (cf. no. 14). The use of this venerable term in modern Orthodox-Catholic dialogue has helped to place relations between our churches on a new footing. . . . The concept of sister churches includes the notion of mutual respect for each other's pastoral ministry. . . . The concept also includes the notion of the co-responsibility of our churches for 'maintaining the church of God in fidelity to the divine purpose, most especially in what concerns unity'" (no. 14). Such an affirmation of the coresponsibility of the two churches contrasts sharply with the Statement (Dublin, 1984) of the Joint Anglican-Orthodox Doctrinal Commission: "The Anglicans do not hold that they are the only true Church, but believe rather, that they are a part of it. The Orthodox, on the contrary, believe that the Orthodox Church is the only true Church of Christ which, in so far as it is the Body of Christ, is neither divided nor divisible." It is no small matter, however, that they see "the Anglicans as brothers and sisters in Christ who seek, together with them, the unity of all Christians in the one Church" (no. 9: cf. EOE I, 453).

The Balamand Document concludes, therefore, "Because of the way in which Catholics and Orthodox once again consider each other in their relationship to the mystery of the Church and discover each other once again as sister Churches, this form of 'missionary apostolate' described above, and which has been called uniatism, can no longer be accepted either as a method to be followed nor as a model of the unity our Churches are seeking."[118]

The first reference to "sister Churches" in the context of the dialogue between the Catholic Church and the *Eastern Orthodox Churches* is found in the *Report of the Second Plenary Session* (Cairo, October 27–31, 1975) of the Joint Commission of the Catholic Church and the Coptic Orthodox Church. It begins by acknowledging an already existing reality, with the purpose of underlining the declared objective, namely, to "investigate . . . what we can do to hasten or to push forward the cause of the union between our two Apostolic sister Churches", a "real unity, a communion in faith, in sacramental life, and in the harmony of mutual relations between our two sister Churches in [the communion of] the one People of God",[119] and to express the certainty of being able to find the means to achieve it.[120] Perplexing, however, is the affirmation that it concerns a process which involves two apostolic Churches of equal dignity and that the full communion which is sought will be founded on the basis of the faith, the traditions, and the ecclesiastical life of the undivided Church of the first four and a half centuries.[121] In practice, this leads to the disappearance of the Coptic patriarchate of Alexandria[122] while, in fact, it is necessary that unity finds, first of all, a "clear and legitimate expression within

---

[118] The Balamand Document (IS, no. 83 [1993], 97a). *Resoconto e raccomandazioni della Consultazione ecumenica CEC-KEK* (Geneva, July 6, 1992): "Oggi si concorda sul fatto che l'unità della Chiesa cattolica romana e della Chiesa ortodossa deve essere considerata in base all'ecclesiologia di comunione tra 'chiese sorelle'" (il *regno-documenti*, 17/92, 521–22).

[119] IS, no. 76 (1991), 17b–18a.

[120] "Since, however, Our Lord Jesus Christ willed that His Church be one, we are confident that a way will be found to achieve union between our two sister Churches" (ibid., 18b).

[121] Cf. ibid., 18b.

[122] "Such a communion once achieved, there will be but one Coptic Church under the leadership of the one Pope of Alexandria and Patriarch of the See of St. Mark" (ibid.). It is worth emphasizing that such a conclusion is cited among the so-called common views.

the structure of this one Coptic Church".[123] For its part, "this one Coptic Church would be in full communion with the other Christian Churches and in particular with the Church of Rome".[124]

The theme of "sister Churches" has provided the background for dialogue during the unofficial consultations as well between theologians of the East and the West, promoted by the "Pro Oriente" Foundation of Vienna. The full union of sister Churches, in communion of faith, sacraments, ministry, and canonical structure, is presented as the final goal in the communiqué of the IV Consultation (September 17, 1978).[125] But already during this phase of inquiry the different Churches can call themselves "sisters", albeit in an imperfect way, in the expectation that at the end they will be so in the full sense of the term, once full communion has been achieved, as is specified in the III Seminar (July 1–5, 1993).[126]

The first one to use the designation "sister Churches" in reference to the communities born of the Reformation and, more directly, in reference to the *Anglican communion* was Paul VI, in his address on the occasion of the canonization of forty martyrs of England and Wales (October 25, 1970).[127] However, as various commentators were quick to clarify, Paul VI used

---

[123] Ibid.

[124] International Joint Commission between the Catholic Church and the Coptic Orthodox Church. *Common Report. Principles, Protocol* (Cairo, June 13–18, 1978; June 23, 1979): IS, no. 76 (1991), 29a. Cf. also ibid., 31a–b. The said principles were approved by Pope John Paul II and by Pope Shenouda III; cf. ibid., 30a.

[125] "Nous sommes d'accord que nous devons travailler pour atteindre une pleine union d'Églises soeurs—en communion dans la foi, dans les sacrements de l'Église, dans le ministère et à l'intérieur d'une structure canonique." The said structure "sera fondamentalement conciliaire", but it presupposes "structures de coordination" among the autocephalous Churches, inasmuch as "les primats de toutes les Églises soeurs ont une responsabilité particulière pour attester et promouvoir l'unité visible de l'Église". A. de Halleux, "Orthodoxes orientaux en dialogue", *Irénikon* 64 (1991), 347: "L'objectif de la réconciliation se trouve ensuite décrit ... comme consistant dans une complète union d'Églises soeurs, avec communion dans la foi, les sacrements, le ministère et dans une structure canonique."

[126] "Les deux parties sont tombées d'accord pour affirmer que la recherche de l'unité doit se faire sur la base d'une ecclésiologie de communion.... Les Églises en pleine communion les unes avec les autres sont des Églises soeurs au plein sens du terme. En dépit du fait que l'Église catholique et les Églises orthodoxes orientales ne sont pas encore en pleine communion, elles sont déjà tellement en commun concernant la foi apostolique et la vie sacramentelle qu'elles peuvent s'appeler l'une l'autre Églises soeurs, bien que d'une manière encore imparfaite": *Irénikon*, "Chronique religieuse", 67 (1994), 200.

[127] "There will be no seeking to lessen the legitimate prestige and the worthy patrimony of piety and [religious] usage proper to the Anglican Church when the Roman

this expression simply "as a hope for the future" [128], insofar as the Anglican communion does not possess apostolic succession and a valid priesthood.

On the other hand, J.-M. R. Tillard is more possibilist with regard to the already existing sisterly relations. To his mind, the question of the validity of the Anglican episcopate impedes only the making of a *definite* pronouncement on the ecclesial status of the Anglican communion, for which reason it is only a *presupposition* that the two Churches cannot be sisters before having reestablished full communion. [129]

From possibilism, one passes on, in the documents on dialogue, to the affirmation of the real condition of sisters, despite the fact that there persist crucial problems yet to be resolved, one of which is the problem of the primacy of Rome. [130] It concerns a condition which is still implicit and virtual, but which is founded on the profound measure of the "real

---

Catholic Church ... is able to embrace the ever beloved Sister in the one authentic communion of the family of Christ" (Ins. VIII, 1067).

[128] Bouwen, s.v. "Churches, Sister", DEM 187b. Cf. Lanne, "L'Orient chrétien au Concile Vatican II et dans la période qui a suivi le Concile", *Seminarium* 15 (1975), 319; R. T. Greenacre, "La signification des Églises orientales catholiques au sein de la communion romaine dans la perspective de "l'Église anglicane unie non absorbée", *Irénikon* 65 (1992): 344–51.

[129] "La primauté romaine", 323–24: "Certes, tant que le dossier de *Apostolicae curae* n'a pas été réouvert, la question de la validité de l'épiscopat anglican empêche Rome de se prononcer avec certitude sur la qualité d'ecclésialité de la communion anglicane", but "l'entrée en communion avec le siège romain, après des siècles de créativité et d'expression propre de la vie de foi, sera donc la reconnaissance du fait que, à supposer que jusque-là elles ne l'aient pas été, les deux Églises deviendront vraiment soeurs. Compte tenu de l'héritage préservé malgré la rupture, il faudra bien admettre que c'est grâce à sa hiérarchie propre que la tradition anglicane aura gardé les traits essentiels faisant d'elle alors cette 'soeur.' Dans ces conditions, impossible pour Rome ne pas recevoir *(receptio)* ni accueillir en la respectant cette ecclésialité, d'ailleurs enracinée dans une structure épiscopale." However, Tillard himself, in another context, makes a distinction between the Orthodox Churches and other Christian communities: "[T]he quality of Sister Churches is reserved for the Churches of the East ... essentially because of their apostolic Eucharist. It is clear, however, that in the 'full and perfect' (cf. *Unitatis redintegratio*, no. 5) Eucharistic communion towards which they are moving, all Christian communities are also called to become Sister Churches of the Church of Rome, and of all the Churches in communion" ("Catholic Church Is at the Heart of 'Communion'", 8).

[130] A–RCC II statement (January 1978): "Although the initial paragraphs of the Venice Statement clearly affirm our mutual faith that all authority in the Church is rooted in Jesus Christ and in the Holy Spirit, the document quickly moves into the most crucial ecumenical problem in our Sister Churches, namely, that of Roman primacy" (*Origins* 7 [1978]: 474b).

though as yet imperfect communion" which already exists, while the two separated Churches advance toward full communion and reconciliation.[131]

In the dialogue between Catholics and Lutherans the recognition of the condition of sisters, with the consequent right to a certain degree of communion, is a kind of presupposition for the dialogue itself [132] and at the same time a reality of the future, when, thanks to a common faith in the fundamental truths, the state of separation will have been overcome through the solution of problems that are still unsettled.[133] The expression is also used, however, to avoid applying the designation *mother* Church to any Church, not even to the Church of Rome, and to underline the

---

[131] A–RCC statement: *Anglican Orders* (May 8, 1990), 9: "Pope Paul VI raised the question of the ecclesial status of the Anglican Communion as he envisaged the future reconciliation of the Anglican and the Roman Catholic churches.... Pope Paul did not call the Anglican Communion a 'sister Church.' Yet by evoking a future embrace of it as the Roman Catholic Church's 'ever beloved sister,' he implicitly suggested that it has the making of a sister church. In this case, ecclesial sisterhood is virtual. It needs to be elicited and actualized." ARCIC II, *The Church as Communion* (Joint Declaration, Dublin, September 1990) (*One in Christ* 26 [1990], 272): The document's objective is to "give substance to the affirmation that Anglicans and Roman Catholics are already in a real though as yet imperfect communion and to enable us to recognise the degree of communion that exists both within and between us" (IS, no. 77 [1991], 87b–88a). "As separated Churches grow towards ecclesial communion it is essential to recognize the profound measure of communion they already share through participation in spiritual communion with God and through those elements of a visible communion of shared faith and sacramental life [which] they can already recognise in one another. If some element or important facet of visible communion is judged to be lacking, the communion between them, though it may be real, is incomplete" (ibid., 95a).

[132] Joint declaration, *Papal Primacy and the Universal Church* (March 5, 1974), no. 33. "Likewise we ask the Roman Catholic Church ... if, in the expectation of a foreseeable reconciliation, it is ready to acknowledge the Lutheran Churches represented in our dialogue as Sister-Churches which are already entitled to some measure of ecclesiastical communion" (LCD V, 23).

[133] JLRCC, joint declaration, *All under One Christ* (Augsburg, February 23, 1980): "Our newly discovered agreement in central Christian truths gives good ground for the hope that in the light of this basic consensus answers will also be forthcoming to the still unsettled questions and problems, answers which will achieve the degree of unanimity required if our churches are to make a decisive advance from their present state of division to that of sister churches" (MV 245). The document, *Unity Facing Us* (Rome, March 3, 1984), of the same commission, also dedicates a paragraph to the "sister Churches" and concludes: "For some time this concept has also been used to describe fellowship that has been regained or aspired to between separated churches, especially in the ecumenical relations between the Roman Catholic and the Orthodox Churches" (IS, no. 59 [1985], 50a).

fact that there exist only sister Churches in the bosom of the *Una sancta*, inasmuch as it is a communion of all the Churches.[134]

The expression "sister Churches" recurs also in the *multilateral dialogue*, although only in passing, as an invitation to the individual local Churches, viewed in the perspective of "conciliar communion", to share in the interests and concerns of other Churches[135] and to "maintain permanent and mutual relations with the sister Churches"[136] in view of the real though imperfect communion among those who believe and are baptized in Christ.[137]

II. THEOLOGICAL FOUNDATION

It is commonly said that the foundation for the reality of "sister Churches" can be traced back to article 14 of the decree *Unitatis redintegratio*, where one is reminded that the Eastern Churches profess the fundamental dogmas of the Christian faith.[138]

---

[134] JLRCC, document *Church and Justification*: "In the documents of Vatican II the designation 'mother church' is not applied to any local church nor even to the Church of Rome, but is strictly reserved for the *una sancta*. This demonstrates that the fellowship of all the churches makes them sisters in its bosom. As the Decree on Ecumenism puts it, there is that 'communion of faith and charity ... which ought to thrive between local Churches, as between sisters'" (IS, no. 86 [1994], 149a, n. 104). Previously, the report entitled "The Office of the Bishop" (March 1988) issued by the official working group of the dialogue between the Church of Sweden and the Roman Catholic diocese of Stockholm, after referring to the constitution of the patriarchates, had clarified that the Churches of the East considered the Bishop of Rome simply "as the patriarch of the West" and that as long as "they lived in that understanding, the patriarchates mutually considered each other to be sister churches" (EOE IV, 2065).

[135] Commission on Faith and Order, the Lima Document (January 1982), *Eucharist*: "It is in the eucharist that the community of God's people is fully manifested. Eucharistic celebrations always have to do with the whole Church, and the whole Church is involved in each local eucharistic celebration. In so far as a church claims to be a manifestation of the whole Church, it will take care to order its own life in ways which take seriously the interests and concerns of other churches" (MV 478–79).

[136] JWG, *The Church: Local and Universal* (1990): IS, no. 74 (1990), 81a.

[137] JWG, *Fourth Official Report* (1975): "Despite all divisions which have occurred in the course of the centuries, there is a real though imperfect communion which continues to exist between those who believe in Christ and are baptized in his name" (IS, no. 30 [1976], 18b).

[138] The text reads, "Nor must we underestimate the fact that the basic dogmas of the Christian Faith concerning the Trinity and the Word of God made flesh from the Virgin Mary were defined in Ecumenical Councils held in the East. To preserve this faith, these Churches have suffered, and still suffer much."

Father Lanne's interpretation of the decree is of vital importance in this regard.[139] First of all, he highlights the importance given in the conciliar document to the idea of fraternity. He does this by referring to two documents which say that the *separated brethren* "justified by faith in baptism are incorporated into Christ; they therefore have a right to be called Christians, and with good reason are accepted as brothers by the children of the Catholic Church", and "for the closer their union with the Father, the Word, and the Spirit, the more deeply and easily will they be able to grow in mutual brotherly love".[140] Having demonstrated this remote foundation, common to every individual Christian, he goes on to attribute to the text a direct affirmation of the fraternity between the Churches of the East and of the West,[141] which, besides being founded on the fraternity among the children of God deriving from baptism, is based also, and above all, on the common priesthood, on the celebration of the Eucharist, and on apostolicity in its three aspects (of origin, of succession, and of doctrine), all of which guarantee a profound and mysterious communion, notwithstanding the absence of canonical communion.[142]

His conclusion, however, seems forced. In actual fact, the decree, in order to facilitate "a prudent ecumenical action",[143] analyzes the "special considerations" of the Eastern Churches and, in the same context, recalls the historical and present reality of these Churches, namely, their concern and care to preserve "in a communion of faith and charity, those family ties which ought to exist between local churches, as between sister Churches".[144] The decree is concerned, therefore, with defining the type

---

[139] "Implications ecclésiologiques", 62–71.

[140] *Unitatis redintegratio*, nos. 3 and 7.

[141] Lanne, "Implications ecclésiologiques", 63: "[A]lors que dans le textes précédents ce qui était visé immédiatement était la fraternité des personnes par l'incorporation au Christ et la communion avec la Sainte Trinité, ici il s'agit directement de la fraternité des Églises d'Orient et d'Occident."

[142] Ibid, 68: "Fraternité sacramentelle et apostolicité (d'origine, de succession et de doctrine) sont donc deux motifs capitaux qui autorisent les catholiques à considérer les Églises orthodoxes comme Églises-soeurs de la leur, puisque ne peut y avoir qu'une seule et unique Église de Jésus-Christ." H. Legrand also writes, "Ainsi donc l'identité dans la foi et les sacrements fonde le fait que nous soyons des Églises-soeurs et cela même requiert le rétablissement de la communion et de l'unité, et déjà une certaine *communicatio in sacris*": "Une éventuelle relance de l'uniatisme pourrait-elle s'appuyer sur Vatican II. Quelques enjeux ecclésiologiques de la crise actuelle autour des Églises unies", *Irénikon* 66 (1993), 25.

[143] *Unitatis redintegratio*, no. 13.

[144] Ibid., no. 14.

of relationship that exists among the Eastern Churches, which certainly
will have to be kept in mind in ecumenical activity; it was not the intention of the Council Fathers—in any case, it cannot be deduced from the
text of the decree—to affirm, as Fr. Lanne has interpreted it, that Catholics are authorized to consider the Orthodox Churches as sister Churches
of their own Church.[145]

Even if mention is made of the fact that on the one hand the Churches
of the East and of the West have lived their own life for many centuries,
remaining united, however, "through fraternal communion of faith and
of sacramental life", and that, on the other hand, they exhort those who
wish to engage in ecumenism to pay due attention to "the type of relations that were in force between them (the Churches of the East) and the
See of Rome before the separation",[146] it cannot be concluded that a
relationship of "sister Churches" between the Catholic Church (or the
Church of the West) and the Orthodox Churches is founded on the decree
Unitatis redintegratio.[147] The expression refers only to the relations among
the Orthodox Churches[148] and not to their relationship with the Catholic

---

[145] Lanne, "Implications ecclésiologiques", 69. H. Legrand also recognizes that in *Unitatis redintegratio*, 14, the expression serves only to describe the relations, past and present,
between the local Churches in the East, but adds later, "Si on ne designe pas directement
les Églises orthodoxes comme des Églises soeurs de la nôtre, on fait beaucoup plus et
mieux dans les numéros 14 à 17: à la lumière du passé commun, qui est resté l'idéal actuel
de l'Orient, on y démontre qu'il est à la fois légitime et requis que l'Église catholique
considère comme des Églises soeurs l'ensemble des Églises orientales, chalcédoniennes ou
pré-chalcédoniennes" ("Une éventuelle relance de l'uniatisme", 23).

[146] *Unitatis redintegratio*, no. 14.

[147] Equally unfounded, it appears, are the affirmation of J. Spiteris ("Il concilio Vaticano
II ha riconosciuto ufficialmente la Chiesa ortodossa come *chiesa sorella*": "La Chiesa ortodossa", 47) and the conclusion of the JLRCC, *Unity Facing Us* (Rome, March 3, 1984),
n. 44: "Recently the concept of 'sister Churches' has become even more important. As an
expression of the fellowship between individual local churches it has a long tradition that
goes right back to the Early Church and was used in this sense by the Second Vatican
Council [UR 14]. For some time this concept has also been used to describe fellowship
that has been regained or aspired to between separated Churches, especially in the ecumenical relations between the Roman Catholic Church and the Orthodox Churches" (IS,
no. 59 [1985], 50a).

[148] Cf. T.S. Stransky: Stormon, 11, no. 29. Tillard too recognizes that the conciliar
decree "n'utilisait le thème des Églises soeurs que pour évoquer les relations fraternelles
qui, selon la tradition orientale, 'doivent exister entre les Églises locales comme entre des
soeurs' (no. 14). L'emploi actuel de l'expression en contexte de retrouvailles oecuméniques
est donc un cas de *receptio* par Rome d'une vision lourde d'implications, proposée par une
autre Église" ("La primauté romaine", 321). Cf. idem, *Chiesa di Chiese*, 361. In fact, Congar

Church, since mutual communion of faith and of sacramental life is lacking: it describes the situation that existed between these two parts of Christianity *before the separation* and provides a formal outline of the state of the Churches that live in mutual communion and autonomy.[149]

On the other hand, such a relationship was clearly ascertained by Paul VI in his papal brief *Anno ineunte*, where the text of *Unitatis redintegratio*, 14, is effectively applied to the "state of sisters" in which "our Churches" (Catholic and Byzantine) lived in the past, and to the current situation in which "they are rediscovering themselves as sisters". The doctrinal foundation remains the same: the already existing communion, thanks to a common baptism, and by virtue of apostolic succession which guarantees the common heritage of priesthood and the Eucharist, through which all men, formed in communion with the Trinity, have become brothers to one another, and the different Churches, having lived for centuries as sisters, have now rediscovered themselves as such.[150] Baptism establishes a communion among all Christians; apostolic succession, the Eucharist, and the priesthood establish a particular communion with the Eastern Churches.[151] Perfect communion has not yet been attained: in fact, there

---

sees in the text a recognition and description of "a form of church life different from that which has prevailed in the West with the dominance of the development of the papacy and in the framework of that kind of ecclesiology of the universal Church" (*Diversity and Communion*, 87).

[149] M. M. Garijo-Guembe, "Schwesterkirchen im Dialog", *Catholica* 48 (1994): 286: "Das Oekumenismusdecret des II. Vatikanischen Konzils verwendet die Bezeichnung Schwesterkirchen für die Beziehung zwischen den orthodoxen Kirchen untereinander (Nr. 14, 1), nicht aber für die Beziehung zwischen der römisch-katholischen Kirche und den orthodoxen Kirchen. Derselbe Text erklärt, warum die römisch-katholische Kirche die orthodoxen Kirchen nicht ausdrücklich als Schwesterkirche bezeichnet. Die Bezeichnung wäre dann möglich, wenn es so wäre, daß 'die Kirchen des Orients und des Abendlandes ... in brüderlicher Gemeinschaft des Glaubens und des sakramentalen Lebens' miteinander verbunden wären. Also: der Text beschreibt die Situation *vor der Trennung* zwischen beiden Teilen der Christenheit, so daß die Bezeichnung 'Schwesterkirchen' eine formelle Bezeichnung für Kirchen ist, die in Kommunion miteinander und in Autonomie leben."

[150] Cf. above, p. 271, note 53. Commenting on the papal brief, Lanne concludes, "Le pape Paul VI ... a fondé la fraternité entre les Églises ... avant tout sur le sacerdoce et l'eucharistie qui établissent entre les deux Églises catholique et orthodoxe, malgré l'absence de communion canonique, une 'communion profonde et mystérieuse'" ("Implications ecclésiologiques", 71).

[151] In the *General Audience* of January 20, 1971, the Pope affirms, "We realize, we Christians ... that we found ourselves in a strange situation, we might call it an absurd one. We

is disagreement over some essential principles of faith; nevertheless, there exists an "almost complete communion" in light of the common participation in the mystery of Christ and his Church,[152] so much so that Paul VI is led to use the designation of sister Churches.[153] Furthermore, as the same Pope would emphasize in his address on the occasion of the tenth anniversary of the cancellation of mutual excommunication from memory, the communion is so deep that very little is lacking to reach the fullness that will make possible the celebration of the Eucharist in common, since there already exists the common heritage of the same sacraments, the same priesthood, and the same episcopate received through the

---

are still separated, we are disunited.... Today perhaps we desire to understand one another.... But we are still far from each other, still lack certain principles which are essential for perfect union, some such principles: complete accord in the same profession of faith and the same bond of charity. This means to say that we are only partially in communion, even though our communion is deep, and, as regards the venerable Eastern Orthodox Churches, it is almost full, but not yet perfect" (IS, no. 13 [1971], 14b–15a).

[152] Paul VI, *Letter to Patriarch Athenagoras* (February 8, 1971): "[C]ommunion which is almost complete—though still short of perfection—deriving from our common participation in the mystery of Christ and his Church" (Stormon, 232, no. 285). Cf. also *Address by Pope Paul VI in the Basilica of St. Peter as He Welcomed Patriarch Athenagoras* (October 26, 1967: Stormon, 174–78, no. 190) and *Discourse to the Delegates of the Commission for Ecumenism* (November 22, 1972: IS, no. 20 [1973], 22–23). Even the Orthodox theologian Meyendorff, citing Paul VI, bases the reality of sister Churches on the already existing communion: "La base théologique de cette affirmation réside, d'après le texte [*Anno ineunte*] dans le mystère de la présence sacramentelle du Christ. Ce mystère 's'opère en chaque Église locale,' et, par conséquent, 'la communion (entre nos Églises), bien qu'imparfaite, existe déjà'" ("Églises-soeurs", 42). This is how Garijo-Guembe emphasizes the development: "Paul VI. verwendete den Begriff 'Schwesterkirchen' für die Kirche des Westens und für die Kirche des Ostens. Die Bezeichnung ergibt sich aus der Tatsache, daß die Mitglieder der beiden Kirchen Kinder Gottes sind und aus der Tatsache, daß in beiden Kirchen dieselben Sakramente gefeiert werden, d.h. die Taufe, das Amt in der apostolischen Sukzession, die Feier der Eucharistie und die anderen Sakramente sind Elemente, die bei beiden Kirchen zu finden sind. Es gibt zwischen beiden Kirchen eine große Gemeinshaft, obwohl sie nicht als vollständige Gemeinschaft zu bezeichnen ist." Curiously enough, the same author, contrary to what he had affirmed earlier (cf. no. 12), affirms, "Die Formulierung bleit auf dem Boden dessen, was schon im Ökumenismusdekret zu finden ist" ("Schwesterkirchen im Dialog", 288).

[153] In his letter to Patriarch Athenagoras (August 8, 1967), Bishop J. Willebrands thanks the patriarch for his contribution "for the reconstitution in full and perfect unity of our two Churches—these Churches which His Holiness the Pope, in the message which I had the joy of reading in his name in the Church of the Holy Spirit, was pleased to call sister Churches, because of the communion which exists between us in the Lord" (Stormon, 164, no. 178).

same apostolic succession.[154] Among the "sister Churches" the bonds of brotherhood are already woven so tightly that whatever concerns the life of one is lived also by the other, through communion in the same Spirit.[155]

The frequent use of the expression "sister Churches" in the Magisterium of *John Paul II* is also based upon the same concepts of "almost complete although still imperfect communion",[156] of "real although not yet full" communion,[157] of "deep communion" in the fundamental elements of faith, for which reason the Catholic Church is bound to the Orthodox Church by very close ties,[158] and also upon the acknowledgment that they have "almost everything in common".[159]

Thus we are witnessing a gradual development of the category of "sister Churches": whereas in *Unitatis redintegratio* it was limited to the rela-

---

[154] Address in the Sistine Chapel after the Reading of the Letter from Patriarch Dimitrios I (December 14, 1975): "The Holy Spirit has enlightened our intelligences and has brought us to see with increased lucidity that the Catholic Church and the Orthodox Church are united by such a deep communion that very little is lacking to reach the fullness authorizing a common celebration of the Lord's Eucharist.... In this way more stress is laid on the fact that we have in common the same sacraments ... and particularly the same priesthood, which celebrates the same Eucharist of the Lord, as well as the same episcopate received in the same apostolic succession to guide the people of God; and also that 'for centuries celebrating together the Ecumenical Councils that have defended the deposit of the faith against all corruption', we have lived 'this life of sister Churches (Brief *Anno Ineunte*)'" (Stormon, 282–83, no. 332). Cf. also Address of Patriarch Dimitrios (November 30, 1977: Stormon, 317, no. 359).

[155] Paul VI, Letter to Patriarch Dimitrios I: "[T]he bonds of brotherhood which are being woven anew, even more closely, between the Old and the New Rome are from now on such that whatever touches the life of one of the two sister Churches enters also into the experience of the other, through communion in the same Spirit" (June 29, 1977: Stormon, 311, no. 356).

[156] Cf. above, pp. 290–91, note 151.

[157] Encyclical *Ut unum sint*, no. 45; cf. nos. 11, 12, 14.

[158] Cf. John Paul II, apostolic letter *Euntes in Mundum*, no. 15: "This Church (Constantinople), like the other Churches, has true sacraments, particularly—by virtue of the apostolic succession—the eucharist and the priesthood, whereby she remains united to the Catholic Church with very close links. And together with the churches mentioned she makes intense efforts 'to perpetuate in a communion of faith and charity those family ties which ought to thrive between local churches as between sisters'" (*Origins* 17 [1987–1988], 717c). Even in the *Address on the Occasion of the Visit of the Orthodox Patriarch of Ethiopia, Abuna Paolos* (June 11, 1993), the Pope underlines: "The deep communion that exists between us, despite the vicissitudes of history, is rooted in the fundamental realities of our Christian faith. For we share the faith handed down from the Apostles, as also the same sacraments and the same ministry, rooted in the apostolic succession. This was strongly stated in the teaching of the second Vatican Council (cf. *Unitatis Redintegratio*, 15)": IS, no. 84 (1993), 151a. Cf. encyclical *Ut unum sint*, no. 50.

[159] *Orientale lumen* 3. Cf. *Ut unum sint*, no. 57.

tions among the Eastern Churches, it is now extended also to the relations between the Orthodox Churches and the Catholic Church, and the requisite foundation of full communion is now replaced by the foundation of real though "not yet perfect" or "incomplete" communion.

Indeed, the very reality of "sister Churches" becomes the point of reference for the reestablishment of full communion and unity through dialogue and the different expressions of fraternity.

III. DOCTRINAL CONSIDERATIONS

In the final analysis, the reality of "sister Churches" might be founded on the ecclesial status of the Orthodox Churches, in virtue of the faith that they have in common with the Catholic Church, regardless of their not yet complete communion with each other.[160] It concerns two presuppositions that are considered as having been already achieved. They nevertheless raise a number of questions and therefore require a few clarifications so as to ascertain whether and in what sense we can continue to speak of "sister Churches".

The recognition of the ecclesial status of the Orthodox Churches[161] was brought about by the Second Vatican Council, above all through the *special consideration* accorded them in the decree *Unitatis redintegratio*, in which it is "solemnly" declared that their spiritual, liturgical, disciplinary,

---

[160] Lanne, "Églises unies ou Églises soeurs: un choix inéluctable", *Irénikon* 48 (1975): 325: "L'Église catholique a déclaré solennellement qu'elle considérait les Églises orthodoxes d'une manière nouvelle. Elle reconnaît en elles de véritables Églises: des Églises soeurs." On the relative importance of the incomplete unity, E. Chr. Suttner has this to say: "Sie werden also vom Konzil im wahren Sinn Kirchen genannt. Dann aber sind sie Schwesterkirchen der katholischen Kirche, auch wenn sie mit ihr nicht in voller Einheit stehen": "Warum getrennte Schwesterkirchen?", *Stimmen der Zeit* 120 (1995): 272.

Curiously enough, Franquesa reverses the relationship between recognizing sister Churches and recognizing the true ecclesial status: "La reconnaissance de l'Église comme une vraie soeur ... exige qu'on reconnaise en elle les qualités de la véritable Église du Christ" ("Paul VI et l'Église orthodoxe", 200). In the same spirit Y. Congar writes, "Quand le pape emploie l'expression 'Églises soeurs' pour parler des Églises orthodoxes ... il reconnaît dans les faits que l'Église de Moscou ou de Constantinople sont des Églises authentiques": *Essais oecuméniques. Le mouvement, les hommes, les problèmes* (Paris, 1984), 75.

[161] We limit ourselves to the Orthodox Churches because it is common opinion that, even after the breach the West "continued to call the Oriental communities that had separated from itself as Churches", even though avoiding the term in referring to the communities dating from the Reformation (cf. Tillard, *Chiesa delle Chiese*, 59–60). As for the ecclesial status of the communities born of the Reformation, the generally shared opinion is that of Louis Bouyer, *The Church of God*, 516: "Strictly speaking, without abandoning what is most essential in the traditional view of the Catholic and Orthodox Church, we

and theological patrimony is fully part of the catholicity and apostolicity of the Church.[162]

One arrives at the same conclusion through the interpretation of *"subsistit in"* in *Lumen gentium* and through the "new concept" of the Church as a communion of local Churches.[163] The action of the Holy Spirit makes itself felt even beyond the confines of communion with the See of Rome, for which reason there is no "ecclesial vacuum" in the separated Churches, but rather the effective presence of one and the same Church of Christ.[164]

---

cannot say either that the Protestant churches are *churches* in the traditional sense or maintain that they are part of the *one* Church." The question arises again: "[I]l decreto sull'ecumenismo parla semplicemente di comunità ecclesiali in riferimento alle chiese della Riforma. Ma è poi così chiaro tutto questo? ... Se da parte romano-cattolica si riconosce che il ministero nelle chiese protestanti ha adempiuto ed adempie 'funzioni essenziali del ministero che Gesù Cristo ha istituito nella sua chiesa'; se inoltre si riconosce la presenza del Signore in queste comunità quando proclamano la sua Parola e celebrano la sua memoria (*anamnesis*) nella Cena, non ci sono allora i requisiti per definirle chiese?": Garijo-Guembe, "Unità nella diversità", 181–83.

[162] De Halleux, "Fraterna Communio", 297–99: "Avec *Unitatis redintegratio*, un pas décisif est franchi: l'Orthodoxie est à présent désignée sous le titre d' 'Églises' orientales, et cette appellation est délibérément fondée sur la reconnaissance de leur ecclésialité authentique.... De la 'considération spéciale' qu'*Unitatis redintegratio* accorde aux Églises d'Orient (nn. 14–18), il ressort qu'elles réalisent toutes les conditions du mystère d'unité qui constitue l'Église du Christ (n. 2). En effet, le concile déclare, à propos de leur patrimoine spirituel et liturgique, disciplinaire et théologique, qu'il fait pleinement partie de la catholicité et de l'apostolicité de l'Église (n. 17, §2)." Cf. encyclical *Ut unum sint*, 50.

[163] H. Legrand, "Une éventuelle relance de l'uniatisme", 27: "Grâce aux perspectives ouvertes par la formule 'subsistit in', désormais très connue, et grâce à l'adoption d'une ecclésiologie de communion entre Églises locales ... l'Église catholique a pu reconnaître les Églises orthodoxes comme des Églises-sœurs." Cereti, "L'enciclica 'Ut unum sint'", 683–84: "[O]rmai possiamo riconoscere che la Chiesa di Cristo è presente (e cioè 'sussiste') anche nelle altre Chiese cristiane.... Il riconoscimento dell'ecclesialità delle Chiese orientali non è mai stato sostanzialmente in discussione: su di esso si fonda per esempio il concilio di Firenze. Essa era stata pienamente riconosciuta dal concilio Vaticano II, che fra le altre cose affermava che 'per mezzo della celebrazione dell'eucarestia del Signore in queste singole Chiese la Chiesa di Dio è edificata e cresce.'" (Vatican II, *Unitatis redintegratio*, no. 15, cited in the encyclical at no. 12.) Cf. also Salachas, "Les Églises sœurs", 321–22.

[164] Tillard, "Catholic Church Is at the Heart of Communion", 8: "The theology of the sister Churches leads the Encyclical to give new vigour to the Council's recognition (*Lumen gentium*, n. 8; *Unitatis redintegratio*, n. 3) of the action of the Spirit outside the organic body of the local Churches gathered around bishops in *communion* with the Roman *Sedes*.... For, because of the elements of sanctification and truth that have their source in the Spirit, even in what is lived in those communities separated from Rome, 'the one Church of Christ is effectively present' (n. 11)."

The question arises, however, of the effective community of faith and of the impact of the incomplete canonical communion with the Successor of Peter.[165]

An *identity of faith* between the Catholic Church and the Orthodox Churches is generally affirmed, on the magisterial level[166] as well as on the theological level.[167] Indeed, it is explicitly emphasized that it is precisely by reason of the same faith and the same apostolic heritage, and possession of the same ministry and Eucharist that the Orthodox Churches are true particular Churches, and that hence they can and must be considered sister Churches,[168] even though there still remain points to be clarified and obstacles to be overcome before arriving at unity in the profession of faith, a necessary condition for the reestablishment of full communion. Despite the two different viewpoints, the Eastern and the Western, there does exist an agreement on the essentials of the faith[169]

---

[165] Even Lanne, one of the most convinced proponents of the reality of sister Churches, is aware of this when he writes, "L'Église catholique reconnaît aux Églises orthodoxes dans leur état présent une ecclésialité qui fonde une communion avec elle que l'on dit parfois 'presque parfaite' en se basant sur l'apostolicité de leur patrimonie propre: Elles sont 'Églises soeurs.' Il reste cependant que cette communion n'est pas complète au plan de la foi et au plan canonique. En particulier, la question même de la nécessaire communion avec le Siège du successeur de Pierre n'est pas résolue": "Les Catholiques orientaux: Liberté religieuse et Oecuménisme", *Irénikon* 65 (1990): 44.

[166] Paul VI, *Address in the Patriarchal Church of St. George*: "[W]e are making further discovery of the profound identity of our faith; and the points on which we still differ ought not to hinder us from seeing this deep unity" (Stormon, 157, no. 172). John Paul II too, in his *Address to the Professors* during his visit to the Pontifical Oriental Institute, does not hesitate in affirming, "But I profess the Christian faith that was also Soloviev's" (December 12, 1993: IS, no. 86 [1994], 100a), and in the *Address at the Conclusion of the Spiritual Retreat* he says with deep conviction that "the same faith unites us" with the Oriental brethren (cf. Ins. XVIII/1, 488).

[167] De Halleux, "Fraterna Communio", 299: "Mais la communion dans les sacrements ne suppose-t-elle pas l'accord dans la même foi dogmatique? La progression du dialogue de la Charité a fait apparaître, dans les déclarations catholiques officielles, l'affirmation répétée d'une communion presque totale entre les Églises catholique et orthodoxe."

[168] Legrand, "Uniatism and Catholic-Orthodox Dialogue", *Theology Digest* 42 (1995): 130: "In light of the common past the Catholic Church can and must consider the Eastern Churches as a whole as Sister Churches, for they are true local or particular churches. This is because we have in common the same apostolic faith, the same heritage from the Apostles (n. 14 [UR]), and the same ministry and eucharist."

[169] Lanne, "Une même foi, une même communion. A propos du dialogue théologique entre Orthodoxes et Catholiques", *Irénikon* 59 (1986): 343: "Personnellement, nous pensons que, de fait, il y a deux 'visions' chrétiennes différentes, l'orientale et l'occidentale,

and even a fundamental identity in the common faith.[170] In any case, despite there being no fuller or complete "doctrinal communion", the Eastern Churches continue to possess, in an imperfect and incomplete measure, the constitutive characteristics of the true Church listed in the Nicene-Constantinopolitan Creed and are therefore true Churches,[171] indeed, true sister Churches.[172] Such a communion of faith, essentially the same, not only establishes a genuine communion, but also could make possible a double communion, with the Catholic Church and with the Orthodox Church.[173]

Equally explicit, however, are the affirmations about the "doctrinal disagreements to be resolved", "true and genuine disagreements in matters of faith" which "hinder full communion between Christians".[174] From this arises the necessity of dialogue in view of an adherence by all to the integral content of the faith, without compromise, and "in acceptance of the whole and entire truth", in order to attain the unity willed by God.[175] It is recognized, therefore, that unity in faith does not yet exist; despite the progress made in dialogue, unity is still a goal to be achieved.[176]

---

mais que ces deux visions s'accordent sur la substance de la foi et que cette foi leur est réellement commune."

[170] Franquesa, "Paul VI et l'Église orthodoxe", 190: "Catholiques et orthodoxes ... ont pris de plus en plus conscience de l'identité fondamentale de leur foi commune."

[171] Peri, "All'alba del terzo millennio", 467–68: "Le caratteristiche costitutive della sola e vera Chiesa fondata da Gesù Cristo, elencate nel simbolo niceno-costantinopolitano (una, santa, cattolica ed apostolica), continuano perciò a connotare, ancorché in misura imperfetta ed incompleta, tali Chiese.... Ciò che le differenzia e divide, tra loro e con Roma, è una riduzione, non una perdita totale dei mezzi sacramentali indispensabili per la salvezza (in tal caso non sarebbero più Chiese, sicché il passaggio dall'una all'altra richiederebbe il ribattesimo di un cristiano convertito quasi fosse un pagano)."

[172] In the Joint Declaration of 1967, Paul VI and Patriarch Athenagoras rejoice over the rediscovery of their Churches as sisters despite the fact that "there still exist points to be clarified and obstacles to be overcome before arriving at the unity in the profession of faith which is necessary for reestablishment of total communion" (Stormon, 181, no. 195).

[173] Cf. E. Zoghby, Tous schismatiques? (Beirut, 1981).

[174] Encyclical Ut unum sint, Introduction and nos. 39 and 36.

[175] Ibid., 18: "The unity willed by God can be attained only by the adhesion of all to the content of revealed faith [in its entirety]. In matters of faith compromise is in contradiction with God who is the Truth." Cf. ibid., 37.

[176] Ibid., 77: "We can now ask how much further we must travel until that blessed day when full unity in faith will be attained.... In view of this goal, all the results so far attained are but one stage of the journey, however promising and positive."

In fact, considerable differences remain, such as those in the field of ecclesiology.[177] Apart from individual questions, the most important of which is that of the primacy of the Bishop of Rome,[178] the basic issue concerns the very concept of the *depositum fidei*, consisting of the truths of the apostolic preaching which were considered essential in the first centuries of the life of the Church, or at least throughout the first millennium. These alone are the essential elements of the *depositum fidei*, professed and lived during the normative period of the faith. The decisions of the so-called general councils celebrated in the West and the *ex cathedra* definitions of the Roman Pontiffs, insofar as they were not adopted by the entire body of bishops, do not form part of the essentials and are

---

[177] I. Bria, "La Koinonia comme communauté canonique", 125–26: "Quoique le pape Paul VI affirme que l'Église catholique est en 'communion presque totale' avec les Églises orthodoxes, des problèmes essentiels se posent encore pour la restauration de l'unité plénière sur une base ecclésiologique dogmatique, sacramentelle et canonique commune." E. Fortino summarizes the controversial points as follows: "Trinitaria (= il problema della conoscenza di Dio, la struttura-essenza della processione del S. Spirito); Ecclesiologia (= infallibilità e giurisdizione universale del vescovo di Roma); Mariologia (= i dogmi mariani dell'Immacolata concezione e dell'Assunzione al cielo; tali dogmi sono accettabili nella sostanza del loro contenuto ma vengono respinti nella forma, cioè come dogmi promulgati dal vescovo di Roma)": "Il dialogo tra cattolici e ortodossi", 11

[178] The question would be worth treating in its own right. We only need to remember the symbolic affirmation of Tillard: the Catholic Church and the Orthodox Church are "two sister Churches, yet 'separated'.... But from the time that the chapter on Roman primacy is opened up, everything is spoiled" (Tillard, *Church of Churches*, 189 and 256–57).

The Eastern position, after so many years of dialogue in charity and truth, is best expressed by Patriarch Bartholomew I: "[L]'idée selon laquelle le Seigneur, en choisissant les douze Apôtres, confia à l'un d'eux la tâche de les gouverner, n'a aucun fondement dans l'Écriture Sainte. L'ordre du Seigneur à Pierre, d'être le berger de ses brebis avait le sens de lui réitérer cet ordre, qu'Il avait donné à tous les Apôtres.... Cela n'avait donc pas le sens de confier à celui-ci un tâche pastorale supérieure vis-à-vis de celle des autres disciples.... Il en découle que chacun de nous, évêques, est tenu personnellement pour responsable de contribuer ou d'entraver la route de la nef de l'Église, de la bonne ou de la mauvaise tenue de cette route" (*Address to the Bishops of Switzerland*, December 14, 1995: *La documentation catholique*, February 4, 1996, no. 3, 135).

On the *original difference* between the East and the West with regard to primacy, cf. A. Garuti, *Il Papa Patriarca d'Occidente?*, 25–28, 243–46, and especially the conclusion: "Nonostante il 'prestigio' di Roma, sempre ritenuta la prima delle sedi patriarcali, e nonostante l'importanza attribuita al suo Vescovo nella proclamazione della fede di Pietro e nel rappresentare l'unità della Chiesa, l'Oriente non sembra avergli mai riconosciuto un vero primato di giurisdizione. In ogni caso la sua autorità era fortemente ridimensionata dalla conciliarità e soprattutto dall'importanza ecclesiologica attribuita all'imperatore e dalla teoria della pentarchia. Per questo egli era considerato il Patriarca d'Occidente, con una potestà nella Chiesa che non andava oltre a quella di un 'primus inter pares'" (269).

not indispensable for ecclesial communion. They are, rather, of secondary importance in the hierarchy of truths and should be considered instead as "theologoumena", which reflect Western theology and upset ecclesial consensus.[179] The Catholic Church cannot, therefore, demand complete agreement on these "dogmas" which she has defined unilaterally, especially when the East is reticent in accepting them, much less impose them with the intention of effecting a reunion;[180] consequently, they should be taken up anew for debate and discussion.[181]

With greater realism, the Orthodox believe that there is no unity of faith with the Catholic Church, and they judge some doctrines and dogmas to be *Roman heresies*. For this reason, although it might seem an exaggeration to affirm that they have passed on from schism to heresy,[182]

---

[179] Tillard, "L'expression de la foi", *Proche-Orient Chrétien* 28 (1978): 198–99: "Nous pouvons même ajouter que ce noyau est suffisant pour que deux Églises se reconnaissent 'en accord substantiel' dans la foi, donc en communion de foi. Par accord substantiel nous entendons ici un accord sur l'ensemble de points sans lequel l'essentiel du *depositum fidei* n'est plus authentiquement transmis.... Les décisions des 'conciles généraux tenus en Occident' même avant la Reforme n'ont pas cette importance. L'absence d'un group imposant d'évêques ... interdit de leur donner, même s'ils sont approuvés par l'évêque de Rome, la même portée qu'aux Conciles des premiers siècles.... Les déclarations, même *ex cathedra*, du Magistère romain doivent être comprises ... comme un exercice extraordinaire du Magistère du corps épiscopal dans l'Église catholique.... Elles ont donc un rang second dans la hiérachie des vérités." Cf. D. Salachas, "Les Églises soeurs", 113; Zoghby, *Tous schismatiques?*, 51–54.

[180] Tillard, "L'expression de la foi", 200: "L'Église catholique ne peut pas exiger un accord *complet* sur les 'dogmes' définis par elle seule, là surtout où l'Orient se montre réticent." Congar (*Diversity and Communion*, 172–77) questions whether a Church, especially the Catholic Church, with union in view, should compel other Churches to "accept" decisions and dogmas which it has defined in their absence; given the sensitivity of the problem, he cites the negative response of many Orthodox and Catholic representatives, especially in relation to the question of primacy.

[181] Cf. Zoghby's Profession of Faith (February 18, 1995), approved by the Synod of the Melchite Church. The Greek-Catholic Archbishop of Baalbeck, Cyril Salim Boustros, published the following comment: "[L]e rétablissement de l'unité entre l'Église catholique romaine et l'Église orthodoxe implique au préalable l'accord sur deux points essentiels: 1. L'acceptation par les Catholiques romains de remettre en cause le caractère oecuménique des conciles réunis en Occident après 1050. Il s'ensuit que les dogmes proclamés par ces conciles sont considérés comme des opinions théologiques de l'Église d'Occident. 2. La reconnaissance par les Orthodoxes de la primauté de l'Évêque de Rome, dans la forme qui existait au premier millénaire": "Relations entre les Communions", *Irénikon* 68 (1995): 370.

[182] D. Ols, "Diversités et communion. Réflexions à propos d'un ouvrage récent", *Angelicum* 60 (1983): "[L]'Église orthodoxe pense, à juste titre, qu'il n'y a pas unité de foi entre elle et l'Église catholique ... Il me semble incontestable que l'on doive reconnaître que l'Église orthodoxe est passée de l'état de schisme à l'état d'héresie. Nous devons en effet

it is undoubtedly too optimistic to maintain that, once every label of "schism" or "heresy" has fallen off, the designation of sister Churches will lead to full and mutual recognition of ecclesial status.[183]

Even the *lack of full communion* with the See of Rome should not stand in the way of considering the Eastern communities as *true* Churches and *true* sisters, because they are of apostolic origin,[184] they continue to possess the original sacramental structures of the Church,[185] and Christ is present in them, too, in virtue of the essential bond between the Eucharist and the Church. According to Tillard, "What is lacking in these Eastern Churches in regard to the Catholic fullness is not, therefore, the very essence of this *communion* but one of its important modalities", in other words, "the *visible* link with the see which has as its function to unite in a *visible* communion all the believing communities".[186] In any case, the ecclesiology of sister Churches makes it possible for the Churches to discover that they share in a relationship of communion, although it is not yet complete.[187]

---

constater que l'Église orthodoxe ne partage la foi de l'Église catholique ni quant à la procession du Saint-Esprit *ex Patre Filioque*, ni quant à la juridiction universelle immédiate et ordinaire du Pape, ni quant à l'infaillibilité personelle du Pape, ni même quant à l'absolue simplicité divine, mais qu'au contraire elle considère ces doctrines comme des hérésies romaines." In fact, already the Greek-Melchite patriarch, Gregorios Jussef, during the discussions of the First Vatican Council, despite protesting his faith in primacy, proposed to limit himself to going back to the doctrine of the Council of Florence, otherwise the Greeks who had been until then called "schismatici, id est seiuncti et separati", "per has definitiones anathemate roboratas... in numero haereticorum relegandi erunt" (J. D. Mansi, LII, 134B).

[183] N. Lossky, "La présence orthodoxe dans la 'diaspora' et ses implications ecclésiologiques, de même que celles des Églises orientales catholiques", *Irénikon* 65 (1992): 355: "Aujourd'hui, l'Église catholique et l'Église orthodoxe ne se traitent plus de 'schismatique' et d' 'hérétique'; elles s'appellent 'Églises soeurs,' donc, se reconnaisent pleinement comme 'Églises.' "

[184] Franquesa, "Paul VI et l'Église orthodoxe", 196: "[L]es Églises d'Orient fondées, directement ou indirectement, par des apôtres sont, en raison de leur origine, des Églises soeurs entre elles et avec l'Église romaine."

[185] C. J. Dumont, "Quelques réflections à propos de la conférence du Métropolite de Myre", *Proche-Orient Chrétien* 30 (1980): 67: "Si toujours Rome a dénié aux Églises d'Orient séparées de sa communion le droit de se dire *l'Église*, toujours aussi elle leur a reconnu le droit de se dire *Églises* et cela en raison de la permanence en elles à des degrés divers de la foi et des structures sacramentelles originelles de l'Église fondée par Jesus-Christ"; de Halleux, "La collégialité dans Église ancienne", 450: "Le décret *Unitatis redintegratio* du dernier concile a permis d'inaugurer un véritable dialogue oecuménique entre Catholiques et Orthodoxes, à titre d'Églises se sachant encore en communion si profonde l'une avec l'autre qu'elles peuvent déjà se considérer comme des soeurs."

[186] *Church of Churches*, 310 and 315.

[187] Cf. Assimakis, "L'Ecclesiologia", 31.

Contrary to what is sometimes said, communion between Churches, and hence the fullness of their ecclesial status, is not realized simply by a mutual recognition of their common faith, priesthood, and sacraments;[188] also necessary are the bonds of "ecclesial government, and communion", that is to say, a presupposed acceptance of the "visible structure" of the Church.[189] Despite the deep bonds that already exist, the parties have not yet reached full communion,[190] "a deep and unquenchable need for the religious order established by Christ", even though "the utmost value should be placed upon at least initial or partial membership in the Church".[191] This too, like unity of faith, still remains a "desired goal of the journey we are making",[192] which will be realized only "when all share in the fullness of the means of salvation entrusted by Christ to his Church", a fullness that is already present in the Catholic Church, in which subsists the one and only Church of Christ.[193]

The most evident proof of the present lack of unity in faith and communion is to be found in the impossibility of celebrating the Eucharist in common. Even though it is the essential element for determining the ecclesial status of a community[194]—for which reason it is believed that through its celebration in the individual Orthodox Churches "the Church of God is built up and grows in stature"[195]—the unanimous conviction is

---

[188] Cf. S. Manna, "Unica fede per la validità dei sacramenti", *Studi ecumenici* 132 (1995): 23.

[189] *Lumen gentium*, no. 14. Cf. Paul VI, *Allocution to the Catholicos Khoren I of Cilicia* (May 9, 1967: Ins. V 219). John Paul II is even more explicit in his *Letter to the Bishops of Europe* (May 31, 1991): after having cited the papal brief *Anno ineunte* of Paul VI, he continues, "The unity which is sought—and must be sought—with these Churches is full communion in one faith, in the sacraments and in the ecclesial government" (IS, no. 77 [1991], 38a). Cf. also the encyclical *Ut unum sint*, no. 9.

[190] John Paul II, *Address to the Delegation of the Ecumenical Patriarchate* (June 29, 1993): "Although deep are the bonds of communion uniting our Churches, we have not yet managed to reestablish full communion among ourselves" (IS, no. 84 [1993], 145a).

[191] Cf. Paul VI, *General Audience* (June 1, 1966: Ins. IV, 790–91).

[192] Encyclical *Ut unum sint*, no. 87.

[193] Cf. ibid., no. 86.

[194] Garijo-Guembe, "Schwesterkirchen im Dialog", 286–87: "Die Feier der Eucharistie wird in verschiedenen Texten des 2. Vatikanums als das wesentliche Element, das die kirchliche Gemeinde zur Kirche macht, bezeichnet. . . . Die Anerkennung der orthodoxen Kirchen und der Kirchen des Orients bedeutet, daß sie—die römisch-katholische Kirche—sich selbst als die wahre Kirche Christi darstellt, wobei sie aber anerkent, daß Kirche Christi auch außerhalb ihrer selbst existiert (vgl. die Formulierung "subsistit in" der Konstitution Lumen gentium Nr. 8,2)."

[195] Cf. *Unitatis redintegratio*, no. 15; encyclical *Ut unum sint*, no. 12.

that it is not yet possible to celebrate it together, a conviction that has been expressed in Catholic[196] and Orthodox[197] circles, and which has been confirmed in the joint declarations.[198]

In order to resolve the serious differences it is necessary to continue the theological dialogue.[199] The objective, however, has not yet been reached, and for this reason: "The reestablishment of eucharistic fellowship during continuing separation in faith is in itself a contradiction since, in spite of common reception of the eucharist, the churches will continue to live in separation from one another."[200]

Since complete identity through profession of the same faith has not yet been achieved, and since perfect participation in the communion of the one and only Church is still lacking,[201] the task remains of taking a closer look at the problem of the ecclesial character of the Orthodox Churches. If they really are particular Churches and as such are part of the Catholic

---

[196]John Paul II, *Discourse to the Roman Curia*: "It [concelebration] cannot but presuppose the fundamental unity of faith which constitutes the core of the ecclesial communion. If it were not so, it would harm the very concept of the Church and the eucharist which we have received from tradition, both Western and Eastern" (June 28, 1985: IS, no. 59 [1985], 3b). Cf. encyclical *Ut unum sint*, nos. 45, 59–78. For earlier attestations cf. Stormon, 376, no. 410; 402, no. 419; 404, no. 422; 410, no. 426; 442, no. 454; 445, no. 459. For the thoughts of Paul VI cf. Stormon, 242, no. 294; 301, no. 346; 320, no. 362; 325, no. 369. Cardinal Willebrands: "The fact that the Churches of the East and the West at a certain moment of their history reached the tragic and scandalous situation of ceasing to celebrate the Lord's Eucharist together means that they considered the differences then existing between them to be grave" (Stormon, 407, no. 423).

[197]Cf., for example, Stormon, 310, no. 354; 357, no. 400; 365, no. 403; 379, no. 411; 410, no. 424; 448, no. 460.

[198]Cf. the Joint Declarations of Pope John Paul II and the Patriarch Dimitrios I (November 30, 1979: Stormon, 367, no. 404) and Bartholomew I (June 29, 1995: IS, no. 90 [1995], 123–24).

[199]John Paul II, *Address to the Delegation of the Ecumenical Patriarchate* (June 28, 1986): "Indeed, if for nearly a millennium our Churches no longer celebrate the Eucharist together ... theological dialogue is therefore indispensable. We will have to clarify misunderstandings, discuss and resolve differences and, finally, proclaim unity in faith" (IS, no. 61 [1986], 114a).

[200]Old Catholic-Orthodox Conversation, joint declaration *Church Community* (Kavala, October 1987): GMR 268.

[201]In the General Audience of January 24, 1968, Paul VI recalls that "l'ecumenismo nostro è anzitutto una questione di carità, ... però la carità non basta a produrre quella completa unione, che deve avere per fondamento una fede eguale e un'adesione concreta alla comunità visibile ed organica, che realizza in pieno il nome di Chiesa di Cristo" (cf. Ins. VI, 724).

Church in which the universal Church is necessarily reflected, in what sense then does the Church of Christ *not subsist in them*?

As mentioned earlier in another context,[202] the *Letter of the Congregation for the Doctrine of the Faith to the Bishops of the Catholic Church on Some Aspects of the Church Understood as Communion* provides a clarification in this regard (*Communionis notio*, May 28, 1992). In fact, it acknowledges that the presence of numerous elements of the Church of Christ in the non-Catholic Christian Churches permits us "to recognise with joy and hope a certain communion, though not perfect". Further on, however, it specifies the nature of this "imperfect communion" and affirms that, "for each particular Church to be fully Church, that is, the particular presence of the universal Church with all its essential elements, and hence constituted *after the model of [in the image of the] universal Church*, there must be present in it, as a proper element, the supreme authority of the Church: the episcopal college *'together with their head, the Supreme Pontiff, and never apart from him.'* Consequently *'we must see* the ministry of the Successor of Peter, *not only as a "global" service, reaching each particular Church from "outside"*, as it were, but as belonging already to the essence of each particular Church from "within".' "[203] With regard to the Orthodox Churches, it recognizes that they "therefore merit the title of particular Churches", but adds nevertheless, "Since, however, communion with the universal Church, represented by Peter's Successor, is not an external complement to the particular Church, but one of its internal constituents, the situation of those venerable Christian communities also means that their existence as particular Churches is *wounded.*"[204]

Not surprisingly, the *Letter* was considered in some circles to have "thrown cold water" on the ecumenical movement,[205] but the problem it has clar-

---

[202] Cf. Garuti, "Ancora a proposito del Papa Patriarca d'Occidente", 40–42.

[203] *Communionis notio* 13.

[204] Ibid. 17.

[205] Lanne, "Présentation du Colloque de Chevetogne 1992", 318. The reasons are explained in the pages that follow (319–20): "Cette affirmation [the wound spoken of in *Communionis Notio*] a profondément affecté la sensibilité oecuménique, en raison surtout ... de l'emploi de la terminologie de Vatican I que Vatican II avait évité de reprendre, de l'apparente négation d'une vraie théologie des Églises soeurs, d'une sorte de sacramentalisation de la papauté mise sur le même pied que l'Eucharistie et, en plus de tout cela, en raison du ton acide qui se dégage du document." The question of primacy "ne touche pas la reconnaissance des Églises orthodoxes comme Églises soeurs". C. Hill, "Récents documents", 65–66: "D'un coup toutes les Églises qui ne sont pas en communion avec Rome sont ainsi privées

ified is of fundamental importance. If the lack of full communion has consequences for "the very ecclesial status of those particular Churches",[206] what is the implication of that wound? In other words, since they lack one of the *internal constituent* elements, in what sense can the Orthodox Churches call themselves particular Churches in actuality?

On the basis of *Communionis notio* one could conclude that they are true particular Churches,[207] and, as such, they exist in and through the universal Church, which, in its turn, exists and is formed through them. Through and in this universal Church, presided over by the Successor of Peter, the Orthodox Churches derive their ecclesial status; since, however, they do not recognize the authority of the Bishop of Rome, they find themselves in an ecclesiologically irregular situation; that is to say, their ecclesial status is wounded. Since they lack full communion—an indispensable condition for any Church to be the Catholic Church in a given place—they do not fully meet the requirements necessary for being sister Churches, especially because they are deprived of that mark of the Catholic Church which consists of being governed by the Successor of Peter and by the bishops in communion with him. They are *true* Churches "in the full sense of the term", but "in an imperfect manner",[208] or "in

---

de leur propre ecclésialité.... Refuser que d'autres traditions chrétiennes aient une valeur ecclésiale refuse en fait qu'elles soient vraiment Églises. J'estime que ceci est en contradiction et avec *Lumen gentium* et avec le Décret sur l'Oecuménisme."

[206] Cf. "La Chiesa come comunione. A un anno dalla pubblicazione della Lettera *Communionis notio*", Congregazione per la dottrina della Fede, *"Communionis notio": Lettera e commenti* (Libreria editrice vaticana, 1994), 88.

[207] Max Thurian, "Comunione ecclesiale ed ecumenismo", in ibid., 75: "Per quanto separate dalla Sede di Pietro, esse sono Chiese particolari, o Chiese sorelle, nelle quali è veramente presente la Chiesa, una, santa, cattolica e apostolica." Congar used the terminology of *authentic Churches*: "Quand le pape emploie l'expression 'Églises soeurs' pour parler des Églises orthodoxes ... il reconnaît dans les faits que les Églises de Moscou ou de Constantinople sont des Églises authentiques" (*Essais oecuméniques*, 75).

[208] B. Schulze, "Il Vaticano II e Paolo VI di fronte al dilemma: Chiese sorelle o Chiese unite?", 96–98: "Se le Chiese ortodosse, dal punto di vista cattolico, sono vere Chiese, non ne segue che lo siano in modo perfetto ... non si nega il carattere di una Chiesa sorella da diversi punti di vista, anche essenziali, ma si nega il riconoscimento perfetto e integro, che è soltanto possibile se una Chiesa accetta tutta la verità cattolica, non escluso il primato del Papa nella successione di Pietro." Ibid., 102: "La comunione canonica e la comunione nell'integra fede, almeno definita, sono elementi ecclesiali essenziali. Se mancano, non si può parlare—e neppure il Vaticano II ne parla—di 'Chiese nel senso pieno del termine.' Una ecclesiologia che comprende e le Chiese cattoliche e le Chiese separate, fondata sulla fraternità, come di Chiese sorelle, rimane sempre più o meno perfetta, in quanto le Chiese più o meno si avvicinano o si allontanano nella comunione di fede e di

an analogous and participatory sense vis-a-vis the *una, catholica, ex qua et in qua existunt*", inasmuch as the term *Church* can be applied to them only "by an analogy of attribution with respect to the one and only Catholic Church *ex qua* and *in qua* they exist".[209] In fact, full incorporation into the Church, which confers the fullness of ecclesial status, is not realized simply by "the bonds of the profession of faith and of the sacraments", but also through the bonds of "ecclesial government and communion", which is to say that it presupposes the acceptance of the "integral structure" of the Church.[210] The one and only Church of Christ, therefore, "subsists in the Catholic Church, which is governed by the Successor of Peter and by the bishops in communion with him",[211] or one might say that it continues to exist from the very beginning and without interruption, as a presence in the Catholic Church, which alone is its complete realization in terms of totality. The Orthodox Churches, in contrast, inasmuch as they possess certain elements of sanctification and of truth—especially apostolic succession and valid Eucharist—do have meaning and importance in the mystery of salvation and are instruments at the service of the Spirit of Christ, and hence they too participate in the proper mission of the Church of Christ, with which they have partial relationship. Nevertheless, these means "draw their salvific value from the fullness ... of the Catholic Church, Christ's one and only Church, which He has constituted the depositary of that fullness". For this reason, the

---

regolarità canonica. L'unica Chiesa di Cristo si edifica e cresce, secondo l'insegnamento del Vaticano II, non nella stessa misura in ciascuna Chiesa, in Oriente e in Occidente." Cf. Max Thurian, "Comunione ecclesiale ed ecumenismo", 75–76.

[209] Cf. L. Chitarin, "L'ecclesiologia di Francis A. Sullivan. Analisi bibliografica", *Ricerche teologiche* 7 (1996): 229.

[210] Cf. above, p. 300, note 189.

[211] *Lumen gentium*, no. 8. The Sacred Congregation for the Doctrine of the Faith in its *Notification Regarding Franciscan Father Leonardo Boff's Book "Church: Charism and Power"* gave the following interpretation of the "authentic meaning" of the conciliar text: "But the Council had chosen the word *subsistit*—subsist—exactly in order to make clear that one sole 'subsistence' of the true church exists, whereas outside her visible structure only *elementa ecclesiae*—elements of church—exist; these being elements of the same church—tend and conduct toward the Catholic Church" (*Origins* 14 [1985]: 685b). The full incorporation of the Catholic faithful into the Church is also compared with the Church's awareness of being "joined in many ways" (*Lumen Gentium*, 16) to non-Catholic Christians, who are "incorporated into Christ" and "are put in some, though imperfect, communion" with the Catholic Church (*Unitatis redintegratio*, no. 3), the "objective basis" of which is constituted by the elements of sanctification and truth present in their communities (encyclical *Ut unum sint* 11).

Orthodox Churches are means of salvation "only because the elements of the one and only Church of Christ which they have conserved belong to the order of salvation". In any case, the said elements "cannot be the subject of the 'subsistence' of the Church itself, because if this were the case, the one and only Church of Christ would be a plurality of Churches, in each of which it *subsists* in an equal measure".[212]

We may conclude, therefore, that although the Orthodox Churches possess elements of ecclesial status, the Church of Christ does not subsist in them: they are Churches, but in an imperfect and analogous manner with respect to the Church, from which they derive their existence and salvific efficacy. Consequently, equally imperfect and analogous is their condition as "sisters".[213]

The recognition, on the Catholic side, of the ecclesial status—though imperfect—of the Orthodox Churches and the euphoria over having rediscovered them as sisters are not reciprocated on the Orthodox side. This is admitted by various Catholic authors who have shown greater openness in the encounters with Orthodoxy and have been staunch supporters of the theology of sister Churches: "Greek theology today firmly maintains that the non-Orthodox do not belong to the Church any more."[214]

In fact, there is a widespread denial especially of the ecclesial status of the Catholic Church;[215] the most they are willing to concede is that she

---

[212] U. Betti, "Chiesa di Cristo e Chiesa cattolica. A proposito di un'espressione della 'Lumen gentium'", *Antonianum* 61 (1986), 726–55: citations on pp. 742–43. Cf. also Garuti, "Relación entre la Iglesia de Cristo y la Iglesia católica", *Curso de actualización teologica organizado por el episcopado colombiano* (Bogotá, 1990), 297–307.

[213] This clarification, however, does not justify the conclusion drawn by Patriarch Alexis II of Moscow, according to whom, after the publication of *Communionis notio*, the Orthodox Church felt that it was considered instead to be a stepsister or, worse, a defective, "sick" Church (Adista, no. 17/93: reported in Adista, February 18, 1995, 12). Similarly unjustified is the reproach directed at Rome by J. Poustooitov that it was not behaving "en Église soeur" inasmuch as it "installe sur le territoire de Russie, par exemple, des structures parallèles"; nevertheless it remains a sister Church which does not behave like one, but rather like a sect: " 'Nation chrétienne' et coexistence des Églises", *Irénikon* 65 (1992): 398.

[214] Assimakis, "L'Ecclesiologia", 22; Manna, "Quale la recezione effettiva seguita ai dialoghi della Commissione mista cattolico-ortodossa?", *Nicolaus* 20 (1993): 69. "La teologia ortodossa mantiene ferma la convinzione che i non ortodossi non appartengono più alla Chiesa."

[215] De Halleux, "Fraterna Communio", 300: "Bref, la reconnaissance catholique de l'ecclésialité de l'Église orthodoxe, telle qu'elle s'exprime dans le décret conciliaire sur l'oecuménisme, n'a pas encore obtenu officiellement sa réciprocité." De Halleux, "Foi,

cannot be excluded from the "sense of the Church" or that, because of the *vestigia Ecclesiae* she conserves, she is "very close to the Orthodox Church".[216] The validity of the Catholic sacraments is also rejected.[217] Perhaps this is the crux of the problem: the Balamand Document itself, even though it recognized the common patrimony of the profession of faith and of participation in the same sacraments, excluding rebaptism as a result,[218] provoked bitter controversy on the Orthodox side.[219] The official declarations should not deceive us: as Spiteris points out, there is a difference between the affirmations made by the highest authorities on the one hand and the position held by the different Churches and, above

---

bapteme et unité. A propos du texte de Bari", *Recueil d'études*, 649: "Il faut espérer qu' ils [Orthodox theologians] en arriveront à constater que l'Église catholique soeur, telle qu'elle se définit et s'efforce de vivre depuis son dernier concile, ne se situe pas à l'extérieur du Corps du Christ, ni sur les parvis du Temple de l'Esprit, mais qu'elle possède, tout en l'exprimant selon sa tradition propre, une ecclésialité tout aussi authentiquement apostolique que celle de l'Église orthodoxe."

[216] G. Galitis, "Gli aspetti ecclesiologici del dialogo", 195: "La Chiesa Ortodossa ha coscienza... di essere ... la Chiesa nel senso vero e pieno della parola.... Cosa avviene, ora, delle comunità che, secondo il punto di vista ortodosso, non posseggono pienamente i suddetti criteri? Non si considerano come Chiese? ... La risposta a tale problema è, in realtà, difficile. Per questo c'è anche una vastissima gamma di risposte da parte ortodossa." Ibid., 197–98: "In conclusione, riguardo al termine Chiesa, possiamo dire che, mentre sappiamo dove'è la Chiesa, non sappiamo dove essa non sia. Possiamo dire, di una comunità, che non possiede integralmente le caratteristiche della Chiesa, ma non possiamo escluderla dal senso di Chiesa. Se dunque si prende in considerazione la parte comune della fede e della tradizione e tutti gli altri punti che sono comuni, gli ortodossi possono, mirando alle cose che uniscono e non a quelle che dividono, riconoscere alle Chiese i *vestigia Ecclesiae*, e non negare ad esse il titolo di Chiesa.... In modo particolare, questo vale per la Chiesa cattolica romana, la cui base biblica, i dogmi fondamentali, la ricchezza liturgica, la tradizione spirituale e, negli ultimi anni, il desiderio di avvicinamento, la portano molto vicino alla Chiesa ortodossa."

[217] Assimakis, "L'Ecclesiologia", 23: "[L]'ortodossia non può accettare la proposta del comune riconoscimento della validità dei sacramenti delle due Chiese dialoganti. Da ciò deriva anche il rifiuto da parte ortodossa di accettare ogni forma di intercomunione." Even when these are recognized by some theologians, it is not a question of having recourse "al principio detto della *economia*, in analogia con quanto fanno i cattolici che ricorrono al principio del *supplet Ecclesia* quando si tratta di sanare certi casi di invalidità che sian tali solo di fatto e senza vera colpa o malizia": L. Sartori, "Battesimo e unità della Chiesa. Un unico battesimo, un'unica Chiesa?", *Studi ecumenici* 13 (1995): 61.

[218] The Balamand Document: "On each side it is recognized that what Christ has entrusted to his Church—profession of apostolic faith, participation in the same sacraments, above all the one priesthood celebrating the one sacrifice of Christ, the apostolic succession of bishops—cannot be considered the exclusive property of one of our Churches. In this context, it is evident that any re-baptism whatsoever is excluded" (no. 13: IS, no. 83 [1993], 97a).

[219] Cf. Y. Spiteris, "La Chiesa ortodossa", 76–80.

all, by some theologians who do not agree with the official declarations of the ecumenical patriarchs[220] on the other.

Another consequence of this is the *rejection of the title of sister*. Spiteris himself, after an interesting "historical retrospect",[221] concludes, "As is evident, the Greek-Orthodox Church is not in a position to recognize the Catholic Church as a sister Church and consequently cannot recognize even the validity of the Catholic priesthood, from which the validity of all other sacraments is derived." [222] His final observation is highly eloquent: "During the period in which Rome polemically claimed to be the mother of all Churches, she was reminded that she was a sister Church. Now that the same Rome uses this expression of fraternity, there are some Orthodox Churches that deny her this title." [223]

In fact, there is no clear consensus in Orthodox circles as to recognizing the "ecclesial status" of the non-Orthodox Churches, including the Catholic Church; for this reason the theology of "sister Churches", even though it represents a step forward and can be considered a sound method for dialogue, does not reflect a reality that has already been achieved, since unity of faith is lacking, which is considered by both sides as the sole necessary condition for reestablishing sacramental and canonical relations.[224]

Not even dialogue has succeeded yet in clarifying the theological and canonical inaccuracies and ambiguities of the category of "sister Churches". The numerous and strong criticisms from Orthodox circles against the various documents published by the relevant joint commission bear

---

[220] Ibid., 47–48: "Da una parte, quindi, possediamo oggi una posizione chiara e unanime della Chiesa cattolica che riconosce ufficialmente la Chiesa ortodossa orientale come *chiesa sorella* e che quindi accetta la validità dei suoi sacramenti; dall'altra per quanto riguarda l'atteggiamento della Chiesa ortodossa circa la validità dei sacramenti della Chiesa cattolica, abbiamo solo alcune affermazioni positive a livello di vertice.... Queste affermazioni, però, non sono vincolanti per gli ortodossi poiché soltanto un concilio ecumenico potrebbe prendere una posizione affermativa o positiva in proposito."

[221] Cf. ibid., 49–78.

[222] Cf. ibid., 78.

[223] Cf. ibid., 82.

[224] Meyendorff, "Églises-soeurs", 44: "Je crois certainement que la théologie des 'Églises soeurs' est la bonne méthode pour le dialogue entre Catholiques et Orthodoxes. Le fait qu' elle ait été adoptée dans le bref *Anno ineunte* constitue un pas en avant très significatif. Il reste pourtant que nos deux traditions sont d'accord pour considérer l'unité de la foi comme condition unique et nécessaire pour l'établissement de relations sacramentelles et canoniques. Cette unité existe-t-elle déjà? ... D'une part, il existe certainement un consensus pour considérer l'Église orthodoxe comme l'Église catholique une. Par contre, il n'existe pas de consensus évident ni sur le statut 'ecclésial' des Non-Orthodoxes, ni sur la meilleure manière de témoigner de la vérité et de promouvoir l'unité des Chrétiens."

testimony to this. The Balamand Document, for example, is criticized for its theological and canonical lack of precision. In particular, they claim that the expression should be used exclusively by an Orthodox Church in relation to another Orthodox Church sharing the same apostolic faith; on the other hand, it cannot be applied to the Catholic Church, which does not as yet profess the fullness of the apostolic faith preserved only in the Orthodox Church, and this does not include recognition of the primacy and infallibility of the Roman Pontiff.[225]

To use the analogy of a choral symphony, while the Catholic circles are singing the praises of the "sister Churches", this is met by a series of discordant notes from the Orthodox side: reproaches against the Catholic Church,[226] ultimatums,[227] and open protestations against mutual recognition between the "sister Churches".[228]

---

[225] W. Hryniewicz, "Reconciliation and Ecclesiology of Sister Churches", *Eastern Churches Journal* 2, no. 3 (1995): 59: "Now, this basic category of Sister Churches is being accused of theological and canonical imprecision. No doubt, the precise significance and concrete implications of this concept are yet to be determined in the dialogue. For some Orthodox critics of Balamand this term is ambiguous and incorrect and can only be used by an Orthodox Church in relation to another Orthodox Church sharing the same apostolic faith. From that point of view, the Orthodox Church and the Roman Catholic Church do not yet profess the same 'apostolic faith', as it is presupposed in the Balamand document (§13); the fullness of apostolic faith has been preserved only in the Orthodox Church and it does not include recognition of papal primacy and infallibility."

[226] Ignazio Hazim, Greek-Orthodox metropolitan of Latakia, "Une vision antiochienne de l'unité de l'Église", *Proche-Orient Chrétien* 28 (1978): 204: "Notre Église-soeur envoyait dans nos pays des légions de missionnaires.... Au lieu de nous aider à nous renouveler, les puissantes Églises d'Occident ont cherché à nous 'convertir' et ont constitué à nos dépens des Églises uniates, latines et protestantes. Est-ce en la divisant que l'on aide une Église, une Église 'soeur' dit-on aujourd'hui, à se rénover?" The same metropolitan adds, "À Antioche désormais une Église ne peut plus être ce qu'elle est appelée à être si elle ne se renouvelle pas avec ses Églises-soeurs du même lieu" (ibid., 206). For his part, the patriarch of Moscow, Alexis II, remarked that, after the duplication of *Communionis notio*, the Orthodox Church feels that it has been treated rather like a stepsister, or at least as a defective and "sick" Church (Adista, n. 17/93: reported in Adista of February 18, 1995, 12).

[227] The monks of Mount Athos, in a letter addressed to Patriarch Demetrios I (December 8, 1993), contend that on account of the " 'ecclésiologie totalitaire' de la primauté romaine" the two Churches "ne sauraient donc être mises sur pied d'égalité et considérées comme 'des Églises soeurs'" and they therefore affirm that "nous sommes obligés de ne jamais accepter l'union ou l'appellation de l'Église catholique comme 'Église soeur' ... tant que les catholiques ne renoncent pas explicitement au *Filioque*, à l'infaillibilité et la primauté du pape" (*Irénikon* 67 [1994]: 513–15).

[228] This was the tenor of a letter from the Synod of the Orthodox Church of Greece to Patriarch Bartholomew (January 1995): cf. *Irénikon* 68 (1995): 126.

On the other hand, it makes no sense any more to bring up the so-called phenomenon of *uniatism/proselytism* and related implications and to ask the respective Churches to clarify their own positions and to put them into practice.[229] The Catholic Church has already recognized the ecclesial status—although imperfect—of the Orthodox Churches, with the soteriological consequences that follow therefrom; now it is the turn of the Orthodox Churches to take an analogous step.

IV. ECUMENICAL IMPLICATIONS

Despite the incomplete unity of faith and communion which *hurts* their very ecclesial status, the Orthodox Churches continue to be presented—as we have seen in the preceding historical overview—as sisters of the Catholic Church in a manner that is indiscriminate,[230] at times ambiguous, and even theologically incorrect. It even seems that this rediscovery has become the panacea for resolving the various doctrinal or canonical questions that are still disputed or for considering them to be resolved already.

---

[229] Lanne, "Aspects ecclésiologiques du dialogue théologique", 188–89: "Les Orthodoxes y voient la négation de la reconnaissance réciproque d'Églises soeurs entre l'Église catholique et l'Église orthodoxe. Un des arguments utilisés autrefois pour justifier le rattachement à la communion romaine de communautés ou de fidèles de l'Église orthodoxe était que seule l'Église véritable dans la pleine communion du siège de Pierre peut procurer le salut: hors de l'Église point de salut. Et cette Église était l'Église catholique romaine. Un des acquis les plus précieux de la redécouverte des relations d'Églises soeurs existant entre l'Église catholique et l'Église orthodoxe est bien de reconnaître l'ecclésialité sotériologique de l'autre partie. Du coté catholique, le décret sur l'oecuménisme de Vatican II est formel (cf. UR 15) et bien des gestes et des textes issus de Rome depuis lors vont dans le même sens. Il reste que, si la légitime liberté rendue aux Églises orientales catholiques ne peut pas mettre en question cette réalité, le décret du même concile Vatican II sur ces Églises orientales catholiques et le développement qui leur est donné, sans que dans le même temps soit prise en considération la théologie des Églises soeurs régissant les relations entre Orthodoxes et Catholique, peut être compris comme un double langage en matière d'ecclésiologie. Pour sortir de l'impasse, nous autres Catholiques devons clarifier nos positions et les traduire dans les faits. Toutefois cela ne sera possible que si nos frères orthodoxes font une démarche semblable et reconnaissent sans ambages non seulement la validité du baptême donné par l'Église catholique, mais que cette dernière procure à ses fidèles le même et unique salut donné par Jésus-Christ que le fait l'Église orthodoxe. Cette double démarche est possible. Elle est nécessaire pour sortir de l'impasse. Y sommes-nous prêts de part et d'autre?"

[230] At times we are tempted to agree with Bishop Zoghby when he writes, "On nous remplit les oreilles de 'communion presque parfaite' entre Rome et l'Orthodoxie, 'd'Églises-soeurs,' de 'communauté de foi', 'd'Église une,' d'ecuménisme, de dialogue.... Mais il ne faut pas exagérer leur portée" (*Tous schismatiques?*, 108–9).

One almost gets the impression that the continual appeal to the reality of "sister Churches" is subject to the conviction that this perhaps is the way that will lead to the reestablishment of full unity in faith and communion, whereas—on the contrary—it is only this reestablishment that will allow us to recognize the full ecclesial status of the Orthodox Churches and thus rediscover them fully as "sisters". There remains, therefore, the task of examining the importance of this unquestionable fact, by pointing out its various implications, for instance, in the field of ecumenism.

Obviously it is not possible to deal with all of them in detail. While the particular questions concerning the concept of "Mother Church",[231] the so-called theology of return,[232] and the problem of "uniatism"[233]

---

[231] Quite a few theologians, even after the "rediscovery" of sister Churches, reject this title. According to Lanne, "Ce vocabulaire était neuf dans la bouche d'un pape; mais aussi la théologie qu'il suppose. Rome ne se posait plus comme la *mater* située au-dessus de toutes les Églises, mais comme la soeur" ("Hommage à Paul VI", 304). Congar poses this question: "Que va devenir dorénavant le thème de Rome disant: *Mater et Magistra?* ... Est-ce que Rome reste *Mater et Magistra* de toutes les Églises, s'il y a des Églises soeurs?", and gives the answer himself: "À plusieurs reprises, dans ces documents, l'Église de Rome et celle de Constantinople se qualifient mutuellement d' 'Églises soeurs....' Comment Rome pourra-t-elle se dire encore 'mére et maîtresse'? Il peut y avoir une soeur ainée, mais les deux viennent du même père: disons que leur apostolicité est égale" (*Essais oecuméniques* 37–38, 108). According to Tillard too: "The only community which has a right to the title of mother" is "the apostolic Church of Pentecost in Jerusalem. The Church of Rome is the first, the *principalior*, the one which presides (from her constitutive relationship to Peter, first of the Apostles, and to Paul). She is not the Mother" ("Catholic Church Is at the Heart of Communion", 8). More recently, de Halleux wrote, "Une ecclésiologie d'Églises soeurs semble exclure que le Siège romain se pose en 'mater et magistra' des Églises orthodoxes, et moins encore en 'caput, fons et origo' de leur ecclésialité. Voilà pourtant ce que paraît exiger une lettre récente de la Congregation romaine pour la Doctrine de la foi aux évêques de l'Église catholique [*Communionis notio*], lorsqu'elle assigne pour objectif au dialogue oecuménique avec 'ces véritables communautés chrétiennes' que sont les 'Églises orientales orthodoxes' (n.17; méritent-elles donc encore d'être appelées Églises soeurs?) que celles-ci puissent reconnaître et voir se réaliser le ministère pétrinien des évêques de Rome 'comme un service apostolique universel présent à l'*intérieur* de toutes les Églises' (n. 18)": "La collegialité dans Église ancienne", 450. Cf. de Halleux, "Fraterna communio", 307.

[232] Hryniewicz, "Reconciliation and Ecclesiology of Sister Churches", 70: "Our Churches should give up their maximalistic claims. Lasting reconciliation cannot consist in the returning of one Church to the other. Reconciliation and reunions are possible only through an act of recognizing each other as Sister Churches within communion of the Churches." The recognition of the elements of truth and sanctification which are present in other Churches and ecclesial communities does not permit us to speak *sic et simpliciter* of "return". It is necessary, however, that they arrive at the fullness of profession of faith and of communion. The Popes who figure among the principal advocates of dialogue and of the rediscovery of "sister Churches" are very clear in this regard. Thus John XXIII invites

can be deferred to an eventual study in the future, it is indispensable that we consider the problems related to the vision of uniqueness and unity of the Church which seems to be subject to the theology of "sister Churches" in present-day ecumenical dialogue between Catholics and Orthodox.

This uniqueness and unity were insisted upon in the past, since they were essential to both the Catholic and the Orthodox traditions. This is why the Catholic Church and the Orthodox Church, despite claiming, each for itself, the exclusive right to be identified with the *una, sancta, catholica*, remained one single Church in law and in fact.[234] Such insistence is undoubtedly not without problems, due to the lack of unity and of government which still divides them.[235] All the more problematic,

those who "ab Apostolica hac Sede seiuncti sunt" to return home (first radio message, *Urbi et orbi*, of October 29, 1958: *Discorsi, Messaggi e Colloqui*, I 8), even speaking explicitly of "reditu ... in communem paternamque domum" (encyclical *Ad Petri Cathedram*, June 29, 1959: ibid., 822) and of the community which "ab ea seiunctae sunt ac nondum pristinam unitatem redintegraverunt" (apostolic exhortation *Sacrae laudis*, January 6, 1962: ibid., IV, 881).

Paul VI too recalls that the Second Vatican Council "ha tra i suoi scopi anche quello di aprire ogni possibile via alla riconciliazione nell'unica Chiesa di Cristo delle varie e venerabili comunità separate" (*Discorso in occasione della cerimonia dell'offerta della reliquia di S. Cirillo*, November 4, 1963: Ins. I/1963, 328) and announces that his visit to the Holy Land has as its purpose "ad eam, unam et sanctam [Catholic Church], Fratres inde seiunctos revocemus" (*Discorso per la chiusura della II sessione del Concilio*, December 4, 1963: ibid., 380). He then denounces the temptation "di mettere da parte i punti controversi; di nascondere, di indebolire, di modificare, di vanificare, di negare, se occorre, quegli insegnamenti della Chiesa cattolica, i quali non sono oggi accettati dai Fratelli separati" (Ins: III 839). In his *Testament* too he admonishes: "Sull'ecumenismo: si prosegua l'opera di riavvicinamento con i fratelli separati, ... ma senza deflettere dalla vera dottrina cattolica" (AAS 70 [1978]: 561). On the positions taken up in the past with regard to "return" cf. Congar, *Essais oecuméniques*, 12–37.

[233] On the relationship between "sister Churches" and uniatism cf. above, p. 282, notes 115ff. John Paul II also recognizes that the Joint Commission "has laid the doctrinal foundation for a positive solution to this problem on the basis of the doctrine of Sister Churches" (encyclical *Ut unum sint*, 60). Various clarifications, however, still need to be made.

[234] L. Bouyer, *The Church of God*, 511–12: "On first sight, there are two Churches: the Catholic Church, whose distinctive sign is communion with the successor of Peter, and the Orthodox Church, which no longer has (or seems to have) this communion. But each claims for itself, in equally exclusive fashion, this identification with the *una, sancta, catholica*, which both confess in the same Credo.... There seems to be only one answer: the Orthodox Church and the Catholic Church, though dreadfully tempted by the spirit of division, remain one Church, in fact and by right, despite contrary appearances."

[235] Ols, "Diversités et communion. Réflexions", 135–36: "On pourrait soutenir qu'entre l'Église catholique et l'Église orthodoxe l'unité existe au plan de la vie sacramentelle.... Mais cela ne suffit pas pour qu'on puisse dire que les Églises catholique et orthodoxe,

however, is the present-day tendency, connected with the theology of
sister Churches, to think that after the great schism the Church of Christ
is divided and does not subsist in its fullness in any of the Churches: the
Catholic Church and the Orthodox Church are two Churches, equally
Catholic and equally Orthodox, because they participate in the same apostolic tradition.[236] Even though each has its own particularity, they find
themselves on a level of equality, or rather, they constitute two parts of
one and the same Church which existed in the first millennium,[237] as
two universal sisters, each endowed with a primacy of its own,[238] and
hence independent of the other, and constituting together a kind of "super-
Church". The two sister Churches are not local Churches, but replace
and constitute the one and only Church of Christ,[239] which is no longer
one but two: from the viewpoint of the theology of *sister Churches* the

---

malgré les apparences, sont une seule et même Église. Il faudrait pour cela unité de gouvernement et unité de foi."

[236] De Halleux, "Fraterna communio", 309: "Compte tenu de ce qu'est l'Église orthodoxe, la conviction que l'Église du Christ subsiste dans l'Église catholique n'exprime qu'une
moitié de la vérité totale. Vraie en ce qu'elle affirme, cette expression deviendrait fausse si
elle entendait contester que l'Église du Christ subsiste semblablement dans l'Église orthodoxe. L'une et l'autre Église sont également catholiques, de même qu'elles sont également
orthodoxes parce que participant de la même tradition apostolique."

[237] Congar, *Diversity and Communion*, 132: "There was not a Church on the one side
and a group which was not the Church on the other. The Church was split in two. Many
of us would hold that on the level of the ancient conception of the Church as a unity of
faith, a sacramental reality and spiritual organism, which the Orthodox retain, it is the
same Church." In an anonymous commentary on the discourse of Patriarch Bartholomew I to the bishops of the Swiss Episcopal Conference (December 14, 1995), we read,
"Ne faudrait-il pas que, de part et d'autre, un effort plus grand soit fait pour que les deux
parties de l'Église Une acceptent de se reconnaître dans leur différence, de se rencontrer
comme 'Églises-soeurs'?": *Istina* 41 (1996): 189. In support of the thesis that the Church of
Christ incorporates both sides, Congar had recourse to the often recurring image of "two
lungs": "Elle respire par ses deux poumons" (ibid., 113). In this connection Ols comments,
"C'est pourquoi l'image des deux poumons est dangereuse: . . . on ne peut absolument pas
prétendre que l'Église en tant qu'institution de salut ait été mutilée par cette sécession, au
sens où, après elle, il lui manquerait quelque chose pour mener à bien sa tâche. Elle con-
serve indubitablement la plénitude de son essence et de ce point de vue la sécession orientale ne la diminue en rien" ("Diversités et communion. Réflexions", 139).

[238] N. Bux, "Le chiese orientali nella Chiesa universale secondo il Concilio Vaticano II", *Communio* no. 123 (May–June 1992), 17: "Non possono invece sussistere due
chiese 'sorelle' universali." Ibid., 23: "Pian piano si è fatta strada una concezione che vede
la Chiesa cattolica e l'insieme delle chiese ortodosse come detentrici di un proprio primato di universalità."

[239] According to Lanne, the apostolic origins and apostolic succession are the foundation for fraternal relations "qui unissent les Églises et qui font qu'elles ne sont qu'une seule
et unique Église de Dieu": ("Implications ecclésiologiques", 68).

local Churches are never actually related to the one Church, but rather to two sister Churches. Every local Church, provided that she is authentically eucharistic, is as such a Church in her fullness. It follows that the Church of Christ is, by her very nature, a confederation of local Churches which together constitute the one and only Church: she no longer exists as one historical reality, but is *in fieri* [in a state of becoming] in the convergence or reunification of the two sister Churches, which is what the dialogue hopes for and promotes. A concrete notion of Church (body of Christ and the new people of God) is replaced by an ideal, to which no verifiable reality today corresponds, and which, even in the hoped-for reunion, would bring together the different Churches without a clear reciprocal bond that goes beyond the so-called juridical harmony, safeguarding the autonomy and self-sufficiency of each.[240]

On the same plane, there is also a distinction between the uniqueness and the unity of the Church. Considering the totality of all Christians, it is affirmed that one single Church (*Ecclesia unica*) already exists, made up of all Christians who, regardless of their local ecclesial community, are incorporated into Christ, in virtue of their baptism, and are united and in communion among themselves. Since, however, many of these communities lack some of the means of grace which are important for communion, the Church is not one (*Ecclesia una*), but "divided" and "disfigured" with regard to her visible form, and it will be possible to rediscover unity only when the various confessional communities will have supplied one another with the elements of full ecclesial status that they now lack or when they will have restored the vibrancy of those communities that are languishing.[241]

---

[240] Cf. Garuti, "Iglesia local e Iglesia universal. Puntas claves en el diálogo ecuménico", *Cuestiones de cristología y ecclesiología*, 323–34.

[241] Tillard, "Une seule Église de Dieu: l'Église brisée", *Proche-Orient Chrétien* 30 (1980): 6: "Puisqu'il n'existe sur terre qu'une seule Église de Dieu, c'est à cette seule Église qu'appartiennent tous ceux que le baptême ... incorpore au Christ." Ibid., 9–12: "À cause des hommes, la seule Église de Dieu sous forme visible (*Ecclesia unica*) n'est pas une (*Ecclesia una*). Elle est brisée.... Certes, demeure en toutes le baptême, avec le 'oui' global de la foi qu'il inclut. Mais chez plusieurs manquent certains des 'moyens de grâce' dont nous avons dit l'importance pour la *communion* ecclésial. L'Église de Dieu en sa forme visible s'en trouve défigurée.... Si la division a ses racines ... en un manque de *communion* dans les valeurs objectives de grâce, la seule Église de Dieu (l'*unica Ecclesia*) ne trouvera son unité que lorsque les communautés confessionnelles se seront donné mutuellement les éléments de pleine ecclésialité qui leur manquent ou auront redonné leur éclat à ceux d'entre eux qui vivotent chez elles."

This tendentious idea, in its various forms, is clearly untenable from the Catholic point of view,[242] because it presupposes that Christ had for centuries left the faithful without a true Church and continues to do so even today. One could even go so far as to ask whether or not the Church of Christ exists: from the affirmation that neither of the two sister Churches can consider herself the exclusive depository of salvation,[243] one must conclude that the Church of Christ, at least in the second millennium, exists only as an ideal, and not in the real and historical sense.

In reality, as we have said repeatedly, Christ's true Church continues to subsist in the Catholic Church alone, because "only one 'subsistence' of the true Church exists, whereas outside of her visible structure only *elementa Ecclesiae*—elements of the Church—exist; these—being elements of the same Church—tend toward and lead to the Catholic Church".[244]

The tendentious idea mentioned above underlies, or is at least favored by, certain expressions related to the reality of sister Churches which are now commonly used in ecumenical parlance, but which should be avoided.

---

[242] As pointed out by Hryniewicz ("Reconciliation and Ecclesiology of Sister Churches", 59–60), the reciprocal recognition of sacraments and of apostolic succession on the Orthodox side, too, "would mean adopting the position that the Orthodox and Roman Catholic Churches, being Sister Churches, constitute together the true Church of Christ. In the opinion of some critics, it would be tantamount to accepting a form of the branch theory, abandoning soteriological and ecclesiological exclusivity, and eventually admitting a possibility of *'communicatio in sacris'*. Once this happens, they fear, doctrinal differences would soon be treated simply as *theologoumena*." In fact, "the divided Church still remains the only Church of the risen Lord in the history of humanity. Any harm done to brotherly relations or even total breaking of them do not destroy the deepest nature of God's gift.... The Church remains one in its ontological dimension. Division affects its visible historic reality. The ontological unity of the Church can persist amidst divisions. Her divine core has never been broken" (ibid., 61–62).

[243] According to Lanne, with *Unitatis redintegratio* (no. 15), which he contrasts with *Orientalium Ecclesiarum*, a *"mutation ecclésiologique"* took place in the Catholic Church, which was substantially taken up and encouraged by Paul VI through his overtures toward the Orthodox, and which subsequently became the guiding inspiration for the documents of the ORCIC. In the new common ecclesiology the "vision théologique selon laquelle chacune des deux Églises se considérait comme l'unique dépositaire de salut" has been left behind. Indeed, "on reconnaît que ce que le Christ à confié à son Église ne peut être considerée comme la propriété exclusive de l'une de nos Églises.... C'est dans cette perspective que les Églises catholiques et les Églises ortodoxes se reconnaissent comme Églises Soeurs": "Présentation du Colloque de Chevetogne 1992", 307–24.

[244] Cf. above, p. 304, note 209.

First among these is the expression *unity of the Church*, underlying which is the mistaken belief that this unity was lost after the Eastern schism[245] and has to be rediscovered, by means of dialogue, through the reconciliation of the sister Churches. Unfortunately, this is the sense in which it reappears in Catholic circles as well, with explicit reference to the unity of the ancient Church which must be restored again between the sister Churches.[246] The expression is frequent, above all, in Orthodox circles[247] and in ecumenical dialogue,[248] in which there is, furthermore, explicit talk of a "future united Church".[249] Consequently, it can be

---

[245] It subsists, on the contrary, "in the Catholic Church as something she can never lose" (*Unitatis redintegratio* 4). The Congregation for the Doctrine of the Faith, in *Mysterium Ecclesiae* (no. 1), June 24, 1973, has also stated explicitly that "(the faithful) are not free to hold that Christ's Church nowhere really exists today and that it is to be considered only as an end which all Churches and ecclesial communities must strive to reach."

[246] Cardinal Willebrands, in his response to the greeting of Patriarch Athenagoras, enumerates, among the principles affirmed by the reciprocal visits, "those concerning the legitimate diversity in unity which the ancient Church lived out ... and which point the way to a restored unity between sister Churches" (Stormon, 226, no. 275. Cf. also Stormon, 465, no. 474). Cardinal Corrado Ursi is even more explicit: "For we have now entered the road leading towards the unity not only of the Holy Churches of Rome and Constantinople, but also of the sister Churches of West and East" (Stormon, 385, no. 333). John Paul II, also, in his address to the "pro Oriente" foundation, instead of "ristabilimento della desiderata piena comunione tra le chiese orientali e la chiesa cattolica" (*Unitatis redintegratio*, no. 14), speaks of "volle Wiederherstellung der Einheit zwischen den orientalischen Kirchen und der katholischen Kirche" (Ins. IX/2, 993).

[247] Patriarch Athenagoras goes so far as to change the official denomination of the Secretariat for the Unity of Christians to "Secretariat for Christian Unity" ("Secrétariat de l'union des Églises") (Stormon, 152, no. 160; 210, no. 250). For other examples cf. Stormon, 222, no. 274; 234, no. 286. Explicit mention is even made of "Unity among the Christian Churches" (Stormon, 30, no. 5; 77, no. 69).

[248] Metropolitan Meliton of Chalcedon, in his Address to the Members of the Joint Commission for Catholic-Orthodox Theological Dialogue (May 28, 1980), affirms that the dialogue was announced by John Paul II and Patriarch Demetrios I "as being directed to the unity of the Church" and on June 28 that same year, during the meeting on the occasion of the feast of Saints Peter and Paul, he describes it as a "decisive factor in building up the unity of Christ's Church" (Stormon, 391, no. 414; 399, no. 417).

[249] Cf. Orthodox Chalcedonian Churches—Orthodox non-Chalcedonian Churches, *The Agreed Statements. Summary of Conclusions* (Addis Ababa, 1971), 3, in *Does Chalcedon Divide or Unite? Towards Convergence in Orthodox Christology*, ed. P. Gregorios, W.H. Lazareth, N.A. Nissiotis (Geneva, 1981), 14. Even in the preface to the Lima Document of the Commission on Faith and Order it is emphasized that a "consensus" has not yet been reached, "understood here as that experience of life and articulation of faith necessary to realize and maintain the Church's visible unity" (MV 468).

ambiguous also to speak of an *undivided* or *divided Church*:[250] it is the Christians who are divided, not the Church as such, wounded though she may be by the division among Christians, but only insofar as the division is "an obstacle to the full realization of its universality within history".[251]

For the same reason one should avoid the expression *our two Churches* (or, as is sometimes the case, *our Churches*), used by Catholics[252] and, above all, by Orthodox,[253] to describe the relations between Rome and Constantinople. Here, too, the underlying idea is that the sole Church of Christ does not yet exist and that she will be realized only after the surmounting of the differences that still exist.[254]

---

[250] John Paul II, apostolic letter *Euntes in mundum*, no. 4: "The fullness of time for the baptism of the people of Rus' thus came at the end of the first millennium, when the Church was undivided.... There was the Church of the East and there was the Church of the West, each of which had developed according to its own theological, disciplinary and liturgical traditions, with even notable differences, but *there existed full communion* with reciprocal relations between the East and the West, between Constantinople and Rome" (*Origins* 17 [1987–88], 713a). Cf. encyclical *Ut unum sint*, no. 52.

[251] *Communionis notio*, 17.

[252] Cf. letter of Cardinal Bea to Patriarch Athenagoras (Stormon, 44, no. 23); letters of Cardinal Willebrands to Patriarch Athenagoras (Stormon, 164, no. 178) and to Patriarch Dimitrios (Stormon, 262, no. 312); Paul VI, letters to Patriarch Dimitrios (Stormon, 314, no. 358); John Paul II, letters to Patriarch Dimitrios (Stormon, 401, no. 418; 445, no. 459), address to the Delegation from Constantinople (IS, no. 78 [1991], 196a), message to Patriarch Bartholomew (December 1995: IS, no. 91 [1996], 57).

[253] We limit ourselves to a simplified list of examples, with references to the sources: Bishop Andrew of Claudiopolis (Stormon, 97, no. 95); Patriarch Athenagoras (Stormon, 140, no. 142; 161, no. 173); Patriarch Dimitrios I (Stormon, 303, no. 248; 322, no. 367; 335, no. 380; 409, no. 424); Metropolitan Meliton (Stormon, 278, no. 330; 310, no. 354; 446, no. 460); Archbishop Stylianos of Australia (IS, no. 53 [1984], 64–65); Metropolitan Damaskinos (IS, no. 68 [1988], 155–56); Metropolitan Bartholomew of Philadelphia (IS, no. 71 [1989], 125–26); Patriarch Bartholomew (IS, no. 85 [1994], 40).

[254] The idea would seem to be present, though in a not very explicit form, in the address of John Paul II to the Catholicos of the Jacobite Malankara Church, Mar Baselius Paulose II: recalling the joint declaration signed in June 1984, he describes it as "*a decisive step* in relations between our two Churches as we move towards unity" (Ins. IX/1, 371). It is explicit, on the contrary, in the letter of Patriarch Demetrios I to Paul VI (December 14, 1975): after having spoken of "our Churches of the elder and the new Rome," the patriarch adds, "The union of our Churches is clearly something that has to be reached by passing through special theological, canonical, and other differences" (Stormon, 289–91, no. 335). In his address to the Catholic Delegation on the occasion of the feast of St. Andrew (November 30, 1986), the same patriarch speaks of "our two Churches" in reference to Constantinople and Rome, only to go on to the designation "Orthodox Churches" and a description of the dialogue as the "work of the union of the Churches" (IS, no. 63 [1987], 9).

Again, and still in the ecumenical field, the Orthodox Churches erroneously consider themselves as the sole Church, and, on the other hand, the Catholic Church is viewed as a particular Church. This manner of speaking implies the tendentious idea—already denounced as unacceptable— that, in fact, the Church of Christ is no longer one, but two: she is said to be a subject transcending the two sister Churches, and [according to this view] only the ensemble of the Churches, Catholic and Orthodox, consitutes the Church.

The existence of a *unique Orthodox Church* (the "Great Orthodox or Byzantine Church"), despite the rather fluctuating terminology, seems to have been taken for granted by now, for instance, in exchanges of letters or messages and in the addresses and greetings during visits. The ambiguity is less frequent on the Catholic side, where the expression is normally avoided: the Catholic Church is contrasted with "the venerable Churches of the East",[255] "the autocephalous Churches of the Orthodox world",[256] "the local Orthodox Churches",[257] or simply "the Orthodox Churches",[258] clearly distinguishing between the different Churches and their respective patriarchates.[259] Often, however, the same persons speak of "the Catholic Church and the Orthodox Churches" as well as of "the Catholic Church and the Orthodox Church".[260] The distinction is more clearly marked with the Eastern Christians, who, besides distinguishing between "Catholic Church" and "Orthodox Church",[261] also make a distinction between "Roman Catholic Church of the West" and "Orthodox

---

[255] Cf. Stormon, 34, no. 9; 41, no. 19; 82, no. 78; 239, no. 285.

[256] Cf. Stormon, 41, no. 19.

[257] Cf. Stormon, 85, no. 86.

[258] Cf. Stormon, 77, no. 71; 122, no. 123; 207, no. 245; 276, no. 328; 304, no. 349. Cardinal Willebrands also speaks of "relations built up ... with the Orthodox Churches in their totality and with each in particular" (Stormon, 406, no. 423).

[259] John Paul II: "I wish to express my respect and deep brotherly charity for all these Churches and their Patriarchs, but above all to the Ecumenical Patriarchate" (Angelus, November 18, 1979: Stormon, 355, no. 397: cf. also 339, no. 418).

[260] Thus Paul VI speaks of "Orthodox Churches" (Stormon, 180, no. 194) and of "Orthodox Orient" or "Orthodox Church" (Stormon, 87, no. 88; 156, no. 171; 175, no. 190; 221, no. 272). Similarly, John Paul II uses the first expression (Stormon, 356, no. 399; 358, no. 401) as well as the second (*Homily for the Millennium of the Baptism of Rus' of Kiev*, July 10, 1988: Ins. XI/3, 78–79; address to the Greek-Orthodox Patriarch Parthenios I: 24/9/ 1990: IS, no. 75 [1990], 152; encyclical *Ut unum sint*, no. 60).

[261] Patriarch Athenagoras (Stormon, 30–31, no. 5; 95, no. 94; 169, no. 186; 179, no. 193); Patriarch Dimitrios I (Stormon, 307, no. 352; 328, no. 374; 334, no. 378; 345, no. 389); Metropolitan Meliton (Stormon, 324, no. 368).

Church of the East",[262] or the Church of Rome and [that of] Constantinople,[263] called, respectively, "the two first Sees of the West and the East".[264] In only one case do they speak contemporaneously of the distinction between the Orthodox Church and the autocephalous Orthodox Churches.[265]

The *joint declaration* of December 7, 1965, in which Paul VI and Patriarch Athenagoras communicated the decision to remove from the record the excommunications of 1054, besides using the pair of terms Catholic Church—Orthodox Church, also makes a sort of identification between the ecumenical patriarchate and the Orthodox Church. They express, indeed, the conviction that the development of brotherly relations between the Roman Catholic Church and the Orthodox Church of Constantinople will be facilitated, and at the same time they say that they feel persuaded to respond to the call of divine grace which is leading the Catholic Church and the Orthodox Church to overcome the differences that still persist.[266]

In the *theological dialogue*, the designation "Joint International Commission for the Theological Dialogue between the Roman Catholic Church and the Orthodox Church" is itself ambiguous, insofar as it presupposes the existence of an Orthodox Church. In fact, one often speaks of "Dialogue between the Roman Catholic and Orthodox Churches",[267] sometimes explicitly presenting the two Churches as the two sections of the

---

[262] Patriarch Athenagoras (Stormon, 86–87, no. 87; 95, no. 94; 140, no. 142).

[263] Patriarch Athenagoras (Stormon, 140, no. 142; 383, no. 173); Patriarch Dimitrios (Stormon, 270, no. 322); Metropolitan Meliton (Stormon, 350, no. 393). The same expression is also found, however, in the papal brief *Ambulate in dilectione* of Paul VI (Stormon, 129, no. 128) and in the corresponding "Topos" of Patriarch Athenagoras (Stormon, 291, no. 129).

[264] Meliton of Helioupolis (Stormon, 132, no. 130).

[265] Communiqué of the Ecumenical Patriarchate on the inception of the Second Vatican Council (Stormon, 43, no. 22).

[266] Cf. Stormon, 127, no. 127. The same identification is found again in the Joint Declaration of October 28, 1967: cf. Stormon, 181, no. 195. The Catholic Church–Orthodox Church correlation will be taken up again in the Joint Declarations of Pope John Paul II and the Ecumenical Patriarch Dimitrios I (November 30, 1979 and December 2, 1987: Stormon, 367–68, no. 404).

[267] Patriarch Dimitrios (Stormon, 309, no. 354; 379, no. 411; cf. 397, no. 416); John Paul II (Stormon, 383, no. 413; 400, no. 418; 474, no. 481). Cardinal Willebrands defines it as a dialogue "between the Catholic Church and the entire Orthodox Church" (Stormon, 405, no. 423).

divided Christianity of East and West[268] which together have decided to embark on the dialogue.[269] In reality, the decision on the Orthodox side was taken by the verious autonomous Churches, which for this purpose established a special pan-Orthodox commission entrusted with the task of preparing for it.[270] The commission is composed of representatives from each of these Churches,[271] as is the practice to this day. It would seem more exact, therefore, to speak simply about "Catholic-Orthodox dialogue"—and by analogy about a "Joint Catholic-Orthodox Commission"—or of "dialogue between the Catholic Church and the Orthodox Churches",[272] possibly specifying that the Orthodox Churches in question are those of the "Byzantine tradition"[273] or those "in canonical communion with the See of Constantinople".[274]

The Church of Constantinople is consistently designated, in both Orthodox and Catholic circles, "the first among the Orthodox Churches",[275] the "holy center of the orthodoxy"[276] which "represents the entire Orthodox world",[277] for which reason she is invested with and "understands its duty of service [*diakonia*] in the present situation towards its sister Orthodox Churches".[278] Consequently, her bishop is the "Bishop of the leading See of the Orthodox East",[279] and as " 'Ecumenical' Patriarch is first among the others"[280] and "the supreme representative of the whole of Orthodoxy".[281]

---

[268] Meliton of Chalcedon, addressing the members of the Joint Commission, speaks of dialogue between "the Roman Catholic and the Orthodox Churches, which represent the two great sections of the divided Christianity of East and West" (Stormon, 387–89, no. 414).

[269] Cf. Stormon, 391, no. 414. The initiative, however, comes from the Ecumenical Patriarchate (cf. Stormon, 283, no. 332).

[270] Cf. Stormon, 283, no. 332.

[271] Cf. the list found in Stormon, 296–97, no. 339.

[272] John Paul II: "With the venerable Orthodox Churches we are on the eve of initiating a theological dialogue.... I wish to express my respect and deep brotherly charity for all these Churches and their Patriarchs" (Stormon, 355, no. 397).

[273] John Paul II, *Address to the Youth* (January 17, 1979: Ins II/I, 82).

[274] Encyclical *Ut unum sint*, no. 52.

[275] Patriarch Dimitrios (Stormon, 259, no. 310). Cf. John Paul II (*L'Osservatore Romano*, 30 giugno–1 luglio, 1995, 7).

[276] Patriarch Dimitrios (Stormon, 366, no. 403).

[277] Patriarch Athenagoras (Stormon, 158, no. 173). Also John Paul II, through the person of Patriarch Dimitrios, greets "all the Churches that you represent" (Stormon, 358, no. 401).

[278] Meliton of Helioupolis (Stormon, 120, no. 122).

[279] Patriarch Dimitrios (Stormon, 290, no. 335; cf. 302, no. 347; 349, no. 392).

[280] John Paul II (Stormon, 377, no. 410).

[281] Cardinal Corrado Ursi (Stormon, 285, no. 333).

In reality, there does not exist one sole "Orthodox Church". In fact, Eastern ecclesiology, "based upon a eucharistic vision of the Church, places ... the emphasis on the reality of the local Church, which has its own autonomy. Given the fundamental equality of all local Churches, in each of which the Church is realized in its totality, a 'primary datum' in the Eastern mentality is that the Church is made up of a multiplicity of local Churches. The only form of ecclesial organization is ... that of clustering around the main Churches, which in turn gives rise to the patriarchates."[282]

As a result of the fundamental equality among all local Churches and among all bishops who preside over them,[283] each of the Orthodox Churches has an internal autonomy of its own. It was only "in response to the needs of the Church's mission" that during the course of history "a hierarchy was established between Churches of earlier foundation and Churches of more recent foundation, between mother and daughter Churches, between Churches of larger cities and Churches of outlying areas", leading eventually to the formation of the pentarchy, whereby "to bishops occupying certain metropolitan or major sees" special prerogatives were attributed "in the organization of the synodal life of the Church".[284] Nevertheless, the institution of "these centers of harmony, thanks to which the living communion of the Churches was concretely manifested",[285] did not and cannot exclude the fundamental equality of all Churches:[286] in accordance with canon 34 of the apostles, the primate

---

[282] Garuti, *Il Papa Patriarca d'Occidente?*, 26. Cf. also 26–29 (the Eastern origins of the title of Patriarch of the West) and 228–34 (the ecclesiological presuppositions of pentarchy). On eucharistic ecclesiology and its effects on the Eastern viewpoint cf. also the following Eastern theologians: O. Clément, *La Chiesa ortodossa*, 62–64; Filaret of Kiev, "Paper", 8–9; Galitis, "Gli aspetti ecclesiologici del dialogo teologico", 193; the Valamo Document (IS, no. 68 [1988], 176b). For relevant clarifications from the Catholic side on the concept of the local realization of the unique Church through the Eucharist cf. Ratzinger, *Church, Ecumenism and Politics*, 7–11; Salachas, *Il dialogo*, 60–63.

[283] Filaret of Kiev, "Paper", 10a: "The Orthodox Church teaches that bishops are equal among themselves. This teaching is based on the fact that each bishop heads the one and the same Catholic Church in a given place, and that no one local Church, including the Roman Church, can be more Catholic than the other." Cf. O–RCC, *An Agreement on the Church*.

[284] The Valamo Document (no. 52: IS, no. 68 [1988], 178). Cf. O–RCC, *An Agreement on the Church*.

[285] Clément, *La Chiesa ortodossa*, 63–64.

[286] O–RCC, *An Agreement on the Church*, no. 6 (BE 85).

was "simply the *primus inter pares*", in order to safeguard the independence and interdependence between the "first" and the other bishops.[287]

In reality, the Orthodox Church today is made up of different Churches, characterized as "national" Churches, "autocephalous" Churches, and "autonomous" Churches, apart from the so-called Churches of the diaspora.[288] Hence there is not *one* "Orthodox Church", but rather, according to its own ecclesiology, reasserted by the dialogue, "a communion of Churches, bound together neither by a centralized organization nor through a single official. [In their capacity] as primates, patriarchs and archbishops do function as signs of the unity of their churches. The ecumenical patriarch of Constantinople does have a priority of honor as 'first among equals'. Nevertheless, the Orthodox churches are unified in love and peace only through communion in faith and sacraments."[289]

After the split between East and West, the presidency over the Orthodox Churches was transferred to the Church of Constantinople, whose patriarch occupies a leading position as *primus inter pares*,[290] with a primacy of honor: not of power, but of service toward the Orthodox communion—something that has been admitted in principle but whose real import has often been the subject of discussion in the Orthodox world itself[291]—and is, in any case, qualified by the pentarchy.[292] His role is much more modest than it is often made out to be, and he does

---

[287] Cf. the Valamo Document (no. 53: IS, no. 68 [1988] 178b).

[288] Cf. G. Zananiri, "Orthodoxes (Églises)", *Catholicisme* X, 284–86; Zananiri, "Orthodoxie", ibid., 286–95; R. G. Robertson, *The Eastern Christian Churches* (Rome, 1990); Lossky, "Ortodossi (Bizantini)", 815–16; C. Dallari, *Chiamati all'unità*, 33.

[289] Institute for Ecumenical Research, *Communion/Koinonia* (Strasbourg, 1990): 18, nos. 24–25. Cf. Lossky, "Orthodoxy", DEM 366–67. It is therefore more of an "Orthodox confederation" than an "Orthodox Church" (Zananiri, "Orthodoxes [Églises]", 284).

[290] Maxime de Sardes, *Le patriarcat oecuménique*, 22: "[L]'Église Orthodoxe a toujours reconnu dans chaque région un premier évêque (Archevêque, Métropolite, Patriarche), de même qu'elle reconnaît dans l'Église universelle un premier évêque. Celui-ci, depuis l'époque du schisme, est l'évêque de Constantinople." Cf. Lossky, "Ortodossia", 820a; Evdokimov, *L'Ortodossia*, 186–87.

[291] K. Ware, "L'exercice de l'autorité dans l'Église orthodoxe", *Irénikon* 55 (1982): 28: "Tandis que la portée précise de la primauté de Constantinople est actuellement en discussion dans le monde orthodoxe, le *fait* de cette primauté est accepté par toutes les Églises orthodoxes autocéphales également, grecques et non-grecques."

[292] Review *Istina* 32 (1987): 337–38, editorial: "L'Orthodoxie souligne que cette primauté de Constantinople n'est pas une suprématie mais un service, un souci exercé au sein d'une structure de concertation et de communion, la pentarchie, à laquelle elle se plaît à reconnaître une origine très ancienne, voire apostolique. Ainsi dans l'Orthodoxie, la

not have the necessary authority because his office is not of divine right and is subject to the decisions of the synod and even of the state.[293] Despite the efforts of the ecumenical patriarchate, this power was gradually fragmented and weakened, as is demonstrated by the continual conflicts with the patriarchate of Moscow and the eparchies of the diaspora, based not merely upon contingent factors but also upon a different ecclesiological viewpoint.[294]

There have been attempts to explain the alternating terminology of "Orthodox Church" and "Orthodox Churches" on the basis of the trinitarian and eucharistic conception of the Church and by making a distinction between the *ontological* order, which entails an absolute equality among all the Churches, and the *hierarchical* order of the universal Church, which implies, on the contrary, a difference in dignity and a certain hier-

---

communion entre les différentes parties de l'Église s'exprime normalement et régulièrement par la voix de ces hiérarques, égaux entre eux, que sont les anciens patriarches."

[293] D. J. Melling, "The Right Path", *Eastern Churches Journal* 2, no. 2 (1995): 172: "The Ecumenical Patriarch's role as senior hierarch of the Orthodox communion is far more fragile than his public image sometimes suggests. To some he may look like the Eastern counterpart of the Pope, and the vigour with which he has exercised and even developed his role in the Orthodox Church may give plausibility to that image, but the fact remains that he is not the linear superior of the chief hierarchs of other autocephalous Churches, but only the first amongst them, and that is something very different. Orthodox tradition, moreover, has never recognized any hierarchical role above that of the local bishop as of divine authority. Any higher layer of authority and responsibility derives from synodical or sometimes even state decision. There is nothing inevitable or immutable in the Primacy of Constantinople. Nor can the Ecumenical Patriarch assert his authority to guarantee the Orthodox Church's acceptance of the policy he espouses."

[294] Clément, *La Chiesa ortodossa*, 64–67: "La moltiplicazione delle 'autocefalie' e l'indebolimento storico della chiesa della nuova Roma hanno reso difficile l'applicazione del *Canone 17* di Calcedonia che conferiva al patriarca di Costantinopoli un certo diritto di appello. Il *Canone 28* dello stesso concilio aveva posto sotto la sua giurisdizione le diocesi missionarie (stabilite nei paesi 'barbari') del Basso Danubio e del Caucaso. Nel XX secolo il patriarcato ecumenico ha voluto dare a questo canone la portata generale di una giurisdizione di diritto su tutta la 'diaspora' ortodossa, accogliendo così, nell'intermezzo fra le due guerre, una importante frazione dell'emigrazione russa in Europa occidentale. Ma il patriarcato di Mosca non ha accettato questa interpretazione. Si tratta in fondo di due approcci ecclesiologici discretamente differenti: Costantinopoli insiste sulla necessità, per la chiesa, di un centro di accordo universale, Mosca invece sull'indipendenza e l'uguaglianza delle chiese autocefale (di cui essa è la più potente) e la sciamatura da 'chiesa-madre' a 'chiesa-figlia.'" On the "misunderstandings" between the Ecumenical Patriarchate and the Orthodox Church of America cf. "Chronique des Églises", *Irénikon* 68 (1995): 112–16.

archical gradation.[295] In fact, Orthodox ecclesiology itself, as corroborated by the facts, does not permit any talk about "the Orthodox Church"; even if on the dogmatic level Orthodoxy considers itself one single reality, the different Churches are autocephalous, that is, institutionally independent, and there is no single voice that can speak with authority for each of them. They themselves insist on saying that the ecumenical patriarch speaks only for the Church of Constantinople and not for the Orthodox Churches in general;[296] some even perceive the need for a ministry of unity in a form different from the one that is actually exercised by the patriarch of Constantinople.[297]

It would seem necessary, therefore, to return to the terminology used by the council, not for fear of jeopardizing ecumenical dialogue,[298] but for doctrinal reasons that are confirmed, moreover, by the facts themselves.

Just to underscore the ambiguity resulting from the use of the term *Orthodox Church* in referring to the Orthodox Churches as a group, it is worth mentioning briefly the error of considering the Catholic Church as a particular Church. The Church of Rome is indeed a particular Church,[299]

---

[295] Maxime de Sardes, *Le patriarcat oecuménique*, 15–25. Chapter II (pp. 53–95) gives a detailed description of ecclesial organization, whereas chapter III in its entirety (pp. 97–154) seeks to demonstrate the primacy of Constantinople.

[296] On the question of autocephaly, especially in relation to the phenomenon of the diaspora, cf. the document "Le problème de l'autocéphalie dans l'Orthodoxie. Quatrième réunion de la Commission interorthodoxe préparatoire (Chambésy, November 7–13, 1993)", *Istina* 39 (1994): 294–314.

[297] Cf. Tillard, "Primacy", 823b.

[298] According to de Halleux, "Fraterna Communio", 297, the decree *Unitatis redintegratio* "omet ou il évite de parler d'Église, au singulier, et de qualifier cette Église d'orthodoxe", inasmuch as the plural designation "répond bien au régime de l'autocéphalie canonique, qui régit actuellement l'Orthodoxie. Mais elle ne tient pas compte de l'unité ecclésiologique profonde que l'Église orthodoxe n'a jamais perdue et pour laquellle elle a depuis peu des organes d'expression visible. Le décret sur l'oecuménisme parlait des Églises orientales, au pluriel, par respect de leur particularité et notamment en fonction du régime patriarcal (n.14 §1). Mais leur opposition grammaticale au singulier monolithique de l'Église catholique pouvait sembler menacer les conditions du dialogue oecuménique entre partenaires égaux."

[299] In this sense it is also the "local" realization of the sole Church (cf. *Lumen gentium*, no. 23; *Christus Dominus*, 11), and hence it is possible to distinguish, in the person of the Pope, the Bishop of the particular Church of Rome and the Pastor of the universal Church: cf. Garuti, *Il Papa Patriarca d'Occidente?*, 253–55. On this level of particular Churches it is also possible to speak of relations between the "Ecumenical Patriarchate and the Church of Rome" (Cardinal Willebrands: Stormon, 216, no. 261).

but not so the Catholic Church, which is by her very nature the *universal* realization of the Church, namely, a body of particular Churches which together participate in the one and only Catholic Church.[300]

However, this simple observation has great significance with regard to the application of the title of "sister Churches". Although originally the expression might have designated the particular Churches of the East in mutual relationship within the bosom of the one and only Church of Christ, after its "rediscovery" it would on occasion be utilized to refer to one particular Catholic Church and one particular Orthodox Church. Indeed, all particular Churches are "sister Churches", even those that are not in full communion, for which reason it makes sense to say that the local Church of Rome is also a sister of any other local Church and vice versa. But it is theologically unacceptable to say that the individual particular Churches, or groups of particular Churches, are sisters[301] of the Catholic Church in her totality (universal Church), composed of all the Churches, each of which is, in her proper place, the very same Catholic Church.

The title is even more unacceptable when used to refer to the "Orthodox Church", which does not exist as such, and to the Catholic Church understood in the universal sense, in which the one and only Church of Christ subsists, and whose Bishop, in his capacity as the Successor of Peter, is head and Pastor of the universal Church. According to such usage, the Catholic Chuch is considered to be a particular Church alongside the other "sister Churches", and this would favor erroneous ideas about the Church understood as communion, ideas which were rejected by the letter *Communionis notio*.

V. CONCLUSION

Having sprung up and developed in the East as a means of designating relations between the local Churches, the expression "sister Churches", in the years immediately following the council, aroused considerable inter-

---

[300] Cf. *Lumen gentium*, no. 23.

[301] Therefore the expression used by Patriarch Dimitrios I on the occasion of the death of Paul VI is incorrect: "The Ecumenical Patriarchate as sister Church shares with its whole soul in the grief of the holy Roman Catholic Church and the entire Roman Catholic world" (Stormon, 327, no. 373–74).

est in the West as well, first in the context of dialogue in charity and then in the context of dialogue in truth. From the analysis carried out against the background of its historical development—on the basis of the letters and messages exchanged between the Roman Pontiffs and the patriarchs or other exponents of the Catholic and Eastern worlds, the joint declarations by the same Pontiffs and patriarchs, as well as the different documents on ecumenical dialogue—the realization has emerged that we are faced with a factual datum of considerable weight and that the use of the term effectively constitutes a reality.[302] It is also undeniable that the expression, contrary to its original meaning, is also used to describe relations between the Catholic Church and the different Orthodox Churches, founded upon a reciprocal unity of faith and communion, described by both as "almost perfect" or "not complete", but in fact judged to be sufficient grounds for acknowledging their ecclesial status.

But it is precisely this foundation that raises a number of questions and requires some clarifications in order to ascertain whether and in what sense we can continue to speak of "sister Churches".

We have seen that, in reality, considerable differences remain between the Catholic Church and the Orthodox Churches or, more acurately, real and proper differences, in matters of faith, for instance in the field of ecclesiology and with regard to the very concept of the *depositum fidei*. For this reason unity in faith does *not* exist, as the Orthodox more realistically maintain, but rather remains a goal. Full communion also remains a goal: despite the deep bonds that already exist, it has not yet been achieved, as is demonstrated by the conviction that it is not yet possible to celebrate the Eucharist together.

Since complete indentity has not yet been realized through the profession of the same faith, and since they lack perfect participation in the communion of the sole Church, the Orthodox Churches are true particular Churches; since, however, they do not recognize the authority of the Successor of Peter, their ecclesiological situation is irregular, or rather, their ecclesial status is wounded. Inasmuch as they possess some elements of sanctification and of truth—especially apostolic succession and a valid

---

[302] For once we could agree with Bishop Zoghby, when he writes, "On nous remplit les oreilles de 'communion presque parfaite' entre Rome et l'Orthodoxie, 'd'Églises-soeurs,' de 'communauté de foi,' d' 'Église une,' d'oecuménisme, de dialogue.... Mais il ne faut pas exagérer leur portée" (*Tous schismatiques?*, 108–9).

Eucharist—they have a meaning and importance in the mystery of salvation. They also have genuine elements of ecclesiality, but the Church of Christ does not subsist in them: they are Churches, but in an imperfect and analogous manner in comparison with the Catholic Church, from which they derive their existence and soteriological efficacy.

It follows that their condition of being "*sister* Churches" is also marked by a "almost full" profession of faith, by an "imperfect" communion, and by their "wounded" ecclesial character, for which reason it is a reality, but an imperfect and analogous one.[303] On the other hand, the position that is encountered at various levels of the Orthodox world is much more drastic, inasmuch as they do not acknowledge the true ecclesial status of the Catholic Church and dispute whether she can be called a sister.

What emerges, finally, is the need to take a close look at some of the implications resulting from an indiscriminate and improper use of the category "sister Churches". Here, too, the problems raised are of a doctrinal nature, but they are of considerable importance for the way in which ecumenical dialogue is conducted and for the evaluation of the documents that proceed from it.

In particular, it has been established that the theology of sister Churches is often connected with a tendentious notion, which is untenable from either the Catholic or the Orthodox point of view. According to this tendentious notion, the Church of Christ has been divided since the great Schism, and she no longer subsists in her fullness in either of the Churches: it is said that two Churches exist, the Catholic Church and the Orthdodox Church, which constitute two parts of the one Church that existed in the first millennium. They exist as two universal sisters, each in possession of her own primate. The Church of Christ no longer exists as *one* in history, but is *in fieri* [in the state of becoming] through the convergence or reunification of the two sister Churches, which is hoped for and promoted by dialogue: at least in the second millennium, she exists only as an ideal and not in a real and historical manner.

From this explicit negation of the existence of the one and only Church of Christ, it follows that we must avoid all those expressions that in some way or other imply or could favor the tendentious notion mentioned above: expressions such as "unity of the Church", "divided Church" or

---

[303] The patriarch of Moscow, Alexis II, also spoke, though in a moment of outburst, of "stepsister" and of being "sick"; cf. above, p. 305, note 213.

"undivided Church", "our two Churches", and the error of considering the Orthodox Churches as one single Church and of understanding the Catholic Church to be a particular Church.

What would be, then, a correct use of the expression "sister Churches", and what significance could it assume?

Although originally the expression may have designated the particular Churches of the East in their mutual relationships within the bosom of the sole Church of Christ, after its "rediscovery", it could be utilized to refer to one particular Catholic Church, including the Church of Rome, and to one particular Orthodox Church in the sense explained above. But it is thelogically unacceptable to say that the individual particular Churches, or groups of them, are sisters of the Catholic Church in her totality (universal Church). Even more unacceptable is the use of the expression to refer to the "Orthodox Church", which does not exist as such, and to the Catholic Church understood in the universal sense, in which the sole Church of Christ subsists. The Catholic Church would thus be considered as a particular Church alongside the other "sister Churches".

INDEX OF PROPER NAMES